HARVARD STUDIES IN CLASSICAL PHILOLOGY

VOLUME 108

HARVARD STUDIES
IN
CLASSICAL PHILOLOGY

VOLUME 108

Department of the Classics, Harvard University
Cambridge, Massachusetts
Distributed by Harvard University Press
2015

THIS BOOK IS PRINTED ON ACID-FREE PAPER, AND ITS
BINDING MATERIALS HAVE BEEN CHOSEN FOR STRENGTH
AND DURABILITY.

LIBRARY OF CONGRESS CATALOGUE NUMBER: 44–32100

ISBN-13: 978-0-674-41754-0

PRINTED IN THE UNITED STATES OF AMERICA

EDITORIAL NOTE

Harvard Studies in Classical Philology is published by the authority of the President and Fellows of Harvard College on behalf of the Department of the Classics. Publication is assisted by the generosity of the Class of 1856, as well as by other gifts and bequests. The guidelines for style and a statement of the editorial policy may be found at http://publishing. classics.fas.harvard.edu.

CONTENTS

"TRUST THE GOD"

THARSEIN IN ANCIENT GREEK RELIGION

MIGUEL HERRERO DE JÁUREGUI

I. DANGER, SALVATION, AND THE EMOTION OF THARSOS

EVERY FEW YEARS new ancient religious texts come to light which contain forms of the Greek verb *tharrein* / *tharsein*, a term generally agreed to be loaded with religious significance. Commentators on these texts adduce some of the best-known parallels of the encouragement formulas in the imperative form, θάρσει.[1] However, there has been little research on what kind of religious experience is implied by *tharsein*: the usual translations—"take heart", "be of good cheer", "do not be afraid", "have courage"—do not convey the full semantic range of the verb, which, when used in religious (not only ritual) situations, implies, above all, being confident that a god will help. The purpose of this paper is, therefore, to analyze the connotations of the verb in religious contexts. On the one hand, it will shed light on specific passages whose meaning becomes more dense and more precise when this verb is given its full value. On the other hand, it aims to illuminate an important dimension of the experiences of danger and salvation in ancient religion. The study of the verb *tharsein* is of relevance to some crucial areas of scholarly inquiry that have recently attracted renewed interest: namely, individual beliefs, emotions, and perceptions of the

---

[1] Firm. Mat. *Err.* 22.1 is the most frequently quoted passage, along with the funerary formula θάρσει, οὐδεὶς ἀθανάτος (cf. Graf and Johnston 2013:208–212). Simon 1936 and Joly 1955 are the studies of reference on the subject. A thorough discussion of the term *tharsein*, with special attention to religious contexts, is Spicq 1978, although it is oriented towards explanation of the New Testament passages. The most recent collection of new documents containing the expression is Chaniotis 2012.

divine; ways of dealing with risk and uncertainty; and the importance of narrative for constructing religious experience in a consistent way.

It is well known that in recent years the study of personal experience of the divine and individual beliefs has enjoyed renewed popularity, after decades of marginalization in favor of a polis-centered approach to Greek religion.[2] As we shall see, even when a whole community is affected by danger and in need of divine help, the epiphanic experience implied by the imperative *tharsei* is almost always personal. The individual is the recipient of salvation, and even when such salvation is collective, it is mediated by one person in privileged contact with the gods.

In addition, the concept of risk, previously studied from anthropological and sociological perspectives, has begun to be exploited as a useful category for analyzing how ancient individuals and communities dealt with situations of uncertainty.[3] The texts we shall encounter show how the promise of salvation from a god helps in confronting a dangerous future and vague or precise threats. Salvation is a broad concept that must be kept distinct from its Christianizing connection with the afterlife, since it has much wider implications in the context of risk or danger: death is just one possible threat, and faith in a blessed afterlife is only one of many (and not even the most popular) possible ways of confronting it. As we shall see, different instances of *tharsein* mirror various forms of risk and safety relevant for ancient religion.

It is perhaps no coincidence that Eidinow, a scholar who specializes in ways of dealing with risk in ancient Greek religion, has recently argued that paying attention to "narrativization" of religious

---

[2]   A pivotal moment seems to have been a 2008 conference to honor the memory of C. Sourvinou-Inwood, where several participants aimed to go beyond her theory of polis-religion: Bremmer 2010, Eidinow 2011, and Kindt 2012:12–35 derive from papers delivered at that conference.

[3]   Eidinow 2007 (pages 13–25 for the theoretical underpinnings of the concept, on which there is abundant bibliography from the last two decades). The Greek *kindynos* embraces both a precise threat and hazardous uncertainty which broadly corresponds to the modern distinction between danger and risk. Risk-calculation is alien to the ancient world, where different strategies were adopted for coping with danger and uncertainty: cf. Henrichs 2009 for Greek tragedy and Beard 2011 for the Roman world.

experience may help to make sense of its several components.[4] In the course of this paper, we will analyze different tales of salvation, which well illustrate this narrative framing of religious experience. Situations of danger and different forms of divine help are the backbone of a narrative pattern in which both individuals and communities are involved—though not necessarily in the same way, as we shall see. The hope of attaining salvation, the trust in a god, and the consequent courage to confront a more or less precise danger, are crucial dimensions in these narratives, and they are all condensed into the verb *tharsein*.

Having set out the wider implications of this study, we should also acknowledge its limits. We must not forget the limitations of lexicography in evaluating religious experiences. Speakers may go outside the normal semantic range of a word or they may distort it. They may also use other expressions as synonyms. Literary tradition may keep alive a meaning or term no longer used or understood in spoken language. However, tracing the appearances of a concept is the most secure way of uncovering its nuances. The Greek word *tharsein*, etymologically connected with the English "to dare" and with the Thracian healing *daimon* Darrhon, means, primarily, "to be confident."[5] An authorized ancient definition helps to specify its meaning: in the *Rhetoric*, Aristotle describes it as an emotion (*pathos*), "on account of which people change their minds and differ with regard to their judgments."[6] He defines it in opposition to fear (*phobos*). The orator who wants to instil fear must show a danger, "the approach of the frightful" (1382a32: τοῦτο γάρ ἐστι κίνδυνος, φοβεροῦ πλησιασμός), and at the same time (1383a5–7) there must be a hope of salvation (δεῖ τινα ἐλπίδα ὑπεῖναι σωτηρίας), since nobody deliberates about hopeless

---

[4] Eidinow 2011.

[5] Cf. Chantraine 1968 s.v.; we shall see cases of θάρσει uttered as a healing word by Asclepius, Jesus, and Apollonius of Tyana. This explains the name of Darrhon, defined by Hesychius (s.v. Δάρρων) as the *daimon* to whom Macedonians pray for the sick (identified with Asclepius in *SEG* 44:546).

[6] Arist. *Rhet.* 1378a20–23; cf. Konstan 2007:33–40. In the last two decades there has been an increasing number of studies on the construction of emotions in ancient Greek culture: bibliography in Konstan 2007, Graver 2007; Chaniotis 2011 and 2012.

things (οὐδεὶς βουλεύεται περὶ τῶν ἀνελπίστων). The inverse definition of *tharsos*, inserted in the same cluster of concepts (*elpis, soteria*), is
given in the same formalized intellectual terms (1383a 16–20):

> τό τε γὰρ θάρσος τὸ ἐναντίον τῷ ⟨φόβῳ, καὶ τὸ θαρραλέον
> τῷ⟩ φοβερῷ, ὥστε μετὰ φαντασίας ἡ ἐλπὶς τῶν σωτηρίων
> ὡς ἐγγὺς ὄντων, τῶν δὲ φοβερῶν ⟨ὡς⟩ ἢ μὴ ὄντων ἢ πόρρω
> ὄντων. ἔστι δὲ θαρραλέα τά τε δεινὰ πόρρω ὄντα καὶ τὰ
> σωτήρια ἐγγύς,

> Confidence is the opposite of fear, and what causes it is the
> opposite of what causes fear; it is, therefore, the expecta-
> tion associated with a mental picture of the nearness of
> what keeps us safe and the absence or remoteness of what
> is terrible: confidence may be due either to the absence of
> what causes alarm or to the near presence of what keeps
> us safe.

The reason for *tharsos* is the consciousness, even at a very intuitive
level, that one's resources are enough to confront the imminent danger
with hope of salvation. Philosophers often consider *tharsos* a permanent virtue.[7] Outside ethical treatises, however, it is usually a sudden
impulse that changes one's mind in a specific situation. As Konstan
and Smoes demonstrate in their studies on courage in ancient Greece
(their findings are confirmed by a TLG search), *tharsos* most commonly
appears in military contexts: soldiers need to be confident that they are
superior to the enemy.[8] There are also interesting cases of *tharsein*'s use
as a quasi-technical legal term guaranteeing immunity from punishment, with the implied nuance: "do not worry, the city is protecting
you."[9] But the expression is not restricted to the extreme cases of life

---

[7] E.g. Democr. fr. 215 DK, Plat. *Prot.* 359a; Aristotle in the *Ethics* treats *tharsos* more as
a virtue than as an emotion; cf. Taylor 2008: 281–294, Garver 1982. On Stoicism, cf. Graver
2007:213–220.

[8] Konstan 2007:129–155; Smoes 1995: 231–239. E.g. Tyrt. fr. 11.2 West, Plut. *Them.* 8.2,
Polyb. 3.54.2, D. S. 19.58.6, 17.25.4. Further examples in Spicq 1978:368–369.

[9] Cf. two Elean decrees of the 6th–5th century BC (*Inscr. Él. Dial.* 9 and 20 Minon)
where individuals are granted legal protection (*tharros, tharren*), along with their families
and properties.

and death. In its transitive uses, very common in epistles, *tharsein* means that the recipient should trust in the benevolence of the letter-writer, i.e. it assuages the implicit concern that he is not benevolent.[10] It need not counter a terrible fear, but just a slight uneasiness (like the English "I'm afraid that ... don't worry"). It may even be used in a very banal sense in normal conversation, as in the case of a character in Plato: "Protagoras spends lots of time inside, so, don't worry (θάρρει), we shall find him inside."[11]

Tharsos, therefore, is not perceived as a specifically religious emotion. This needs to be noted since there has sometimes been a scholarly tendency to see a hidden religious meaning in all its instances (e.g. novels or comedy, as we shall see). Confidence (and fear) can, of course, be felt in secular contexts. Its interest within the context of religious experience lies precisely in the fact that a common emotion becomes an encounter with the divine when a god is the agent who instils *tharsos.* Doubtless, divine protection presupposes an extreme threat: death, illness, or destruction. Nonetheless, the religious *tharsein* implies the same components as the general emotion described by Aristotle: the god's help in countering an approaching danger (often a situation of military need) is promised and the mortal, conscious of that help, will hope for salvation and feel *tharsos.* Since it is the presence of a god that provokes the experience of *tharsein,* it is no wonder that in religious contexts the verb is most frequently found in the imperative form, spoken by a god or a divinely inspired man. In these contexts, it means not only "take heart!", but "take heart, for there is a god with you!" Just as in legal contexts when the polis ensures immunity, the verb *tharsein* also acquires a technical ring when it expresses divine protection. The mortal can be confident because he trusts the god.

II. *THARSEIN* AS A RELIGIOUS TERM

With this conceptual paradigm in mind, let us now examine the sources in which *tharsein* appears as a religious term. These can be grouped into

---

[10] Spicq 1978:367n2 gives several examples from papyri (e.g. *P. Oxy.* 1468.9, 1872.4).

[11] Plat. *Protag.* 311a6. This conversational *tharsei* appears often in Theocritus' *Idylls*: 15.13, 15.56, 15.73.

four categories: inscriptions in funerary contexts; inscriptions from sacred spaces; records of priestly utterances; and religious literature.[12] The most important pieces of evidence, dating from Imperial times, have been studied separately in some depth, but there has not yet been a comprehensive treatment of all the evidence, nor a study of why and how *tharsein* is used in different contexts. I omit for the moment the early poetic instances in which *tharsein* appears in relation to the divine, but, as we will see later, it is in the poetic tradition that the interpretative key to these later instances lies.

II.1 Funerary Inscriptions and Gold Tablets

The formula θάρσει, (name), οὐδεὶς ἀθάνατος ("take heart, X, nobody is immortal") occurs frequently, in diverse variants, in Imperial funerary inscriptions from all over the Roman Empire, but especially from the Eastern regions, from which it spread to the West and to Rome.[13] The funerary contexts of these inscriptions are pagan, Jewish, and Christian, so the formula is independent of religious affiliation. Correspondingly, the meaning of the formula is not identical in every case, and scholars have debated for a century about the contradictory beliefs that it seems to imply, even when due allowance is made for the importance of convention in funerary inscriptions. In some contexts the deceased is given a standard consolation; a reminder that everybody is subject to death.[14] The hope of afterlife is not present, and sometimes it is even explicitly denied. These cases, then, may

---

[12] With this division I do not claim to definitively classify all the possible evidence, although I know no case that would not fit into at least one of these sets. I only give the most representative examples of each one, without any attempt at exhaustiveness.

[13] Graf and Johnston 2013:208–212. Sometimes only *tharsei* appears, and other grounds for the consolation follow (e.g. "after your death, your husband will follow you to Hades" *EBGR* 2001:151; cf. also note 49 below). There are also instances with synonyms like εὐψύχει or μὴ λυπῆς, and some modifications of the formula (e.g. the Christian innovation "nobody is immortal on earth": cf. Spicq 1978:370n4). Many examples and bibliography are listed in Lattimore 1962:231, 253, 256; Park 2000:47–62; Blumell 2011:166.

[14] This is the most common meaning of the pagan θ.o.α. inscriptions and alike: cf. Lattimore 1962:250–256. Park 2000:47–63 shows that this is also the case in most Jewish instances. Human mortality is a key topos of the letters of condolence preserved in Greek papyri (cf. Chapa 1998).

be interpreted as straightforwardly profane consolations. However, in many other instances, particularly (but not only) in the Christian examples, the inscriptions aim to give encouragement to the dead person as he embarks upon his *post-mortem* existence.[15]

The latter is clearly the case in eleven gold lamellae with this formula found in Palestinian graves of the second to third century AD. Buried with the corpse, these leaves were intended to accompany the deceased.[16] We cannot know if they belonged to a specific religious group, since they are compatible with pagan, Jewish, or Christian contexts. However, the use of a gold tablet as a *vademecum* for the after-life has affinities with the "Orphic" lamellae of earlier centuries, as Graf and Johnston have recently suggested.[17] The connection seems to be reinforced by the fact that four tablets, instead of the personal name, address the deceased as "noble," Eugene. Rather than an appellative for deceased women, this title may apply to the soul in the feminine, as is the case in several Orphic gold tablets.[18] As we shall see, although in the published Orphic leaves there is no *tharsei* formula, the poetic texts which they contain present the sort of situations in which it is frequently found, so it is plausible to think that this exhortation to the deceased derived from earlier eschatological poetry.

---

[15] This was demonstrated by Simon 1936 (Simon 1981:vi–vii acknowledges that he followed the advice of Franz Cumont for this, his first article; Cumont 1942:76 applies his conclusions to a Roman pagan inscription under a funerary relief of the Dioscuri). In these cases, the "nobody is immortal" seems to refer just to the body.

[16] Graf and Johnston 2013:208–212 edit all Palestinian lamellae in an appendix of their new edition of the Orphic gold tablets. The first lamellae were published by Siebourg 1905; cf. Blumell 2011 with the last published lamella and earlier bibliography; Torallas Tovar 2013 shows that the equivalent formula μὴ λυπῆς appears also in some mummy cartonages (SB I 3514–3155 = *C. Étiq. Mom.* 231 TM 40311–40312), which suggests that the θ.ο.α. formula may also have been written on papyri and on clothes buried with the deceased for eschatological purposes.

[17] Graf and Johnston 2013:208–212. Kotansky 1991:116 had already linked them with earlier tablets which had healing and eschatological purposes.

[18] In three gold tablets from Thurii (*Orph. Fragm.* 488–490 Bernabé) the soul claims to come "pure from the pure" (ἐκ καθαρῶν καθαρά) and to be of divine lineage (ὑμῶν γένος ὄλβιον εὔχομαι εἶναι). This is the standard formula for proclaiming the nobility of one's lineage in epic (cf. Herrero de Jáuregui 2011a). In *Orph. Fragm.* 477.9 Bernabé, the heavenly lineage is indicated by a nickname, "Asterios," which could have the same function as Eugene.

II.2 Entering Sacred Space

Different forms of the verb *tharsein* or words with the same root also appear in inscriptions situated in sacred places, apparently marking the entrance into the *temenos*. For instance, a poetic inscription from Lindos of the third century AD says:[19]

> You have set foot on a path filled with true virtue leading to Olympus. Therefore enter the sanctuary confidently (εἴσιθι θαρραλέως), stranger, if you are pure. But if you bring harm, leave this harmless temple and go off, wherever you wish, away from the sanctuary of Pallas.

A prose inscription from Commagene (first century BC) is similar in its content:[20]

> Those whose minds are pure of unrighteous living and who eagerly pursue pious deeds, let them look confidently (θαρροῦντες ἀποβλεπέτωσαν) on the countenances of the gods, let them tread (ἐπιβαινέτωσαν) in the benign footsteps of the blessed immortals and let them by honoring us conduct a good life on a happy path (εὐδαίμοσιν ἀτραποῖς) to the fulfillment of their hopes (εἰς ἐλπίδας ὁδηγείτωσαν ἰδίας).

These two examples are sufficient for understanding what *tharsein* implies in these contexts.[21] Fear in approaching the sacred is a widespread, not to say universal, experience, and being in the presence of the deity requires confidence that one will not be punished for impurity. These inscriptions underline the presence of the god inside the *temenos* and aim to distinguish the pure from the impure; those who dare to enter from the rest. Let us note that in these two instances the

[19] LSS no. 91.23–26. Cf. Dickie 2004a:582.

[20] Text (following H. Waldmann's edition of 1974) and references in Dickie 2004a:583–584 (his translation).

[21] The inscriptions with the "enter with confidence" formula are studied by Dickie 2004a:581–587, who is concerned "with the form, not the content" (p. 580): the present study seeks to complement his work by studying the content. Cf. Chaniotis 2012 on the "fear of god" alluded to in several inscriptions.

spatial conception extends beyond the physicality of the *temenos*: the *sacra via* is equated to the path of life, and entrance into the temple is associated with living in the company of the gods.

II.3 Liturgical Exhortations

The third category of evidence consists of *testimonia* in which priests of different cults exhort the participants to *tharsein*. In some of them, in fact, the priestly proclamation seems to convey a message very similar to that in the aforementioned inscriptions, inviting the pure and/or initiated to come, i.e. to enter a sacred sphere where they officiate. As Dickie has demonstrated, Julian's caricature of Jesus as an initiator in *Caesars* imitates the pagan priestly proclamations in formal expressions like "whoever is a sinner ... let him proceed in full confidence (ἴτω θαρρῶν), for I shall straightaway make him pure with this water here ..."[22]

Other ritual exhortations may have had a different sense. As some scholars have pointed out, there is reason to suppose that the *tharsei* of the funerary inscriptions was taken from burial liturgies.[23] However, it is well known that in Christianity and in several mystery cults encouragement in confronting death is not restricted to the funerary ritual. Although there is actually little information from the inside, on account of the secrecy surrounding mysteries, there is evidence that in the ordeals imposed on initiates by various mystic cults *tharsei(te)* was the exhortation used to encourage them to confidently bear that terror or pain.[24] In addition, as an extension of encouragement against fear, *tharsein* seems to have implied confidence in a happy afterlife, as is apparent in a famous testimony by the late Christian apologist Firmicus Maternus (*De err. prof. rel.* 22.1: Forbes' translation modified):

---

[22] Iul. *Caes.* 38.3361a–b. Cf. Dickie 2004a:579–580. Some of the "dice" and "alphabetical oracles" from Asia Minor in Imperial Age, collected by Nollé 2007, contain similar expressions in order to insufflate trust in their users (Chaniotis 2012:206n3).

[23] Graf and Johnston 2013:211, based on IG XIV 2342 and on some Latin inscriptions where the formula appears in Greek. For its use in Christian liturgy, cf. note 37.

[24] Merkelbach 1995: 164–165, 345. On the "terror and relief" experiences of the mysteries, the *locus classicus* is Plutarch fr. 168 Sandbach. Mithraism is also well-known for submitting initiates to proofs of pain and terror (cf. Gordon 2009:308–310).

Let us advance also another *symbolum*, in order that the
crimes of polluted thought may become clear; one which
must be described in detail, to let everyone agree on the
corruption brought to the law of the divine plan by the
devil's perverse imitation. On a certain night a statue is
laid flat on its back on a bier, where it is bemoaned with
cadenced lamentations. Then when the worshipers
have satisfied themselves with the due plaints, a light is
brought in. Next a priest anoints the throats of all who
were mourning, and once that is done he whispers in a
low murmur: "Take heart, you initiates! The god has been
saved. There will be salvation from sufferings for us"
(θαρρεῖτε, μύσται, τοῦ θεοῦ σεσωσμένου / ἔσται γὰρ ἡμῖν
ἐκ πόνων σωτηρία).

Firmicus does not say to which mysteries this *symbolon* belongs, and
there has been some debate about the question; Osiris, Attis, and
Eleusis being the most popular candidates.[25] In the search for this cult,
scholars have collected references in other texts which show clearly
that *tharsein* was part of the *legomena* of mystic cults already in classical times, whether or not they are the source of Firmicus' *symbolon*.
Joly drew attention to its presence among other unmistakably mystical
terms related to the afterlife in Plato's *Phaedo*: "a man who dedicates his
life to true philosophy should be confident when he is going to die and
have good hope (θαρρεῖν μέλλων ἀποθανεῖσθαι καὶ εὔελπις εἶναι) that
there will be the greatest goods there when he dies."[26] This terminology

[25] Simon 1936 proposed Osiris, while Joly 1955 preferred Eleusis: both postulated
a common origin for the funerary formula θ.ο.α. implying afterlife and for Firmicus'
symbolon (which is an improbable assumption). Cumont 1949:404 related the *symbolon*
to Pythagoreanism on the grounds of its resemblance to Carm. Aur. 64 (discussed below),
which is also implausible. Podeman Sorensen 1989, after a wave of scholarship in favor
of Attis, has tipped the balance again in favor of Osiris cult on the basis of similarities
between Firmicus' ritual and Osirian texts. The cult, however, could already be under
Christian influence (cf. note 100).

[26] Plat. *Phaed.* 63e–64a; cf. also 88b, 114d, 115e, where *tharrein* refers to hope in the
afterlife. Joly 1955:168–169 thought exclusively of Eleusinian influence. However, the
utterance may (also) come from Orphic/Bacchic mysteries, to which the *Phaedo* alludes in
69c, and which also seem to have used the term, as we shall see.

was very probably part of mystical discourses in Eleusinian and Bacchic rites, with which Plato was undoubtedly familiar. Either as a result of their influence or independently, other cults (e.g. Trophonius' oracle in Lebadea) also seem to have included an exhortation to *tharsein*.[27]

II.4 Religious Literature

In my fourth category of evidence I include literature from different religions of Imperial times which aims to present an accurate and serious account of how the gods intervene in human lives. In these cases, the word is mainly related to the manifestation of the divinity (epiphany), which often aims to fill men with confidence against different kinds of fear. The most immediate fear is that inspired by the awesome presence of the god himself, and his θάρσει implies his benevolence.[28] In an inscribed aretalogy of Isis in Maronea (1st–2nd century BC) we find the same expression of confidence in approaching the sacred that characterizes inscriptions marking the entrance into the *temenos*:[29]

> I am convinced that you will be absolutely with me (πείθομαι δὲ πάντως σε παρέσεσθαι). For if you came when called about my salvation (σωτηρία), how could you not come in a matter concerning your own honor? I will therefore proceed in confidence with respect to what is left

[27] Bonnechere 2003:206–208 sees a parody of a Lebadean *legomenon* in the repetition of θάρρει in an initiatory context in Aristoph. *Nub.* 141, 422, 427, 436, 490 (just before the parody of the Trophonian descent in 506–608), and in Luc. *Menipp.* 22; Byl 2007:21–22 sees many passages of the *Clouds*, including these, as reflections of Eleusinian initiation. Parodies like these reflect, in my opinion, generic mystical language rather than a specific cult.

[28] The god who will never ease the mind of men who experience his presence is the god Pan, often identified with Phobos (cf. Borgeaud 1988:88–116). A Hellenistic epigram to Pan (IG IX² 1, 253, commented on by Chaniotis 2012:206–207) says: "who can approach you with confidence (προσπελάσαι θαρρῶν), even if bringing you sacrificial animals? You are by nature entirely wild (πάμπαν ἀγρεῖος ἔφυς)." Cf. also Call. *Ep.* 44 Pf. = *AP* 12.139.

[29] *I. Thrac. Aeg.* 205. Cf. Grandjean 1975:42–43; Chaniotis 2011:269–270. The mention of divine encouragement in Isidorus' *Hymn to Isis* (SEG 8.550.18: ὀλίγοισι δὲ θάρσος ἔδωκε, cf. Vanderlip 1972:49) seems closer to the following examples where a god encourages his troubled devotees in military matters.

(θαρρῶν οὖν πορεύομαι πρὸς τὰ λοιπά), knowing that it is the mind of god that praises, and the hands of man write.

The inscribed character of this text increases its resemblance to the aforementioned inscriptions: the act of speaking and writing is also assimilated to a spatial journey in which one crosses the boundary into the sacred "in confidence."[30] At the same time, the declaration of trust in the god gives the text a divine authority notwithstanding the human mediation.

Divine assistance, however, often goes beyond benevolent presence, and is actively helpful in times of trouble. One of the most typical instances of this kind of *tharsein* is provided by the so-called Lindian Chronicle, an inscription of the 1st century BC which, in the last part, recalls three local epiphanies of the goddess Athena. The first epiphany took place when Darius' Persian army was besieging the city:[31]

> On account of the lack of water, the Lindians, being worn down, were of a mind to surrender the city to the enemy. During this time, the goddess, standing over one of the rulers in his sleep, called upon him to be bold (ἐνὶ τῶν ἀρχόντων ἐπιστᾶσα καθ' ὕπνον παρεκάλει θαρσεῖν), since she was about to ask her father for the much-needed water for them. After he had seen the vision, he announced to the citizens the command of Athena.

The Chronicle goes on to say that they requested a truce for five days. On the fifth it rained over the acropolis, and the Persians understood that the city was protected by the gods and made a truce. Several local written sources are cited as authorities for this tale, as for the other accounts in this inscription dedicated to glorification of the Lindian

---

[30] A sovereign could use this kind of vocabulary in granting protection so that people would be encouraged to speak, like Octavius to the Rhosians (*IGLS* 718.93): "As I am going to do everything possible for you all the more gladly on account of Seleucus, address me with confidence concerning the matters you desire" (θαρροῦντες περὶ ὧν ἂν βούλεσθε πρός με ἀποστέλλετε). Cf. Raggi 2004:134.

[31] *I. Lindos* 2 D 1, edited and commented by Higbie 2003, who notes on page 143 that the writing of -ρσ- in θαρσεῖν contrasts with -ρρ- in γέρρα in B23: this may reflect the influence of epic, where -ρσ- is regularly kept, on the original accounts of the epiphany.

past. It is a traditional epiphanic tale, like that in Herodotus about the dream of Egyptian King Sethos, when he was threatened by an Arabian invasion: "sleep came over him and it seemed to him that the god, standing over him, told him to have courage (ἐν τῇ ὄψι ἐπιστάντα τὸν θεὸν θαρσύνειν)."[32] An even closer parallel is provided by Plutarch, who cites a stele reporting that when the Cyzicenians were attacked by Mithridates Athena helped them: in a dream the goddess stood beside (παραστᾶσα) Aristagoras, the clerk of the town; "I have come," she said, "leading the Lybian fluteplayer against the Pontic trumpeter. Tell the citizens to have courage (θαρρεῖν)."[33] Tales of this kind, as we shall see, owe much to the epic tradition, and even when they are summarized in a later prose account, a poetic scene in all probability underlies the epiphanic tale.

However, this use of the verb *tharsein* in epiphanic contexts is not restricted to traditional poetry or archaizing history. It is also found in the literary presentations of two major religious figures of Imperial times: Apollonius in Philostratus' *Life* and Jesus in the Gospels. The *Life of Apollonius* presents him as a *theios aner*, who behaves and speaks as one who is divinely inspired.[34] It is not surprising, therefore, to find him speaking with these words to a woman who is afraid that a daemon will kill her son (3.38.3): "take heart, for he will not kill him when he reads this" (θάρσει, οὐ γὰρ ἀποκτενεῖ αὐτὸν ἀναγνοὺς ταῦτα). And he produced a letter from his pocket and gave it to the woman. It was addressed to the spirit with threats and rebukes." Apollonius' power, it is implied, is superior to the daemon, and his help in the spiritual fight should bring *tharsos* to the woman. In another passage he announces his healing powers to the Ephesians with this term, when he cures the city from a plague (4.10.1): θαρσεῖτε, ἔφη, τήμερον γὰρ παύσω τὴν

---

[32] Hdt. 2.141.3. Cf. Higbie 2003:281.

[33] Plut. *Lucullus* 10.2. Cf. Higbie 2003:274

[34] On late antique *theioi andres*, cf. Anderson 1994, esp. pages 76-85 on "the rhetoric of revelation." For our purposes the debate around the historical or fictional nature of Philostratus' work (or the Gospels) is not relevant, since it is impossible (and largely unimportant) to know whether Apollonius (or Jesus) really uttered *tharsei* or any similar word. The "truthful fiction" that Philostratus aims to construct (cf. Francis 1998) marks his work as religious literature.

νόσον ("take heart, for today I will end the plague"). It is noteworthy that the utterance θάρσει itself does not bring about the healing, which will come later following the defeat of another daemon. Rather it aims to act upon the souls of the addressees, filling them with confidence that the miracle will come owing to the exceptional power of the speaker. The imperative θάρσει acts upon the soul of the addressee as a persuasive word (πιθανὸς λόγος) rather than as an enchantment (ἐποιδή), and the grounds on which it persuades (as in shown in the γάρ clauses) are that the speaker is invested with divine authority.[35] In 7.38 Apollonius is in prison and shows Damis that he can free himself from his chains "inmediately" (ἄρτι), saying "I have given you a proof of my own freedom, so take heart (θάρρει)," whereby Damis "first understood that Apollonius' nature was godlike and more than human." In other passages Apollonius addresses people with imperatives and the participle of *tharsein*, in a similar tone to the aforementioned priestly proclamations: He instructs his followers ἴτε θαρροῦντες (5.43.2), explicitly appropriating the utterance made by the Eleans to participants in the Olympic games. Even more clearly, when installed in Asclepius' sanctuary, he tells the governor of Cilicia that if he has noble thoughts he can "approach the god in confidence and make any prayer you want" (1.12: χώρει θαρρῶν παρὰ τὸν θεόν καὶ εὔχου ὅ τι ἐθέλεις). Dickie has rightly said that "since he performs a priestlike role in the sanctuary, he is made to speak in the manner of a priest."[36]

The imperative of *tharsein* is again loaded with the authority of the divine in some key passages in the Gospels where Jesus shows his divinity: Matthew 9:2: "take heart, child, your sins are forgiven" (θάρσει, τέκνον· ἀφίενταί σου αἱ ἁμαρτίαι); Matthew 9:22: "take heart,

---

[35] Cf. Laín Entralgo 1956:88–105, 152 for the distinction between these two therapeutic terms. In the instances where θάρσει is uttered in healing contexts (Hom. *Il.* 15.254, Isyllus 74, discussed below), it is always justified by divine authority, not used as a magical word. This is perhaps the reason that θάρσει does not appear with particular frequency in Epidaurian *iamata* or in magical papyri: cf. note 52 *infra*.

[36] Cf. Dickie 2004a:584, where he also comments on the encouragement which Apollonius gives a pipe-player (*VA* 5.21: "if you can exhibit all this, Canus, have no fear about playing (θαρρῶν αὔλει), since Euterpe will be with you"): "he speaks in the register of a religious official telling the worshipper that he may approach the god in full confidence of winning his help if he fulfills the requirements imposed by the gods."

daughter, your faith has saved you" (θάρσει, θύγατερ· ἡ πίστις σου σέσωκέν σε);[37] Matthew 14:27 (= Mark 6:50): "they all saw him and trembled. But he spoke to them and said: take heart, it is me, do not fear" (θαρσεῖτε, ἐγώ εἰμι· μὴ φοβεῖσθε); John 16:33: "take heart, I have vanquished the world" (θαρσεῖτε, ἐγὼ νενίκηκα τὸν κόσμον); Luke 23:43 (D):[38] "take heart! today you will be with me in Paradise" (θάρσει. σήμερον μετ' ἐμοῦ ἔσῃ ἐν τῷ παραδείσῳ). All these sentences issue from the lips of Jesus except one (Mark 10:49), in which he delegates his divine word when summoning a blind man who is invoking him: "Jesus said 'call him'; and they called the blind man telling him: 'take heart, wake up, he calls you.'" (στὰς ὁ Ἰησοῦς εἶπεν, φωνήσατε αὐτόν. καὶ φωνοῦσιν τὸν τυφλὸν λέγοντες αὐτῷ, θάρσει, ἔγειρε, φωνεῖ σε). In the only appearance of the word in Acts (23:11), it is also Christ who speaks to Paul: "the next night the Lord appeared to him (ἐπιστὰς αὐτῷ) and said, 'take heart! (θάρσει) for as you gave testimony of me in Jerusalem, you must bear witness to me in Rome.'" The imperative θάρσει in these passages from the Gospels, as in those from the *Life of Apollonius*, is a marker of divinity, an epiphanic utterance that comes only as the spoken word of God at a close physical distance. By contrast, the imperative θάρσει never appears in the New Testament epistles, despite their abundant hortatory passages.[39]

---

[37] Commentators agree that Matthew added θάρσει in 9:2 and 9:22 (in the equivalent passages in Mark 2:5, 5:34; Luke 5:20, 8:48 the word is absent). According to Simon 1936:200 the addition of θάρσει shows that it was already in use as a liturgical utterances at the time of the writing of his Gospel, as in the mysteries. However, the only proof of *tharsein* in Christian liturgy (funerary context) is in the 4th cent. AD: John Chrys. *Orat. de Sanctis Bernice et Prosdoce*, PG 50.2.364), and a Coptic apocryphal Gospel (Simon 1936:205–206). Matthew's addition may simply be due to the wish to underline Jesus' divine authority.

[38] This is a variant reading according to the Beza Codex: the vulgate version has ἀμήν σοι λέγω, which is also an authoritative expression often uttered by Jesus. The juxtaposition with τήμερον makes it similar to Philostr. *VA* 4.10 as a prophetic announcement on the day of salvation. It follows a declaration by the addressee that he is fearful of God (Luke 23:40).

[39] Spicq 1978:367–371 is more complete than the several entries for *tharsos / tharrein* in the New Testament dictionaries, or the commentaries to these Gospel passages. For the Pauline letters, cf. note 43 *infra*.

This presence of θάρσει in the Gospels is doubtless due to the epiphanic connotations of the term in the Hellenistic environment in which they were written. However, we should not forget another important reason, namely, that the imperative θάρσει also serves as a translation of the Hebrew (*'al* + a form of *yârê*) in the Septuagint. In these passages, the people of Israel, whether invoked directly or through metonymy as "Jerusalem," are told to maintain courage in some difficult situation (e.g. before the Red Sea in Exodus 14:13). The collective exhortation to courage is typical of military harangues, but in the Bible the justification is always religious, and is thereby assimilated to prophetic exhortations: God is on their side.[40] Some individuals are also exhorted to *tharsein,* in contexts of a very dangerous, deadly threat, against which God's help will protect them.[41]

Given this Scriptural background, it is unsurprising that *tharsein* was adopted in the religious lexicon of Hellenistic Judaism, especially by Philo, and by Christian authors.[42] In their works, the philosophical virtue of *tharsos* is given a religious signification as a permanent trait of the faithful Jew or Christian. In the Pauline corpus, there are two examples. The Epistle to the Hebrews (13:6) says: "we can say with confidence (θαρροῦντας): 'the Lord is my help, I will not be afraid.'" The confidence to speak about the god which was a punctual state of the mind in the aforementioned Isis' aretalogy is now a perennial characteristic of the Christian. Likewise, the Second Epistle to the Corinthians (5:6–8) expresses trust in God's promise of a better

---

[40] Some exhortations are in the plural (θαρσεῖτε), addressed to the people of Israel in times of distress: Exod. 14:13, 20:21; Jth. 7:30; Hag. 2:5; Zech. 8:13, 8:15; Bar. 4:5, 4:21, 4:27. This tone of military exhortation is similar to the prophetic passages that address Sion or the whole universe with θάρσει in order to give hope in God's future help: Joel 2:21–22; Zeph. 3:16; Bar. 4:30. I follow Rahlfs' text of the Septuagint.

[41] 1 Kings 17:13 (Elijah to a widow); Esther 5:7; Jth. 11:1–3 (a king to a suppliant woman); Tob. 5:10 (an angel to Tobiah); Dan. 6:17 (King Dareius to Daniel, in an ironic sense); it is also uttered as a kind of blessing between close relatives: Tob. 7:17, 8:21, 11:11; 4 Macc. 13:11, 17.4; in Gen. 35:17 (a midwife to Rachel) it is uttered in the moment of the transition to death. Eccles. 19:10 is the only passage in which it has a non-religious sense: "stay quiet."

[42] Cf. *Joseph and Aseneth* 15.2.3.5; *Henoch* 102.4. Phil. *Vit. Mos.* 2.252; Phil. *Rer. Div.* 22, 28; *Spec.* 1.270. For the presence of *tharrein* in Patristic literature (e.g. Clem. Alex. *Protr.* 2.121.2 Stählin), cf. Lampe s.v.

afterlife with these words: "So we are *always* confident (θαρροῦντες οὖν πάντοτε), and we know that while we are at home in the body we are away from the Lord, for we walk by faith, not by sight. Yes, we are confident (θαρροῦμεν), and we would rather be away from the body and at home with the Lord."[43]

The convergence of religion and popular philosophy in the term *tharsein* is by no means restricted to Judaism and Christianity. Ethical texts may acquire religious overtones, as when Epictetus, after hearing all the correct answers from his disciple, tells him to "go in confidently and remembering everything" (ἄπ[ε]ιθι λοιπὸν ἔσω θαρρῶν καὶ μεμνημένος τούτων).[44] The roughly contemporary *Tabula of Cebes* contains an allegorical image where "Self-Control and Perseverance encourage those who arrive to be confident (παρακαλοῦσιν τοὺς παραγινομένους ἐπὶ τὸν τόπον θαρρεῖν) and not to shrink back, saying that they must persevere yet a little longer and then they will come to the good path." An exhortation to *tharsein* with a language so close to initiatory utterances has led some scholars to suppose that the *Tabula* is a mystical text with an eschatological meaning—which seems unlikely.[45] As we shall see, earlier poetic texts such as Empedocles' fragments or the Pythagorean *Golden Verses* already include such exhortations within the broader image of philosophical knowledge as an initiatory process.

Similarly, non-philosophical literature may have made use of the sacred resonances of the imperative θάρσει for a range of purposes,

---

[43] The many commentators on this passage (e.g. Thrall 2004:385; cf. Lindgard 2005:185–188 with bibliography) stress the relation to Stoic courage before death. Spicq 1978 focuses instead on the eschatological context, relating it to PGM IV, 718-724 P-H. This epistle also provides the two other attestations of the verb in the Pauline letters, in the description of Paul's relation to the addressees: 2 Cor 10:1–2 (θαρρῶ εἰς ὑμᾶς) perhaps in relation to *parrhesia* (cf. note 98); 2 Cor. 7:16 (ἐν παντὶ θαρρῶ ἐν ὑμῖν).

[44] Epict. *Diss.* 1.30.5. Cf. Graver 2007:213–220 on Epictetus' *tharrein* compared to Cicero's *confidere*.

[45] *Ceb. Tab.* 16.3; also in 30.2: "what the Daimon commands those entering Life to do; to be confident (θαρρεῖν)." Joly 1963:46–47 sees these passages as cryptically referring to the afterlife, in consonance with his theory that the whole work is a mystical Pythagorean text. Fitzgerald and White 1983:148–149, 159–160 are more cautious (like Joly's reviewers, cf. *CR* 14, 1964:38–39), and interpret these texts in the light of Stoic recommendations to *tharrein*.

from solemnity to parody. Authors like Aristophanes, Theocritus or Lucian clearly imitate the *tharsein* of mysteries and priestly proclamations.[46] In many other literary texts an exhortation θάρσει is uttered in contexts of confrontation with death or to express the hope in divine help, which may sometimes echo its religious use.[47] Indeed, where para-religious language is most conspicuous, it may cause confusion about the true nature of the text, as happened above all with the Greek novel: Merkelbach, following up Kerényi's idea, always considered the Greek novel as a mystically encrypted text written by initiates for initiates, and the ubiquitous presence of *tharsein* in Greek novels would be a consequence of this mystical language. Mainstream scholarship, however, has not pursued this extreme thesis. It is much more probable that the novel just uses the atmosphere and aesthetics of mystery cults for its literary purposes, rather than taking the ritual as a script to follow.[48] Hence, the exhortations to *tharsein*, which are appropriate for the dangerous situations undergone by the characters, need not be interpreted as purposive mystical utterances.

Tharsein, therefore, is present in a great variety of religious contexts, not always evidently related to each other, and sometimes even in apparent contradiction: fear of the god and entrance into the *temenos*; hope for immortality and consolation for death; manifestation of divine power and delegation of such power to a mortal; written recording on stone and liturgical oral performance; private, public, and

---

[46] Theocr. *Epigr.* 19 (*AP* 13.3); Luc. *Alex.* 38; cf. Dickie 2004a, 579–587. Cf. also note 27 *supra* for passages with *tharrein* in Aristophanes and Lucian which have been seen as parodies of mystical *legomena*.

[47] Soph. *El.* 174: θάρσει μοι, θάρσει, τέκνον· ἔτι μέγας οὐρανῷ / Ζεύς, ὃς ἐφορᾷ πάντα καὶ κρατύνει. Joseph. *AJ* 7.266 is similar to the θάρσει of the historical books of the Old Testament.

[48] Merkelbach 1962:100, 141, 173, 212, 231; he insisted on this idea in later works: 1988:52–53, 175; 1995:362. Henrichs 2006 evaluates Kerényi's and Merkelbach's positions. For a sound position on the novel and mystery cults, see Burkert 1987: 66–67, and Dowden 2005. Chariton's *Chaereas and Callirhoe* 3.6.4, for example, plays humorously with the poetic and religious tradition of the epiphanic θάρσει which assuages fear of the manifest god (cf. Dickie 2004b:168). Going further than Merkelbach, and with even less success, Keuls 1969 proposed extending his theory to New Comedy, so that Menander's *Dyskolos* would follow the script of an Orphic-Dionysiac mystic cult: on page 217 she interprets the θάρρει of *Dysc.* 692 along these lines.

literary contexts, relating to pagan, Jewish and Christian beliefs. The common ground, however, for these diverse situations is the formal paradigm indicated above: the god gives protection from a precise danger or an imprecise risk—even that caused by the frightening proximity of the divine—and the trust in this god allows the mortal to be confident. In these Hellenistic and imperial contexts the precise sense of the words seems to be taken for granted, as if the simple utterance of the word brought with it all its implications. By contrast, we shall see that in poems from archaic and classical times the scenes in which the term *tharsein* is employed are fully developed, offering an opportunity for considering all the nuances of the term. In fact, some of the instances examined above (e.g. the Lindian Chronicle) derive directly or indirectly from earlier poetry.[49] The trust in divine help expressed by *tharsein* is heavily mediated by the poetic tradition, which is a powerful agent of religious experience. Poetry had been the privileged medium for religious discourse in archaic times and even later; in later religion, it served as a key referent and model for shaping the representation of the divine, up to late antiquity. Indeed, the study of the term *tharsein*, will prove once again that Herodotus was right about Homer and Hesiod having taught the Greeks what the gods are like.[50]

III. HOMER

There has been scarce work on *tharsein* as a religious emotion in Homer. Only Kullmann in a book of 1956 discussed how gods instill *tharsos* (and other emotions) into men among other examples of "Wirken der Götter," within the context of the lively contemporary debate on the free will of mortals vs. divine determination. In the divine "Paränesis," whereby courage is instilled in mortals without necessarily forcing them to act in a certain way, Kullmann saw a Homeric effort to

---

[49] Of course, many late texts play with the presupposed knowledge of earlier poetry: e.g. *CIG* 6438 (εὐψύχει, Μίδων, οὐδεὶς ἀθανάτος. καὶ ὁ Ἡρακλῆς ἀπέθανε) is a clear reference to *Il.* 18.117–118: "even Heracles died." For some funerary epigrams containing the verb *tharsein*, see Merkelbach and Stauber I 6/02/32, IV 20/11/06, 21/12/02.

[50] Hdt. 2.53; *a contrario*, the same is said by Xenophanes (B 14–16 DK).

incorporate "magical" conceptions within a "higher" religious ideology.[51] Despite its outdated terminology, Kullmann's formulation is still useful in drawing attention to the fact that in Homer, as we shall see, *tharsein* results from trust in divine help, not from any magic power with which it is associated. Yet there is no need to postulate a magical use of *tharsein* prior or contemporary to Homer or to maintain that Homer "invented" its religious use.[52] There are also many important passages and relevant questions pertaining to Homeric *tharsein* which Kullmann did not consider. Furthermore, although a divine θάρσει always occurs in epiphanic contexts, the frequent studies of epiphany up to this day have focused so exclusively on what mortals perceive as the image of the god that the circumstances of the utterance from a god, and mortals' reactions to it, have not been explored.[53]

There are fifteen instances of the utterance θάρσει in Homer and a few other expressions in which an imperative is accompanied by a *thars-* word.[54] It is always the starting word of a solemn speech, and in a

[51] Kullmann 1956:68–82 on the "göttlicher Impuls"; page 73: "der Ausdruck wird aus der volkstümlichen Sprache stammen. Er dient nur zur Charakterisierung göttlichen Wirkens"; page 78: "bei jedem einzelnen Eingreifen der Gottheit die Freiheit des Menschen nicht gänzlich ausscheiden"; page 119 on Paränesis: "für den vor Homer noch keine Vorbilder gab, und den wir daher als spezifisch homerisch ansprechen müssen." Of the Homeric passages analyzed below, he discusses *Il.* 5.115–126 (pages 71, 120) and *Il.* 15.247–258 (pages 122–123).

[52] *Tharsein* does not appear in the hexametrical incantations studied in different articles by Faraone (e.g. 1996). Nor, even in later times, did the Homeric passages with *tharsein* acquire any prominence among Homeric lines reused for magic and healing purposes (cf. Collins 2008): in PMG VII. 200, *Il.* 10.383 appears among many others. *Il.* 24.171–175, Iris' exhortation to Priam beginning with *tharsei*, is written on a Roman grafitto (2nd–3rd cent. AD) with apotropaic purposes: cf. Faraone 1996:84–85, and Collins 2008:226–227. The fact that the whole passage is written shows that the first word by itself is not automatically effective as an ἐποιδή, but needs to be grounded in the entire episode to be persuasive (cf. note 35 *supra*).

[53] On epiphany, cf. Versnel 1987, Turkeltaub 2007, Platt 2011, with earlier bibliography and the monograph *Ill. Class. Stud.* 29 (2004), with, among other studies, Graf 2004 and Dickie 2004b.

[54] θάρσει: *Iliad* 4.184, 8.39, 10.383, 15.254, 18.463, 22.183, 24.171; *Odyssey* 2.372, 4.825, 8.197, 13.362, 16.436, 19.546, 22.372, 24.357. θάρσει also appears in one variant of a Ptolemaic papyrus of *Od.* 5.183 where Calypso encourages Odysseus after he expresses his fear of the journey. The verb fits well in the context and may reflect an ancient poetic variant. The other imperatives are *Il.* 5.124 (θαρσῶν νῦν μάχεσθαι), *Il.* 1.85 (θαρσήσας μάλα

metrically prominent position, at the beginning of the hexameter, since as the epic genre demands, such encouragement appears in extreme situations faced by heroes "sitting on the edge of death." [55] However, we must recall that we are not dealing with specifically religious terminology. *Tharsos* means self-confidence, and it appears in contexts of danger or apparent weakness, where fear would be the expected reaction. [56] All this is in agreement with the Aristotelian definition that sees it as a result of a rational calculation of the relative strength to confront a threat. The encouragement presupposes that the speaker possesses the power and authority to instill the confidence that the addressee lacks. It is crucial, therefore, to distinguish between mortal and divine instillers of *tharsos*: mortals need to base their encouragement on some rational ground, while gods may instill *tharsos* by their mere presence, which is an obvious bolster to confidence.

When a mortal says θάρσει to another mortal it is the knowledge specific to the particular situation that enables him to alleviate the addressee's fear: Menelaus knows where he has been injured so he eases Agamemnon's mind (*Il.* 4.184); Penelope is told in a dream by Odysseus that he is alive (*Od.* 19.546), and by her sister that Athena is accompanying Telemachus on his trip (*Od.* 4.825);[57] Telemachus calms Eurycleia by claiming that his journey is inspired by a god (*Od.*

εἰπέ). There is a very similar expression also in *Od.* 7.50, quoted below. The commentaries on these passages (and on those in the *Homeric Hymns* quoted below) do not analyze the term beyond pointing to the parallels. The metrical analysis of Hasenohr 1988 shows that these imperatives belong to a very ancient layer in the Homeric poems, even "un trait de style poétique de l'indoeuropéen commun" (page 91). Apart from the imperatives in paraenetic direct speech, the action of the god can be reported as a past event with θαρσύνω (*Il.* 16.242, *Od.* 24.448) or with θάρσος + verbs like δῶκε (*Il.* 5.2), ἐνῆκεν (*Il.* 17.570), βάλε (*Il.* 21.547), ἐνέπνευσεν (*Od.* 9.381), θῆκε (*Od.* 1.321, 3.76, 6.140).

[55] Turkeltaub 2007:68. The exceptions are the three instances in which one god addresses another (*Il.* 8.39, 18.463, 22.183) where, since both interlocutors are immortals, θάρσει takes the banal tone of friendly conversations (cf. note 11 *supra*); in the only case where it is not in initial position, *Od.* 8.197, the verb is not used as an encouragement in the face of a lethal threat, but as encouragement in the sporting contests on Scherie (cf. *Il.* 23.682 for a similar case with θαρσύνω).

[56] Beck 1987, Zaborowski 2002.

[57] Although the dream is inspired by Athena, the speakers are human. In Homer, dreams have ambivalent authority because they are not always right, as Penelope says (*Od.* 19.560–570): even when they are messages from gods they may deceive (*Il.* 2.36–37). In

2.372); and Odysseus is in a strong enough position to calm Dolon (*Il.* 10.383), to save Medon's life (*Od.* 22.372) or to ease Laertes' mind about his enemies (*Od.* 24.357), just as Eurymachus is in a powerful position to assure Penelope that he will care about Telemachus (*Od.* 16.436), or Achilles to reassure Calchas of his protection against any other Achaean (*Il.* 1.35). In the cases of a god speaking to another god we find the same superiority of knowledge in the speaker: Zeus knows what his real plans are, and his twice repeated θάρσει to Athena is based on that knowledge (*Il.* 8.39, 22.183). Similarly, Hephaestus is in superior position when he accedes to Thetis' supplication and assures her that he will make Achilles' arms (*Il.* 18.463).[58]

By contrast, when a god addresses a mortal, the asymmetry which results from the epiphanic presence of a superior power needs no further justification. There are three instances in the *Iliad* and one in the *Odyssey* worth examining in detail. In the first Diomedes has been hurt. So he prays saying (*Il.* 5.115–117):[59]

κλῦθί μευ αἰγιόχοιο Διὸς τέκος Ἀτρυτώνη,
εἴ ποτέ μοι καὶ πατρὶ φίλα φρονέουσα παρέστης
δηΐῳ ἐν πολέμῳ, νῦν αὖτ᾽ ἐμὲ φῖλαι Ἀθήνη·

Hear me now, Atrytone, daughter of Zeus of the aegis
if ever before in kindliness you stood by my father
in the terror of fighting, be my friend now also, Athena.

And Athena restores his forces and then appears to him (*Il.* 5.123–126):

ἀγχοῦ δ᾽ ἱσταμένη ἔπεα πτερόεντα προσηύδα·
θαρσῶν νῦν Διόμηδες ἐπὶ Τρώεσσι μάχεσθαι·
ἐν γάρ τοι στήθεσσι μένος πατρώϊον ἧκα
ἄτρομον, οἷον ἔχεσκε σακέσπαλος ἱππότα Τυδεύς·

---

later literature there is greater faith in encouraging epiphanies through dreams (cf. notes 31–33 *supra*), although they still may be ambiguous to interpret (Artemid. 5.94).

[58] In later literature there are some cases in which the addressee of a θάρσει rejects the speaker's implicit superiority, e.g. in Amycos' answer to the Dioscuri in Theocr. *Idyll* 22.57 and Hector's to the chorus in Eur. *Rhesus* 16. In both cases the response θαρσῶ seems to mean "I don't need your reassurance."

[59] Translations from Lattimore, with slight changes of my own.

And standing close beside him she spoke and addressed him
in winged words:
Be of good courage now, Diomedes, to fight with the Trojans,
since I have put inside your chest the strength of your father
unwavering, such as the horseman Tydeus of the great shield
had.

The effect of these words on Diomedes is instantaneous: he goes
back to the battle (*Il.* 5.134–143) and the Trojans are uncertain whether
he is a god himself or a god is behind him (5.177–191). The second
instance expands this pattern: Hector has been struck by Ajax with
a rock that has almost killed him. He has fainted and is slowly recov-
ering when Apollo appears—with the same epiphanic formula used
for Athena in the previous example (15.247: ἀγχοῦ δ' ἱστάμενος)—and
speaks words that have a spectacularly restorative effect (15.254–270):

θάρσει νῦν· τοῖόν τοι ἀοσσητῆρα Κρονίων
ἐξ Ἴδης προέηκε παρεστάμεναι καὶ ἀμύνειν
Φοῖβον Ἀπόλλωνα χρυσάορον, ὅς σε πάρος περ
ῥύομ', ὁμῶς αὐτόν τε καὶ αἰπεινὸν πτολίεθρον.
ἀλλ' ἄγε νῦν ἱππεῦσιν ἐπότρυνον πολέεσσι
νηυσὶν ἔπι γλαφυρῇσιν ἐλαυνέμεν ὠκέας ἵππους·
αὐτὰρ ἐγὼ προπάροιθε κιὼν ἵπποισι κέλευθον
πᾶσαν λειανέω, τρέψω δ' ἥρωας Ἀχαιούς.
Ὣς εἰπὼν ἔμπνευσε μένος μέγα ποιμένι λαῶν.
ὡς δ' ὅτε τις στατὸς ἵππος ἀκοστήσας ἐπὶ φάτνῃ
δεσμὸν ἀπορρήξας θείη πεδίοιο κροαίνων
εἰωθὼς λούεσθαι ἐϋρρεῖος ποταμοῖο
κυδιόων· ὑψοῦ δὲ κάρη ἔχει, ἀμφὶ δὲ χαῖται
ὤμοις ἀΐσσονται· ὃ δ' ἀγλαΐηφι πεποιθὼς
ῥίμφά ἑ γοῦνα φέρει μετά τ' ἤθεα καὶ νομὸν ἵππων·
ὣς Ἕκτωρ λαιψηρὰ πόδας καὶ γούνατ' ἐνώμα
ὀτρύνων ἱππῆας, ἐπεὶ θεοῦ ἔκλυεν αὐδήν.

"Take heart! such an avenger I am whom the son of Cronos
sent down from Ida, to stand by your side and defend you,
Phoebus Apollo of the golden sword, who in time before this

have also defended you and your sheer citadel.
So come now, urge your cavalry in great numbers
to drive their horses against the hollow ships. Meanwhile
I shall go before you and make the entire path for the horses
smooth before them, and turn back the Achaean fighters."
Thus speaking he breathed huge strength into the shepherd
     of the people.
And as when some stalled horse which has been fed on corn
     at the manger,
breaks free of his rope and gallops thundering over the plain
to his accustomed bathing place in a sweet-running river;
in the pride of his strength he holds high his head and the
     mane flows
over his shoulders, sure of his glorious strength, his swift
     knees
carry him to the loved places and the pasture of horses,
so Hector rapidly moving his feet and his knees went
onward, rousing the horsemen when he heard the god's
     voice.

As the poet underlines, Apollo, by the very act of speaking (262: ὡς
εἰπὼν; 270: ἐπεὶ θεοῦ ἔκλυεν αὐδήν), instills confidence (267: πεποιθώς)
and great strength (262: μένος μέγα) in Hector. The god opens a path
for the Trojan hero, who hastens with swift knees from the banks of
the river back into the battle.[60] Immediately, fear sizes the Achaeans
when they see that Hector "has got to his feet once more, and eluded
the death spirits" (287: αὖτ' ἐξαῦτις ἀνέστη κῆρας ἀλύξας), since they
understand that "a god has rescued and saved him" (290: ἐρρύσατο καὶ
ἐσάωσεν).

---

[60] In *Il.* 21.302–304 Achilles, thanks to the strength that Athena has given him, is able
to move his knees with such speed that even the river cannot stop him. Mackie 1999
shows that in *Iliad* 21 the river Scamander is depicted as one of the infernal rivers, and
Achilles' swift feet saving him is consistent with that image: cf. note 84 *infra* on the swift
feet necessary for acquiring salvation in Hades in the gold tablets. Hector's near-death
experience by the river in *Iliad* 14–15 is depicted as a liminal moment close to Hades, cf.
Herrero de Jáuregui 2011:44n21.

The third instance is Iris' speech telling Priam to go to the Achaean camp (*Il.* 24.169–174, 181–183):

στῆ δὲ παρὰ Πρίαμον Διὸς ἄγγελος, ἠδὲ προσηύδα
τυτθὸν φθεγξαμένη· τὸν δὲ τρόμος ἔλλαβε γυῖα·
θάρσει Δαρδανίδη Πρίαμε φρεσί, μὴ δέ τι τάρβει·
οὐ μὲν γάρ τοι ἐγὼ κακὸν ὀσσομένη τόδ' ἱκάνω
ἀλλ' ἀγαθὰ φρονέουσα· Διὸς δέ τοι ἄγγελός εἰμι,
ὅς σευ ἄνευθεν ἐὼν μέγα κήδεται ἠδ' ἐλεαίρει
. . . .
μὴ δέ τί τοι θάνατος μελέτω φρεσὶ μηδέ τι τάρβος·
τοῖος γάρ τοι πομπὸς ἅμ' ἔψεται Ἀργειφόντης,
ὅς σ' ἄξει εἷός κεν ἄγων Ἀχιλῆϊ πελάσσῃ.

The messenger of Zeus stood beside Priam and spoke to him
gently, and but shivering took hold of his limbs:
"Take heart, Priam, son of Dardanos, do not be frightened.
I come to you not eyeing you with malevolent intent
but devising your good. I am a messenger
of Zeus, who far away cares much for you and feels pity
. . . .
Let death not be the concern of your heart, you need have no
    fear,
such is the escort who shall go with you to guide you,
    Argeiphontes,
who will lead you till he brings you to Achilles."

The aim of the initial θάρσει here is not just to put Priam's mind at ease about the godly presence.[61] Iris' words also have an invigorating effect upon the old man, who immediately gives orders for the preparation of his chariot. He then seeks Hecuba's opinion. She opposes the idea, but he insists he will go anyway, saying (24.220–224):

---

[61] Priam is the only Homeric character who actually experiences fear when encountering a god. The poet uses a traditional concept in epiphanic scenes (*Il.* 20.130–131: even Achilles would hypothetically be afraid to see a god face to face) to characterize him as a frightened old man in contrast with other heroes who speak with familiarity with the gods. Cf. Turkeltaub 2007:59.

εἰ μὲν γάρ τίς μ' ἄλλος ἐπιχθονίων ἐκέλευεν,
ἢ οἳ μάντιές εἰσι θυοσκόοι ἢ ἱερῆες,
ψεῦδός κεν φαῖμεν καὶ νοσφιζοίμεθα μᾶλλον·
νῦν δ', αὐτὸς γὰρ ἄκουσα θεοῦ καὶ ἐσέδρακον ἄντην,
εἶμι καὶ οὐχ ἅλιον ἔπος ἔσσεται.

If it had been some other who ordered me, one of the
mortals,
one of the soothsayers, or priests, or diviners,
I might have called it a lie and rather have rejected it.
But now, since I myself heard the god and looked straight
upon her,
I am going, and this word shall not be in vain.

Priam's words not only show the effect that the god's voice has had in
him, but also contrast divine speech with that of mortals, a key distinction in this kind of exhortation to confidence.

In the *Odyssey* only Athena instills *tharsos* in mortals, and in most
cases indirectly, whilst in disguise or through dreams in which human
figures are speakers.[62] There is just one direct instance in *Od.* 13.358-
362, when Odysseus, having finally arrived in Ithaca, prays to the
nymphs of the nearby cave concluding with a petition to Athena:

"χαίρετ'· ἀτὰρ καὶ δῶρα διδώσομεν, ὡς τὸ πάρος περ,
αἴ κεν ἐᾷ πρόφρων με Διὸς θυγάτηρ ἀγελείη
αὐτόν τε ζώειν καί μοι φίλον υἱὸν ἀέξῃ."
τὸν δ' αὖτε προσέειπε θεὰ γλαυκῶπις Ἀθήνη
"θάρσει, μή τοι ταῦτα μετὰ φρεσὶ σῇσι μελόντων·"

"I salute you: I will also give you gifts, as I used to before,
if Athene the Spoiler, Zeus' daughter, benevolently grants

---

[62] In two other passages Athena, in disguise as a mortal, exhorts Odysseus. In *Od.* 7.50–
51, a boy tells him to enter Alcinous' palace: "you go inside fearing nothing in your spirit
(κίε μηδέ τι θυμῷ τάρβει); for the confident (θαρσαλέος) man accomplishes more in every
action, even if he is a stranger coming from elsewhere." And Odysseus enters the palace
"with swift pace" (7.135: καρπαλίμως, cf. note 84). In 8.197 a Phaeacian (Athena) encourages him in his sporting contest (σὺ δὲ θάρσει τόνδε γ' ἄεθλον), upon which Odysseus
rejoices (8.199: γήθησεν). On the Phaeacians as a potential source of danger, cf. Rose 1969.

that I go on living here myself, and sustains my dear son."
Then in turn the goddess grey-eyed Athene addressed him:
"Take heart, let none of these matters trouble your mind."

Like Diomedes' prayer in the *Iliad*, Athena responds with a θάρσει that eases Odysseus' mind. A typical poetic pattern of a prayer asking for protection and benevolence when entering a potentially hostile space, answered by a formulaic exhortation to confidence, seems reflected in these Homeric instances—a poetic pattern which in ritual terms may correspond to an accepted supplication.[63] Personal benevolence is a key element in all these passages. Apollo and Iris tell Hector and Priam, respectively, that the gods have benevolent intentions towards them; Athena's θάρσει in response to prayers by Diomedes and Odysseus respectively assures them that she is (once again) φίλα φρονέουσα and πρόφρων towards them. There is also a personal relationship between the speaker and the addressee, regardless of whether the speaker is divine; this goes hand in hand with the anthropomorphism of the Homeric gods. The trust demanded by a θάρσει means that the speaker is presenting him- or herself as guarantor of its truth. Such a commitment is not gratuitous, but derives from personal affection towards the addressee which seems essential to a valid θάρσει in the Homeric examples. An intimate relationship is sometimes emphasized through familiar vocatives after the initial θάρσει: Zeus addresses Athena as Τριτογένεια φίλον τέκος, Telemachus calls Eurycleia μαῖα. The intimacy between speaker and addressee may be implicit in the context: Menelaus speaks to his brother, Odysseus to his father; just before receiving Thetis, Hephaestus recalls that he is particularly indebted to her (*Il.* 18.394–409); and Penelope is encouraged in dreams by her sister and her husband. When it is not obvious, the benevolent disposition is recalled by the speaker: Odysseus spares the life of Medon because he is dear to his son; and even when

---

[63] Cf. *Od.* 7.75, in which Odysseus must ask Arete to be φίλα φρονέησα, like Athena in Diomedes' prayer. An accepted supplication had a juridical value in which immunity was ensured (Gould 1973, Naiden 2006), and θάρσει may well have been one standard response for accepting it (cf. Hdt. 9.76, D. S. 32.23.1, Plut. *Vit. Coriol.* 23.9, Judith [Septuagint] 11:1–3). For the legal value of *tharsein* as assuring immunity, cf. Eur. *Hec.* 345, with note 9 *supra*.

Eurymachus is uttering a false θάρσει to Penelope, he reminds her of his personal relationship with Odysseus as proof that he would always defend Telemachus. In fact, the utterance itself presupposes a friendly disposition and a personal bond between speaker and addressee: thus when Odysseus hears a Phaeacian (Athena) uttering the word θάρσει "he rejoiced in finding a kind friend" (*Od.* 8.199). There is only one exception: Odysseus' θάρσει to Dolon is not accompanied by any expression of personal affection nor any other external justification; it comes as no surprise that it does not entail salvation.[64]

If the mortal and divine uses of θάρσει are similar in presupposing a close affection of the speaker towards the addressee, the same cannot be said of their effects. The most striking specific feature of the divine exhortations is their immediate effectiveness. The θάρσει of a god is always true; it is immediately accomplished; there is no possibility of failure. By contrast, a mortal who utters θάρσει may be lying, as Odysseus lies to Dolon, and Eurymachus to Penelope;[65] or he may just be unable to fulfill his promises because destiny has proved superior: in *Il.* 18.325–326 Achilles laments that his encouraging (θαρσύνων) of Patroclus' father was an "empty utterance" (ἅλιον ἔπος). The shared knowledge of this fallibility means that a θάρσει from a mortal does not necessarily generate the desired confidence in the addressee: when Menelaus reassures Agamemnon that he has not been fatally injured, the latter responds with a hesitating optative, "hopefully will it be as you say" (*Il.* 4.189); Dolon keeps trembling after Odysseus' θάρσει; Penelope doubts that everything will turn out well despite Odysseus' appearance to her in a dream (*Od.* 19.560–570), and she keeps weeping after hearing Eurymachos' false words (*Od.* 16.449–450); Phemius and Medon go out of the dining-hall and even after Odysseus' words they "still feared death" (*Od.* 22.380). By contrast, the effect of the divine

---

[64] However, as if his previous θάρσει hindered Odysseus from killing Dolon, it will be Diomedes who kills the Trojan, so that Odysseus preserves his role of "good cop." Yet the false θάρσει of the *Doloneia* seems to have struck the Greek audience as exceptional, since it is prominent in the *Rhesus*: Odysseus says it as a false password (685), and Athena says it also falsely to the Trojans (646), in the only unambiguously false θάρσει from a god that I know of in Greek literature.

[65] The poet explicitly underlines that Eurymachus is θαρσύνων falsely (*Od.* 16.448).

tharsei on Hector, Diomedes or Odysseus is instantaneous, not as result of any "magical" intrinsic power in the word, but precisely because of the speaker's divine nature, which guarantees the desired outcome. So, too, with Priam who tells Hecuba that the goddess' word cannot be a vain ἅλιον ἔπος (*Il.* 24.224). Indeed, the θάρσει of a god is, in Austin's terminology, a speech-act, a word which is effective in the very moment it is uttered.[66] Furthermore, it functions as a speech-act in two ways; not only does the internal addressee have absolute confidence that he can trust the god, but also the external audience of the poem knows that the word of a god cannot be a ἅλιον ἔπος, and that what is being said is now guaranteed within the narrative. The same applies to all cases of θάρσει when uttered by a god in later literature.[67]

IV. RELIGIOUS POETRY

The Homeric scenes in which a god instructs a mortal to *tharsein* portray, albeit in ways sometimes refracted for narrative purposes, a certain type of religious experience which the audience understood. It is no surprise, therefore, that the term also appears in poetry which explicitly claims to bear a religious message. Such poetry is often influenced by Homer, but perhaps also derives from independent traditions of religious poetry—with which Homer may have been familiar. Indeed, it is possible that in some cases Homer was drawing on the value of *tharsein* in religious contexts, for his own "secular" purposes.[68] In any case, there are a few instances of θάρσει uttered by a god in religious poetry of classical times that bridge the gap between Homer and the evidence from Imperial times examined previously. The term appears

---

[66] Austin 1964. Cf. notes 35 and 52 *supra* for the distinction between the immediate persuasion that a divine *tharsei* achieves and the magical effect of other healing words.

[67] The only exception in note 64 *supra*. In cases like Hdt. 1.120 the god did not really encourage, but the interpreters falsely thought he had. In Artemidorus 5.94, the interpreter has misunderstood the truth of the divine encouragement.

[68] E.g. the scenes of Hector's near-death experience or Priam's trip to the Achaean camp, which incorporate elements from katabatic poems: cf. Herrero de Jáuregui 2011:51n43 and 44n21.

in three types of poetry which, again, are intimately related to each other: epiphanic, katabatic, and initiatory poetry.[69]

IV.1 Epiphanic Poetry

Although not usually used as generic label, for present purposes, it is useful to single out epiphanic poetry as a special category. Some poems do not merely narrate epiphany as a past event, but rather re-enact that epiphany in the present moment of poetic performance. The aim of invoking the god's presence makes a narrative hymn different from an epic song that happens to tell of an epiphany, although the boundary is admittedly fluid. The *Homeric Hymns* have frequently been analyzed from this perspective,[70] and it comes as no surprise that the clearest examples of an epiphanic θάρσει similar to those in the *Iliad* and the *Odyssey* are found in *Hymn* 5, to Aphrodite and *Hymn* 7, to Dionysus.[71] In the former, after making love with Anchises, the goddess wakes him up and shows herself in her complete splendor. He is afraid and supplicates her (187–188: γουνάζομαι, ἐλέαιρε). And just like Athena when supplicated by Odysseus, Aphrodite answers Anchises' supplication (192-197) with θάρσει, "for you are dear to the gods indeed" (ἐπεὶ ἦ φίλος ἐσσὶ θεοῖσι).

In *Hymn* 7 to Dionysus, after the pirates have been turned into dolphins, the god turns to the terrified pilot, the only sailor who had recognized his divinity (53–57):

κυβερνήτην δ' ἐλεήσας
ἔσχεθε καί μιν ἔθηκε πανόλβιον εἶπέ τε μῦθον·
Θάρσει † δῖ' ἑκάτωρ τῷ ἐμῷ κεχαρισμένε θυμῷ·
εἰμὶ δ' ἐγὼ Διόνυσος ἐρίβρομος ...

But for the helmsman, the god took pity on him
and held him back, and gave him the highest blessings,
saying:

---

[69] Cf. Dickie 2004b:178–179 for the proximity of epiphany and initiation, Martín Hernández 2005 for the links between initiation and katabasis.

[70] Cf. e.g. Garcia 2002.

[71] *Hymn* 3.462 offers a typical scene of welcome to a strange land in which *tharsos*, instilled by Apollo in disguise, is the key emotion (ὥς φάτο, καὶ σφιν θάρσος ἐνὶ στήθεσσιν ἔθεκεν).

Take heart, good sailor, who are dear to my heart.
I am Dionysus the mighty roarer ...

In both hymns, θάρσει is the first word of the epiphanic discourse of the god(dess), who reveals him/herself and assuages the fear provoked by the encounter with the divinity. An explicit expression of personal attachment (φίλος, κεχαρισμένε) is the guarantee that there are no grounds for fear. As in the Homeric examples, a solemn initial θάρσει sets the tone of benevolent revelation from above, a revelation of the god's personality, and of the privileged bond of friendship that ensures protection and happiness.[72]

That this was a technical way of initiating an epiphanic discourse is clear from the earliest literary adaptations of the epic tradition. A Dionysiac epiphany is portrayed in Euripides' *Bacchae* when the god appears to his maenads (604–607):

βάρβαροι γυναῖκες, οὕτως ἐκπεπληγμέναι φόβωι
πρὸς πέδωι πεπτώκατ'; ἤισθεσθ', ὡς ἔοικε, Βακχίου
διατινάξαντος †δῶμα Πενθέως· ἀλλ' ἐξανίστατε†
σῶμα καὶ θαρσεῖτε σαρκὸς ἐξαμείψασαι τρόμον.

Barbarian women, thus struck by fear have you fallen to the ground? It seems you felt Bacchus shaking Pentheus' house to pieces. But raise up your bodies and take heart, to counter the trembling of your flesh.

Translation Seaford, modified

It is not necessary to look for a direct ritual subtext in this passage, but it seems very probable that Euripides has drawn on the tradition of epiphanic scenes, giving Dionysus the characteristic utterance for countering the fear caused by the god's arrival.[73] A similar appeal to the poetic tradition of epiphany is evident in Moschus' *Europa*, when Zeus

---

[72] Caesar's θάρσει to his pilot when he is crossing the sea in Plutarch's *Vit. Caes.* 38 may be seen as a literary echo of *Hymn* 7 (cf. Simon 1936:191 relating Plutarch's passage to Acts 27:25).

[73] Seaford 1996:200, in keeping with his ritual reading of the *Bacchae*, connects it with the *symbolon* transmitted by Firmicus. Merkelbach 1962:213 also links this passage to the mysteries.

reveals himself saying (154–155): "Take heart (θάρσει), maiden, do not fear the billows. I am Zeus himself." [74]

The importance of epiphany, however, went far beyond literary convention, as we saw in the instances from religious literature of classical, Hellenistic, and Imperial times. Traditional poetry kept alive the epiphanic ring of the imperative θάρσει to suggest a divine manifestation in favor of individuals, families, and cities. A famous case is Isyllus' *Paian*, recorded in an inscription at Epidaurus from early Hellenistic times (ca. 280 BC). [75] It ends with a hexametric section telling of the encounter between Isyllus as a sick child and Asclepius, in a scene that blends traditional elements of supplication and epiphany (69–80): [76]

> τῶι τύγα ποστείχοντι συνάντησας σὺν ὅπλοισιν
> λαμπόμενος χρυσέοισ', Ἀσκλαπιέ. παῖς δ' ἐσιδών σε
> λίσσετο χεῖρ' ὀρέγων, ἱκέτηι μύθωι σε προσαντῶν·
> "ἄμμορός εἰμι τεῶν δώρων, Ἀσκληπιὲ Παιάν,
> ἀλλά μ' ἐποίκτειρον." τὺ δέ μοι τάδε ἔλεξας ἐναργῆ·
> "θάρσει· καιρῶι γάρ σοι ἀφίξομαι—ἀλλὰ μέν' αὐτεῖ—
> τοῖς Λακεδαιμονίοις χαλεπὰς ἀπὸ κῆρας ἐρύξας
> οὕνεκα τοὺς Φοίβου χρησμοὺς σώζοντι δικαίως
> οὓς μαντευσάμενος παρέταξε πόληι Λυκοῦργος."

---

[74] Merkelbach 1962:331 interprets Moschus' *Europa*, too, as a mystical text and therefore sees this utterance as a ritual phrase. It seems rather to echo texts like the *Hymn to Aphrodite*, as commentators on both poems have pointed out.

[75] A similar instance in *Orac.* 431 P–W (cf. D. S. 8.29, Paus. 10.15.2): when Attalos I, King of Pergamon in the 3rd cent. BC, asked the Delphic Oracle how long his dynasty would reign, the answer was: θάρσει, Ταυρόκερως, ἕξεις βασιληίδα τιμὴν / καὶ παίδων παῖδες, τούτων γε μὲν οὐκέτι παῖδες (take heart, bull-horned, you will have royal honor / and your children's children, but their children no more). θάρσει invests the oracle with the aura of a divine revelation, in response to a question that implicitly asks for protection. Thus the solemnity of epic diction is put into the service of political historiography, as is also shown by βασιληίδα τιμήν, an epic expression used both in this oracle and Isyllus' poem 59 (cf. Hes. *Theog.* 462, *Orph. Fragm.* 11 Bernabé: Suárez de la Torre 2000).

[76] Fantuzzi's translation, modified. The inscription is edited and commented on in detail by Kolde 2003. On pages 198–209 she relates these lines to the similar Homeric passages with θάρσει and the epiphanic ἦλθε (with a god as subject). The expression of line 63 ἐγ κείνοισι χρόνοις (*in illo tempore*) contributes to the mythicization of the episode, in a manner similar to the Lindian Chronicle, whose poetic sources may have been similar to this text.

Ὡς ὃ μὲν ᾤχετο ἐπὶ Σπάρτην· ἐμὲ δ' ὦρσε νόημα
ἀγγεῖλαι Λαχεδαιμονίοις ἐλθόντα τὸ θεῖον
πάντα μάλ' ἐξείας· οἳ δ' αὐδήσαντος ἄκουσαν
σώτειραν φήμαν, Ἀσκλαπιέ, καί σφε σάωσας.

The god came in the moment when the boy from Bosphorus came in ill, and you came as he approached shining with your golden arms, Asclepius. And when he saw you he prayed, stretching out his hands, and he touched you with suppliant words. I am have no share in your gifts, Asclepius Paian, have pity on me. And you told me clearly: "Take heart! I will come to you in due course, just wait here, but I first must save the Spartans from dire destruction. For they justly observe the decrees of Phoebus which Lycurgus imposed upon the city after consulting the oracle." After speaking these words he went off to Sparta, and my mind urged me to go and report the epiphany to the Spartans, all of it, word for word. They listened to the prophecy of salvation I spoke, Asclepius, and you saved them.

The imperative θάρσει and the line that follows are the only direct answer to Isyllus' supplication, but they are enough to convey future healing and protection. The poet adapts the traditional formula to his needs—the glorification of Asclepius not only as Isyllus' healer, but as Sparta's savior. Thus the salvation of the whole city is expressed through an individual epiphany. Isyllus hears a θάρσει that, in reality, is directed to the Spartans: he understands the unimportance of his own future healing (not mentioned any more), and instead of waiting as instructed, he goes to the Spartans to transmit them the "saving word" (80: σώτειραν φημάν). Individual healing and collective rescue from defeat are two forms of salvation (σωτηρία), both of which are announced by the traditional epiphanic formula.

IV.2 Katabasis

A second category of religious poetry in which *tharsein* appears is the descent to Hades. The theme of the heroic journey to the land of the dead goes back to traditional tales as ancient as Sumerian literature. Since the Greeks spoke of dying as "going to Hades," accounts of such journeys were readily linked to the process of death. Katabasis poetry was, therefore, potentially steeped in religious affiliations, particularly when performed in funerary rites or those which pre-performed a kind of descent to the underworld. It is probable that some of the poetic *legomena* of the mysteries were in fact katabatic poems, in which mythical journeys to Hades were turned into models for initiation. The encouragement θάρσει is particularly appropriate in the face of the deadly terrors of Hades, and therefore it suits the context of katabatic poetry in which the hero receives divine help.[77] Very little of these poems has been preserved, but we may reconstruct them through later literary versions, parodies and indirect references, in some of which the expected imperative appears. A clear instance is Aristophanes' *Frogs*, when, in his descent to Hades, Dionysus is frightened by the sight of the monster Empousa (302–308) and Xanthias mocks him: "Take heart! (θάρρει), everything's working out fine ... Empousa is gone ... and the fear for this one here has made you brown!" It is not too risky to suppose that this and similar examples parody the exclamation made by the divine guide of heroes and the souls to the Underworld (Hermes in most cases) in the serious katabatic poems.[78] The encounter with a monster like Empousa offers a possible setting where θάρσει would be very appropriate.[79]

---

[77] Dio Chrys. *Or.* 1.75 tells that Heracles ἐθάρρησε in presence of the goddess Basileia when led by Hermes on an allegorical journey which seems to have been inspired by katabatic tales. On katabasis in general, cf. Clark 1976. Alberto Bernabé points out to me that in a tiny scrap of papyrus containing Bacchyildes' dithyramb 25 f Maehler (lines 3 and 5) one may read ν]εκρὸν and θ]άρσει. Since the poem tells the myth of Orpheus, it is plausible that these words belonged to an encouragement (by a god) to go down to Hades in search of Eurydice.

[78] Cf. also *Pax* 725–726, Luc. *Dear. Iud.* 3.2. Perhaps the *Hymn to Hermes* 301–302 plays with the same scatological / eschatological theme as the *Frogs*, making Apollo mock (κερτομέων) Hermes by telling him θάρσει, after his lack of self-control has made the infant god loosen his sphincter. Apollo says exactly what Hermes usually says, θάρσει, just as he orders him to do what Hermes usually does, to lead the way—which he cannot do, of course, since he is being carried by Apollo.

[79] On the encounter with a female monster as a typical Hades-horror in descents, cf. Clark 2009. Apart from the actual encounter, the looming threat of a monstrous

Another witness to the presence of *tharsein* in the poetic tradition of katabasis comes in the *Aeneid*, in which the Sibyl, upon hearing the bark of Hecate's dogs as she is about to enter the underworld, utters some expressions closely linked to mystical formulas (6.255–263):

> ecce autem primi sub limina solis et ortus
> sub pedibus mugire solum et iuga coepta moueri
> siluarum, uisaeque canes ululare per umbram
> aduentante dea. "procul, o procul este, profani,"
> conclamat uates, "totoque absistite luco;
> tuque inuade uiam uaginaque eripe ferrum:
> nunc animis opus, Aenea, nunc pectore firmo."
> tantum effata furens antro se immisit aperto;
> ille ducem haud timidis uadentem passibus aequat.

> See now, at the dawn light of the rising sun
> the ground bellowed under their feet, the wooded hills
>   began
> to move, and at the coming of the goddess, dogs seemed to
>   howl
> in the shadows. "Away! away! you that are uninitiated!"
> shrieks the seer, "withdraw from all the grove!
> And you, rush on the road and unsheathe your sword!
> Now, Aeneas, is the hour for courage, now for a dauntless
>   heart!"
> So much she said, and plunged madly into the opened cave;
> he, with fearless steps, keeps pace with his advancing guide.

Scholars have not failed to recognize that *procul o procul este* echoes the ritual utterances which ordered the profane to keep away. This and other examples have been attributed to Eleusinian imagery, and notably to an initiatory poem on the katabasis of Heracles.[80] I would like to add that *nunc animis opus, Aenea, nunc pectore firmo* echoes the θάρσει

---

apparition is typical of the underworld (cf. Hom. *Od.* 11.633–635) and makes θάρσει suitable at any moment (see the Vergilian example below).

[80] Cf. Bremmer 2009, who updates Norden's classical commentary (1936). Cf. also Clark 1976 and 2009 on a probable Heraclean model for Vergil.

(νῦν) that was probably uttered in the katabasis poem(s) which Vergil used as his model(s). Precisely when the threatening dogs and the goddess appear, courage is needed. And, upon hearing such an exhortation Aeneas advances with self-confident step into the Underworld.[81] It was not only epic heroes who had to go down to Hades. In some cults, initiates, too, thought they would reach a happy place in Hades. The pseudo-Platonic dialogue *Axiochus* says: "the followers of Dionysus and Heracles, in their descent to Hades, were first initiated and obtained courage for the journey there (τὸ θάρσος τῆς ἐκεῖσε πορείας) from the Eleusinian goddess." A ritual scene of supplication to Persephone answered by an encouraging θάρσει can easily be imagined.[82] On the narrative level, in the Orphic gold tablets the epic scenes and formulae are given a religious sense in a context in which the soul of the initiate is the hero descending into Hades. Three from Thurii (fourth century BC) depict the scene of the soul arriving as a suppliant (ἱκέτις ἥκω) to Persephone with the hope that the goddess will be benevolent (πρόφρων). The epic scenes of arrival and supplication are reshaped to depict an encounter with the Queen of the Underworld.[83] Correspondingly, the self-confident steps of the hero who enters courageously into an unknown and dangerous land become those of the soul who is sure of reaching salvation.[84] Though not preserved in the published leaves, the exhortation θάρσει is likely to have been uttered

---

[81] The Sybil's oracle in *Aen.* 6.95 also echoes the tone of divine authority that allows an oracular θάρσει to announce salvation: *tu ne cede malis, sed contra audentior ito / qua tua te Fortuna sinet, uia prima salutis* ... The confident steps seem to have been characteristic of the hero descending to Hades, cf. notes 60 *supra* and 84 *infra*.

[82] [Plat.] *Axi.* 371e. Cf. note 63 *supra* for θάρσει as a typical answer to ritual supplication.

[83] *Orph. Fragm.* 489–490 Bernabé. Parmenides' goddess, upon welcoming him, is also said to be πρόφρων (fr. 1.22 DK). The scene in these tablets is akin to Odyssean supplications upon arriving in a strange and possibly dangerous land such as Scheria (*Od.* 5.445–450, 7.146–152): cf. Herrero de Jáuregui 2013. As we saw in note 62 *supra*, Athena instills *tharsos* into Odysseus when he enters the land of the Phaeacians.

[84] *Orph. Fragm.* 488.6 Bernabé: "I have reached the desired crown with swift feet (ποσὶ καρπαλίμοισι)." The "swift feet," as in *Iliad* 15.269 for Hector, or in *Od.* 7.135 (καρπαλίμως) for Odysseus, express the strength and the confidence required for embarking on a risky path. On this hexametric *symbolon*, cf. Santamaría 2011. *A contrario*, monosandalism is widely recognized as a representing a link to the world of the dead (Ginzburg 1989:213–231).

in these scenes by some divine or divinely inspired voice in the eschatological poems on the descent of the soul. This is the probable origin of the formula in the "Eugene" gold tablets and inscriptions from Imperial times.

IV.3 Initiatory Poetry

In close relation to the previous two themes, a third possible context of religious poetry was a ritual of initiation. The poetic *legomena* of mystery cults sometimes depicted or echoed a descent to the underworld, and retold epiphanic encounters with the god, with or without a previous prayer, where references to *tharsein* are plausible, as has been suggested in connection with Plato's language in the *Phaedo*.[85] However, unlike the epiphanic poetry that was sung publicly or recorded in stone, this was poetry sung privately for the few chosen—and is therefore lost. The only trace we have is the mystic tone which didactic poetry adopts when it wants to present its message as the result of a religious experience, where the divinely inspired knowledge is transmitted to the chosen disciple.[86] We can focus on two poetic texts in which θάρσει expresses that special revelation.

The (neo-)Pythagorean gnomic *Carmen Aureum*, traditionally considered a product of the Imperial Age, has been dated as early as the fourth century BCE by its latest commentator.[87] Whatever the dating of the extant version, it is inspired by earlier poetry of the same style. As in all gnomic literature, the speaker claims to have a superior wisdom that he transmits to men through exhortations. The first sixty lines are recommendations addressed in the second person in usual gnomic style. Close to the end, the tone suddenly changes (62–66):

> Ζεῦ πάτερ, ἦ πολλῶν γε κακῶν λύσειας ἅπαντας,
> εἰ πᾶσιν δείξαις, οἵωι τωι δαίμονι χρῶνται.

---

[85] Cf. note 26 *supra*. On Orphic eschatological/ritual poetry in Eleusis, cf. Graf 1974.

[86] A single disciple is much more common than a group of disciples in the tradition of didactic poetry (Hesiod and Perses, Theognis and Cyrnos). Initiatory poetry (Empedocles and Pausanias, Orpheus and Musaeus) follows that trend, with the chosen disciple being opposed to *hoi polloi*: cf. Obbink 1993:79–89.

[87] Thom 1995:35–59.

ἀλλὰ σὺ θάρσει, ἐπεὶ θεῖον γένος ἐστὶ βροτοῖσιν,
οἷς ἱερὰ προφέρουσα φύσις δείκνυσιν ἔκαστα.

Father Zeus, you would surely deliver all from many evils,
if you were to show all what kind of *daimon* they have.
But you take heart, for mortals have a divine origin,
to whom Nature displays and shows each sacred object.

There is a prayer to Zeus, and an encouragement based on the divine origin of men and on the assurance that sacred things (ἱερά) will be revealed (δείκνυσιν). Whether or not the poem had a ritual application, its form in this final part is that of revelatory poetry, which assures the interconnection between divine and human affairs, and particularly between the addressee of the poem (the reader) and the divine source of knowledge. The utterance θάρσει must be understood as a marker of that change of tone, from gnomic wisdom to a mystical revelation from above.[88]

The second instance is a fragment of Empedocles (B 3.6–10 DK) which, whatever its exact position in his poem(s) may have been, clearly belongs to the early part of his revelation:

μηδέ σέ γ' εὐδόξοιο βιήσεται ἄνθεα τιμῆς
πρὸς θνητῶν ἀνελέσθαι, ἐφ' ὧι θ' ὁσίης πλέον εἰπεῖν
<u>θάρσει</u>, καὶ τάδε τοι σοφίης ἐπ' ἄκροισι θοάζε.
ἀλλ' ἄγ' ἄθρει πάσηι παλάμηι, πῆι δῆλον ἔκαστον,
μήτε τιν' ὄψιν ἔχων <u>πίστει</u> πλέον ἢ κατ' ἀκουήν
ἢ ἀκοὴν ἐρίδουπον ὑπὲρ τρανώματα γλώσσης,
μήτε τι τῶν ἄλλων, ὁπόσηι πόρος ἐστὶ νοῆσαι,
γυίων <u>πίστιν</u> ἔρυκε, νόει δ' ἧι δῆλον ἔκαστον.

Do not be compelled to take up garlands of glory and honour from men, on the condition that you speak over-stepping propriety; <u>take heart</u>, and then sit on the high

---

[88] The neo-Platonist philosopher Hierocles, in his commentary on the poem, sees *tharsei* as the starting point of a new path: ἀλλὰ σὺ θάρσει ὡς τὴν ὁδὸν ἐξευρηκὼς τῆς ἀπολύσεως τῶν κακῶν: "But you take heart, because he has found the way of the liberation from evils" (*In Aureum Carmen* 25.12). Cf. Thom 1995:205–212 on the striking similarity between the final lines of the poem and some of the Orphic gold leaves.

throne of wisdom! But come, observe with every power in
what way each thing is clear, without holding any seeing
as more reliable compared with hearing, nor the echoing
ear above the clarities of the tongue; and do not keep back
trust at all from the other parts of the body by which there
is a channel for understanding, but understand each thing
in the way in which it is clear.

Trans. Wright, modified

The transmission of B 3 DK, mainly through a lengthy quotation in
Sextus Empiricus, is extremely complicated, and line 3.8 beginning
with θάρσει has also been subject to discussion. The first word is read
by Diels, Kranz, and others as a dative ("recklessly"), but recent scholarship has convincingly argued that an imperative that makes this
line an independent sentence is a superior reading.[89] A more difficult
problem is Empedocles' addressee, who has been thought to be either
Pausanias or the Muse herself (in Sextus' quotation it follows an invocation to the Muse, B 3.1–5 DK).[90] In this latter case, without parallels,
θάρσει would require a banal sense such as "come on."[91] However, this
trivialization is not usual in Empedocles and the superiority presupposed by the speaker who says θάρσει contrasts with the solemn and
humble tone of his other invocations to the Muse (B 131 DK). It would
be more suitable if it were addressed to Pausanias, with Empedocles as
medium of the gods, or even as a divine authority himself, somewhat
as in the *Golden Verses*. In the light of the other instances of θάρσει,

---

[89] Trépanier 2004:64–65, going back to the ancient punctuation by Karsten 1852,
which best suits the contexts of the citations by Clement and Proclus. Further arguments
in Gagné 2006:101n66, referring to the religious dimension of *tharsei*. Another plausible
emendation, widely accepted, is πιστήν for πίστει, which does not alter the sense (Wright
1981:161).

[90] Cf. Trépanier 2004:214n94: "Pausanias has been suggested by Karsten, Gomperz,
Wilamowitz, Reinhardt, Wright, Inwood; the Muse by Bergk, Diels, Kranz, Bollack." Some
of them of course read θάρσεῖ as dative. Trépanier himself "see(s) no way of deciding"
(2004:65). Only Hardie 2013:238 supports, from an approach parallel to my own in this
point, an imperative uttered by the Muse to Empedocles.

[91] Trépanier 2004:65 compares it with the ἄγε of B 3.9 DK, but there are no parallels for
that usage. Even in the conversational instances of θάρσει (cf. note 11) the speaker is in a
position of superior knowledge that enables him to ease the mind of the addressee.

however, I find it even more probable to take it as an imperative uttered by the Muse to Empedocles in answer to his previous invocation: the encouragement of the deity to the mortal fits perfectly with the usual contexts of epiphanic and religious connotations, with a response to a prayer in which the Muse has been asked to come (B 3.1–5 DK), and with the beginning of a divine discourse. In this case, Sextus' only omission would be the lines announcing the change of speakers, i.e. the answer of the Muse to Empedocles; an omission that is even easier to explain than changing between two different addressees (first an invocation to the Muse and then a didactic address to Pausanias). In a manner which resembles the Parmenidean and Hesiodic models, a mystical utterance from a god opens a religious revelation.[92] As Renaud Gagné has shown, in counterbalance to the *phobos* which fills all of Empedocles' poem(s) as a key instrument of *Neikos*, it is only natural that Empedocles should make *tharsos* the opposite principle that will guide him on his way back to the divine realm.[93] The addressee, chosen by the god, is encouraged before entering a theoretical sacred space, the "peaks of wisdom" (a metaphorical Etna?): θάρσει exhorts Empedocles to start a potentially dangerous journey for which much self-confidence and trust in the divine revelation is needed: in the lines that presumably followed (fr. B 3.10–13) πίστις is invoked twice, and in fr. B 4 Pausanias seems to be reminded of that: "and it is indeed the habit of mean men to disbelieve (ἀπιστεῖν) what is authoritative, but do you learn as the assurance of my Muse (πιστώματα Μούσης) urges, after the argument has been divided within your breast."[94] Again, *tharsein* is linked to trust, a trust

---

[92] The following lines of B 3 (10–13) could also be addressed by the Muse to Empedocles, rather than by Empedocles to Pausanias as is usually assumed (e.g. Obbink 1993, Trépanier 2004). Cf. Herrero de Jáuregui 2013 for comparison of a supplication scene in Empedocles, with the *Odyssey* and the Orphic gold leaves.

[93] Cf. Gagné 2006 for a convincing defense of the reading φόβῳ in fr. 115 DK as the primordial cause of the *daimon*'s fall: the exhortation to *tharsos* not only previews the terrors which the *daimon* has to face in his katabasis-like trip to this world, and situates the divine revelation of knowledge within an initiatory frame, but also opposes the principle of *phobos*. The alternation between *phobos* and *tharsos* was a frequent element of mystical experience, cf. note 24 *supra*.

[94] Empedocles' πίστις is often linked to the image of an inner path (e.g. B 133), and the πιστώματα are "the objective reliable signs that justify confidence" (Verdenius 1948:12; Wright 1981:163)

that can be transmitted from the original revelation (from the Muse to Empedocles) to subsequent recipients of divine encouragement (Pausanias).

V. CONCLUSION: THE RELIGIOUS VALUE OF *THARSEIN*

In epiphanic poetry the primary dimension in the θάρσει utterance is the divinity of the speaker, in katabasis it is the protection offered when entering a dangerous space, and in initiatory poetry it is the divine choice of a particular addressee as recipient of revelation. However, all the instances examined share the fundamental features of the experience of *tharsein* explained by Aristotle and shown clearly in the Homeric scenes. Thus the analysis of the poetic cases of *tharsein* in archaic, classical and early Hellenistic times explains why the verb was used widely in religious contexts of the Imperial period. The power of poetic tradition to reflect and shape religious experience across the centuries is seen clearly in the continuity of meaning between the earliest Homeric cases and the evidence from late antiquity that was reviewed at the beginning: θάρσει in epitaphs and in funerary gold tablets, as an encouragement in confrontation with death, has clear correspondences with the poems of katabasis; encouragement before entering a sacred space, which is patent in the inscriptional evidence, is found in the poetic scenes of supplication when arriving in a dangerous place, and in those where the god approaches and assuages the fear of proximity of the divine; the revelatory θάρσει that shows the divine nature of the speaker in the Septuagint, the New Testament, or the *Life of Apollonius*, is already found in the traditional epiphanic scenes of hexametric poetry; and *tharsein*'s connection with the language of the mysteries goes back to the (probably poetic) *legomena* of some early cults. All these dimensions are closely linked with each other by a cluster of notional correspondences and similar images, as well as in relation to other terms like ἐλπίς, πείθομαι/πίστις and σωτηρία. They can be used in different contexts and within different beliefs (e.g. about immortality). And of course literature, from Homer to the novel and from comedies to philosophical texts, may use these themes freely for its own purposes, be they serious or parodic, without the need to slavishly follow any ritual or narrative model or being "mystical texts" that only initiates can understand.

However, the implications of *tharsein* as a religious emotion remain much the same in all these contexts, since it always presupposes a narrative frame in which the god speaks as a helper in a specific risky situation. The instances we have reviewed follow the same pattern as the Homeric scenes, with a clear predominance of direct speech: even the written inscriptions echo oral utterances. It is most frequently found in the imperative, either θάρσει or another imperative, generally of a spatial verb (e.g. ἴθι), accompanied by a *thars*- word. Religious *tharsos* is instilled verbally, an utterance of one person to another at a close physical distance (παρίστημι is the characteristic verb in the examined epiphanies). It is not by chance that the ancient definition of *tharsos* appears in a treatise, the *Rhetoric*, whose subject is how an orator can instill emotions in the audience. The effect of θάρσει may be instant, but derives from its persuasive power for the specific situation, rather than any automatic magic associated with it. The utterance θάρσει, therefore, is not only a mark of divinity, but at the same time also a mark of divine anthropomorphism: on the one hand, only with divine power can one utter θάρσει as a speech-act that has immediate consequences, as an epiphanic sign of uncontested authority; but on the other hand, the god adopts very human language, and addresses a mortal with an utterance used often among men, which furthermore implies a personal relation between speaker and addressee that becomes actualized within the narration of events that culminate in the god's help. A god who says θάρσει is close enough to the addressee, physically and spiritually, to speak his own language without any mediation or translation. It is therefore most uttered by gods who act and look like mortals such as Apollo, Asclepius or Athena, or to men who have divine nature or are at least divinely inspired, such as Jesus, Apollonius or the Biblical prophets. Supreme gods like Zeus[95] or

---

[95] Only in Moschus' literary account of his turning into a bull is Zeus "human" enough to utter θάρσει. Apart from this case, in which Zeus is not really bringing σωτηρία, he delegates the actual epiphany: it is Apollo who, following Zeus' instructions, says θάρσει to Hector in *Il.* 15.254, just as in the Lindian Chronicle Athena intercedes on his behalf when he saves the Rhodians.

Yahweh, or the inaccessible and ineffable One, do not say θάρσει: lower gods who speak like mortals and to mortals do.

Besides, if uttering θάρσει implies divine authority and personal affection on the part of the speaker, a god or a god-inspired mortal, the confidence acquired upon hearing it implies trust on the part of the addressee. The association with πείθομαι (to be convinced) in some of the aforementioned texts is revealing: self-confidence comes from trust in the helping power of the god. The conviction that causes *tharsos* is not a blind faith or a purely intellectual belief in a rational proposition, but an emotional reaction of trust in a specific person: trust in the reality of the epiphany, in the divine authority of the speaker, and in the sure fulfillment of the promise. This trust can be prolonged in the chain of transmission of the original epiphany: the first addressee tells others (e.g. Isyllus to the Spartans) who must also trust the account. When the epiphany is recorded in written texts (e.g. the inscriptions of Isyllus or the Lindian Chronicle, the Gospels), the readers many centuries later are also required to trust the truth of the original epiphany and of the original θάρσει, which may apply also to themselves if the feel co-involved in the original narrative of salvation.

The various narrative patterns around *tharsein* have two constant elements: on the one hand, the threat (*kindynos*), either a specific danger or an uncertain risk; on the other hand, salvation (*soteria*), a permanent solution against that threat. The range of meanings of salvation depends on the specificity of the threat, which, as we have seen, is variable: the most common one, death, can be feared in a certain moment or as a definitive end, and "salvation from death," correspondingly, can have a wide array of forms, often very similar to one another (e.g. Hector's healing by Apollo seems a wondrous resurrection to the Achaeans). The imperative *tharsei* may equally encourage the addressee to overcome an illness and go on living, or to overcome death and go on living in a blessed afterlife.[96]

---

[96] As Kotansky 1991:116 and Faraone 2009 show, there is a clear continuity between inscribed amulets for attaining salvation from illness in this life and those which guarantee protection from death or condemnation in the afterlife. The θάρσει utterances of Jesus in the Gospels show that the same terms can be used in a similar way in both contexts.

Tharsein, therefore, implies two complementary dimensions: in all cases the addressee is granted a "passive" relief from fear; but often there is also an active dimension in which the addressee receives the strength and confidence to start something risky by himself.[97] In Homer, such an enterprise can be going into the battle (Diomedes, Hector), entering a dangerous space (Priam into the Achaean camp, Odysseus into Ithaca or Alcinous' palace), or speaking (Calchas before the assembly).[98] As in Homer, in religious contexts, whether it is embarking on the afterlife, transmitting the teaching of the god (Empedocles, Isis' aretalogist, Paul in the New Testament), or entering sacred space, such action is generally conceived in spatial terms, as taking a step forward with the help of the god. This step forward is decisive and irreversible, it makes the mortal different from his earlier being: having gone through danger is an initiatory experience in which the help of the god will be the key to success and transformation.

Of course, some philosophical schools like Stoics or Epicureans aimed to go beyond the narrative frame around the poles of danger and salvation that produced all sorts of unique experiences, and produced a theorization of *tharrein* as a permanent virtue to be practiced along the whole life—and not to fear death, for nobody is immortal, as some funerary inscriptions say with the same formula of the gold tablets that give access to an afterlife. Others, like Jews and Christians, arrived at the same result by substituting the individual and local narratives with an all-embracing universal narrative of salvation that made *tharsos* (and other connected concepts like *elpis* or *pistis*) permanent religious virtues to be practiced not only individually, but also collectively.

This provides a final key to the understanding of the value of *tharsein* in Greek religion. Most often, it enlightens an individual religious experience, framed in a personal narrative that can be compared,

---

[97] Zaborowski 2002:275–285; Hasenohr 1988:92.

[98] In addition, Priam and Odysseus must speak in the dangerous spaces they are entering. Telemachus in *Od.* 3.76 receives *tharsos* from Athena to speak in Nestor's presence. Nagy 1999:260–261 shows that the firm link between being confident and speaking potentially dangerous words is already present in Thersites' name. Protection from a hero (Achilles to Calchas) or a god ensures immunity and is a ground for *tharsos*. Later texts link *tharsos* with *parrhesia* (Epict. *Diss.* 3.22.96).

but not identified, with other ones. In the examined instances, it must be noted that encouragement from a god is almost always in the singular, addressed to a specific chosen person who is the recipient of personal divine benevolence. Instead, a collective θαρσεῖτε or ἴτε θαρροῦντες may appear in exhortations from a divine-inspired man, or a priest, to other men. When a god wants to encourage a whole city, he chooses one person as addressee and messenger of his θάρσει, as in the tales of Isyllus or the Lindian chronicle. Collective epiphanies, in fact, are extremely rare in Greece.[99] Only the Euripidean Dionysus of the *Bacchae* uses θαρσεῖτε to encourage his maenads, who form as a chorus with a collective identity. By contrast to maenadism, in most mysteries, rather than establishing a collective bond with the group of *mystai*, the god shows his benevolence personally to each one. The singular θάρσει seems more adequate in the majority of cults.[100] Initiation into "the mysteries of philosophy" follows this model of one particularly chosen recipient of revelation, as we have seen in Empedocles or the Pythagorean Golden Verses. Instead, the plural is often found in the Septuagint and in the Gospels: God's people, Jew or Christian, receive a collective revelation, not only individual ones, and as such they have a much stronger identity than the loose communities of participants in mystery cults—although they borrow much of the Greek mystical terminology.

Thus the experiences of *tharsein* in Greek religion turn out to be strongly individual, rather than collective—to a much greater degree than in Christianity. It is not by chance that the Homeric scenes in which a god tells a specific hero θάρσει contain the essential elements of later usages of the imperative formula. The experience of epiphany and the relation of affection and trust between god and mortal expressed

---

[99] Graf 2004:122 (on Isyllus). Athena's appearance to many of the citizens of Ilion took the form of individual dreams (Plut. *Lucullus* 10.2.4).

[100] See Burkert 1987:30–65 on the importance of the individual in Greek mysteries. As Dickie 2004a shows, the usual form of priestly appellation is individual (ὅς τις … ἴτω) rather than the collective ἴτε. The collective priestly exhortation in Firmicus' *symbolon* may already be subject to Christianizing influence. *Contra* Chaniotis 2011:268–269 puts this late text as an example of the collective experience of initiates which he thinks would form "emotional communities" in mystery cults.

by *tharsein* remained mainly individual throughout antiquity. And it is remarkable that, as the examined instances show, such experiences did not take place (only) in marginal cults, but in central spheres of the life of cities and people, and did not occur in opposition to collective religion, but in total consistency with it. This runs counter to the main trends of scholarship on Greek religion in recent decades, which have focused mainly on collective rituals and identities, and have often labeled the elements of personal religion as "deviating," "magic," or "marginal." The analysis of an emotion like *tharsein*, however, may provide a different perspective on Greek religion whereby the individual and collective dimension are not considered necessarily separate or opposite, but complementary. The cases of the Homeric heroes, Isyllus, the Lindian Chronicle, Apollonius, or the public inscriptions in temples show clearly that a strong personal relation with a god does not preclude an equally strong sense of collective identity and public interest: on the contrary, a benevolent god may grant salvation—from an immediate danger or from the uncertain risks of life—to the individual, but this may also entail the salvation of the entire community.

Universidad Complutense de Madrid

WORKS CITED

Anderson, G. 1994. *Sage, Saint and Sophist: Holy Men and their Associates in the Early Roman Empire.* London.

Austin, J. L. 1964. *How to Do Things with Words.* Oxford.

Beard, M. 2011. "Risk and the Humanities: *Alea Iacta Est.*" In *Risk*, ed. L. Skinns, M. Scott, and T. Cox, 85–108. Cambridge.

Beck, W. 1987. "θαρσαλέος", "θαρσ(έω)", "θάρσος / θράσος", "θάρσυνος", "θαρσύνω" in *Lexicon des frühgriechischen Epos;* Lieferung 12: ἐπαμύντωρ - θαῦμα, ed. B. Snell and M. Meier-Brügger, 973–976. Göttingen.

Blumell, L. H. 2011. "A Gold Lamella with a Greek Inscription in the Brigham Young University Collection." *Zeitschrift für Papyrologie und Epigraphik* 177:166–168.

Bonnechere, P. 2003. *Trophonios de Lebadée.* Leiden.

Borgeaud, P. 1988. *The Cult of Pan in Ancient Greece.* Chicago.

Bremmer, J. N. 2009. "The Golden Bough: Orphic, Eleusinian and Hellenistic-Jewish Sources of Virgil's Underworld in *Aeneid* VI." *Kernos* 22:183–208.

———2010. "Manteis, Magic, Mysteries and Mythography: Messy Margins of Polis Religion?" *Kernos* 23:13–35.

Burkert, W. 1987. *Ancient Mystery Cults*. Cambridge MA.

Byl, S. 2007. *Les Nuées d'Aristophane: Une initiation à Eleusis en 423 avant notre ère*, Paris.

Chaniotis, A. 2011. "Emotional Community through Ritual: Initiates, Citizens, and Pilgrims as Emotional Communities in the Greek World." In *Ritual Dynamics in the Ancient Mediterranean*, ed. A. Chaniotis, 263–290. Stuttgart.

———. 2012. "Constructing the Fear of Gods: Epigraphic Evidence from Asia Minor." In *Unveiling Emotions: Sources and Methods for the Study of Emotions in Ancient Greece*, ed. A. Chaniotis, 205–234. Stuttgart.

Chantraine, P. 1968. *Dictionnaire étymologique de la langue grecque*. Paris.

Chapa, J. 1998. *Letters of Condolence in Greek Papyri*. Florence.

Clark, R. J. 1979. *Catabasis: Vergil and the Wisdom-Tradition*. Amsterdam.

———. 2009. "The Eleusinian Mysteries and Vergil's 'Appearance of a Terrifying-Female-Apparition-in-the-Underworld' Motif in *Aeneid* 6." In *Mystic Cults in Magna Graecia*, ed. G. Casadio-P. Johnston, 190–203. Austin.

Collins, D. 2008. "The Magic of Homeric Verses." *CP* 103.3:211–236.

Cumont, F. 1942. *Recherches sur le symbolisme funéraire des romains*. Paris.

———. 1949. *Lux perpetua*. Paris.

Dickie, M. W. 2004. "Sacred Laws and Priestly Proclamations." *CQ*, n.s., 54:579–591.

———. 2004b. "Divine Epiphany in Lucian's Account of the Oracle of Alexander of Abonuteichos." *Illinois Classical Studies* 29:159–182.

Dowden, K. 2005. "Greek Novel and the Ritual of Life: An Exercise in Taxonomy." In *Metaphor and the Ancient Novel* (Ancient Narrative Supplementum 4), ed. S. Harrison, M. Paschalis, and S. Frangoulidis, 23–35. Groningen.

Eidinow, E. 2007. *Oracles, Curses, and Risk Among the Ancient Greeks*. Oxford.

———. 2011. "Networks and Narratives: A Model for Ancient Greek Religion." *Kernos* 24:9–24.

Faraone, C. 1996. "Taking the Nestor's Cup Inscription Seriously: Conditional Curses and Erotic Magic in the Earliest Greek Hexameters." *CA* 15:77–112.

———. 2009. "A Socratic Leaf-Charm for Headache (*Charmides* 155b-157c): Orphic Gold Leaves and the Ancient Greek Tradition of Leaf Amulets." In *Myths, Martyrs, and Modernity: Studies in the History of Religions in Honour of Jan N. Bremmer*, ed. J. Dijkstra, J. Kroesen, Y. Kuiper, 145–166. Leiden.

Fitzgerald, M., and J. T. White. 1983. *The Tabula of Cebes*. Chico.

Francis, J. A. 1998. "Truthful Fiction: New Questions to Old Answers on Philostratus' 'Life of Apollonius.'" *AJP* 119:419–441.

Gagné, R. 2006. "L'esthétique de la peur chez Empédocle." *Revue de philosophie ancienne* 24.3:83–110.

Garcia, J. F. 2002. "Symbolic Action in the *Homeric Hymns*: The Theme of Recognition." *CA* 21.1:5–39.

Garver, E. 1982. "The Meaning of θάρσος in Aristotle's *Ethics*." *CP* 11:228–233.

Ginzburg, C. 1989. *Storia notturna: Una decifrazione del Sabba*. Milan.

Gordon, R. 2009. "The Mythraic Body: The Example of the Capua Mithraeum." In *Mystic Cults in Magna Graecia*, ed. G. Casadio and P. Johnston, 290–313. Austin.

Gould, J. P. 1973. "Hiketeia." *Journal of Hellenic Studies* 93:74–103.

Graf, F. 1974. *Eleusis und die orphische Dichtung Athens in vorhellenistischer Zeit*. Berlin.

———. 2004. "Trick or Treat? On Collective Epiphanies in Antiquity." *Illinois Classical Studies* 29:111–130.

Graf, F., and S. I. Johnston. 2013. *Ritual Texts for the Afterlife: Orpheus and the Bacchic Gold Tablets*. 2nd ed. London.

Grandjean, Y. 1975. *Une nouvelle aretalogie d'Isis à Maronée*. Leiden.

Graver, M. R. 2007. *Stoicism and Emotion*. Chicago.

Hardie, A. 2013. "Empedocles and the Muse of the Agathos Logos." *AJP* 134:209–246.

Hasenohr, G. 1988. "Deux formules d'encouragement chez Homère: μὴ δείδιθι et θάρσει". In *Logopédies: Mélanges de philologie et de linguistique grecques offerts à Jean Taillardat*, ed. J. Hasenohr, M. Casevitz, O. Masson, J. L. Perpillou, and F. Skoda, 83–92. Paris.

Henrichs, A. 2006. "Der antike Roman. Kerényi und die Folgen." In *Neuhumanismus und Anthropologie des griechischen Mythos: Karl Kerényi im europäischen Kontext des 20. Jahrhunderts*, ed. R. Schlesier and R. S. Martínez, 57–70. Locarno.

———. 2009. "Inszeniertes Risiko: Rituelle Krisenbewältigung und provozierte Ritualkrisen in der griechischen Tragödie." In *Ritual als provoziertes Risiko*, ed. R. Schlesier and U. Zellmann, 97–108. Würzburg.

Herrero de Jáuregui, M. 2011. "Priam's Catabasis: Traces of the Epic Journey to Hades in *Iliad* 24." *TAPA* 141.1:37–68.

———. 2011a: "Dialogues of Immortality from Homer to the Gold Leaves." In *The Orphic Gold Tablets and Greek Religion: Further Along the Path*, ed. R. G. Edmonds III, 265–284. Cambridge.

———. 2013. "Salvation for the Wanderer: Odysseus, the Gold Leaves, and Empedocles." In *Philosophy and Salvation in Greek Religion*, ed. V. Adluri, 1–29. Berlin.

Higbie, C. 2003. *The Lindian Chronicle and the Greek Creation of their Past.* Oxford.

Joly, R. 1955. "L'exhortation au courage (ΘΑΡΡΕΙΝ) dans les Mystères." *Revue des études grecques* 68:164–170.

———. 1963. *Le Tableau de Cebes et la philosophie religieuse.* Collection Latomus 41. Brussels.

Karsten, S. 1838. *Empedoclis Agrigentini Carminum reliquiae.* Amsterdam.

Keuls, E. 1969. "Mystery Elements in Menander's *Dyskolos.*" *TAPA* 100:209–220.

Kindt, J. 2012. *Rethinking Greek Religion.* Cambridge.

Kolde, A. 2003. *Politique et religion chez Isyllos d'Epidaure.* Schweizerische Beiträge zur Altertumswissenschaft 28. Basel.

Kotansky, R. 1991. "Incantations and Prayers for Salvation on Inscribed Greek Amulets." In *Magika Hiera: Ancient Greek Magic and Religion*, ed. C. Faraone and D. Obbink, 107–137. New York.

Konstan, D. 2007. *The Emotions of the Ancient Greeks.* Toronto.

Kullmann, W. 1956. *Das Wirken der Götter in der* Ilias. Berlin.

Laín Entralgo, P. 1958. *La curación por la palabra en la antigüedad clásica.* Madrid (ed. and trans. by L. J. Rather and John M. Sharp as *The Therapy of the Word in Classical Antiquity.* New Haven, 1970.)

Lattimore, R. 1962. *Themes in Greek and Latin Epitaphs*. Urbana.

Lampe, G. W. H. 1961. *A Patristic Greek Lexicon*. Oxford.

Lindgard, F. 2005. *Paul's Line of Thought in 2 Corinthians 4:16-5:10*. Tübingen.

Mackie, C. 1999. "Scamander and the Rivers of Hades." *AJP* 120:485–501.

Martín Hernández, R. 2005. "La muerte como experiencia mistérica: Estudio sobre la posibilidad de una experiencia de muerte ficticia en las iniciaciones griegas." *Ilu: Revista de ciencias de las religiones* 10:85–105.

Merkelbach, R. 1962. *Roman und Mysterium in der Antike*. Munich.

———. 1988. *Die Hirten des Dionysos: Die Dionysos Mysterien der römischen Kaiserzeit und der bukolische Roman des Longus*. Stuttgart.

———. 2005. *Isis regina - Zeus Sarapis: Die griechisch-ägyptische Religion nach den Quellen dargestellt*. Munich.

Nagy, G. 1999. *The Best of the Achaeans*. 2nd rev. ed. Baltimore.

Naiden, F. S. 2006. *Ancient Supplication*. London.

Nollé, J. 2007. *Kleinasiatische Losorakel: Astragal- und Alphabetchresmologien der hochkaiserzeitlichen Orakelrenaissance*. Munich.

Norden, E. 1957. *P. Vergilius Maro Aeneis Buch VI*. 4th ed. Darmstadt.

Obbink, D. 1993. "The Addressees of Empedocles." *Materiali e discussioni per l'analisi dei testi classici* 31:51–98.

Park, J. S. 2000. *Conceptions of Afterlife in Jewish Inscriptions*. Tübingen.

Platt. V. 2011. *Facing the Gods: Epiphany and Representation in Graeco-Roman Art, Literature and Religion*. Cambridge.

Podeman Sorensen, J. 1989. "Attis or Osiris? Firmicus Maternus *De Errore* 22." In *Rethinking Religion: Studies in the Hellenistic Process*, ed. J. Podeman Sorensen, 73–86. Copenhagen.

Raggi, A. 2004. "The Epigraphic Dossier of Seleucus of Rhosus: A Revised Edition." *Zeitschrift für Papyrologie und Epigraphik* 147:123–138.

Rose, G. P. 1969. "The Unfriendly Phaeacians." *TAPA* 100:387–406.

Santamaría, M. A. 2011. "I Have Reached the Desired Crown with Swift Feet (*OF* 488.6)." In *Tracing Orpheus: Studies of Orphic Fragments in Honour of Alberto Bernabé*, ed. M. Herrero de Jáuregui, A. I. Jiménez San Cristóbal, E. R. Luján, R. Martín Hernández, S. Torallas Tovar, 213–218. Berlin.

Seaford, R. 1996. *Euripides. Bacchae: With an Introduction, Translation and Commentary*. Warminster.

Siebourg, M. 1905. "Zwei griechische Goldtänien aus der Sammlung C. A. Niessen in Köln." *Archiv für Religionswissenschaft* 8:390–410.

Simon, M. 1936. "θάρσει οὐδεὶς ἀθάνατος: Études de vocabulaire religieux." *Revue de l'histoire des religions* 1936:189–206. (= Simon 1981:63–81).

———. 1981. *Le christianisme antique et son contexte religieux.* Scripta Varia I. Tübingen.

Smoes, E. 1995. *Le courage chez les grecs, d'Homère à Aristote.* Paris.

Spicq, C. 1978. *Notes de lexicographie neotestamentaire.* 2 vols. Fribourg.

Suárez de la Torre, E. 2000. "En torno a la fórmula βασιληΐδα τιμήν y variantes." In *Actas del X Congreso Español de Estudios Clásicos* 1, 631–646. Madrid.

Taylor, C. W. 2008. "Wisdom and Courage in the *Protagoras* and the *Nicomachean Ethics*." In *Pleasure, Mind, and the Soul: Selected Papers in Ancient Philosophy.* Oxford.

Thom, J. C. 1995. *The Pythagorean Golden Verses: With Introduction and Commentary.* Leiden.

Thrall, M. 2004. *The Second Epistle to the Corinthians 1–7.* International Critical Commentary. London.

Torallas Tovar, S. 2013. "Egyptian Burial Practices in Late Antiquity: The Case of Christian Mummy Labels." In *Cultures in Contact: Transfer of Knowledge in the Mediterranean Context*, ed. S. Torallas Tovar and J. P. Monferrer-Sala, 15–26. Cordoba.

Trépanier, S. 2004. *Empedocles: An Interpretation.* London.

Turkeltaub, D. 2007. "Perceiving Iliadic gods." *HSCP* 103:51–82.

Vanderlip, V. F. 1972. *The Four Greek Hymns of Isidorus and the Cult of Isis.* Toronto.

Verdenius, W. J. 1948. "Notes on the Presocratics." *Mnemosyne* 4.1:8–14.

Versnel, H. S. 1987. "What Did Ancient Man See When He Saw a God? Some Reflections on Greco-Roman Epiphany." In *Effigies Dei: Essays on the History of Religions*, ed. D. van der Plas, 42–55. Leiden.

Wright, M. R. 1981. *Empedocles: The Extant Fragments.* New Haven.

Zaborowski, R. 2002. *La crainte et le courage dans l'Iliade et l'Odyssée.* Warsaw.

ANCIENT TEXTS: EDITIONS USED
(the editions of the inscriptions are cited in the notes)

Aristophanes: Wilson, N.G. 2008. *Aristophanes Fabulae I*. Oxford.

Aristotle *Rhetoric*: Ross W. D. 1959. *Aristotelis Ars Rhetorica*. Oxford.

Empedocles: Diels, H., and W. Kranz. 1966. *Die Fragmente der Vorsokratiker.* 12th ed. Zurich.

Epictetus: Schenkl, H. 1916. *Epicteti Dissertationes ab Arriano digestae.* 2nd. ed. Leipzig.

Euripides *Bacchae*: See Seaford 1996.

Firmicus Maternus: Turcan, R. 1982. *Iulius Firmicus Maternus: De errore profanarum religionum.* Paris.

Herodotus: Hude, C. 1963. *Herodoti Historiae.* Oxford.

Hierocles: Köhler F. G. 1974. *In Aureum Carmen: Hieroclis in aureum Pythagoreorum carmen commentarius.* Stuttgart.

Homer and *Homeric Hymns*: D. B. Monro, T. W. Allen. 1920. *Homeri Opera.* 3rd ed. Oxford.

Isyllus: See Kolde 2003.

Julian, *Caesares*: Lacombrade, C. 1964. *L'empereur Julien. Oeuvres complètes,* vol. 2.2. Paris.

Moschus' *Europa*: Gow, A.S.F. 1952. *Bucolici Graeci.* Oxford.

New Testament: Nestle, E., and B. Aland. 1993. *Novum Testamentum Graece.* 27th Standard Edition. Stuttgart.

Plato: Burnet, J. 1900-1907. *Platonis opera.* Oxford.

Plutarch *Lucullus*: Ziegler, K. 1969. *Plutarchi vitae parallelae.* Leipzig.

Philostratus *Life of Apollonius*: Jones, C. P. 2005. *Philostratus: The Life of Apollonius of Tyana.* Cambridge, MA.

[Pythagoras] *Carmen Aureum* : See Thom 1995.

Septuagint: Rahlfs, A. 1935. *Septuaginta.* 8th ed. Stuttgart.

Sophocles *Electra*: Lloyd-Jones, H., and N. Wilson. 1990. *Sophoclis Fabulae.* Oxford.

Tabula of Cebes: See Fitzgerald White 1983.

Vergil *Aeneid*: Mynors, R. A. B. 1972. *Publii Vergili Maronis Opera.* Oxford.

ACUSILAUS OF ARGOS AND THE BRONZE TABLETS

JORDI PÀMIAS

De Acusilao spissa caligine circumfusa sunt omnia.
Müller and Müller 1841:xxxvi

I. PRELIMINARY REMARKS

A RECENT TREND in the study of early Greek historiography has focused on the relationship between orality and literacy.[1] To what degree does oral tradition linger in the first historical accounts and to what extent does it help explain the conditions of the production and consumption of such literary records? In what way does the introduction of a new technology such as alphabetic writing shape the construction and transmission of past events? Moreover, what is the attitude of the first historians (the so-called logographers) vis-à-vis the oral tradition and how does the use of writing contribute to and develop their authorial self-consciousness?

Nowadays it is safely taken as a *verité acquise* that no clear-cut dichotomy separates orality and literacy in late Archaic and Classical Greece. Any evolutionary model that emphasizes the shift into subsequent intellectual paradigms has proved hazardous for understanding a culture in transit from full orality to partial literacy. Rather, as Fowler

Parts of this paper have been read by, or discussed with, colleagues at different stages of my research: Markus Asper, Charles Delattre, Lowell Edmunds, Robert Fowler, José Luis García Ramón, Klaus Geus, and Glenn Most. I am greatly indebted to them for their valuable insights and criticism. I am also grateful to the referee of *HSCP* for helpful comments and suggestions.

[1] The "oral revolution" that has long been crucial to the understanding of ancient Greek epic attained acceptance in historiography with a certain delay (see Luraghi 2001a:3). On the origins and development of Greek prose, see Asper 2007.

has clearly explained, "literate" and "oral" mentalities were different stages of development within whole societies.[2] Thus, in the same manner as an *entwicklungsgeschichtliches Prinzip* leading from myth to reason has proved uncomfortable for many Hellenists,[3] so too a progressive construct going from orality to literacy has been severely criticized.[4] As late as the second half of the fifth century BCE, historians like Herodotus and Thucydides built their literary monuments relying primarily on oral traditions. Indeed, neglect of written records shows that such sources were not primarily considered a suitable material to reconstruct the past. Such an indifference to documents needs to be explained not by any absence of written records but rather by a cultural choice, as was argued by Momigliano.[5]

II. ACUSILAUS AND THE IDOLATRY OF THE DOCUMENT

Projected against this background, the logographer and genealogist Acusilaus of Argos appears as a disconcerting figure. According to the testimony provided by the Byzantine lexicon Suda, Acusilaus had transcribed divine and heroic genealogies from some bronze tablets that his father had unearthed from somewhere in his home. Probably this story was included in the proem to his *Genealogies*.[6]

Ἀκουσίλαος· Κάβα υἱός· Ἀργεῖος ἀπὸ Κερκάδος πόλεως οὔσης Αὐλίδος πλησίον. ἱστορικὸς πρεσβύτατος· ἔγραψε δὲ γενεαλογίας ἐκ δέλτων χαλκῶν, ἃς λόγος εὑρεῖν τὸν πατέρα αὐτοῦ ὀρύξαντά τινα τόπον τῆς οἰκίας αὐτοῦ.

Acus. test. 1 Fowler = *FGH* 2T1 = Suda,
s.v. Ἀκουσίλαος, ed. Adler

---

[2] Fowler 2001:99.
[3] As the question mark in the title of Buxton 1999 shows.
[4] See, for instance, Andersen 1987; Thomas 1992.
[5] Momigliano 1990:29–53; cf. Momigliano 1966. See Thomas 1989:89: "Ancient historians' relative neglect of written evidence is not simply explained by the paucity or inadequacy of ancient documents." See also Rhodes 2007:56. Still in the fourth century BCE: see Thomas 1989:88–93.
[6] Cf. Fowler 1996:78; Fowler 2001:105. See below, n. 14.

Acusilaus was the son of Kabas. He was Argive from the city of Kerkas, which is near Aulis. He was the most ancient of historians. He wrote *Genealogies* based on bronze writing-tablets which, according to one account, his father discovered after he had dug up some place in his house.

Trans. Toye

Thus, Acusilaus does not show any sign of rejecting written records, which apparently sets him apart from his contemporaries.[7] The accounts of ancient historians tend to absorb, and therefore to make disappear, traces of the documentation used by the author, while the modern historian by contrast tries to reconstruct the facts from the documents.[8] The rhetoric of the document contrasts with the rhetoric of ancient historians, which derives from epic poetry and constructs the character of the historian as the authoritative narrator.[9] With the impressive authority of his presumable fabrication aimed at bolstering the Argive national genealogy, Acusilaus appears oddly close to the modern idolatry of the document.

Such an extraordinary account, whatever its relation to "truth," has not attracted the attention that it in my opinion deserves. Rather, the testimony has been dismissed by a tradition of modern (and rationalizing) scholarship that has confined itself to stating the spurious nature of this pseudo-biographic testimony without taking into account its cultural significance. Indeed, this autobiographic anecdote has been passed over in silence (Jacoby), or dismissed as an attempt to circumvent criticism (Fowler), or considered a forgery of Hellenistic (Tozzi) or Imperial (Schwartz) scholarship.[10] However, no evidence suggests that

---

[7] According to Christian Jacob (1994:181), the story of the bronze tablets provides Acusilaus' *Genealogies* with the seal of intertextuality, while at the same time emphasizing the crucial value of reading and writing at the end of the Archaic period: by means of the "epigraphic" discovery of his father Acusilaus would have initiated a new era of textual production that relies upon the authority of a preexistent text, guarantee of antiquity, and upon the critical exercice of rewriting.

[8] See Nicolai 2007:13–14.

[9] See Marincola 1997:6.

[10] Schwartz 1893:1222–1223; Jacoby 1957:375; Tozzi 1967:605; Fowler 2001:104–105: "Acusilaus' claim to have copied his genealogies from bronze tablets ... is a cop-out." More skeptical is Mazzarino 1990:61, 547.

the "epigraphic" discovery of Acusilaus' father could not constitute the basic narrative framework of the *Genealogies* and thus have the function of providing authenticity to the work.[11] In fact, the formula that introduces the episode of the bronze tablets (ἃς λόγος εὑρεῖν ...) points, in my opinion, to the proem of Acusilaus' work. The phrase should not be translated as "according to one account," as Toye has it.[12] Comparison with parallel uses in ancient preambles shows that the term (λόγος), and its verbal counterpart (ὧδε/τάδε λέγει),[13] serve to designate and introduce the work at the very commencement of the book.[14]

As for the content of the tablets' story, scholars tend to overlook the fact that the production and diffusion of a piece of fiction, false as it might be, provides valuable evidence of the mentality that has forged it and passed it on, since it reveals spontaneous associations in the mind of individuals who share a cultural model. Therefore, Acusilaus' claim to have copied the genealogies from bronze tablets can be useful to explore and may unveil cultural perceptions of literacy and oral tradition. Moreover, a reappraisal of Acusilaus' testimonium 1 can be helpful to better understand the way in which Acusilaus tries to construct his authorial self-consciousness.

---

[11] Skepticism about the authenticity of Acusilaus' work stems from an isolated account (Acus. test. 7 Fowler = *FGH* 2T7: τὰ γὰρ Ἀκουσιλάου νοθεύεται), which in turn has led to doubts about the genealogist's claim to have based his work on the bronze tablets found by his father (although Fowler's restoration of the sequel to Acus. frag. 11 would introduce another reference to the forgery: ἐν τοῖς [ἀναφερο]μένοις ε[ἰς αὐτόν]). The fact, however, that Acusilaus was well known to Plato (Acus. test. 10 Fowler = *FGH* 2T10 and frag. 6a Fowler = *FGH* 2F6a) makes it difficult to believe that Acusilaus' *Genealogies* were already a forgery in Plato's time (see Tozzi 1967:585).

[12] The word does not point either to an external tradition ("che è tradizione ..." in the translation of Giannantoni 1969), i.e. independent from Acusilaus' own statement.

[13] On the formula ὧδε/τάδε λέγει, see Porciani 1997:34–37.

[14] Cf. Heraclit. *FVS* 22B1: τοῦ δὲ λόγου τοῦδ' ἐόντος ἀεὶ ἀξύνετοι γίνονται ἄνθρωποι ... (with Koenen 1993:96: "Die ... Tradition, am Anfang eines Werkes auf die vorliegende Niederschrift des Buches zu verweisen"; "Beziehen sich die ersten Worte deutlich auf das konkrete Buch"; cf. also Conche 1986:31): Io *FVS* 36B1 (= *FGH* 392F24a): ἀρχὴ δέ μοι τοῦ λόγου ...; and Diog. Apoll. *FVS* 64B1: ἀρχὴ δὲ αὐτῶι τοῦ συγγράμματος ἥδε· λόγου παντὸς ἀρχόμενον δοκεῖ μοι χρεὼν εἶναι τὴν ἀρχήν ... On Greek historiographic proems, see Porciani 1997:44–69.

III. ACUSILAUS, THE TABLETS,
AND THE BRONZE MYTHOLOGY

It is my goal to examine the biographic account of Acusilaus' tablets anew, trying to understand its minor components and to recast them into a broader cultural background. Indeed, minor (and contingent) elements prove to be the more significant within a story as long as they are preserved by an accidental history of textual transmission. So, the following questions shall be addressed: why are the tablets made of bronze? Why were the tablets buried and eventually dug up? Why is Acusilaus' father made responsible for their discovery? Why does the Argive Acusilaus appear to be closely connected to Aulis?

In order to fully understand the significance of the tablets' story it is, in my opinion, crucial to see it in its proper cultural context, which entails unveiling the complex significance of bronze and its technology in Archaic and Classical Greece, as well as the cultural constructs surrounding it. It is agreed that metal and metallurgy in Ancient Greece have an ambiguous status, as Graf has explained.[15] The contrasting ideological representations of metallurgy in many cultures may be related with the sacred character of metal and thus with the eccentricity and marginality of its manipulation.[16] More particularly on Greek bronze, however, I would like to stress at this point my debt to the study of Camassa, on "Calcante, la cecità dei Calcedoni e il destino dell'eroe del bronzo miceneo."[17] In this article, the Italian scholar scrutinized the links relating Calchas' name and mythology to the cultural representations of bronze and its techniques, as well as to the cities Chalcedon and Chalcis, broadly known in antiquity for their bronze mines. The origins of the Greek word for bronze (χαλκός) are still unclear to modern linguistics, but a seminal article of Maass (1888) sustained the etymological identity of the toponym Chalcedon (Χαλκηδών/Καλχηδών) and Chalcodon (eponym of Chalcis) with the

---

[15] See Graf 1999.
[16] So Eliade 1977; cf. Forbes 1971:71–80. On the intersection between magic and technology, see the cautious remarks of Blakely 2007.
[17] Camassa 1980a; cf. Camassa 1983.

Kurzname Calchas (Κάλχας/Χάλκας). At any rate, and leaving aside the controversial etymological speculations on the name of Calchas,[18] the importance of Chalcedon for the mineral deposits is stressed, among others, by the author of the Aristotelian *Mirabilia*, who shall be used to better understand the complex mythology of bronze—and eventually Acusilaus' testimonium 1.

Δημόνησος ἡ Καλχηδονίων νῆσος ἀπὸ Δημονήσου τοῦ πρώτου ἐργασαμένου τὴν ἐπωνυμίαν εἴληφεν … ἔστι δὲ αὐτόθι χαλκὸς κολυμβητὴς ἐν δυοῖν ὀργυιαῖς τῆς θαλάσσης· ὅθεν ὁ ἐν Σικυῶνί ἐστιν ἀνδριὰς ἐν τῷ ἀρχαίῳ νεῷ τοῦ Ἀπόλλωνος … οἱ δὲ τὸν χαλκὸν ὀρύττοντες ὀξυδερκέστατοι γίνονται, καὶ οἱ βλεφαρίδας μὴ ἔχοντες φύουσι· παρὸ καὶ οἱ ἰατροὶ τῷ ἄνθει τοῦ χαλκοῦ καὶ τῇ τέφρᾳ τῇ Φρυγίᾳ χρῶνται πρὸς τοὺς ὀφθαλμούς.

Arist. *Mirab.* 834b

Demonesus, the island of the Chalcedonians, received its name from Demonesus, who first cultivated it … In the same place there is also copper, obtained by divers, two fathoms below the surface of the sea, from which was made the statue in Sicyon in the ancient temple of Apollo … Those who dig the copper become very sharp-sighted, and those who have no eyelashes grow them: wherefore also physicians use the flower of copper and Phrygian ashes for the eyes.

Trans. Dowdall

Pseudo-Aristotle thus implicitly describes the inhabitants of Chalcedon as being ὀξυδερκέστατοι, "sharp-sighted." Such a property is much more astonishing as this city was famously known in antiquity as the "city of the blind" *par excellence*.[19] This designation was commonly

---

[18] Etymological *liaison* of Calchas with χαλκός is deemed suspect by Saladino 1990:931. But see now Russo and Barbera 2008:52–58.

[19] Cf. Hdt. 4.144: Καλχηδονίους τοῦτον τὸν χρόνον τυγχάνειν ἐόντας τυφλούς· οὐ γὰρ ἂν τοῦ καλλίονος παρεόντος κτίζειν χώρου τὸν αἰσχίονα ἑλέσθαι, εἰ μὴ ἦσαν τυφλοί; Str.

explained by means of a trivial rationalization: when the Megarians decided to settle a colony at the Bosporus, they chose Chalcedon instead of the land just across the sea, where later was founded the opulent Byzantium—that is to say, they overlooked a much more convenient and prosperous site.

The prominent disagreement between blindness and sharp-sightedness concerning the inhabitants of Chalcedon has called for a "structural" approach. We shall be able to understand such a contradiction by taking both notions (blindness and sharp-sightedness) as being a "coppia anfibologica, regolata dall'ambigua grammatica del mito," since both blindess and sharp-sightedness can designate "la stessa realtà fisica, vale a dire l'anomalia funzionale degli organi preposti alla vista nel manipolatore dei metalli."[20] Indeed, studies on ancient mythology of metals and metallurgists have long pointed to a persistent feature: individuals and groups dealing with metalworking are associated with conspicuous alterations of visual organs or with particular sight properties. In Greece, the most obvious cases are the monophthalmic Cyclopes,[21] the evil-eyed and sharp-eyed Telchines, and the keen-sighted Lynceus.[22] Whether by deficiency or excess, the visual capacities of the metalworkers are deemed extraordinary and

---

7.6.2: τυφλοὺς καλέσαντα τοὺς Χαλκηδονίους, ὅτι πρότεροι πλεύσαντες τοὺς τόπους, ἀφέντες τὴν πέραν κατασχεῖν τοσοῦτον πλοῦτον ἔχουσαν [sc. Βυζάντιον], εἵλοντο τὴν λυπροτέραν.

[20] See Camassa 1980a:35. Cf. Deonna 1965:115–116: "Un organe du corps, tête, oeil, main, etc., envisagé ou figuré seul, suffit à évoquer ou représenter le corps entier. En l'isolant ... on intensifie sa puissance fonctionnelle, ceci d'autant plus quand il s'agit d'organes qui normalement sont doubles ou multiples, et que l'on ramène ainsi à l'unité ... N'en avoir qu'un seul [sc. oeil], ou mille, comme le soleil, n'en avoir qu'on, ou trois, comme le Cyclope, est pareil."

[21] On the connection between monophthalmy and manipulation of metals, see Detienne and Vernant 1974:89n99. See also Piccirilli 1978:926.

[22] On the sharp-sightedness of the Telchines, see Suet. Blasph. p. 54, ed. Taillardat (ὀξυδερκέστατοι; cf. Brelich 1958:335–336: similarities between Cyclopes and Telchines ὀξυδερκέστατοι). On the Telchines and the malocchio, see Brillante 1993. On sharp-sighted Lynceus and his connection to metalwork, see Sch. Lyc. 553; Palaeph. 9; Hyg. Fab. 14.12–13 (cf. Macrì 2009:102–104). As for Orion's blindness and his cure by the metal god Hephaestus and his assistant Cedalion in Lemnos, see Eratosth. Cat. 32 (cf. Renaud 2004:263–288).

abnormal—which may be taken as a sign of the exceptionality and ambiguity of their cultural and social status.[23]

The Pseudo-Aristotelian appellation ὀξυδερκέστατοι concerning the Chalcedonians can thus be viewed as a specular projection of their purported blindness and, therefore, as symmetrical and strictly equivalent to it. A correspondence of the miner with the seer, whose physical blindness is the price for his acuity and perspicacity in mantic or divinatory matters, can easily be observed.[24]

Provided with abnormal visual capacities, the Chalcedonians have the same attributes that can be credited to Calchas, the prominent seer of the Troian myth, who is also related to the foundation of Chalcedon and whose name was again related (albeit *volksetymologisch?*) to χαλκός, "bronze."[25] Parallelisms with other mythical personalities may help explain connections of Calchas with clairvoyance and mantic capacities: consider, for instance, Lynceus, the hero provided with sharp eyesight and at the same time a prominent miner;[26] or the monophthalmic lawgiver Lycurgus, whose close connections with metals have also been pointed out.[27] Indeed, this notion lingers on in "historical" accounts, like the Herodotean story of the bronzesmith who dug up and exhumed from the courtyard of his forge a coffin with Orestes' bones, thus accomplishing the mandate of the Delphic oracle.[28] According to Camassa, it was the metallurgical aspect of Calchas and his ὀξυδερκία that allowed him to enter the sphere of divination when the social changes of post-Mycenean Greece brought about a revolution in the social consideration of bronze metallurgy.[29] Be that as it may, the mythology of Calchas can also be traced with certainty to several

---

[23] See Graf 1999.

[24] On Tiresias' blindness as a price for his mantic acuity, see Brisson 1976:31–33.

[25] Hsch.Mil. *FGH* 390F1.21: Χαλκηδὼν δὲ ὠνόμασται τὸ χωρίον, ὡς μέν τινές φασιν, ἀπὸ τοῦ Χαλκηδόνος ποταμοῦ, ὡς δὲ ἕτεροι ἀπὸ τοῦ παιδὸς Κάλχαντος τοῦ μάντεως ὕστερον τοῦ Τρωικοῦ πολέμου γενομένου. Cf. Camassa 1980a:28–32; Rossignoli 2004:131–132. On Calchas' ὀξυδερκία, see for instance Apollod. *Epit.* 6.4.

[26] Cf. above n. 22.

[27] See Piccirilli 1978:928.

[28] Hdt. 1.68: Ἐγὼ γὰρ ἐν τῇδε θέλων [ἐν] τῇ αὐλῇ φρέαρ ποιήσασθαι, ὀρύσσων ἐπέτυχον σορῷ ἑπταπήχεϊ ... ἄνοιξα αὐτὴν καὶ εἶδον τὸν νεκρὸν μήκεϊ ἴσον ἐόντα τῇ σορῷ.

[29] See Camassa 1980a:48–51.

sites intimately associated with bronze metallurgy, such as Chalcis in Euboea.[30] It is hardly a coincidence that Chalcis exerted its influence over the neighboring Aulis, where Calchas plays a major role in the panhellenic tradition of the Troian expedition.[31]

If seen against this background, the biographic account of Acusilaus of Argos (test. 1) transmitted by the Suda takes on a new significance. Two pieces of information included in the lexicographical entry now need to be taken into account: the bronze nature of the tablets unearthed by Acusilaus' father; and the fact that the tablets are not discovered somewhere else but dug up from the soil: ἔγραψε δὲ γενεαλογίας ἐκ δέλτων χαλκῶν, ἃς λόγος εὑρεῖν τὸν πατέρα αὐτοῦ ὀρύξαντά τινα τόπον τῆς οἰκίας αὐτοῦ (cf. the Aristotelian text quoted above: οἱ δὲ [sc. the Chalcedones] τὸν χαλκὸν ὀρύττοντες). This coincidence is most significant as both elements are not indispensable for the economy of the narrative. After all, Acusilaus had many other choices at his disposal to raise a plausible claim for the possession of superhuman knowledge to trace Argive history back to its cosmological origins (for Hesiod, see below; inscriptions as storage of ancient wisdom seem to be a common feature in fictitious texts).[32] Contingent and arbitrary details within a story, and the very fact that they have resisted the accidental process of textual transmission, point to their

---

[30] Chalcis was well-known in antiquity for innovations in bronze metallurgy. See Pliny *NH* 6.21.64 (*antea uocitata est ... Chalcis aere ibi primum reperto*); Str. 10.3.19; Steph. Byz. s.v. Χαλκίς; s.v. Αἴδηψος. Cf. Mele 1981; too skeptical: Bakhuizen 1981 (cf. Jourdain-Annequin 1984:414).

[31] See the condensed account of Stephanus Byzantius (s.v. Αὐλίς): πόλις Βοιωτίας κατὰ Χαλκίδα, εἰς ἣν ἠθροίσθησαν οἱ Ἕλληνες. Associations of Chalcas to Euboea: Camassa 1980b; Rossignoli 2004:130–133.

[32] Forgeries of decrees seem to be a recurrent phenomenon in fourth-century Athens (cf. Thomas 1989:84–93). As for the publishing (but not unearthing) of an inscription containing ancient knowledge, Euhemerus' *Hiera Anagraphe* could also serve as a comparative example. In general, "references to ancient records discovered in temples ... are a commonplace of impostors' literature" (West 1994:294). The artifice is old: the prologue of the Gilgamesh epic invites us "to go to Uruk, unlock the copper chest that contains Gilgamesh's own record of his adventures on a lapis lazuli tablet, and read it for ourselves" (West 1997:601). On falsification and religious pseudepigrapha, see Speyer 1977. On bronze legal documents in Rome and their symbolic aspects, see Williamson 1987.

originality and reliability, inasmuch as they should always be seen, and prevail, as *lectiones difficiliores*.

For all its unexpectedness and oddity, however, a *lectio difficilior* awaits an explanation. The biographic statement through which Acusilaus claims to have obtained the Argive national genealogies can be compared with other transcendental experiences from other cultural contexts. Poets, prophets, and legislators are thought to have undergone preternatural experiences that would entitle their claims to authoritative speech.[33] A closely comparable figure is the epic poet Hesiod, who in some respects appears as a model for his *Doppelgänger* Acusilaus (see below § VI). Hesiod became a poet after his mystic encounter with the Muses, who initiated him into the art of poetry. Through this experience the poet was enabled to acquire an exceptional status and to rise above his purely human capacities to reach a level of divinatory poetry that could celebrate both future and past (Hes. *Th.* 32: τά τ' ἐσσόμενα πρό τ' ἐόντα). In a similar vein, Acusilaus depicted himself as inheriting a transcendental knowledge from his father, who gained access to divinatory wisdom by contact with unearthed bronze. Indeed, digging up and extracting the bronze tablets, scarcely a "rationalization" or "historization" of the mantic acuity and ὀξυδερκία associated with the metalworker's activity described above, enables Acusilaus' father to obtain a knowledge that is as precluded to humans as the understanding of the future: that is, the divinatory penetration of a far-reaching genealogical past up to the cosmological beginnings.[34]

---

[33] See Most 2006:xiii.

[34] For the all-embracing knowledge of past and future as a divinatory matter, and their symmetrical equivalency, see Detienne 1994:49–70. Μνημοσύνη ("Memory") is aimed both forward and backward and therefore implies the capacity to observe τά τ' ἐόντα τά τ' ἐσσόμενα πρό τ' ἐόντα. That is why the same phrase (τά τ' ἐσσόμενα πρό τ' ἐόντα) can be attributed both to the prophet (Calchas: Hom. *Il.* 1.70) and to the poet (Hesiod: Hes. *Th.* 32).

IV. ACUSILAUS, SON OF KABAS

The succinct biographical entry of Suda provides still another piece of information that may be relevant for our purposes, viz. the name of Acusilaus' father, Kabas (Ἀκουσίλαος· Κάβα υἱός). This name has not so far attracted the attention of modern scholars.[35] Its form, however, clearly suggests a non-Greek origin. In a recent article dealing with the etymology of the name Kabeiroi and its cognates, Beekes has argued against a semitic origin, as scholars ever since Scaliger had proposed. Instead, Beekes points to a Pre-Greek, Anatolian etymology.[36] Leaving aside the ultimate origin of this word, if the name Kabas is taken as a secondary form (or *Kurzform*) of Kabeiros (see below) and is lined up with Kabeiroi and with other words of the same family, connection with metal and its manipulation again emerges. Like other groups of comparable deities, such as the Telchines and the Dactyloi, the Kabeiroi are also closely related to metallurgy.[37] Indeed, connections of the Kabeiroi with metals and smiths are many and manifold, as Hemberg in his comprehensive monography on *Die Kabiren* has specified.[38] Greek mythology relates them genealogically to the metallurgical god *par excellence*, Hephaestus—as Acusilaus himself shows in one of his fragments.[39] Since genealogy in Greece does not convey a historical

[35] But see Müller and Müller 1841:xxxvii. The manuscripts of Diogenes Laertius (1.41) provide a textual variant for the name of Acusilaus' father Kabas (Σκάβ[ρ]ας; cf. test. 11a Fowler = *FGH* 2T11a). For this variant, cf. Kelmis/Skelmis (Call. frag. 100 Pfeiffer; Hemberg 1952:50).

[36] Beekes 2004. Cf. Nilsson 1967:670.

[37] Brisson 1981:85: "Or, comme Héphaistos, dont ils sont les descendants, les Cabires sont des métallurges." Cf. Burkert 1985:281: "Guilds of craftsmen, especially smith guilds ... may be seen in the background" (in Lemnos); "This points to guilds of smiths analogous to those of the Lemnian Hephaistos" (in Thebes); cf. Vollkommer-Glökler 1997:821: "Auch als Schmiede fungieren sie." Another etymology, suggested by Georges Dossin, relates the Kabeiroi with the Sumerian word for bronze, *kabar*. Again, if this hypothesis is correct, "on peut ... proposer pour le nom des Cabires le sens premier de 'métallurgiste, forgeron'" (Dossin 1953:200). Iconography seems to point to the same direction, according to Daumas (1998:44–45 and 118).

[38] Hemberg 1950:168–169 and 285–286.

[39] See Acus. frag. 20 Fowler = *FGH* 2F20 = Str. 10.3.21: Ἀκουσίλαος δ' ὁ Ἀργεῖος ἐκ Καβειροῦς καὶ Ἐφαίστου Κάμιλλον λέγει· τοῦ δὲ τρεῖς Καβείρους, οἷς νύμφας Καβειρίδας. Cf. Hemberg 1950:163–166.

relationship, as Thomas among others has stressed,[40] but often a metaphorical or conceptual one, Acusilaus, like many other authors, is most likely to have potrayed them as metallurgical deities.[41] Yet, genealogical inheritance is not the only metallurgical aspect of the Kabeiroi. A lexicographical gloss of Hesychius identifies the Kabeiroi with crabs.[42] As Brisson has aptly shown, this crustacean has some significant points in common with Hephaestus.[43] On the one hand, its oblique gait and sideways movement recalls the god's lameness; on the other hand, its claws evoke the blacksmith's pincers (Greek καρκίνοι, "crabs"). In addition, the daimones who make metal (Daktyloi, Telchines, and Kabeiroi) are placed in regions that were historically rich in ore, and particulary, as Blakely puts it, "the Kabeiroi appear often at sites located on the metals trading route, visited by the Phoenicians."[44]

The groups of gods related to metallurgy (Telchines, but also Daktyloi and Kabeiroi) combine other attributes. Aside from their familiar relationship with magic and sorcery,[45] a category that has proved to be extremely controversial,[46] these daimones are often depicted as πανοῦργοι, "mischievous, knavish."[47] The word κόβαλος, "impudent knave, mischievous goblin," has been compared with the name Kabeiroi (cf. also κόβειρος); and the meaning "knave" is also confirmed by comparison with another word, κάβαξ, which perfectly

---

[40] Thomas 1989:175–179.

[41] Cf. Pherecyd. frag. 48 Fowler = *FGH* 3F48 = Str. 10.3.21: ἐκ δὲ Καβειροῦς τῆς Πρωτέως καὶ Ἡφαίστου Καβείρους τρεῖς καὶ νύμφας τρεῖς Καβειρίδας· ἑκατέροις δ' ἱερὰ γίνεσθαι; Hesych. s.v. Κάβειροι ... λέγονται δὲ εἶναι Ἡφαίστου παῖδες; St. Byz. s.v. Καβειρία.

[42] Hesych. s.v. Κάβειροι· καρκίνοι. πάνυ δὲ τιμῶνται οὗτοι ἐν Λήμνῳ ὡς θεοί. Cf. Collini 1990:248n54.

[43] Brisson 1981:85.

[44] Blakely 2007:58–59.

[45] See the straightforward wording of Hemberg 1950:286: "Mit dem Schmieden hängt die Zauberei zusammen." For a "classic" approach to this issue, see Delcourt 1982. Graf 1999:325, too, has insisted on the stability of the tradition linking "metalworking, sorcery, and the Mother [sc. Goddess]" from Archaic Greece to the Byzantines.

[46] Blakely 2007.

[47] Cf. Suda s.v. Τελχῖνες· πονηροὶ δαίμονες. ἢ ἄνθρωποι φθονεροὶ καὶ βάσκανοι; Hesych. s.v. Τελχῖνες· βάσκανοι, γόητες, φθονεροί. See Hemberg 1950:286: "Dämonen, die als Zauberer gedacht wurden, haben sich leicht zu πανοῦργοι, d. h. Bösewichten, die allerlei schlimme Dinge tun können, entwickelt."

fits "die neckische Kabiren."[48] The latter word is close to the anthroponym of Acusilaus' father, Kabas, whose name can be considered a *Kurzform* of Kabeiros. Theophoric names based on Kabeiros are not exceptional in Greek, with almost all of them attested in Boeotia and Euboea.[49]

If this argument is correct, Acusilaus' father could be imagined as taking part in the same wave of migrations that brought the cult of the Kabeiroi to Thebes and Hesiod's father from Kyme in Aeolis to Ascra in Boeotia.[50] So, the account of Acusilaus' life and his familiar origins seems to replicate Hesiod's biography, who can be seen, again, as a model for the construction of Acusilaus' as an author. Therefore, it is not necessary to see the Kabeiroi exclusively as a paradigm for a class of smith-shamans or a guild of smiths (as Burkert would put it)[51] and Kabas as their leading representative. Rather, and aside from their paradigmatic relevance for ancient craftsmen and blacksmiths, the Kabeiroi offer themselves as professional models for the Archaic sage, in the same way, as Blakely has shown, the Daktyloi did.[52]

V. ACUSILAUS, AN ARGIVE FROM AULIS

Birthplace has become a *locus classicus* in the controversy over Acusilaus of Argos.[53] Athough ancient sources unanimously agree that Acusilaus was an Argive, the place of origin given by the lexicographer Suda is Boeotia, and more precisely the polis Kerkas in the vicinity of Aulis (ἀπὸ Κερκάδος πόλεως οὔσης Αὐλίδος πλησίον). This location has long been

---

[48] Beekes 2004:471–472. Cf. Suda / *EM* / Phot. s.v. κάβαξ· πανοῦργος.

[49] See *LGPN* III.B: Καβείρας, Καβειρίχα, Καβείριχος, Καβειρώ, Καβιρῖνος, Καβίριος, Καβιρίχα, Καβίριχος, Κάβιρος, Καβιρώ (Boeotia); *LGPN* I: Καβιρίχα, Κάβων (Euboea); *LGPN* III.A: Καβιρίας (Triphylia); *LGPN* II: Καβείριχος (Athens). Cf. Marchand 2011:351–352.

[50] See Schachter 2003:112–113. Cultural and commercial contacts between Euboea and Aeolic Kyme have been noticed (Rossignoli 2004:131).

[51] See Burkert 1985:281.

[52] According to Blakely (2007:66), the Daktyloi offered "cosmological and professional models for the Presocratic sages," which should lead to "a new perspective on the larger puzzle of the magician smith within the Greek tradition." Since earlier investigations had assumed the relevance of the Daktyloi for smiths, this approach has obscured "the sophistication of the daimones as an intellectual type."

[53] See, for instance, Müller and Müller 1841:xxxvi–xxxvii.

considered suspicious and, therefore, different attempts at correction have been put forth.[54] The last proposal has been made by West,[55] who has conjectured Ναυπλίας instead of Αὐλίδος (relying ultimately on a conjecture by Robert).[56] Again, in my opinion, textual evidence needs to be seriously taken into account without apriorisms. Before rejecting the *lectio recepta* and instead of hazarding a conjecture, those elements that are apparently inconsistent should be explained.

The polis Kerkas mentioned by Suda has not been identified by modern archaeology.[57] Probably the name had faded into oblivion already in late antiquity, as is suggested by the fact that the lexicographer provides supplementary information as a point of reference to locate it (οὔσης Αὐλίδος πλησίον). The site may be thus located in the vicinity of Aulis, at the coastal region of Boeotia across Chalcis (Str. 10.1.2). As a matter of fact, when defining the position of Aulis, authors like Strabo (9.2.8), Livy (45.27), or the lexicographer Stephanus Byzantius (s.v. Αὐλίς· πόλις Βοιωτίας κατὰ Χαλκίδα) take the city of Chalcis as a point of reference. Both sites are separated by a narrow strait, the Euripus canal (Pliny *NH* 4.21.63: *Euboea et ipsa auolsa Boeotiae, tam modico interfluente Euripo, ut ponte iungantur*). Indeed, in 411 the town of Chalkis was connected with the mainland by a bridge (cf. D.S. 13.47; Str. 9.2.8; Solin. 11.24).[58] So, although Acusilaus takes Argos as a focal point for his genealogical work, and ancient documentary evidence terms him as an Argive, he is said to come originally from the Boeotian (or Euboean?) coastline, at any rate from the area of Aulis or its environs. This additional piece of evidence proves to be relevant, since the location happens again to hover over a leading center of bronze and mantic mythology (Calchas at Aulis) and in the vicinity of bronze deposits (Chalcis in Euboea, well known in antiquity for its

---

[54] Cf. Kordt 1903:64–67. See Mazzarino 1990:547: "La errata localizzazione 'vicino Aulide' ... potrebbe anche derivare da autoschediasma o penetrazione glossematica." The φράτρα of the Κερκάδαι is attested for Argos (inscription of Imperial date), but again connection to Boeotia awaits explanation (Vollgraff 1909:183–185, 196).

[55] Cf. Fowler 2000, app. crit. ad loc.

[56] Cf. Piérart 1997:349n56.

[57] See Piérart 2004:600.

[58] See Cawkwell 1978:47.

innovations in the field of bronze craftsmanship).[59] The biographic piece of information about the "extraction" of the bronze tablets by Acusilaus' father needs to be observed in its proper context, i.e. in a particular landscape characterized by intense metallurgical activity and, more particularly, by bronze extraction and production.[60] The episode can thus be recast as part of the complex ideological sphere of bronze mythology as described above (§ III).

Indeed, it can hardly be a coincidence that Acusilaus, and the metallic discovery of his father, are located in an area that is heavily charged with bronze resonances and full of mining and metallurgic activities.

VI. ACUSILAUS AND THE CONSTRUCTION OF THE AUTHOR

Acusilaus' precise location in the vicinity of Aulis recalls another literary and biographic tradition, namely the Hesiodic, and confirms the analogies between both authors. (Other correspondences between Acusilaus and Hesiod have been suggested above at §§ III and IV.)[61] It may be significant for our purposes to remark that Aulis is mentioned

---

[59] Cf. Str. 10.3.19: περιθέσθαι δ' ὅπλα χαλκᾶ πρώτους ἐν Εὐβοίᾳ· διὸ καὶ Χαλκιδέας αὐτοὺς κληθῆναι; Pliny NH 4.21.64: Chalcis aere ibi primum reperto; St. Byz. s.v. Χαλκίς· τινὲς δὲ Χαλκιδεῖς φασι κληθῆναι διὰ τὸ χαλκουργεῖα πρῶτον παρ' αὐτοῖς ὀφθῆναι; St. Byz. s.v. Αἴδηψος· πόλις Εὐβοίας ... ἦν δὲ καὶ σιδηρᾶ καὶ χαλκᾶ μέταλλα κατὰ Εὔβοιαν ... οἱ γὰρ Εὐβοεῖς σιδηρουργοὶ [καὶ] χαλκεῖς ἄριστοι. Ἐπαφρόδιτος δὲ μαρτυρεῖ ἐκεῖ χαλκὸν πρῶτον εὑρεθῆναι. See n. 30.

[60] For a broad perspective on the role of Euboea (especially Chalcis) in the development of bronze technology and its trading, see Boardman 1980:42–43. On the traces of bronze metallurgy to be found in mythical Euboean traditions, see Mele 1981.

[61] Connections of Acusilaus with epic poetry, and Hesiod, are stressed by Calame 2004:232–236, 241–243. Parallelisms had long been observed by modern scholarship (cf. Kordt 1903:67–75: "Caput III: Hesiodus et Acusilaus"). Another similar, symmetrical feature in Acusilaus' and Hesiod's biography may be the epigraphical (lead) tablets held near Hipocrene containing a copy of Works and Days (Paus. 9.31.3–5). A good example of the continuity between Hesiod's Theogony and Acusilaus' cosmology are frag. 1 Fowler (= FGH 2F1) (to be compared with Hes. Th. 337–340) and frag. 6d Fowler (= FGH 2F5) (to be compared with Hes. Th. 116–120). This continuity was not overlooked by Plato: Ἡσιόδῳ δὲ καὶ Ἀκουσίλεως ὁμολογεῖ (u. l. ξύμφησιν) (Pl. Smp. 178b = Acus. frag. 6a Fowler = FGH 2F6a). When it comes to genealogies, by contast, Acusilaus seems to rewrite, or correct, the Hesiodic tradition (for Pelasgus, for instance, see Apollod. 2.1.1 [2.2] = Acus. frag. 25a Fowler = FGH 2F25a). Cf. Mazzarino 1990:67–69.

in one of Hesiod's few first-person statements (*Op.* 651–655) where the poet says that he visited Aulis and crossed the Euripus to Chalcis in Euboea. Jacoby justified the *déplacement* of the birthplace of the Argive Acusilaus with pregnant precision: "die versetzung nach Boiotien erfolgte um Hesiods willen."[62]

It is well known that Hesiod is the first Western author to supply us with his name and indications about his life in his work. Parallelism with Hesiod may give a clue to better appreciate the way in which Acusilaus understood personal references and made use of them to build his authorial identity. Acusilaus' personal statement about his father's discovery does not need to be taken as autobiographical and literal but rather metaphorical and notional. Modern scholarship has insisted on the fact that Archaic authors, like "Homer" and "Hesiod," as historical and biographical realities, are to be distinguished from the figure of the author fabricated within the text.[63] Thus, first-person references, like the story about the bronze tablets, should encourage us to approach in a more sophisticated way the autobiographical functions that such statements serve. Indeed, Acusilaus' biographic indications about the "epigraphic" extraction of his father is concomitant with the ideological representation of his cosmogonical and genealogical wisdom, namely a lore of ineffable antiquity that, having been excluded from humans, requires authorization from transcendental forces. Compared to Homer and Hesiod, Acusilaus' fetishization of the written document would confer the authority of age, replacing the need for a poetic tradition.

In conclusion, another aspect of Acusilaus' biography that has not been positively explained hitherto will now be addressed. Indeed, his contact with a secret and unfathomable wisdom can perfectly account for the tradition, attested by Hermippus, according to which Acusilaus

---

[62] Cf. Jacoby 1957:375.

[63] Cf. Lefkowitz 1981. For Homer, see West 1999:364: "'Homer' was not the name of a historical poet, but a fictitious or constructed name." Graziosi (2002), too, belives that discussions of the figure of Homer, whatever their relation to "truth," provide valuable insights for understanding the significance of the Homeric poems. For Hesiod, see Most 2006:xii–xxv (cf. Clay 2003:181).

was incorporated in the lists of the prominent Wise Men of Greece.[64] As a matter of fact, Acusilaus of Argos is one of the few authors that were included in both of the two great collections of fragments of the last century: the *Fragmente der Vorsokratiker* of Diels and Kranz and the *Fragmente der griechischen Historiker* of Jacoby. And yet, whereas as a mythographer and a genealogist nobody challenges Acusilaus' presence in the first volume of the *FGH*, his contribution to Archaic cosmological thought is downplayed, and some scholars would even exclude his name from the history of Greek philosophy *tout court*.[65] If he is viewed, however, as a "Presocratic" sage or mystic having access to a divinatory, preternatural wisdom, the work of Acusilaus ought not to be labeled "a step backwards, not forwards, in Greek historiography," as Hermann Fränkel once put it.[66] Rather the "primitive level of his thought and language" merely suggests that Acusilaus is to be assigned to an earlier date. With the invention of an impressive authority for his message by means of the story of the bronze tablets, Acusilaus appears to be closely related to a theological-priestly tradition and to a mythic approach to the time of origins. Indeed, as Mazzarino masterfully argued, Acusilaus resembles the Archaic writers, such as the sages and *Wundermänner* Epimenides of Crete or Pherecydes of Syros, that bear witness to the "transformazione religiosa connessa con il movimento iniziatico" of the sixth century BCE.[67]

UNIVERSITAT AUTÒNOMA DE BARCELONA

---

[64] See Fowler 2001:105: "The implication that his text contained lore of indescribable antiquity might have been what gave him the reputation of a mystic or sage." The main source is Hermipp. Hist. *FGH* 1026F10 (= frag. 6 Wehrli), though Hermippus should have relied on earlier traditions (Bollansée 1999:171).

[65] Kirk, Raven, and Schofield 1983:20: "Acusilaus ... was a genealogist who might well have given a summary and of course unoriginal account of the first ancestors ... He is almost entirely irrelevant to the history of Presocratic thought, and scarcely deserves the space accorded him in Diels/Kranz."

[66] Fränkel 1975:348.

[67] See Mazzarino 1990:58–70. Cf. Casadio 1999:44n12: "F. Jacoby, H. Fraenkel, A. Lesky e H. Herter ... lo collocano nel V secolo dopo l'empirico, razionalista Ecateo. L'anticonformista geniale S. Mazzarino ... con lucido argomentare, rovescia il rapporto tra i dui libri di Genealogie [sc. Hecataeus' and Acusilaus'] e assegna Acusilao e. g. al 550 a. C." See also Montanari 2002:130: "The simple and perhaps even really arid qualities

WORKS CITED

Andersen, Øivind. 1987. "Mündlichkeit und Schriftlichkeit im frühen Griechentum." *Antike und Abendland* 33:29–44.

Asper, Markus. 2007. "Medienwechsel und kultureller Kontext: Die Entstehung der griechischen Sachprosa." In *Philosophie und Dichtung im antiken Griechenland: Akten der 7. Tagung der Karl und Gertrud Abel-Stiftung am 10. und 11. Oktober 2002 in Bernkastel-Kues*, ed. Jochen Althoff, 67–102. Stuttgart.

Bakhuizen, S. C. 1981. "Le nom de Chalcis et la colonisation chalcidienne." In *Nouvelle contribution à l'étude de la société et de la colonisation eubéennes*, 161–173. Naples.

Beekes, R. S. P. 2004. "The Origin of the Kabeiroi." *Mnemosyne* 57:465–477.

Betegh, Gábor 2002. "On Eudemus Fr. 150 (Wehrli)." In *Eudemus of Rhodes*, ed. István Bodnár and William W. Fortenbaugh, 337–357. New Brunswick.

Blakely, Sandra. 2007. "Pherekydes' *Daktyloi*: Ritual, Technology, and the Presocratic Perspective." *Kernos* 20:43–67.

Boardman, John. 1980. *The Greeks Overseas: Their Early Colonies and Trade*. 2nd ed. London. (Orig. pub. 1964, Baltimore.)

Bollansée, Jan 1999. *Hermippos of Smyrna: Die Fragmente der griechischen Historiker Continued*. Part Four, *Biography and Antiquarian Literature*, ed. G. Schepens. *IVA: Biography. Fascicle 3*. Leiden.

Brelich, Angelo. 1958. *Gli eroi greci: Un problema storico-religioso*. Rome.

Brillante, Carlo. 1993. "L'invidia dei Telchini e l'origine delle arte." *Aufidus* 19:7–42.

---

of the narrative and the subject matter in the fragments, seemingly naive at times ... would argue against associating A[cusilaus] with the movement for a rationalist interpretation of myths." Cf. also Fowler 2001:105n17. In fact, Eudemus' account (frag. 150 Wehrli = Acus. frag. 6b Fowler = *FGH* 2F6b) of the most ancient cosmogonies and theogonies quotes Acusilaus after Orpheus, Homer, and Hesiod and before Epimenides and Pherecydes (see Betegh 2002:353: "Poets and prose writers discussed by Eudemus constitute a well defined, self-consistent group for Aristotle: they are the 'theologians,' those ancient authors who concerned themselves with mythical narratives about the gods and their genealogy"). On "sages and philosophers," see now Ustinova 2009:177–217. Finally, one ought not to overlook the fact that the entry of Suda defines Acusilaus as ἱστορικὸς πρεσβύτατος.

Brisson, Luc. 1976. *Le mythe de Tirésias: Essai d'analyse structurale*. Leiden.

———. 1981. "Artisan: Dieux et artisans; Héphaistos." In *Dictionnaire des mythologies et des religions des sociétés traditionnelles et du monde antique (A-J)*, ed. Yves Bonnefoy, 83–85. Paris.

Burkert, Walter. 1985. *Greek Religion*. Trans. John Raffan. Cambridge, MA.

Buxton, Richard, ed. 1999. *From Myth to Reason? Studies in the Development of Greek Thought*. Oxford.

Calame, Claude. 2004. "Le funzioni di un racconto genealogico: Acusilao di Argo e la nascita della storiografia." In *La città di Argo: Mito, Storia, tradizioni poetiche*, ed. Paola Angeli Bernardini, 229–243. Rome.

Camassa, Giorgio. 1980a. "Calcante, la cecità dei Calcedoni e il destino dell'eroe del bronzo miceneo." *Annali della Scuola Normale Superiore di Pisa* 10:25–69.

———. 1980b. "Calcante euboico e Poseidon Geraistos." *Parola del passato* 35:371–375.

———. 1983. *L'occhio e il metallo: Un mitologema greco a Roma?* Genoa.

Casadio, Giovanni. 1999. "Eudemo di Rodi: Un pioniere della storia delle religioni tra Oriente e Occidente." *Wiener Studien* 112:39–54.

Cawkwell, G. L. 1978. "Euboea in the Late 340's." *Phoenix* 32:42–67.

Clay, Jenny Strauss. 2003. *Hesiod's Cosmos*. Cambridge.

Collini, Paolo. 1990. "Gli dèi Cabiri di Samotracia: Origine indigena o semitica?" *Studi classici e orientali* 40:237–287.

Conche, Marcel. 1986. *Héraclite. Fragments*. Paris.

Daumas, Michèle. 1998. *Cabiriaca: Recherches sur l'iconographie du culte des Cabires*. Paris.

Delcourt, Marie. 1982. *Héphaistos ou la légende du magicien*. 2nd ed. Paris. (Orig. pub. 1957.)

Deonna, Waldemar. 1965. *Le symbolisme de l'oeil*. Paris.

Detienne, Marcel. 1994. *Les maîtres de vérité dans la Grèce archaïque*. 2nd ed. Paris. (Orig. pub. 1957.)

Detienne, Marcel, and Jean-Pierre Vernant. 1974. *Les ruses de l'intelligence: La mètis des grecs*. Paris.

Dossin, Georges. 1953. "Les Cabires à Lemnos: Rapports des Séances de la Société 'Théonoé'; Séance du 7 mai 1951." *La nouvelle Clio* 5:199–202.

Eliade, Mircea. 1977. *Forgerons et alchimistes*. 2nd ed. Paris. (Orig. pub. 1956.)

Forbes, R. J. 1971. *Studies in Ancient Technology*. Vol. 8. 2nd ed. Leiden. (Orig. pub. 1956.)

Fowler, Robert L. 1996. "Herodotos and His Contemporaries." *JHS* 116:62–87.

———. 2000. *Early Greek Mythography*. Vol. 1, *Texts*. Oxford and New York.

———. 2001. "Early *Historiē* and Literacy." In Luraghi 2001b, 95–115.

Fränkel, Hermann. 1975. *Early Greek Poetry and Philosophy: A History of Greek Epic, Lyric, and Prose to the Middle of the Fifth Century*. Trans. Moses Hadas and James Willis. Oxford. (Orig. pub. as *Dichtung und Philosophie des frühen Griechentums: Eine Geschichte der griechischen Epik, Lyrik und Prosa bis zur Mitte des fünften Jahrhunderts*. New York, 1951.)

Giannantoni, Gabriele. 1969. *I Presocratici: Testimonianze e frammenti*. Bari.

Graf, Fritz. 1999. "Mythical Production: Aspects of Myth and Technology in Antiquity." In Buxton 1999, 317–328.

Graziosi, Barbara. 2002. *Inventing Homer: The Early Reception of Epic*. Cambridge.

Hemberg, Bengt. 1950. *Die Kabiren*. Uppsala.

———. 1952. "Die Idaiischen Daktylen." *Eranos* 50:41–59.

Jacob, Christian. 1994. "L'ordre généalogique: Entre le mythe et l'histoire." In *Transcrire les mythologies*, ed. Marcel Detienne, 169–202. Paris.

Jacoby, Felix. 1957. *Die Fragmente der griechischen Historiker*. Erster Teil, *Kommentar*. Leiden.

Jourdain-Annequin, Colette. 1984. "La colonisation eubéenne: Métallurgie, mythe, société." *Dialogues d'histoire ancienne* 10:414–417.

Kirk, G. S., J. E. Raven, and M. Schofield. 1983. *The Presocratic Philosophers: A Critical History with a Selection of Texts*. 2nd ed. Cambridge. (Orig. pub. 1957.)

Koenen, Ludwig. 1993. "Der erste Satz bei Heraklit und Herodot." *Zeitschrift für Papyrologie und Epigraphik* 97:95–96.

Kordt, Arnold. 1903. *De Acusilao*. Basel.

Lefkowitz, Mary R. 1981. *The Lives of the Greek Poets*. Baltimore.

Luraghi, Nino. 2001a. "Introduction." In Luraghi 2001b, 1–15.

——, ed. 2001b. *The Historian's Craft in the Age of Herodotus*. Oxford.

Maass, Ernst. 1888. "Mythische Kurznamen." *Hermes* 23:613–621.

Macrì, Sonia. 2009. *Pietre viventi: I minerali nell'immaginario del mondo antico*. Turin.

Marchand, Fabienne. 2011. "Rencontres onomastiques au carrefour de l'Eubée et de la Béotie." In *Philologos Dionysios: Mélanges offerts au professeur Denis Knopfler*, ed. Nathan Badoud, 343–376. Geneva.

Marincola, John. 1997. *Authority and Tradition in Ancient Historiography*. Cambridge.

——, ed. 2007. *A Companion to Greek and Roman Historiography*. Vol. 1. Malden, MA.

Mazzarino, Santo. 1990. *Il pensiero storico classico*. Vol. 1. 2nd ed. Bari. (Orig. pub. 1965–1966).

Mele, Alfonso. 1981. "I Ciclopi, Calcodonte e la metallurgia calcidese." In *Nouvelle contribution à l'étude de la société et de la colonisation eubéennes*, 9–33. Naples.

Momigliano, Arnaldo. 1966. "Storiografia su tradizione scritta e storiografia su tradizione orale: Considerazioni generali sulle origini della storiografia moderna." In *Terzo contributo alla storia degli studi classici e del mondo antico*, 13–22. Rome.

——. 1990. *The Classical Foundations of Modern Historiography*. Berkeley.

Montanari, Franco. 2002. "Acusilaus." In *Brill's New Pauly*. Vol. 1, ed. Hubert Cancik and Helmuth Schneider, 129–130. Leiden and Boston.

Most, Glenn W. 2006. *Hesiod. Theogony, Works and Days, Testimonia*. Cambridge.

Müller, Carl, and Theodor Müller. 1841. *Fragmenta Historicorum Graecorum*. Vol. 1. Paris.

Nicolai, Roberto. 2007. "The Place of History in the Ancient World." In Marincola 2007, 13–26.

Nilsson, Martin P. 1967. *Geschichte der griechischen Religion*. Vol. 1. 3rd ed. Munich. (Orig. pub. 1941.)

Piccirilli, Luigi. 1978. "Due ricerche spartane." *Annali della Scuola Normale Superiore di Pisa* 8:917–947.

Piérart, Marcel. 1997. "L'attitude d'Argos à l'égard des autres cités d'Argolide." In *The Polis as an Urban Centre and as a Political Community*, Acts of the Copenhagen Polis Centre. Vol. 4, ed. Mogens H. Hansen, 321–351. Copenhagen.

———. 2004. "Argolis." In *An Inventory of Archaic and Classical Poleis*, ed. Mogens Herman Hansen and Thomas Heine Nielsen, 599–619. Oxford.

Porciani, Leone. 1997. *La forma proemiale: Storiografia e pubblico nel mondo antico*. Pisa.

Renaud, Jean-Michel. 2004. *Le mythe d'Orion: Sa signification, sa place parmi les autres mythes grecs et son apport à la connaissance de la mentalité antique*. Liège.

Rhodes, P. J. 2007. "Documents and the Greek Historians." In Marincola 2007, 56–66.

Rossignoli, Benedetta. 2004. *L'Adriatico greco: Culti e miti minori*. Rome.

Russo, Federico, and Massimiliano Barbera. 2008. "Calcante in Italia: Alle radici di un mito." *Considerazioni di Storia ed Archeologia* 1:43–70 [= Russo, Federico, and Massimiliano Barbera. 2009. "Archeologia di un mito: Calcante in Italia." In *Lycophron: Éclats d'obscurité; Actes du colloque international de Lyon et Saint-Étienne. 18–20 janvier 2007*, ed. Christophe Cusset and Évelyne Prioux, 347–375. Saint-Étienne].

Saladino, Vincenzo. 1990. "Kalchas." In *LIMC* V/1, 931–935. Zürich.

Schachter, Albert. 2003. "Evolutions of a Mystery Cult: The Theban Kabiroi." In *Greek Mysteries: The Archaeology and Ritual of Ancient Greek Secret Cults*, ed. Michael B. Cosmopoulos, 112–142. London.

Schwartz, Eduard. 1893. "Akusilaos (3)." In *RE* I/1, 1222–1223. Stuttgart.

Speyer, Wolfgang. 1977. "Religiöse Pseudepigraphie und literarische Fälschung." In *Pseudepigraphie in der heidnischen und Jüdisch-christlichen Antike*, ed. Norbert Brox, 195–263. Darmstadt. (Orig. pub. 1967.)

Thomas, Rosalind. 1989. *Oral Tradition and Written Record in Classical Athens*. Cambridge.

———. 1992. *Literacy and Orality in Ancient Greece*. Cambridge.

Toye, David L. 2009. "Akousilaos of Argos (2)." In *Brill's New Jacoby*, ed. Ian Worthington. Leiden.

Tozzi, Pierluigi. 1967. "Acusilao di Argo." *Rendiconti / Istituto Lombardo, Accademia di Scienze e Lettere, Classe di Lettere, Scienze morali e storiche* 101:581–624.

Ustinova, Yulia. 2009. *Caves and the Ancient Greek Mind. Descending Underground in the Search for Ultimate Truth*. Oxford.

Vollgraff, Wilhelm. 1909. "Inscriptions d'Argos." *Bulletin de correspondance hellénique* 33:171–200.

Vollkommer-Glökler, Doris. 1997. "Megaloi Theoi." In *LIMC* VIII/1, 820–828. Zürich and Düsseldorf.

West, Martin L. 1994. "*Ab ovo*: Orpheus, Sanchuniathon, and the Origins of the Ionian World Model." *CQ*, n.s., 44:289–307.

———. 1997. *The East Face of Helicon: West Asiatic Elements in Greek Poetry and Myth*. Oxford.

———. 1999. "The Invention of Homer." *CQ*, n.s., 49:364–382.

Williamson, Callie. 1987. "Monuments of Bronze: Roman Legal Documents on Bronze Tablets." *Classical Antiquity* 6:160–183.

"JUST DESSERTS"

REVERSALS OF FORTUNE, FECES, FLATUS, AND FOOD IN ARISTOPHANES' *WEALTH*

KAREN ROSENBECKER

"It's a strange world. Some people get rich and others eat shit and die."[1]

Hunter S. Thompson

A RISTOPHANES' FINAL COMEDY, *Wealth,* explores one of humanity's great existential conundrums: why do wicked people prosper while the just ones suffer? This question has driven Chremylus, the last of Aristophanes' heroic oldsters, to Delphi in order to ask whether the way to get ahead is to become unjust, given the obvious inversion of merit to reward.[2]

The exploration of the oracle's opaque answer, that Chremylus should attach himself to the first man he meets, results in the familiar

An earlier version of this paper was presented at the annual meeting of the Southern Section of the Classical Association of the Middle West and South in St. Louis, MO, in March 2004. Throughout the many revisions since then, I have received invaluable advice and support from April Spratley, Mae Smethurst, and Connie Rodriguez. Wilfred Major provided a particularly insightful critique of the penultimate draft, and I am grateful for the recommendations given by the readers and editors at *HSCP* as to how I could improve it still more. All mistakes and infelicities that remain, be they large or small, are completely my own. The texts of all plays and fragments of Aristophanes are quoted from N. G. Wilson's Oxford Classical Text of Aristophanes (Oxford, 2007); scholia are cited from *Scholia in Aristophanem III4a and III4b* (ed. D. Holwerda, Groningen, 1994 and 1996) and *Aristophanes Scholien* (ed. F. Dübner, Paris, 1842). Comic fragments from authors other than Aristophanes are cited as per R. Kassel and C. Austin's *Poetae Comici Graeci* (Berlin, 1986–2001). All English translations of the Greek are my own, unless otherwise noted.

[1] Thompson 1988:11.

[2] The question (εἰ χρὴ μεταβαλόντα τοὺς τρόπους | εἶναι πανοῦργον, ἄδικον, ὑγιὲς μηδὲ ἕν, | ὡς τῷ βίῳ τοῦτ' αὐτὸ νομίσας ξυμφέρειν, 36–38) was asked so that Chremylus could furnish advice to his son (35).

comic scheme to remake the world,[3] but the unexpected way in which Aristophanes unfolds this familiar trope marks *Wealth* as unique, particularly in terms of scatological humor. Here in his last extant play, Aristophanes presents his audience with an on-stage Athens nearly identical to the real world they occupy, a city in which the immediate concerns are the ubiquitous nature of poverty and the inequitable distribution of material resources,[4] instead of disputes over the shenanigans of corrupt politicos or the problems of an endless war. However, against this backdrop of daily hardships in a hand-to-mouth world, Aristophanes challenges his audience's assumptions and expectations concerning both their *polis* and his comedy through non-stop inversions and revisions of presumed norms. This article explores the program of reversals in *Wealth*, specifically how the opening episode— the re-presentations of the gods Wealth and Zeus *Soter*—creates the backdrop against which the poet reworks two mainstays of his genre: the role of sympotic activity[5] and of humor involving crepitation and scatophagy. Throughout the play, the presence of flatus, feces, and even urine in place of food and wine continues the play's inversion of expected and assumed customs and, in one pivotal scene, may even facilitate the success of Chremylus' scheme and the transformation of the on-stage world. Far from being disposable, off-color antics that serve only as personal insults or trite and tired clowning,[6] the role of

---

[3] Cf. similar schemes by Dikaiopolis (*Ach.* 130–134), Peisetairos (*Av.* 162–186), Trygaios (*Pax* 50–149, 289–300), Lysistrata (*Lys.* 96–128), Dionysus (*Ran.* 66–114), and Praxagora (*Eccl.* 204–212).

[4] For an overview of the conditions in Athens, see Strauss 1987:42–63. The aftermath of the Peloponnesian War created similar economic problems for other cities as well; e.g. in 371, demands for debt forgiveness and the redistribution of land led to violent riots in Argos (Diod. Sic. 15.57–58 [ed. P. J. Stylianou, Oxford, 1999]). In general, small farmers, like Chremylus and the chorus, were the most seriously affected, see David 1984:3, 19–20.

[5] Here sympotic activity is defined as the presence of desirable food, the ability to feast, access to wine, opportunities for sexual encounters, and participation in komiastic revelry. For a list of these as hallmarks of an ideal world, see *Ach.* 195–202, 247–279; *Av.* 128–142; *Pax* 338–345, 520–538; *Eq.* 1384–1395.

[6] In discussing the play, Henderson 1991:104–107 states that the use of "obscenity in *Plutus* shows a parallel change in character and function" similar to the play's disappointing departure from the earlier form of the genre. The scatological humor that does remain is characterized by "blunt, hackneyed crudities" and serves in the main

scatological humor in *Wealth* pushes these familiar jokes beyond their typical context and ultimately imbues them with a metaphorical sense that is surprisingly modern.

I. TRAPPED IN A TOPSY-TURVY WORLD

At the opening of the play, Aristophanes foregrounds the inversion and revision of expected norms even before a word of dialogue is spoken, by first presenting this topsy-turvy Athens visually.[7] Chremylus and his servant Cario enter bedecked in festal garlands but following a blind and filthy old man instead of a procession of revelers.[8] Comic speculation and threats verbally underscore the puzzling and contrary nature

---

as personal invective or slapstick. This assessment of the quality of the play's humor mirrors much of the scholarly assessment of the play's overall merits. In particular, Sommerstein 1984:314 points to a general decline in Aristophanes' literary faculties; MacDowell 1995:249, 327 points to the lack of impact of the political and social events within the *polis* upon the on-stage world, and to a lack of energy and a carelessness characteristic of old age; Halliwell 1997:202 discusses what he terms the "loose connection" of the *parodos* and choral passages to the action; Dover 1972:204–208 and 194n7 sees Cario as the predecessor of the clever slave of Menander's comedy but refers to *Wealth* as "clumsy in detail"; Bowie 1993:269 mentions the loosening of the bond between citizen and state; McLeish 1980:156 goes so far as to speculate that *Wealth* may have been composed after a stroke. These observations all correspond, on a general level, to the changes that ancient scholars themselves observed in comedy of the period, specifically the lack of political criticism (Platonius *De differentia comoediarum* 10–11 [ed. R. Kassel and C. Austin, Berlin, 1986–2001]) and the shift away from gross obscenity and toward innuendo (Arist. *Eth. Nic.* 4.8, 1128a22–25 [ed. I. Bywater, Oxford, 1920]). For more on scholarship critical of the merits of *Wealth*, see Sfyroeras 1996:231–232 and Olson 1990:223n1. Despite suffering a poor initial reception from modern scholars, *Wealth* was preeminent among Byzantine scholars and popular with audiences in the Renaissance and beyond; the play was variously translated and adapted in Jacobean England, and received a production at Trinity College sometime between 1626 and 1638, see Smith 1998:170–172.

[7] For an analysis of how costumes and props delineate the play's theme of inversion, see Groton 1990. Revermann 2006:261 observes that, in particular, Aristophanes' use of stage movements, costumes, and props allow the play's vision of utopia to unfold in a manner that is "problematized without being rendered undesirable." See also Hughs 2012:146–164 on how styles of acting might have emphasized the visual contradictions.

[8] In terms of the signs of a festive processional, the wreaths that Chremylus and Cario wear are specifically mentioned (20, 22), as is the sacrificial meat that Cario carries (227). Aristophanes continues to comment on the figure's shabby appearance (οὕτως ἀθλίως διακείμενος, 80; αὐχμῶν βαδίζεις, 84). Stone 1981:365 also suggests Wealth's costume may be nothing but a ragged *himation*.

of these events[9] and reach a crescendo when the old man is revealed to be the god Wealth himself, a discovery perhaps meant to shock Aristophanes' audience,[10] especially since the Athenians in particular may have been accustomed to the representation of the god Wealth as the young and beautiful son of Demeter.[11] The conception of Wealth as blind, however, did exist "not in cult but ... in poetic and popular imagination,"[12] specifically in the *skolia* of Timocreon and Hipponax, who depict the god as both blind and mean-spirited.[13] Yet here, too, Aristophanes re-frames that figure. Far from being the source of man's

---

[9] Specifically that following a blind man is doing the opposite of what is expected (i.e. the sighted should lead the blind, [13–15]). Compton-Engle 2013:155–170 suggests the dynamics of this opening scene may parody the opening of Sophocles' *Oedipus at Colonus*.

[10] In fact, Aristophanes has Chremylus and Cario register surprise at Wealth's miserable state (80).

[11] Particularly so because of the centrality of the Eleusinian Mysteries in Athenian culture. Wealth is named as a son of Demeter (Hes. *Th.* 969–974 [ed. F. Solmsen, R. Merkebach, and M. L. West, Oxford, 1990]) or as an attendant deity in celebrations for the Two Goddesses (*Hymn. Hom. Dem.* 486–489 [trans. M. Crudden, Oxford, 2009]; Ar. *Thesm.* 295–310). The god may also be depicted on the great Eleusinian frieze as a young boy holding a cornucopia and the revelation of his birth may be part of the *dromena* presented for those about to be initiated, see Clinton 1992:91–95.

[12] Cf. Sommerstein 2001:5–8. Another possibility for Aristophanes to misdirect the audience's expectations about the nature and appearance of the god Wealth may stem from Cratinus' *Ploutoi*, which featured an eponymous chorus of Wealth Gods, but the date of the play is uncertain. See also Revermann 2006:263, 307–308.

[13] Timocreon claims the god is both blind (ὦ τυφλὲ Πλοῦτε, 1) and a source of trouble for men (διὰ σὲ γὰρ πάντ' αἰὲν ἀνθρώποις κακά, 3–4), an opinion that Aristophanes will refute (143–146; cf. *PMG* 731 and Σ *ad* Ar. *Ach.* 532). Hipponax also comments on the god's blindness and hard-heartedness (Πλοῦτος—ἐστι γὰρ λίην τυφλός, 1; δείλαιος γὰρ τὰς φρένας, 4; cf. Hippon. 36 in *IE1* and Σ *ad* Ar. *Plut.* 87). Prior to the *agon*, Blepsidemus' reaction at the revelation that Wealth is in fact blind ("you're saying he really is blind?", τυφλὸς γὰρ ὄντως ἐστί; 403) shows that Aristophanes expected some of his audience to be aware of that tradition. See Sommerstein 2001 *ad* 203 for a more detailed discussion of the lyric fragments and the depiction of Wealth; for the tradition of a blind Wealth in iambic poetry, see Sfyroeras 1996:233–235. It is also worth noting that the comic poet Archippus, a contemporary of Aristophanes, had a comedy titled *Wealth* attributed to him as well; two fragments from that play would seem to speak of a decline in morality, but the larger context for these comments is uncertain and it is impossible to tell how closely his conception of Wealth may have paralleled that of Aristophanes (Archipp. 37, 38; cf. Σ *Vesp.* 418 and *Av.* 1648). In terms of contemporary prose, Plato both confirms (*Resp.* 8.554b5–6 [ed. S. R. Slings, Oxford, 2003]) and denies (*Leg.* 1.631c4–5 [ed. J. Burnet, Oxford, 1922]) a blind Wealth as it suits his arguments.

problems, this Wealth, despite his deplorable state, is the sole source of all man's benefits and moreover is actually the wellspring of Zeus' power.[14] Wealth's blindness, as Aristophanes re-presents it, is not a physical reflection of the god's misanthropic spirit, it is the literal cause of his seemingly senseless bestowal of riches upon the unjust.[15] Curing Wealth of his blindness will not only restore his benefits to the good folk of Athens, it will punish the god Zeus as well. Here in this initial scene, Aristophanes also introduces a new and repulsive vision of the Father of Gods and Men that is directly juxtaposed to the kindly Wealth. Although direct representations of Zeus never occur on the dramatic stage, in comedy it is neither uncommon nor problematic to enact both his overthrow and the promotion of mortals to a status that rivals or dominates his.[16] The typical description of Zeus in Aristophanic comedy is that of a god who is uninterested in the affairs of men and who becomes active only when the hero's plan affects him.[17] By contrast in *Wealth*, Aristophanes presents a monarchic Zeus (τυραννίδα, 124) who actively envies the just men of Athens (φθονῶν, 87; οὕτως ... φθονεῖ, 92), men whose moral, ethical, and even political decency (σοφούς καὶ κοσμίους, 89; χρηστοῖσι, 92) contrasts sharply with his malice.[18] In fact, it is Zeus himself who has blinded Wealth so that

---

[14] Chremylus and Cario sketch the all-encompassing nature of Wealth's power through direct claims (127–129) and a catalogue of his effects (130–197). By their logic, Wealth alone is the source of all things both good and bad (μονώτατος γὰρ εἶ σὺ πάντων αἴτιος καὶ τῶν κακῶν καὶ τῶν ἀγαθῶν, 182–183) and it is for his blessings that mortals sacrifice to Zeus (θύουσι δ' αὐτῷ διὰ τίν', 133).

[15] Sommerstein 1984:314–315 notes that Aristophanes' description of the rich as being unjust is itself a reversal of his usual association of the rich with the good.

[16] In other examples, Peisetairos becomes the new ruler of heaven (*Av.* 1748–1765), Trygaeus receives an apotheosis (*Pax* 1316–1357), and Socrates deconstructs and denies Zeus (*Nub.* 367–411).

[17] Prometheus alerts Peisetairos to Zeus' displeasure and the upcoming divine embassy only after the divine blockade is in effect (*Av.* 1515–1536); Hermes warns Trygaeus of Zeus' anger as the rescue of Peace begins (*Pax* 371–373).

[18] Given 2009:112–113 argues that "[this] is an extreme type of malevolence" that stands in contrast to the typical role of the gods as divine opponents in Aristophanes and that also stands in contrast to the φθόνος of the gods in tragedy, where the emotion arises in the divine as the result of human transgression. Although it is impossible to reconstruct to a certainty the fourth-century Athenian view on the nature of Zeus, there is ample background for the popular imagination found in epic and lyric poetry: Zeus

Wealth may never again visit those same just mortals whom he loves.[19] This deliberate cruelty by a god against those who worship him violates the ethos of reciprocity of treatment,[20] one of the cardinal moral principles of Greek culture, and thereby provides another instance of a surprising reversal of expected norms. The envious and punitive Zeus delineated in this opening scene of *Wealth* also stands in stark relief to the god in his role as Zeus *Soter* (Zeus the Preserver), an incarnation that had become increasingly popular in early fourth-century Athens.[21] In this role as protector and deliverer, Zeus as *Soter* was conceived of as a god whose beneficence was directed at the individual rather than at the *polis*, and was a deity whose role would appeal to the impoverished people both on and off the stage.

By establishing an angry and envious Zeus to contrast with a blind but moral Wealth, Aristophanes foregrounds the pattern of revisions and reversals of the norm that he will expand upon throughout the play. This program is especially evident in the atypical role of sympotic activity in the first half of *Wealth*. In many of his comedies, the escalating presence of food and wine usually mark the progress of the hero's scheme to remake the world and possess the good life s/he desires; indeed, the consumption of food and wine often seems to help facilitate the success of the hero's plan.[22] In terms of the link between foodstuffs

---

keeps order, demands that men work and maintain honesty in their dealings with one another, and commands that they honor the gods and respect the rites of ξενία. When men fail to do these things, punishment will follow; cf. Lloyd-Jones 1971:28–37.

[19] The assumption of enmity between Wealth and Zeus may stem from the Hesiodic tradition in which Zeus hides the bounty of the earth from humans, see Konstan and Dillon 1981:373n3. However, this mythological "backstory" is not invoked by Aristophanes to explain the extreme level of Zeus' hostility towards mortals in *Wealth*; see n. 20 below.

[20] Sommerstein 2001 ad 93–94 addresses the active hostility of Zeus at the outset of the play. Bowie 1993:271–75 also discusses this ethical breach in light of the cultural imperative of reciprocity. The scholia preserve a blunt assessment: ἐκ τούτου οὐδὲ ἀγαθὸς εἴη. See also Given 2009n26.

[21] All references to Zeus *Soter* in Aristophanes' plays date from 411 and later (cf. *Ran.* 738, 1433; *Eccl.* 79, 761, 1045; *Plut.* 877, 1175, 1186, 1189). Pausanias also attests to the presence of shrines in the Piraeus for both Zeus *Soter* and Athena *Soteira* by the fourth century (cf. Paus. 1.1.3 [trans. W. H. S. Jones, Cambridge, MA, 1918]). For a discussion of the rise of the cult of Zeus *Soter*, see Parker 1996:240–241.

[22] See n. 27 below.

and being wealthy, the association of one with the other is so strong that, in previous plays, Aristophanes had coined the word πλουθυγιεία ("wealthy-healthiness") to express the state of economic well-being based on a plentiful and healthy diet.[23] So, too, in *Wealth* is a state of affluence defined as absence of need and access to desirable food, as well as the acquisition of money and honors.[24] In addition to the direct naming of foodstuffs as a hallmark of possessing riches, man's desire for wealth is akin to eating. The words used to describe the satiety of pleasures (πλησμονή, 189; μεστός, 188 and 193) are terms that also apply to being physically filled with food. Moreover the phrase "no one ever gets full of you" (οὐδὲ μεστὸς σοῦ γέγον' οὐδεὶς πώποτε, 188; σου δ' ἐγένετ' οὐδεὶς μεστὸς οὐδεπώποτε, 193) both introduces and concludes the list of pleasures, honors, and edibles that being rich entails.

However, in *Wealth*, the good folk of Athens are food-insecure in the extreme.[25] Given the absence of food entailed by the lack of wealth, Aristophanes cannot use sympotic activity to mark Chremylus' progress towards the remaking of the world[26] nor to assist in the correction of the problem that has stymied this particular iteration of Athens.[27]

[23] The term πλουθυγιεία is a neologism coined by Aristophanes (cf. *Vesp.* 677; *Eq.* 1091; *Av.* 731) and used exclusively by him. The connotations of the term are discussed by Wilkins 1996:46.
[24] The catalogue of bounty creates a juxtaposition of the honors with foodstuffs. Note, too, the commensurate escalation of the marks of personal distinction—honor, battles, ambition, a generalship (191–192)—as the food mentioned also spans a range of desirability. Hunger is assuaged by the presence of staple foods, such as barley mash and porridge (192), while sweets, flat-cakes, and figs (190–191) suggest the possibility of a feast or even an erotic encounter. For a discussion of foodstuffs as synonymous with sexual organs and activities, see Henderson 1991:22, 118, 129, 134, 144, 160, 200.
[25] Chremylus and the chorus are described as reduced to eating thyme (τῷ δεσπότῃ ταὐτὸν θύμον φαγόντες, 253; θύμων ῥίζας διεκπερῶντες, 283), a wild plant not cultivated per se, but gathered from its naturally occurring patches as a food of last resort; cf. Dalby 1996:26. The general paucity of food is also stressed by Cario's description of the "tidbit of meat" (κρεάδιον, 227) that he received from the sacrifice at Delphi. Later in the *agon*, Poverty's insistence that Wealth is an evil is met by arguments that foreground the horrors of endemic hunger and food shortages (503–504, 535–539, 542–544, 562).
[26] As when the restoration of peace to Dikaiopolis' deme is illustrated by the return of the Rural Dionysia and the reappearance of desirable food items at his market (*Ach.* 247–279, 719–894).
[27] Examples of Aristophanic heroes using food, wine, or feasting in order to defeat their foes and effect universal change include Dikaiopolis "arming" himself for dinner to

Moreover, access to food is particularly crucial in *Wealth* because food is portrayed as the material axis of the relationship between men and gods. This premise, that the gods actually depend on human sacrifice for sustenance, is also invoked in *Birds* and is even used as a pressure point by Peisetairos during his negotiations with the divine embassy.[28] Here in *Wealth*, a similar logic is advanced by Chremylus, who claims the foundation of Zeus' supremacy is that mortals sacrifice to him in order to obtain wealth (θύουσι δ' αὐτῷ διὰ τίν', 133). However, given the inverted nature of the world in *Wealth*, when the good make their offerings Zeus provides resources to the undeserving (93–94). Consequently, the decent folk of *Wealth* are caught in a metaphysical contradiction: although sacrificial foodstuffs should be a tool to influence the gods, the ritual process produces a result that is the opposite of what is expected.

II. THE SEMANTICS OF SCATOLOGY AND STERCORAL "CURES"

In an on-stage Athens so defined by inverted expectations and contrarian divine order, to effect change would also seem to require surprising and inventive methods. Aristophanes carries this idea to a delightfully offensive extreme as the handling, production, and consumption of flatus, feces, and urine—substances that are surely the opposite of food[29]—become the hallmarks and in some cases the means by which Chremylus and Cario change their world. But in order for episodes of scatological humor to take on such an unaccustomed function, Aristophanes must alter the typical role played by these sorts of jokes. Humor relying on crepitation is of course *de rigueur* in Aristophanes, and the usual context for flatulence is fairly predictable: characters pass gas due to their coarse and uncouth nature; they may

---

counter Lamachus arming himself for war (*Ach.* 1081–1142), Sausage Seller's successful redistribution of food *qua* political graft (*Eq.* 1096–1215), Trygaeus "waging peace" by inviting the men of Athens on a city-wide holiday (*Pax* 713–717, 871–909), Peisetairos using cooking as a tool in his negotiations with the divine embassy (*Av.* 1579–1689).

[28] For a discussion on this point, see Dunbar 1995 on *Av.* 186.

[29] Just as the ruin of Trygaeus' agrarian life is reflected in the substitution of dung beetle for steed, feces for oatcakes, and urine for water (*Pax* 1–81).

also fart owing to fear, in order to express happiness and contentment, or as a display of arrogance and aggression.[30] However, within the catalogue of Wealth's power and desirability, there is an example of farting that is puzzling given the usual context of the act. When Cario makes a reference to the general Agyrrhius, he asks, "doesn't Agyrrhius fart because of it (wealth)?" (Ἀγύρριος δ᾽ οὐχὶ διὰ τοῦτον πέρδεται; 176). Modern interpretations as well as comments in the scholia have explained this fart variously as an expression of Agyrrhius' arrogant satisfaction with his own position, as a declaration of his contempt for those less fortunate, or even as evidence for his indulgent lifestyle.[31] In regard to these particular suggestions, Major rightly notes that this reasoning about Agyrrhius' fart is problematic.[32] Given Agyrrhius' high social status and role as a political figure, Aristophanes may not be alluding to Agyrrhius' happiness, contempt, or even his overfed lifestyle; instead his flatulence is a metaphor for public speaking and oratory and therefore it marks Agyrrhius as an example of a typology Major terms "the babbling butt."[33] Although Aristophanes doubtless intended to insult Agyrrhius by mentioning his flatulence, Major's interpretation suggests that crepitation may not merely be an indicator of a character's emotional state and coarse social background, farting may also connote other activities such as political speech and legislative activities.[34] In this way, when Agyrrhius

---

[30] For examples of this pattern and examples of these contexts for crepitation in Aristophanes and his contemporaries, see Henderson 1991:195–199.

[31] Sommerstein 2001 *ad* 176 suggests that Agyrrhius farts because he "hasn't a care in the world," citing parallel examples in Dover 1968 on *Nub.* 9, which list instances of farting to show "lively insouciance." However, the context for the episodes of flatulence cited by Dover is less ambiguous than the context for Agyrrhius' fart; see Major 2002:550.

[32] Agyrrhius' familial background and social status set him apart from the typical demographic of the flatulent (i.e. rustic, aggressive buffoons). See Major 2002:550 and Sommerstein 2001 *ad* 176 for a discussion of Agyrrhius' social background, Holzinger 1979 *ad* 176 for the history of the problems with the scholiasts' comments on Agyrrhius' fart.

[33] See Major 2002:551 for a discussion of the parallels between political speech and flatulence as evidenced in Aristophanes' contemporaries.

[34] Agyrrhius is an ideal target for this implication; his introduction of pay for attending the *Ekklesia* (*Ran.* 367 and Σ *ad Ran.* 367) and his time in prison for failure to repay public debt (Dem. 24.134–135) must have rendered him a well-known, if infamous, public figure.

farts for wealth (176), he is also sharing in the system that oppresses the good people of Athens.

This instance of expanding the expected context for fart jokes is in itself an inversion and suggests an expanded context of interpretation for this type of humor. A second example of flatus used in this sort of extended context occurs during the *agon* as Chremylus and his neighbor Blepsidemus must confront the personification of Poverty who has come to stop their plans to restore Wealth's sight. Chremylus successfully counters Poverty's insistence that Wealth is actually an evil by recounting the horrors of chronic deprivation, conditions so harrowing and oppressive that they seem the results of divine malevolence (500, 503–504, 535–539, 542–544, 562). As Poverty is subsequently banished from the stage, Blepsidemus sees her off by saying:

νὴ Δί', ἐγὼ γοῦν ἐθέλω πλουτῶν
εὐωχεῖσθαι μετὰ τῶν παίδων
τῆς τε γυναικός, καὶ λουσάμενος
λιπαρὸς χωρῶν ἐκ βαλανείου
τῶν χειροτεχνῶν
καὶ τῆς Πενίας καταπαρδεῖν.[35]

613–618

Yes indeed! As for me, I want to be rich and to feast in celebration of it, along with my kids and wife! I want to emerge sparkling clean from the bath, and then go blow a fart in the face of Poverty and her partisans!

In this instance, Blepsidemus' flatus is unquestionably an example of farting as an act of aggressive self-assertion performed by a character in a hostile situation,[36] but Blepsidemus also envisions his fart as being

---

[35] I have retained the proper name Πενίας here (Wilson reads πενίας). Poverty's exit can begin only at line 610 and Chremylus is still addressing her in lines 610–613. Given that, I think it is reasonable, and in keeping with the dramatic flow of the scene, to imagine that Blepsidemus is taunting her defeated and receding form as she exits the stage.

[36] καταπέρδομαι also marks aggressive flatulence at *Pax* 547 and *Vesp.* 618. For the centrality of self-assertion throughout the extant comedies, see Dover 1972:31–41. Blepsidemus' fart may also be interpreted as an example of passing gas in order to express glee over his emancipation from poverty (cf. Dover: 1968 on *Nub.* 9). In terms

the result of sumptuous dining, as εὐωχεῖσθαι (614) denotes celebrations that unite both revelry and feasting. Torchio suggest that the use of εὐωχεῖσθαι here is even more significant as this particular verb indicates that the celebration Blepsidemus envisions goes beyond the wish for a feast and marks the inception of a "land of plenty."[37] This image creates a strong contrast between mortals enjoying a celebratory feast and a divine figure being left with nothing but odiferous contempt, and thus Blepsidemus' fart punctuates the reversal of the oppressive circumstances endured by the just men of Athens so far. Unlike Agyrrhius, whose farts marked him as part of the corrupt system that hoarded wealth away from the *demos*, Blepsidemus breaks wind to mark the liberation of the just folk from that system.

This pattern—expanding the normal context for a joke, then using that transformed context so that the joke becomes both insult and illustration of the characters' movement towards "curing" the topsyturvy world—also holds true for humor regarding excrement. In terms of the typical comic exploitation of feces, the consumption of dung and depictions of characters in a state of incipient defecation seem to be regarded as fundamentally humorous.[38] Moreover, humor involving the handling of feces also serves to ridicule and refute the target of these insults, and as such it is not surprising that Aristophanes' heroes monopolize insults of this nature.[39] This context for jokes that hinge

---

of scatological humor used to prompt a character's exit, this episode has a parallel in Trygaeus confusing and banishing the Armorer by threatening to convert his breastplate into a chamber pot (*Pax* 1226–1239).

[37] Torchio 2001 *ad* 613–618. For uses of εὐωχέομαι in reference to celebratory feasts that indicate the entrance into or the existence of a "land of plenty," cf. *Ach.* 1009, *Lys.* 1224, *Eccl.* 716–717, *Ran.* 85.

[38] Note Strepsiades' mean-spirited merriment at the news a lizard had shat into Socrates' mouth (*Nub.* 169–174), the humor assumed in the protracted depiction of Blepyrus' constipation (*Eccl.* 313–371), and the assertion that a man in desperate need of easement is a very funny sight (Eub. fr. 52.3–6).

[39] Henderson 1991:7–11 outlines the general principle of the power dynamic created between the character making the joke, his target, and the audience; the point is also observed with specific reference to scatological humor, 187. Edwards 1991:164–165 notes this dynamic is particularly foregrounded in the cases of Sausage Seller (*Eq.* 997–998), Philocleon (*Vesp.* 625–626), Trygaeus (*Pax* 1235–1237), and Dionysus (*Ran.* 1074–1076), who in particular monopolize scatological humor within their respective comedies.

on the production or handling of dung is certainly applicable to *Wealth* as well, but here, too, Aristophanes both exploits this expected role of feces and extends that familiar context in order to transform the comic applications of feces. During the choral *parodos*, creative and atypical uses of feces figure prominently in the verbal duel between Cario and the members of the chorus. Cario, whose performative identity shifts from one figure of divine menace to another, attempts repeatedly to assign a servile role to the old farmers. Instead of allowing Cario's incarnation of the Cyclops to lead them as if they were his hapless flock, the chorus retaliate and summarily blind the monster (300–301). Cario swiftly turns himself into Circe and then invokes her mystical ability to transform men into swine, a transformation so complete that the pigs will even eat dung from her hands (302–305). In response, the chorus slips from being swine to again imitating Odysseus and his men (312), going so far as to rub Circe's nose in the dung as if she were a goat (μινθώσομέν θ' ὥσπερ τράγου τὴν ῥῖνα, 313–314), so that she is left gaping in a docile haze and blithely following the rest of the pigs (314–315).[40]

In general, the eating of feces is considered a typical characteristic of animals, especially pigs, and consequently scatophagous activity by humans is depicted as crude behavior more characteristic of beasts than of man.[41] In this passage Aristophanes is employing both of these connotations: the eating of dung by animals to highlight their lower nature, and the eating of dung by men to illustrate their coarse and socially inferior qualities, a status that is reflective of the contempt in which the gods hold mortals in this play. However, these scenes in the *parodos* also establish the use of feces as a curative and corrective substance, a usage perhaps based on folk remedies in animal husbandry, but one that also echoes the centrality of excreta in

[40] The phrase ἔπεσθε μητρὶ χοῖροι (308, 315) not only describes Circe's tractability but it also may be a play on either a child's oft-repeated refrain or meant as an insult towards the uneducated (i.e. children will be as ignorant as their parents); cf. Σ *ad* 308 and 315, Holzinger 1979 *ad* 313–314.

[41] For a discussion of scatophagous humor in general, see Henderson 1991:192–194. On the motif of animals as men and men as animals being an expression of a world-turned-upside-down, see Rothwell 2007:20–21.

Greek medical practices.[42] This second and peculiar use of feces in the *parodos*, its application to a goat's nose, is cited by the scholia as being therapeutic for respiratory ailments.[43] Consequently, when the chorus restore themselves to their roles as men, they mark the subjugation of the divine figure of Circe with an application of shit that acts as both a token of contempt and a remedy for divine oppression.

In the second half of *Wealth*, it is the production and consumption of feces, flatus, and urine—in keeping with their expanded context as un-food, symbol of servile status, and curative—that facilitates the restoration of Wealth's sight and marks the subservience of the oppressive divine hierarchy instituted by Zeus. As the skewed relation of merit to reward is corrected by Wealth's restored sight, sympotic activity at last begins to appear as the on-stage world is enriched. After the missing choral *parabasis*, Cario reappears and begins his account of the healing of Wealth with an urgent and insistent call for wine (ταχέως ταχέως φέρ' οἶνον, 644). Thus far in *Wealth*, wine had been mentioned only briefly in the choral *parodos* as part of the description of the fictive Cyclops (295–301). But, wine is the "home-brew" of Greek Old Comedy and the great gift of the god Dionysus to mortals, a link that Aristophanes drew upon when he dubbed his genre "wine song."[44] Consequently, the extreme delay in the presence of wine in *Wealth* punctuates the previous abysmal conditions, just as the demand for it now marks the return of the successful heroes, the enrichment of Chremylus' house, and the subsequent correction of the heretofore-skewed world order.[45]

[42] Stercoral cures and prescriptions are found throughout Egyptian medical writings, especially the Kahun and Ebers papyri (Pinch 1994:108–134; Halioua and Ziskind 2005:176–177, 215n33). Although Arango 1989:48–49 argues that feces were likely omnipresent ingredients in Greek and Roman folk medicine, the Hippocratic corpus treats feces as a powerful diagnostic tool, rather than as a medicinal additive; see n. 48 below.

[43] The explanation for this technique is that the feces induce sneezing (πταρμὸν χινεῖν), which in turn cures blocked or runny nasal passages. Later citations suggest that mint is a magic charm (τὴν ἴυγγα), but this citation would seem to confuse μίνθη, the mint plant, with μίνθος, human excrement.

[44] Cf. τρυγῳδία, *Ach.* 499, 500. For more on the connotations of τρύξ in drama, see Hall 2006:328–355.

[45] In this episode, Aristophanes also uses a gesture of high metatheater to show the enrichment of the house. At 788, Chremylus' wife reemerges from the house with a tray

It is not the presence or drinking of wine, however, that has facilitated the restoration of Wealth's sight.[46] As Cario narrates the events in
the temple of Asclepius leading up to the healing of Wealth, it becomes
clear that another substance has helped to correct the pattern of
inversion. The pivotal scene in which Wealth is cured, as it is narrated
by Cario, highlights two distinct episodes of farting: one that represents the expected humor of flatulence, the other that continues
Aristophanes' transformation of flatus into a substance that has world-
altering properties. During their incubation, Cario copies the priest,
who had been pilfering food from the sacred table and altar, and makes
for a pot of porridge belonging to another suppliant. The owner of the
pot, a Little Old Lady, attempts to ward off the assault upon the pot
(672–683). In an astounding feat of mimesis, Cario hisses like the sacred
snake of Asclepius and bites her hand, which then allows him to eat his
fill, but causes the Little Old Lady to crepitate out of fear (ὑπὸ τοῦ δέους
βδέουσα δριμύτερον γαλῆς, 693). Shortly thereafter, when Asclepius and
his daughters appear, Cario also farts (μέγα πάνυ ἀπέπαρδον, 698–699),
but not from fear. Instead, his flatulence comes from his stomach being
bloated with porridge (699), and he represents his flatulence as the god
draws near as a laughing matter (γελοῖον δῆτά τι ἐποίησα, 697–698).
The reaction of Asclepius' divine attendants is likewise humorous: Iaso
blushes and Panacea holds her nose (701–703). Just as the Little Old
Lady's flatus was rank (693), Cario's is too, but here he compares his,
negatively of course, to frankincense (οὐ λιβανωτὸν γὰρ βδέω, 703), an
aromatic incense typically offered to the gods as part of ritual worship.[47]

Despite the humor of the scene, Cario's fart is the direct precursor
to the healing of Wealth and may even be the substance that sets the
cure in motion. In describing his breech of decorum, Cario muses that

---

of καταχύσματα to shower on Wealth and presumably to throw to the audience; *Pax*
959–962 suggests this sort of stunt was not atypical, but here in *Wealth* the sweets remain
on the plate as an illustration of the increasing means of the house.

[46] Contrast with how the drinking of wine provides the inspiration for the overthrow
of Paphlagon (*Eq.* 108) and with Dercetes' certainty that Dikaiopolis' *spondai* will cure his
blindness (*Ach.* 1018–1036).

[47] All other mentions of frankincense in Aristophanes tie it directly to ritual (cf. *Nub.*
426; *Vesp.* 96, 861; *Ran.* 871, 888; *Plut.* 1114; Dalby 2000:114–116).

Asclepius seems to accept this odiferous votive offering. The aroma did not bother the god in the least because, as a physician, he is used to tasting stool (σκατοφάγον, 706). In framing this joke, Aristophanes plays with acknowledged medical practices of the period involving the close examination of both feces and urine as a diagnostic tool.[48] But in calling Asclepius a σκατοφάγος, Aristophanes is also playing with the overlap between comic depictions of scatophagous behavior and the low status often accorded to physicians.[49] In addition, this episode alludes back to the curative effects of feces cited in the choral *parodos* when the chorus stopped the fictive Circe with a dollop of shit on her nose (cf. 313–315), but most importantly, Asclepius' "consumption" of Cario's flatus does what all the previous sacrifices could not: it unblocks the ritual process and prompts a god to act in a way that benefits the good folk of Athens. Upon partaking of Cario's flatus, the god arranges it so that Neoclides the blind and corrupt orator is subject to a painful cure and thereafter cannot perjure himself before the assembly (724–725).[50] Wealth, on the other hand, is treated with great care during the cure and is tended to by Asclepius, Panacea, and two of the sacred serpents (727–736). Cario then ends his account by summing up the speed of Wealth's recovery: before his mistress could guzzle ten glasses of wine, the god could see again (737–738). This second mention of wine

---

[48] The scholia preserves the comment διότι οἱ ἰατροὶ ἐκ τοῦ τὰ σωμάτων κενώματα βλέπειν καὶ οὖρα τοὺς μισθοὺς λαμβάνουσιν. Hippocrates considers a close inspection of excreta to be of central importance in diagnoses (cf. *Prog.* 2.11–16); the color, shape, and consistency of stools (*Prog.* 11.1–30), the sound and occasion of flatulence (*Prog.* 11.31–42), and the amount and appearance of urine (*Prog.* 12.1–39) are all used to gauge patient health; e.g. description of the plague in *Epid.* 3, which may also be the plague of Thuc. 2, contains sixteen case studies in which the color, quantity, and smell of feces and urine figure prominently in charting the progression of the disease (*Epid.* 3.17.1–353 [all trans. W. H. S. Jones, Cambridge, MA, 1923]).

[49] In particular coarseness of manner (ἄγροικον ... τὸν θεόν, 705; cf. 305; *Pax* 48). Chang 2008:220–226 notes that attitudes towards physicians in Classical Greece were often ambivalent, observing that the lack of state regulation of medical practices and the hands-on nature of the job resulted in physicians being regarded with suspicion and in the practice of medicine being regarded as messy and distasteful manual labor.

[50] It is worth noting that we are never told whether Asclepius restores Neoclides' sight, only that he "cures" the man's politics. For more on Neoclides' political machinations, see *Eccl.* 254, 398.

brings the narration full circle and alludes to the burgeoning *komos* that will celebrate the world moving to its newly restored moral order.

III. "ORDER UP!": SERVING "JUST DESSERTS" TO THE MOST DESERVING

In the final episodes of *Wealth*, Aristophanes depicts a level of enrichment for the just folk of Athens that is the inverse of their previous state of scarcity, beginning with a visual tableau that reframes the opening scene of the play. At the head of the procession returning from the temple of Asclepius are, once again, Wealth followed by Chremylus. Here, though, the wreaths and celebratory language now match the mood portrayed on stage.[51] The bounty that Wealth has bestowed upon Chremylus is indeed remarkable, ranging from the predictable elements of monetary wealth such as silver and gold, to an overabundance of food.[52] The house is now transformed, in effect, into the new temple of restored wealth, and because the traditional sacrificial process can now work, the god Wealth is able to respond reciprocally to the offerings of the just, thereby enriching them as well.

Whether we are to understand the second half of *Wealth* as representing a true utopia or as one beset by ironies and inconsistencies has long been a topic of debate.[53] What is certain is that the four "intruder scenes"[54] that round out *Wealth* illustrate the correction

---

[51] The celebration is specifically indicated by the fact that the immense crowd thronging about the returning heroes are wreathed for celebration (750–752, 757) and overjoyed by Wealth's presence (753).

[52] The full list includes white barley in the bins, dark and fragrant wine in the amphorae, lots of oil and figs in the loft, bronze and silver dishes, an ivory oven, and the fact that servants now cleanse themselves with garlic after defecating (807–818). This last item highlights an association between material wealth and pleasant circumstances for defecation (cf. *Ach.* 81–83).

[53] For an overview of the "ironic" and "anti-ironic interpretations" of *Wealth*, see Ruffell 2006; Konstan and Dillon 1981:378n10, 386n20. As part of this debate, McGlew 1997:49–50 suggests that finding irony in the play depends on audience reception, rather than on any unambiguous evidence in the text.

[54] The scenes pair the Just Man and the Informer (823–958), the Old Woman and the Gigolo (959–1094), Hermes and Cario (1099–1170), and the Priest of Zeus *Soter* and Chremylus (1171–1190).

of the heretofore-skewed world order, as the on-stage Athens finally moves from poverty to feast and celebration. The first two intruder scenes show the swift, but not unproblematic, reshaping of the human world through the appearance of food, wine, and revelry. The scene with the Just Man and the Informer plays out the most obvious effect of Wealth's sight: that the good shall be enriched and the unjust shall be impoverished. In fact, by just as much as the Just Man now finds himself rich (825), the Informer now finds himself ruined and wracked by hunger (850–854, 873). That Chremylus is roasting an abundance of tuna inside his newly opulent house serves to emphasize the Informer's lost wealth and power, as his accusations of gastronomical and political malefaction now fall on deaf ears (893–900).[55] In the following intruder scene, the entrance of the Gigolo, drunk and decked out for a *komos*, and his ensuing mock-flirtation with the Old Woman (1039–40, 1048, 1055–1069) makes it clear that celebrations have proceeded apace throughout this on-stage Athens, although neither character is able to fully enjoy the *komos*.[56] Far from being sympathetic to the complaints of either, Chremylus first torments the Old Woman[57] but then enforces the "contract" between them and uses a sympotic metaphor to explain to the Gigolo that since rational moral order has been restored, the young man must uphold his end of the bargain: the Gigolo drank the

---

[55] This scene exploits the connection between tuna and shady politics; cf. Paphlagon's *pisca*-political appetites (*Eq.* 353–355) and the accusations of tyranny leveled against those who consume too much fish (*Vesp.* 489–499). For a longer discussion of the union of politics and fish, see Davidson 1998:278–308.

[56] In terms of their conflicting desires, the Gigolo longs to be rid of his former meal ticket (993–1005, 1076–1079), but the Old Woman is loath to release him (1032, 1095–1096). However, their reversed circumstances are not as clear-cut as those of the Just Man and the Informer. The Old Woman speaks of her wealth strictly in terms of buying the Gigolo's affections (981–986, 999–1002), but it does not seem that the new distribution of wealth has left her poor; instead she has been stripped of the illusion of beauty that her wealth had provided. The Gigolo's newly enriched life (1003–1005) allows him to "see" his former paramour's true age (1042–1043) yet not to be rid of her (1084–1094) since she is still due his attentions for goods provided (1028–1030, 1084–1086). See also Sommerstein 1984:324–325 on the problematic nature of the scene.

[57] Chremylus' insults are based on the well-established link between women and food in Aristophanes; see Henderson 1991:144. Pütz 2007:62–65 discusses the parodies of sympotic games played by Chremylus and the Gigolo at the expense of the Old Woman.

Old Woman's "wine," now he must drink the "lees" as well, even if they are old and rotten (1084-1086).

The final two intruder scenes reveal that the effects of the new world order have at last reached the gods themselves. The interactions of Cario and Hermes, and of Chremylus and the Priest of Zeus *Soter*, present the long-awaited reversal of power between human and god and show that the newly enriched mortals are not only free from divine persecution but are now also superior to the very same gods who had treated them so poorly for so long. This contrast is highlighted by the reification of an image from the end of the *agon*, that of mortals feasting in a "land of plenty," free from want while the gods are left with a product of the bowels (cf. 613-618). Here in these last two intruder scenes, flatus, urine, and feces are offered as food to the gods both to insult them and to express their new position as subservient to the whims and will of mortals.

Prior to the healing of Wealth, Cario had been the food-obsessed slave, concerned with his belly to such an extent that for him, wealth manifested itself first and foremost through the presence of food (cf. 190-193, 802-822). Now Hermes will take this role from him. Much as Cario brought news of the healing of Wealth, Hermes arrives bringing news of the woes on Olympus: Zeus is furious that no sacrifices are being offered to the gods anymore, and Hermes is himself now starving and looking for new employment (1107-1119, 1146-1170). After reminding Hermes that this neglect at the hands of the mortals is of the gods' own creation (1116-1117), Cario uses a series of aural puns based on the god's complaints of deprivation to drive home the extent to which Hermes is now receiving his comeuppance. When Hermes despairs over the loss of the sacrificial ham (κωλῆς, 1128), Cario tells him to "ham it up" all he likes (ἀσκωλίαζ', 1129). When the god bemoans the innards denied him (σπλάγχων τε θερμῶν, ὧν ἐγὼ κατήσθιον, 1130), Cario says it does sound as if his gut is troubling him (ὀδύνη σε περὶ τὰ σπλάγχν' ἔοικέ τις στρέφειν, 1131). Finally, when Hermes cries out for strong wine (οἴμοι δὲ κύλικος ἴσον ἴσῳ κεκραμένης, 1132), Cario responds by telling him to drink "this" and then get out (ταύτην ἐπιπιὼν ἀποτρέχων οὐκ ἂν φθάνοις, 1133).

The text of the play is, of course, opaque as to what substance or prop ταύτην may refer. We learn at 1168–1170 that Cario may have emerged from the house carrying offal (τὰς κοιλίας, 1169), but even so, ταύτην cannot refer to τὰς κοιλίας. What, then, could Cario be offering Hermes as the climax of his taunts at 1133? Translators, commentators, and scholiasts have, in general, suggested three answers.⁵⁸ The most common suggestion is that ταύτην is meant to refer to a χύτρα or κύλιξ that Cario was holding when he re-emerged from the house.⁵⁹ Although the gender and number of either noun would agree with ταύτην, that wine would be onstage for so long and not be commented on is unusual.⁶⁰ More importantly, if this exchange is meant to tease Hermes about his state of deprivation, then offering him wine is not in keeping with the rest of the humor that exploits denial, lack, and a reversal of fortune.

Even though the presence of wine on stage would be a potent symbol of the restored world, it has also been suggested that ταύτην refers to a substance that has been offered to deities twice at this point in the play: a fart (πορδή). This reading is supported by a scholiast's gloss on ταύτην as πορδήν, which explains that Cario farted just before he spoke 1133.⁶¹ Further support for this reading may come from understanding that Cario interprets Hermes' stomach trouble as gas pains rather than hunger pangs, and then responds to that allusion by farting himself.⁶² Although interpreting ταύτην as πορδήν would fit in

⁵⁸ A fourth possibility is that the demonstrative here stands for ψωλήν (cf. ταυτηνί, *Lys.* 956), but given that the tenor of the scene is culinary rather than sexual, this seems unlikely.

⁵⁹ Understanding ταύτην as referring to a χύτρα was suggested by Rogers 1907 *ad* 1133; Olson 1989 agrees. Henderson 2002 suggests ταύτην refers to a κύλιξ in response to Hermes mourning the loss of his own (οἴμοι δὲ κύλικος, 1132; cf. Halliwell 1997 ad loc.). In contrast, Torchio 2001 leaves the line ambiguous, translating it as "tracanna questa" and providing no notation at 1097 to indicate that Cario enters with any prop.

⁶⁰ Cario returns to the stage at 1097, but the prop is first referred to at 1133. Note the near immediate identification of wine upon the entrances of Amphitheos (*Ach.* 175, 184), Dikaiopolis (*Ach.* 1198, 1203), and Nicias (*Eq.* 99, 101).

⁶¹ Σ *ad* 1133 ταύτην· Παίζει· αὐτίκα γὰρ τῷ Ἑρμῇ λόγῳ ἀπέπαρδε. Θ. ἥν ἔπαρδεν.

⁶² ὀδύνη ... ἔοικέ τις στρέφειν, 1131; cf. *Pax* 175; *Thesm.* 484. Holzinger 1979 *ad* 1131 cites examples from other comic writers that pair ὀδύνη and στρέφειν as shorthand for incipient crepitation, stating that 1131 "handelt der Vers vor einer πορδή."

with the pattern of marking contempt and subservience with feces and flatus, to read the line in this manner is impossible to do with certainty, especially given that Cario instructs Hermes to "drink" (ἐπιπινών, 1133) the substance in question.[63]

A third possibility is suggested by Sommerstein, who observes that there is a parallel between Cario emerging from the house with a prop that is initially unidentified and an episode in *Birds* in which Peisetairos likewise emerges from the house with a prop that is only much later named as a night-stool.[64] In fact, Sommerstein suggests that Cario may have come on stage with both a chamber pot and the offal, an idea that, again, is impossible to prove, but is in keeping with the play's rigorous program of reversals and juxtapositions. This interpretation would also allow for a clear meaning for ἐπιπινών (1133). If Sommerstein's reading is correct, Cario would be offering Hermes urine to drink while he himself is holding the sweetbreads taken from the triple sacrifice preformed when Wealth entered Chremylus' house (cf. 819–820). This scene, then, would act as a reification of two extremes envisioned by Blepsidemus in the *agon*: a mortal enjoying wealth and congenial feasting, while a god is offered excreta (cf. 613–618).[65]

Hermes, however, is not the king of the gods and although his mortification and demotion to house servant (1170) are satisfying

---

[63] ἐπιπινών could be used here metaphorically (i.e. "quaffing" the fart) but such a use would be a *hapax legomenon*.

[64] Peisetairos emerges from the house (*Av.* 1495) but the prop is first identified when he hands it to Prometheus (δίφρον, *Av.* 1552). Although Sommerstein takes the prop to be a night-stool, Dunbar 1995 on *Av.* 1308, 1552 understands it as a regular stool, rather than a commode. For a longer discussion in support of Cario returning with a δίφρον *qua* chamber pot, see Sommerstein 2001 *ad* 1133. I would suggest that the prop in question may be more properly identified as an ἀμίς (cf. *Vesp.* 807, 858, 935, 940, 946; *Thesm.* 633) or σκωραμίς (cf. *Eccl.* 371) thereby matching the gender of ταύτην and being something immediately recognizable to the audience as neither a wine jar nor a chair.

[65] Although Sommerstein's conjecture is appealing, it should be noted that jokes about drinking urine are in fact rare in Aristophanes. Only the monstrous dung beetle is offered urine to drink (*Pax* 49). Ar. fr. 269 does mention pissing in a wine jar, but whether the contents would then be passed off as wine is unclear. Urine is, of course, not the only material to be found in a chamber pot, but there can only be speculation as to the precise nature of the contents that Aristophanes meant for his audience to envision Hermes drinking.

developments, he is not the god most responsible for the injustices that Chremylus and those like him have suffered. The final intruder scene between Chremylus and the Priest of Zeus *Soter* shows the ultimate inversion of the old exploitative order and the extent to which eating excrement has acquired its new metaphorical meaning. As the last interloper, the Priest of Zeus *Soter* brings the news that, thanks to the reallocation of material wealth, he is now starving because no one needs to sacrifice or ask for help from the priests anymore (1172–1181, cf. 1112–1116); instead people now throng to the temples only when they need to defecate (πλὴν ἀποπατησόμενοι γε πλεῖν μύριοι, 1184). This joke at the expense of the corrupt religious official is heightened by Chremylus' unsympathetic response that the Priest take his official cut from those offerings (οὔκουν τὰ νομιζόμενα σὺ τούτων λαμβάνεις; 1185). The punchline may lose something in translation, but in advising the proxy of Zeus *Soter* to take a share from the feces left behind by the just folk of Athens, Chremylus literally offers the corrupt gods, and those who benefit from their malfeasance, the substance that they have metaphorically force-fed to decent mortals.[66]

These final two intruder scenes once again reframe the expanding meaning of scatological humor. By using the consumption of flatus, feces, and urine to mark the subservient status of the gods, Aristophanes creates a new metaphorical meaning for scatophagy. Here at the close of *Wealth*, to "eat shit" has come to mean something akin to the meaning of the phrase in modern American slang, where it describes an unequal relationship from the perspective of a subordinate who must endure unpleasant situations created by more powerful

---

[66] It is worth noting that this scene between Chremylus and the Priest of Zeus may help support the interpretation that Cario offers Hermes πορδή or the contents of a chamber pot at line 1133. The structural parallels between the scenes (i.e. a messenger arrives with news of how the restoration of wealth has affected Zeus [1106–1116, 1172–1175]; the messenger is more concerned with their own suffering [1120–1135, 1174–1175] and requests admission to the house [1146–1147, 1188–1189], the messenger is taunted and offered something unpleasant to consume [1125–1138, 1185], but then is allowed to join in the festivities [1169–1170, 1186–1190]) create a correspondence between the two. Given those similarities, it is possible that the unspecified substance (ταύτην, 1133) is also something parallel to the feces alluded to Chremylus (1185).

agents.[67] A widely circulated folk etiology for the phrase places its origins with the United States Army where the expression began as "eat, shit, and die" and was used to describe the role of the soldier at its most basic; the phrase was then generalized to describing the essential activities of man. The point at which it was altered to "eat shit and die" is lost in the annals of American slang, but the change is understandable given the ubiquitous use of the noun "shit" to describe unpleasant circumstances.[68] Whatever its origins may be, the phrase "eat shit and die" was well in place in the popular vernacular by the end of the 1980s when journalist Hunter S. Thompson used it to preface his account of the gross inequities he observed in the social and political climate in America during that decade.[69]

For the ancient Greeks, the necessity of enduring these same sorts of existential insults and inequities is part of the normal relationship between men and the gods. Perhaps the best example of this cultural principle is the parable of the two urns of Zeus, which warns that

[67] Variations on this expression include "shitburger" and "shit sandwich." That these variants bear the same meaning as "eat shit" can be observed in a joke commonly attributed to the American comedian Jonathan Winters: "Life is a shit sandwich. But if you've got enough bread, you don't taste the shit" (quotingquotes.com/3871 [accessed 02/01/14]). For the commonly cited background for the development of the phrases "eat shit" and "eat shit and die," see the entries at wikipedia.org/wiki/Shit (accessed 02/01/14).

[68] As the noun "shit" and the verb "shit" are homonyms, to mistake one for the other, especially when hearing the words, would be natural. The development of the phrase "eat shit and die" from the original "eat, shit, and die" represents an amphibology similar to the now famous "eats, shoots, and leaves," in which the ambiguity of verb "shoots" and noun "shoots" also created a new meaning for the phrase. For background on "eats, shoots, and leaves," see Lynn Truss Gotham's *Eats, Shoots & Leaves: The Zero Tolerance Approach to Punctuation* (Gotham 2004).

[69] More existential variants of the phrase "eat shit and die" include "shit happens" and the bowdlerized version "it happens," which are used to acknowledge that bad things often happen for no discernable reason. Much as with the phrase "eat shit and die," the origin of this expression "shit happens" is difficult to trace. The movie *Forrest Gump* (Paramount Pictures, 1994) creates a moment for the titular character to coin the phrase sometime in the late 1970s or early 1980s, thereby helping to inspire the ubiquitous bumper sticker, but this is a Hollywood-created etiology. *The Yale Book of Quotations* categorizes "shit happens" as a modern proverb and traces the first in-print use of the expression to an item titled "UNC-CH Slang" and dated to 1983 (see *Modern Proverbs* entry 83, 2006 ed.).

Zeus may mingle libations from both the urn of blessings and the urn of sorrows for men, or that he may pour them only from the urn of sorrows.[70] Consequently, difficulties in life arise from the divine mix that is part of the very workings of the universe. Since suffering at the hands of a superior cannot be avoided (i.e. all lives have a portion from the urn of sorrows), it is no surprise that seeing an average man with a crazy scheme go on to achieve spectacular success is central to the appeal of Aristophanic comedy. For humans who find themselves "living in a world populated by superhuman agents," as well as being subject to their social and political betters, comedy provides a chance at revenge, an opportunity to "hit back" at all oppressors, both human and divine.[71] However, even within the broad latitude for insult provided by Old Comedy, Aristophanes cannot bring the figure of Zeus onto the stage, as direct representation of the god was conventionally disallowed in both tragedy and comedy. That said, Aristophanes can insult the god by proxy through the rude treatment accorded the Priest of Zeus *Soter* and by sketching the downfall of Zeus as a *fait accompli*. At 1189, we learn that the god himself, weary of these fecal offerings, has already come of his own accord into Chremylus' temple of the restored Wealth (1189–1190).[72]

---

[70] δοιοὶ γάρ τε πίθοι κατακείαται ἐν Διὸς οὔδει | δώρων, οἷα δίδωσι· κακῶν, ἕτερος δὲ ἐάων. | ᾧ μὲν κ' ἀμμίξας δώῃ Ζεὺς τερπικέραυνος, | ἄλλοτε μέν τε κακῷ ὅ γε κύρεται, ἄλλοτε δ' ἐσθλῷ· | ᾧ δέ κε τῶν λυγρῶν δώῃ, λωβητὸν ἔθηκεν, | καί ἑ κακὴ βούβρωστις ἐπὶ χθόνα δῖαν ἐλαύνει, | φοιτᾷ δ' οὔτε θεοῖσι τετιμένος οὔτε βροτοῖσιν. (*Il.* 24.527–533, [ed. D. B. Monro and T. W. Allen, Oxford, 1920]). This attitude is not a simply a Homeric *gnome.* Solon's interview with Croesus is an extended example of the fluctuations in the fortunes of mortals caused by the gods alternating the good with the bad (Hdt. 1.30–33); it ends with a final admonition that "the god(s) utterly overturn many after first granting them prosperity" (πολλοῖσι γὰρ δὴ ὑποδέξας ὄλβον ὁ θεὸς προρρίζους ἀνέτρεψε (Hdt. 1.33.11–12 [ed. C. Hude, Oxford, 1927]). Similarly, the Herald sent to announce Agamemnon's victorious return admonishes the chorus that no one can live forever without experiencing some pain and suffering (Aesch. *Ag.* 553–554). The metaphor of Zeus' urns is also echoed in Socrates' image of the mortal soul as a charioteer who is given two horses to drive, one good and one bad (Pl. *Phdr.* 246e–247b).

[71] Dover 1972:31; for his discussion of the centrality of human self-assertion to Aristophanic comedy, see also Dover 1972:31–39.

[72] There is a long-standing question as to whether ὁ Ζεὺς ὁ σωτήρ (1189) should indicate Wealth (i.e. "the real Zeus the Preserver") rather than the god Zeus. Rogers 1907 ad loc. suggests that 1189 must refer to Zeus, but Olson 1989 posits that the audience would

This final scene, in which the Priest of Zeus the Preserver and the ubiquitous yet unseen god receive their "just desserts," illustrates the last movement of the wholesale reordering of society that began with the rediscovery of Wealth. Not only has Aristophanes shown his audience an Athens free from poverty, but he has also presented one in which the nature of how wealth operates has been redefined. In creating this newly enriched Athens at the expense of those who had exploited her decency and morality, Aristophanes has expanded upon the theme of reversals throughout *Wealth* both by re-presenting the natures of Wealth and Zeus *Soter*, and also by reframing the expected context for jokes involving feces, urine, and flatus. At the close of the play, to leave the gods to consume excreta or inhale flatus is more than an indicator of coarseness of character and more, even, than a gesture of ridicule; it has become a metaphor that illustrates how thoroughly the world has been remade, one that helps to place the just mortals in control and one that gives the gods a chance to literally and figuratively eat shit.

LOYOLA UNIVERSITY NEW ORLEANS

WORKS CITED

Arango, A. 1989. *Dirty Words: Psychoanalytical Insights*. Northvale, NJ.

Bowie, A. M. 1993. *Aristophanes: Myth, Ritual and Comedy*. Cambridge.

Chang, H. 2008. "Rationalizing Medicine and the Social Ambitions of Physicians in Classical Greece." *Journal of the History of Medicine and Allied Sciences* 63:217–244.

Clinton, K. 1992. *Myth and Cult: The Iconography of the Eleusinian Mysteries*. Stockholm.

Compton-Engle, G. 2013. "The Blind Leading: Aristophanes' *Wealth* and *Oedipus at Colonus*." *CW* 106:155–170.

---

understand that it was Wealth to whom Chremylus was referring. However, Sommerstein 2001, much like Rogers, argues that since 1191–1192 read "we are going to install Wealth" (τὸν Πλοῦτον), the audience would understand that Wealth is not being referred to as Zeus the Savior in 1189; if he were, Aristophanes would have simply used the pronoun αὐτόν. For more on the history of the varying interpretations of these lines, see Holzinger 1979 ad loc., Torchio 2001 ad loc., Konstan and Dillon 1981:383n16.

Dalby, A. 1996. *Siren Feasts: A History of Food and Gastronomy in Greece*. London.

———. 2000. *Dangerous Tastes: The Story of Spices*. Berkeley.

David, E. 1984. *Aristophanes and Athenian Society of the Early Fourth Century B.C.* Leiden.

Davidson, J. 1998. *Courtesans and Fishcakes: The Consuming Passions of Classical Athens*. New York.

Dover, K. J. 1968. *Aristophanes. Clouds*. Oxford.

———. 1972. *Aristophanic Comedy*. Berkeley.

Dunbar, N. 1995. *Aristophanes. Birds*. Oxford.

Edwards, A. 1991. "Aristophanes' Comic Poetics: Τρύξ, Scatology, Σκῶμμα." *TAPA* 121:157–179.

Given, J. 2009. "When Gods Don't Appear: Divine Absence and Human Agency in Aristophanes." *CW* 102:107–127.

Green, W. C. 1892. *The* Plutus *of Aristophanes*. Cambridge.

Groton, A. 1990. "Wealth and Rags in Aristophanes' *Plutus*." *CJ* 86:16–22.

Halioua, B., and B. Ziskind. 2005. *Medicine in the Days of the Pharaohs*. Cambridge.

Hall, E. 2006. *The Theatrical Cast of Athens: Interactions between Ancient Greek Drama and Society*. Oxford.

Halliwell, S., trans. 1997. *Aristophanes Birds, Lysistrata, Assembly-Women, Wealth*. Oxford.

Henderson, J., 1991, *The Maculate Muse: Obscene Language in Attic Comedy*. 2nd ed. Oxford.

———, trans. 2002. *Aristophanes IV: Frogs, Assemblywomen, Wealth*. Cambridge, MA.

Holzinger, K. 1979. *Aristophanes' Plutos*. New York. (Orig. pub. Vienna, 1940.)

Hughs, A. 2012. *Performing Greek Comedy*. Cambridge.

Konstan, D., and M. Dillon. 1981. "The Ideology of Aristophanes' *Wealth*." *AJP* 102:371–394.

Lloyd-Jones, H. 1971. *The Justice of Zeus*. Berkeley.

MacDowell, D. M. 1995. *Aristophanes and Athens: An Introduction to the Plays*. Oxford.

Major, W. 2002. "Farting for Dollars: A Note on Agyrrhios in Aristophanes *Wealth* 176." *AJP* 123:549–557.

McGlew, J. 1997. "After Irony: Aristophanes' *Wealth* and its Modern Interpreters." *AJP* 118:35–53.

McLeish, K. 1980. *The Theatre of Aristophanes*. London.

Olson, S. D. 1989. *Aristophanes. Plutus*. Bryn Mawr, PA.

———. 1990. "Economics and Ideology in Aristophanes' *Wealth*." *HSCP* 93:223–242.

Page, D. L. 1962. *Poetae Melici Graeci*. Oxford.

Parker, R. 1996. *Athenian Religion: A History*. Oxford.

Pinch, G. 1994. *Magic in Ancient Egypt*. Austin.

Pütz, B. 2007. *The Symposium and Komos in Aristophanes*. Exeter.

Revermann, M. 2006. *Comic Business: Theatricality, Dramatic Technique, and Performance Contexts of Aristophanic Comedy*. Oxford.

Rogers, B. 1907. *The Plutus of Aristophanes*. London.

Rothwell, K. 2007. *Nature, Culture and the Origins of Greek Comedy: A Study of Animal Choruses*. Cambridge.

Ruffell, I. 2006. "A Little Ironic, Don't You Think?: Utopian Criticism and the Problem of Aristophanes' Late Plays." In *Playing Around Aristophanes: Essays in Honor of the Complete Edition of the Comedies of Aristophanes by Alan Sommerstein*, ed. L. Kozak and J. Rich, 65–104. Cambridge.

Sfyroeras, P. 1996. "What Wealth Has to Do with Dionysus: From Economy to Poetics in Aristophanes' *Plutus*." *GRBS* 36:231–261.

Smith, B. 1998. "Comedy." In *Ancient Scripts & Modern Experience on the English Stage, 1500–1700*, 134–198. Princeton.

Sommerstein, A. H. 1984. "Aristophanes and the Demon Poverty." *CQ*, n.s., 34:314–333.

———. 2001. *Aristophanes. Wealth*. Warminster.

Stone, L. M. 1981. *Costume in Aristophanic Comedy*. New York.

Strauss, B. 1987. *Athens after the Peloponnesian War: Class, Faction and Policy 403–386 B.C.* Ithaca, NY.

Thompson, H. S. 1988. *Generation of Swine: Tales of Shame and Degradation in the '80s*. New York.

Torchio, M. 2001. *Aristofane. Pluto*. Turin.

West, M. L. 1989. *Iambi et Elegi Graeci*. 2nd ed. Oxford.

Wilkins, J. 1996. "Eating in Athenian Comedy." In *Food in European Literature*, ed. J. Wilkins, 46–56. Exeter.

CRITO'S CHARACTER IN PLATO'S *CRITO*

YOSEF Z. LIEBERSOHN

I. INTRODUCTION

ANALYZING THE WHOLE of any of Plato's dialogues within the limits of an article is no longer possible. This is true even of a relatively short dialogue such as the *Crito*. This paper will focus on what might seem to be a marginal issue, but is, as I hope to show, rather one of the most important issues to be considered in analyzing Plato's dialogues: determining what exactly is the character of each player *in a specific dialogue*.[1]

The *Crito* is a conversation between Socrates and Crito, where each of the interlocutors tries to persuade the other to act in a certain way. Crito tries to persuade Socrates to escape from jail and Socrates tries to convince Crito to stop trying to persuade him to run away. Throughout the dialogue Socrates is the one who dominates the conversation, and we are to assume that Socrates knows his interlocutor's personality and what one may call "frame of mind"—including his explicit and implicit views—and designs his strategy accordingly. Understanding Crito's character is therefore a necessary step in analyzing the *Crito* and deciphering its message. I shall argue that Crito as he appears in Plato's

---

All English translations, unless otherwise mentioned, are taken from Vol. 1 of Plato's works in the Loeb series, translated by H. N. Fowler (1914) with some necessary modifications.

[1] The words "*in a specific dialogue*" are important and need to be emphasized. The characters appearing in Plato's dialogues have their own personalities that are shaped by Plato in accordance with the specific dialogue in which they appear. Thus, Crito, Critias, Meletus may appear in more than one dialogue, but they are fictitious characters (albeit based on historical people), and Plato can present them in each dialogue as he pleases, to suit the context. While Crito appears in other dialogues too, Crito in the *Crito* may not be better understood from studying Crito in the *Apology*, the *Phaedo*, or the *Euthydemus*. On this issue see my paper Liebersohn 2005:306–307. See also n. 39 below.

Crito is designed as a complex personality with regard to friendship, the state, and above all justice. Disentangling this complexity can not only solve some problems raised in the secondary literature, but can also throw new light on the exact status and significance of the speech of the Laws that occupies the greater part of the dialogue, and lead eventually to an understanding of the dialogue in its entirety.

II. IS CRITO A PHILOSOPHER?

The importance of deciphering Crito's personality and world-view before proceeding to the discussion between him and Socrates (actually *in order* to be able to deal with it) is prominently expressed in two books wholly dedicated to analyzing the *Crito*.

Weiss 1998 and Stokes 2005 each dedicate a whole chapter to a description of Crito.[2] Weiss' view is plainly expressed by the title of one of the sections in her book "The Unphilosophical Crito" (pp. 43–49). Weiss bases her description mainly on evidence she finds in the *Crito* itself, pointing to three facts in support of her view.

(1) "Crito is seen to regard Socrates' impending death as calamitous." As she comments, this is not a philosophical view.

(2) "Crito does not wish to take counsel; he wants only to be obeyed."

(3) "Socrates avoids using the term 'soul' in Crito's presence, referring instead to 'that which becomes better by the just and is destroyed by the unjust.'"

If this description is accepted, one would infer what Weiss does infer, that Crito is wholly ignorant of philosophy, or even stupid.[3] The *Crito*, especially the Laws' speech, is accordingly seen as aimed at the non-

---

[2] I take these books as representative of recent secondary literature, especially because they dedicate a declared and self-standing discussion to Crito's character, which is my main subject in this paper (Weiss 1998:43–49; Stokes 2005:23–35). This is not to dismiss any other discussions that appear in articles and chapters in books dealing with Plato in general, and some of these, indeed, will be mentioned in due course.

[3] Weiss 1998:43–49. The fact that Socrates does not use the term ψυχή in his conversation with Crito is considered by Weiss to be proof of "Crito's total estrangement from philosophy" (43n12). For a similar view, see Fox 1956:227. For a discussion of Weiss'

philosophical citizen who should keep the laws for non-philosophical reasons.[4] I shall address Weiss' evidence in detail, but before doing so, I wish to turn to a view quite different from that of Weiss. Stokes regards Crito as an ordinary intelligent man, who perhaps is not a perfect and devoted philosopher, but still "likes to listen, and is glad to learn."[5]

A third view I would like to propose is that Crito, far from being stupid, and far from being a layman with regard to philosophy,[6] is in fact well acquainted with philosophical arguments as used by Socrates. One need only recall the whole passage 49a4–c11 to accept that Crito is quite familiar with philosophical discussions, including philosophical terminology and premises.[7] On the other hand, it cannot be denied that he frequently advances vulgar opinions and uses philosophical terms unphilosophically. Thus, as against his "preference for death over justice," he believes that "in no circumstances must one act unjustly,"[8] and against his "not wishing to take counsel"[9] when Socrates suggests

---

opinion, see immediately below. See also my paper "The Place of ψυχή in Plato's *Crito*" (Liebersohn 2015).

[4] Weiss' view towards the Laws' speech as not representing Socrates' own position is known in scholarship as "the separation thesis" (first termed by Brickhouse and Smith 2006). For a list of other "separationists," see Weiss 1998:5–6. For an opposed view—"the integration thesis"—see Dasti 2007. Though it is not my intention to argue this point here I may add that in my view this very dispute between "separationists" and "integrationists," based on the division between Socrates' own position, namely what he says in his own name, as against imaginary speakers brought by him (such as the Laws in the *Crito*), does not seem to be very useful, since even when speaking in his own name one should remember that he speaks to someone and at least some of his arguments or statements could, therefore, be *ad hominem*. See, for example, my paper, Liebersohn 2011, where I argue that what Vlastos 1991 has called "Socrates' Rejection of Retaliation" should not be referred to Socrates but is an *ad hominem* argument directed at Crito and his special problem.

[5] Stokes 2005:30. Stokes uses, though with a certain reservation, other dialogues too.

[6] As against both Young 1974 (especially p. 6, and see also n. 25 below) and Colaiaco 2001:202.

[7] A question such as τὸ δὲ εὖ καὶ καλῶς καὶ δικαίως ὅτι ταὐτόν ἐστιν, μένει ἢ οὐ μένει; ("And does this hold good or not, that to live well and honorable and justly are the same thing?", 48b7–8) simply cannot be referred to one who is "totally estranged from philosophy." Moreover at 44c6–d5 Crito even seems to agree that one is to prefer the opinion of the *epieikestatos* ("most reasonable man") rather than that of the Many. On this issue, see my discussion pp. 110–112 below.

[8] 45a1–3 and 49b7 respectively. Here I use the 1979 tanslation by Woozley.

[9] On "preference for death over justice" and "not wishing to take counsel," see Weiss' first and second arguments above against considering Crito a philosopher.

to investigate with him, his answer is "I will try" (49a3).[10] It is my claim that the apparent discrepancy in Crito's expressions is *not* to be ascribed to Crito's ability or inability to philosophize or to his education, but rather to the circumstances in which he finds himself. This is clearly emphasized by the multiple references made both by Crito and Socrates to "then" and "now."[11] In other words, in regular circumstances Crito is a follower of Socrates, and accepts how terms such as *dikaion* ("right") and *andreia* ("courage"), to mention but two examples, are used by Socrates. When circumstances change, however, all these philosophical perceptions and insights are put aside. Indeed, the greater part of Socrates' effort in the *Crito* is to remove this discrepancy in Crito's character.[12] Plato has created Crito as a "*then* and *now* character" in the *Crito*. This essential feature of the character is in danger of

[10] A similar view is found in the 1999 article by Verity Harte. Harte is aware of these two somewhat inconsistent sides in Crito's character, and conjectures: "One might suggest that Crito is confused" (p. 131). In the end Harte takes Crito to represent the ordinary Athenian citizen whose "value system might be described as involving 'kinship values'" (p. 140). In this sense Harte's view is closer to that of Stokes 2005, but not too far from that of Weiss 1998.

[11] E.g. 43b7–8 (πρότερον–νῦν: "hitherto," "in this present misfortune"); 44d2 (αὐτὰ δὲ δῆλα τὰ παρόντα νυνὶ ...: "for this very trouble we are in now shows ..."); 46b4 (οὐ νῦν πρῶτον ἀλλὰ καὶ ἀεὶ: "not only now but always"); 46b6–7 (τοὺς δὴ λόγους οὓς ἐν τῷ ἔμπροσθεν ἔλεγον οὐ δύναμαι νῦν ἐκβαλεῖν: "and I cannot, now ... discard the arguments I used to advance"); 46d2–3 (ἢ πρὶν μὲν ἐμὲ δεῖν ἀποθνῄσκειν καλῶς ἐλέγετο, νῦν δὲ ...: "or were we right before I was condemned to death, whereas it has now ..."). In general the entire passage 46b1–47a5 is wholly dedicated to this principal of countermanding Crito's discrepancy between "then" and "now." Had Crito not fallen victim to this discrepancy, Socrates would not have emphasized his own consistency throughout his life.

[12] To take but one example: At 46e3–47a2 we read: σὺ γάρ, ὅσα γε τἀνθρώπεια, ἐκτὸς εἶ τοῦ μέλλειν ἀποθνῄσκειν αὔριον, καὶ οὐκ ἂν σὲ παρακρούοι ἡ παροῦσα συμφορά ("For you, humanly speaking, are not involved in the necessity of dying to-morrow, and therefore present conditions would not lead your judgment astray"). Weiss 1998:43n11 refers to this passage. Criticizing the view of Young (1974) who sees here an "ironic proof that Socrates recognizes that Crito is not able to have unclouded judgment at this moment and stick to Socratic principles", Weiss writes: "The irony in this passage is even greater ... because Crito has never really embraced Socratic principles at all." In my view Socrates' remark rather reflects the complicated situation in which Crito finds himself and Socrates' attempt to encourage Crito to return to his philosophical self. In Weiss' interpretation Socrates' remark would have no purpose.

being lost when elements of this or that Crito from other dialogues (all based on the same historical figure) are introduced into this dialogue. The "*then* and *now* character" solves not a few problems long ago raised by scholars, as will now be demonstrated. It will also provide a better understanding of the whole of the *Crito*, as will be shown later.

III. WHAT IS JUSTICE?

Strangely, there is in the *Crito* no discussion of the sort so prevalent in other dialogues of Plato, where the central term used in the dialogue takes on a personality of its own and calls forth an independent discussion in the form of "what is *X*."[13] This absence is even stranger here, since justice is not merely a term that appears in the *Crito*,[14] but is the notion at the heart of the conversation. Even more important, it is a notion over which Socrates and Crito are sharply divided.[15] At 48b10–d6 Socrates appears to begin a new discussion that continues to the end of the conversation, on "whether it is just[16] for me to try to escape from here without the permission of the Athenians, or not just" (πότερον δίκαιον ἐμὲ ἐνθένδε πειρᾶσθαι ἐξιέναι μὴ ἀφιέντων Ἀθηναίων ἢ οὐ δίκαιον). Yet this new discussion is actually only the last stage of a long process starting two pages before, at 46b1, after Crito's second speech.[17] It is in this speech that Crito uses for the first time a cognate of "justice."[18] We shall discuss Crito's various uses of justice and its

---

[13] See e.g. *Euth.* 5c9–d7; *Phileb.* 12c5; *Men.* 71d5; *Theaet.* 145e9, 146b11; *Lach.* 190e3; *Hipp. Maj.* 287d3; *Rep.* 331d2–3.

[14] In the *Crito* there are no less than 48 appearances of *dik-* and derivatives in the sense of "just, right" and the like.

[15] This question has indeed been raised and addressed by scholars. See Stokes 2005:91–94. Harte, whose paper is devoted to the different meanings of justice suggested in the *Crito*, notices the absence of a discussion concerning "what is justice" but seems not to give it much significance: "Neither Socrates nor Crito spells out their respective conceptions of justice. But an impression of the difference between them can be extrapolated from what each of them says" (1999:132).

[16] Fowler 1914 translates "right."

[17] It is no accident that Socrates begins his reply not with "justice", but with "rightness" (ὀρθότης, 46b2).

[18] 45c6–7: Ἔτι δέ, ὦ Σώκρατες, οὐδὲ δίκαιόν μοι δοκεῖς ἐπιχειρεῖν πρᾶγμα, σαυτὸν προδοῦναι, ἐξὸν σωθῆναι ("And besides, Socrates, it seems to me the thing you are

cognates later on, but for the moment it will suffice to hypothesize that Socrates understands Crito's usage, and that all the stages of his refutation are now organized around the axis of justice. If so, however, the absence of any discussion of the nature of justice might seem puzzling.

The answer is actually quite simple if my main hypothesis is correct: a discussion concerning justice is unnecessary since Crito knows very well what justice means for Socrates. The whole discussion at 49a4–c11 is steeped with the concepts of justice and injustice; but even earlier in the conversation Socrates has made use of justice and Crito has not asked what justice is. Crito knows what justice is for Socrates, and his problem lies precisely in adhering to this meaning of justice in the special circumstances in which he finds himself. The present situation may have Crito being governed by a popular notion of justice (on which later), but he is still well aware of the other—philosophical— meaning of this term. As for Socrates, it is evidently contrary to his aims to open a discussion on the question "what is justice." It is sufficient for his purposes to leave in the background the right and philosophical meaning of justice (from Socrates' point of view, of course, but a meaning hardly unfamiliar to Crito), and to conduct the discussion on the basis of the popular notion currently governing Crito.

IV. DEATH: MENTIONING AND INSINUATING

One of Weiss' arguments for claiming that Crito is not a philosopher is as follows: "Crito is seen to regard Socrates' impending death as calamitous ... Crito's attitude is unphilosophical" (1998:43). In my opinion the fact that Crito regards Socrates' impending death as calamitous is only evidence for one side of Crito's character, namely that side that has succumbed to the present conditions and is concerned with the danger of losing both a friend and his own reputation among the Many. Yet a careful examination of Crito's reference to the evaluation of death, rather than to death as a mere fact, reveals some points of interest. At

---

undertaking to do is not even just—betraying yourself when you might save yourself"). Here also what I have translated "just" is translated by Fowler 1914 as "right."

44d1–5 Crito responds to Socrates' attempt to deny the importance of the Many:

Ἀλλ' ὁρᾷς δὴ ὅτι ἀνάγκη, ὦ Σώκρατες, καὶ τῆς τῶν πολλῶν δόξης μέλειν. αὐτὰ δὲ δῆλα τὰ παρόντα νυνὶ ὅτι οἷοί τ' εἰσὶν οἱ πολλοὶ οὐ τὰ σμικρότατα τῶν κακῶν ἐξεργάζεσθαι ἀλλὰ τὰ μέγιστα σχεδόν, ἐάν τις ἐν αὐτοῖς διαβεβλημένος ᾖ.

But you see it is necessary, Socrates, to care for the opinion of the Many, for this very trouble we are in now shows that the Many are able to accomplish not by any means the least, but almost the greatest of evils, if one has a bad reputation with them.

Almost all commentaries interpret the words τὰ μέγιστα τῶν κακῶν ("the greatest of evils") as hinting at death. If this is the case, why not mention death explicitly? It cannot simply be an issue of style, since at 48a10–11 Socrates mentions death explicitly: "ἀλλὰ μὲν δή," φαίη γ' ἄν τις, "οἷοί τέ εἰσιν ἡμᾶς οἱ πολλοὶ ἀποκτεινύναι ("But one might, of course, say that the Many can put us to death").[19] Moreover, what Socrates puts into the mouth of this fictitious questioner is exactly what Crito has argued much earlier at 44d1–5. It is my contention that Crito, as Socrates' follower, is careful not to place too much weight on death: note the word "almost" (*schedon*) which Crito adds after "the greatest." It is, however, precisely death that informs his present *sumphora*. His "compromise" is to mention death in a roundabout manner. In short, Crito's choice reflects the tension between "then" (Crito as Socrates' follower) and "now" (Crito as an Athenian citizen who is troubled by the idea of losing a friend and his own good reputation among the Many). This is exactly why Socrates will later reformulate the same argument, but with two modifications. First, death will be mentioned explicitly. Second, it will be mentioned neither by Crito nor by Socrates, but by an imaginary fictitious questioner.

---

[19] Crito's response is enthusiastic (48b1): Δῆλα δὴ καὶ ταῦτα· φαίη γὰρ ἄν, ὦ Σώκρατες ("Yes, that too is clear; one would say that").

Socrates formulates for Crito what he—Crito—would have formulated himself had he not been wavering between "now" and "then."

V. THE MANY OR THE MOST REASONABLE MEN

Throughout our dialogue Crito delivers two speeches, and it is only through these two speeches that Socrates can fully understand Crito's conflict of interests. This information, indeed, serves Socrates in his treatment of Crito and his problems. For my limited purpose in this article I shall concentrate on Crito's first speech and Socrates' response (44b6–d10).

At 44b6–c5 Crito offers two reasons for encouraging Socrates to escape, namely his friendship with Socrates and his concern for his own good reputation among the Many. Socrates, however, easily but subtly discovers that the second point is what really motivates Crito, his care for his good reputation among the Many. He does this by mentioning in his response only Crito's argument from reputation and wholly ignores the issue of friendship. Thus we read (44c6–d2):

ΣΩ. Ἀλλὰ τί ἡμῖν, ὦ μακάριε Κρίτων, οὕτω τῆς τῶν πολλῶν δόξης μέλει; οἱ γὰρ ἐπιεικέστατοι, ὧν μᾶλλον ἄξιον φροντίζειν, ἡγήσονται αὐτὰ οὕτω πεπρᾶχθαι ὥσπερ ἂν πραχθῇ. ΚΡ. Ἀλλ᾽ ὁρᾷς δὴ ὅτι ἀνάγκη, ὦ Σώκρατες, καὶ τῆς τῶν πολλῶν δόξης μέλειν …

SOC. But, my dear, Crito, why do we care so much for what the Many think? For the most reasonable men, whose opinion is more worth considering, will think that things were done as they really will be done. CR. But you see it is necessary, Socrates, to care for the opinion of the Many …

Crito is here put to the test; had friendship really been what motivated him he should have protested against its omission. Crito does not protest, and Socrates concentrates from now on solely on the reputation motif.[20] Socrates' efforts at this stage focus on drawing a sharp

---

[20] For the relations between these two reasons in Crito's world-view, see also Weiss 1998:40 and n. 2 above for further references. See also West 1989.

distinction between the Many and the *epieikestatoi* ("most reasonable men"). This is carried out in two stages. First (at 44c6–9) Socrates simply dismisses the Many in favor of the *epieikestatoi;* incidentally, this move would not have been made had Socrates had no hope of Crito being able to accept such a distinction. Crito, indeed, does accept the distinction: in his reply he does not dismiss the opinion of the *epieikestatoi,* but rather *adds* the opinion of the Many. This is clearly emphasized by the word *kai* ("as well," 44d1).[21] The *kai* indicates that in principle Crito does appreciate the superiority of the opinion of the *epieikestatoi;* the reason for taking the opinion of the Many into account here is that this has caused the special circumstances in which Crito finds himself (a death punishment awaiting Socrates with all its consequences, including the loss of Crito's own good reputation among the Many). Given these circumstances, one has—in Crito's opinion, of course—to consider *also* the opinion of the Many.[22] In other words, Crito has two different outlooks, one when Socrates' life and his own reputation among the Many are safe, and the other when Socrates' life and his own reputation among the Many are in danger. Socrates' second attempt is based exactly on an assumption that Crito accepts such a distinction, and that Crito *also* considers the opinion of the Many only due to the current special circumstances.

At this stage Socrates appears to feel that one more "push" can make Crito return to the right way. Now (at 44d6–10) Socrates tries to sharpen the distinction between the *epieikestatoi* and the Many by focusing on each group's ability and power. As against the ability possessed by the Many to take *one*'s life, Socrates introduces what for him is—and, we assume, has also been for Crito—the superior ability of the *epieikestatoi* to make a man wise (or "prudent," *phronimos*). The

---

[21] Fowler 1914 (above) and Woozley 1979 both ignore the word *kai* in their translations. Treddenick 1961 correctly translates: "You can see for yourself, Socrates, that one has to think of popular opinion *as well*" (emphasis mine).

[22] This is clearly emphasized by Crito's' words αὐτὰ δὲ δῆλα τὰ παρόντα νυνὶ ὅτι ... (44d2–3, "your present position is quite enough to show that ..."; Tredennick's translation). Moreover, in his response at 46b1 (to be discussed shortly) Socrates begins with a kind of a *protreptikos logos* which focuses exactly on this point, namely the tension between "then" and "now," and tries to remove it.

ability of the Many is thus to be seen as inferior and should be paid no attention. Socrates does not entirely fail to influence Crito. At 44e1, Crito answers ταῦτα μὲν δὴ οὕτως ἐχέτω ("Well, let that be so"),[23] and immediately starts his long speech trying to discover what could deter Socrates from accepting his offer to escape. This response (ταῦτα μὲν δὴ οὕτως ἐχέτω) which "is used to indicate acceptance," as Stokes has justly noted,[24] teaches Socrates how serious Crito's problem is in deciding between these two criteria, namely, Socrates' teaching and the opinion of the Many.[25] Crito's response (ταῦτα μὲν δὴ οὕτως ἐχέτω) does acknowledge Socrates' statement at least in principle, but the long speech that immediately follows on this acknowledgement, a speech in which Crito is trying to guess what could deter Socrates from accepting his offer to escape, testifies very clearly to the fact that this confirmation is still very far from expressing Crito's real feelings, and that it is rather the other criterion—the opinion of the Many—that dominates him, or at least does not let him adhere to his philosophical training.

VI. JUSTICE, RIGHT, AND THE LAWS' SPEECH

As has already been observed, Socrates does not initiate a discussion concerning "what is justice,"[26] although justice plays a crucial part throughout the dialogue.[27] The term "justice" and cognates appear frequently in the speech of the Laws. I shall argue that only by assuming that Crito is vacillating between two meanings of justice—the popular and the philosophical—can the Laws' speech be fully understood and its exact aim be clarified. It is my contention that the Laws' speech does not set out to teach Crito anything concerning justice (Crito is well aware of what justice is and what it should be) but is intended to turn Crito away from the popular meaning of justice that he now uses

---

[23] Woozley 1979's translation.

[24] Stokes 2005:216n72.

[25] This as against Young's view (1974:6): "Crito is one of the Many. The dialogue *Crito* makes this clear." Crito is, indeed, taking care of the Many, but this does not mean that he is simply one of them.

[26] See p. 107 above.

[27] See n. 14 above.

because of his *sumphora* and back to its philosophical meaning. This is done by taking Crito's current, popular, concept of justice and using it against Crito himself.

Crito is the first in this dialogue to use a cognate of the term "justice." This should reveal what Crito really means by using this term, since he is taking the initiative.[28] The first mention appears at 45a1: ἡμεῖς γάρ που δίκαιοί ἐσμεν σώσαντές σε κινδυνεύειν τοῦτον τὸν κίνδυνον καὶ ἐὰν δέῃ ἔτι τούτου μείζω ("since we are just [*dikaioi esmen*] to run this risk in saving you, and even a risk greater than this if necessary"). If here we are not sure what *dikaioi* exactly means, we find somewhat later, at 45c6–9, another mention of 'just' that gives us some information concerning its content:

Ἔτι δέ, ὦ Σώκρατες, οὐδὲ δίκαιόν μοι δοκεῖς ἐπιχειρεῖν πρᾶγμα, σαυτὸν προδοῦναι, ἐξὸν σωθῆναι, καὶ τοιαῦτα σπεύδεις περὶ σαυτὸν γενέσθαι ἅπερ ἂν καὶ οἱ ἐχθροί σου σπεύσαιέν τε καὶ ἔσπευσαν σὲ διαφθεῖραι βουλόμενοι.

And besides, Socrates, it seems to me the thing you are undertaking to do is not even just [*dikaion*]—betraying yourself when it is possible to be saved.[29] And you are eager to bring upon yourself just what your enemies would wish and what those were eager for who wished to destroy you.

What Crito understands by the terms *dikaioi* and *dikaion*, so it seems, has something to do with saving friends and with not doing the will of enemies. In other words, Crito is here motivated by the popular notion of justice, "to help friends and to harm enemies." In the secondary literature, however, these terms, *dikaioi* and *dikaion*, are interpreted as not referring to justice. Already Adam 1888 in his commentary on 45a1 translates "it is right that we" and on 45c6 he comments: "it is not correct to translate δίκαιον here as 'just': it is 'right', 'moral.'" It is not

---

[28] Crito would of course be aware of Socrates' usual usage, but he may hope that the conventional view of justice that currently concerns him may also sway Socrates if he uses it first.

[29] Fowler 1914 translates "you might" and Woozley 1979 "when saving it [sc. your life] is possible."

hard to guess what brought Adam to this conclusion, which, by itself and without taking the drama into account, is right.[30] There are other appearances of this term in other places in the dialogue that necessarily should refer to justice in its strict and philosophical meaning (e.g. 45a6–46a9 passim). Indeed, most scholars and translators followed Adam's insight, among them Fowler's translation cited above.

Here I come to my main argument: Crito's use of "just" and cognates, at least at this point in the conversation, is in the popular sense. The fact that afterwards Socrates and Crito can have a philosophical conversation concerning "justice," and indeed use "justice" in the strict and philosophical meaning of the word is no problem at all. It rather reflects the "*then* and *now* tension" in which Crito finds himself, and at the same time it also corroborates our hypothesis concerning this very tension. When Crito tries at 45c6–9 to convince Socrates to escape jail he uses a popular and unphilosophical meaning of "justice"; when he responds to Socrates at 47c8–48a10, and especially at 49a4–e3, the meaning of this term is philosophical.[31] Socrates is doing nothing but trying to return Crito to the philosophical meaning of "justice," and this is the point of the Laws' speech.

In order to see how the Laws' speech fights fire with fire in response to Crito's popular meaning of justice, we should first examine how Crito expects to achieve his aim. His material means include the use of connections and money. His rhetorical means are directed at Socrates himself, in an attempt to persuade him to exploit the opportunity created to escape from jail and save his life. Crito's long speech 44e1–46a9[32] is wholly devoted to trying to convince Socrates to accept the offer to escape. It is principally divided into two main parts. The first (44e1–45c5) seeks and refutes possible reasons for Socrates not

---

[30] Adam's conclusion is no doubt based on the standard interpretation of the linguistic facts of the usage of *dikaios + einai + infin.*, which are codified in *LSJ*'s entry on *dikaios* under heading C.

[31] In all the places where the term *dikaion* and derivatives are used in a philosophical meaning it is Socrates who initiates and handles the discussion. The only places where Crito uses *dikaion* or a derivative on his own initiative are at 45a1 and 45c6 cited above.

[32] Crito makes two speeches. The first is at 44b6–c5, but it is a kind of an emotional outburst, *pace* Stokes 2005:27–28. Although it teaches Socrates what really motivates Crito (see p. 110–111 above) it is irrelevant to our present argument.

accepting Crito's offer. These are Socrates' concern for his friends after his escape, and Socrates' apprehensions regarding places of refuge. The second part (45c6–46a9) is aimed at trying by rhetorical manipulations to persuade Socrates to accept the offer to run away. The two main themes are Socrates' apparent neglect of his children, and his claim to have virtue (ἀρετή). When we turn to the Laws' speech we find exactly these themes.[33] In other words, all the themes used by Crito to persuade Socrates to escape are now used by the Laws to persuade Socrates not to escape.[34] Let us have a look at two examples. In Crito's speech we find the argument concerning Socrates' children: πρὸς δὲ τούτοις καὶ τοὺς ὑεῖς τοὺς σαυτοῦ ἔμοιγε δοκεῖς προδιδόναι, οὕς σοι ἐξὸν καὶ ἐκθρέψαι καὶ ἐκπαιδεῦσαι οἰχήσῃ καταλιπών (45c10–d2, "And moreover, I think you are abandoning your children, too, for when you might bring them up and educate them, you are going to desert them and go away"). Against this argument the Laws present a counter argument (54a2–7):

ἀλλὰ δὴ τῶν παίδων ἕνεκα βούλει ζῆν, ἵνα αὐτοὺς ἐκθρέψῃς καὶ παιδεύσῃς; ... ἢ τοῦτο μὲν οὔ, αὐτοῦ δὲ τρεφόμενοι σοῦ ζῶντος βέλτιον θρέψονται καὶ παιδεύσονται μὴ συνόντος σοῦ αὐτοῖς;

But perhaps you wish to live for the sake of your children, that you may bring them up and educate them? ... will they be better brought up and educated if you are not with them than if you were dead?

The same goes for the argument concerning virtue (ἀρετή). Crito was the first to make use of this argument: χρὴ δέ, ἅπερ ἂν ἀνὴρ ἀγαθὸς καὶ ἀνδρεῖος ἕλοιτο, ταῦτα αἱρεῖσθαι, φάσκοντά γε δὴ ἀρετῆς διὰ παντὸς τοῦ βίου ἐπιμελεῖσθαι (45d7–9) ("and you ought to choose as a good

---

[33] This has already been noticed by Harte 1999:134–137. Yet Harte sees here an alternative suggested to Crito where his principle of taking care for his friends and relatives should be expanded to include the laws and the state. On Harte's view, see also n. 38 below.

[34] Socrates may be hinting to this at 50b6–7, just before the beginning of the Laws' speech: πολλὰ γὰρ ἄν τις ἔχοι, ἄλλως τε καὶ ῥήτωρ, εἰπεῖν ("for one might say many things, especially if one were an orator"). On this point, see Weiss 1998:84–95.

and brave man would choose, you who have been saying all your life that you cared for virtue"). The Laws have their answer too: λόγοι δὲ ἐκεῖνοι οἱ περὶ δικαιοσύνης τε καὶ τῆς ἄλλης ἀρετῆς ποῦ ἡμῖν ἔσονται; (53e6–54a2, "What will become of our conversation about justice and virtue?").

The message is clear.[35] If the opinion of the Many is one's criterion for justice, one must accept that the Many, in the form of the Laws, are stronger than one individual.[36] Crito uses every means he can find in order to achieve his aim, but so does the polis (as presented by the Laws). Crito, who came very early to Socrates' cell quite sure of his success in smuggling Socrates out of jail, finds himself at the end of the conversation with nothing to say. In other words, Socrates' retort to the Laws does not represent any kind of frustration or an attempt to teach Crito a new meaning of "justice."[37] Its aim is to subvert the device by which Crito tries to make Socrates run away, namely through speeches and rhetoric. By using the same device, the Laws show Crito that speeches and generally rhetoric are not the way to reach the right decision. This interpretation explains Crito's response whereby he neither agrees nor disagrees (οὐκ ἔχω λέγειν: "I have nothing to say," 54d9). He cannot decide, since both speeches—his own and that of the Laws—used the same themes but ended with opposite results. When an *aporia* is reached a different method should be looked for. Rhetoric apparently proves to be unhelpful.[38]

---

[35] The Laws' speech is by no means exhausted by this one point.

[36] Here rhetoric has been treated as only an example of the means at one's disposal. However, just how important rhetoric was in a democracy where speeches are prominent in public life is beyond the scope of this article.

[37] As against both the "separationists" and the "integrationists"; see n. 4 above.

[38] My view here is very similar to that of Harte 1999 but because of our different starting points we reach different conclusions. Both of us agree that Crito's concept of justice is that of the Many, namely one's obligation to do whatever one can in order to help one's friend (τοὺς μὲν φίλους εὖ ποιεῖν, τοὺς δ' ἐχθροὺς κακῶς: "to benefit friends and harm enemies"). We further agree that the Laws' speech does not present a different concept of justice *qua* justice. We are divided concerning the aim of the Laws' speech. Harte emphasizes the domain of those to whom Socrates should be obliged. While Crito spoke of Socrates' duty mainly towards his friends and family, the Laws—adopting this same concept of justice—expand it to include also the state on the ground of its greater importance even than his parents: "The Laws conception of justice can also be construed

VII. CONCLUSION

Crito was Socrates' friend from the same demos. This is undeniable, but most scholarly literature goes a step further and assumes that Crito was *only* Socrates' friend. This may have been correct as a historical fact, but the real Crito should be sharply distinguished from the Crito who appears in Plato's *Crito*. Here the dramatist (Plato) has the freedom to shape his characters according to the aim of the dialogue.[39] Crito in the present dialogue vacillates between two meanings of justice, and this is because of what he regards as his double *sumphora*, namely losing his good friend and his own good reputation among the Many. In fact, because of this *sumphora* he is obsessed by the popular meaning of justice, and represses the philosophical meaning. It is Socrates' aim to restore this philosophical meaning to its rightful place, as that which is the criterion of justice in every case. Crito in this dialogue is designed to represent the man who knows what is right and how a good man should behave, but fails to apply this knowledge when the moment of truth arrives. This is what makes Crito's complicated character so interesting and human. It is the sort of thing that makes Plato's dialogues always relevant.

Bar-Ilan University

---

in terms of concentric circles. But their circles extend further than Crito's, insofar as they include the political community in which Socrates resides ... The Laws argue that the political community is owed allegiance of the same kind, but to a greater degree, than one's family and friends" (p. 135). Thus for Harte the Laws' aim is to present an alternative domain for justice: "While Crito's value system might be described as involving 'kinship values'; he treats the justice of an agent's action in terms of their relation to a specific community of family and friends ... The Laws' value system may be described as 'civic'; they treat the justice of an agent's action in terms of their relation to the political community" (p. 140). I have no quarrel with Harte concerning what the Laws regard as justice and what they do with it, namely their including in it Crito's domain but expanding it to include the polis as well. But I take it as the device by which the Laws succeed in defeating Crito. In other words my view emphasizes rather the essence of Crito's concept of justice.

[39] As already emphasized at the beginning of this paper, a character should always be analyzed in context, and not across all the dialogues in which he appears. See n. 1 above.

WORKS CITED

Adam, J. ed. 1888. *Plato. Crito*. Cambridge.

Brickhouse, T. C., and N. D. Smith. 2006. "Socrates and the Law of Athens." *Philosophy Compass* 1:564–570.

Colaiaco, J. A. 2001. *Socrates against Athens: Philosophy on Trial*. New York.

Dasti, M. R. 2007. "The *Crito's* 'Integrity.'" *Apeiron* 40:123–140.

Fox, M. 1956. "The Trials of Socrates: An Interpretation of the First Tetralogy." *Archiv für Philosophie* 6:226–261.

Harte, V. 1999. "Conflicting Values in Plato's *Crito*." *Archiv für Geschichte der Philosophie* 81.2:117–147

Liebersohn, Y. Z. 2005. "Art and Pseudo-Art in Plato's *Gorgias*." *Arethusa* 38:303–329.

———. 2011. "Rejecting Socrates' Rejection of Retaliation: Gregory Vlastos, Socrates' Morality, Plato's Dialogues and Related Issues." *Maynooth Philosophical Papers* 6:45–56.

———. 2015. "The Place of ψυχή in Plato's *Crito*." *Illinois Classical Studies* 40.1:1–20.

Stokes, M. C. 2005. *Dialectic in Action: An Examination of Plato's Crito*. Swansea.

Treddenick, H., trans. 1961. *Crito*. In *The Collected Dialogues of Plato*, ed. E. Hamilton and H. Cairns. Princeton.

Vlastos, G. 1991. "Socrates' Rejection of Retaliation." In *Socrates, Ironist and Moral Philosopher*, 179–199. Cambridge.

Weiss, R. 1998. *Socrates Dissatisfied*. Oxford.

West, E. 1989. "Socrates in the *Crito*: Patriot or Friend?" In *Essays in Ancient Greek Philosophy*. Vol. 3, *Plato*, ed. J. Anton and A. Preus, 71–83.

Woozley, A. D. 1979. *Law and Obedience: The Argument of Plato's Crito*. Chapel Hill.

Young, G. 1974. "Socrates and Obedience." *Phronesis* 19:1–29

STAGING THE DIVINE

EPIPHANY AND APOTHEOSIS IN CALLIMACHUS *HE* 1121–1124

ALEXANDROS KAMPAKOGLOU

I. INTRODUCTION

IN THIS PAPER it will be argued that Callimachus *HE* 1121–1124 refers to an actual statue of Berenice the consecration of which marked her deification. The epigram is accordingly an important source for the court rituals and ceremonies that enveloped such occasions, and should be associated with the apotheosis of Ptolemaic rulers. Callimachus alludes to the discourse of divine epiphanies in order to represent the deification of Berenice as such. The discussion will conclude by exploring the reasons that occasioned Berenice's assimilation to the Charites and so re-evaluate the information that the epigram can impart about the identity of the Berenice mentioned.

II. OCCASION AND DATE OF COMPOSITION

Τέσσαρες αἱ Χάριτες, ποτὶ γὰρ μία ταῖς τρισὶ κείναις
ἄρτι ποτεπλάσθη κῆτι μύροισι νοτεῖ.
εὐαίων ἐν πᾶσιν ἀρίζηλος Βερενίκα,
ἆς ἄτερ οὐδ' αὐταὶ ταὶ Χάριτες Χάριτες.

The Graces are four: in addition to The Three, one
   has just been cast and still breathes of perfumes.
Blest among all is radiant Berenike,
   without whom even the Graces lack grace.

Trans. Nisetich 2001:176

The epigram offers information about the setting up of the statue of Berenice, some of the ritual acts performed on it, and the predicates that Callimachus attributes to the deified woman. Still, it imparts no information concerning its context of performance. While it remains unclear whether the epigram itself was ever carved on the base of a real statue, an attractive hypothesis is that the epigram was in fact performed or recited when such a statue was first consecrated: Callimachus could have participated with his poem in a court ceremony that celebrated the deification of Berenice and included the dedication of her statue.[1]

Recent discussions of the epigram have preferred to see the statue as a textual metaphor conveniently conjured up by Callimachus to offer his praise to Berenice II as inspiration for and guardian of his poetry, especially of the second part of the *Aetia* (see below, Section VII).[2] In contrast, one can analyze the epigram based on the premise that Callimachus was referencing an actual statue of Berenice. In this case it has generally been assumed that the statue was established in the proximity of statues depicting the three Charites. This assumption, however, is based solely upon the demonstrative κείναις in the first line of the epigram,[3] and the text does not prevent one from assuming that the Charites are instead evoked as epiphanic goddesses. The sight of Berenice's statue awakes in Callimachus such feelings of admiration that he compares her charm and beauty to that of the Charites and declares her to be one of them, perhaps because this image of Berenice was fashioned in a style reminiscent of statues of the Charites. This would sustain more palpably the comparison or assimilation to the Charites that Callimachus suggests.

While contemplating this less common perspective, it remains necessary to examine the accepted possibility that a statue of Berenice

---

[1] For the possibility that Hellenistic epigrams were performance events, see Bing's (2000:146–148) judicious remarks; cf. also Van Bremen 2007:350–352.

[2] Petrovic and Petrovic 2003; Acosta-Hughes and Stephens 2012:222–223.

[3] In the first line κείναις does not necessarily refer to actual statues; so Petrovic and Petrovic 2003:195. It could refer to the widely known three Charites and so throw into relief the creation of the new fourth Charis; cf. also LSJ[9] s.v. ἐκεῖνος 2 "to denote well-known persons etc."

was placed in the vicinity of statues depicting the three Charites. The statue of Berenice was both newer than the other three and specifically sculpted in order to be placed in their setting. At the same time, the first couplet metaphorically assimilates Berenice to the Charites. In line two ποτεπλάσθη can be understood in both senses: a statue of Berenice has been created to complement those of the three Charites and, analogously, Berenice has ascended as a fourth member to the group of deities.[4] The epigram, then, would function on two levels that allow the integration of both the statue and Berenice herself. It is difficult to reach a conclusion about the actual form of such a statuary group. Most likely, it would be a complex of statues of the three Charites represented together and an independent statue of Berenice; a statuary complex that depicted the Charites as a tetrad does not agree with the first line of the epigram. It is equally difficult to define the location of the statues as described by Callimachus, or of the statues of the three Charites more specifically, if they antedated that of Berenice.

Some scholars have suggested that the epigram marks the institution of a cult of Berenice as temple-sharing goddess with the Charites.[5] However, in view of the absence of any evidence about the cult of the Charites in Ptolemaic Alexandria,[6] one should assume with Barigazzi (1966:81) that their statues served decorative rather than cultic purposes. This interpretation does not exclude the possibility that ritual acts were performed on the statues,[7] or that they may have been associated with the shrine of a major god (such as Aphrodite) rather than with an autonomous cult of the Charites.

As will be argued below, there is no evidence to suggest that assimilation to the Charites was repeated with any other member of the Ptolemaic dynasty. It was a unique honor, in contrast to the usual

[4] Callimachus' epigram reworks a common theme: an outstanding mortal is added to a fixed group of divinities (e.g. Charites, Muses): cf. e.g. Plato (FGE 13) Ἐννέα τὰς Μούσας φασίν τινες· ὡς ὀλιγώρως | ἠνίδε καὶ Σαπφὼ Λεσβόθεν ἡ δεκάτη. For the Charites as a fixed group, see Section III below.

[5] Cf. e.g. Robert 1946:115n3; Meillier 1979:150; rightly contra, Barigazzi 1966:81.

[6] Cf. Visser 1938:32. Visser is wrong to claim that Philotera is identified with Charis in the Ectheosis Arsinoes (fr. 228.47 Pf.). Charis there is Hephaestus' wife, as in Iliad 18.382.

[7] For a critique of the distinction between cult and dedicatory images in a ritualized context, see Day 2010:264–266 with references.

identification of Ptolemaic queens with Aphrodite and other goddesses of the Greek and Egyptian pantheons.[8] An interesting parallel, however, for the introduction of a royal lady into a group of minor deities is provided by a third-century epigram tentatively attributed to Posidippus of Pella (*SH* 978 [= *113 AB = *FGE* anon. 151a]).[9] This epigram describes a fountain or *nymphaeum*. Details of the monument as well as its context of consecration remain unclear. It seems certain, however, that it included an image—the Greek text refers ambiguously to εἰκόνες, which can refer to independent statues or to relief-paintings— of Queen Arsinoë II Philadelphos or Queen Arsinoë III Philopator in the midst of the Kreniades nymphs (*SH* 978.11–12) and that the monument somehow associated the queen with these goddesses (*SH* 978.14–16): Arsinoë is supposed to be (or to become) one of the Nymphs.[10] The selection of the nymphs was predicated on the character of the monument, which originally surrounded a fountain.[11] In view of the scarcity of springs in Alexandria, the monument threw into relief the queen's interest in the well-being of her people and her role as benefactor of the populace. If the Arsinoë praised here was indeed Philadelphus' sister, her association with water nymphs could be a further aspect of her assimilation to marine Aphrodite.[12]

With the exception of this epigram, water nymphs do not regularly figure in Hellenistic poetry or cult (see, however, Callimachus frr. 65–66 Pf. = Harder = 164–165 Massimilla) and so there is no reason to assume that Arsinoë was venerated in cult as a water nymph. This holds true also for the Charites in Callimachus' epigram (see, however, Callimachus frr. 3–7[14] Pf. = 3–7b Harder = 5–9[18] Massimilla), strengthening the analogy between the two cases. Outside Orchomenos, where they had an independent ancient cult, the cult of the Charites in most

---

[8]   Compare the list provided by Tondriau 1948. For the meaning carried by the queen's assimilation to Aphrodite, see Gutzwiller 1992:367–368; Carney 2000:30–37.

[9]   See Fraser 1972: vol. 1, 609–611 and vol. 2, 860–861n412 with older bibliography; see also next note.

[10]   Cf. Settis 1965:248–250; Cazzaniga 1966:488–490; Ronchi 1968:59–63. Differently, Giangrande 1973:68–73 and Page 1981:468, who do not accept the assimilation of Arsinoë to the Nymphs as evidence for the establishment of a cult of her as a Krenias nymph.

[11]   Cf. Barigazzi 1966:81.

[12]   Cf. Fraser 1972: vol. 2, 861.

Greek cities was generally incorporated into that of more important feminine deities, especially Aphrodite or Hera (e.g. at Argos, Pausanias 2.17.3).[13] In view of the close literary association of the Charites with Aphrodite and the royal status of Berenice (see below, Section IX), it is difficult to ignore as irrelevant the usual assimilation of Ptolemaic queens to Aphrodite. It is possible that the statues of the Charites along with that of Berenice were placed in a shrine of Aphrodite. Berenice, then, would be associated with the Charites and through them with the cult of Aphrodite, the favorite Ptolemaic goddess.[14]

This leads to a more difficult question: why did the court represent Berenice as a Charis and not as Aphrodite, as was common practice with Ptolemaic queens? The answer to this question depends to a certain degree on the poetic tradition into which Callimachus inscribes his epigram and secondly on the specific occasion that offered the context for the dedication of the statue of Berenice. As will be shown below, this choice also relates to the identity of the Berenice being praised.

III. BERENICE AS CHARIS

The comparison or assimilation of Berenice to the three Charites is meant to praise her charm and beauty. This much can be said with certainty irrespective of whether Callimachus refers to actual statues of the goddesses or, more likely, to the goddesses themselves. One ought not to lose sight of another aspect latent in this juxtaposition: Berenice exceeds the limits of human comparison and only goddesses can effectively function as models for her beauty. Within the socio-religious ambience in which Callimachus composed his poetry, it is difficult not to associate this aspect of the epigram with the deification of members of the Ptolemaic family and the dynastic cult at large. Callimachus' praise features both flattery of Berenice's vanity and her

---

[13] See Schwarzenberg 1966:4–24.

[14] One can compare an inscribed base from Aphrodisias (*IAph2007* 12.7 = MAMA vol. 8, 416, 1st–3rd centuries CE) that preserves the names of the three Charites. Robert 1965:116 surmised that the statues originally accompanied the cult-statue of Aphrodite, an association represented in local coins.

representation as a goddess. The audience was probably attuned to both aspects and associated them in their appreciation of the epigram.

A telling parallel often mentioned in modern discussions of this epigram can shed light on the function of Callimachus' praise discourse. *HE* 995a–b (= 39 Sens), an elegiac couplet that has been attributed to Asclepiades or Posidippus,[15] concerns an image that represents Berenice, either the wife of Soter or of Euergetes, as Aphrodite. The poet's focus is entirely on the similarity between queen and goddess and the difficulty of telling them apart. This confusion is a device to convey the poet's flattery to an aging queen, probably Berenice I, and support her identification with Aphrodite.[16] The difficulty in establishing identities thus becomes difficulty in establishing ontological categories: is Berenice a goddess rather than human? And if so, what is the appropriate way to praise her? Even if one cannot securely associate this epigram with her posthumous cult as Berenice I-Aphrodite, the gradual assimilation of Berenice I to Aphrodite seems to have begun during her lifetime.[17] Flattery and claims of dynastic divinity again go hand in hand.

Viewed against this background, Callimachus' epigram does not fail to bring home to the reader the various, and certainly interrelated, levels of signification of its praise discourse. Apart from the praise of Berenice's physical beauty, the comparison to the Charites unequivocally suggests this trait as a sign of her divine status.[18] This aspect of Callimachus' praise is supported by an old poetic tradition that utilized the comparison to goddesses in general and the Charites in particular to suggest the divine or heroic status of mortal women. One of the highest compliments that a poet could pay to a mortal woman is that she rivals the immortal goddesses in beauty (e.g. Hesiod frr. 23a.10, 16; 36.3; 180.14 M–W ἢ εἶδος ἐρήριστ' ἀθανάτῃσι; 129.5; 252.2

---

[15] Cf. Wilamowitz 1924:216n1; Sens 2011:265.

[16] Cf. Nastos 2006:302–304; Sens 2011:263. For the cult of Berenice I-Aphrodite, see Fraser 1972: vol. 1, 240, 666–667; Gutzwiller 1992:363–365; Carney 2000:33.

[17] Cf. Gow and Page 1965: vol. 2, 143; Nastos 2006:303; Sens 2011:263–264.

[18] For beauty as manifestation of power and divinity, see Carney 2000:35.

ἢ εἶδος Ὀλυμπιάδεσσιν ἔριζεν).[19] In the same vein, poets can also claim
that the beauty imparted on a specific woman is equal to that of the
Charites: Χαρίτων ἀμαρύγματ᾽ ἔχουσα (e.g. Hesiod frr. 43a.4; 70.38
M-W) or Χαρίτων ἄπο κάλλος ἔχουσα (Odyssey 6.18; Hesiod fr. 215.1
M-W).[20] Several Hellenistic and later epigrams make use of the motif
of a woman—in Straton even of a boy—becoming or being the fourth
Charis in order to emphasize her beauty: e.g. anon. AP 5.95 (Τέσσαρες
αἱ Χάριτες, Παφίαι δύο καὶ δέκα Μοῦσαι· | Δερκυλὶς ἐν πάσαις· Μοῦσα,
Χάρις, Παφίη); AP 5.70 (4 σὺν σοὶ δ᾽ αἱ Χάριτες τέσσαρές εἰσι, Φίλη);
Straton (AP 12.181.1-2 Ψεύδεα μυθίζουσι, Θεόκλεες, ὡς ἀγαθαὶ μὲν |
αἱ Χάριτες, τρισσαὶ δ᾽ εἰσὶ κατ᾽ Ὀρχομενόν·). An interesting variation, which imitates Callimachus᾽ poem, is provided by Meleager HE
4162-4165 on a statue of Zênophila: Meleager praises the artistry of
the statue by comparing Zênophila first to one of the three Charites
and then to Charis herself (HE 4163 τίς μίαν ἐκ τρισσῶν ἤγαγέ μοι
Χάριτα ~ 4165 δῶρα διδοὺς καὐτὰν τὰν Χάριν ἐν χάριτι). These parallels suggest that the Charites, whatever the specific demands that the
immediate context placed upon them, fulfilled first and foremost the
role that poetic tradition had accorded them as paragons of divine
beauty. This element, together with the sweet fragrance that the statue
of Berenice exudes, reminds one of motifs recurrent in narratives
of divine epiphanies so much so that one can argue that Callimachus
views the consecration of the statue of Berenice as a kind of epiphany
(cf. below, note 45). Flattery of Ptolemaic vanity, religious politics, and
literary traditions are brought together under the overarching theme
that epiphanic discourse provides to suggest that Berenice, a member
of the ruling family, has moved to another level of existence and so has
become a companion of deities.

---

[19] See especially Jax 1933:6, 65; Lieberg 1962:13–34. For the male version of this motif,
see Boedeker 1974:70–71. One is reminded of Calypso᾽s supercilious proclamation (Odyssey
5.212–213): οὐ δέμας οὐδὲ φυήν, ἐπεὶ οὔ πως οὐδὲ ἔοικε | θνητὰς ἀθανάτῃσι δέμας καὶ
εἶδος ἐρίζειν. One should also compare the Homeric Hymn to Aphrodite (93–95): Anchises
compares Aphrodite, disguised as a mortal girl, to a number of goddesses and nymphs,
among whom one finds also the Charites.
[20] Cf. Jax 1933:40–42, 62, 65–67. For Hellenistic variations of this theme, cf. e.g. Hedylus
HE 1825–1830; Meleager HE 4210–4215, 4228–4231, 4398–4407; Pompey the Younger GP
3961–3965; FGE anon. 42. See also Petrovic and Petrovic 2003:187–189.

IV. DEIFICATION AS SPECTACLE AND RITUAL EXPERIENCE

The assimilation of Berenice to the Charites is a form of deification. Berenice is not simply compared to the Charites on account of her attractiveness. She is represented as the source of their divine charm.[21] This is the more remarkable as it is usually the Charites or another god (e.g. Athena, *Odyssey* 6.235, 8.19, 23.162; Aphrodite, *Works and Days* 65; Charis, Pindar *Olympian* 6.76) who bestow *charis* on mortals and not the other way around; cf. especially Meleager *HE* 4216–4217 (Ζηνοφίλα κάλλος μὲν Ἔρως, σύγκοιτα δὲ φίλτρα | Κύπρις ἔδωκεν ἔχειν, αἱ Χάριτες δὲ χάριν), 4154–4155 (Ζηνοφίλα, σοὶ σκῆπτρα Πόθων ἀπένειμαν, ἐπεί σοι αἱ τρισσαὶ Χάριτες τρεῖς ἔδοσαν χάριτας). The way Callimachus has constructed his epigram provides an insight into the theatrical character that such court events assumed in Ptolemaic Alexandria.[22] The narrative voice adopts the role of the spectator who reacts to a new setting. This literary device is also found in Theocritus 15 and Herodas 4 and can be traced as far back as Aeschylus' *Theôroi* (frr. 78a**–82 Radt).[23] Grammatically absent from the text, the narrator engages only ambiguously in the *ekphrasis* of Berenice's statue; he gives a testimony rich in deictic elements that enables the reader to recreate a textual universe in which he or she is identified with the viewing poet. This is achieved through the organic combination of temporal (ἄρτι, κῆτι), olfactory (μύροισι νοτεῖ), and visual markers (1124). To read the epigram is to witness the epiphany of the new goddess.

The consecration of the statue of Berenice not only marks her deification but also constitutes her first epiphany as a new Charis.[24] In terms of ritual practice, Callimachus' epigram is also meant to make

---

[21] Cf. Petrovic and Petrovic 2003:188.

[22] The theatrical character of royal appearances is noted by Plutarch *Demetrios* 41.5–8; see also Chaniotis 1997:235–242, 250–252; Strootman 2007:260.

[23] Cf. Headlam and Knox 1922:xliii–xliv; Cunningham 1971:128. For the Hellenistic culture of viewing, see Goldhill 1994 esp. 216–223.

[24] Cf. Platt 2011:47 "images themselves have the potential to be viewed as *epiphanic embodiment of the deities they represent*" (my emphasis). Cf. also Day 2010:233. Regarding the consecration of divine images as epiphanies, Platt 2011:64 compares Zeus' promise in the *Homeric Hymn to Dionysus* (10) that mortals will consecrate many statues of the new god in temples. For this hymn, see West 2011.

the epiphany happen: by enumerating her divine attributes (beauty, fragrance, happiness, and stature), he confers them upon her image, which is the focus of the ritual performed. In this manner, Callimachus shapes the way in which his audience experiences the epiphany of the goddess believed to be present in the guise of her statue.[25] More specifically, the catalogue-like enumeration of these attributes directs the audience's attention to those elements that will help them recognize the divine status that Berenice has attained. In both these respects, Callimachus' epigram unmistakably recalls the epiphanic function of hymns.[26] As Platt has demonstrated, "hymns confer ... powers upon the deity they celebrate, and in defining divine identity, generate the very being whose presence they evoke." Further, "the central *argumentum* ... of each [hymn] is concerned with the establishment of definitive *eidea* through narratives ... in which humans learn to read correctly the *semata* of divine presence."[27] In this way, the ritual behind the apotheosis of Berenice goes beyond mere propaganda and turns the claims of royal divinity into "tangible reality for both spectators and participants."[28] The statue of Berenice is no more just a statue: thanks to Callimachus' hymnic epigram and to the ritual acts it undergoes, it becomes "a living embodiment of the divine, inhabiting the same space as the viewer-worshipper."[29]

Similarly, the epiphanic discourse of Callimachus' *Hymn* 5 systematically effaces the distinction between the ancient statue of Athena and the goddess herself.[30] First, the ritual bathing of the cult image of Athena is associated with Athena's bathing after physical toil, giving us a first instance of the conceptual interchangeability between the goddess and her image (5–12). Secondly, the exhortation that the

---

[25] Cf. Platt 2011:72–74.

[26] For the polysemic genre discourse of the epigram, see Petrovic and Petrovic 2003:194. For similarities between epigrams and hymns, see Day 2010:246–254.

[27] Platt 2011:74 and 64, respectively.

[28] Strootman 2007:259.

[29] Platt 2011:77–78. For the identification of statues with gods, see also Scheer 2000:45–66; Platt 2011:89 and 100.

[30] For the epiphanic discourse of this hymn, see especially Hunter and Fuhrer 2002:159–161; Vestrheim 2002:180–183; Platt 2011:175–180. For the importance of epiphanic discourse in Hellenistic literature, see Hunter and Fuhrer 2002:146.

persona loquens addresses to the male spectators (51–52) occasions the transition to the myth about the blinding of Teiresias (57–136). The threat that underlies the rhetorical employment of this episode unequivocally equates seeing Athena bathing with seeing her statue being bathed and casts every male spectator as a potential Teiresias. The arrival of the image of the goddess is clearly seen as an epiphanic event.[31] The hymn intimates the danger entailed in viewing a god without his or her approval and offers a protective lens through which epiphany can be experienced: gods cannot be seen directly, but only through the medium of poetry that evokes them. In this regard, Callimachus both in his hymn and in his epigram offers guidance to his audience as to how to experience the divine revelation, adopting at the same time a privileged position as an intermediary between god-monarchs and the court audience in the communicational spectrum of the performance. This trope self-referentially indicates Callimachus' privileged role in the Ptolemaic court.

The statues of the Charites, if real, could have been statues permanently placed *in situ* or portable images made of lighter materials like those used in the various pageants included in Philadelphus' Grand Procession or set up in his lavish pavilion. Judging from Callixeinus' description (*FGrH* 627F2), one notes that in several cases the inclusion of statues of the Ptolemies in the midst of statues of gods was a naïve but explicit way to indicate their deification.[32] Already before the Ptolemies, Philip II of Macedon had advanced such claims by placing his statue next to that of the twelve Olympian gods (Diodorus 16.92.5).[33] Theocritus (17.13–27) reflects a similar spatial arrangement when he represents the deified Ptolemy I feasting alongside his progenitors and the rest of the Olympian gods.[34]

---

[31] See also Bulloch 1985:3–4. For similar prohibitions in processions involving cult images, see Scheer 2000:60–61.

[32] For the statues in Philadelphus' procession, see Rice 1983 passim; Strootman 2007:322.

[33] Cf. Weber 1993:48 with note 4; Carney 2000:25; Strootman 2007:306.

[34] One notes the detailed emphasis on the arrangement of the thrones in this scene; see Hunter 2003:112–113. For the ritual importance of royal thrones in Hellenistic times, see also Strootman 2007:338–340. Thrones were associated with the king's charisma and could be venerated on their own: note the presence of the wreathed thrones of Soter

Although Callimachus describes a static scene, the inclusion of perceptual markers invites the reader to join these pieces of information in a narrative sequence that represents *in nuce* the actual ritual of consecration (see below, Sections V and VI). This technique is typical of inscriptions, and it is quite likely that Callimachus follows inscriptional tradition. As Joseph W. Day (1989: 23) has shown in the case of funerary inscriptions, "epitaphs were ... regularly structured to memorialize the funeral, but for strangers who had not been present." Similarly to these early inscriptions, Callimachus provides the statue of Berenice with "a poetic voice that perpetuates verbally" its consecration and so her deification, by reducing the ceremony to its bare essentials.[35] The oscillation between these two modes (i.e. description of the new statue and narration of the ritual) is a device that one finds again in Posidippus' *hippika* and allows the poet to make up for the brevity of the epigrammatic form.[36] Assuming that the epigram was inscribed on the base of the statue, it would recreate the original experience of epiphany as personal wonder for every future spectator. Besides, those who read the epigram are bound to identify with the poet and cast themselves in the same role as divinely favored viewers of the epiphany of the goddess.[37] The vocal aspect of the Ptolemaic ceremony is thus imagined to be repeated in perpetuity with every new reading of Callimachus' epigram "as oral praise poetry" for the deified royal.[38]

From this vantage point, one can revisit the meaning of the two first lines of the epigram and re-evaluate the assimilation of Berenice to the Charites from a ritual point of view. I argue that the assimilation of Berenice to the Charites reworks what Day has termed the "come-with-the-Charites" motif.[39] The temporal indications in the second

---

and Berenice I in the Grand Procession of Philadelphus (Athenaeus 5.202a–b); cf. Rice 1983:116–118. For the aniconic veneration of thrones, see Gaifman 2012:108–110 and 163–169. For the role of thrones in mystic cults and rituals, see Edmonds 2006.

[35] Cf. Day 1989:24–25.

[36] See especially Del Corno 2002:64 and Bingen 2002:185 on 74 AB.

[37] For epiphanies as wonders meted out to those favored by the gods, see Platt 2011:56–57. For the identification of the reader with the praise poet in inscribed epitaphs, see Day 1989:26–27.

[38] Cf. Day 1989:27; 1994:41; 2010:274–275.

[39] Cf. Day 1994:59–63; 2010:246–254.

line (ἄρτι … κῆτι) imply not only that the statue of Berenice has been recently sculpted but also that Berenice has recently become one of the Charites. In this sense, ἄρτι ποτεπλάσθη κῆτι … νοτεῖ can be seen as an indication of the recent epiphanic advent of Berenice along with the Charites that coincides with, if it is not actually reified through, the consecration of the new statue. Day (2010:267) argues that the "arrival-with-the-Charites" motif is a transformation of offertory *chaire* addressed to gods in hymns and epigrams. Berenice is, thus, "invited" to take pleasure in her new statue, which has been skillfully wrought and so possesses *charis*. This ambiguity with regard to *charis* allows Callimachus to reflect both the divine role that Berenice has assumed and the artistry of her statue. Indirectly, through the latter the poet also praises Berenice's beauty. Inasmuch as the *charis* of the statue pleases both Berenice and mortal viewers it becomes a channel of contact between the new goddess and Callimachus, and through the poet his audience.[40] The *charis* that the poet feels at the sight of the statue is an indication of the presence of the goddess with her companions—that is, the *charis* of the statue as conveyed to the viewer and reader within the specific ritualized experience evoked is represented as the result of Berenice's beneficent divine presence and so of her enhancement of the sculptor's art.[41] In this light, the assimilation of Berenice to the Charites suggests that the viewers of the statue, the readers of the epigram, and the new deity are involved in a circuit of mutual benefactions and that the statue is the medium for this communication. The statue— and the epigram—is a *charis* offered to Berenice; every re-reading of Callimachus' epigram offers *charis* afresh to the goddess, inviting her to reciprocate by offering *charis* to the reader.[42] In this regard, Berenice appears as a beneficent figure, a quality intriguingly pertinent if the Berenice praised was, as I will argue is more than likely, a member of the family of Ptolemy III Euergetes.

---

[40] Compare the address to the Charites in the *Aetia* epilogue; see below, Section VI.

[41] My discussion of this aspect of the epigram is indebted to the analysis of Day 2010:266–271.

[42] Cf. Day 2010:274–275, especially 275 "reading not only reenacted the original ritual in speech, but also successfully framed the experiences of hearers and viewers as reper-formances of that ritual's *charis* effects."

V. ANOINTMENT WITH OIL

Callimachus notes that the statue of Berenice is still wet with aromatic oils (κῆτι μύροισι νοτεῖ).[43] The temporal adverb κῆτι suggests that the anointment of Berenice's statue happened once and that it was not repeated as part of a ritual carried out periodically. However, the possibility cannot be excluded that her statue would be thenceforth anointed on important celebrations, perhaps on the anniversary of her death, if she were dead, or even on a daily basis. Egyptian manuals indicate that the anointment with aromatic oils of the statues of gods by a specifically designated priest was part of the so-called "daily ritual."[44] Given that there is no known cult of Berenice as Charis, it is unlikely that this was performed daily on her statue. It remains unclear whether the anointment took place during the consecration of her statue. However, within the ritual that the epigram presupposes, the anointment comes to play a role congruent with Berenice's divine profile: the aroma that her statue diffuses is reminiscent of the fragrance that emanates from divine bodies and accoutrements.[45] Gods anoint themselves (e.g. Hera at *Iliad* 14.170–175) and their clothes (e.g. *Homeric Hymn to Demeter* 277–278) with ambrosial oil;[46] this act offers the divine equivalent of the human habit of using perfumes and oils

---

[43] For μύρον ("scented oil") and its uses in cosmetics, see Olson and Sens 2000:227–228.

[44] Sternberg-el-Hotabi 1988 esp. 402–404; cf. *Lexikon der Ägyptologie* s.v. Kult B 842–843. For the anointment of statues with scented oils in Hittite cleansing rituals, see Fappas 2010:135–138. For the anointment of Assyrian stones and tablets, see Daiches 1913:3.

[45] Cf. Schmid 1923:179 and Petrovic and Petrovic 2003:183. In literature, divine epiphanies are indicated by the sweet fragrance that deities or divine objects diffuse: see especially Lohmeyer 1919 and Platt 2011:56; for the motif, cf. e.g. Theognis 8–9; Euripides *Hippolytus* 1391; Virgil *Aeneid* 1.402–405; Milton *Paradise Lost* 3.135–137, 5.284–287. Aristoxenus of Tarentum reports that Alexander's body gave off a sweet fragrance (Plutarch *Alexandros* 4). Hamilton (1969:11) notes that it is unclear whether Aristoxenus thought of Alexander as a god or a hero. He prefers the latter view. Still, after Alexander's deification such distinctions would have become obsolete; cf. Hauben 1989:447n41. Similarly, the deified Arsinoë II is called "[suave] de parfums" (Sauneron 1960:90, line 18) on the base of a statue from Alexandria depicting her sitting between her consort and Amun-Re. The statue marked her deification.

[46] Cf. Roscher 1883:39–40.

to anoint body and clothes.[47] This use of ambrosia is supposed to give divine bodies an attractive look, a sweet fragrance, and even help gods preserve their immortality.[48]

As her beauty suggests her to be a goddess reminiscent of the Charites, the sweet fragrance of Berenice's statue is another sign of her divine status and so constitutes one of the σήματα of her epiphany.[49] The anointment must have also had a ritual significance, suggesting Berenice's distancing from the mortal world and her acquisition of divine status.[50] This combination of interpretations of the olfactory imagery lends strength to the reading of the epigram as a narrative about the epiphany of the deified Berenice,[51] artistically transforming the consecration of her statue into a religious drama that stages her epiphany.

VI. OIL AS RITUAL OFFERING AND THE DEIFICATION OF BERENICE

The anointment of the statue of Berenice is associated with cultic practice in both Greek and Egyptian religions. Scholars have pointed out that the anointment of statues of gods was a very old habit practiced

---

[47] Similarly the anointment with oils of the hair of statues parallels the use of aromatic oils for hair; e.g. *Iliad* 19.126; Aristophanes *Ecclesiazusae* 1117–1118; *Ploutos* 529. See also Williams 1978:43–44 and Olson and Sens 2000:227–228.

[48] Cf. Roscher 1883:51–54 and Lohmeyer 1919:12–13.

[49] The kinaesthetic means employed in temple rituals in order to intimate to the worshippers the epiphany of the god, present in his or her statue, are discussed by Tanner 2006:47–48 and Platt 2011:78, 89. For signs that were supposed to help mortals recognize divine beings, see Platt 2011:57–58, 67.

[50] Bowie (1993:29) notes that the anointment of statues often had "the practical purpose of protecting them, but here too there is a religious element involved"; cf. also Hock 1905:51; Scheer 2000:58; Bettinetti 2001:147. Phidias, for instance, ordered oil to be poured over the chryselephantine statue of Zeus at Olympia ὥστε ἀθάνατον ἐς δύναμιν αὐτὸ φυλάσσεσθαι (Photius *Bibliotheca* p. 293 b 1 Bekker); oil was poured over wooden images at Ephesus (Pliny *Natural History* 16.214) and at Chaeroneia to preserve them (Pausanias 9.41.7). For oil as preservative of ivory, see Pliny *Natural History* 13.23.

[51] According to Plutarch (*Antonios* 26.3–4), when Cleopatra dressed as Aphrodite sailed to visit Antonius at Tarsos (41 BCE), incense was spread from her barge towards the crowds on the banks of river Kydnos in order to suggest her epiphany as a goddess; see also Chaniotis 1997:241–242 and Strootman 2007:303.

throughout the ancient world.[52] The custom is often mentioned by both Greek and Roman authors.[53] Several sources also refer to the anointment with oil of stones and *stelae* at crossroads or of shrines and temples, usually followed by their adornment with a wreath.[54] This was often castigated by Christian authors as a sign of pagan beliefs.[55] Theophrastus (*Characters* 16.5) mockingly mentions the same practice in his description of the superstitious man.[56] The anointment of cult statues, funerary *stelae*, and sacred stones reflects the same religious belief: the anointed objects were supposed to mark the possible presence of a divine spirit or of the soul of the departed. The anointment of these items signifies their separation from the world of mortals and their consecration to the divine world.[57]

Support for this conclusion is not found only in Greek or Latin literature. Although classical authors mention such practices, they hardly ever give a reason for them. Frazer (1918: vol. 2, 72–77; cf. also 1898: vol. 5, 354–355; 1914: vol. 5, 36) noted the parallel with the monolith (*mazzebah*) of Bethel and its anointment by Isaac in *Genesis* 28:10–22. Isaac set up the stone that he had slept on the previous night as a pillar and anointed it with oil, declaring it to be the "house of God." It is clear that for Isaac the spirit of God will be resident in the stone (καὶ ὁ λίθος οὗτος, ὃν ἔστησα στήλην, ἔσται μοι οἶκος θεοῦ. Cf. also *Genesis* 31:13).[58]

---

[52] See e.g. Allen, Halliday, and Sikes 1936:419; Massimilla 1992:253–254; D'Alessio 2007: vol. 2, 385n45; cf. also Crawley 1908:553–554; Bowie 1993; Bettinetti 2001:137–140; Petrovic and Petrovic 2003:183.

[53] Cf. e.g. Cicero *In Verrem* 2.4.77; Lucian *Deorum concilium* 12; Proclus *In Platonis Rempublicam commentarii* 1.42.5 Kroll; Artemidorus 2.33. One should also take into account the numerous Hellenistic inscriptional inventories from the island of Delos which attest to the ritual cleansing and anointment of cult statues; cf. Bettinetti 2001:144–147.

[54] Pausanias 10.24.6; Lucian *Alexandros* 30; Apuleius *Florida* 1.1; Minucius Felix *Octauius* 3. Pausanias (2.6.3) mentions that oil was poured in front of the temple of Athena after Epopeus had prayed to her. Similarly 55.9–11 *LSAM* from Cnidos (ca. 350 BCE) may suggest that oil was poured over altars as an offering to the gods. For the identification of sacred stones and altars in ancient religions, see Benzinger 1905:558; Smith 1957:201–204.

[55] Cf. e.g. Arnobius *Aduersus nationes* 1.39.

[56] See Diggle 2004:357–358 on 5 with further references and Gaifman 2012:119–123.

[57] For anointment as a form of consecration or re-consecration, see Hock 1905:51–52; Daiches 1913:3; Herter 1975:202; and Gladigow 1985–1986:121.

[58] Cf. Frazer 1918: vol. 2, 59: "Originally the deity seems to have been conceived as actually resident in the stone"; cf. also Delitzsch 1887:378–379; Driver 1904:267–268;

Smith (1957:233) explained this act as a form of homage to the deity that at the same time was believed to bring divine life to the stone anointed.[59] Von Rad (1972:285–286) compared some lines from *Exodus* (30:25–32) and especially *Leviticus* (7:10–12) where God prescribes to Moses the consecration by anointment of ritual items and priests. The Septuagint text throughout uses the verb ἁγιάζω, the full implications of which become evident only when one compares the original Hebrew text. The verb used in the original (*qadash*) is cognate with the noun *qodesh* which denotes "separateness" and "sacredness."[60] In other words, sacredness is perceived as setting something apart from the human world by making it ritually clean.[61] One is reminded at this point of the similar injunctions laid out for places or people hit by a lightning bolt in Greek religion.[62]

It has been suggested that the cleansing, anointment, and wreathing of Aphrodite by the Charites in the *Homeric Hymn to Aphrodite* (61–63) and the *Cypria* (frr. 5–7 West) reflects temple rituals during which the priests anointed and wreathed Aphrodite's cult statue.[63] Another well-known example concerns the stone situated over the tomb of Neoptolemus at Delphi (Pausanias 10.24.6). This was anointed with oil and wreathed daily. The analogy with the Hebrew practice suggests that anointment served the same aims in Greek religion as well. The anointment of the statue of Berenice, then, if connected with this religious belief, implies its consecration, meaning the separation of Berenice from the mortal world and her elevation to the world of the gods. Furthermore, as Smith (1957:436) argued, the anointment of a sacred stone, and by extension of a statue, with oil or blood is a theurgic process that brings divine life to the stone or statue anointed. At the same time, this act of anointment is the first offering to the god

---

Benzinger 1905:558; Smith 1957:203–205; Vawter 1977:313–314; Hamilton 1995:245–247; Arnold 2009:255. For the belief in the presence of gods in Greek statues, see Bettinetti 2001:9.

[59] Cf. also Smith 1957:232, 383–384, and especially 436.

[60] Cf. Edwards 2007:1142.

[61] Cf. Smith 1957:150; von Rad 1972:285 "anointing as a means of separating for and dedicating to the god." See also Fappas 2010:282–301 with bibliography.

[62] Cf. Usener 1901:8–11.

[63] Cf. Càssola 1975:580. See also Scheer 2000:54–66.

depicted and as such constitutes a rudimentary epiphany.[64] This interpretation becomes stronger if one sees it in connection with the assimilation of Berenice to the Charites and notes that only statues of gods and monarchs were ritually scented.[65]

In one of the very few literary representations of Ptolemaic apotheoses in Hellenistic poetry, Theocritus has fashioned a mythic account about the deification of Berenice I (15.106-108): Aphrodite drops ambrosia on the queen's chest thus making her immortal. This scene has an intercultural parallel in the immortalizing effect that anointment with oil was supposed to have in Egyptian funerals: the priest anointed the statue or the mummy of the pharaoh in order to make him immortal. The anointment was believed to re-enact the anointment of Osiris by his son Horus.[66] Although there is no mention of ambrosia in Callimachus' epigram, the anointment of the statue could have a similar symbolic and religious meaning signifying Berenice's accession to the divine world. It is further possible that statues or figurines representing the Charites were placed around that of Berenice to suggest their role in her deification and their welcoming of her in their group.

The anointment of the statue then is a narrative theme given in its simplest form that sets the basis for the epiphany of the new goddess in the company of her companions. In Theocritus, it is Aphrodite who drops ambrosial oil on Berenice I's chest. The epigram does not provide any such information, but one could surmise that the Charites assumed such a role. One can bring this into connection with *Aetia* 1 fr. 7.13-14 Pf. = Harder = fr. 9.13-14 Massimila:[67]

---

[64] Cf. Smith 1957:436.

[65] For the scenting of divine and royal images, see Petrovic and Petrovic 2003:183 with notes 20, 22. That the anointment of Berenice's statue was part of the consecration ritual was surmised first by Wilamowitz and subsequently accepted by Gow and Page 1965: vol. 2, 172. Petrovic and Petrovic 2003:182 challenge the evidence on which this interpretation has been based. Hesychius (ι 696 Latte: ἰντύεσθαι κοσμεῖν. φαιδρύνεσθαι), as was argued by Hock 1905:49-50, seems to imply that ritual κόσμησις of cult statues, part of which was also their anointment with oils or wax (cf. Bettinetti 2001:144-160), was also practiced at their consecration.

[66] Cf. Assmann 2001:408-418 and Kampakoglou 2013b:306-311. For Theocritus 15.106-108, see Hunter 1993:132-134; Stephens 2003:153-155.

[67] Cf. also Acosta-Hughes and Stephens 2012:222-223.

ἔλλατε νῦν,⌋ ἐˌλέˌγοισι ˌδ'ˌ ἐνιψήσασθˌεˌ λιπώσˌας
χεῖρˌας ἐμˌοῖς, ἵνα μοˌι πουλὺ μένωσˌιˌν ἔτος.

Callimachus asks the Charites to come to him in order for them to touch his elegiacs with their anointed hands.[68] As he explicitly states, this will allow his poetry to be preserved for a long time. This is a kind of poetic immortality, although the poet does not talk about eternity but rather about the long duration or longevity of his poetry. The Charites, personifications of poetic artistry and talent, confer upon Callimachus' poem a divine attribute, suggested above all by the divine oil which they place on his lines. The oil of the Charites bestows charm to his lines, thus endowing them with ongoing attractiveness.[69]

VII. THE STATUE OF BERENICE AS A METAPOETIC METAPHOR

In the fifth book of the Palatine Anthology, where it has been preserved, Callimachus' epigram is part of a sequence of epigrams that can be traced back to the opening section of the amatory book of Meleager's Garland.[70] Gutzwiller (1998:284) has shown that the opening sequence of Meleager's amatory book as preserved in AP 5.134–149 includes metaphors that have specific metapoetic assonances. These assonances allude to the proemial epigram that introduced Meleager's anthology (Meleager HE 3926–3983). In the light of this consideration, Acosta-Hughes and Stephens (2012:222) have recently argued that Meleager probably read Callimachus' epigram in a metapoetic manner. It is uncertain, however, whether Meleager's reading reflects the poem's original context of composition and performance. In the same way in

---

[68] For ἐνιψήσασθˌεˌ Massimilla (1992:254–255) and Harder (2012: vol. 2, 135–136) compare Theocritus 17.36–37. For the motif, see also Massimilla 1994:323 and Hunter 2003:128.

[69] Cf. Pfeiffer 1949 and Harder 2012 ad loc. One is also reminded of Rhianus HE 3200–3201: Ὡραί σοι Χάριτές τε κατὰ γλυκὺ χεῦαν ἔλαιον, | ὦ πυγά, κνώσσειν δ' οὐδὲ γέροντας ἐᾷς. Cf. also HE 3221–3223: ... ἤντησαν ταὶ λιπαραὶ Χάριτες, | καί σε ποτὶ ῥοδόεσσιν ἐπηχύναντο χέρεσσιν, | κοῦρε, πεποίησαι δ' ἡλίκος ἐσσὶ χάρις.). The anointment of the boys with the sweet oil of the Charites enhances their attractiveness.

[70] Cf. Gutzwiller 1998:282–287. See also Cameron 1993:29.

which Meleager (*HE* 4232–4233) claims to prefer Hêliodôra's whisper to the lyre of Apollo, suggesting that she assumes the role that traditionally went to inspiratory deities, Berenice is represented as a source of divine grace and poetic skill, a power of artistic inspiration.[71] Since Berenice II is the only bearer of this name whom we know Callimachus to have celebrated in his poetry and so to be able to claim such a prestigious role as inspirer of his poetry, the identification of the subject of the epigram with her in this reading seems inevitable and quite likely.[72]

Along similar lines, Petrovic and Petrovic (2003:198–204) have suggested that the occasion for the composition of the epigram under discussion was the completion of Callimachus' *Aetia*. In view of Berenice II's prominent position in the second half of the *Aetia* and her probable connection with the three Charites in the *Aetia* epilogue (fr. 112 Pf.), the association is not improbable (see also below, Section IX).[73] However, the possibility that this epigram accompanied the second edition of the *Aetia*, as Petrovic and Petrovic (2003:198) suggest, requires the introduction of a further alternative that I have not examined so far—that is, that the statues of the three Charites and that of Berenice were textual fiction.[74] The closer study of Posidippus' epigrams has alerted scholars to the possibly fictive character of statues in Hellenistic epigrams,[75] and this is a scenario that needs to be borne in mind for the epigram under discussion. As I have shown above, Callimachus recalls ritual acts of consecration. So, even if the statue of Berenice were textual, each reader would still recognize the discourse and recreate the consecration ritual by reading the epigram. In this manner, the completion of the *Aetia* would mark the apotheosis and epiphany (through Callimachus' text) of Berenice as goddess of artistic inspiration. Callimachus would allude to the immortality that poetry can confer,

---

[71] Cf. Gutzwiller 1998:285; Petrovic and Petrovic 2003:199–202.

[72] Cf. Petrovic and Petrovic 2003:194–198; Acosta-Hughes and Stephens 2012:222–224.

[73] Callimachus praised Berenice also in elegies that do not seem to have formed part of the *Aetia*; frr. 385–391 Pf. and possibly *PHorak* 4; see, however, D'Alessio 2007: vol. 2, 798–799n18.

[74] The analogy between poems and statues is characteristic of praise discourse and is found before Callimachus in Pindar's *Nemean* 5.1–2. See Kampakoglou 2011:137–139 with bibliography.

[75] Cf. Porter 2011.

modifying the traditional motif to hint at Berenice's divine hypostasis. It is even possible to envisage a court ceremony coordinated in such a way that the establishment of the statue of Berenice-Charis coincided with the official presentation of the *Aetia* to the court, reflecting Berenice's patronage of Callimachus.

Although no one would object to seeing Berenice II generally as the divine inspirer and protector of Callimachus' poetry, the specifics of the interpretation offered by Petrovic and Petrovic (2003:194–204) necessitate a series of assumptions that cannot be exclusively accepted unless one agrees a priori with their speculative contextualization of the epigram either as a "prologue" to the second half of the *Aetia* or on the *sillybos* attached to the poem's papyrus roll. For instance, it is not obvious why one should connect the mention of the three Charites in this context specifically with the *aetion* for their Parian cult in the first book of the *Aetia* (frr. 3–7[14] Pf.) especially when their role can be explained more persuasively from the point of view of literary conventions (see above, Section III). Equally difficult is their interpretation of κῆτι μύροισι νοτεῖ (*HE* 1122). The anointment of the statue of Berenice, even if it was only textual and so a metaphor for book four or books three and four of the *Aetia* taken together, cannot allude to the *Coma Berenices*. Such a connection ignores the juxtaposition between λιτά ("plain oils") and γυναικεῖα μύρα ("scented oils used by married women") or *ungenta nuptae* and *multa uilia* (fr. 110.77–78 Pf. ≈ Catullus 66.77–78; cf. Marinone 1997:198–204). The two categories of oils throw into relief Berenice II's double image as a warrior goddess like Athena (cf. Posidippus 36 AB for Arsinoë II) and a goddess of marriage and feminine attraction like Aphrodite.[76] Furthermore, since the lock does not partake of the μύρα that Berenice II uses as a married woman (γυναικείων δ' οὐκ ἀπέλαυσα μύρων ≈ *omnibus expers unguentis nuptae*) the connection with a statue which is explicitly said to be anointed with μύρα is infelicitous (see also below, Section IX). Against this background, Berenice II's anointment with plain oil during

---

[76] For Berenice II's association with Athena, see Clayman 2011; 2012. For the athletic aspect of λιτά, see Marinone 1997:199. For a similar juxtaposition of oils and their respective connotations, see Callimachus' *Hymn* 5.15–17; cf. Bulloch 1985:124–125.

her virginity (Callimachus fr. 110.77–78 Pf. ≈ Catullus 66.75–78) recalls that of Athena in Callimachus' *Hymn* 5.13–17 and that of athletes before performing. Despite the magical and religious significance that Ulf (1979:228, 232–233) and Sansone (1988:97, 102) have suggested for the anointment of athletes with oil (that is, as a means to increase their strength and enhance their performance), this use can hardly account for the anointment of a statue of Berenice represented as a Charis. Similarly, the metaphoric meaning of *charis* as "poem" (e.g. Theocritus 16) is not enough by itself to suggest that "Berenice" was ever used as a title either for the second part or for specific books of the *Aetia* so as to explain the anointment of Berenice's statue in connection with the habit of anointing with cedar oil new papyrus rolls to protect them from destruction. In the light of these objections, connection with the *Aetia*, albeit an attractive hypothesis, cannot be viewed as conclusive evidence either for identifying the Berenice praised or for explaining the anointment of her statue.

VIII. THE ATTRIBUTES OF BERENICE

The first half of the epigram assumes the form of an epiphany of the new Charis to Callimachus. The identity of the new goddess is revealed for the first time in the second half of the epigram, which employs more prominent signs of hymn discourse with the *aretalogia* of the deified Berenice.[77] Interestingly, both of Berenice's attributes appear again in connection with other members of the Ptolemaic dynasty. This coincidence raises the question of whether they had any specific significance with regard to the representation of the Ptolemies as deified monarchs.

VIII.1 εὐαίων Βερενίκα

Berenice is first called εὐαίων, which is usually rendered "happy in life" or just "happy, fortunate" (cf. LSJ⁹ s.v.). The only other occurrences in Callimachus' poetry are in *Hymn* 4 (292) and 5 (117). In *Hymn*

---

[77] See especially Norden 1923:143–176. For divine epithets in dedications and their connection with statues, see Day 1994:54.

4, it modifies Hekaergê, one of the three virgins that the Hyperboreans sent as *theôroi* to Delos.[78] In this context, the adjective refers to the election of the three girls as *theôroi* and euphemistically to their death at Delos.[79] εὐαίων corresponds to εὔμοιροι in 295 for the young men who escorted the three virgins to Delos.[80] As ἀκλεές in the same line also suggests, both adjectives ought to be seen in connection with the establishment of their posthumous cult (296–299). The three virgins and the three young men are fortunate in that they die in the service of Apollo and more importantly in that they change ontological status, becoming divinities supervising the transition of young men and women to adulthood (cf. also Herodotus 4.33–34; Pausanias 1.43.4). This use, then, is quite relevant to the interpretation of Callimachus' epigram. In both cases, εὐαίων refers to the establishment of divine honors for the Hyperborean maidens and Berenice.

The adjective has a similar meaning in its other Callimachean occurrence, although the connotations here are more sinister. Athena tries to console (117) Chariclô, because she has blinded her son, Teiresias: ὀλβίσταν δ' ἐρέει σε καὶ εὐαίωνα γενέσθαι | ἐξ ὀρέων ἀλαὸν παῖδ' ὑποδεξαμέναν, "happiest of women and blessed she (sc. Aktaiôn's mother) shall call you / since you received a blind son from the mountains" (tr. Bulloch). With a certain dose of exaggeration, Athena claims that, in comparison with Aktaiôn's mother, Chariclô should consider herself not only blissful to the highest degree but also εὐαίων because Athena, differently from Artemis, spared the life of her son Teiresias. Even in her cruel treatment of Chariclô, Athena preferentially singles out her companion: for the same transgression, Chariclô receives as

---

[78] See also Larson 1995:118–121; D'Alessio 2007: vol. 1, 167n101.

[79] The manner of one's death suggests whether one was happy in life or not (cf. e.g. Herodotus 1.30–31: ἀπέθανε κάλλιστα [30.5]); for "good" death, see Sourvinou-Inwood 1995:326. In the pessimistic Greek culture, where life was an affliction likely to be full of misfortunes, death, especially at a young age, was often seen as a charitable, if not beneficent, act on the part of the gods demonstrating their sympathy for the deceased: e.g. *Odyssey* 15.245–246; Menander fr. 111 Thierfelder-Körte; *Certamen* 75–80 etc.; cf. Lattimore 1962:258–260; Garland 2001:8–10; Asheri 2007:102. If one adds to this conceptual background the establishment of a heroic cult or the apotheosis of the deceased, one can see the reason for the use of this specific adjective in *Hymn* 4 and the epigram.

[80] Cf. Mineur 1984:231–232.

an option what Autonoê and Aristaios will not be granted even after several sacrifices and prayers (107–109). Again this use underlines Berenice's special position as beneficiary of divine good will. The ancient scholia render the adjective as μακαρία (Scholia to *Hymn* 4.292b in Pfeiffer 1953: vol. 2, 73). In classical Greek, μακάριος indicates that "a condition is felt to be above the ordinary or to be striking in some way. The stress appears to be on the uniqueness of this condition." [81] There is also a vague implication of divine favor. Differently from the cognate μάκαρ, which is used predominantly of gods, μακάριος modifies solely mortals. [82] On the other hand, Hesychius (ε 6688 Latte) renders εὐαίων as ἀγήρως, εὔμοιρος. The first gloss implies the divine status attained: everlasting youth is the attribute par excellence of immortal gods. If Hesychius is right, the use of εὐαίων would be an indication of the divine status that Berenice has attained. This is essentially the opinion of Wilamowitz, who believed that εὐαίων describes divine happiness in contradistinction to human happiness (εὐδαιμονίη). [83] Even so, one fails to find any such evidence. Hesychius' second gloss lacks such implications. It alludes to a good lot or fortune (cf. e.g. *Suda* s.v. εὐμοιρία). The compound suggests a person that has a happy life or a person whose happiness lasts all his or her life. In contrast to the mutability of the human condition, a feature commonly stressed in classical literature, imperturbability or complete happiness during one's lifetime comes very close to the state of the gods, who were eternally happy (cf. e.g. Simonides *PMG* 521; Aeschylus

[81] See De Heer 1969:56; cf. also 31–32 and 83–87.

[82] Cf. De Heer 1969 previous note and 4–11, 21–25, 28–31, 51–55, 81–82, 99–100. It also describes the blessed dead who have attained certain privileges in their afterlife or men who were deemed to be especially fortunate (i.e. wealthy, wealth being also a gift meted out by the gods to their favorites); cf. e.g. Hesiod *Works and Days* 379; Solon fr. 13.9 W². For the contextual association of εὐαίων with wealth, cf. Sophocles fr. 592.3 Radt.

[83] So also Barigazzi 1966:71. As Owen (1939:78) rightly noted, the confusion seems to have arisen from the interpretation of the adjective in passages such as *Ion* 126 = 142 εὐαίων εἴης. Most editors do not accept that the adjective can have an active meaning ("conferring happiness") but take it universally as passive ("supremely happy"); cf. e.g. Paley 1872–1880: vol. 2, 18 and 448; Wilamowitz 1926:92; Keyßner 1932:132–135, 165–166; and Lee 1997:173.

Agamemnon 553–554; Herodotus 1.5.4).[84] Still, such people were not believed to become or be gods. εὐαίων presupposes, often implicitly, the favor that gods have shown to a specific mortal person. This can be seen more clearly in a funerary epigram by Leonidas of Tarentum (*HE* 2028–2031). The Cretan Pratalidas is εὐαίων because various gods favored him during his lifetime with excellence in several different fields: pederastic love, hunting, and music (cf. Solon fr. 23 W²). Leonidas uses ἐγγυαλίζω, which is often employed for divine favors.[85] These gifts constitute the pinnacle of mortal bliss, a state that separated Pratalidas from the rest of the mortals as a divine favorite but did not render him deified or divine either during his lifetime or after his death.[86]

In a few cases, εὐαίων can be used as an attribute of gods, especially Apollo (Euripides *Ion* 126 = 142) and Dionysus (Philodamus Scarpheus, *Paean in Dionysum*).[87] In *Ion*, the adjective refers primarily to Apollo, who as Paean can give a happy life to mortals, although the text is not specific enough (see note 83). In Philodamus' *paean*, Paean, identified here with Dionysus, is asked to protect Delphi and to procure ὄλβος which will render life happy for its inhabitants. Philodamus is probably referring to material possessions and wealth (εὐαίωνι σὺν ὄλβῳ). Similarly, in Sophocles' *Philoctetes* (829), Hypnos is addressed as

---

[84] Cf. e.g. Dodds 1960:128 "It is a strong word, implying *permanent* happiness such as man attributes to the gods" (my emphasis).

[85] Cf. Gow and Page 1965: vol. 2, 324 on *HE* 2029.

[86] Cf. also inscriptional epitaphs: *IG* II² 6214; *Demos Ramnountos* II 260 [= *SEG* 43: 88]; *IK Kyme* 51.

[87] In Aeschylus' *Persae* (711 βίοτον εὐαίωνα Πέρσαις ὡς θεὸς διήγαγες), it is Darius who as a god confers upon his subjects the attribute of being εὐαίων—that is, the gift of spending a happy life; see Broadhead 1960:178–180 and Garvie 2009:283–284. Darius is compared to a god or was even perhaps perceived as such by his subjects after his death (cf. Σ 157 Dindorf τοὺς βασιλεῖς θεοὺς καλοῦσιν οἱ Πέρσαι with Hall 1996:121 and Garvie 2009:99–100). Cf. also Sophocles' *Trachiniae* (80–81) with Davies (1991:73) and the *iunctura* δυσαίων ὁ βίος that Euripides fashioned on Sophocles' model: *Supplices* 960 with Collard 1975: vol. 2, 346; cf. also *Helen* 213 αἰὼν δυσαίων with Kannicht 1969: vol. 2, 78. In the same manner, but from the opposite point of view, in *Bacchae* the chorus speaks about the boons that the cult of Dionysus has to offer and which bring happiness to mortals (424–426). In *Iphigenia in Aulis* 543–551 εὐαίων is connected with prudence in love.

εὐαίων. The members of the chorus ask Hypnos to offer some relief to Philoctetes so they can scamper away with his bow.[88]

In Callimachus' epigram, the reference to Berenice's happiness is followed by a line that elaborates on its essence.[89] Berenice is the recipient of divine favor, and thanks to it she has attained the highest degree of mortal good fortune: deification (see also above, note 79).[90] One notes that, in his description of the apotheosis of Queen Berenice I, Theocritus (17.46) explicitly singles out divine favor and interest as the motives for Aphrodite's intervention. Callimachus, however, innovates in slightly twisting the traditional motif: not only apotheosis renders Berenice fortunate, but also her ability to confer *charis* upon the Charites, themselves goddesses.

This picture is not altered when one compares the use of the same adjective for Ptolemy III Euergetes (Eratosthenes fr. 35 Powell) and his son, Ptolemy IV Philopator (*SH* 979 = *FGE* anon. 151b). Eratosthenes uses the adjective in his address to the former (35.13–15 Powell). Ptolemy is considered to have reached the peak of human happiness, because he presented his son with those things that bring joy to the Muses and kings, a probable allusion to Hesiod (*Theogony* 80–93). Eratosthenes refers to the care that Euergetes showed for the training of his successor. Even so, it is the means or the wealth with which Zeus has blessed Ptolemy that allows the king to bestow such a lavish education on his son (cf. Callimachus *Hymn* 1.84–86; Theocritus 17.105–130). The blossoming of the arts and sciences in the Museum, supported by the munificence of the king, is another factor that will enable the young prince to become a model king, when the time comes for him to succeed his father.[91]

---

[88] In an unpublished Attic inscription (*SEG* 39:235; ca. 400–350 BCE), Dionysios asks the local hero Kallistephanos to grant him πλοῦτον καὶ εὐαίων᾽ ὑγίειαν in return for his offerings.

[89] Cf. Norden 1923:159 with n. 2 and Bulloch 1985:228n2.

[90] One could compare Cadmus' mortal daughters who were deified after their death. In Pindar's *Olympian* 2, their deification exemplifies the alternation of good and bad fortune, a main characteristic of human condition. Their deification is a sign of their good fate, despite the grievous mishaps that befell them during their life (21–37).

[91] Cf. Wilamowitz 1941:64.

Similar sentiments are expressed in an epigram or elegy (*SH* 979 = *FGE* anon. 151b) preserved in what appears to have originally been a copy of a school anthology (*P.Cairo* inv. JE 65445 = MP³ 2642). The poem celebrates the foundation of a temple to Homer by Ptolemy IV Philopator. The king is praised for his good fortune (2, ἐϋαίων Πτολεμ[), in that Homer appeared to him in his sleep. This apparition moved him to build the temple.[92] The epigram finishes with the eulogy of the king's parents: Euergetes and Berenice II are praised for raising Philopator to be a king excellent both in war and the arts. The passage is too close to Eratosthenes' praise for this to be a coincidence. It is quite likely that both poets echo a standard motif in royal praise. However, one should not exclude the possibility that the later poet is alluding to Eratosthenes' epigram.[93]

VIII.2 ἀρίζηλος Βερενίκα

Scholars do not agree about the etymology and thus the meaning of the second adjective attributed to Berenice. It can mean that Berenice is greatly envied because of her good fortune to become one of the Charites (LSJ⁹ s.v. II: synonym of ἀριζήλωτος ["much to be envied"]; Hesychius s.v. α 6920). Alternatively, it can mean that she is famous or illustrious, referring in all probability to her royal status or pedigree (DGE s.v. 2 "preclaro, famoso"; Hesychius α 7207; cf. also α 7211; α 4101; α 7208). The second gloss is more plausible on etymological grounds. Still, it is far from certain that this was the (only) way in which the word was understood by Callimachus' audience—although this is the most likely case.

Another question concerns the implications that the use of the same adjective for Berenice I in Theocritus 17.57 and for Ptolemy I in a Callimachean fragment of uncertain place (fr. 734 Pf.) could have for the interpretation of the epigram under discussion.[94] Pfeiffer (1949: vol. 1, 467 note on fr. 734 "de mortuis in Olympum receptis") connects the

---

[92] Cf. Lloyd-Jones and Parsons 1983:494. For the Egyptian provenance of this motif, see Bourgeaud and Volokhine 2000:53

[93] Cf. Barigazzi 1966:71–72.

[94] Cf. Hunter 2003:142.

use of the adjective with the status of the person mentioned. It implies the deification of deceased members of the Ptolemaic family. However, Pfeiffer does not accept that its use in this epigram necessarily implies that the Berenice praised was dead ("de Magae filia tum uiua"). The issue is whether there are any connotations of divinity in the use of this adjective and whether such connotations can be corroborated by previous usage. Explicit divine associations are rare.[95] Hesiod's use (*Works and Days* 6, ῥεῖα δ' ἀρίζηλον μινύθει καὶ ἄδηλον ἀέξει [sc. Ζεὺς ὑψιβρεμέτης]) suggests that the conspicuousness or illustriousness denoted by ἀρίζηλον is a divine gift. This squares nicely with Callimachus' previous representation of Berenice as recipient of divine favor.

There is only one case in Greek literature where the use of the adjective is explicitly connected with a characteristically divine attribute, the size of divine bodies. In the description of one of the two cities on Achilles' shield, Homer describes the presence of Ares and Athena among the two armies and their representation on the shield (*Iliad* 18.518–519): καλὼ καὶ μεγάλω σὺν τεύχεσιν, ὥς τε θεώ περ | ἀμφὶς ἀριζήλω· λαοὶ δ' ὑπολίζονες ἦσαν. The difference in stature between the two gods and the mortal warriors around them is pictorially represented on the shield by the difference in the size of their respective bodies. Homer refers to a traditional belief that gods were generally larger than mortals, a divine attribute usually mentioned in scenes of divine epiphany along with radiance and ambrosial fragrance: cf. e.g., *Iliad* 4.443; *Homeric Hymn to Aphrodite* 173–174; *Homeric Hymn to Demeter* 188–189.[96] The use of this adjective in this context echoes that belief and does not of itself point to a divine status. It is through the context that we can associate the adjective with the divine status of Ares and Athena, evidence altogether missing from Callimachus' text. Yet it is possible in view of Berenice's epiphany that this adjective refers to the size of her statue as a sign of Berenice's divinity.[97] The adjective can

[95] Cf. Voigt in *LfgrE* s.v. ἀρίζηλος.

[96] For the physical differences between gods and mortals, see especially Richardson 1974:207–211 and 252–253.

[97] On the size of the statues of gods and the connection with this mythological belief, cf. Carney 2000:28–30 and Platt 2011:89. Size was also part of the Homeric ideal of beauty.

semantically fluctuate between the two senses in which it has been traditionally understood based on the level of signification that each reader chooses: the statue is of conspicuous size, a sign of Berenice's divinity,[98] but Berenice is also conspicuous in figurative terms thanks to her royal and divine status.

IX. IDENTIFICATION WITH THE CHARITES AND THE IDENTITY OF BERENICE

Although there is no explicit indication of Berenice's royal status in the epigram, she was likely a member of the royal family.[99] Most scholars would identify her with the consort of Ptolemy III (Berenice II).[100] Generally, identification with a member of Euergetes' family (his wife, sister, or daughter) is to be preferred for reasons that will become apparent below and in view of Callimachus' silence over Berenice I in his surviving poetry. Some scholars have found evidence in favor of the identification with Berenice II in the information given by Athenaeus (15.689a) that the trade of perfumes and especially of a specific Cyrenean kind thrived under the reign of Berenice II.[101] Presumably, Berenice the Great, whom Athenaeus mentions, is the consort of Ptolemy III and not her grandmother the wife of Ptolemy I, although

---

Women of the heroic era were believed to be larger than normal women; cf. Jax 1933:8–9, 68–70. In this regard too, Berenice is different from contemporary mortal women.

[98] Cf. Day 2010:269 "Artists, translating aspects of that cultural sense of divine appearance into their craft, made images look like epiphanic gods in terms of size (or display) and especially beauty and radiance." For a different interpretation of ἀρίζηλος in connection with Berenice's statue, see Schmid 1923:177.

[99] Four members of the royal family bore this name during Callimachus' lifetime (ca. 320–240 BCE): Berenice I (*PP* 14497), queen consort of Ptolemy I; Berenice Syra (*PP* 14498), daughter of Ptolemy II Philadelphus and of his first wife Arsinoë I, and queen consort of Antiochus II; Berenice II (*PP* 14499), daughter of Magas of Cyrene and queen consort of Ptolemy III Euergetes; Berenice (*PP* 14500), daughter of Ptolemy III Euergetes and Berenice II.

[100] Jouguet 1938; Pfeiffer 1949: vol. 1, 468 on fr. 734; Gow 1952: vol. 2, 336; Lieberg 1962:28–29; Gow and Page 1965: vol. 2, 175; Meillier 1979:149–150; Weber 1993:268 with note 1; Kakaridos 1997:336; Hunter 2003:142; Acosta-Hughes and Stephens 2012:223n56. For identification with Berenice I, see Schmid 1923:177.

[101] Cf. Gow and Page 1965: vol. 2, 172 on 1122; Herter 1975:201–205; Kakaridos 1997:335; Massimilla 2010:502; Harder 2012: vol. 2, 846.

this is not clear. Scholars have connected Athenaeus' testimony with the so-called "nuptial rite" in Catullus 66.[102] Catullus' rite cannot persuasively account for the anointment of the statue of Berenice in Callimachus' epigram.[103] The deified lock asks wives to offer their unguents to it as libation before they sleep with their husbands (82–83): *quam iucunda mihi munera libet onyx, / uester onyx, casto colitis quae iura cubili.*[104] This injunction is brought into connection with marital felicity as the lock juxtaposes chaste and adulterous wives, threatening that it will not accept any libations from the latter (84–86). The lock's wish in lines 87–88 implies that the veneration of Berenice's lock and the offering of unguents to it are associated with marital stability and accord: *sed magis, o nuptae, semper concordia uestras, / semper amor sedes incolat assiduus.* In this context, unguents are seen as a means of enhancing feminine attraction. In *Iliad* 14, before seducing Zeus, Hera anoints her clothes, body, and hair with ambrosial oil, the sweet fragrance of which fills the whole cosmos (171–175).[105] Similarly, in the *Homeric Hymn to Aphrodite* (61–62), before sleeping with the mortal Anchises, Aphrodite anoints herself and her dress with ambrosial oil.[106] In both cases, anointment boosts the attractiveness of the goddesses, rendering them irresistible to their respective lovers. The marital associations, albeit present in both scenes, are more explicit in *Iliad* 14, as the union of Zeus and Hera is connected by the narrator with their first union (14.295–296), a theme of importance for Ptolemaic royal

---

[102]Lines 79–88 of Catullus' poem that describe the rite do not correspond to anything on *POxy* 2258, which preserves the Greek text. Catullus followed a later version of the *Coma* after its incorporation in the *Aetia*: this version included the nuptial rite and omitted lines 94a–b that are missing from Catullus' version. Cf. Pfeiffer 1949: vol. 1, 120–121; Fordyce 1961:339; Gutzwiller 1992:382; Marinone 1997:41–49; Thomson 1998:460–461; Rossi 2000:299–301; D'Alessio 2007: vol. 2, 530; Massimilla 2010:503–506; Harder 2012: vol. 2, 846–847. For a different interpretation, according to which lines 79–88 were added by Catullus, see Acosta-Hughes and Stephens 2012:229–233.

[103]Cf. also Herter 1975:202; Meillier 1979:150.

[104]The lock addresses married women, not just newly-wedded wives; cf. Marinone 1997:205; Thomson 1998:461.

[105]Cf. Janko 1992:174–175.

[106]Cf. Faulkner 2008:142–143; Richardson 2010:230–231. Cf. also *Odyssey* 18.193–194: Aphrodite anoints herself before joining the dance of the Charites. For χορός as the *locus* of feminine attraction and its relation to Aphrodite, see Boedeker 1974:43–63.

marriages.[107] By dedicating oils, perfumes, and unguents to the lock, wives are offering to the new divinity part of their sexual power over their husbands. They can hope in return for a divine boosting of the feminine attraction that cements marriages. By insisting on the difference in quality between the unguents used by maidens and those used by married women (Callimachus fr. 110.77–78 Pf. ~ Catullus 66.77–78),[108] the lock insinuates the erotic appeal that anointment with unguents and oils has and emphasizes that important role it holds in the sexual life of married women.[109] The lock is an avatar of Berenice II and a form of Aphrodite as is clearly indicated by the cultic context within which the queen is to offer her sacrifices (Catullus 66.89–92); this association hints at the imminent apotheosis of Berenice II as Aphrodite, the goddess of marriage.[110] The royal marriage is the model to which ordinary women can aspire, and it is in achieving this ideal that the lock can help them. Marital felicity, a standard *topos* in Ptolemaic public discourse (e.g. Theocritus 17.38–44), was seen in pharaonic ideology as guarantee for the stability and prosperity of the kingdom.[111]

The details about the offering of the libations to Berenice II's lock are not specified.[112] The lock suggests private libations without specifying if the oil is poured over an image or an altar as was usually the case with oil libations.[113] By analogy with wine libations, one may suppose that part of the oil was poured out for the lock, while the remaining consecrated oil was used by women to anoint their body and hair. In this manner, married women would both offer the lock its share of quality unguents but also recreate the process of anointment

---

[107]Cf. Mori 2008:96–97.

[108]Cf. Marinone 1997:198–204; Thomson 1998:459–460; D'Alessio 2007: vol. 2, 530; Harder 2012: vol. 2, 845–846.

[109]Cf. Gutzwiller 1992:381.

[110]For Berenice II as Aphrodite, see Tondriau 1948:21.

[111]Cf. Koenen 1983:160–165; 1993:61–64; Pomeroy 1990:30–32; Gutzwiller 1992:364–369; Rossi 2000:301–312; Harder 2012: vol. 2, 847.

[112]The motif used for the apotheosis of Berenice II's lock is common in narratives about the deification of abducted mortals; cf. Vérilhac 1982: vol. 2, 325–330; Kampakoglou 2013b:313–325. In a way, the lock is like a deceased mortal and so libations of oil are the appropriate way to honor it; cf. Stengel 1910:129.

[113]Cf. Burkert 1985:71.

that the deified lock cannot participate in any longer. Similarly, problems surround Berenice II's official libations at Aphrodite's festivals (89–92). Did the queen anoint a statue of Aphrodite? Or did she pour oil over the goddess' altar at Cape Zephyrium from which the lock was abducted? Berenice offers libations to her divine aspect, encouraging her cult by her subjects.[114] Her role is paradigmatic. Assuming that Berenice II was already deified by that time, one notes the same sort of ritual reflexivity that Patton (2009) has examined in detail. As she argues (171), "gods practice those forms of religion that are specific to their own particular form of worship." If this is so in our case, the cult of Berenice II-Aphrodite included libations of perfumes and scented oils, which could have been used for the anointment of her statues or altars. The analogy with the use of anointment in the *Coma Berenices* intimates that in Callimachus' epigram Berenice's sexual potency and desirability are manifested through her sweet fragrance. Sexual attractiveness along with beauty and sweet scent are divine attributes that shape the epiphany of the new goddess. Even so, it is very difficult to see how Callimachus' epigram could fit in the frame provided by Catullus' details: there is no mention of Aphrodite and the marital context is uncertain.[115]

The selection of the Charites can perhaps be explained by the fact that Berenice II wanted to avoid the implications that her identification with Aphrodite would create, as the goddess was generally associated in the mind of the public with her predecessor, Arsinoë II, and to a lesser degree with her namesake grandmother, Berenice I. It has been recently pointed out that in order to reinforce her precarious public position, first during her long engagement to Ptolemy III and

---

[114]This kind of ritual reflexivity is paralleled in the Mendes Stela, where Arsinoë II is represented twice among the local gods and with her sacrificing husband; cf. Quaegebeur 1988:43. Before Arsinoë II, Ramesses II was represented offering libations to his deified self, a statue bearing the name Ramessu-meramen the God; see Habachi 1969 passim.

[115]Jouguet (1938) proposed that the epigram was composed right after Berenice II's arrival at the Ptolemaic court, probably around the same time as her nuptials. This scenario could be supported by some evidence that points to an association of the Charites with marriage. Schwarzenberg 1966:20–22. Cf. also Euripides *Hippolytus* (1148 συζύγιαι Χάριτες) with the discussion of Bushala 1969; *Etymologicum magnum* s.v. Γαμηλία with Rocchi 1980:20 and n. 14.

then during his absence in Syria, Berenice II fashioned her public image on the model of Hathor, the Egyptian equivalent of Aphrodite.[116] This assimilation appears more clearly in Callimachus' *Coma Berenices*, which alludes to Egyptian myths about the locks of Isis and Hathor.[117] One cannot exclude the possibility that the Charites were selected precisely because they belonged to the same conceptual framework as Aphrodite but retained their individuality as independent goddesses of physical and artistic charm.[118] The example of other Ptolemaic queens suggests that the queen can be identified with or assimilated to more than one goddess at the same time, a fact facilitated by the various ways in which Egyptian goddesses and gods were combined or viewed as aspects of the same deity.[119] It is not impossible, then, that the Charites were considered as another possibility at some point at a prior time or in tandem with Hathor and Aphrodite.[120] It ought to be borne in mind that Berenice does not become just one of the Charites but, as it were, the personification of divine *charis*, although this is not explicitly stated. The idea is paralleled in *FGE* anon. 14 (τρεῖς εἰσὶν Χάριτες· σὺ δὲ δὴ μία ταῖς τρισὶ ταύταις | γεννήθης, ἵν' ἔχωσ' αἱ Χάριτες Χάριτα). In this light, Évelyne Prioux (2007:207–210) may be right to suggest that we should see Berenice's assimilation to the Charites as a political allegory: the Charites as a group stand for χάρις—that is, the feeling of mutual respect and gratitude that unites the sovereign as benefactor· of his people and his subjects as receivers of his benefactions. In this manner, the honors paid to Berenice and the selection of these goddesses reflect a basic principle of Ptolemaic kingship.

[116] See Llewellyn-Jones and Winder 2011:247–269.

[117] Selden 1988:344–348; cf. also Clayman 2011:239–242. For the identification of Aphrodite with Hathor in Ptolemaic times, see Fraser 1972: vol. 1, 197 with note 50 (= vol. 2, 332).

[118] It is possible, but rather unlikely, that this similarity between the Charites and Aphrodite hides behind Hephaestus' two wives: Charis in *Iliad* 18.382 and Aphrodite in *Odyssey* 8.266–269; cf. Hainsworth 1988:364 and West 2011:34, 37.

[119] Cf. Selden 1998:349–351.

[120] The interpretation of Berenice II's Hathoric image is based on Callimachus' *Coma Berenices* and temple reliefs from after the second Syrian war; cf. Llewellyn-Jones and Winder 2011. The exact date of the epigram, if it refers to Berenice II, cannot however be established with any certainty.

Apart from this epigram, there could be some slight evidence that Callimachus again associated Berenice II with the Charites in the extremely lacunose epilogue of the *Aetia* (fr. 112.1–4 Pf. = Harder = 215.1–4 Massimilla). Even so, the identity of the queen mentioned there and her exact relationship with the Charites is far from certain:

> . . .] . . ιν ὅτ' ἐμὴ μοῦσα τ[. . . .]άσεται
> . . .]του καὶ Χαρίτων [. . . . .]ριᾳ μοιαδ' ἀνάσσης
> . . .]τερης οὔ σε ψευδον[. . . . .]ματι
> πάντ' ἀγαθὴν καὶ πάντα τ[ελ]εσφόρον εἶπεν . . . [. .].[

Scholars agree that Callimachus addresses a feminine personage about whom Hesiod said that she was always good and fruitful. The queen mentioned in line two has been tentatively identified with either Arsinoë II or Berenice II, with most scholars seeing the latter as the most likely candidate.[121] This identification is perhaps strengthened by the fact that the last *aetion* narrated just before the epilogue deals with Berenice II's lock (fr. 110 Pf. = 110–110f Harder = 213 Massimilla). Goffredo Coppola believed that Callimachus addressed Cyrene, the eponymous heroine of his native country.[122] This would square nicely with the probable mention of Berenice II, also a native of Cyrene.

The reason for the inclusion of the Charites, however, remains unclear. It certainly looks back to the first *aetion* of the first book which concerned the Parian cult of the three goddesses in a programmatic ring composition.[123] Some scholars see this as a reference to a specific location in Cyrene called the "hill of the Charites" where the river Cinyps had its springs.[124] There might, however, be more to this than is usually assumed. Archaeologists have posited that the Theran colonists who founded Cyrene brought with them to their new home the Theran

---

[121]Pfeiffer 1949: vol. 1, 124 on fr. 112.2; Massimilla 1992:514; D'Alessio 2004: vol. 2, 541n67; Acosta-Hughes and Stephens 2012:223; Harder 2012: vol. 2, 859–860 on fr. 112.2–3.

[122]Coppola 1930:273–281 and 1935:174–175; cf. Massimilla 2010:513–514.

[123]Cf. Pfeiffer 1949 and Harder 2012 on fr. 112.2.

[124]Callimachus fr. 673 Pf. (ἢ ὑπὲρ αὐσταλέον Χαρίτων λόφον) [= Σ Pindar *Pythian* 5.31]. D'Alessio 2007: vol. 2, 770n144, mentions also Herodotus 4.175 and Nonnus *Dionysiaca* 13.340.

cult of the Charites, an offshoot of their cult at Orchomenos.[125] One could perhaps posit the existence of an old and traditional cult of the three Charites at Cyrene. The special connection that the Cyreneans would have felt that the Charites had with their native land might have been the reason why the court or Callimachus associated Berenice II with them. This connection must remain an attractive hypothesis as there is no evidence, inscriptional or literary, to prove either the existence of this Cyrenean cult or that Berenice II ever took an active interest in the dissemination of the cult of the Charites in her new country.

However, the secondary position of the Charites, who were usually relegated to be the handmaids of more important goddesses,[126] not to mention their hypostasis as a trinity, renders identification with the Charites not prestigious enough for the profile of a Ptolemaic queen and especially of Berenice II.[127] Even so, Berenice II's predecessor, Arsinoë II, was associated with water nymphs or represented as one of them (see Section II above). *SH* 978.14, σύγκληρον νύμφαις κατὰ πᾶν ἔτος, which some scholars have seen as an allusion to the establishment of a cult of Arsinoë II as a Krenias nymph, has not been

---

[125] All our literary evidence for the cult of Charites in Cyrene derives from the ancient scholia on Pindar's *Pythian* 5 (31); cf. Vitali 1932:57. The existence of a Theran cult of the Charites is posited on the basis of *IG* XII,3 1312 Κ(h)άριτες. For the connections of the Theran cult of the Charites with Orchomenos and with Cyrene, see Gaertringen 1899:182 and 1901:216, 218; Farnell 1909: vol. 5, 429 with note 146; Inglese 2008:209–214.

[126] Plutarch (*Antonios* 26.1–3) reports that in 41 BCE when Cleopatra VII sailed to visit Antonius at Tarsos she was adorned like Aphrodite, while her ladies-in-waiting were dressed like Nereids and Charites; cf. also Strootman 2007:302–303. For the Charites as handmaids of major goddesses, and especially of Aphrodite, see Jax 1933:66; Schwarzenberg 1966:14–15. For Aphrodite as the queen of the Charites, cf. Colluthus 16.

[127] The assimilation of Berenice II to the nymph Cyrene, which Tondriau (1948) mentions on the suggestion of Couat (1882:235n1), relies on an allegorical interpretation of Callimachus' *Hymn to Apollo*; cf. also Williams 1978:1–2; see, however, Barbantani 2011:190–191 and Prioux 2011:211. Obviously, as the eponymous nymph of a kingdom part of the Ptolemaic empire, Cyrene enjoyed a more prestigious status than the three Charites. For the parallelism between Berenice II and Athena in Callimachus' poetry, see Herter 1975:197–203 and Clayman 2011:233–237.

universally accepted as conclusive evidence.[128] Even those who do accept this interpretation are puzzled by the identification of Arsinoë II with minor nymphs. It is usually explained as a heroization—that is, as the first step in the process that led to her ultimate apotheosis as Aphrodite. Similar reasoning regarding the selection of the Charites is less convincing in the case of Berenice II. From Catullus' version it is clear that the catasterism of her lock is the first step towards her assimilation to Aphrodite as goddess of marriage.

Ptolemaic kings and queens were as a rule identified with or assimilated to unique gods or goddesses—that is, they did not become members of a collective group of gods or goddesses such as the Muses and the Charites, unless there was a specific political reason for it.[129] One presumes that gods and goddesses who were venerated collectively as a group could never claim or receive the same degree of importance and attention as an independent deity. On the other hand, it would not be inappropriate for the young Berenice or even for Euergetes' sister, Berenice Syra, to become a member of a group of goddesses that attend upon Aphrodite, the goddess associated in the artistic and public sphere with important Ptolemaic queens such as Berenice I and Arsinoë II.

---

[128] See especially Cazzaniga 1966:488–490 and Ronchi 1968:59–63; see, however, Barigazzi 1966:81–82; Giangrande 1973; Page 1981 on *FGE* anon. 151a; and Lloyd-Jones and Parsons 1983 on *SH* 978.14.

[129] Arsinoë III, sister and consort of Ptolemy IV Philopator, was represented on Thespian coins, and possibly even venerated at Thespiae, as the Tenth Muse; Schachter 1986:165–166. This honor was probably conferred upon her by the local authorities in recognition of her involvement in the re-organization of the Mouseia; see Feyel 1942:103–117. For a reference to an Arsinoë in a Thespian context, cf. also *SH* 959.4. Callimachus may have referred to Arsinoë II or Berenice II as the Tenth Muse in the beginning of the first book of the *Aetia*. The London scholia (fr. 1.41 Pf. [page 7] = fr. 2a.1 Harder [page 129]) preserve the lemma δεκάς which was interpreted by the scholiast as a reference to Arsinoë II or even mistakenly to Arsinoë III; cf. Schachter 1986:165–166n4 and Cameron 1995:141–142. However, the interpretation is far from certain not only because of the lacunose state of the gloss, but also because the scholiast raises the possibility that the numeral can equally refer to the nine Muses plus Apollo: η Ἀρσιν(όη) δυω ... | ἦν ἄνω(θεν?) ἢ ὅτι δ(ε)κάτη(ν) | Μοῦσαν ἐκδ(ε) .... ( ); cf. D'Alessio 2007: vol. 2, 279n29; Harder 2012: vol. 2, 106–107. More likely, Callimachus did not specify the identity of this tenth person in the original text.

An alternative, previously undiscussed candidate for the subject of the epigram is Berenice, the daughter of Ptolemy III and Berenice II. Her death at a very young age in 238 BCE coincided with the synod of the Egyptian priests at Canopus (*OGIS* 56). The decree of this synod reports the priests' decision to confer divine honors upon the young princess. Her death was paralleled to the disappearance of Tefnut (*OGIS* 56.55–56), considered to be the daughter of Re and usually identified with Hathor and through her with Sothis (= Sirius). Berenice became a temple-sharing goddess with Osiris at the temple that her parents had founded for him at Canopus. Her cult statue received the cultic name "Berenice queen of the maidens" (*OGIS* 56.61 Βερενίκη ἄνασσα παρθένων), which, according to scholars, recalls similar titles attributed to Hathor at Dendara.[130] Interestingly, her parallelism with Hathor-Tefnut brings her close to the public profile of her mother who was an avatar of Hathor, giving us an Egyptian equivalent for the close connection between the Charites and Aphrodite in Greek mythology.

Berenice "the Younger" is an attractive candidate for this epigram although she has not received proper attention. The time of her death does not pose any serious problems. The date of Callimachus' death is approximately dated in 240 BCE so this would not speak against the proposed identification. Also it seems that her significance for the public profile of the royal family was such that even after her death she was represented along with the rest of Euergetes' family at the monumental complex of statues erected at Thermos.[131] In the light of such an honor, it is not unlikely that she could have been praised with an epigram by Callimachus. The exact age of Berenice at the time of her death is not known. Dating her conception right after the marriage of her parents in 246 BCE would allow for an age up to 7 years old. However, the order of birth of Ptolemy III's six children is not known

---

[130] Cf. Pfeiffer 2004:177.

[131] *IG* IX, I² I:56, e.1–3 preserves the arrangement of the statues on the exedra. The monument was consecrated by the Aetolian League in return for Ptolemy III's benefactions (cf. *IG* IX, I² I:56, i.1). The exact date of the monument is not known. Huss (1975:319–310) dates it shortly after the end of the Demetrian war in the late 230s BCE; other scholars place it in the time between 224–222 BCE; more recently Bennett (2002:142) has suggested 239 or early 238 BCE before the death of Berenice.

and cannot be securely concluded from the exedra at Thermos. Arsinoë III, the queen consort of Ptolemy IV Philopator and Berenice's sister, was probably the older of the two daughters. Even if Berenice was born in 239 BCE, as Bennett (2002:145) has suggested, this would not speak against her representation as a Charis. She seems to have had an independent statue on the Thermos exedra, although it is unclear how she was actually depicted. The Canopus decree makes clear that her Egyptian statues depicted her as a young woman, something also suggested by her comparison to Tefnut, who was represented as an adult deity. More likely, and irrespective of her actual age at the time of her death, she was represented idealistically as a young woman. The funerary stele of Nikopolis Sarapionos from Smyrna (*PM* 329; epigram: McCabe, Smyrna 260) supports the conflation of ages and roles in funerary monuments in Hellenistic times. Nikopolis died at the age of two but was represented as a young woman with her own attendant.[132] Berenice's young age could make her identification with the Charites perhaps more reasonable. The association of (very) young men and women with the Charites is well attested in the Roman period, especially in the context of funerary imagery:[133] e.g. Theophilê (*CIRB* 130.18; ca. 50 BCE–50 CE); Charitôn, eight years old (*IGUR* vol. 3, 1294.1; reign of Antoninus Pius); Phlaouia (1404 Peek; 2nd–3rd centuries CE); Menophilos, eight years old (*IGUR* vol. 3, 1275.2; undated). The lapidary style of most archaic and classical funerary inscriptions allows no certainty about the antiquity of this theme. Callimachus' epigram could reflect the early stages of this tradition. On the other hand, Tadeusz Zielinksi (1924) argued that the association of the Charites with the underworld and death is an ancient element of their cult that antedates their association with Aphrodite and *erôs*. In their chthonic role, the Charites are connected with the physical cycle of life and death. Zielinski (1924:160–163) placed special emphasis on the connection between *chthonia charis* and the cult of heroes. According to his

---

[132] See Zanker 1993:221; Bobou 2006: 169–170.

[133] Cf. especially Robert 1946 and Vérilhac 1982: vol. 2, §§ 7 and 22. For the chthonian associations of the Charites, see Zielinski 1924; Schwarzenberg 1966:9–10; Rocchi 1980:24–25.

argument, the tomb of the heroized dead was a source of *charis* for his people who enjoyed his benefactions and protection. It is possible that the assimilation of Berenice to the Charites—and generally of deceased young persons to these deities—reflects this aspect of the cult of Charites. It is very difficult, and perhaps not prudent in the case of Ptolemaic imagery, to dissociate literary conventions from religious ideas. One can compare the representation of deceased maidens as Hades' bride (e.g. Leonidas of Tarentum *HE* 2563–2566; Meleager *HE* 4680–4681); in effect, this motif casts them in the role of Persephone, situating them in a specific religious and mythological system of beliefs. How seriously such assimilations are to be taken depends on the original circumstances of composition. At any rate, the Ptolemaic court could have invested this religious idea with a new life in order to serve the public image of the royal family. This interpretation, if relevant to our case, would also imply that Berenice becomes a beneficent goddess supporting the role of her parents as benefactors of Egypt.[134] As Pfeiffer (2004:172–173, 265–266) has suggested, Berenice's identification with Tefnut could have alluded to the heliacal rising of Sothis and its influence on the annual rising of the Nile. This would give us another instance of her association with royal benefactions on a cosmic level.[135]

In addition to the above interpretation, the association of the deceased person with the Charites combines an amatory theme with the traditional praise of the virtues of the deceased person.[136] Such imagistic connections between *erôs* and death are typical of Hellenistic epigrams and Callimachus in particular (cf. e.g. *HE* 1057–62: abduction by *erôs* combined with abduction by death). The Charites, then, could have been selected because of their connection with the funerary tradition and Aphrodite, their relevance to the public profile of the Euergetae, and in view of Berenice's age. One can compare the

---

[134]For the title "Euergetes" and its ideological implications, see Muccioli 2013:178–193.
[135]Cf. Kampakoglou 2013a:132; 2013b:322–324.
[136]Cf. also Leonidas *HE* 2014–2023; Pompey the Younger *GP* 3961–3965; and Julian *AP* 7.599–600. For the praise of the deceased, see Lattimore 1962:290–299; Vérilhac 1982: vol. 2, 3–79. For comparison to heroes or gods as part of funerary praise, see Lattimore 1962:97–106; Vérilhac 1982: vol. 2, 26–28, 321–332.

apotheosis of Princess Philotera, Philadelphus' sister (fr. 228.43–45 Pf.). In the *Ectheosis Arsinoes*, the deified Philotera appears as a member of Demeter's entourage––an appropriate selection if her sister, Arsinoë II, was identified with Demeter.[137] Although Philotera's actual role in the *Ectheosis* is not clear, it seems that she welcomed the deified Arsinoë II to the world of the gods. If the Berenice praised by Callimachus is the youngest daughter of Ptolemy Euergetes, then the statue could have had a funerary character and could have been associated with her post-humous deification.

However, one should not press the factor of age too much either for Berenice II or her daughter. The artistic representation was not necessarily accurate or truthful. For instance, if the identification of Arsinoë II with Helen in *Idyll* 18 is correct, Theocritus represented the mature queen as a young woman.[138] In this sense, the comparison to the Charites could also include flattery that would have worked for every one of the queens or princesses mentioned above.[139]

Another possible, although perhaps less likely, candidate is Euergetes' sister, the second wife of Antiochus II.[140] Berenice Syra's role in Hellenistic court poetry had been uncertain for quite some time until the discovery of Posidippus' Milan Papyrus. Thompson (2005:274–279) and Criscuolo (2003:328–330) have made a strong case in favor of identifying the Berenice whose victories Posidippus praises in epigrams 78, 79, 82, 88 AB with the daughter of Philadelphus and of his first wife Arsinoë I.[141] According to this interpretation, in the years

[137] Cf. Tondriau 1948:18–19.

[138] The identification of Helen with Arsinoë II is supported by Theocritus 15.110. Cf. Griffiths 1979:88; Basta Donzelli 1984.

[139] Cf. Sens 2011:263 on Asclepiades *HE* 995a–b (= 39 Sens).

[140] Cf. Prioux 2007:208n61.

[141] I am not entirely convinced that all these victories ought to be attributed solely to Berenice Syra and not to her sister-in-law Berenice II. On the other hand, I agree with Clayman's (2012:124–127) reading of terms such as παῖς or παρθένος not as denomina-tors of biological age or social status but as a reworking of epinician conventions. From an epinician point of view, the emphasis on Berenice's virginity is to be associated with the athletic virility of virgins like Artemis and Cyrene. In *Pythian* 9, virginity and quasi-masculinity allow Cyrene to claim her position in epinician poetry as foil to the victor. Apollo's attraction to her parallels the attraction of the audience to the victorious athlete. For the attractiveness of the victor, see Scanlon 2002:219–226; Papakonstantinou

between Arsinoë II's death (270 or 268 BCE)[142] and her departure for the
Seleucid court (252 BCE) Berenice as the most senior princess assumed
at her father's side the ceremonial role that her deceased step-mother
had left vacant. Furthermore, there is some evidence that this Berenice
received divine honors after her death (246 BCE). According to one
interpretation, Euergetes cut coins that suggested her apotheosis in
a manner reminiscent of her step-mother Arsinoë II.[143] Like her step-
mother, Berenice Syra was also considered to have been abducted by
the Dioscuri.[144] The use of the same apotheosis myth could imply that
Berenice Syra's representation as a Charis was deemed as a suitable way
to link her to the deified Arsinoë II-Aphrodite either on the occasion
of her impending wedding to Antiochus II or posthumously after her
apotheosis. As has already been shown, the selection of the Charites
can be explained in terms of both these scenarios.

Another question that can have a bearing on the problem of
Berenice's identity is whether she was dead or alive at the time of the
consecration of her statue. As argued above, the epigram marks the
deification of Berenice and assumes the form of an epiphanic narrative. The Mendes Stela[145] and the Canopus decree (*OGIS* 56) unequivocally suggest first that the apotheosis of Arsinoë II and Berenice "the
Younger" were attained by means of the (Egyptian) rituals performed
on their bodies and secondly that the erection of their statues and the
establishment of their respective cults took place after their funerals.
Part of these rituals was the anointment of the statue of the deceased
person. The anointment of the statue of Berenice in Callimachus'

2012:1658–1659. Similarly, Berenice's maidenhood emphasizes her epinician credentials,
while it also underlines her desirability as victor and royal consort; cf. Kampakoglou
2011:125–126. For Berenice as an Amazon-like queen, see also Kampakoglou 2013a:118–
120 with further bibliography.

[142] Cf. Grzybek 1990:104–112.

[143] Mørkholm 1991: Plate XIX, image 307; cf. Hazzard 2000:114–115; Criscuolo 2003:329n76;
and Prioux 2011:223. The identification of Berenice is not secure: Mørkholm (1991:106)
identifies her with Queen Berenice II.

[144] For this motif, see Acosta-Hughes 2012:167–168; Kampakoglou 2013b:317–324.

[145] Cf. Roeder 1959:177–188.

epigram could be part of the same ritual.[146] Although the anointment of the statue is not enough by itself to prove that Berenice was dead at the time, the apparent deification of Berenice could imply that she was already dead. Hellenistic poets provide indications of a heroic or semi-divine status for the Ptolemies, but they refrain from representing them as actual gods during their lifetime.[147] This, however, should not be taken for granted. One should keep in mind that differently from the members of the families of Soter and Philadelphus, historical and archaeological evidence proves that Euergetes and his consort were deified early during their own lifetimes.[148] Even so, one would look in vain for such explicit traces in contemporaneous court poetry—see, however, Asclepiades *HE* 995a–b (= 39 Sens) above. The *Coma Berenices* suggests indirectly through the καταστερισμός of Berenice II's lock that the court intended to confer upon the queen divine honors.[149] The roughly contemporary *Victoria Berenices* and *Elegia in Magam et Berenicen* eschew, as far as the limited remnants allow one to say, any such allusions. These considerations could lead one to believe that Berenice was dead at the time of her apotheosis. This fact would leave one with only two appropriate options: either Euergetes' daughter or his sister, both of whom received divine honors after their death.

---

[146]Cf. Kampakoglou 2013b:306–311. Bowie (1993:30–31) mentions two late Roman examples, where the inscriptions on the dead men's tombs invite their friends and relatives to anoint their statue with wine or oils mixed with wax and adorn them with flowers: *CIL* vol. 6, 9797.6 and *CIL* vol. 8, 9052.13. The purpose for this is not specified. Apart from the practical side of preserving the statue, one could venture a religious interpretation along the lines suggested by Fappas 2010:282–301.

[147]According to Theocritus 17.50, Berenice I became a temple-sharing goddess with Aphrodite after her death. Similarly, in the *Ectheosis Arsinoes* (fr. 228 Pf.) Callimachus represented Queen Arsinoë II as being snatched away by the Dioscuri and being carried to Cape Zephyrium, where she was honored as Arsinoë II-Aphrodite; cf. Fraser 1972: vol. 1, 239–240. In Theocritus 17.16–19, Ptolemy I appears after his death feasting on Olympus alongside Heracles and Alexander the Great. He had already appeared as Atum in the so-called Satrap Stela before his death; cf. Grzybek 1990:77–80.

[148]Cf. Quaegebeuer 1989:95–99.

[149]Cf. Koenen 1993:168; Hauben 2011:362.

X. CONCLUSIONS

In this paper, I have argued that Callimachus' epigram for Berenice presupposes a consecration ritual that marked the apotheosis of Berenice as a Charis and her first epiphany along with the other three Charites. Against this ritual context, the anointment of her statue intimates her accession to the divine world and alludes to motifs regarding the bestowal of immortality. The identity of the Berenice praised remains one of the epigram's most difficult interpretative *cruces*. Callimachus' epigram presupposes a specific occasion for the assimilation of Berenice to the Charites. This event is not known: whilst examining several different scenarios, I have raised the possibility that the epigram is connected with the posthumous apotheosis of either Berenice "the Younger" or, perhaps less likely, Berenice Syra. There can be no doubt that in a Callimachean poem dating from the 240's a Berenice without any further qualification would have been identified by default with Berenice II. Be that as it may, the case of Posidippus' "Berenices" has alerted modern readers to the slippery ground on which our assumptions about Hellenistic poetry and its *laudandi* or *laudandae* are based. Thompson (2005) has rightly drawn attention first to the fact that, had it not been for the discovery of the Milan Papyrus, we would still ignore all the Olympic victories won by Ptolemaic queens; and secondly that court poets could have turned their attention to members of the royal family other than the king and queen. We know so little about the Ptolemaic court to exclude other candidates. The embarrassment that the use of the same name for various members of the Ptolemaic dynasty causes to modern readers was apparently shared by ancient readers. The marginal note on *P.Lille* 83 shows that some readers may have failed to identify correctly the Berenice of the *Victoria Berenices* and so needed to be reminded of her pedigree.[150] Similarly, the mysterious δεκάς in the first book of the *Aetia* (fr. 2e.2a, 1 Harder, vol. 1, 129) suggests that identifying queens was

---

[150]Fr. 60d.54, 2 Harder (vol. 1, 218) θυγάτηρ τῶ]ν θεῶν ἀδελφῶν, οἵ ε[ἰσιν Πτολεμαῖος καὶ Ἀρ]σινόη ὧν ἀνηγόρευ[ον τὴν Βερενίκην. ἦν δὲ ἐπ'] ἀληθείας θυγάτηρ Μ[άγα τοῦ θείου τοῦ Ε]ὐεργέτου. For a different identification of the Berenice in the *Victoria Berenices*, see Criscuolo 2003.

not always easy. If Callimachus' epigram was actually inscribed on the base of a statue, as I have argued, the environs of the statue and the form of Berenice would have helped with her identification. The problems began when this contextualizing frame was lost. It is more likely than not that already from the moment of its inclusion in Meleager's anthology readers without any knowledge of the epigram's original context of composition and performance connected it with Berenice II. If this epigram was composed in order to be associated, in whatever way, with the *Aetia*, then Berenice was indeed Euergetes' consort. But if it was not, none of the other Berenices can be excluded a priori. The possibility of alternative identifications ought to be raised for methodological reasons, especially in view of our present state of knowledge, even if Berenice II is generally seen as the most likely candidate for our epigram.

TRINITY COLLEGE, UNIVERSITY OF OXFORD

WORKS CITED

Acosta-Hughes, B. 2012. "Les Dioscures dans la poésie alexandrine: Caractère et symbolique." In *Mythe et pouvoir à l'époque Hellénistique*, ed. C. Cusset, N. Le Meur-Weissman, and F. Levin, 155–169. Hellenistica Groningana 18. Leuven.

Acosta-Hughes, B., and S. Stephens 2012. *Callimachus in Context from Plato to the Augustan Poets*. Cambridge.

Acosta-Hughes, B., L. Lehnus, and S. Stephens, eds. 2011. *Brill's Companion to Callimachus*. Leiden.

Allen, T. W., W. R. Halliday, and E. E. Sikes, eds. 1936. *The Homeric Hymns*. 2nd ed. Oxford.

Arnold, B. T. 2009. *Genesis*. Cambridge.

Asheri, D. 2007 = [Commentary on Herodotus, Book I]. In D. Asheri, A. Lloyd, and A. Corcella. *A Commentary on Herodotus Books I–IV*, ed. O. Murray and A. Moreno with a contribution by M. Brosius. Oxford.

Assmann, J. 2001. *Tod und Jenseits im alten Ägypten*. Munich.

Barbantani, S. 2011. "Callimachus on Kings and Kingship." In Acosta-Hughes, Lehnus, and Stephens 2011, 178–200.

Barigazzi, A. 1966. "Due epigrammi ellenistici." In *Atti dell'XI Congresso di Papirologia*, 69–85. Milan.

Basta Donzelli, G. 1984. "Arsinoe simile ad Elena (Theocritus *Id*. 15.110)." *Hermes* 112:306–316.

Bastianini, G., ed. 2002. *Un poeta ritrovato: Posidippo di Pella; Giornata di studio, Milano 23 novembre 2001.* Milan.

Bennett, C. 2002. "The Children of Ptolemy III and the Date of the Exedra of Thermos." *Zeitschrift für Papyrologie und Epigraphik* 138:141–145.

Benzinger, I. 1905. "Stone and Stone-worship." In *Jewish Encyclopedia*. Vol. 11, 556–559. New York.

Bettinetti, S. 2001. *La statua di culto nella pratica rituale greca.* Bari.

Bing, P. 2000. "Text or Performance / Text and Performance: Alan Cameron's *Callimachus and His Critics*." In *La letteratura ellenistica: Problemi e prospettive di ricerca*, ed. R. Pretagostini, 139–148. Rome.

Bingen, J. 2002. "Posidippe: Le poète et les princes." In Bastianini 2002, 47–59.

Bobou, O. 2006. *Statues of Children in the Hellenistic Period.* DPhil diss., Oxford University.

Boedeker, D. D. 1974. *Aphrodite's Entry into Greek Epic.* Mnemosyne Supplement 32. Leiden.

Bourgeaud, P., and Y. Volokhine. 2000. "La formation de la légende de Sarapis." *Archiv für die Religionsgeschichte* 2:37–76.

Bowie, A. 1993. "Oil in Ancient Greece and Rome." In *The Oil of Gladness: Anointing in the Christian Tradition*, ed. M. Dudley and G. Rowell, 26–34. London.

Braun, J. 1932. *De Theraeorum rebus sacris.* Halle.

Broadhead, H. D., ed. 1960. *The Persae of Aeschylus: Introduction, Critical Notes, and Commentary.* Cambridge.

Bulloch, A., ed. 1985. *Callimachus. The Fifth Hymn: Introduction and Commentary.* Cambridge.

Bulloch, A., et al., eds. 1993. *Images and Ideologies: Self-definition in the Hellenistic World.* Berkeley.

Burkert, W. 1985. *Greek Religion: Archaic and Classical.* Oxford.

Bushala, E. W. 1969. "Συζύγιαι Χάριτες, *HIPPOLYTUS* 1147." *TAPA* 100:23–29.

Cameron, A., ed. 1993. *The Greek Anthology from Meleager to Planudes.* Oxford.

———. 1995. *Callimachus and his Critics.* Princeton.

Carney, E. 2000. "The Initiation of Cult for Royal Macedonian Women." *CP* 95:21–43.

Càssola, F., ed. 1975. *Inni omerici.* Milan.

Cazzaniga, I. 1966. "De papyro 65445 apud Cairense Museum servata, v. 140–154." *Parola del Passato* 21: 487–493.

Chaniotis, A. 1997. "Theatricality beyond the Theater: Staging Public Life in the Hellenistic World." *Pallas* 47: 219–259.

Clayman, D.L. 2011. "Berenice and her Lock." *TAPA* 141:229–246.

———. 2012. "Did Any Berenike Attend the Isthmian Games? A Literary Perspective on Posidippus 82 AB." *Zeitschrift für Papyrologie und Epigraphik* 182:121–130.

Collard, C., ed. 1975. *Euripides.* Supplices: *Introduction and Commentary.* 2 vols. Groningen.

Coppola, G. 1930. "*Callimachus senex.*" *Rivista di Filologia e di Istruzione Classica* 8:273–291.

———. 1935. *Cirene e il nuovo Callimaco.* Bologna.

Couat, A. 1882. *La poésie alexandrine sous les trois Ptolémées (324-222 av. J.-C.).* Paris.

Crawley, A. E. 1908. "Anointing." In vol. 1 of *The Encyclopaedia of Religion and Ethics,* ed. J. Hastings, 549–555. Edinburgh and New York.

Criscuolo, L. 2003. "Agoni e politica alla corte di Alessandria: Riflessioni su alcuni epigrammi di Posidippo." *Chiron* 33:311–333.

Cunningham, I. C., ed. 1971. *Herodas.* Mimiambi: *Introduction, Commentary, and Appendices.* Oxford.

Daiches, S. 1913. *Babylonian Oil Magic in the Talmud and in the Later Jewish Literature.* London.

D'Alessio, G. B., ed. 2007. *Callimaco.* 4th ed. Milan.

Davies, M., ed. 1991. *Sophocles.* Trachiniae: *Introduction and Commentary.* Oxford.

Day, J. W. 1989. "Rituals in Stone: Early Grave Epigrams and Monuments." *Journal of Hellenic Studies* 109:16–28.

———. 1994. "Interactive Offerings: Early Greek Dedicatory Epigrams and Ritual." *HSCP* 96:37–74.

———. 2010. *Archaic Greek Epigram and Dedication: Representation and Reperformance.* Cambridge.

De Heer, C. 1969. ΜΑΚΑΡ – ΕΥΔΑΙΜΩΝ – ΟΛΒΙΟΣ – ΕΥΤΥΧΗΣ: *A Study of the Semantic Field of Happiness in Ancient Greek to the End of the 5th century B.C.* Amsterdam.

Del Corno, D. 2002. "Posidippo e il mestiere di poeta." In Bastianini 2002, 61–66.

Delitzsch, F. 1887. *Neuer Kommentar über die Genesis.* Leipzig.

Diggle, J., ed. 2004. *Theophrastus.* Characters: *Introduction, Translation, and Commentary.* Cambridge.

Dodds, E. R., ed. 1960. *Euripides.* Bacchae: *Introduction and Commentary.* 2nd ed. Oxford.

Driver, S. R. 1904. *The Book of Genesis: Introduction and Notes.* London.

Edmonds, R. G. 2006. "To Sit in Solemn Silence? 'Thronosis' in Ritual, Myth, and Iconography." *AJP* 127:347–366.

Edwards, M.-J. 2007. "The Vocabulary of Religion." In *A History of Ancient Greek: From the Beginning to Late Antiquity,* ed. A.-F. Christidis, 1074–1079. Cambridge.

Erskine, A., and L. Llewellyn-Jones, eds. 2011. *Creating a Hellenistic World.* Swansea.

Fappas, I. 2010. Ἔλαιον εὐῶδες, τεθυωμένον: Τα αρωματικά έλαια και οι πρακτικές χρήσης τους στη μυκηναϊκή Ελλάδα και την αρχαία Εγγύς Ανατολή (14ος–13ος αι. π.Χ.). Chania.

Farnell, L. R. 1896–1909. *The Cults of the Greek States.* 5 vols. Oxford.

Faulkner, A., ed. 2008. *The Homeric Hymn to Aphrodite: Introduction, Text, and Commentary.* Oxford.

Feyel, M. 1942. *Contribution à l'épigraphie béotienne.* Le Puy.

Fordyce, C. J., ed. 1961. *Catullus: A Commentary.* Oxford.

Fraser, P. M. 1972. *Ptolemaic Alexandria.* 3 vols. Oxford.

Frazer, J. G., ed. 1898. *Pausanias' Description of Greece: Translation and Commentary.* 6 vols. London.

———. 1911–1915. *The Golden Bough: A Study in Magic and Religion.* 3rd ed. 8 parts in 12 vols. London.

————. 1918. *Folklore in the Old Testament: Studies in Comparative Religion, Legend, and Law.* 3 vols. London.

Gaertringen, H. von. 1899. "Neue Ausgrabungen auf Thera." *Archäologischer Anzeiger* 4:181–191.

————. 1901. "Die Götterkulte von Thera." *Klio* 1:212–227.

Gaifman, M. 2012. *Aniconism in Greek Antiquity.* Oxford.

Garland, R. 2001. *The Greek Way of Death.* 2nd ed. London.

Garvie, A. F., ed. 2009. *Aeschylus.* Persae: *Introduction and Commentary.* Oxford.

Giangrande, G. 1973. "Hellenistic Fountains and Fishermen." *Eranos* 71: 68–83.

Gladigow, B. 1985–1986. "Präsenz der Bilder – Präsenz der Götter: Kultbilder und Bilder der Götter in der griechischen Religion." *Visible Religion* 4–5:114–133.

Goldhill, S. 1994. "The Naïve and Knowing Eye: *Ecphrasis* and the Culture of Viewing in the Hellenistic World." In *Art and Text in Ancient Greek Culture,* ed. S. Goldhill and R. Osborne, 197–223. Cambridge.

Gow, A. S. F. 1952. *Theocritus: Translation and Commentary.* 2nd ed. 2 vols. Cambridge.

Gow, A. S. F., and D. L. Page, eds. 1965. *The Greek Anthology: Hellenistic Epigrams.* 2 vols. Oxford.

Griffiths, F. T. 1979. *Theocritus at Court.* Mnemosyne Supplement 55. Leiden.

Grzybek, E. 1990. *Du calendrier macédonien au calendrier ptolémaïque: Problèmes de chronologie hellénistique.* Basel.

Gutzwiller, K. 1992. "Callimachus' *Lock of Berenice*: Fantasy, Romance, and Propaganda." *AJP* 113:359–385.

————. 1998. *Poetic Garlands: Hellenistic Epigrams in Context.* Berkeley, Los Angeles, and London.

Habachi, L. 1969. *Features of the Deification of Ramesses II.* Glückstadt.

Hainsworth, J. B. 1988. "Commentary on *Odyssey* 5–8." In vol. 1 of *A Commentary on Homer's* Odyssey, ed. A. Heubeck, S. West, and J. B. Hainsworth, 249–385. Oxford.

Hall, E., ed. 1996. *Aeschylus.* Persians: *Introduction, Translation, Commentary.* Warminster.

Hamilton, J. R., ed. 1969. *Plutarch.* Alexander: *A Commentary.* Oxford.

Hamilton, V. 1995. *The Book of Genesis*. Vol. 2, *Chapters 18-50*. Grand Rapids, MI.

Harder, A., ed. 2012. *Callimachus*. *Aetia*. 2 vols. Oxford.

Hauben, H. 1989. "Aspects du culte des souverains à l'époque des Lagides." In *Egitto e storia antica dall'ellenismo all'età araba*, ed. L. Criscuolo and G. Geraci, 440-467. Bologna.

———. 2011. "Ptolémée III et Bérénice II, divinités cosmiques." In *More than Men, Less than Gods: Studies on Royal Cult and Imperial Worship*, ed. P. P. Iossif, A. S. Chankowski, and C.C. Lorber, 357-388. Leuven.

Hazzard, R. A. 2000. *Imagination of a Monarchy: Studies in Ptolemaic Propaganda*. Phoenix Supplement 37. Toronto.

Headlam, W., and A. D. Knox, eds. 1922. *Herodas. The Mimes and Fragments*. Oxford.

Herter, H. 1975. "Die Haaröle der Berenike." In *Kallimachos*, ed. A. Skiadas, 186-206. Darmstadt. (Orig. pub. Stuttgart, 1971.)

Hock, G. 1905. *Griechische Weihgebräuche*. Munich.

Hunter, R. L. 1993. *Theocritus and the Archaeology of Greek Poetry*. Cambridge.

———. 2003. *Encomium of Ptolemy Philadelphus*. Berkeley.

Hunter, R. L., and T. Fuhrer. 2002. "Imaginary God? Poetic Theology in the *Hymns* of Callimachus." In *Callimaque: Sept exposés suivis de discussions*, ed. F. Montanari and L. Lehnus, 143-175. Entretiens sur l'antiquité Classique 48. Vandoeuvres-Geneva.

Huss, W. 1975. "Die zu Ehren Ptolemaios' III. und seiner Familie errichtete Statuengruppe von Thermos (*IG* IX 1,1Q,56)." *Chronique d'Égypte* 50:312-320.

Inglese, A. 2008. *Thera arcaica: Le iscrizioni rupestri dell'agora degli dei*. Rome.

Janko, R. 1992. *The Iliad: A Commentary*. Vol. 4, *Books 13-16*. Cambridge.

Jax, K. 1933. *Die weibliche Schönheit in der griechischen Dichtung*. Innsbruck.

Jouguet, P. 1938. "Reine et poète (à propos d'une épigramme de Callimaque)." *Bulletin de l'institut d'Égypte* 20: 131-135.

Kakarikos, K. 1997. "Commentary on Callimachus Epigram 51 Pf." In *Τα Επιγράμματα του Καλλιμάχου: Εισαγωγή, κείμενο, μετάφραση, σχόλια*, ed. P. Pagonari-Antoniou, 334-338. Athens.

Kampakoglou, A. 2011. *Studies on the Reception of Pindar in Hellenistic Poetry*. DPhil diss., Oxford University.

————. 2013a. "Victory, Mythology, and the Poetics of Intercultural Praise in Callimachus' *Victoria Berenices*." *Trends in Classics* 5:111–143.

————. 2013b. "Glimpses of Immortality: Theocritus on the Apotheosis of Queen Berenice I." *Rivista di Filologia e di Istruzione Classica* 141:300–334.

Kannicht, R., ed. 1969. *Euripides*. Helena. 2 vols. Heidelberg.

Keyßner, K. 1932. *Gottesvorstellung und Lebensauffassung im griechischen Hymnus*. Stuttgart.

Koenen, L. 1983. "Die Adaption Ägyptischer Königsideologie am Ptolemäerhor." In *Egypt and the Hellenistic World: Proceedings of the International Colloquium Leuven 22–26 May 1982*, ed. E. Van't Dack et al., 143–190. Leuven.

————. 1993. "The Ptolemaic King as a Religious Figure." In Bulloch et al. 1993, 25–115.

Larson, J. 1995. *Greek Heroine Cults*. Madison, WI.

Lattimore, R. 1962. *Themes in Greek and Latin Epitaphs*. Urbana.

Lee, K. H., ed. 1997. *Euripides*. Ion: *Introduction, Translation, and Commentary*. Warminster.

Lieberg, G. 1962. *Puella divina: Die Gestalt der göttlichen Geliebten bei Catull im Zusammenhang der antiken Dichtung*. Amsterdam.

Llewellyn-Jones, L., and S. Winder. 2011. "A Key to Berenike's Lock? The Hathoric Model of Queenship in Early Ptolemaic Egypt." In Erskine and Llewellyn-Jones 2011, 247–269.

Lloyd-Jones, H., and P. Parsons, eds. 1983. *Supplementum Hellenisticum*. Berlin and New York.

Lohmeyer, E. 1919. Vom göttlichen Wohlgeruch. SB Heidelberg Philosophische-Historische Klasse Abhandlung 9. Heidelberg.

Marinone, N. 1997. *Berenice da Callimaco a Catullo*. 2nd ed. Bologne.

Massimilla, G., ed. 1992. *Callimaco*. Aetia: *Libro primo e secondo*. Pisa.

————. 1994. "L'invocazione di Callimaco alle Cariti nel primo libro degli Aitia (fr. 7, 9–14 Pf.)." In *Proceedings of the 20th International Congress of Papyrologists*, ed. A. Bülow-Jacobsen, 322–325. Copenhagen.

————. 2010, ed. *Callimaco*. Aetia: *Libro terzo e quarto*. Pisa.

Meillier, C. 1979. *Callimaque et son temps: Recherches sur la carrière et la condition d'un écrivain à l'époque des premiers Lagides*. Lille.

Merkelbach, R., and M. L. West, eds. 1967. *Fragmenta Hesiodea*. Oxford.

Mineur, W. H. 1984. *Callimachus. Hymn to Delos: Introduction and Commentary*. Mnemosyne Supplement 83. Leiden.

Mørkholm, O. 1991. *Early Hellenistic Coinage from the Accession of Alexander to the Peace of Apamea (336-188 B.C.)*. Ed. P. Griersonand and U. Westermark. Cambridge.

Mori, A. 2008. *The Politics of Apollonius Rhodius'* Argonautica. Cambridge.

Muccioli, F. 2013. *Gli epiteti ufficiali dei re ellenistici*. Historia Enzelschriften 224. Stuttgart.

Nastos, I. S., ed. 2006. *Ασκληπιάδου του Σαμίου επιγράμματα*. Heraklion.

Nisetich, F. 2001. *The Poems of Callimachus: Introduction, Translation, Notes, and Glossary*. Oxford.

Norden, E. 1923. *Agnostos Theos: Untersuchungen zur Formengeschichte religiöser Rede*. Leipzig and Berlin.

Olson, S. D., and A. Sens, eds. 2000. *Archestratos of Gela: Greek Culture and Cuisine in the Fourth Century BCE: Text, Translation, and Commentary*. Oxford.

Owen, A. S., ed. 1939. *Euripides. Ion: Introduction and Commentary*. Oxford.

Page, D., ed. 1981. *Further Greek Epigrams*. Rev. R. D. Dawe and J. Diggle. Cambridge.

Paley, F. A., ed. 1872-1880. *Euripides with an English Commentary*. 3 vols. London.

Papakonstantinou, Z. 2012. "The Athletic Body in Classical Athens: Literary and Historical Perspectives." *The International Journal of the History of Sport* 29.12:1657–1668.

Patton, K. C. 2009. *Religion of the Gods: Ritual, Paradox, and Reflexivity*. Oxford.

Petrovic, I., and A. Petrovic. 2003. "Stop and Smell the Statues: Callimachus' Epigram 51 Pf. Reconsidered (Four Times)." *Materiali e discussioni per l'analisi dei testi classici* 51:179–208.

Pfeiffer, R., ed. 1949-1953. *Callimachus*. 2 vols. Oxford.

Pfeiffer, S. 2004. *Das Dekret von Kanopos (238 v. CHR.): Kommentar und historische Auswertung*. Munich.

Platt, V. 2011. *Facing the Gods: Epiphany and Representation in Greco-Roman Art, Literature, and Religion*. Cambridge.

Pomeroy, S. B. 1990. *Women in Hellenistic Egypt: From Alexander to Cleopatra*. Detroit.

Porter, J. I. 2011. "Against λεπτότης: Rethinking Hellenistic Aesthetics." In Erskine and Llewellyn-Jones 2011, 271–312.

Powell, J. U., ed. 1925. Collectanea alexandrina: Reliquiae minores poetarum graecorum aetatis ptolemaicae, 323–146 A.C. Oxford.

Prioux, É. 2007. Regards alexandrins: Histoire et théorie des arts dans l'épigramme Hellénistique. Leuven.

———. 2011. "Callimachus' Queens." In Acosta-Hughes, Lehnus, and Stephens 2011, 201–224.

Quaegebeur, J. 1988. "Cleopatra VII and the Cults of the Ptolemaic Queens." In Cleopatra's Egypt: Age of the Ptolemies, ed. R. A. Fazzini and R. S. Bianchi, 41–54. Brooklyn, NY.

———. 1989. "The Egyptian Clergy and the Cult of the Ptolemaic Dynasty." Ancient Society 20:93–113.

Radt, S., ed. 1985. Tragicorum Graecorum Fragmenta, vol. 3: Aeschylus. Göttingen.

Rice, E. E. 1983. The Grand Procession of Ptolemy Philadelphus. Oxford.

Richardson, N. J., ed. 1974. The Homeric Hymn to Demeter. Oxford.

———, ed. 2010. Three Homeric Hymns: To Apollo, Hermes, and Aphrodite. Cambridge.

Robert, L. 1946. "Épigramme de Thasos." In Hellenica: Recueil d'épigraphie, de numismatique et d'antiquités grecques, vol. 2, 114–118. Paris.

———. 1965. "Statue des Graces." In Hellenica: Recueil d'épigraphie, de numismatique et d'antiquités grecques, vol. 13, 116–119. Paris.

Rocchi, M. 1980. "Contributi allo culto delle Charites (II)." Studii clasice 19:19–28.

Roeder, G. 1959. Die ägyptische Götterwelt. Zurich.

Ronchi, G. 1968. "Il papiro cairense 65445 (vv. 140–154) e l'obelisco di Arsinoe II." Studi classici e orientali 17:56–75.

Roscher, W. H. 1883. Nektar und Ambrosia. Leipzig.

Rossi, L. 2000. "La Chioma di Berenice: Catullo 66, 79–88, Callimaco e la propaganda di corte." Rivista di Filologia e di Istruzione Classica 128:299–312.

Sansone, D. 1988. Greek Athletics and the Genesis of Sports. Berkeley.

Sauneron, S. 1960. "Un document égyptien relatif à la divinisation de la reine Arsinoé II." Bulletin de l'institut français d'archéologie orientale 60:83–109.

Scanlon, T. F. 2002. *Eros and Greek Athletics.* Oxford.

Schachter, A. 1981–1994. *Cults of Boiotia.* 4 vols. BICS Supplement 38. London.

Scheer, T. S. 2000. *Die Gottheit und ihr Bild: Untersuchungen zur Funktion griechischer Kultbilder in Religion und Politik.* Zetemata Heft 105. Munich.

Schmid, W. 1923. "Ἀρίζηλος Βερενίκα." *Philologus* 78:176–179.

Schwarzenberg, E. 1966. *Die Grazien.* Bonn.

Selden, D. L. 1998. "Alibis." *Classical Antiquity* 17:289–412.

Sens, A. 2011, ed. *Asclepiades of Samos: Epigrams and Fragments Edited with Translation and Commentary.* Oxford.

Settis, S. 1965. "Descrizione di un ninfeo ellenistico." *Studi classici e orientali* 14:247–257.

Smith, W. R. 1956. *The Religion of the Semites: The Fundamental Institutions.* New York. (Orig. pub. Edinburgh, 1889.)

Sourvinou-Inwood, C. 1995. *'Reading' Greek Death: To the End of the Classical Period.* Oxford.

Stengel, P. 1910. *Opferbräuche der Griechen.* Leipzig.

Stephens, S. 2003. *Seeing Double: Intercultural Poetics in Ptolemaic Alexandria.* Berkeley.

Sternberg-el-Hotabi, H. 1988. "Das tägliche Tempelritual." In *Texte aus der Umwelt des Alten Testaments: Rituale und Beschwörungen,* ed. D. Manfried, vol. 2, 391–404. Gürtersloh.

Strootman, R. 2007. *The Hellenistic Royal Court, Court Culture, Ceremonies, and Ideology in Greece, Egypt, and the Near East 360–330 bce.* PhD diss., University of Rotterdam.

Tanner, J. 2006. *The Invention of Art History in Ancient Greece: Religion, Society, and Artistic Rationalisation.* Cambridge.

Thompson, D. J. 2005. "Posidippus, Poet of the Ptolemies." In *The New Posidippus: A Hellenistic Poetry Book,* ed. K. Gutzwiller, 269–283. Oxford.

Thomson, D. F. S., ed. 1997. *Catullus: A Textual and Interpretative Commentary.* Phoenix Supplement 34. Toronto.

Tondriau, J. L. 1948. "Princesses ptolémaïques comparées ou identifiées à des déesses (IIIème–Ier siècles av. J. C.)." *Bulletin de la société d'archéologie d'Alexandrie* 37:12–33.

Ulf, C. 1979. "Die Einreibung der griechischen Athleten mit Öl." *Stadion* 5:220–238.

Usener, H. 1901. "KERAUNOS." *Rheinisches Museum für Philologie* 60:1–30.

Van Bremen, R. 2007. "The Entire House is Full of Crowns: Hellenistic *agones* and the Commemoration of Victory." In *Pindar's Poetry, Patrons, and Festivals*, ed. S. Hornblower and C. Morgan, 345–375. Oxford.

Vawter, B. 1977. *On Genesis: A New Reading*. London.

Vérilhac, A.-M. 1978–1982. ΠΑΙΔΕΣ ΑΩΡΟΙ: *Poésie funéraire*. 2 vols. Athens.

Vestrheim, G. 2002. "The Poetics of Epiphany in Callimachus' Hymns to Apollo and Pallas." *Eranos* 100:175–183.

Visser, C.E. 1938. *Götter und Kulten im ptolemäischen Alexandrien*. Amsterdam.

Vitali, L. 1932. *Fonti per la storia della religione cyrenaica*. Padua.

Von Rad, G. 1972. *Genesis: A Commentary*. Tr. J. H. Marks. London.

Weber, G. 1993. *Dichtung und höfische Gesellschaft*. Hermes Einzelschriften 62. Stuttgart.

West, M. L. 2011. "The First *Homeric Hymn to Dionysus*." In *The Homeric Hymns: Interpretative Essays*, ed. A. Faulkner, 29–43. Oxford.

Wilamowitz-Moellendorff, U. 1924. *Hellenistische Dichtung in der Zeit des Kallimachos*. 2 vols. Berlin.

———, ed. 1926. *Euripides. Ion*. Berlin.

———. 1941. "Ein Weihgeschenk des Eratosthenes." In *Kleine Schriften: Hellenistische, spätgriechische, und lateinische Poesie*, vol. 2, 48–70. Berlin.

Williams, F., ed. 1978. *Callimachus*. Hymn to Apollo. Oxford.

Zanker, P. 1993. "The Hellenistic Grace *Stelai* from Smyrna: Identity and Self-image in the *Polis*." In Bulloch et al. 1993, 212–230.

Zielinski, T. 1924. "Charis and Charites." *CQ* 18:158–163.

MUSES, METAPHOR, AND METAPOETICS IN CATULLUS 61

CHRISTOPHER ECKERMAN

I. INTRODUCTION

A T THE BEGINNING OF CATULLUS 61, the narrator invokes Hymenaeus and thereafter celebrates Hymenaeus' majestic power. As the poem proceeds, the narrator addresses numerous personages, including unwed Roman girls (36), the bride (82), boys (114), the groom's previous *concubinus* (124), the groom (135), the bride's *praetextatus* (175), and Roman matrons (179), urging them to play a part in the marriage ceremony in various ways.[1] The numerous invocations add vividness to the ode, since the reader envisions several people participating in the ritual.[2] After the apostrophe to Hymenaeus, the narrator exhorts the bride to come forth from her chamber and follow the *deductio* to her husband's home (76–118). Once she has begun the *deductio*, the *fescennina iocatio* occurs (119–143), and the narrator offers "words of wisdom" for the bride (144–163). When the poem ends, as an *epithalamium*, the narrator positions the bride, Vinia, in the groom's bedchamber and tells the groom, Torquatus, to enter.[3] The narrator closes the ode by providing "gnomic wisdom" and hoping for a male to be born from the union of the bride and groom. As this brief description suggests, c. 61

---

[1] The narrator also calls on the bridal bed (107). For discussion, see Fedeli 1983:6. Translations in the paper are mine, unless otherwise noted.

[2] So too Thomsen 1992:126, "I strongly doubt that c. 61 was sung at Vinia's and Manlius' wedding, as it proclaims. But I insist that the poem, even if it was never performed in real life, can be performed in the imagination, and that the text should be analyzed accordingly."

[3] On the identity of the groom, see Thomsen 1992:32–34.

is a complex poem, with the narrator invoking numerous personages.[4] One invocation, however, remains problematic.

Several interpretive difficulties have arisen in relation to the end of the ode, where the narrator says:

> claudite ostia, virgines:
> 225 lusimus satis. at, boni
> coniuges, bene vivite et
> munere assiduo valentem
> exercete iuventam.

> Close the gates, maidens: we've played enough. But, good spouses, live well and exercise your flourishing youth with your constant gift (i.e. sex).[5]

The *virgines*, the *ostia*, as well as the subject and meaning of *lusimus* in 224 and 225 have been variously interpreted and have, accordingly, provided hermeneutic cruces within the ode. The lack of consensus concerning these phenomena may suggest that Catullus is doing something here that has gone unnoticed previously. I shall argue that Catullus wants his audience to recognize the *virgines* as the Muses and that, if they do so, the other interpretive difficulties are easily overcome. In support of this interpretation, I use the broader literary context of the poem, as well as comparanda from Catullus and Vergil and from Pindar and Bacchylides.

---

[4] Scholars regularly note that the ode exemplifies the phenomenon known as *die Kreuzung der Gattungen*, characteristic of Hellenistic literature, though the phenomenon can be traced back to archaic Greek poetry. Opinion is divided as to whether Catullus successfully mixes these elements: see Fedeli 1983:3; Thomsen 1992:11–12. On the "parts" of the ode, see Thomsen 1992:26–27.

[5] For *munus* as a euphemism for sexual intercourse, see, with reference to primary sources and secondary bibliography, Kroll 1960:122; Habinek 2005:136.

II. PREVIOUS INTERPRETATIONS

The *virgines* have been interpreted previously as three discrete groups of people. Fedeli and Syndikus link the *virgines* of line 224 with the *integrae virgines* of 36–40 who are exhorted to sing the hymenaeus:[6]

> vosque item simul, integrae
> virgines, quibus advenit
> par dies, agite in modum
> dicite "o Hymenaee Hymen,
> 40   o Hymen Hymenaee."

> You too similarly together, untouched virgins, for whom
> there comes a like day [i.e. of marriage], come on in mea-
> sure, say, "O Hymenaeus Hymen, O Hymen Hymenaeus."

Alternatively, believing the *ostia* (224) to be the *Haustur* of the groom, Friedrich suggests that the *virgines* of 224 are domestic slaves who attend the home of the groom. Friedrich does not link the *virgines* of 224 with the *integrae virgines* of 36–37, as Fedeli and Syndikus would have it, for two particular reasons: he believes that the *integrae virgines* are friends of the bride who would have remained at the house of the bride when she leaves to begin the *deductio* (77) and he thinks that the *ostia* must be closed from inside the groom's house; this would preclude the possibility that women from outside the household are evoked here.[7]

---

[6] Fedeli 1983:144: "In c. 61 the maidens are certainly present in the ὕμνος κλητικός, where, following the poet's invitation, they intone the songs in Hymen's honour. I have already expressed, with regard to ll. 36–45, my opinion for the solution of the doubt roused by l. 224: I think that, on the model of Theocritus—who attributes the whole epithalamium to the maidens—in the finale of his wedding song Catullus addresses the maidens who have sung the hymenaeus and have accompanied him during the various phases of the ceremony, thus connecting the end of the poem to the beginning also from this angle"; Syndikus (1990:48): Die Mädchen waren seit Vers 36 nicht mehr erwähnt worden, aber es besteht kein Grund, hier an jemand anders zu denken."

[7] Friedrich 1908:269: "Mit *virgines* können unmöglich die *integrae virgines* von v. 36 gemeint sein, die sich in Hause der Braut eingefunden haben, um der bisherigen Gespielin vor der deductio Lebewohl zu sagen. Jedenfalls ist es undenkbar, daß sie an dieser selbst teilgenommen haben. Und endlich: die Haustür mußte doch schließlich von innen geschlossen werden. *Virgines* können nur Sklavinnen des Hauses sein."

Friedrich is right to note that it is difficult to assume that young girls who are friends of the bride are closing the door of the groom's house or *thalamus*.[8] It is equally problematic, however, to assume that the *virgines* of 224 are slaves of the groom, since nothing in the ode suggests that the *virgines* are slaves. Rather, the word *virgines*, as Thomson remarks,[9] denotes lofty status in Latin poetry, and it would be strange for slave girls, who regularly were used as their Roman masters desired sexually, to be referred to here as *virgines*. Accordingly, dismissing the position of Friedrich, Mangelsdorff suggests that the *virgines* are the bride's friends, "entsprechend dem griechischen Ritus, nicht etwa zu den Sklavinnen," but he does not link them with the *integrae virgines*.[10] Thus, Fedeli, Friedrich, and Mangelsdorff offer discrete interpretations of the *virgines*, while, most recently, Thomson, having considered the problem, dismisses the question of the *virgines* at line 224 as "antiquarian" and "of little significance" and does not take a stance on their identity.[11] We must know who the *virgines* are, however, if we wish to understand the ode and interpret it competently.

III. *VIRGINES* AS MUSES

Catullus uses *virgo*/*virgines* as a reference to the Muse(s) twice elsewhere, and these Catullan parallels corroborate the suggestion that the *virgines* are the Muses at 61.224. In c. 1, the programmatic dedication of Catullus' *libellus* to Cornelius Nepos, Catullus apostrophizes the Muse when he prays that his poetry book be long-lived: ⟨o⟩ *patrona virgo,* / *plus uno maneat perenne saeclo* ("O patron, virgin, may [it] last through the ages for longer than one age," 9–10). The noun *virgo* here belongs to the "high" or "elevated" style and refers to the poet's Muse.[12] By making his patron the Muse, Catullus declares his socio-economic and artistic status: he

---

[8] On the *ostia* as the groom's *thalamus* door, see Fedeli 1983:142.

[9] 1997:199.

[10] Mangelsdorff 1913:43.

[11] Thomson 1997:363. In their commentaries, Fordyce and Quinn do not comment on the *virgines*.

[12] Thomson 1997:200; so too, e.g., Fordyce 1961:87.

is a man who has no human patron, only a divine one.[13] As others have recognized, Catullus here leans on the programmatic introduction of Meleager of Gadara's *Garland*, which also begins with an invocation to a muse.[14] The connection of c. 1's *virgo* with a Muse, then, is clear. Catullus refers to the Muses as *virgines* similarly in c. 65, a dedication letter that purportedly accompanied Catullus' translation of Callimachus' *Lock of Berenice*, c. 66, to Q. Hortensius Hortalus.[15] The narrator begins the poem saying: *etsi me assiduo defectum cura dolore / sevocat a doctis, Hortale, virginibus, / nec potis est dulcis Musarum expromere fetus / mens animi* ("Though I am worn out with constant grief, Hortalus, and sorrow calls me away, apart from the learned virgins, nor can my mind put forth the sweet offspring of the Muses," 1–4). Because of the grief that has arisen from the death of his brother, the narrator is physically separated (*sevocat*, 2) from the "learned virgins"[16] and is not able (*nec potis est ... mens animi*, 3) to put forth the "sweet offspring" (*dulcis fetus*) of the Muses. The description of the Muses as "learned" will become a *topos* of Latin poetry.[17] The presence of *virgo/virgines* in cc. 1 and 65, then, shows that Catullus uses *virgines* as a denotation for the Muses, just like other Roman authors, who follow the Greek practice, beginning with Pindar (*Isthmian* 8.127), of referring to the Muses as *parthenoi*.[18]

IV. RING COMPOSITION

An invocation to the Muses at the end of c. 61 allows us to recognize ring composition, already recognized as an important formal technique

---

[13] Cf. Fordyce 1961:87, "If the reading is right, the *patrona virgo* must be the (or a) Muse, one of the *doctae virgines* of 65.2, who is the poet's *patrona* as in [Sulpicia] 11 ('precibus descende clientis et audi') the poet is Calliope's *cliens*; the characteristically Roman notion of *cleintela* appears in 34.1."

[14] Μοῦσα φίλα, τίνι τάνδε φέρεις πάγκαρπον ἀοιδάν; *A.P.* 4.1.1; See, e.g., Fordyce 1961:83; Quinn 1973:88; Van Sickle 1981; Knox 2011:157.

[15] On the addressee, cf. Fordyce 1961:325; Quinn 1973:351.

[16] On "learned virgins," see Fordyce 1961:178; Quinn 1973:197.

[17] Cf. [Tib] 3.4.45, Ov. *Tr.* 2.13, *Met.* 5.255; see too Fordyce 1961:325.

[18] On the Muses in Greco-Roman literature, see, with reference to further bibliography, Spentzou and Fowler 2002.

within three of Catullus' other *carmina maiora* (63, 64, 68b).[19] In the first stanza, the narrator invokes Hymenaeus as a "cultor" of Mt. Helicon (his *sedes*) and as the offspring of the Muse Urania:[20]

> Collis o Heliconii
> cultor, Uraniae genus,
> qui rapis teneram ad virum
> virginem, O Hymenaee Hymen,
> O Hymen Hymenaee

> O haunter of Mt. Helicon, offspring of Urania, you who take the tender virgin to her man, O Hymeanaeus Hymen, O Hymen Hymenaeus!

With reference to Mt. Helicon and Urania, the narrator activates the importance of the Muses at the beginning of the poem. When the narrator tells the Muses to close the *ostia* at the end of the poem, then, he structurally recollects the references to the Muse Urania and Mt. Helicon that he uses in this first stanza.

The ring composition of odes 63, 64, and 68b has led scholars to analyze these poems structurally, noting thematic relationships between the internal rings.[21] The ring composition in c. 61, however, differs from that in the other *carmina maiora*, due to the manner in which the *deductio* moves from the home of the bride to the home of the groom, a "linear" spatial movement from point A to point B.[22] The

---

[19] As Traill 1988:365 remarks, "That Catullus used ring composition as a structural device is not seriously disputed." See, with reference to further bibliography, Thomson 1961; Schäfer 1966:95–107; Wiseman 1974:59–76; Skinner 2011b:43–44.

[20] On the Hellenistic conceit of Hymen as the offspring of Urania, see Fedeli 1983:25–26.

[21] Traill 1988 passim notes five features characteristic of Catullan ring composition, based on cc. 63, 64, and 68b: (1) corresponding sections correspond in theme but not necessarily in length; (2) thematic correspondence is not always exact or properly balanced; (3) centers are clearly marked off from adjacent sections by verbal repetitions; (4) centers are clearly demarcated by a radical change in subject matter or ethos; (5) in sections flanking the center, people hurry towards or away from the object of interest in the center.

[22] Catullus' practice of "linear" ring-composition in c. 61, then, adds a twist to the phenomena that Traill catalogues (see preceding note) as characteristic of Catullan ring-

spatial linearity of the ode is paralleled by the narrative's temporal linearity, which moves the ode forward in time with no "flash-backs" or "flash-forwards." The spatial and temporal linearity are further paralleled by the invocations that recur throughout the ode, as the narrator invokes one person or group after the next. While one could argue that personages evoked later in the ode form rings with personages evoked earlier, Catullus does not construct obvious thematic rings throughout c. 61. Rather, he constructs ring composition particularly with the Muses at the beginning and the end of the ode.

Catullus' ring composition, with Urania and Mt. Helicon at the beginning of the poem and with the Muses at the end of the poem, recalls the *Theogony* 33–34, where Hesiod asserts:

> καί μ' ἐκέλονθ' ὑμνεῖν μακάρων γένος αἰὲν ἐόντων,
> σφᾶς δ' αὐτὰς πρῶτόν τε καὶ ὕστατον αἰὲν ἀείδειν

> And [the Muses] commanded me to sing of the race of the
> blessed ones that live always, and they ordered me to sing
> of themselves always first and last.

By using ring composition and positioning the Muses first and last in c. 61, Catullus recalls Hesiod's famous dictum πρῶτον ... ὕστατον. Moreover, he positions himself as a poet in the same tradition as Hesiod, who has a close relationship with the Muses.[23] Catullus' ring composition, then, marks the poem as participating in a high literary register because Catullus follows Hesiod's dictum. But it is not only Hesiod's *Theogony* that Catullus' ring composition recalls, since Callimachus too constructs a close relationship with the Muses in the *Aetia*. By integrating the Muses at the end of c. 61, then, Catullus also aligns himself with Callimachean poetics.[24]

---

composition in the odes in which the technique was previously noted. Thomsen 1992:85 has suggested that ring composition can be found in lines 83–88 of c. 61 also: "Lines 83–88 constitute a block with ring composition: 87–8 ~ 83." Thomsen does not explain what he means by ring composition here, however, and I fail to see a ring.

[23] For discussion of the Hesiodic passage, see West 1966:158–167.

[24] The beginning of the *Aetia* (fr. 2 Pfeiffer) includes a passage where Callimachus envisions himself transported in a dream from Alexandria to Mt. Helicon. There Callimachus asks the Muses numerous questions, which form the etiologies of books 1 and 2.

V. *LUDERE* AS POETIC TERM

The phrase *lusimus satis* (225) has been interpreted in multiple discrete manners: as a reference to the end of the *deductio* described text-internally,[25] as a reference to the first line of the epithalamium proper,[26] or, as Lieberg rightly interprets it, as a reference to Catullus' poetic composition.[27] Wagenvoort first drew attention to the importance of *ludere* and its derivatives as poetic terms, and *ludere* at 61.225 should be inscribed within this semantic matrix.[28] As Lowrie notes, "Poetic play (*ludus, ludere, iocum*) denotes two related things: stylistic elegance of the Alexandrian variety and erotic poetry. The *locus classicus* for this association is Catullus 50, and the *double entendre* is rife in Latin elegy."[29] When Catullus says that he and the Muses have "played enough," he refers both to the composition of the ode, which is marked throughout with Alexandrian learnedness,[30] and to the erotic subject matter of the ode.[31]

One can read the ode as a meditation on and exhortation to sexuality, since the narrator stresses the importance of sex and the procreation of children. Moreover, the narrator also lightheartedly

[25] E.g. Fedeli 1983:142: "In the last strophe Catullus urges the maidens to close the thalamus' door: the *ludus* is over and the poem ends with the traditional wish to the bride and the groom to *bene vivere* and practice erotic exercises assiduously."

[26] Lieberg 1975:357 notes that it recalls the first line of the text-internal epithalamium (*ludite ut lubet*, 204); see too Lieberg 1974:220.

[27] 1975:356–357: "Daß Catull durch die Entsprechung von *claudite ostia, virgines* V. 224 und *claustra pandite ianuae* V. 76 die Trennung von einleitendem Hymnus V. 1–75 und anschließender Beschreibung der Feier unterstrichen hat, ist von Fedeli zu Recht hervorgehoben worden. Hingegen hat er nicht gesehen, wie der Dichter in der Entsprechung von *lusimus satis* V. 225 und *ludite ut lubet* V. 204 Anfang und Ende des eigentlichen Epithalamiums aufeinander bezieht, indem er in der Sinnverschiebung vom erotischen *ludite* zum poetologisch gemeinten *lusimus* das Epithalamium seines Liedes als dichterischen *lusus* kennzeichnet, dazu bestimmt, den *lusus amatorius* zu preisen." Burgess 1986:577 suggests, "*ludere* is used by Catullus possibly of poetic composition at 61.225."

[28] Wagenvoort 1956 (= Wagenvoort 1935).

[29] 1997:41; Lowrie's text reads Catullus 59, a typographical error for Catullus 50.

[30] For c. 61, see, e.g., Fedeli 1983:25, 32, 34, 41, 70, 81, 107, 122, 149–152. For Catullus' practice more broadly, see, with reference to further bibliography, Knox 2011.

[31] Catullus uses *ludere* in an explicitly erotic manner when he tells the bride and groom to play as they wish: *ludite ut lubet* (204), i.e. have as much sex as they want.

refers to the sexual habits of the groom with his previous *concubinus*, and, as a *praeceptor amoris*, he offers "words of wisdom" to the bride on sexual topics, exhorting Vinia not to refuse her husband when he desires her sexually, lest Torquatus find sexual gratification with other partners. In Thomsen's words, "Carmen 61 is erotic from beginning to end."[32]

In addition to its erotic connotations, *ludere* connotes Alexandrian aesthetics and technical learning, and should be classified among words such as *lepidus, libellus,* and *nugae* in c. 1, which align Catullus with Callimachean aesthetics.[33] By using *ludere*, Catullus also directs attention to c. 61's metrical structure, which consists of rather complex lyric stanzas comprising glyconic and pheracratean *kôla*.[34] In c. 50, to Catullus' fellow poet, Calvus, the narrator twice uses *ludere* in reference to the pleasure received from composing poetry:

> Hesterno, Licini, die otiosi
> multum lusimus in meis tabellis,
> ut convenerat esse delicatos:
> scribens versiculos uterque nostrum
> 5   ludebat numero modo hoc modo illoc
> reddens mutua per iocum atque vinum.

Yesterday, Licinius, at leisure, we played a lot on my tablets, since we had agreed to be dandies. Each of us, writing little verses, was playing now in this meter, now in that, giving back and forth, while drinking wine and laughing.

Catullus 50 has received extended attention as a programmatic poem, and, as Burgess notes, "the repeated verb *ludere* (lines 2 and 5) ... specifies that these are light verses."[35] In c. 68, Catullus similarly uses *ludere*

---

[32] 1992:40.

[33] On Catullus and Callimachus, see, with reference to further bibliography, Knox 2011.

[34] On Catullus' *kôla*, see Syndikus 1990:12–13; Kroll 1960:107.

[35] 1986:577.

to refer to his poetic output, which has fallen off due to grief at his brother's death:

> 15   tempore quo primum vestis mihi tradita pura est,
>   iucundum cum aetas florida ver ageret,
>   multa satis lusi: non est dea nescia nostri,
>   quae dulcem curis miscet amaritiem:
>   sed totum hoc studium luctu fraterna mihi mors
> 20   abstulit.

At the time when first a white dress was given to me, when my youth in its flower was keeping jocund spring-time, I wrote merry poems enough; not unknown am I to the goddess who mingles with her cares a sweet bitterness. But all care for this is gone from me by my brother's death.

Trans. Cornish

Here *lusi* (line 17) denotes poetry that is playful. As noted above, the poetics of *ludere* can include metrical sophistication, and it is no surprise that when Catullus asserts here that he can no longer "play" poetically, he does so in a poem written in comparatively simple elegiac distichs rather than in a lyric meter.[36] Vergil and Horace also use *ludere* in relation to literary composition, and Catullus' *ludere*, accordingly, participates in a well-attested, prominent poetic *topos*.[37]

---

[36] Given the erotic connotations of *ludere*, moreover, some commentators have found a reference here to the narrator's own erotic activities in addition to a description of his poetic output. Thomson (1997:476) suggests, "I played the lover" for *lusi*.

[37] Vergil uses *ludere* in relation to poetic composition in the *Eclogues*, where, at 1.9–10, Tityrus declares, *ille meas errare boves, ut cernis, et ipsum / ludere quae vellem calamo permisit agresti* ("He allowed my cows to roam, as you see, and he allowed me *to play* what I wish on the reed"). Here Tityrus' play on the reed overlaps metaphorically with Vergil's composition itself in this programmatic eclogue. Similarly, *Eclogue* 6 opens: *Prima Syracosio dignata est ludere versu / nostra nec erubuit silvas habitare Thalea* ("My Muse first deigned *to play* in Sicilian strains, and blushed not to dwell in the woods"), and, at the programmatic ending of the *Georgics* (4.565), Vergil says: *carmina qui lusi pastorum audaxque iuventa, / Tityre, te patulae cecini sub tegmine fagi* ("I who *played* the songs of shepherds and bold in youth, sang of you, Tityrus, under the canopy of a spreading beech tree"). Developing the *topos*, Horace asserts: *Poscimus, si quid vacui sub umbra / lusimus tecum, quod et hunc in annum / vivat et pluris, age dic Latinum, / barbite, Carmen* ("I pray you, if I have ever in an

With *lusimus satis* in c. 61, Catullus may also refer to his own play with his readers, who may first expect the *virgines* of line 224 to refer to the *integrae virgines* evoked earlier at lines 36–37. In fact, what for some readers may seem to be a rather jarring reference to the Muses at 224 is paralleled by Catullus' practice elsewhere. As Fordyce notes on c. 1, "even with the defining *patrona, virgo* is curiously unexplicit. When Catullus begins a poem with an address to *deae* (68.41), his meaning is obvious: *deae*, in that position, can only be the Muses."[38] As Fordyce's rumination on Catullus' reference to the Muse in c. 1 exemplifies, it is something of a Catullan mannerism to make oblique references to the Muses. He may call them *virgines* or he may call them simply *deae*, expecting his reader to know who the "goddesses" are, just as Homer does in the first line of the *Iliad*, with his apostrophe to the Muse as θεά, "goddess."

The reference to the Muses as *virgines* in c. 61, then, may be viewed as a further instance of *doctus* Catullus exhibiting his poetic sophistication. I would argue, however, that Catullus always disambiguates his *virgines* when he wants them to be recognized as Muses; just as he adds *patrona* to *virgo* in c. 1 and *doctis* to *virginibus* in c. 65 to qualify the otherwise ambiguous *virgo/virgines*, so too in c. 61 he adds the programmatic verb *lusimus* to trigger a poetic connection with the *virgines*, thereby demarcating them as the Muses. Moreover, *lusimus satis* mirrors *satis lusi* in c. 68.17, where the narrator uses the same words to refer to his poetic output. The placement of *satis* after *lusimus* in c. 61, then, invites the reader to interpret *claudite, ostia, virgines: lusimus satis* pragmatically as a single unit: it is now time for the *virgines* to close the gates, the *ludus* has happened "enough." Catullus logically links the *virgines*, the

---

idle hour *played* with you beneath the shade something that I hope may live for this year and longer, come, my Greek lyre, sing a Latin song," Hor. *Od.* 1.32.2, tr. Rudd). Thus *ludere* can denote poetic composition explicitly (*Ecl.* 6.1), or it can denote poetic composition metaphorically through the play on the reed that accompanies poetry and is described in poetry (*Ecl.* 1.9–10, *Geo.* 4. 565; Hor. *Od.* 1.32.2). On *ludus* in Vergil and Horace, see Habinek 2005:136–148. *Ludus* is a programmatic term in prose too; see, e.g., Pliny the Younger's *Epistle* 7.9.9.

[38] 1961:87.

ostia, and the *ludus*; it would make little sense for him to be poetically "playing" with any *virgines* other than the Muses.

It would indeed be peculiar for Catullus to refer to the performance of the wedding hymn as a *ludus* if he were invoking girls participating in the ritual, since, as scholars such as Panoussi (2011) have shown, Catullus takes great pains to construct a solemn ritual environment in c. 61. Accordingly, for the narrator to rupture that solemnity by telling girls who participate in the formal occasion that they have been "playing" may be inappropriate."[39] Furthermore, it would make no sense for the narrator to credit text-internal "maidens" with any role in the composition of the poetic play that *lusimus* denotes, but it makes good sense for the narrator to credit the Muses. Catullus' use of *ludere* here, then, is not suitable to express the performance of and participation in a formal wedding hymn, but it does align neatly with his use of *ludere* in cc. 50 and 68, where it denotes poetic play.[40]

VI. THE *OSTIA*

Controversy also surrounds the *ostia* in line 224, which are interpreted as either the door(s) to the groom's home or the door(s) to his bedchamber. Friedrich believes that Catullus' *ostia* refers to the door of the house, while Fedeli, Kroll, and Syndikus suggest that *ostia* refer to the *thalamus* door.[41] Fedeli, assuming that the *virgines* are the "maidens" invoked early in the ode (36–40), suggests that it is a Catullan innovation to have the "maidens" close the door of the *thalamus*. He notes that it was the task of the θυρωρός in Greece and probably that of the *pronuba* in Rome to close the *thalamus* door. This leads Fedeli to conclude, "Catullus' particular, therefore, has no correspondence either in Greek or in Roman ceremonies."[42] Since Catullus' ritual, as

---

[39] See below, however, for the ramifications of rupturing the solemnity of the ode with an apostrophe to the Muses.

[40] As Habicht 2005:132 notes, "calling poetry *ludus* implies no hostility toward it; rather it associates the poetry in question with relaxation, culture, and the arts in general."

[41] Friedrich 1908:279; Kroll 1960:122; Fedeli 1983:142; Syndikus 1990:48.

[42] Fedeli 1983:143.

Fedeli understands it, has no "particular" correspondence to known practice, Fedeli interprets the passage as an example of Catullan innovation. But, since there is no evidence for maidens ritually closing the door of the groom's house or the door of the groom's bedchamber, the otherwise unparalleled nature of this hypothesized ritual provides no evidence in its favor.

There is another peculiarity that should be noted in relation to scholars' previous interpretations of the *ostia* and wedding ritual. Thomsen notes, "As for the epithalamion, there is no doubt concerning the convention: bride and groom are established in the bridal chamber—with the door closed—when this song (or speech) is begun; we are familiar with this convention from various poetic sources as well as from the rhetors."[43] Accordingly, if *claudite ostia* (224) referred to the closing of the door of the groom's house, an epithalamium should follow, not precede, the closing, but scholars agree that c. 61 includes an epithalamium that comprises nine stanzas (114–183), which precede the imperative *claudite ostia*.[44] The identity of the *ostia*, then, in addition to that of the *virgines*, remains disputed and problematic in relation to Greco-Roman wedding ritual.

The noun *ostia* itself is peculiar and not an obvious choice in reference either to the door of the house or to the door of the bedchamber. As Ellis notes, "*ostia*, with a singular meaning, hardly belongs to the age of Catullus."[45] Moreover, when the narrator urges the bride to leave her home and begin the *deductio*, he says *claustra pandite ianuae / virgo adest* (76–77). Catullus here uses *ianua* when he wishes to refer to the door of a house, and we might have expected him to use *ianua* again in line 224 if he wished to describe the door of the groom's house. Both because *ostia* is not elsewhere used in "the age of Catullus" as a literal door and because Catullus uses *ianua* when he wants to refer to a literal door both in this ode and in c. 67 (where the door plays a prominent role), I suggest that Catullus does not use *ostia* here as a literal door, either a front door or a *thalamus* door.

---

[43] Thomsen 1992:36.
[44] See Thomsen 1992:27.
[45] 1889:239.

Following the interpretation of the *virgines* as the Muses, we should interpret the *ostia* as metaphorical gates separating the human world of the poet from the immortal realm of the Muses. Elsewhere in Latin literature, *ostia* may reference the liminal space between earth and the underworld. In Plautus' *Trinummus*, the old man Philto says to his interlocutor, the slave Stasimus, *apage, Acheruntis ostium in vostrost agro* ("Wow! The entrance to Acheron is on your farm!", 525). In the *Georgics* (4.467), Aristaeus refers to Orpheus as making his way through the *alta ostia Ditis* ("the lofty portals of Dis") on his way to the underworld. In the *Aeneid* (8.667), Virgil again uses the same phrase, when Hephaestus depicts the *alta ostia Ditis* on Aeneas' shield. In Latin poetry, then, *ostia* may mark the transference between human and divine realms, and Catullus' use of *ostia* at 61.224 to denote metaphorical gates that separate him and the Muses resonates with these uses.

VII. CATULLUS' GREEK LYRIC PREDECESSORS

Readers familiar with Greek epinician poetry will further note that gates may serve as metapoetic symbols. In *Olympian* 6, Pindar celebrates a victory won in the mule-cart race, using road and gate imagery to connect his ode to his patron's victory on the Olympic hippodrome. Pindar refers to his poetic activity as a process of opening "gates of song" (πύλας ὕμνων, 27); by opening his poem's gates he recollects the gates of the hippodrome that were opened to mark the beginning of the mule-cart race.[46] Pindar would not use gates as a metapoetic symbol for closure, since starting gates are not relevant to the conclusions of equestrian competitions. It is suitable, however, for Catullus to use gates as metapoetic symbols for closure since they resonate with the closing of the groom's home after the *deductio*. We should not seek, however, to align Catullus' metapoetic gates with any particular gates of the groom's envisioned home.

Catullus' engagement with Greek poetry and his rich, allusive style are widely recognized, and Catullus developed his invocation to the

---

[46] This has previously gone unnoted.

Muses at the end of the ode based on analogous Greek poetic practice.[47] A particularly apt comparandum that may be cited to help us interpret Catullus' *ostia* comes from Bacchylides. In ode 5 Bacchylides invokes Calliope, telling her to bring her chariot to rest (176–178):

λευκώλενε Καλλιόπα,
στᾶσον εὐποίητον ἅρμα
αὐτοῦ

White armed Calliope, station your well-made chariot here.

Bacchylides 5 is 200 lines long, and this invocation, at line 176, comes close to the end, just as Catullus' invocation of the Muses comes close to the end of c. 61. Accordingly, we may conclude that both Catullus and Bacchylides use the *Abbruchsformel*, "break-off formula," to turn their odes in a new direction.[48] In Bacchylides 5 and in Catullus 61 that direction is closure, and both poets use metaphor to express the need for closure. By closing the *ostia*, the Muses bring Catullus' poem to an end, just as the Muse Calliope brings Bacchylides' poem to an end by stationing her well-made chariot. Moreover, since the poems do end shortly after Bacchylides and Catullus ask the Muse(s) to bring their odes to an end, the Muses appear in the odes as colleagues, happy to follow the behest of their poets. This rhetorical maneuver constructs poetic authority for both Catullus and Bacchylides who thereby link themselves closely with the Muses.

Steiner argues that in c. 68 Catullus makes an allusion to a simile in Pindar's *Olympian* 10, and she suggests that once Catullus' audience recognizes the allusion to *Olympian* 10 in c. 68, they will recognize numerous other thematic parallels.[49] Analogously, I suggest that

---

[47] On Catullus' rich allusivity in general, see, with reference to further bibliography, DeBrohun 2011; on c. 61, see Thomsen 1992:13–14; Fedeli 1983 passim.

[48] Pindar also uses the *Abbruchsformel* (e.g. *Pythian* 11.38, *Nemean* 16.8). On Bacchylides 5, see, with reference to further bibliography, Maehler 2004:106–129; Cairns 2010:75–100, 216–247.

[49] Steiner 2004:276: "Readers who note the source of Catullus' conceit then move on to the more obviously pressing problems that this notoriously complex poem (or set of poems) poses. But I want to argue that the Pindaric simile is only the most direct of

if Catullus' audience activates Bacchylides 5 as an intertext for c. 61, verbal, structural, and thematic similarities between the two poems will be apparent. First, there are thematic similarities between an athletic victor, who wins his competition and receives an epinician ode, and the groom, Manlius Torquatus, who wins his bride and receives this Catullan epithalamium. Second, Bacchylides also uses the Muses in ring composition, integrating the Muses at both the beginning and the end of his poem. Moreover, just as Catullus constructs himself and the Muses as fellow composers of c. 61, Bacchylides too gives credit to goddesses for the construction of his ode, saying that he wove his hymn "with the deep-girdled Kharites" (σὺν Χαρίτεσσι βαθυζώνοις ὑφάνας ὕμνον, 9–10). Finally, the myth of Bacchylides 5 ends on the climactic note of Herakles wishing to marry a sister of Meleager, and of Meleager informing Herakles that Deianeira remains unmarried (165–175). The theme of marriage, accordingly, plays a prominent role in Bacchylides 5, just as it does in c. 61.[50]

VIII. REPERCUSSIONS FOR PERFORMANCE SCENARIO

The interpretation of the *virgines* as the Muses may affect the manner in which we envision the performance of the ode. Scholars regularly suggest that Catullus constructs c. 61 in such a manner that a chorus of boys and a chorus of girls are to be envisioned as its performers. For example, Thomsen asserts, "there is a chorus in c. 61, but this is not apparent until lines 36ff. Either Catullus presupposed that his readers

a whole series of glances towards *Olympian* 10 that Catullus 68 includes, and that the Roman poet has drawn on his Greek predecessor in more wholesale fashion. The influence of *Olympian* 10, I specifically suggest, manifests itself in three principal areas: in Catullus' treatment of his ostensible theme, the celebration of the benefactor's deed; in his choice and presentation of one of the chief mythical paradigms in his text, Herakles; and in his reflections on time's passage and the poet's ability to stay its course. Of course this approach risks privileging one set of references in Catullus' densely allusive work, bypassing the borrowings from Homer, Euripides, Callimachus, and a host of Hellenistic sources that others have documented."

[50] Pindar and Bacchylides both use *Abbruchsformeln*, and we need not assume that Catullus' metaphor in c. 61 depends on a specific allusion to Bacchylides 5. Readers of Catullus familiar with Bacchylides 5, however, will have a richer appreciation for Catullus' metapoetics than those who do not.

would consider it self-evident that a wedding song includes a chorus, or he provides his reader with a crucial piece of evidence in a capricious way, to surprise him."[51] Interpreting the *virgines* of 224 as the *integrae virgines* of 36, Fedeli suggests that *lusimus satis* ("we've played enough") is "related to the poet as well as the chorus of *puellae integrae*, rather than being a plural *maiestatis*." Fedeli correctly rules out the plural *maiestatis*, but, as argued in this paper, the denotation of "we" (in *lusimus*) should include the Muses rather than the *integrae puellae* of lines 36–37. Catullus does not construct a chorus in the ode, then, as Fordyce has noted.[52] Unless something in the ode encourages them to realign their assumptions, most readers will align the narrator with "Catullus," and the narrator refers to "himself" in the singular on two occasions; this encourages us to envision the narrator as singular.[53]

IX. VERGIL'S CATULLUS

As commentators have noted, at the end of the third *Eclogue*, Vergil alludes to Catullus 61.224.[54] At the end of an amoebean contest, Palaemon, the chosen judge, tells Damoetas and Menalcas, the two competitors, to stop competing with one another.

> non nostrum inter vos tantas componere lites:
> et vitula tu dignus et hic—et quisquis amores

---

[51] 1992:242–243.

[52] Fordyce 1961:237 believes that there is no chorus in the ode, but that Catullus constructs himself as leader of an imaginary chorus. Lines 36ff. do not support the argument that a chorus of girls participates in the ode. Rather, the narrator addresses girls who are present during the performance of the mimetic ode, asking them "too" to sing the hymenaeus refrain. Pragmatically, Catullus' audience will interpret this passage as an exhortation for the girls to sing along with the narrator who has sung the hymenaeus refrain previously up to this point (4–5). In relation to *item simul* (36), Thomsen (1992:245) asserts, "From *item* it appears that the boys have sung prior to the girls who are now requested to sing ... From *simul*—certainly when following, as it does here, upon 'also' + *item* whereby *simul* acquires the meaning 'at the same time *as others*.'" Alternatively, we should interpret the phrase as meaning "at the same time *as another*," i.e., the narrator; so too e.g. Cornish (Loeb tr.), who translates: "ye too with me."

[53] Singular: 180, 209; *scimus* (plural) at 139 seems to refer to the wedding party.

[54] Cf. Coleman 1977:128.

110 aut metuet dulcis aut experietur amaros.
claudite iam rivos, pueri: sat prata biberunt.

It is not for me to settle such great strife. Both you and he
deserve the yearling—and he also, whoever will fear sweet
loves or will taste bitter loves. Now close the irrigation
channels, boys; the meadows have drunk enough.

At line 111, the *pueri* refer to the competitors, and the switch from
"maidens" (*virgines*) to "boys" (*pueri*) provides, from Catullus 61 to
Eclogue 3, a twist on Vergil's source text. Vergil's allusion to Catullus is
relevant to the argument put forth here in two respects. First, Vergil
alludes to Catullus in the last line of the poem and accordingly uses
the line as an *Abbruchsformel*, since the poem ends at the same time
that Palaemon tells the competitors "to close the irrigation channels."
Second, Vergil's use of metaphor also shows that he recognizes metaphor behind his Catullan source text. As Servius directs us at line 111,
"*iam cantare desinite, satiati enim audiendo sumus.*" The "irrigation channels," then, serve as metaphors for the amoebean songs that Damoetas
and Menalcas have been singing while performing their art. Vergil
and Catullus both use metaphor that relates to the immediate context
of the poems, then, since, in Catullus' poem, the *ostia* resonate with
various doors of the groom's house (as previous scholars have noted),
while in Vergil's eclogue, the rivers of song also relate to the agricul-
tural labor that Damoetas and Palaemon perform.[55] Vergil does much
the same at the end of *Eclogue* 10.[56]

X. CONCLUSION

Readers should connect Catullus' *virgines* at 61.224 with the Muses,
while the *ostia* should be interpreted as metaphorical "gates" that,
when shut, also shut Catullus' ode. Just as Bacchylides 5 ends shortly

---

[55] As Coleman 1977:128 notes, "Palaemon's injunction marks a return to the workaday world."

[56] *haec sat erit, divae, vestrum cecinisse poetam, / dum sedet et gracili fiscellam texit hibisco, / Pierides* (70–72). Here *sat* is like Catullus' *satis* in *carmen* 61; the Muses are first called *divae* (and *Pierides* two lines later), and the poetic act is metaphorized as basket-weaving.

after Bacchylides exhorts the Muses to provide his ode with closure, so too, by using the *Abbruchsformel*, Catullus ends his ode shortly thereafter. Catullus notes that his and the Muses' "play" has gone on long enough (*lusimus satis*) and thereby constructs himself as a poet who collaborates with the Muses. As Wagenvoort points out, *ludere* as a poetic term "is a relative idea: what reserves of meaning it contains with respect to literary appreciation can only be decided by an accurate interpretation of the context."[57] In the context of c. 61, then, it connotes the ode's erotic subject matter and its complex lyric meter, as well as denotes Catullus' composition in general and the facility with which he composed the ode with his colleagues, the Muses. With the interpretation of the *virgines* as the Muses in c. 61, ring composition becomes an even more important formal characteristic of Catullus' poetic technique in the *carmina maiora*.

By invoking the Muses (*virgines*) and by noting his own role in the composition of the ode (*lusimus satis*), Catullus positions himself as a poet, in the process of composing, in the manner that Greco-Roman poets do from the archaic period onward. As Murray notes, modern critics often view god-given inspiration and poetic craft/technique as incompatible, but the early Greek poets themselves envision poetics as inclusive of both inspiration and craft:

> The one—poetic inspiration—accounts for poetic activity in terms of a temporary visitation from some external, or seemingly external, force; the other in terms of permanent qualities inherent in the poet. The beginnings of both of these ideas are, I suggest, discernible as early as Homer, and failure to distinguish between them has clouded our understanding of ancient views of poetic creativity.[58]

With his apostrophe to the Muses, Catullus constructs a relationship of inspiration with them, and with *ludere* he integrates a verb that, within his own corpus, triggers associations with poetic craft. Catullus thereby positions himself comfortably within Greco-Roman discourse that

[57] Wagenvoort 1956:42.
[58] Murray 1981:89.

emphasizes the conjoined nature of poetic inspiration and poetic craft. Catullus develops himself as a "dependent" of the Muses in c. 1 when he refers to the Muse as his "patron" (⟨o⟩ *patrona virgo*, 9). There, however, the call to the Muse is importantly an appeal for the protection of Catullus' already-completed *libellus* rather than an appeal for poetic inspiration. As Murray recognizes, "the point at which the appeal [to the Muses] ceases to be genuine is, of course, problematic."[59] We cannot know whether Catullus believes the Muses play a prominent role in his composition, but there is good reason to think that the appeal to the Muses is chosen more to position Catullus within the matrix of Greco-Roman literary history than to stress his piety.[60]

Catullus elevates the poetic register of c. 61 with his apostrophe to the Muses, before he "breaks into" the ode and flippantly draws attention to how easy it has been for him to compose it. Scholars generally assume that c. 61 is a literary creation that was not intended for performance at the wedding ceremony of Manlius Torquatus and Vinia,[61] but they do assume that c. 61 was composed in celebration of a real wedding.[62] The language of "play" during composition, however, marks the poem as a piece of literary fun, much like the literary fun Catullus shares with his fellow neoteric poet, Calvus, in c. 50. Accordingly, Catullus' invocation of the Muses at the end of the ode marks an abrupt change for the reader: *doctus* Catullus foregrounds his own talent by referring to the composition of c. 61, an extremely sophisticated ode, as mere play, and the names Manlius Torquatus and Vinia may, accordingly, simply be placeholders. Otherwise, Catullus might not so easily rupture the solemnity of the wedding ritual at the ode's end. This suggests that c. 61 is book poetry; accordingly, c. 61 very well may not have been composed for a "real" wedding. One is reminded of

---

[59] 1981:90.

[60] See, too, Murray 1981:90.

[61] Against performance, for example, are: Fedeli 1983:5; Thomsen 1992: 124–126 (with reference to further bibliography); Panoussi 2011:276.

[62] E.g. Syndikus (1990:1): "Catulls Gedicht auf die Hochzeit eines Manlius Torquatus und einer Junia oder Vinia Aurunculeia ist wie einst die Hochzeitsgedichte der Sappho zu einem realen Anlaß geschrieben"; Quinn 1973:264–265: "written apparently in honour of a real marriage."

Quintilian's famous complaint of Ovid being *nimium amator ingenii sui*.[63] Ovid was not without Roman precedent.[64]

UNIVERSITY OF OREGON

WORKS CITED

Burgess, D. 1986. "Catullus c. 50: The Exchange of Poetry." *AJP* 107:576–586.

Cairns, D. L. 2010. *Bacchylides. Five Epinician Odes* (3, 5, 9, 11, 13). ARCA 49. Oxford.

Coleman, R. 1977. *Vergil. Eclogues.* Cambridge.

DeBrohun, J. B. 2011. "Catullan Intertextuality: Apollonius and the Allusive Plot of Catullus 64." In Skinner 2011a, 293–313.

Ellis, R. 1889. *A Commentary on Catullus.* Oxford.

Fedeli, P. 1983. *Catullus' Carmen 61.* Amsterdam.

Fordyce, C. J. 1961. *Catullus.* Oxford.

Friedrich, G. 1908. *Catulli veronensis liber.* Leipzig.

Habinek, T. 2005. *The World of Roman Song: From Ritualized Speech to Social Order.* Baltimore.

Knox, P. 2011. "Catullus and Callimachus." In Skinner 2011a, 151–171.

Kroll, W. 1960. *C. Valerius Catullus.* 4th ed. Stuttgart.

Lieberg, G. 1974. "Observationes in Catulli carmen sexagesimum primum." *Latinitas* 22:216–221.

———. 1975. "Paolo Fedeli: Il carme 61 di Catullo." *Gnomon* 47:354–358.

Lowrie, M. 1997. *Horace's Narrative Odes.* Oxford.

Maehler, H. 2004. *Bacchylides: A Selection.* Cambridge.

Mangelsdorff, E. 1913. *Das lyrische Hochzeitsgedicht bei den Griechen und Römern.* Hamburg.

Murray, P. 1981. "Poetic Inspiration in Early Greece." *JHS* 101:87–100.

Panoussi, V. 2011. "Sexuality and Ritual: Catullus' Wedding Poems." In Skinner 2011a, 276–292.

Quinn, K. 1973. *Catullus: The Poems.* London.

---

[63] *Inst.* 10.1.88, "too much in love with his own talent."

[64] For productive comments on a previous version of this essay, I would like to thank Lowell Bowditch, Sander Goldberg, and the anonymous referee.

Schäfer, E. 1966. *Das Verhältnis vom Erlebnis und Kunstgestalt bei Catull.* Wiesbaden.

Skinner, M., ed. 2011a. *A Companion to Catullus.* Malden, MA.

——— 2011b. "Authorial Arrangement of the Collection: Debate Past and Present." In Skinner 2011a, 35–53.

Spentzou, E., and D. Fowler. 2002. *Cultivating the Muse: Struggles for Power and Inspiration in Classical Literature.* Oxford.

Steiner, D. 2004. "Catullan Excavations: Pindar's *Olympian* 10 and Catullus 68." *HSCP* 102:275–297.

Thomsen, O. 1992. *Ritual and Desire: Catullus 61 and 62 and Other Ancient Documents on Wedding and Marriage.* Aarhus.

Thomson, D. F. S. 1961. "Aspects of Unity in Catullus 64." *CJ* 57:49–57.

———. 1997. *Catullus, Edited with a Textual and Interpretive Commentary.* Toronto.

Traill, D. 1988. "Ring Composition in Catullus 63, 64 and 68b." *CW* 81:365–369.

Van Sickle, J. 1981. "Poetics of Opening and Closure in Meleager, Catullus, and Gallus." *CW* 75: 65–75.

Wagenvoort, H. 1956. "Ludus Poeticus." In *Studies in Roman Literature, Culture and Religion*, 30–42. Leiden. (Orig. pub. 1935 in *Les etudes classiques* 4:108–120.)

West, M. L. 1966. *Theogony.* Oxford.

Wiseman, T. P. 1974. *Cinna the Poet and Other Roman Essays.* Leicester.

THE GREEK LETTERS ASCRIBED TO BRUTUS

CHRISTOPHER P. JONES

AUTHORS FROM PLUTARCH to the Suda mention Greek letters allegedly written by Brutus the "Tyrannicide." Plutarch gives the most circumstantial account (*Brutus* 2.5–8). "(Brutus) was practiced in (speaking) Latin for exposition or disputation, but (when writing) in Greek here and there he is remarkable for using compressed and Laconic brevity in his letters" (Ἑλληνιστὶ δὲ τὴν ἀποφθεγματικὴν καὶ Λακωνικὴν ἐπιτηδεύων βραχυλογίαν ἐν ταῖς ἐπιστολαῖς ἐνιαχοῦ παράσημός ἐστι). The biographer quotes three examples of this brevity, one in a letter to the Pergamenes, one to the Samians, and another "about the Patarans."[1] He ends his discussion: "This therefore is the style of his remarkable notes" (τὸ μὲν οὖν τῶν παρασήμων γένος ἐπιστολίων τοιοῦτόν ἐστιν).

Plutarch's indications correspond closely to a collection of seventy letters that survives in a large number of manuscripts, thirty-five of them allegedly written by Brutus and thirty-five in reply. In the manuscripts they come in a variety of sequences, and only two, E and L, have them in the order of the printed editions, the so-called "vulgate"; almost all have the first letters in the same order before diverging after no. 10 or 16.[2] Most of Brutus' letters are addressed to cities in the province of

---

As always, I am grateful for the careful and constructive criticism of Glen W. Bowersock, and I have also profited from the comments of Tom Keeline. This article was about to go to press when I learned that the same subject had been treated by P. Goukowsky, "Les lettres grecques de Brutus: Documents authentiques ou forgerie?," in N. Barrandon, F. Kirbihler, eds., *Les gouverneurs et les provinciaux sous la République romaine* (Rennes, 2011) 273–290. His conclusions are in several respects similar to mine.

[1] Ziegler 1964:137 excises περὶ Παταρέων in 2.8, but the letter, though addressed to the Lycians generally, is about the Patarans.

[2] Torraca 1959:xlvii–lv.

Asia and within Lycia, which at this time was nominally free but allied to Rome; some are addressed to the "Bithynians" and "Lycians" in general; only one is to an individual. Plutarch's observation that Brutus "here and there" uses a Laconic style fits the collection, for while many of the letters are indeed terse, such as the three that he quotes, two run to over a hundred words (nos. 8 [55], 30 [39]): the average length is about forty-five words, not counting the initial salutation of the form "Brutus to the Pergamenes." Later than Plutarch but still in the second century, the *grammatikos* Phrynichus quotes a "critic" named Marcianus as considering the letters of "the Italian Brutus" superior to those of Plato and Demosthenes. One of the third-century Philostrati, in a brief treatise on correct letter-writing, praises the letters of Brutus "or his scribe" as well as those of the emperor Marcus for their succinctness of style.[3]

In the following I aim to show that the letters of Brutus, though not the responses, are authentic. I begin (Section I) with a discussion of the Mithridates who claims to have composed the replies. In this section I also survey the modern reception of the collection and the debate as to its authenticity. I then (Section II) construct a chronology of the eighteen months or so covered by the letters (approximately early 43 to mid-42). My longest section (III) consists of a text, translation, and commentary for each of Brutus' letters. Finally (Section IV) I argue for the authenticity of Brutus' letters, though not of course of those composed by Mithridates. In an Appendix I give a text and translation of Mithridates' preface.

I. MITHRIDATES AND HIS COLLECTION

Many manuscripts begin with a dedication addressed by a certain Mithridates to his cousin or nephew (*anepsios*), "King Mithridates."[4] He explains that he greatly admires the letters for their style and for what

---

[3] On Phrynichus, see Photius *Bibliotheca* 101a15–27; cf. Nogara 1991. On the younger Philostratus, see Kayser 1870–1871: vol. 2, 257–258.

[4] On the reading, see Torraca 1959:xxviii–xxxi. *Anepsios* is often taken to mean "nephew" (so also Torraca 1959:xxxi); LSJ[9] give only the meaning "cousin," but Demochares the nephew of Demosthenes is called *anepsios* by Athenaeus *Deipnosophistae* 252F (*FGrHist* 75 F 1), *adelphidous* by [Plutarch] *Vitae X Oratorum* 847C (*FGrHist* 75 T 1).

they reveal about Brutus' character, and has undertaken to compose replies to them, consulting histories of the period to learn the circumstances of the parties involved. Brutus, he says, wrote a huge number of letters either in his own hand or using the services of a secretary, but "published only those that were written skillfully (*euphorōs*)." (This seems to imply that Mithridates was using an already existing selection that he took to come from Brutus himself). He ends by enumerating the difficulties involved in writing such fictitious responses, but hopes that his "slight essay" will please his royal namesake.

There has been much discussion of the identity of these two Mithridates. Assuming that the collection of letters and replies came into being sometime between the death of Brutus and the date of Plutarch's biography, that is, approximately in the first century CE, the addressee might be one of several kings: Mithridates, the boy-king appointed to rule Commagene by Augustus in 20 BCE; Mithridates, the ruler of the Bosporan kingdom, who after a troubled reign was sent under guard to Rome and lived there until the time of Galba; the Iberian Mithridates who ruled Armenia (with an interruption under Gaius and Claudius) from 35 to 69; his nephew, king of the Iberi, known from an inscription dated to 75; or he might be some unknown king, not necessarily one still reigning over a kingdom.[5] With the addressee uncertain, the writer is even less identifiable. The fact that the collection opens with letters addressed to Pergamon might suggest a connection with Mithridates of Pergamon, the supporter of Caesar on whom the Dictator bestowed the kingdom of Bosporus, but this Mithridates was killed before he could claim his reward, and left no known descendants.[6]

Richard Bentley's classic exposure of "Phalaris" cast a shadow over all letters attributed to known persons such as Plato and Demosthenes.[7] In his *Dissertation on the Letters of Phalaris* of 1697 he expressly linked the letters of Brutus with those of Phalaris:[8]

---

[5] For the Commagenian king, see *PIR* M 637; for the Bosporan, see *PIR* M 635; for the Iberian, see *PIR* M 644; for his nephew, see *OGIS* 379; *SEG* 20.112; *PIR* M 638.

[6] For the fundamental study of Mithridates, see Hepding 1909; see further bibliography in Sherk 1969:281–284; Jones 1974:202, 204–205.

[7] Rightly observed by Goldstein 1968:3.

[8] Bentley 1883:583.

> All these are the forgeries and impostures of the Sophistae:
> they searched a little into the histories of the person they
> designed to personate, and so adapted their letters to
> their circumstances. This was in great credit among them,
> to follow the character of the person well, and suit the
> affairs of their times. A man got reputation by it, and it was
> owned at first by the true authors; but in time they were
> forgot, and the personated characters kept the titles. They
> made it an exercise to counterfeit thus, much as Ovid when
> he wrote Epistles in the names of heroes and heroines. So
> *Mithridates* tells you in the prologue to *Brutus's* epistles,
> that he made feigned answers from the persons and critics
> [*sic*: "cities"?] that Brutus had wrote to; though any man
> that hath νοῦς and sagacity will perceive that there is a
> double and triple sham in that story.

By "triple sham" Bentley appears to mean that the anonymous author
took the pseudonym "Mithridates," composed the letters of Brutus,
and then pretended that his replies were replies to authentic letters.
In the second edition of the *Dissertation* Bentley cited Erasmus, who
had dismissed the letters of Brutus, Phalaris, and others as "declamations": in Bentley's translation, "Those epistles that somebody has left
us, in the name of Brutus, and of Phalaris, and of Seneca, and St. Paul,
what else can they be reckon'd than little poor declamations?" (*Porro
epistolae, quas nobis reliquit nescio quis Bruti nomine, nomine Phalaridis,
nomine Senecae et Pauli, quid aliud censeri possunt quam declamatiunculae?*).[9]
Bentley now slightly softened his position on "Mithridates": "Some of
the Greek sophists had the success and satisfaction to see their essays
in that kind pass with some readers for the genuine works of those they
endeavoured to express ... One of them indeed, has dealt ingenuously,
and confessed that he feigned the answers to *Brutus*, only as a trial of
skill."[10]

---

[9] Erasmus *Letter* 1206 (Allen and Allen 1922:501) (written to Beatus Rhenanus in
1520); cf. Bentley 1883:76. On Erasmus' comment, see Achelis 1917–1918.

[10] Bentley 1883: 79.

The debate over Brutus' letters went on fitfully in the nineteenth and twentieth centuries, with some arguing strongly in favor and others strongly against.[11] In 1936 Smith examined them very skeptically before coming to an ambiguous conclusion: "That we have not a complete collection of Brutus' genuine letters there seems little doubt."[12] In 1962 Torraca produced a very serviceable edition and an Italian translation (apparently the only one in a modern language), and took a mixed view of authenticity, defending some of Brutus' letters and rejecting others.[13]

In 1986 Rawson argued that the letters could not be genuine: "one needs only to look at the various epistles that survive on stone from Roman generals to Greek cities, including those from Octavian and Antony which are from just the right period for useful comparison, to see how implausible the exaggeratedly brief, unremittingly gnomic and antithetic notes attributed to Brutus are; they are almost empty of precise historical content."[14] As for the comparison with letters from Roman magistrates to the Greek cities, bland missives such as one of Augustus to Sardis, in which he thanks the city for sending an embassy of congratulation, are no parallel to notes demanding money and supplies, or threatening retribution for disloyalty.[15] A letter of Augustus to a certain Stephanus, written in the triumviral period, is a better parallel: at forty-six words (discounting the salutation) it is almost exactly the average length of one of the letters of Brutus, and Joyce Reynolds notes its "curt and authoritative" language.[16] Brutus in his last months was under great stress of every kind, including shortness of time and money. In a letter to Cicero written while on campaign in 43, he says, "Anxiety and vexation make it impossible for me to write at length, nor do I have to" (*scribere multa ad te neque possum prae*

---

[11] Overviews in Torraca 1959:v–ix; Moles 1997:143–144.

[12] Smith 1936:203.

[13] Torraca 1959; cf. Smith 1936. Supporters of authenticity include Rostovtzeff 1953:1579n110.

[14] Rawson 1986:107.

[15] Oliver 1989, no. 7. Cf. also Reynolds 1982, no. 4, the very brief letter of a Roman (?) general to Aphrodisias, possibly Julius Caesar.

[16] Reynolds 1982, no. 10, comparing the letter of Augustus to Norbanus Flaccus, Josephus *Antiquitates Judaicae* 16.166; cf. also the letter of Flaccus to Sardis, *Antiquitates Judaicae* 16.171.

sollicitudine ac stomacho neque debeo). His brevity vexed Cicero, who wrote in reply to another message, "Your short letter—I say 'short,' but it was not really a letter at all. Does Brutus only write me three lines in times like these? Better nothing at all" (*breves litterae tuae—breves dico? Immo nullae. Tribusne versiculis his temporibus Brutus ad me? Nihil scripsisses potius*).[17] As for Rawson's argument that the letters are "almost empty of precise historical content," on the contrary they can almost all be assigned to particular periods of Brutus' activity in 43 and 42, and some contain very precise information indeed.

The latest discussion of the problem known to me is by Moles (1997).[18] On his analysis, "the function of [Plutarch *Brutus*] 2.5–8 is extremely complex and such complex ambiguity is ... not untypical of Plutarch's art." This passage "seems straightforward," but "[its] full meaning only becomes clear later [i.e. in 53.6–7], or through re-reading." Specifically, *parasēmos* can mean "counterfeit" as well as "marked," "conspicuous." Plutarch's use of this adjective thus hints at a meaning different from his apparent one, and "the reader whose suspicions have been aroused" finds them confirmed in chapter 53. Here Plutarch says that a note (*epistolion*) attributed to Brutus concerning the death of Porcia, "if it is one of the authentic ones," implicitly contradicts a tradition about her suicide preserved by Nicolaus of Damascus (*FGrHist* 90 F 99) and Valerius Maximus (4.6.5).[19] According to Moles, "Ring structure contributes vitally to the creation of meaning," and having already suggested that the Greek letters are inauthentic by his use of *parasēmos* in chapter 2, Plutarch gives the key to his latent meaning there by this reference to the existence of inauthentic ones. Moles' conclusion is: "In so far as there remains any authenticity question about the Greek letters attributed to Brutus, this analysis of

---

[17] *Ad Brutum* 1.13.2 (Shackleton Bailey 1980, no. 20), 1.14.1 (SB 22), with Shackleton Bailey's translation. On *tribus* Shackleton Bailey 1980:245 comments "probably not to be taken literally," but the letter was evidently very short.

[18] Moles 1997:143–148. Reitzenstein 2012:437, with bibliography in n. 41, leaves the question open.

[19] On the question of spurious Latin letters preserved in the Cicero–Brutus correspondence, see Shackleton Bailey 1980:10–14. Plutarch does not indicate whether the letter he refers to was in Latin or Greek, but if addressed to Brutus' friends in Rome, it was presumably in Latin.

2.5–8 disposes of any lingering appeals to the incontestable value of Plutarch's evidence on the side of the authenticity of even a few of the letters; rather it is his evidence which drives home the case for the spuriousness of the entire collection." By the reverse application of the same logic, Moles also argues that Plutarch's statement about Brutus' letter concerning the death of Porcia, "if it is one of the authentic ones," "does not in fact cast doubt on the letter—rather the reverse. Plutarch actually thinks the letter genuine, but cannot admit it."[20]

Though Moles argues that Plutarch's use of *parasēmos* both for Brutus and for his *epistolia* hints at the inauthenticity of the letters, this does not accord with the author's usage. When he uses the word other than in the substantive neuter plural ('marks', usually insignia of office), he can mean 'counterfeit' of coinage (*quomodo adulator ab amico internoscatur* 65B). When applying it to persons he can mean 'debased' (*De liberis educandis* 43C, coupled with *adokimoi* of slaves used as teachers), or 'insincere' (*Alexander* 48.3, coupled with *soloikos* of a person's behavior),[21] but he uses it in a sense close to that of the neuter plural, 'marked, conspicuous', when he advises that the politician not be "conspicuous for what causes envy by luxury and expense" (τοῖς εἰς τρυφὴν καὶ πολυτέλειαν ἐπιφθόνοις παράσημος, *Praecepta gerendae reipublicae* 823B). Though in all cases where he applies it to persons the word seems to have an unfavorable tinge, in the *Brutus* 'debased' or 'insincere' would have no meaning, and the sense must again be 'conspicuous'.

Moles also points to Plutarch's word *epistolion*, since "like other ancient writers, he often uses diminutives to convey distance or irony," but he has neglected the context. Earlier in the chapter Plutarch says that Brutus was laconic "here and there" (*eniachou*) in the Greek letters (*epistolai*), and he cites three, none of which exceeds thirty-five words. When he adds, "This therefore is the style of his remarkable notes (*epistolia*)," he is referring to those he has just mentioned and those like them, not, as Moles maintains, to "the letters in general." As already

---

[20] Moles 1997:160.
[21] Hamilton 1969:133 translates, "in bad taste and in a manner that did not ring true."

noted, the average letter is about forty-five words long, and two letters are over a hundred.

In favor of Plutarch's acceptance of the authenticity of Brutus' letters (there is no way of telling whether he knew of Mithridates' replies) is the fact that they so strongly contradict the picture that he himself draws of his subject. Especially in his treatment of the fall of Xanthos, Plutarch is concerned to minimize the guilt of Brutus and to throw the blame on the Lycians, whereas the letters make Brutus say such things as "their city serves as the tomb of their madness" (no. 17 [25]) and "all of them we have considered deserving of complete destruction" (no. 22 [43]). If Plutarch had doubted the authenticity of the letters, he would surely have taken the discrepancy between them and his own view of Brutus as the crowning proof: as it is, he does nothing of the sort, but merely avoids mentioning the Greek letters in the narrative part of the *Life*.

II. CHRONOLOGY

The letters involve two years (43 and 42) and three principal actors: Brutus himself, Cassius, and Cornelius Dolabella, Caesar's consul suffect of 44, who steadfastly opposed Brutus and Cassius until his death in Syria in mid-43.[22] Brutus arrived in Dyrrachium by January 43, by which time Cassius was perhaps already in Cilicia and Dolabella in Asia. After campaigning against Gaius Antonius, Brutus returned to Dyrrachium by April (Cicero *Ad Brutum* 2.3 [Shackleton Bailey 1980, no. 2]) and was encamped in Candavia, two or three days along the Via Egnatia from Dyrrachium, by mid-May (Cicero *Ad Brutum* 1.6 [Shackleton Bailey 1980, no. 12]). By this time Dolabella had recently left Asia; in July Cassius trapped him in Laodicea *ad mare* (modern Latakia), where he was either killed by one of his own soldiers (Appian *Bella civilia* 4.62.267) or took his own life (Dio *Historia Romana* 47.30.5).[23]

---

[22] For summaries, see Magie 1950:418–426; Pelling 1996:5–8. Detailed citation of ancient sources in Drumann–Groebe 1899–1929: 2.105–128 (Cassius), 2.491–497 (Dolabella), 4.33–38 (Brutus); cf. also Fröhlich 1899 (Cassius); Münzer 1900 (Dolabella); Gelzer 1918 (Brutus).

[23] Münzer 1900:1305–1308; Broughton 1952, 2.317, 344.

For the rest of the campaigning season of 43, Brutus' movements are uncertain: he defeated the Thracian Bessi, for which he received the title of *imperator*, and according to Dio visited Asia both before and after this campaign.[24] During the following winter (43/42) he prepared for the next campaigning season. In Plutarch's words (*Brutus* 28.3), "he now crossed over into Asia with his army, which was by this time splendid, and started to equip a fleet in Bithynia and around Cyzicus, while he himself going by land began to bring over (*kathistato*) the cities, to negotiate with the dynasts, and to write to Cassius to return from Egypt to Syria." The two met in Smyrna at the beginning of 42, and decided to raise further funds and material as Cassius attacked Rhodes and Brutus the cities of Lycia. Having attained their objectives, in the course of which Brutus destroyed the Lycian capital of Xanthos, they met again in Sardis about the middle of the year, and from there crossed together to Macedonia. In October the Caesarian forces led by Antony defeated them at Philippi, and both committed suicide.

Fitting Brutus' letters into this chronology raises a number of uncertainties. One is the length of time that it would take for a letter to pass between him and an addressee, especially when he was still in Europe. A letter-carrier from Macedonia or Thrace might have taken an overland route for much of the way, or have shortened it by crossing from a port such as Neapolis near Philippi to a coastal city of Asia such as Alexandria Troas. This makes distances almost impossible to gauge, but conservatively assuming a distance of 500 miles from Dyrrachium to a northerly city such as Pergamon, or one from a point further east to an inland city such as Tralles, a letter going at approximately fifty miles per day would have taken some ten days to reach its destination.[25] Moreover, letters might have arrived when the situation they addressed had already changed: for example, Brutus' several letters to the Trallians urging them to break with Dolabella do not show that Dolabella was still in the city when the letters arrived (though the replies composed

---

[24] Dio 47.24.2, 25.2, followed by Groebe against Drumann in Drumann–Groebe 1899–1929, 4.37n4.

[25] On the speed at which letters could travel, Kolb 2000:321–332, reckoning an average of about 50 miles a day for regular transport, with much higher speeds for emergencies.

by Mithridates presuppose that every letter arrived on time). Whatever the other difficulties, there seems no chronological obstacle in the way of supposing that Brutus could have sent the thirty-five extant letters.

III. TEXT, TRANSLATION, AND COMMENTARY ON BRUTUS' LETTERS

I take the letters in clusters according to whether they can be assigned to particular times in 43 or 42; for some even an approximate date must remain uncertain. Within each cluster I usually group together letters written to an individual city or league, giving first a brief sketch of the historical background, then a text and translation, and thirdly a discussion of problems; for this purpose I have ordered the letters sequentially, giving the vulgate number in parentheses. When translating, I have consistently rendered the first person plural as a true plural and not as the "royal we," since it is not clear when Brutus is speaking in his own name and when in the name of both himself and Cassius. In some places I have expanded vague expressions such as *tauta*, "these things," indicating such expansions by means of parentheses. To avoid tedious repetition, I have not used a phrase such as "if genuine" when referring to the letters. My Greek text follows that of Torraca, with a few minor changes. I have numbered the letters so far as possible in chronological order, indicating Torraca's numbers in parentheses (since I have only reproduced Brutus' letters, not Mithridates' replies, all of Torraca's numbers are odd).

1. Campaigning season, 43

1.1 Pergamon

The correspondence with the Pergamenes opens the collection in most of the manuscripts, but the vulgate order is erroneous, as nos. 1 (1) and 2 (7) imply a time when the city was still supporting Dolabella, nos. 3 (3), 4 (5), and 5 (9) a time when it was supporting Brutus. Plutarch cites no. 1 (1), placing it at the beginning of the campaign of 43, in which he seems to be correct (*Brutus* 2.6). No. 5 (9) is written from Abdera or a point further east, when Brutus had reached Thrace.

1 (1). Βροῦτος Περγαμηνοῖς. Ἀκούω ὑμᾶς Δολοβέλλᾳ χρήματα δεδωκέναι. ἃ εἰ μὲν ἑκόντες ἔδοτε, ὁμολογεῖτε ἀδικεῖν· εἰ δὲ ἄκοντες, ἀποδείξατε τῷ ἐμοὶ ἑκόντες δοῦναι.

Brutus to the Pergamenes. I hear that you have given money to Dolabella. If you did so willingly, you admit to doing wrong: if unwillingly, prove it by giving willingly to me.

2 (7). Βροῦτος Περγαμηνοῖς. Δολοβέλλας ἐστὶν ἡμῖν μὲν πολέμιος, ὑμῖν δὲ φίλος, ᾧ εἰς ἅπαν καὶ καθ' ἡμῶν ὑπουργεῖσθε. τί δῆτα ἂν ἔποιτο τοῖς τὰ αὐτὰ ἐκείνῳ ἑλομένοις εἰ μὴ ἁλόντας ἴσα πολεμίοις πάσχειν; οὐδὲ γὰρ μετάνοιαν δοτέον τοῖς οὐ πρὶν ἢ ἐς τὸ παντελὲς ἀποκαμεῖν μετανοοῦσι.

Brutus to the Pergamenes. Dolabella is our enemy and your friend, and you assist him in every way and against us. What then might be the consequence for those who choose to side with him other than that, once captured, they should suffer no less than enemies? One should not give (room for) repentance to those who only repent once they are completely exhausted.

3 (3). Βροῦτος Περγαμηνοῖς. Τὰ χρήματα ἡμῖν εἰς ὃν ἐπετάξαμεν καιρὸν μὴ πέμψαντες, οὐδὲν ἄλλο εἰ μὴ τὸ δοκεῖν μετὰ τοῦ βεβιάσθαι ταῦτα παρασχεῖν ὠφέλησε. ὥστε διχόθεν ὑμᾶς βεβλάφθαι, καὶ τῷ τὸ ἀνάλωμα κατ' ἴσον ὑπομεῖναι (δώσετε γὰρ τοσούτῳ κάκιον ὅσῳπερ ἄκοντες) καὶ τῷ ἣν εἰκὸς ἀντὶ τῶν ὑπουργηθέντων φέρεσθαι χάριν ὑμᾶς ἀφῃρῆσθαι· οὐ γὰρ χρὴ τὴν τῶν προθύμων ὑπηκόων παρρησίαν νέμεσθαι τοὺς οὐκ ἂν εἰ μὴ μετὰ ἀνάγκης ταῦθ' ἡμῖν παρασχόντας.

Brutus to the Pergamenes. By not sending the money by the deadline we ordered you gained nothing except the appearance of providing it under compulsion. You seem therefore to have harmed yourselves twice over, both by undergoing the expense nevertheless (since your gift will be made all the worse by your reluctance), and by losing the credit that you might reasonably have gained in return for your services; for those who provide this (money) (only) when compelled should not enjoy the same liberty[26] as subjects (who are) sincere.

4 (5). Βροῦτος Περγαμηνοῖς. Τὰ χρήματα ὑμῶν ἐκόμισαν οἱ πρέσβεις, ὡς μὲν πρὸς ἣν ᾐτιᾶσθε ἀσθένειαν πλείω, ὡς δὲ πρὸς ἣν ᾐτούμεθα χρείαν ὀλίγα. φυλάττεσθε οὖν μὴ καὶ δύνησθε πλεῖον οὗ προσποιεῖσθε καὶ βούλησθε ἔλαττον οὗ δύνασθε.

Brutus to the Pergamenes. Your ambassadors have brought the money, which is more than (was to be expected considering) the distress that you alleged, but little relative to what we asked. Be careful lest your capacity is greater than you pretend, and your willingness less than your capacity.

5 (9). Βροῦτος Περγαμηνοῖς. Ψήφισμα ὑμέτερον οἱ πρέσβεις ὑμῶν ἀπεκόμισάν μοι ἐν Ἀβδήροις τὴν ἀπ᾽ Ἰταλίας στρατιὰν ἐπισκοπουμένῳ, δεξάμενος δὲ τῆς μὲν βραδυτῆτος ὑμᾶς ἐμεμψάμην (Περγαμηνοὺς γὰρ ταῦτα φρονεῖν ἐκ πολλοῦ ἂν ἐβουλόμην καὶ ἔδει), ἐπήνεσα δὲ τῆς εἰς τὰ ἄλλα προθυμίας καὶ τῆς δωρεᾶς τῶν διακοσίων ταλάντων, δι᾽ ἧς πάλαι ἄκοντες δοῦναι Δολοβέλλᾳ τὰ πεντήκοντα ἐπεδείξασθε.

Brutus to the Pergamenes. Your ambassadors gave me your decree in Abdera when I was reviewing the army from Italy. On receiving it I faulted you for your tardiness, for it has long since been my wish, and the Pergamenes' obligation, to take this position. Still, I thanked them for their general support, and especially for the gift of the two

---

[26] LSJ⁹ s.v. παρρησία 3, "freedom of action."

hundred talents, which shows that it was against your will that you previously gave Dolabella fifty.[27]

One argument against this group is chronological: Brutus arrived in Asia after Dolabella's departure from it, and hence there was no time for him to write to Pergamon reproaching them for their support of his enemy.[28] As already noted, there is no reason to suppose that Brutus only wrote after arriving in Asia, since he was in correspondence with informants there long before: a letter that he sent to Cicero in mid-April from Candavia, west of Lake Ochrid, shows that he had already had news about Dolabella's movements in the province (*Ad Brutum* 1.6.3 ([Shackleton Bailey 1980, no. 12]). Letter no. 9, indicating that the Pergamene ambassadors met him at Abdera, implies that he had previously contacted their city while at some point further west.

Another argument against authenticity is that Brutus could not have received an army from Italy when Lepidus and the republicans were raising money and troops there for the confrontation with Antony. But this is belied by a letter that Cicero sent to him in mid-April: "You say that you are in want of two necessities, reinforcements and money. It is hard to make any suggestion. No financial resources occur to me as available for your use other than those which the senate has decreed, namely that you should borrow money from civic bodies. As to reinforcements, I do not see what can be done. So far from assigning you anything from his own army or levies Pansa is not happy that so many volunteers are joining you."[29] Letter no. 5 (9) therefore reveals a fully plausible situation: that Brutus, having written to Pergamon from Dyrrachium or at some stage on his march east, reached Abdera in Thrace, where he held a review of volunteers from Italy and met the ambassadors from Pergamon.

Like other cities named in this correspondence, Pergamon had reason to be loyal to the memory of Julius Caesar. Its leading citizen,

---

[27] That is, by their larger "gift" to Brutus they proved that they had not wanted to help Dolabella.

[28] Thus Magie 1950:1274–1275, following Smith 1936:200–201.

[29] *Ad Brutum* 2.4.4 [Shackleton Bailey 1980, no. 4]; translation in the text by Shackleton Bailey 2002:217.

Mithridates, reputedly a bastard son of Mithridates Euergetes, brought forces to him during the Alexandrian War of 47, and won many privileges for his city. A fragmentary letter of Caesar to the city, written in 48 or later, survives from Smyrna; one from Caesar's proconsul of Asia, Servilius Isauricus, found in Pergamon, probably contained a favorable decision concerning the city's Asclepieion. It is not therefore surprising that the Pergamenes gave financial support to Dolabella. If they gave a larger sum to Brutus, that could have been a response to greater pressure; Brutus' remark, "It shows that you earlier gave Dolabella fifty (talents) reluctantly" sounds ironic.[30]

1.2 Tralles

These four letters must be among the earliest, perhaps contemporary with those to Pergamon, since they assume the presence of Dolabella in the region of Tralles; as already noted, it is not necessary to suppose that Brutus wrote them from somewhere in Asia rather than from Europe, nor that all of the letters found Dolabella still in Tralles.

> 6 (51).   Βροῦτος Τραλλιανοῖς. Εἰ μὲν ἐν τῇ ὑμετέρᾳ στρατο-
> πεδεύειν Δολοβέλλαν ἀνεχόμενοι οἴεσθε μηδὲν ἀδικεῖν
> με, οὐκ ὀρθῶς φρονεῖτε· εἰ δὲ νομίζετε ὧν ἂν τοὺς ἑαυτῶν
> πολεμίους ἀφελώμεθα, τούτων ὑμῖν ὡς ὄντων οἰκείων
> παραχωρήσειν, αὐτίκα πλανᾶσθαί μοι δοκεῖτε. ἢ εἴργετε
> οὖν αὐτὸν τῆς σφετέρας, ἢ ὅλως μηδ' ὑφ' ἡμῶν ἀδικεῖσθαι
> φάσκετε ὧν ἂν ἔχειν αὐτοὶ Δολοβέλλαν ἀφελόμενοι, ἀλλὰ
> μὴ ὑμῖν παραχωρεῖν ἀξιῶμεν.

> Brutus to the Trallians. If you think that by tolerating Dolabella's encampment on your territory you do me no injury, you are mistaken; but if you think that we will concede to you as your property whatever we take from our own enemies, you seem to me in a fundamental error. Either keep him away from your territory, therefore, or do not allege that we have done you any wrong at all if we

---

[30] For Mithridates of Pergamon, see above, n. 6. For the letter of Caesar, see Sherk 1969, no. 54 (Caesar), no. 55 (Servilius Isauricus); better edition of no. 55 in Habicht 1969, no. 1.

decide to keep for ourselves, rather than giving over to you, what we take from Dolabella.[31]

7 (53).   Βροῦτος Τραλλιανοῖς. Καὶ πρόσθεν ὑμῖν ἐπέστειλα ὅτι ἁμαρτάνετε Δολοβέλλαν ἐν τῇ ὑμετέρᾳ στρατοπεδεύοντα περιορῶντες, καὶ τὸ παρὸν ἴστε, εἰ μὲν ὡς οἰκείας αὐτῷ παραχωρεῖτε, οὐδ' ἂν εἰ πρὸς ἡμῶν ἀφαιρεθείητε, ὧν ἐκείνῳ ὡς ἀλλοτρίων ἐξέστητε ἡμῖν ὡς ἰδίων ἀντιποιησόμενοι· εἰ δὲ ὡς φίλῳ ἐν τῇ ὑμετέρᾳ στρατοπεδεύειν δίδοτε, κοινωνεῖν αὐτῷ τῆς ἐπὶ τῷ πολέμῳ τύχης ἀρξάμενοι οὐδὲ ἡμῖν ἀκούσιοι πολέμιοι φανεῖσθε.

Brutus to the Trallians. I wrote to you before that you do wrong to connive at Dolabella's encampment on your territory. Now too you must realize that, even if you are deprived of it by us, you will not dispute with us as (if it were) yours what you conceded to him as (if it were) another's.[32] If you are allowing him to encamp on your territory as a friend, that will show that you have begun to share with him in the fortunes of war, and are not reluctant to be our enemy.

8 (55).   Βροῦτος Τραλλιανοῖς. Ἠγγέλθη μοι Μηνόδωρον ὑμέτερον πολίτην, ξένον καὶ φίλον Δολοβέλλᾳ τῷ ἡμετέρῳ πολεμίῳ, καὶ πρότερον ὑμᾶς μὴ εἴργειν αὐτὸν ἐν τῇ ὑμετέρᾳ στρατοπεδεύοντα πεῖσαι, καὶ νῦν ὅπως καὶ αὐτὸν καὶ τὴν στρατιὰν αὐτοῦ τῇ πόλει δέξησθε συμβουλεύειν. ἐγὼ δὲ ὡς μὲν οὐδὲν ὀνήσει Δολοβέλλαν, εἰ καὶ ταῦτα καὶ ἔτι πλείω τούτων ποιῆσαι προσαχθείητε ὑπὸ Μηνοδώρου ἢ καὶ εἴ τις ἄλλος πείσειεν, οὐκ ἀγνοῶ, οὐδὲ μὴν οὔτε Μηνόδωρον ἡ Δολοβέλλᾳ φιλία καὶ ξενία. οὐ μὴν ἀλλ'

---

[31] Translation uncertain: the genitive ὧν is perhaps a genitive of reference, "with respect to such things as, having taken them from Dolabella, we decide to keep ourselves and not to concede to you."

[32] The meaning seems to be, "if you let Dolabella camp on your territory, you will have implicitly conceded that it is no longer yours; consequently, if I seize it from Dolabella, there will be no reason for me to return it to you."

οὐχ ὅπως κολάσαιμί τινας σκοπῶν ἐφεδρεύειν οἶμαι τοῖς
ἑνὸς ἑκάστου ἁμαρτήμασιν. ἵνα μέντοι μηδὲν κολάσεως
ἄξιον ἁμαρτεῖν ἀναγκασθῆτε, κελεύω ὑμᾶς Μηνόδωρον
φυγαδεῦσαι τῆς πατρίδος τοῦ ἰδίου λυσιτελοῦς ἕνεκα, εἴ
γέ τι λυσιτελεῖν ἔμελλεν αὐτῷ τὴν πατρίδα πωλοῦντι,
Δολοβέλλαν δὲ μήτε τῇ πόλει δέχεσθαι τῆς τε γῆς ἐξελάσαι,
βιαζόμενον δὲ ὅπλοις ἀμύνασθαι· ἢ ἀπειθοῦντας οὐχ ὑπὸ
Μηνοδώρου ταῦθ' ὑμᾶς οἰήσομαι προαχθέντας πεισθῆναι,
ἀλλ' αὐτοὺς Μηνοδώρῳ τούτων ἀφορμὴν δοῦναι
ἐθέλοντας.

Brutus to the Trallians. It has been reported to me that
Menodorus, your citizen and a host and friend of our
enemy Dolabella, previously persuaded you not to keep
him out when he was encamping on your territory, and
is now advising you to allow him and his troops into your
city.[33] I am quite sure that it will not help Dolabella if you
are induced by Menodorus to do this or even more (than
this), or if anyone else persuades you (to do so), nor indeed
will his position as friend and host of Dolabella (profit)
Menodorus. Nonetheless, (just) because I am considering
how to punish certain persons, I do not think I have to
observe the errors of every individual.[34] And yet, so that
you may not be forced to do anything calling for punishment, I order you to exile Menodorus from his homeland
for (his) own good, if indeed it was likely to be for his own
good that he sold his homeland; (and I order you) not to
receive Dolabella into your city but to expel him from your
territory, and if he uses force of arms, to fight him off. But
if you disobey, I shall infer, not that you were persuaded
by Menodorus to act as you have, but that you yourselves
willingly gave Menodorus the occasion for such behavior.

---

[33] For this classic distinction between polis and chōra, e.g. Robert 1984:480–481 = Robert
1987:468–469.

[34] δεῖν has perhaps dropped out after ἐφεδρεύειν: so implicitly Hercher 1873:187
(advigilandum censeo).

9 (57). Βροῦτος Τραλλιανοῖς. Χρήματα ὅσα Δολοβέλλας κατέθετο παρὰ Μηνοδώρῳ τῷ ἑαυτοῦ ξένῳ εἴ τέ τινας ἄλλας παρακαταθήκας, παρὰ τῶν τέκνων αὐτοῦ κομισάμενοι τῶν διαδεξαμένων αὐτοῦ τὴν οὐσίαν μετὰ τὴν ἐκείνου φυγὴν ἀναπέμψατε πρός με· εἰ δέ τι μὴ εἶναί φατε, αὐτοὺς τοὺς ἄνδρας μετὰ τέκνων καὶ γυναικῶν· οὐ γὰρ δίκαιον τοῖς τῶν ἐμῶν πολεμίων φίλοις ἢ καὶ ξένοις περαιτέρω τοῦ μηδὲν αὐτοὺς παθεῖν λυσιτελῆσαι τὴν ἡμετέραν ἐπιείκειαν.

Brutus to the Trallians. All moneys or any other objects of trust that Dolabella deposited with his host Menodorus, you must recover from (Menodorus') sons on whom his property devolved after his exile, and send them to me. If you say that there is nothing, (send) the men themselves with their children and women. It is not right that those who are the friends, or indeed the hosts, of my enemies should, in addition to suffering no harm themselves, profit from my moderation.

The presence of Dolabella in eastern Caria is shown by an inscription from Tabai, only about four or five days away from Tralles. This, honoring a citizen whose name is now lost, shows that he was an "assessor (*synedros*) of imperator Dolabella, was appointed [perhaps as an ambassador] several times under the most difficult circumstances, went as an ambassador to cities, to those of the leaders [the Romans] who had crossed over as consuls, and to dynasts, and as hipparch marshaled the cavalry corps in difficult circumstances." The word "assessor" implies that Dolabella exercised judicial functions. The "most difficult circumstances" may well refer to the same troubled time as the two letters of Brutus mentioning Menodorus, when cities of western Caria were forced to choose between pressure from Dolabella and from the tyrannicides.[35]

---

[35] L. and J. Robert 1954:102–105, no. 6 (previously L. Robert 1937:322–328). On Dolabella's constitutional position while in Asia, Kreiler 2008:45–46.

The Menodorus whom Brutus accuses of supporting Dolabella is very possibly the Menodorus mentioned by Strabo as a leading citizen of Tralles. "A learned man and generally venerable and steady, he held the priesthood of Zeus Larisaeus. He was overthrown by a faction (κατεστασιάσθη) of the friends of Domitius Ahenobarbus, who killed him for allegedly having caused the fleet to be disloyal, which he (sc. Ahenobarbus) took on trust from informers." This Domitius Ahenobarbus must be the man who commanded a fleet in the service of Brutus in 42, but in 40 transferred his allegiance to Antony. Consul in 32, he was one of the commanders of the fleet of Antony and Cleopatra, but went over to Octavian shortly before Actium, and died soon thereafter.[36] Strabo's statement refers either to Ahenobarbus' earlier command, or more probably to his later one: in either case, Menodorus appears to have been a staunch supporter of the Caesarian cause as represented by Caesar's heir, and could well have used his influence in Tralles to support Dolabella in 43. He is a good example of those leading citizens, such as Mithridates in Pergamon and Asclepiades of Cyzicus, on whom the generals of the late republic relied for support in the cities of the East. The name of a younger Menodorus, perhaps his son, now emerges in an inscription referring to help that Augustus gave to Tralles after the great earthquake of 26.[37]

By a curious coincidence, similar letters survive from Tralles concerning citizens loyal to Rome in the time of the first Mithridatic War. In both letters Mithridates writes to his satrap, Leonippus, ordering him to arrest a certain Chaeremon. The second runs: "King Mithridates to Leonippus, greeting. Chaeremon son of Pythodorus has previously effected the escape of the fugitive Romans with his son to Rhodes, and now, learning of my proximity, he has taken refuge in the temple of the Ephesian Artemis. From there he continues to communicate with the Romans, the common enemy of mankind. His confidence

---

[36] Strabo *Geography* 14.1.42, C. 649 (my translation). For Ahenobarbus, see Suetonius *Nero* 3; Münzer 1903; Broughton 1952, 2.365, 373, 382, 421; Herrmann 1974.

[37] On such local supporters, see Bowersock 1965:5–11; Robert 1966:418–423 = 6.42–47. On Mithridates, see above, n. 7. On Asclepiades, see below, 24n48. For the suggestion that the Menodorus of the letters is Strabo's Menodorus, see Magie 1950:1275n55. For the younger Menodorus, see Jones 2011:114.

in face of the offenses he has committed is the starting point of the movement against us. Consider how you may by all means bring him to us, or how he may be kept under arrest and in imprisonment until I am free of the enemy." These letters incidentally show that letters sent by an enemy of the Roman people could still be found after the end of hostilities and be recorded for posterity.[38]

2. Autumn–winter, 43/42

After reporting the execution of Gaius Antonius, which occurred late in 43 or early in 42,[39] Plutarch relates that Brutus brought his army over from Macedonia to Asia, and "began to prepare a fleet in Bithynia and around Cyzicus" (*Brutus* 28.3). This forms the background of five letters addressed to "the Bithynians" (presumably the Bithynian *koinon*) and two to Cyzicus.[40]

2.1 Bithynia

> 10 (59). Βροῦτος Βιθυνοῖς. Μηδενὶ δοκείτω χαλεπὸν εἰ πολλὰ εἰσπράττομεν πολλῶν δεόμενοι· τούτων γὰρ ἡμεῖς ἔργα ἀποδίδομεν. εἰ δὲ τὸ τῶν εἰσφορῶν πλῆθος βαρύνεσθε, μεμνῆσθαι χρὴ πόσοι πόνοι σὺν τοῖς διδομένοις ὑφ᾽ ἡμῶν ἀναλίσκονται. παντὶ γὰρ δῆλον ὅτι τοῦ παρασκευαζομένου ὁ ταῖς παρασκευαῖς τοῦ πολέμου χρώμενος πλεῖον κάμνει, ἄλλως τε καὶ ὑμῶν μὲν τῆς οἰκείας φροντίδος ἑκάστῳ, ἡμῖν δὲ τῆς ἁπάντων προνοεῖν ἀνάγκη.

Brutus to the Bithynians. Let no-one think it harsh if we requisition much when we need much, since we are giving actions in return. If you are burdened by the weight of tribute, you should remember how many efforts we are making together with what you give. It is perfectly obvious that one who uses the means (to make) war labors more than the one who provides them, especially since each of

---

[38] Welles 1934:294–299, nos. 73/74, with his translation of no. 74.

[39] Plutarch may be wrong in placing the death of C. Antonius after that of Cicero: cf. Groebe in Drumann–Groebe 1899–1929, 4.36n8.

[40] On the correspondence with the Bithynians, see Deininger 1966.

you has only himself to take thought for, while we must take thought for everyone.

11 (61). Βροῦτος Βιθυνοῖς. Ἀκύλαν ἐμὸν φίλον ἔπεμψα πρὸς ὑμᾶς κατασκευάσοντά μοι ναῦς στρογγύλας πεντήκοντα καὶ μακρὰς διακοσίας, τοσαύτας δὲ καὶ Δολοβέλλᾳ πυνθάνομαι ὑμᾶς παρασχῆσθαι. ὀρθῶς οὖν ποιήσετε ναύτας καὶ ἐρέτας εἰς ταῦτα τὰ πλοῖα, ἄχρι ἂν πρὸς ἐμὲ ἀνακομισθῇ, παρασχόντες τῷ Ἀκύλᾳ καὶ σιτηρέσιον τούτοις μηνῶν τεσσάρων. τῶν γὰρ εἰς τὴν ναυπηγίαν δεόντων ξύλων καὶ τῆς τούτων παρακομιδῆς ἐπὶ θάλατταν καὶ τεχνιτῶν εὖ οἶδ' ὅτι οὐδὲν ἀμελήσετε, μηδὲ Δολοβέλλᾳ ἐλλιπόντες.

Brutus to the Bithynians. I have sent my friend Aquila to equip fifty cargo-ships for me and two hundred warships, since I hear that you provided the same number to Dolabella. You will do as you ought, therefore, in providing Aquila with the sailors and rowers for these ships until they are delivered to me, and four months' wages for the crews. As for the timber needed for constructing the ships, its conveyance to the sea, and the workmen, I am sure that you will not be at all negligent, not having failed Dolabella either.

12 (63). Βροῦτος Βιθυνοῖς. Ἔγραψέ μοι Ἀκύλας πολλήν τινα ὑμῖν ῥαθυμίαν ἐγκεῖσθαι τῆς εἰς τὰ πλοῖα ὑπουργίας, ἐγὼ δὲ ἐκεῖνον σφόδρα ἐμεμψάμην τῆς ἀνεξικακίας, πειθόμενον ἐπιστολῶν μοι τῶν καθ' ὑμῶν, ἃς παρ' ἕκαστα πέμπων οὐ παύεται, δεῖν μᾶλλον ἢ νεῶν, κἂν εἰ σὺν ταῖς κατ' αὐτοῦ πρεσβείαις δέοι· οὐ γὰρ οἷόν τε διὰ τούτων ἐκείνας καταρτισθῆναι. ὑμᾶς δὲ ὑπομνήσαιμ' ἂν ἡδέως καὶ νῦν καὶ ἔπειτα τοῦ μὴ ἄκοντας ἡμῖν ἀλλ' ἑκόντας καὶ εἰς ταῦτα καὶ εἰς τὰ ἄλλα πάντα ὁμοίως συναγωνίζεσθαι· ἐκ τῶν παρόντων γὰρ καὶ περὶ ἐκείνων ῥάδιον τεκμαίρεσθαι.

Brutus to the Bithynians. Aquila has written to me that you are afflicted with considerable procrastination in assisting with the ships, and I have rebuked him strongly for his tolerance, believing (as he does) that I need letters incriminating you, which he continues to send in detail, rather than ships, even if I needed them together with your embassies incriminating him.[41] The latter [i.e. ships] cannot be built by means of the former [i.e. letters]. I would like to remind you both now and for the future to join our struggle willingly and not unwillingly, both in the present circumstances and in all future ones; for it is easy to infer from the present (ones) what those will be.

13 (65). Βροῦτος Βιθυνοῖς. Οἱ ἄκοντες ἡμῖν ὑπηρετοῦντες οὐχ ἃ μὴ βούλονται παρέχειν κερδαίνουσιν (ἀγαπητὸν γὰρ ἂν ἦν αὐτοῖς τοῦτό γε) ἀλλὰ τὴν ἐπ' ἐκείνοις χάριν, ἥτις ἂν αὐτοῖς ὠφείλετο ὑφ' ἡμῶν, ἀποβάλλουσι. κατασκευάσαντες οὖν τὰς ναῦς ὅνπερ τρόπον ἐπεστείλαμεν σὺν τοῖς ἐρέταις καὶ τῷ ὀφειλομένῳ σιτηρεσίῳ πέμψατε, ἢ ἀναγκασθήσεσθε οὐκ ἐπὶ τούτοις ἄχθεσθαι, ἀλλ' ὧν ἂν ὑπολίπωμεν χάριν ἡμῖν εἰδέναι.

Brutus to the Bithynians. Those who assist us against their will do not profit from what they do not wish to provide (they would be only too happy to do that):[42] instead they lose the gratitude that would be owing to them from us. So equip the ships as we ordered you, and send them together with the rowers and the due provision-money. Otherwise you will be obliged to thank us for whatever we leave you with, rather than to grumble at these things [i.e. what you are now having to give].

14 (67). Βροῦτος Βιθυνοῖς. Τὰ πλοῖα ἐγὼ πάντα ὅσων μοι ἔδει ἐν θαλάσσῃ ἔχω, παρασχόντων μοι Μακεδόνων καὶ

---

[41] Obscure: perhaps "I need ships more than letters from either you or Aquila, even if the ships come accompanied by complaints from you against him."
[42] I.e. they do not profit from keeping for themselves what they are expected to give to others, since any such profit is outweighed by the consequences of their reluctance.

Λεσβίων καὶ Φοινίκων. ὑμεῖς οὖν ἐπεὶ παρὰ τοὺς χειμῶνας αἰφνιδίως ἐπιπεσόντας ὑστερήσατε, τετρακόσιά μοι τάλαντα εἰς τὸ ἐπιβατικὸν αὐτῶν συγκομίσατε· νομίζω γὰρ εἰς μηδὲν ὑμῖν τούτων αἴτιον τὸν χειμῶνα γεγονέναι, ἐθελησάντων δὲ ὑμῶν ἐνοχλῆσαι.

Brutus to the Bithynians. I have all the ships I needed at sea, provided to me by the Macedonians, Lesbians, and Phoenicians. Since you were delayed by the sudden occurrence of storms, collect four hundred talents for the expenses of manning them. I do think, not that the storm was the reason for these actions of yours, but that you were happy for it to hinder you.

These five letters are long (none of them is less than fifty words) and detailed, and move from comparative mildness through a growing impatience to a demand for four hundred talents instead of the ships that have not arrived. They have been doubted on various grounds, one being that, when Dolabella was in Asia in early 43, he could not have received help from the Bithynians, as the republican Tillius Cimber was governing the province. But almost nothing is known about the chronology or location of Cimber's resistance: in mid-April, Brutus heard that "Dolabella has been cut to pieces and put to flight (*caesum fugatumque*) by Tillius and Deiotarus," but though this defeat may have hastened Dolabella's departure from Asia, the Bithynians could have aided him earlier in the year.[43] Another argument is that the Bithynian *koinon* did not have the competence to order the constituent cities to contribute to a war-effort; moreover, it only met once a year, and therefore could not have engaged in a sustained correspondence with Brutus. But in the circumstances of impending war neither Dolabella nor Brutus was likely to consider either the constitutional limitations of the Bithynian *koinon* or its regular schedule of meetings.[44] The Aquila of nos. 11 and 12 [61,

---

[43] For this argument, see Smith 1936:201. On Dolabella's defeat, see Cicero *Ad Brutum* 1.6.3 (Shackleton Bailey 1980, no. 12), translation in the text by Shackleton Bailey 2002:243; cf. Broughton 1952:349.

[44] For this argument, see Deininger 1966:365–69.

63], who to judge by the designation of "friend" is perhaps an agent or client of Brutus, is otherwise unknown. Q. Aquila was a junior officer in Caesar's fleet during the African campaign of 46, and would have been a suitable person to superintend the building of ships for Brutus, but if he is the same he must have gone over to the anti-Caesarian cause.[45]

2.2 Cyzicos[46]

15 (35). Βροῦτος Κυζικηνοῖς. Τὰ ἀπὸ Βιθυνίας ὅπλα παραπέμψατε μέχρι Ἑλλησπόντου, ἢ κατὰ γῆν ἐπιθέμενοι ἢ κατὰ θάλατταν, αἴσθοισθε δ' ἂν αὐτοὶ τῆς ῥᾴονος αὐτῶν κομιδῆς. εἰ μέντοι βραδύτερον ἢ δεῖ ἡμῖν ἔλθοι ὡς ἂν εἰ καὶ παράπαν φθαρείη ἢ καὶ ὑπὸ τοῖς πολεμίοις γένοιτο, ὑφ' ὑμῶν ἠδικῆσθαι δόξομεν.

Brutus to the Cyzicenes. Escort the armaments from Bithynia as far as the Hellespont, either loading them on land or by sea; you can determine which is the easier means of transport. If they reach us more slowly than they ought, and equally (?) if they are completely lost or indeed fall into enemy hands, we will hold that you have done us an injury.

16 (37). Βροῦτος Κυζικηνοῖς. Ἐκομίσθη τὰ ὅπλα καὶ εἰς ὃν ἐβουλόμεθα καιρόν. τῆς οὖν λειτουργίας ταύτης ἐν δέοντι γενομένης, ἀντιδίδομεν ὑμῖν τὴν Προκόννησον σὺν ταῖς ἐν αὐτῇ λιθουργίαις.

Brutus to the Cyzicenes. The armaments arrived, and by the time we wished. Since you performed this service in good time, in return we give you Proconnesos with its stone-quarries.

---

[45] [Anonymous] *Bellum Africum* 62.2, 63.2, 67.1; Broughton 1952:303. Pontius Aquila, tribune in 45 and one of the "tyrannicides," is out of the question, since he fell at Mutina (Münzer 1953a): Cicero (*Philippics* 12.20) mentions a *primus pilus* Aquila who received money from L. Antonius, and who might be identical with Caesar's naval officer (Münzer 1953b).

[46] Another letter to Cyzicos (no. 30 [39]: see below) was presumably written in 42.

Brutus' gift of Proconnesos to the Cyzicenes in reward for their services is mentioned nowhere else, and was presumably soon revoked by the triumvirs.[47] Like Pergamon, Cyzicus had been a fervent supporter of Julius Caesar, and, as happened in Pergamon, a leading citizen called Asclepiades brought troops to his aid in the Alexandrian War of 47. Again like Mithridates of Pergamon, Asclepiades must have earned privileges for his city, probably during Caesar's stay in Asia in 46.[48] It might seem surprising that Brutus relied so heavily on a city favored by Caesar, and that Cyzicus was so forthcoming with its help: possibly a faction had prevailed in favor of the tyrannicides, rather as the Caesarian Menodorus of Tralles was overthrown by supporters of Antony.

3. Early campaigning season, 42

The largest group of interconnected letters concerns the operations of Cassius in Rhodes and of Brutus in Lycia, presumably at the start of the campaigning season in 42; they imply that Cassius finished his operations before Brutus, as also does the narrative of Appian (*Bella civilia* 4.81, 341).

3.1 The Lycian League (Lycians)

Like the letters to Pergamon, those to the Lycian league are out of order in the vulgate. Nos. 17 (25) and 18 (27) represent a time after the fall of Xanthos but before the formal capitulation of the Lycian league;[49] nos. 19 (21) and 20 (23) show the league co-operating with Brutus in the attack on Rhodes.

> 17 (25). Βροῦτος Λυκίοις. Ξάνθιοι τὴν ἐμὴν εὐεργεσίαν
> ὑπεριδόντες τάφον τῆς ἀνοίας ἐσχήκασι τὴν πατρίδα,
> Παταρεῖς δὲ πιστεύσαντες ἑαυτοὺς ἐμοὶ οὐδὲν ἐλλείπουσι
> διοικοῦντες τὰ καθ᾽ ἕκαστα τῆς ἐλευθερίας. ἐξὸν οὖν καὶ
> ὑμῖν ἢ τὴν Παταρέων κρίσιν ἢ τὴν Ξανθίων τύχην ἑλέσθαι.

---

[47] On Proconnesos and its marble, see Danoff 1974; Karagianni 2012.

[48] *Inscriptiones Graecae ad Res Romanas Pertinentes* 4.159, with J. and L. Robert 1964:180–181, no. 227; cf. Jones 2010:117–118.

[49] Cf. Appian, *Bella civilia* 4.82 (345), "the Lycian league (*koinon*) sent ambassadors to Brutus promising its alliance and to contribute whatever it could."

Brutus to the Lycians. The Xanthians despised my good-will, and their city serves as the tomb of their madness, whereas the Patarans, who entrusted themselves to me, enjoy every degree of liberty in the administration of their affairs. It is therefore in your power too to choose between the decision of the Patarans and the fate of the Xanthians.

18 (27). Βροῦτος Λυκίοις. Ξανθίων τοὺς διαφυγόντας οἱ ὑποδεξάμενοι ὑμῶν οὐδὲν μετριώτερον πείσονται Ξανθίων, Παταρεῦσι δὲ καὶ Μυρεῦσι καὶ Κωρυκίοις καὶ Φασηλίταις, κἂν ἄλλο τι εὖ ποιεῖν ὑποδεξάμενοι αὐτοὺς ἐθέλωσιν, ἐπιτρέπω, ἵνα ὀρθῶς αὐτοῖς βεβουλεῦσθαι φίλους ἡμᾶς ἀλλὰ μὴ πολεμίους ἑλόμενοι ἔργῳ αἴσθωνται ὁρῶντες Ξανθίους.

Brutus to the Lycians. Those of you who shelter the refugees from Xanthos will get no milder treatment than the Xanthians. As for the peoples of Patara, Myra, Corycos and Phaselis, if they decide to do them a further kindness after receiving them, I give them leave (to do so) in order that, on seeing the Xanthians, they may understand from the facts that they made the right decision in opting to make us friends rather than enemies.

19 (21). Βροῦτος Λυκίοις. Ὅσα ὑμῖν ἐστὶ μηχανικὰ ὄργανα τειχομαχίας ἢ ναυμαχίας, ἐπὶ Καῦνον⁵⁰ παραπέμψατε Κασσίῳ, τῷ συνάρχοντί μου πορθοῦντι Ῥόδον, θᾶττον ἡμερῶν τριάκοντα ἀφ᾽ ἧς ἂν ἡμέρας τὴν ἐπιστολὴν ταύτην δέξησθε, ἵνα μὴ τοῖς κατ᾽ ἐκείνων ἡμῖν παρεσκευασμένοις ἀναγκασθῶμεν χρήσασθαι καθ᾽ ὑμῶν.

Brutus to the Lycians. Whatever equipment for sieges or sea-warfare you have you must send to Caunos within no more than thirty days from receipt of this letter for (the use of) my colleague Cassius, who is ravaging Rhodes.

---

⁵⁰ Καύνου mss., Καῦνον ms. Q (fifteenth century), presumably by inadvertence or conjecture, surely rightly: cf. no. 15 (35) above, τὰ ὅπλα παραπέμψατε μέχρι Ἑλλησπόντου.

Otherwise we shall be forced to use against you what we have prepared for use against them.

20 (23). Βροῦτος Λυκίοις. Αἱ μηχαναὶ ὑμῶν μετὰ τὸν πόλεμον, ὡς ἡ παροιμία, ἐκομίσθησαν. ἀλλ᾽ ὑμᾶς γε ἐπαινοῦμεν· οὐ γὰρ ὑστερήσατε εἰς ἣν ἐκελεύσαμεν προθεσμίαν, Κάσσιος δὲ ἔφθασεν.

Brutus to the Lycians. Your engines arrived after the war, as the saying is, but we thank you, since you did not miss the deadline we imposed, but Cassius anticipated it.

These letters show Brutus acting with cold calculation and brutal frankness. They present a stark contrast with one of the three principal sources, Plutarch. His account is designed to extenuate Brutus' conduct in his dealings with Xanthos, which was completely destroyed with huge loss of life (*Brutus* 30–32), and with Patara. According to Plutarch, whereas Cassius took Rhodes and "did not manage affairs kindly," Brutus "asked" the Lycians for money and an army, but "the demagogue Naucrates" persuaded the cities to revolt (*aphistasthai*).[51] Though he tried to win over the region with kindness, the most obstinate of the Lycians resisted and finally fled into Xanthos. When those inside the city set fire to the Roman siege-engines, a wind rose that ignited the nearby houses, and "Brutus, fearing for the city, gave orders for the fire to be put out and help to be given." However, "a fearful and irrational impulse to madness suddenly seized the Lycians, which one could best compare to a love of death, and while the Romans tried to extinguish the fire, they themselves threw reeds and brushwood down on them, and the fire spread. Thereupon Brutus rode around outside, calling for help, and stretched out his arms begging the Xanthians to spare and save the city." The "tragic sight" moved Brutus to tears, and "he offered a reward to any of his soldiers who could bring in a Lycian still living: and they say only a hundred and fifty failed to avoid being saved" (an

---

[51] The treaty struck between Rome and the Lycians in 46 (Mitchell 2005; *SEG* 55.1452), lines 78–79, now reveals this "demagogue" as present when the treaty was ratified in Rome (cf. Mitchell 2005:239–240), so that he must have been one of the leading citizens of Xanthos, a Caesarian heading the opposition to Brutus in 42.

awkward circumlocution for "were saved"). By contrast, the account of Appian has none of these pathetic scenes, and ends with the bald statement, "After saving as many of the sanctuaries as he could, Brutus took only slaves from among the Xanthians and from the citizens [literally, "males"] a few free women and not even a hundred and fifty men at most" (*Bella civilia* 4.76–80, 321–337). Dio's account is briefer still, but he too represents the event as a regular siege leading to the capture of the city and the mass suicide of the inhabitants (*Historia Romana* 47.34). Of the four cities mentioned in no. 18 (27), Corycos is the Lycian city later known as Olympos, not the better-known Cilician Corycos: it is hard to imagine a sophist lighting on this site when composing an imaginary letter. Caunos (no. 19 [21]) had a major port within the province of Asia, just over the western border of Lycia, and about fifty kilometers from the northern tip of Rhodes. It was the obvious place for sheltering ships and other material for use against the island. [52]

3.2 Patara, the port-city of Xanthos

All sources agree that Patara surrendered soon after the fall of Xanthos. In Plutarch's account (*Brutus* 32), Brutus hesitates to attack the city, fearing the same "desperation" (*aponoia*) as he had met at Xanthos, but he captured some Pataran women and set them free without ransom. These, the wives of leading citizens, returned to Patara, "described Brutus as a man of the greatest moderation and justice," and so persuaded their husbands to surrender the city. The accounts of Appian (*Bella civilia* 4.81, 339–343) and Dio (*Historia Romana* 47.34.4–6) do not differ as to the basic facts, though again they lack the pathetic coloring.

> 21 (17). Βροῦτος Παταρεῦσιν. Δαμάσιππον Ῥοδίων ναύ-
> αρχον μετὰ τὴν Ῥοδίων ἅλωσιν φυγόντα μετὰ δυεῖν
> καταφράκτων ἐπυθόμην παρὰ Ἑρμοδώρου τοῦ Σαμίου
> ἐμπόρου πεφηνέναι ἐν τῷ μεγίστῳ ὑμετέρῳ λιμένι.
> καταχθῆναι μὲν οὖν αὐτὸν ἐκεῖσε οὐδὲν ἁμάρτημα
> ὑμέτερον ἡγοῦμαι εἶναι, καταχθέντα δὲ εἰ περαιτέρω ποι

---

[52] For the two Corycoi, see Jüthner 1922a, 1922b; for the Lycian Corycos (Olympos), see *Barrington Atlas* 65D5; Adak 2004; Şahin and Adak 2007: 275–277, with Map 3 at end. For Caunos, see *Barrington Atlas* 65A4.

τῆς γῆς ὑμῶν ἀποδρᾶναι ἐάσετε, καὶ ἀδικίας καὶ ἀνανδρίας
ὑμῶν καταγνώσομαι.

Brutus to the Patarans. Damasippos, the Rhodian admiral,
so I have learned from Hermodoros the Samian captain,
fled with two cataphracts after the fall of Rhodes and
appeared in your largest harbor. The fact that he put in
there I do not consider any fault of yours: but if, after he
has put in, you allow him to escape further to any other
place on earth, I will count it against you both as injury
and as treachery.

Brutus' phrase, ἐν τῷ μεγίστῳ ὑμετέρῳ λιμένι, seems more likely
to be particularizing, "the largest of your harbors," rather than
descriptive, "your very large harbor." Many cities had plural harbors,
and though the Patarans' main harbor was certainly very large, they
could well have had other ones.[53] The name of the Rhodian *nauarchos*,
"Damasippos," is rare, and the *Lexicon of Greek Personal Names* knows of
only two examples in the Aegean islands, this one and a Damasippos
son of Socrates who appears on a list from Rhodes dated ca. 68 BCE.
Hermodoros, a "potamonym" derived from the Lydian river, is widely
attested in coastal Asia Minor, and another Hermodoros is known from
Samos.[54]

3.3 Myra

Myra in south-eastern Lycia receives two very threatening letters,
which imply a time after the fall of Xanthos; the first (no. 22 [43]) is
written before the Patarans' surrender and the second (no. 23 [45]) after
it, when the league was now allied with Brutus. According to Appian
(*Bella civilia* 4.82 [344]), Lentulus Spinther obtained the surrender of
Myra by breaking the chain that enclosed its port of Andriace.

---

[53] *Tituli Asiae Minoris* 2.1.142; Radke 1949:2556. For inscriptions from the reigns of
Nero and Vespasian referring to lighthouses of Patara, see *SEG* 2007.1672; for cities with
multiple harbors, see Robert 1960.

[54] For "Damasippos" on Rhodes, see *Inscriptiones Graecae* 12.1.46, line 185. For Hermodoros, see Athenaeus *Deipnosophistae* 606 C.

22 (43). Βροῦτος Μυρεῦσι. Ξάνθιοι ἁλόντες ἐλεεῖσθαι ὑφ’ ἡμῶν ἱκέτευον, ἦν δὲ οἶμαι χαλεπὸν τῆς ἐλπίδος τοῦ πολέμου κοινωνοῦντας φεύγειν τὰ πάθη, καὶ τὴν ἐκ τῆς νίκης ἡδονὴν θηρωμένους ἴσῃ εἰσχρῆσθαι τῇ διαμαρτίᾳ πρὸς τὸ ἄλυπον. καὶ τούτους οὖν ἐπιτηδείους παντελοῦς ἀπωλείας ἐθέμεθα, καὶ τοῖς ἄλλοις ἀποκηρύττομεν, εἰ μὴ εὐθέως ἡμᾶς δέχοιντο, μηδενὶ τὴν ἡμετέραν γνώμην ἐπιεικεστέραν τῆς ἐκείνων τύχης ἔσεσθαι.

Brutus to the Myrans. The Xanthian captives begged us for pity, but it was difficult, I think, that having shared in the hope of war[55] they should avoid its sufferings, and having sought the joy of victory should use the same mistake to (gain) impunity. We have accordingly judged them to be deserving of complete annihilation, and we forewarn the others, if they do not admit us immediately, that none of them will find our judgment more merciful than the fate of (the Xanthians) was.

23 (45). Βροῦτος Μυρεῦσι. Ἡ συμμαχία ὑμῶν ἧκεν ἤδη νενικηκόσιν ἡμῖν. τοῦ μὲν οὖν μηδ’ ὅλως τὸ βράδιον ἀφικέσθαι ἄμεινον, πρὸς μέντοι τὴν τοῦ πολέμου ὑπουργίαν ὁμοίως ἧτε ἄχρηστοι· ἡ γὰρ ἐν πολέμῳ βραδυτὴς ἴσον ἔχει τῷ μηδ’ ὅλως γενομένῳ τὸ ἄπρακτον.

Brutus to the Myrans. Your assistance has come when we are already victorious. To have arrived too late is better than not having arrived at all, but as far as assisting in the war-effort you have been no less useless. Arriving late in wartime is as fruitless as doing nothing at all.

3.4 Caunos

Brutus's two letters to Caunos imply that the city was cooperating with him, presumably in the campaign against Rhodes, but only reluctantly:

---

[55] That is, who had anticipated the defeat of the Romans.

this may refer to the war-equipment that he had ordered the Lycians to send there (no. 19 [21]).

24 (19). Βροῦτος Καυνίοις. Εὐνοεῖν μὲν ἡμῖν πρεσβευόμενοι προσποιεῖσθε, τὰ δὲ ἔργα εἰς οὐδὲν ὧν ἐχρῆν ἐσπουδακότας ἐλέγχει. ὁρᾶτε οὖν μὴ καὶ ἡμεῖς τῇ διὰ τῶν ἔργων πεισθέντες δυσμενείᾳ μᾶλλον ἢ τὴν ἐκ τῶν λόγων ἡδονὴν θηρώμενοι ὡς ἐχθροῖς ὑμῖν προσενεχθῶμεν.

Brutus to the Caunians. By sending ambassadors you pretend to be friendly, but your actions prove that you are not eager to do anything you ought. So be careful, or I may believe more in the malevolence of your actions than I find pleasure in your words, and so may treat you as enemies.

25 (31). Βροῦτος Καυνίοις. Αἱ μὲν κατ' ὄψιν ὑπουργίαι τῶν ὑπηκόων κολακείας καὶ φόβου τὸ πλέον μεμοίρανται, τὸ δὲ προθύμως εἰς ὃ ἂν ἐπιστέλλωμεν ὑπακούειν πολλὴν ἐνδείκνυται βεβαιότητα. καὶ ὑμεῖς οὖν ὑπὲρ ὧν ἐγράψαμεν διασκέψασθε πότερον ὑμῶν καὶ τὰς ἄλλας ὑπουργίας δι' ἀνάγκην ἁπάσας ἢ δι' εὔνοιαν χρὴ δέχεσθαι. πίστις γὰρ αὐτάρκης τῆς ἀεὶ βεβαιότητος φανεῖται τὸ διηνεκῶς ὑμῶν εἰς τὰς χρείας ἕτοιμον.

Brutus to the Caunians. Services performed by subjects when under observation are in general composed of flattery and fear, whereas ready willingness to perform our every command shows great reliability. You therefore must consider what we wrote, (and) whether I should understand your other services too (to have been) performed out of necessity or out of goodwill. It will seem an incontrovertible proof of your unfailing reliability if you are constantly ready to answer our needs.

3.5 Rhodes

Though the Rhodians appear in several of the letters, they receive only one, in which Brutus advises them to contrast the fates of Xanthos and Patara, and to deliberate for their own good. This implies a time after the fall of Xanthos but before or during Cassius' campaign. The Rhodians, like the Lycians, had supplied ships to Dolabella in early 43, and when Lentulus Spinther tried to bring them over to the republican cause their *boulē* refused to declare Dolabella an enemy (Appian *Bella civilia* 4.60 [258], 61 [264]; Lentulus in Cicero, *Ad familiares* 12.15.2–3 [Shackleton Bailey 1977, no. 406]). Brutus' letter must therefore be directed to the same body, which not surprisingly still hoped to avoid entanglement with the republicans.

26 (11). Βροῦτος 'Ροδίοις. Ξανθίους ἀποστάντας ἡμῶν χειρωσάμενοι ἡβηδὸν ἀπεσφάξαμεν, τήν τε πόλιν αὐτῶν κατεπρήσαμεν· Παταρεῦσι δὲ προσθεμένοις ἡμῖν τῶν τε φόρων ἄφεσιν ἐδώκαμεν, ἐλευθέρους αὐτοὺς καὶ αὐτονόμους συγχωρήσαντες εἶναι, εἰς ἐπισκευήν τε τῶν ὑπὸ τοῦ χρόνου καταλελυμένων παρ' αὐτοῖς πεντήκοντα τάλαντα ἐχαρισάμεθα. ὑμῖν οὖν βουλευομένοις περὶ ἑαυτῶν πάρεστιν ὁρᾶν ὄψει εἴτε χρὴ πολεμίους ἡμᾶς ὥσπερ Ξάνθιοι, εἴτε φίλους καὶ εὐεργέτας ὅνπερ τρόπον Παταρεῖς αἱρεῖσθαι.

Brutus to the Rhodians. When the Xanthians revolted from us, we subdued them, slew the adult population, and burned their city down; but when the Patarans surrendered to us, we gave them remission of tribute, allowed them to be free and autonomous, and granted them fifty talents to repair any of their buildings weakened by age. You too, therefore, when you deliberate about yourselves, can see with your own eyes whether you should choose us to be your enemies, as the Xanthians did, or to be your friends and benefactors, as the Patarans did.

3.6 Cos

Plutarch ends his account of the affairs of Lycia and Rhodes as follows: "Cassius had about the same time forced all the Rhodians to surrender the gold and silver that they owned individually (from which about eight thousand talents were collected), and fined the city publicly with another five hundred, whereas (Brutus) exacted a hundred and fifty talents from the Lycians, and without doing them any further harm left for Ionia" (*Brutus* 32.4; cf. Appian *Bella civilia* 4.82 [345]).[56] One letter to Cos (no. 27 [13]) comes from this time, and two others (nos. 28 [15], 29 [29]) may do so as well, though they may belong rather to the last stage of the war, when Brutus was mustering his allies in the Aegean.

27 (13). Βροῦτος Κώοις.   Ῥόδος μὲν ἤδη δεδούλωται Κασσίῳ, πόλις αὐθαδέστερον αἰσθομένη τῆς οἰκείας ἰσχύος ἢ βεβαιότερον, Λυκία δὲ ἡμῖν ὑπήκοος πᾶσα, ἡ μὲν πολέμῳ καμοῦσα, ἡ δ' ἐκ τῆς ἀνάγκης ὠφελημένη τὸ ἀβίαστον· ἑκοῦσα γὰρ εἵλετο ἃ μετ' οὐ πολὺ ἔμελλε μὴ βουλομένη. καὶ ὑμεῖς οὖν ἕλεσθε ἢ πολέμῳ βιασθέντες δοῦλοι ἢ ἑκουσίως ἡμᾶς δεξάμενοι φίλοι γενέσθαι.

Brutus to the Coans. Rhodes, a city that estimates its strength with more temerity than assurance, has already been enslaved by Cassius. All of Lycia is subject to us, part of it succumbing in war, part out of necessity earning immunity, for it chose to do voluntarily what it was destined soon to do involuntarily. You too therefore must choose to become slaves under the pressure of war, or to admit us voluntarily and become our friends.

28 (15). Βροῦτος Κώοις. Οὐδὲν οὔτε θαλάττης ἄνευ νεῶν οὔτε ἀγεωργήτου γῆς ὄφελος. πονήσατε οὖν περὶ τὰ σκάφη ὡς εἰ τῶνδε εἴητε ἄποροι, μηδὲν ἠπειρωτῶν πλέον ἐκ θαλάττης ὀνησόμενοι.

Brutus to the Coans. There is no profit from the sea without ships, nor from the land if it is untilled. So put effort into (providing) the vessels, since, if you are not able

---

[56] Pelling 1996:7, "the figure of 150 talents for Lycia is hard to believe."

to provide these, the sea will be as much good to you as (if you were) mainlanders.[57]

29 (29). Βροῦτος Κώοις. Οἱ πεμφθέντες ἐπὶ τὴν παρ' ὑμῶν συμμαχίαν ἀπήγγειλάν μοι τὰς ναῦς ὑμῶν ἄρτι κατασκευάζεσθαι· εἰ δὲ εἰς τὸν τοῦ πολέμου καιρὸν παρασκευάζεσθε, εἰς τί χρήσεσθε ταῖς παρασκευαῖς οὐκ οἶδα. τί γὰρ πλέον ἰσχύος ἀκαίρου, ἧς παντελὴς ἀσθένεια τὸ ἄχρηστον;

Brutus to the Coans. Those whom I sent to get your assistance have reported to me that your ships are only now under construction. If you are preparing them for the time of the war, I cannot see what use you expect to make of your preparations. For what is the use of untimely strength, which amounts to absolute weakness by being unused?

4. Summer–early fall, 42

After their campaigns against Lycia and Rhodes, Brutus and Cassius met in Sardis about the middle of 42, and deliberated before their final departure from Asia and the decisive campaign of Philippi (Plutarch *Brutus* 34–35; Dio *Historia Romana* 47.35.1). They left the province by transporting their forces from Abydos to Sestos in the Dardanelles (Appian *Bella civilia* 4.82 [345]). In Plutarch's words, once arrived in Thrace "Brutus had now made subjects of most of the nearby provinces, and if any city or dynast had been exempted, he collected all to the sea off Thrace" (*Brutus* 38.1), presumably using Maronea or another of the maritime cities as his base. This seems the background for a letter addressed to Cyzicos in the Hellespont and of some very short letters to cities situated in or on the Aegean.

---

[57] Apparently, "if you do not provide these, you will pay so dearly that you will no longer be a maritime community."

4.1 Cyzicos

30 (39). Βροῦτος Κυζικηνοῖς. Οἱ πρέσβεις ὑμῶν συνέτυχόν μοι ἀπιόντι ἐπὶ τὸν πόλεμον καὶ παρεῖσθαι τῆς συμμαχίας ἱκέτευον, ἀσθένειαν αἰτιώμενοι καὶ τὸ ἀπορεῖν τὰ κοινά. δίκαιον μὲν οὖν ἦν, πλησίον ἤδη τῆς χρείας κατεπειγούσης, καὶ εἰ πρότερον οὐκ ἔδοτε, κἂν νῦν ἐπιπέμψαι. πλέον γὰρ ἂν ἐτίμα τὴν λειτουργίαν ὑμῶν ὁ καιρός. ἐπεὶ δὲ ἐοίκατε τὴν κακίω τοῦ πολέμου προσλαβεῖν ἐλπίδα, τῇ μὲν ἀσθενείᾳ ὑμῶν ἣν αἰτιᾶσθε ἥδομαι (τοὐναντίον γὰρ ἂν ἠχθέσθην ἀκούων ἰσχύειν ὑμᾶς κακοὺς ὄντας), τοὺς δὲ ἄνδρας ὑμῶν συμμάχους μὲν οὐκέτι, ὑπουργοὺς δὲ καὶ ἄκοντας ἔξω. λέληθε δὲ ὑμᾶς οὐδαμῶς ὡς δεινὸν τῆς ἐκ τοῦ πολέμου μετασχεῖν νίκης, εἰ γένοιτο, τοὺς τὸ ἐφ᾽ ἑαυτοῖς εἰς πᾶσαν ἡμᾶς ἀσθένειαν προδόντας.

Brutus to the Cyzicenes. Your ambassadors met me as I was leaving for the war and begged to be exempted from the alliance, excusing you on the ground of your impoverishment and your lack of public funds. The need being so urgent, it would be proper for you to send further help even now, even if you did not give it before, because the timing would make the service more valuable. But since you seem to entertain an unfavorable expectation of the war, I am pleased by the impoverishment you allege (since on the contrary I would have been annoyed to hear that you were wealthy, treacherous as you are). Your fighting men I will no longer consider allies, but subordinates and recalcitrants. You surely must be aware that it would be strange (for you) to share in any victory in war that may occur, when to the best of your ability you have betrayed us into the utmost impoverishment.

4.2 Smyrna, Miletus, Samos

31 (41). Βροῦτος Σμυρναίοις. Τὸ πρόθυμον τῶν ὑπηκόων διηνεκὲς μὲν ὂν βεβαιότητα δηλοῖ πρὸς τοὺς ἡγεμόνας,

ἐλλεῖπον δὲ καὶ τὸν ὅτε ἑτοίμως ὑπουργεῖ χρόνον δι᾽ ἀσθένειαν ἐλέγχεται τὴν ἑαυτοῦ μᾶλλον ἢ γνώμην ὑπουργοῦν. σπουδάσατε οὖν ἐκπληρῶσαι ὅσα ὑμῖν ἐπέστειλα πρὸς τὸν πόλεμον, ὡς εἰ νῦν κακοὶ φανεῖσθε, μηδ᾽ ἣν πρόσθεν ἐπορίσασθε μαρτυρίαν ἔτι οἰσόμενοι· οὐ γὰρ χρὴ δοκεῖν ἕξειν τὰ ἴσα μὴ ὁμοίους ἀεὶ φανέντας.

Brutus to the Smyrnaeans. Unfailing zeal on the part of subordinates shows loyalty towards their leaders, but if it fails it is proved to have been obeying because of its own weakness rather than by design, even when it did so readily. Make an effort, then, to perform all I ordered you for (the purpose of) the war, since if you prove treacherous now you will no longer receive the credit that you earned before: for it cannot be expected that those who do not prove always consistent will get an equal reward.[58]

32 (47). Βροῦτος Μιλησίοις. Οὐδὲ χρημάτων πένεσθαι πόλει συγγνωστόν, ἐκ πολλοῦ γὰρ ὀφείλει φυλάττεσθαι τὸ ἄπορον· τὸ δὲ ἐν τοσούτῳ πλήθει μηδ᾽ ἄνδρας ὑμᾶς ἔχειν γενναίως ἀγωνιουμένους φῆσαι, παντελῶς ἴστε οὐ τύχης ἐνδεεῖς ἀλλὰ τῆς σωτηρίου γνώμης ἐλεγχόμενοι. εἰ δὲ μήτε ὅσα πρὸς ἰσχὺν παρασκευάζεσθε μήτε ὅσα εἰς ἀρετὴν ἀσκεῖτε, ἀδίκως ἴστε πόλις λεγόμενοι.

Brutus to the Milesians. It is not pardonable for a city to be poor in funds, since it should plan long in advance against poverty. But as for claiming not to have men who will fight bravely when your population is so large, you must know that that absolutely proves you to lack, not means, but a policy for survival. If you are not prepared in respect to strength nor trained in respect to courage, I must say that you do not deserve the name of city.

---

[58] I.e. those who are not consistently loyal are not rewarded equally with those who are.

33 (49). Βροῦτος Μιλησίοις. Εἰ μὲν ἔστιν ὑμῖν ὅπλα ἐν κοινῷ, μὴ χρώμενοι τούτοις ἁμαρτάνετε, μία γὰρ ἰσχὺς ὅπλων τὸ χρῆσθαι· εἰ δὲ καὶ τῆς κατασκευῆς αὐτῶν ἀμελεῖτε, μεμφθέντες ἂν εἰ καὶ ἔχοντες μὴ ἐχρῆσθε, πόσῳ μεμπτότεροι μηδὲ ἔχοντες;

Brutus to the Milesians. If you have arms in the public stock, you are wrong not to use them, since use is the one advantage of arms. But if you also neglect to manufacture them, considering that you would be blamed for not using them when you had them, how much more blameworthy are you for not even having them?

34 (69). Βροῦτος Σαμίοις. Αἱ βουλαὶ ὑμῶν ὀλίγωροι, αἱ ὑπουργίαι βραδεῖαι. τί τούτων τέλος ἐννοεῖσθε;

Brutus to the Samians. Your deliberations are negligent, your services slow. What do you expect will be the result?

4.3 Damas

Only one letter has an individual as its addressee. It urges a certain Damas either to send help or to make his position clear. "Damas," a hypocoristic or short form of a longer name such as "Damasistratos," seems to be unknown. He can hardly be the Rhodian Damasippos who put in at Patara after the fall of Rhodes (no. 21 [17]), but is perhaps a local dynast: thus the same citizen of Tabai who served as an assessor to Dolabella went on embassies to "dynasts."[59] According to Plutarch, Brutus "negotiated with the dynasts" (τοῖς δυνάσταις ἐχρημάτιζε, *Brutus* 28.3) after leaving Italy in 44, and also summoned "any city or dynast who had been exempted" (παρεῖτο) in the months before Philippi (*Brutus* 38.1). This letter could come from either time.

35 (33). Βροῦτος Δαμᾷ. Ὅπλων καὶ χρημάτων χρεία. ἢ πέμπε ἢ ἀποφαίνου.

---

59 Citizen of Tabai: above, n. 35.

Brutus to Damas. Arms and money are needed. Either send (them) or make your position clear.

IV. ARE BRUTUS' LETTERS AUTHENTIC?

The problems raised by the collection can never be solved in their entirety, and a final decision as to the authenticity of the letters ascribed to Brutus will vary with individual inclinations to credulity or skepticism. But it is paradoxical that ancient readers such as Plutarch, the "critic" Marcianus, and a member of a highly literary Athenian family should have had no doubt about the authenticity of these letters (even though they allowed for the possibility of an amanuensis), whereas modern scholars can pronounce with decision that they are sophistic exercises. The modern impression may be due in part to the practice of printing Brutus' letters and the supposed replies as if there were no difference between them, whereas Mithridates states clearly that the replies are his own invention.[60]

In the commentary (Section III), I have argued that there is nothing in the historical content of the letters that contradicts their authenticity. A different question concerns their style. How likely is it that a commander such as Brutus, writing in a period of emergency, would have used a form of "Laconian brachylogy" sometimes so compressed as to make his meaning ambiguous? It is perhaps this feature that led ancient critics such as Mithridates and the younger Philostratus to suggest that he employed an amanuensis, to whom they perhaps supposed that he indicated his general meaning, and then left him to put it into compressed but stylish Greek. Such assistants are abundantly attested in the history of ancient letter-writing: Caesar is said to have been able to write letters on horseback, and to have used two or more amanuenses simultaneously (Plutarch *Caesar* 17.7).

Caesar's amanuenses clearly wrote at dictation, and if Brutus did have such an assistant, he too could have used the person merely as a scribe, for like other Romans of his time he was a Hellenophile and fully

---

[60] The *Thesaurus Linguae Graecae* deepens the impression by separating Mithridates' letter ("Epistula Mithridatis") from the body of the letters.

fluent in Greek. He was trained in philosophy by a brother of Antiochus of Ascalon, Aristos, who sometimes lived in his house (Plutarch *Brutus* 2.3), and he had spent part of his student days in Athens.[61] The salient question is why he should have adopted a style of "Laconian brachylogy" rather than a more expansive one. Not all of the letters are in fact very laconic: the two letters concerning Menodorus of Tralles, for example (nos. 8 [55], 9 [57]), run to over fifty words each, and are comparable to the letters of Mithridates VI about Chaeremon. But as well as being a Hellenophile, Brutus was a Laconophile. His estate at Lanuvium had a "Eurotas" and a "Persian Portico" (named after the portico set up at Sparta after the Persian Wars), and he may have called the whole estate "Lacedaemon."[62]

Ancient theorists of style were interested in the effect of brachylogy. Thus "Demetrius" in his tractate *On Style*: "Small *cōla* are used also in cases of intensity [*deinotēs*, a word used by Mithridates of Brutus' style], for it is more intense to say much in a short space and more vigorous. That is why the Spartans are given to brevity (*brachylogia*), because of vigor. Orders are given tersely and briefly, and every master speaks to his slave in monosyllables" (7).[63] "The Spartans were given to brevity, for brevity is more intense and imperious, but lengthy speech suits supplication and begging" (242). So also the younger Philostratus: "The elegance of (letter-writing) should lie in avoidance of figures of speech, for if we use them we will seem to be showing off, and it is puerile to show off in a letter. In briefer letters I permit the polishing of a period (*kuklon apotorneuein*), so that brevity can show off in this respect at least, being entirely limited as to sound-effect" [or reading πᾶσαν, "being limited as to all (other) sound-effects"].

---

[61] It is perhaps worth remarking how frequently words with the root δικ-, referring to (in)justice or injury, occur in Brutus' letters: nos. 1, 17, 35, 39, 41, 51, 57.

[62] On Brutus' student days, see Aurelius Victor *De viris illlustribus* 82.1. On his estate, see Cicero *Ad Atticum* 15.9.1 (Shackleton Bailey 1965–1970, no. 387), with Shackleton Bailey's commentary, 1967–1970, 6.256; Gelzer, 1918:974–975.

[63] Demetr. *Eloc.* 241–242 (Chiron 1993:68). Cf. the centurion in the *Gospel of Matthew* 8:9: "For I am a man under authority, with soldiers under me; and I say to one, 'Go,' and he goes, and to another, 'Come,' and he comes, and to my slave, 'Do this,' and he does it" (Revised Standard Version).

Brutus was not therefore aiming simply at linguistic bravura, like Caesar with his famous *ueni, uidi, uici,* but at a style that was all the more "intense" for being brief. Brevity could also be effective in conveying menace, as when Brutus tells the Lycians to help Cassius, "so that we are not compelled to use against you the materials prepared by us against them" (no. 19 [21]). It is also likely that messages such as these were brought by personnel, solders or trusted civilians, who would amplify them verbally and report back on what they had seen. Thus when Brutus writes to the Trallians, "It has been reported to me that Menodorus previously persuaded you ... and is now advising you" (no. 8 [55]), or to the Coans (no. 29 [29]), "Those whom I sent to get your assistance have reported to me ...," these reports could well have come from messengers whom Brutus himself had sent to the cities.

Another motive for brevity was lack of time. As already noted, Brutus writing to Cicero in 43 says that "anxiety and vexation make it impossible for me to write at length, nor do I have to," and Cicero wrote in reply to another message, "Your short letter—I say 'short,' but it was not really a letter at all. Does Brutus only write me three lines in times like these? Better nothing at all."[64] As well as being amplified by messengers or representatives, it is possible that such brief notes made their effect by being read out in public or posted up, not in paper form but on a whitened board (*leukōma, album*). If that happened, they would have met the intended purpose not so much by their explicit content but by the compressed, enigmatic language with its menacing implications.[65]

The very gruffness, amounting almost to brutality, that emerges from certain of the Greek letters is perhaps one of the strongest arguments in their favor. This is not the "moderate and just" Brutus of Plutarch, the "honorable man" of Shakespeare's *Julius Caesar*: this is the hard, practical Roman known from the letters of Cicero, for instance in the matter of his agent Scaptius. In writing to Atticus to complain

<hr/>

[64] Cicero *Ad Brutum* 1.13.2 (Shackleton Bailey no. 20), 1.14.1 (Shackleton Bailey no. 22), all with Shackleton Bailey's translation. Cf. the brief and menacing letters of Bar Kokhba, Yardeni 2000:66–69, nos. 166–182.

[65] For the use of wood for inscriptions, see Eck 1998; on inscriptions as "symbolic writing," see Beard 1985:139–141.

about Brutus' extortionate demands on the Salaminians of Cyprus, Cicero says: "Brutus, who writes about me so kindly to you, is apt in his letters to me to take a brusque, arrogant, ungracious tone even when he is asking a favor" (*qui de me ad te humanissimas litteras scripsit, ad me autem, etiam cum rogat aliquid, contumaciter, adroganter,* ἀκοινωνήτως *solet scribere*).[66] "Brusque, arrogant, ungracious" exactly describes these letters addressed to Greek communities in Brutus' last months.

The formation of the collection remains a mystery. Mithridates appears to have started from a collection of thirty-five letters, which he supposed Brutus to have published. Though Brutus certainly published works of his own, philosophic treatises as well as speeches, he could hardly have published these letters amid the press of war. The most probable source is someone who had access to copies of the originals made before they were sent off, that is, someone on Brutus' own staff or among his Greek friends. One such friend is the rhetor Empylos who published a short work *On the Killing of Caesar*. Perhaps more likely is another rhetor, Strato, who helped Brutus commit suicide and later accompanied Augustus at Actium.[67] At some unknown date, but probably in the reign of Augustus, yet another rhetor, the famous Potamo of Mitylene, composed an *Encomium of Brutus* as well as an *Encomium of Caesar* (perhaps Julius Caesar rather than Augustus).[68]

Cicero in the *Verrines* refers to companies of *publicani* maintaining registers of letters sent and received, *libri litterarum missarum* or *adlatarum*, which he was able to consult before preparing his brief (*Verrines* 2.3.167). Apart from the many archives of correspondence preserved on papyrus, such as those of the estate-manager Zeno of Caunos, some papyri contain letter-registers similar to those mentioned by Cicero. A notable instance from the last years of the third century CE is the roll containing letters to and from Apollinarius, *stratēgos* of the Panopolite nome, which sometimes display a sharpness

---

[66] Cicero *Ad Atticum* 6.1.7 (Shackleton Bailey 1965–1970, no. 115) with Shackleton Bailey's translation. Cf. Badian 1996, "Arrogant, rapacious, calculatingly ambitious, Brutus yet professed a deep attachment to philosophy."

[67] Empylos: Plutarch *Brutus* 2.4: *FGrHist* 191. Strato: Plutarch *Brutus* 52.3, 53.1; Münzer 1931.

[68] Suda s.v. Ποτάμων, 4.181–182 Adler.

reminiscent of the letters of Brutus. Thus the procurator Aurelius Isidorus minces no words when writing to Apollinarius: "Well and truly, and continuing right up to the present moment, you have been proved guilty, both by the monthly accounts sent in to my office and by the second survey carried out before the *Decemprimi* of the nome under your rule, of acting to the detriment of the most sacred Treasury, and the same I have myself inferred from the reports drawn up in my office. At another time I might have pardoned what has occurred; but now, in order that both you yourself and equally they may render account of such behaviour, do you imprison all the *Decemprimi* in the city, and confine them there until the arrival of my lord Domnus, the most eminent Catholicus. I bid you farewell, for many years." A register of sent letters survives from the Fayum in the third century BCE. Like those in the present collection, it contains only the names of the addressee in the dative and no formula of greeting or farewell, for example:

> To Amōeēs. Having read the account of the safflower-growing land, I find that you have not sown any part (of it). I swear by all the gods, if on immediate receipt of this letter you do not [the last few words are missing].[69]

A feature of Brutus' letters that tells against their being composed by Mithridates or some other impersonator is their lack of order: there is a tendency to group them by recipient, but while some of those groups, such as the letters to the Bithynians (nos. 10–14 [59–67]) are in chronological order, others such as those to Pergamon (nos. 1, 7, 3, 5, 9 [1–9]) and to the Lycian league (nos. 19, 20, 17, 18 [21–27]) are clearly not. This same lack of order is observable in the Latin correspondence of Cicero and Brutus. If Mithridates wrote his prefatory letter and his imaginary replies in the first century of the Christian era, as seems likely, then Plutarch and others might have had the original version, or may have known the letters in Mithridates' compilation and simply ignored his additions.

---

[69] For Panopolis, see Skeat 1964, no. 2 lines 68–71, with Skeat's translation. For the Fayum, see Preisigke 1915:341, no. 4369b36–40.

Such an unabashed interest in Brutus' writings is not surprising, despite his role as the chief conspirator against Julius Caesar. One of Horace's earliest *Satires* alludes without embarrassment to Brutus' role as a tyrant-slayer; Cornelius Nepos, writing early in the reign of Augustus, speaks with equal freedom of Atticus' close friendship with Brutus and of the aid he gave to him, his family, and his friends. Two well-known incidents in the reign of Tiberius suggest that public commemoration of Brutus was at that time suspect. When Junia, the half-sister of Cato and Brutus's mother, died in the year 22, the busts of Brutus and Cassius were conspicuous by their absence from her funeral procession, and in 25 the historian Cremutius Cordus was condemned for having called the same two "the last of the Romans." But these are public events at Rome in the reign of a suspicious Caesar and offer little guidance to what was permitted in literature; Cordus claimed that many had recounted the deeds of Brutus and Cassius, mentioning them "with honor." Nearly a century later, the atmosphere had changed. The eminent equestrian Titinius Capito set up portraits of Brutus, Cassius, and Cato at home, though he was not able to do so in public.[70] His contemporary Plutarch designed his biography of Brutus so as to put his hero in as favorable a light as possible.

Other arguments against the authenticity of the letters are not strictly answerable, in so far as they depend in large part on subjective judgment. Erasmus, and after him Bentley, considered them declamatory or sophistic. But their style is not at all declamatory, and Bentley's imagined scenario, whereby "the Sophistae searched a little into the histories of the person they designed to personate, and so adapted their letters to their circumstances," seems to come from his own fertile imagination; though the schools of rhetoric emphasized the composition of imaginary speeches, treatises such as those of the rhetorician Theon suggest that imaginary letters were a very minor part of the curriculum.[71]

---

[70] See Horace *Satires* 1.7.32–35. For Junia, see Tacitus *Annals* 3.76. For Cremutius Cordus, see Tacitus *Annals* 4.34. For Titinius Capito, see Pliny *Letters* 1.17.

[71] Theon *Prog.* 2.115.22 ed. Spengel. I hope to return to this subject elsewhere.

Rawson considered the letters "exaggeratedly brief, unremittingly gnomic and antithetic," and therefore impossible for a Roman general. But that was not the impression they made on Plutarch, who quotes the first letter in the series (no. 1 ([1]), one of the most compressed and "antithetic," in full. Nor is it possible to separate those letters that have the closest relation to actual circumstances from those that are "gnomic and antithetic." Thus Brutus' first letter concerning Menodorus of Tralles, one of the longest in the series (no. 8 [55]), uses several antitheses, one of which serves as the closing threat:

ξένον καὶ φίλον / τῷ ἡμετέρῳ πολεμίῳ

ἐν τῇ ὑμετέρᾳ / τῇ πόλει

τοῦ ἰδίου λυσιτελοῦς ἕνεκα / εἴ γέ τι λυσιτελεῖν ἔμελλεν

φυγαδεῦσαι τῆς πατρίδος / τὴν πατρίδα πωλοῦντι

ἀπειθοῦντας οὐχ ὑπὸ Μηνοδώρου ταῦθ' ὑμᾶς οἰήσομαι προαχθέντας πεισθῆναι / ἀλλ' αὐτοὺς Μηνοδώρῳ τούτων ἀφορμὴν δοῦναι ἐθέλοντας.

In conclusion, the Greek letters ascribed to Brutus in the manuscripts, as opposed to the replies written by the unidentifiable Mithridates, contain nothing that impugns their authenticity, at least as far concerns the historical situation. They also contain details that it is hard to imagine a "sophist" or other fabricator inventing out of his imagination: the names "Damasippos" for a Rhodian admiral and "Menodoros" for a prominent Trallian, the reference to the minor Lycian town of Corycos as having surrendered along with Myra, Patara, and Phaselis. The Laconic compression also suits one who had a Greek education and owned an estate called "Lacedaemon." Above all, the tone of the letters, "brusque, arrogant, ungracious," befits the real Brutus rather than the mild student of the Academy so memorably depicted by Plutarch.

APPENDIX: THE LETTER OF MITHRIDATES

Μιθριδάτης βασιλεῖ Μιθριδάτῃ τῷ ἀνεψιῷ χαίρειν.

(1). Τὰς Βρούτου ἐθαύμασα πολλάκις ἐπιστολάς, οὐ μόνον δεινότητος καὶ συντομίας χάριν, ἀλλὰ καὶ ὡς ἡγεμονικοῦ φρονήματος ἐχούσας χαρακτῆρα· ἐοίκασι γὰρ οὐδὲν νομίζειν καλόν, εἰ μὴ καὶ μεγαλοψυχίας ἔχοιτο. ἐγὼ δ' ἃ μὲν περὶ τῶν τοιούτων φρονῶ λόγων οὐδ' ἐν τῷδε ἀξιῶ διαμφισβητεῖν· ἀποφαίνοντος δὲ σοῦ δυσαποκρίτως αὐτὰς ἔχειν, ᾠήθην δεῖν πεῖραν ποιήσασθαι τῆς ἀντιγραφῆς καὶ πορίσασθαι λόγους, οἵους εἰκὸς ἦν ἕκαστον ἀποκρίνασθαι τῶν ἐπεσταλκότων. ἦν δὲ δυσεύρετος ἡ ἐπιβολὴ κατ' ἄγνοιαν τῆς τότε περὶ τὰς πόλεις τύχης τε καὶ γνώμης· οὐ μὴν ταύτῃ γε ἀνῆκα τὴν ὁρμήν, ἀλλὰ τὰ μὲν ἐξ ἱστοριῶν ἐπιλεξάμενος, τὰ δὲ ταῖς δευτέραις καὶ τρίταις ἐπιστολαῖς ὑποσημαίνεσθαι περὶ τῶν προτέρων συνεὶς οὐχ ἥκιστα παρέζευξα καὶ τὸν ἐξ ἐπινοίας κατάλογον.

(2). φύσει δέ πως δυσχερὲς ἀποβαίνει τὸ εἰς ἀλλοτρίαν συνδραμεῖν εὐστοχίαν, ὁπότε καὶ ἰδίαν χαλεπὸν ἀναλογῆσαι. ὁ γοῦν Βροῦτος μυρίας ὡς εἰκὸς ἄνδρα πολλοῖς ἔθνεσι πολεμοῦντα διαπρεσβευσάμενος ἐπιστολάς, εἴτε ἰδίας εἴτε τινὸς τῶν εἰς ταῦτα μισθοῦ δοκίμων, μόνας ἐξέδωκε τὰς εὐφόρως γραφείσας διὰ τὸ ἀρκέσαι ταῖς ὀλίγαις μόλις τὴν διόρθωσιν. ὁπότε οὖν ἐκεῖνος ἠσθένησεν ἑαυτὸν ἐν πᾶσι μιμήσασθαι, πῶς οἷόν τε ἡμᾶς ἑτέρῳ ἐξομοιωθῆναι καὶ τῇ κατὰ σφᾶς ὁμοτονῆσαι προθέσει;

(3). ἀλλά πως γλυκὺ πάθος ἐλπίς, οὐ τῇ ἐπιτυχίᾳ δελεάζουσα μόνον, κολακεύουσα δὲ καὶ τὸ ἀπότευγμα, δι' ἣν οὐδενὸς ἄλλου λείπεσθαι δικαιῶ μάλιστά σοι χαριεῖσθαι. ἐπεὶ κἀκεῖνό με οὐ λέληθεν, ὅτι ὃ μὲν πολλοῖς ἀνδράσι καὶ δήμοις γράφων εἰκότως ἑνὸς ἐξείχετο χαρακτῆρος, ὃ δὲ ὑπὲρ πολλῶν διαλεγόμενος, ἐὰν μὲν ἀλλάσσῃ τὸν τύπον, ἀποπεπλανῆσθαι δόξει τοῦ σκοποῦ, τῇ δὲ αὐτῇ προσέχων ἰδέᾳ καὶ ἀπίθανος φανήσεται καὶ ἕωλος.

(4). ἔτι πρὸς τούτοις ἐνθυμητέον, ὡς ἡγεμόνος μὲν ἴδιον οἴονταί τινες τὰ γέμοντα ὑπεροψίας ἐπιστέλλειν τοῖς ὑπηκόοις, ἡμῖν δ' ἡ αὐθάδης ἀντιγραφὴ κατάγνωσιν ὡς ἠλιθίοις φέρει, τὸ δὲ ταπεινὸν οὐκέτ' ἀναλογεῖ πρὸς τὴν ὁμοίαν ἀπόκρισιν. ὅμως δ' οὖν τὰ δυσχερῆ καίπερ τοσαῦτα ὄντα προεκλογισάμενος οὐδὲν ἧττον ὑπέστην τὸ ἔργον, βραχὺ μὲν ἐμαυτῷ γύμνασμα συντάξας, σοὶ δὲ οὐ μέγα κτῆμα, ἀλλὰ τοῖς πολλοῖς τάχα καὶ εὐκαταφρόνητον· φιλεῖ γὰρ τὰ πρὸ τῆς πείρας θαυμαστὰ μετὰ τὴν ἐκ τοῦ συντελέσματος γνῶσιν ῥᾴδια εἶναι παραθεωρεῖσθαι.

Mithridates to his cousin King Mithridates, greetings.

(1). I have often admired the letters of Brutus, not only for their intensity[72] and compression, but because they show the stamp of a leader's mind: for they seem to consider nothing honorable that is not also combined with magnanimity. I do not think this is the place to argue my own opinion on such topics, but when you expressed the opinion that the letters were hard to answer, I thought I ought to make a try at replying to them, and at finding the arguments that each of the writers might plausibly have used when answering. My ignorance about the situation and feelings of the individual cities made the undertaking difficult, but even so I did not give up the attempt. I gathered some materials from histories, and others, so I observed, were suggested by the second and third letters referring to the previous ones, so that to no small degree I could subjoin the arguments that I had reached by inference.

(2). It is somehow intrinsically difficult to match the felicitous language of another, considering that it is difficult even to attain one's own. Brutus of course, as a man making war against many regions, conducted diplomacy

[72] For this sense of *deinotēs*, see LSJ s.v. III.

through countless letters, whether written by himself or by someone skilled at doing such things for pay, but published only those that were skillfully written, since he was barely able to polish a few. Considering therefore that he himself was not up to an absolutely consistent style, how was it possible for me to take on the semblance of another and do justice to my intention?

(3). But hope is a pleasant feeling, and as well as enticing by (the prospect of) success, it flatters failure too, and it leads me to claim to be as good as anybody in my attempt to give you very great pleasure. I am also aware that someone writing to many men and to many peoples naturally maintains a single style, but someone arguing on behalf of many, if he varies his style, will appear to have failed in his aim, while by adhering to the same style he will seem both implausible and tiresome.

(4). This too needs remembering: that some people consider it the mark of a leader to write to his subjects in language brimming with pride, while if I reply insolently I will be condemned for my folly: and yet humility is inconsistent with a reply in kind. Still, after considering in advance the difficulties, numerous as they are, I have nonetheless undertaken the task, composing a slight essay for my own benefit and no great treasure for yours, and one perhaps contemptible in most people's eyes. For what looks admirable before the attempt, when observed after completion, is all too easy to despise.

HARVARD UNIVERSITY

ABBREVIATIONS

Barrington Atlas. R. J. A. Talbert, ed. 2000. *Barrington Atlas of the Greek and Roman World.* Princeton.

FGrHist. F. Jacoby. 1923–1958. *Die Fragmente der griechischen Historiker.* Repr. Leiden 1954–1969.

LSJ[9]. H. G. Liddell, R. Scott, and H. S. Jones. 1996. *A Greek-English Lexicon.* 9th ed. Oxford.

OGIS. W. Dittenberger, ed. 1903–1905. *Orientis Graeci Inscriptiones selectae.* Leipzig.

PIR. E. Groag, A. Stein, et al., eds. *Prosopographia Imperii Romani.* Berlin.

RE. G. Wissowa, et al., eds. 1893–1980. *Paulys Realencyclopädie der classischen Altertumswissenschaft.* Stuttgart.

SEG. J. J. Hondius et al., eds. *Supplementum Epigraphicum Graecum.* 1923–. Amsterdam.

WORKS CITED

Achelis, T. O. 1917–1918. "Erasmus über die griechischen Briefe des Brutus." *Rheinisches Museum* 72:633–638.

Adak, M. 2004. "Lokalisierung von Olympos und Korykos in Ostlykien." *Gephyra* 1:27–51.

Allen, P. S., and H. M. Allen, eds. 1922. *Opus epistolarum Des. Erasmi Roterdami.* Oxford.

Badian, E. 1996. "Iunius Brutus (2), Marcus." In *The Oxford Classical Dictionary* (3rd ed.), ed. S. Hornblower, 788. Oxford.

Beard, M. 1985. "Diversity and Expansion in the Arval Acta." *Papers of the British School at Rome* 53:114–162.

Bentley, R. 1883. *Dissertation on the Epistles of Phalaris.* Ed. W. Wagner. London.

Bowersock, G. W. 1965. *Augustus and the Greek World.* Oxford.

Broughton, T. R. S. 1952. *The Magistrates of the Roman Republic.* 2 vols. New York.

Chiron, P. 1993. *Démétrios. Du style.* Paris.

Danoff, C. 1974. "Prokonnesos." In *RE Supplementband* 14:560–561.

Deininger, J. 1966. "Brutus und die Bithynier. Bemerkungen zu den sog. griechischen Briefen des Brutus." *Rheinisches Museum* 109:356–372.

Drumann, W., and P. Groebe. 1899–1929. *Geschichte Roms in seinem Übergange von der republikanischen zur monarchischen Verfassung.* 6 vols. Berlin.

Eck, W. 1998. "Inschriften auf Holz: Ein unterschätztes Phänomen der epigraphischen Kultur Roms." In *Imperium Romanum: Studien zur Geschichte und Rezeption*, ed. P. Kneissl and V. Losemann, 203–217. Stuttgart.

Fröhlich, F. 1899. "C. Cassius Longinus." In *RE* 3:1727–1736.

Gelzer, M. 1918. "M. Iunius Brutus." In *RE* 10:973–1020.

Goldstein, J. A. 1968. *The Letters of Demosthenes.* New York.

Habicht, Ch. 1969. *Die Inschriften des Asklepieions.* Altertümer von Pergamon 8.3. Berlin.

Hamilton, J. R. 1969. *Plutarch, Alexander: A Commentary.* Oxford.

Hepding, H. 1909. "Mithridates von Pergamon." *Athenische Mitteilungen* 34:329–340.

Hercher, R. 1873. *Epistolographi Graeci.* Paris.

Herrmann, P. 1974. "Cn. Domitius Ahenobarbus, Patronus von Ephesos und Samos." *Zeitschrift für Papyrologie und Epigraphik* 14:257–258.

Jones, C. P. 1974. "Diodoros Pasparos and the Nikephoria of Pergamon." *Chiron* 4:183–205.

———. 2010. "Ancestry and Identity in the Roman Empire." In *Local Knowledge and Microidentities in the Roman Empire*, ed. T. Whitmarsh, 111–124. Cambridge.

———. 2011. "An Inscription seen by Agathias." *Zeitschrift für Papyrologie und Epigraphik* 179:107–115.

Jüthner, J. 1922a. "Korykos 3." In *RE* 11.1451–1452.

———. 1922b. "Korykos 4." In *RE* 11.1452–1453.

Karagianni, A. 2012. "The Harbor of Proconnesus in Greco-Roman and Early Byzantine Times." http://e-a-a.org/TEA/archive/TEA_36_WINTER_2011_2012/rep4_36.pdf (accessed December 20, 2012).

Kayser, C. L. 1870–1871. *Flavii Philostrati opera auctiora.* 2 vols. Leipzig.

Kolb, A. 2000. *Transport und Nachrichtentransfer im römischen Reich.* Berlin.

Kreiler, B. M. 2008. "Bemerkungen zu den Statthaltern der Provinz Asia am Ende der Republik." *Gephyra* 5:33–50.

Magie, D. 1950. *Roman Rule in Asia Minor.* 2 vols. Princeton.

Mitchell, S. 2005. *Papyri Graecae Schøyen (PSchøyen 1).* Papyrologica Florentina 35. Florence.

Moles, J. L. 1997. "Plutarch, Brutus and Brutus' Greek and Latin Letters." In *Plutarch and his Intellectual World,* ed. J. Mossman, 141–168. London.

Münzer, F. 1900. "P. Cornelius Dolabella." In *RE* 4.1300–1308.

———. 1903. "Cn. Domitius Ahenobarbus." In *RE* 5:1327–1331.

———. 1931. "Straton (16)." In *RE* 4A:315.

———. 1953a. "Pontius Aquila." In *RE* 22:34–36.

———. 1953b. "Pontius Aquila." In *RE* 4A:36.

Nogara, A. 1991. "Una testimonianza sulle *Epistole greche* di Bruto nella *Bibliotheca* di Fozio." *Aevum* 65:111–113.

Oliver, J. H. 1989. *Greek Constitutions of Early Roman Emperors from Inscriptions and Papyri.* Memoirs of the American Philosophical Society 178. Philadelphia.

Pelling, C. B. R. 1996. "The Triumviral Period." In *Cambridge Ancient History,* vol. 10 (2nd ed.), ed. A. K. Bowman, E. Champlin, and A. Lintott, 1–69. Cambridge.

Preisigke, F. 1915. *Sammelbuch griechischer Urkunden aus Ägypten.* Vol. 1. Strasbourg.

Radke, G. 1949. "Patara." In *RE* 18.2.2555–2561.

Rawson, E. 1986. "Cassius and Brutus: The Memory of the Liberators." In *Past Perspectives: Studies in Greek and Historical Writing,* ed. I. S. Moxon, 101–119. Cambridge.

Reitzenstein, D. 2012. "Der Lykische Bund, die Städte des Xanthostals und Rom in späthellenisticher Zeit." In *Communautés locales et pouvoir central dans l'Orient hellénistique et romain,* ed. C. Feyel et al., 429–450. Nancy.

Reynolds, J. M. 1982. *Aphrodisias and Rome: Documents from the Excavation of the Theatre at Aphrodisias.* London.

Robert, J., and L. Robert. 1964. "Bulletin épigraphique." *Revue des études grecques* 77:127–259.

Robert, L. 1937. *Etudes anatoliennes: Recherches sur les inscriptions grecques de l'Asie Mineure.* Paris.

———. 1960. "Λιμένες." *Hellenica: Recueil d'épigraphie, de numismatique, et d'antiquités grecques* 11/12:263–266.

———. 1966. "Inscriptions d'Aphrodisias: Première partie." *L'Antiquité Classique* 35:377–432.

———. 1984. "Documents d'Asie Mineure." *Bulletin de Correspondance Hellénique* 108:457–532.

———. 1987. *Documents d'Asie Mineure.* Paris.

———. 1989. *Opera minora selecta: Épigraphie et antiquités grecques.* Vol. 6. Amsterdam.

Robert, L., and J. Robert. 1954. *La Carie: Histoire et géographie historique avec le recueil des inscriptions antiques.* Paris.

Rostovtzeff, M. I. 1953. *The Social and Economic History of the Hellenistic World.* Rev. P. M. Fraser. Oxford.

Şahin, S., and M. Adak. 2007. *Stadiasmus Patarensis: Itinera Romana Provinciae Lyciae.* Gephyra Monographien 1. Istanbul.

Shackleton Bailey, D. R. 1965–1970. *Cicero's Letters to Atticus.* 7 vols. Cambridge.

———. 1977. *Cicero. Epistulae ad familiares.* 2 vols. Cambridge.

———. 1980. *Cicero. Epistulae ad Quintum Fratrem et M. Brutum.* Cambridge.

———. 2002. *Cicero. Letters to Quintus and Brutus.* Cambridge, MA.

Sherk, R. K. 1969. *Roman Documents from the Greek East.* Baltimore.

Skeat, T. C. 1964. *Papyri from Panopolis.* Dublin.

Smith, R. E. 1936. "The Greek Letters of M. Junius Brutus." *CQ* 30:194–203.

Torraca, L. 1959. *Marco Giunio Bruto. Epistole greche.* Collana di Studi greci 31. Naples.

Welles, C. B. 1934. *Royal Correspondence in the Hellenistic Period: A Study in Greek Epigraphy.* New Haven.

Yardeni, A. 2000. *Textbook of Aramaic, Hebrew and Nabataean Documentary Texts from the Judaean Desert.* Jerusalem.

Ziegler, K. 1964. *Plutarchus. Vitae Parallelae.* Vol. 2, Fasc. 1. Leipzig.

ANOTHER SORT OF MISOGYNY

AENEID 9.141–142

Jefferds Huyck

> sunt et mea contra
> fata mihi, ferro sceleratam exscindere gentem
> coniuge praerepta; nec solos tangit Atridas
> iste dolor, solisque licet capere arma Mycenis.
> 140 "sed periisse semel satis est": peccare fuisset
> ante satis, penitus modo non genus omne perosos
> femineum. quibus haec medii fiducia valli
> fossarumque morae, leti discrimina parva,
> dant animos ..."[1]

140 sed *FPR* : set *M* : si *d*   periisse *F¹M¹P* : perisset *F* : perisse *MR*   satis semel *Rufinianus*   fuisse *F* (*corr. F¹*)   141 mohonon *F* (*corr. F¹*) : non modo *R* : modo nunc *Tiberius Claudius Donatus in interpr.* (*coni. Markland*) : modo nec *recc.*   perosos *FM²R, Arusianus* : perossos *MP* : perosus *F⁴M⁶r, Charisius* : perosum *adn, Porphyrio*

The difficulty of construing the words *penitus* ... / *femineum* (141–142), whether with *non* or the variant *nunc*, has long been noted by commentators. One of them, Philip Hardie, has suggested that "the text may be corrupt."[2] My object here, after sketching the problem and reviewing existing approaches, is to commend a cure. A previously undetected model in *Iliad* 9 will offer support.

I am grateful to Fiachra Mac Góráin and Harvey Yunis for their helpful criticisms.

[1]   So Mynors 1969:310. The apparatus depends on the fuller reports of Geymonat 1973:500. For the variant *modo nunc*, see p. 254 with n. 42 (Tiberius Claudius Donatus) and n. 16 (Servius). For *perosum*, see n. 43.

[2]   Hardie 1994:101.

I. THE PROBLEM

Turnus is rallying his men, who are shaken and fearful after witnessing the miraculous transformation of the Trojan ships. Defiant from his opening words, when he comes to consider the "theft" of Lavinia, he grows indignant. Things reach a boil in line 140.[3] The hero allows an imaginary interlocutor to plead for the Trojans, only to rebuff him. "But it's enough (for them) to have perished[4] *once*," says his straw man;[5] to which Turnus scornfully replies, "(Then) it should have been[6] enough (for them) to pursue their adulteries[7] *beforehand*" (the logically emphatic word *ante* being spotlighted at the beginning of its verse). Since the Trojans that he has to do with are still very much alive, Turnus detects a mawkish exaggeration in *periisse* and immediately punishes the fault with *peccare*, implicitly equating Aeneas' "theft" of Lavinia with Paris' theft of Helen. Now comes the crux (141–142): *penitus modo non* (v.l. *nunc*) *genus omne perosos / femineum*. Critics have proposed at least six interpretations of this phrase, minor variations excepted, and twice resorted to conjecture. Not all of these approaches need detain us here, but three deserve a hearing:[8]

Most commentators translate roughly as follows: "(Then) it should have been enough (for them) to pursue their adulteries *beforehand*,

---

[3] Paratore–Canali (1982:152) on line 140: "lo sviluppo oratorio del discorso, con le obiezioni e le relative risposte, tocca qui il culmine."

[4] The first meaning of *periisse* is "to be ruined" (*OLD* s.v. *pereo* 5), but the poet is deliberately flirting with the literal sense "to have died"; cf. Liv. 42.23.10 *perire ... semel* ("once and for all"); Plaut. *Mostell.* 375 *disperii. — bis periisti? qui potest?*

[5] Highet (1972:88 with n. 71) stresses the artificiality of this objection, "the most intrusive piece of rhetoric in the whole *Aeneid.*"

[6] A jussive subjunctive denoting an unfulfilled obligation in past time, e.g. Cic. *Fin.* 4.57 *saltem aliquid de pondere detraxisset* ("should have taken"). For the contrafactual idea, one would have expected *satis erat*, e.g. Cic. *Prov. cons.* 26 *rei publicae satis erat* ("would have been enough"). "Aber nie steht der Konjunktiv des Plusquamperfekts als Potentialis der Vergangenheit" (Kühner–Stegmann 1976: vol. 1, 180).

[7] *OLD* s.v. *pecco* 3b, "of offenses against the sexual code."

[8] Three more approaches are acknowledged in various connections below, i.e. the interpretations of Conte (n. 10), Dingel (p. 253), and Tiberius Claudius Donatus (p. 253–255). Wagner (1861:348) is cited here simply for the sake of completeness: "*penitus ... Femineum*: Accusativus cum Infinitivo, quo utebantur mirabundi atque indignabundi." So too the conjecture of Hoffmann 1853:887–889: *modo enim ... perosis*.

deeply hating (thenceforth) almost all (*modo non ... omne*)[9] the race of women." But Turnus' kindly limitation "almost all" is hardly compatible with his indignant injunction to "utter hatred" (*penitus ... perosos*).[10] On one view, "it is more proper for Turnus to require the Trojans, who it should be remembered had their wives, mothers, sisters, and daughters with them, to hate *almost the whole* race of women, than to hate *the whole race*."[11] That explanation, though, "eine sonderbare Pedanterie," collapses under its own weight.[12]

The second approach is due to Markland. He proposed to replace *non* with *nunc* (the reading, since conjecturally restored, of the late-antique commentator Tiberius Claudius Donatus)—and not just in Vergil's text, but in the interpretation of Servius.[13] By allowing the Trojans to hate unreservedly (*modo nunc ... perosos*), that scheme avoids the previous difficulty, but only by creating another. So far from helping to fix the force of the participle, the words *modo nunc* seem rather to confuse it. Markland himself explains "modo nunc penitus perosi sint omne genus femineum," i.e. "(Then) it should have been enough (for them) to pursue their adulteries *beforehand*, provided that they *now* hate the

---

[9] For *modo non*, "all but, very nearly," see *OLD* s.v. *modo*[1] 1d.

[10] Though translating in this vein, both Page (1900:261) and Hardie (1994:101) censure the limiting phrase. Conte (2009:264) attempts to skirt the problem by explaining "immo satis fuisset propter feminam unam ante peccare eos qui, etsi acerbissime edocti, tamen genus omne femineum nondum (*modo non*) abominati sunt," i.e. "... who, despite having been taught by the bitterest experience, have not yet learned to loathe the entire race of women"; but it is hard to see how *modo non* could mean "not yet." Alternatively, an anonymous reader of this paper suggested taking *modo* in the sense "just now" (*OLD* s.v. *modo*[1] 5) and rendering "for those who just now (in the Helen business) did not utterly despise the female race (as they should have), to sin previously would have been enough"; but (1) the point of the participial phrase is now elusive, and (2) even if "the Helen business" is the whole Trojan War, at least seven years have passed since then, too many to permit the characterization "just now" (cf. *Aen.* 1.23 *veterisque ... belli*).

[11] Henry 1881:820.

[12] "Pedanterie": Dingel 1997:89. The explanation of Madvig (1873:31n1) is briefer, but not better: "prope (quod natura non ferat) omne genus femineum." Turnus remains caught between consideration and contempt.

[13] The conjecture of Markland (1728:284)—supported, as he thought, by the variant *modo nec*—was adopted by Peerlkamp (1843:165) and Ribbeck (1862:124). "Requiritur illud oppositum praegressis *semel* et *ante*," says Peerlkamp. For the text of Donatus, "late 4th-early 5th cent. AD?" (*OCD*[3]), see p. 254. For Servius, see n. 16.

whole race of women." Statements of past propriety, though, are not naturally subject to present stipulations, and the resulting sentiment is awkward and illogical. Others, accordingly, understand "(si) modo ... perosi essent" ("if only they hated"),[14] but there is no room here for conviction. The Latin is unclear.

A third approach—to detach *modo* from *non* and render "(Then) it should have been enough (for them) to pursue their adulteries *before-hand*, if only they didn't deeply despise the whole female sex"—is the weakest of the lot (regardless whether *perosos* can be taken in a contra-factual sense).[15] In the previous two schemes, woman-hating was viewed as a *cure* for woman-stealing; now woman-stealing has become an *instance* of woman-hating.[16] This interpretation is consistent with modern conceptions of rape considered as a violent sexual act, but it does not sort with more casual ancient attitudes towards mythological abduction. If Aphrodite's sanction counts for anything, Paris stole Helen because he *liked* her. In any case, the misogynistic aspect of rape does not seem to have been uppermost in the Roman mind. "The emphasis in the law relating to *raptus* generally centered on the damage that the household suffered, rather than on the personal hurt and injury done to the victim."[17] A further criticism applies equally to all three approaches: Turnus despises the Trojans and believes it is his peculiar destiny "to wipe out the evil nation" (137 *ferro sceleratam exscindere gentem*); he has no interest in stipulating (*modo*) the terms of their redemption.

Since the discussion to this point has turned largely on the words *modo non* (*modo nunc*), it is important to note that the participle *perosos*

---

[14] So e.g. Conington 1883:172 (though he inclines to *modo non*).

[15] Williams (1973:288) raises this possibility ("if only ... female sex") only to discount it. "This is an obscure sentence," he says, "of which the meaning is very doubtful."

[16] Servius likewise seems to equate woman-stealing with woman-hating, though his interpretation is hard to understand: "modo omne genus femineum non eos penitus perosos decebat, (*Schol. Dan.*) propter quod ante perierunt," i.e. "only it would have been proper that they not hate the entire female race, on account of which (attitude) they perished before," where "propter quod" presumably means "quare" (cf. Servius on *Aen.* 4.127, 5.31, 81, etc.), not "propter quod genus." The sentiment remains doubtful, however, and Markland (1728:284) plausibly conjectured "nunc" for "non": "aliter non video quomodo huic loco constet sensus."

[17] Brundage 1987:48.

(elsewhere in Vergil at 6.435 *lucemque perosi / proiecere animas*) presents difficulties of its own:

(1) After *fuisset ... satis* we would expect a dative, not an accusative.[18] There is no objection to a subject accusative per se; compare *Ecl.* 7.33–34 *haec te liba, Priape, quotannis / exspectare sat est.* But its position is key. If the expressions "Priapum haec exspectare sat est" and "haec exspectare sat est Priapo" are virtually equivalent, it does not follow that one could say, "haec exspectare sat est Priapum" or, by extension, "haec exspectare sat est, pauperem hortum custodientem."[19]

(2) The familiar observation that the perfect participles of deponent and semi-deponent verbs frequently express an action contemporaneous with that of the main verbs[20] cannot very well be extended to cover *perosos*, of which all three approaches require a future reference. Commentators speak of the "timeless" quality of the participle, but without adducing parallels.

(3) Regardless whether it comes concentrated or in a dilute solution, the hatred that Turnus requires in the first two approaches is *gratuitous*. It is understandable why the hero would wish the Trojans to avoid other men's women, or simply to avoid stealing them, but there is no reason in the world why he should then wish them to don hair shirts and "deeply detest" womankind. Turnus is angry and in a mood to exaggerate, but his injunction to misogyny, let alone the celibate existence that (with the reading *modo nunc*) he supposes misogyny to guarantee, seems oddly puritanical and out of sync with pagan sensibilities.[21] Indeed, the very idea of *enjoining* hatred is strange, the more so when the *detestandum* is a basic human want. One might just as well tell a pickpocket to "hate money." "Thou shalt not covet ...": the Tenth Commandment by comparison is a pattern of tact.

[18] So, somewhat more tentatively, Fordyce in his unpublished commentary on *Aeneid* 9, cited by Hardie 1994:101.

[19] Since *predicate* accusatives (and even datives; cf. Sil. *Pun.* 16.492–493) cannot be grammatically alienated from their infinitives, one would expect their placement to be less constrained; thus, not only Ov. *Met.* 13.319 *cum sit satis esse fidelem*, but also Mart. 2.18.7 *esse sat est servum* (v.l. *servo*).

[20] See e.g. Kühner–Stegmann 1976: vol. 1, 759–760.

[21] On pagan sensibilities, see Brown 1988:26–32; cf. Barrett 1966:172–173 (on Eur. *Hipp.* 79–81).

II. A CURE

I believe that Vergil wrote,

"sed periisse semel satis est": peccare fuisset
ante satis. ⟨pereat⟩, penitus modo, nunc genus omne
femineum!

"But it's enough (for them) to have perished *once*," (someone will say). (Then) it should have been enough (for
them) to pursue their adulteries *beforehand.* May the whole
womanish[22] race perish[23] *here and now,* provided[24] (that it
perish) *for good!*[25]

What was once "the whole race of women" is now "the whole
womanish race"—that is, the Trojans themselves. As we shall see, scattered critics since antiquity have suspected that the phrase *genus ...
femineum* conceals Trojans, but without quite managing to coax them

---

[22] For *femineus* in the sense "womanish, cowardly," cf. 12.52–53 (Turnus scorns Aeneas)
longe illi dea mater erit, quae nube fugacem / feminea tegat; Ov. *Met.* 12.610 (you would have
preferred, Achilles, to be killed by Penthesilea rather than that timid wife-snatcher) *si
femineo fuerat tibi Marte cadendum;* Stat. *Theb.* 7.677–678 *quid femineis ululatibus ... /
terrificas, moriture, viros;* Sil. *Pun.* 13.16–17 *gentis / femineam Tyriae labem* (i.e. the inability to fight in
foul weather).

[23] Compare especially Cat. 66.48 *ut Chalybon omne genus pereat!* (translating Callim. *Aet.*
4, fr. 110.48 Χαλύβων ὡς ἀπόλοιτο γένος) and Sen. *Controv.* 1.5.2 (a rapist) *constituatur in
conspectu publico, caedatur diu, toto die pereat qui tota nocte peccavit* (so Junius Gallio, the
friend of Ovid). The form *pereat* occurs just once elsewhere in Vergil's corpus: *nunc pereat
Teucrisque pio det sanguine poenas,* says Juno, petulantly, of Turnus (10.617).

[24] This use of *modo* (in the sense *dummodo* with an ellipse of the verb) is inherently
sharp and "oratorical." There are many examples in Cicero, e.g. *Rosc. Am.* 138 *decerne,
modo recte; Phil.* 2.103 *valeant tabellae, modo Caesaris, non tuae.* Cf. [Brut.] ap. Cic. *Ad Brut.*
1.17.4 *servitutem, honorificam modo, non aspernatur;* Sen. *Prov.* 2.2 *quis autem, vir modo et
erectus ad honesta, non est laboris adpetens iusti; OLD* s.v. *modo*[1] 4; *TLL* 8.1302.47. A motive to
the elliptical use (not elsewhere in Vergil, with the possible exception of the paradosis)
lay in the highly charged rhetoric of Turnus' speech (see n. 5). Compare the still more
intricate phrasing of Lucan, 1.201–202 *en, adsum ... / Caesar, ubique tuus (liceat modo, nunc
quoque) miles,* where the limiting clause "reads forward."

[25] For *penitus* in the sense "utterly" (*OLD* s.v. 5), cf. Lucr. 1.262 *haud igitur p. pereunt
quaecumque videntur,* 1.226 *p. perimit;* Cic. *Fin.* 1.49 *plerique ... se ipsos p. perdiderunt;* Vulg. *II
Sam.* 14.14 *ne p. pereat qui abiectus est.*

forth. Although the process of corruption envisioned here is not unduly complicated, the supporting arguments are many and will take some time to evolve: (1) the traditional slur of eastern effeminacy is well established in the *Aeneid* and, indeed, elsewhere employed by Turnus himself; (2) Roman invective regularly represented adultery (140 *peccare*) and effeminacy (141–142 *genus ... femineum*) as compatible impulses: single hearts could accommodate both; (3) the words *pereat, penitus modo* are neatly suited to Turnus' argument and his emotional state; (4) lines 140–141 have a specific model in the tirade that Achilles delivers in *Iliad* 9; (5) the loss of *pereat* before *penitus* is explained by haplography; (6) the position of the stopgap *perosos* at the end of its verse in the traditional text was predictable after the loss of *pereat*; (7) the stopgap itself might have been readily supplied from a passage in Ovid; (8) metrical features entailed by the proposed conjecture, though less common, are sufficiently apt; and finally (9) we now have a smooth transition to the next point where one was lacking before.

"The whole womanish race": the Trojans are repeatedly character-ized as soft and effete by their opponents in the *Aeneid*. In Book 4, King Iarbas dismisses Aeneas as "that Paris with his effeminate crew." In Book 12, amid further abuse of "the effeminate Phrygian," Turnus sneers at his hair "curled with hot irons and drenched in myrrh."[26] Later in Book 9, the Rutulian Numanus Remulus refers to the newcomers as "really Phrygian-ettes, not Phrygians" (doubly derisive, as Servius notes, since even the masculine form may connote softness).[27] It is no surprise, then, when Juno makes it a condition of her acquiescence to the Trojan takeover that the Latins remain "men" in full possession of their Italian "manliness."[28] The effeminate easterner is, of course, a byword in classical literature. Compare Livy's discussion of the question *what if Alexander the Great had*

---

[26] 4.215–217 (Iarbas) *et nunc ille Paris cum semiviro comitatu, / Maeonia mentum mitra crinemque madentem / subnexus, rapto potitur.* 12.98–100 (Turnus wishes) *loricam ... lacerare ... / semiviri Phrygis et foedare in pulvere crinis / vibratos calido ferro murraque madentis.*

[27] 9.614–617 *vobis picta croco et fulgenti murice vestis, / desidiae cordi, iuvat indulgere choreis, / et tunicae manicas et habent redimicula mitrae. / o vere Phrygiae, neque enim Phryges,* etc. Servius: "ipsos vituperaverat *Phryges* (9.599), nunc ad maiorem iniuriam *Phrygias, non Phryges* dicit." For *Phryges* as a term of reproach, see Fordyce 1977:117.

[28] 12.824–827 *neu Troas fieri iubeas Teucrosque vocari / aut vocem mutare viros aut vertere vestem. / ... / sit Romana potens Itala virtute propago.*

invaded Italy? "Even if he had enjoyed some initial success, he would have often felt the lack of Persians and Indians and the unwarlike peoples of Asia and admitted he had waged war with *women.*"[29] Livy goes on to allude to a remark supposedly made by Alexander the Molossian as he was crossing over into Italy—that he "was entering, as it were, the men's quarters, whereas Alexander the Great, in invading Persia, had entered the women's."[30] There is no need to multiply examples.[31] The imputation of effeminacy is easy in itself and well suited to Turnus' disdainful tone.

Doubtless, coming after the mention of adultery in the preceding line (140 *peccare*), a reference to "the womanish race" will strike some modern readers as abrupt or inappropriate—but only, I think, because ancient mores were different from our own. That womanishness may consist with womanizing is sufficiently shown by the character of Paris, to whom the words *peccare ... ante* refer. One thinks first and foremost of Paris' portrayal in *Iliad* 3, a pastiche of dandyism, empty menace, inglorious flight, and adulterous sex. In the eyes of his rival Iarbas, Aeneas is a *second* Paris, part seducer and part fop (4.215–217 *ille Paris cum semiviro comitatu / ... rapto potitur*; note also Juno's characterization, with a different emphasis, 7.321 *Paris alter*). Similarly in the speech of Numanus Remulus, though the target is Trojan effeminacy, the backdrop is Trojan adultery (9.600 *nostra sibi bello conubia poscunt*). Nor is this combination of qualities merely "mythological." As several recent studies have emphasized,[32] the effeminate adulterer was a distinct type in Vergil's day.

> It is not at all unusual ... for the same man to be castigated both for effeminacy or interest in other men and for being an adulterer ... This was simply part of the Roman sexual stereotype: effeminate men were thought to be more interested in sex of any kind than were more rugged types.[33]

---

[29] Liv. 9.19.10 *saepe ... Persas et Indos et imbellem Asiam quaesisset et cum feminis sibi bellum fuisse dixisset.*

[30] So Gell. *NA* 17.21.33 *quasi in andronitin ... quasi in gynaeconitin.*

[31] For more on this rich theme, see Oakley 2005:255–256.

[32] See e.g. Frazel 2009:140–147. Frazel's notes provide a conspectus of recent scholarship.

[33] Richlin 1983:91–92.

As one might expect, such accusations were especially prominent in political invective. Verres, Clodius, and Antony are all tarred in this way by Cicero,[34] and no less a soldier than Julius Caesar is said to have maintained the twofold tradition of his Trojan forebears. Catullus mocks Caesar and his lieutenant Mamurra not only for their womanizing but (in the very next verse) for their pathic relations with men. According to the elder Curio, Caesar was "every woman's man and every man's woman."[35] Small wonder, then, if he was a dandy like Paris. Caesar's preference for long-sleeved tunics recalls the taunt of Remulus: "your tunics have sleeves."[36] The lesson is clear: if *moechocinaedi*[37] shocked, they did not surprise. By Roman standards, the malicious association of adultery and effeminacy was nothing if not conventional.

The desire to discover Trojans in the phrase *genus ... femineum* is not a new one. In his commentary on *Aeneid* 4, Austin says simply, "Turnus calls the Trojans *genus femineum*"—evidently an oversight.[38] Dingel, the most recent commentator on *Aeneid* 9, suggests that in saying "almost all" the race of women Turnus is permitting the Trojans to make an exception for *themselves*.[39] But "that is one twist too many."[40] Tiberius

---

[34] For Verres, see *Verr.* 2.192 *vir inter mulieres, impura inter viros muliercula*, 5.81 (all-women parties, not excepting the host and his son). For Clodius, see *Har. resp.* 44; *Clod. fr.* 21–23 Crawford (transvestism in service of adultery); *Dom.* 139 *qui contra fas et inter viros saepe mulier et inter mulieres vir fuisset.* Antony: *Phil.* 2.44–45 (pathic homosexuality), 48 (adultery). For other Romans so aspersed, see Richlin 1983:88–91; Corbeill 1996:150n58. The elder Seneca goes so far as to attribute both faults to the *generality* of Roman youth, *Controv.* 1, *praef.* 9 *expugnatores alienae pudicitiae, neglegentes suae*; see Williams 1999:149.

[35] Cat. 57.8–10 *non hic quam ille magis vorax adulter, / rivales socii puellularum. / pulchre convenit improbis cinaedis* (cf. 2 *pathicoque*, 6 *morbosi*); Suet. *Iul.* 52.3 *omnium mulierum virum et omnium virorum mulierem.* Suetonius treats each charge separately: 50.1–52.1 (adultery), 49.1–4 (pathic homosexuality). Accused in his youth of having yielded his favors to King Nicomedes, Caesar was derided by his consular colleague Bibulus as "the Bithynian queen" (49.2); "the virginity of Venus' descendant was polluted in Bithynia," wrote Cicero (49.3 = Cic. *Ep. fr.* 17.5, trans. Shackleton Bailey). More economical criticism made Caesar simply "a woman" (22.2 *negante quodam per contumeliam facile hoc ulli feminae fore*).

[36] On sleeves, see Suet. *Iul.* 45.3 *lato clavo ad manus fimbriato*; *Aen.* 9.616 *et tunicae manicas ... habent*; cf. Dingel 1997:231. On other dandyism, see Suet. *Iul.* 45.2; Plut. *Caes.* 4.9; Dio Cass. 43.43.2–5. See also Richlin 1983:92–93; Corbeill 1996:159–169.

[37] Lucil. 1058 *inberbi androgyni, barbati moechocinaedi.*

[38] Austin 1963:78.

[39] Dingel 1997:89.

[40] Hardie 1999:386.

Claudius Donatus, for his part, was so intent on finding a reference to the Trojans that he seems to have contrived an instance of aposiopesis to get it (2.206.13–20):[41]

> *penitus modo nunc* (coni. Georges : *non* V)[42] *genus omne, perosos, femineum!* vel nunc intereant (*post corr.* Georges : *interea ut* V) penitus quos exitium suum ad bonam vitam formare non valuit. supra posuit *si qua Phryges prae se iactant* (9.134) et in appellatione Phrygum occultum convicium dixit, hic autem, dum loquitur, vehementer exarsit, quod ipsum intellegitur ex eo, quod in apertam iniuriam ruit dicendo perosos et femineum genus.

> At least *now* may they utterly perish, whom their own ruin could not incline to an upright life. Earlier in his speech (Turnus) said "if the Phrygians boast any (oracles)" and used the name Phrygians as a veiled insult. Here, however, he has become violently angry while speaking, as can be plainly seen from the fact that he launches into outright defamation, calling (the Trojans) hateful[43] and a womanish race.[44]

Donatus read *nunc*, not *non*, but in other respects his text was the same as ours.[45] He appears, therefore, to have understood Turnus as saying, roughly, "At least *now* may the hateful and womanish race utterly—," at which point the hero succumbs to his exasperation, and the unspoken word, left hanging in the air since *periisse* in line 140,

---

[41] The standard edition (Georges 1906) is cited by volume, page, and line numbers.

[42] The following words "vel nunc" clearly justify the correction. Reports that suggest Donatus acknowledged both readings are misleading.

[43] The passive sense of *perosus* is not attested before Tertullian (*TLL* s.v. 10.1608.47), but it was current in Donatus' time. Compare his remark on *Aen.* 12.517 *exosum nequiquam bella Menoeten*, i.e. "Menoetes ... perosa habens bella" (2.613.5–6). Instead of *perosos* in our passage, some manuscripts show the variant *perosum* (adn, Porphyrio). If the change was deliberate, *perosum* must have been intended as passive, though one can only guess how its author proposed to construe the sentence as a whole.

[44] Compare Servius' remark (n. 27) on the progression of abuse in Remulus' speech.

[45] With the exception of *omne*, every word of the lemma is accounted for in the note: *modo* (i.e. "vel") *nunc, penitus, perosos, femineum genus*—and since the metrical properties of *omne* make it uniquely qualified to stand before *perosos*, it too, in effect, is accounted for.

is "perish" ("intereant"). That may be ridiculous, but it could well be "right." One wonders whether Donatus might not have been influenced by a commentator who relied on a different text. Consider, again, the proposed conjecture:

> "sed periisse semel satis est": peccare fuisset
> ante satis. ⟨pereat⟩, penitus modo, nunc genus omne
> femineum!

By saying *peccare fuisset / ante satis*, Turnus has already implied that the Trojans should "die again."[46] Now, with brutal frankness, he drives the point home. Note how the phrase *penitus modo* mocks the grandiosity of *periisse*. The Trojans didn't really "die." They were not in fact "destroyed." They simply suffered a setback. This time, though, they will perish "for good."

It is true that Turnus fails to translate his threat into action, but that flaw is already embedded in his speech.

> Indeed he does call on his men to storm the Trojan camp (146–147), adding the argument *facile* (148–155). But then, instead of leading the charge in person, he remarks that it is getting rather late, and postpones the operation to the next day (156–158). This is a serious blunder ... Vergil intended this to show Turnus's immaturity of character and his inadequacy as a tactician.[47]

The Rutulian may soar to new heights of passion in 140–142, but in the end he is merely elaborating the boast he made just a few lines before, that he is fated "to wipe out the evil race" (137). Besides, if his empty bravado is a fault, it is a fault, as will appear, with impeccable credentials.

Before attempting to trace the course of corruption, we need to consider a Homeric model for lines 140–141. Vergil's commentators

---

[46] So Servius: "ex quo colligitur quotiens peccaverunt, totiens eos perire debere." Likewise Markland 1728:284.

[47] Highet 1972:88. The "feeble conclusion" to Turnus' speech (158) is noted by Hardie 1994:103.

regularly note correspondences between Turnus' speech and the bitter rant with which Achilles favors the ambassadors in *Iliad* 9 (308–429). The most obvious point of contact is the argument that the Atridae are not alone in loving their wives: ἦ μοῦνοι φιλέουσ' ἀλόχους μερόπων ἀνθρώπων | Ἀτρεῖδαι; (340–341; cf. *Aen.* 9.138–139). To maintain the parallel, both heroes are tempted to the same exaggeration: just as Briseis is Achilles' ἄλοχος (336), so Lavinia is Turnus' *coniunx* (138). The same tone informs both speeches: curt and staccato, indignant, almost spitting. Note especially the succession of outbursts in which Achilles declares, among other things, that he will not be fooled twice by Agamemnon (375–377):

οὐδ' ἂν ἔτ' αὖτις
ἐξαπάφοιτ' ἐπέεσσιν· ἅλις δέ οἱ. ἀλλὰ ἔκηλος[48]
ἐρρέτω· ἐκ γάρ εὐ φρένας εἵλετο μητίετα Ζεύς.

About the short sentence ἅλις δέ οἱ, the commentators are silent, but since its meaning is nearly the same—"It is enough for him ⟨to have committed one offense⟩"[49]—it seems likely that it inspired *peccare fuisset / ante satis* (140–141). Homer's clipped sentences appear also to have influenced Vergil's phrasing ("*sed periisse semel satis est.*" *peccare fuisset / ante satis. pereat ...*)[50] and perhaps even his choice of consonants (ἐξαπάφοιτ' ἐπέεσσιν, cf. *periisse ... peccare ... pereat, penitus*). But the proposed conjecture allows us to extend the parallel. With ἅλις δέ οἱ. ἀλλὰ ἔκηλος | ἐρρέτω, compare *peccare fuisset / ante satis. pereat, penitus modo.*[51] In colloquial speech the sense of *pereat* often approximates that

---

[48] There is heavy irony in ἔκηλος, "at one's ease, unmolested." In combination with ἐρρέτω, it seems to mean "He can go to hell for all I care." Compare the Latin use of *valeat*, e.g. Cat. 11.17 *cum suis vivat valeatque moechis.*

[49] So Hainsworth 1993:111, who compares the idiom ἦ οὐχ ἅλις ὅττι ...; (*Il.* 5.349, etc.).

[50] Hainsworth 1993:111: "The violent enjambments and short phrases admirably express Akhilleus' withering contempt ... Verses with two major breaks of sense, like 376, are extremely rare in the *Iliad*." Hardie 1994:98 (characterizing the Latin speech as a whole): "there are few end-stopped lines as the words pour forth." Note also the unusual concentration of verses with elision in the fifth or sixth foot: 9.129, 131, 145; cf. Norden 1926:455–456.

[51] The "perfect" correspondence *penitus pereat* entails an unparalleled metrical anomaly (see n. 57).

of ἐρρέτω ("to hell with him"),[52] and nothing precludes that nuance here.[53] Again, Turnus' stipulation *penitus modo* shows precisely that he wanted to rule out a non-literal interpretation of the verb. Note that whereas Achilles views his adversary as chiefly one man, Turnus throughout his speech views his as the Trojans collectively.[54] If therefore the subject of ἐρρέτω is Agamemnon, it is consistent with his argument that the subject of *pereat* is "the whole womanish race." A further correspondence with the Iliadic speech may now be discerned in Turnus' idle threat to destroy the Trojans "here and now" (*pereat ... nunc genus omne / femineum*). Achilles resorts to the same kind of angry bluster when after scorning Agamemnon's offers, he tells Odysseus— in a rambling, anacoluthic vaunt—that he will see his ships sailing off "first thing tomorrow" (9.356–361 νῦν δ' ... | αὔριον ... | ὄψεαι ... | ἦρι μάλ' Ἑλλήσποντον ἐπ' ἰχθυόεντα πλεούσας | νῆας ἐμάς). As neither threat is actually carried out, each "should be taken as a hyperbolical sign of the speaker's fury."[55] Even in his embarrassments, Turnus is "another Achilles."[56]

The cause of the corruption was homoeoarchon (*PEREAT PENITVS*).[57] Once *pereat* dropped out, a word with verbal force would have been required as a stopgap, and in view of its many problems (of case, of

---

[52] Cf. Plaut. *Pers.* 281 *dico ut perpetuo pereas* ("I tell you—to roast in hell"); Ter. *Ad.* 133–134 *si tibi istuc placet, / profundat perdat pereat; nil ad me attinet* ("let him spend his last dime and be damned!"); Cic. *Verr.* 2.5.104 *pereat Cleomenes una!* ("Let C. hang with the rest!" trans. Greenwood); *Fam.* 8.15.2 *peream, si ...* ("I'll be darned if ..."); Hor. *Epod.* 12.16 *pereat male quae ...*; *Copa* 34 *a pereat cui sunt prisca supercilia*; TLL 10.1331.62. The semantic grading of such expressions—from "mild oath" to "imprecation" to literal "injunction"—will naturally depend on the context. In this regard, the distinctions of Cunliffe 1963:159 (s.v. ἔρρω 2) are instructive.

[53] Hardie (1994:98) notes that the language of Turnus' speech "is blunt and at times colloquial." See his comments on 9.135 *sat ... datum*, 153 *luce palam*, 154–155 *cum Danais rem ... / esse*, 154 *faxo*.

[54] Cf. 128 *Troianos ... his*, 130 *Teucris*, 134 *Phryges*, 136 *Troes*, and especially 137 *sceleratam exscindere gentem*. Likewise in 140–141, both *sed periisse semel satis est* and *peccare fuisset / ante satis* imply a dative like *eis* ("for them").

[55] So Hainsworth 1993:110, with reference solely to Achilles' speech.

[56] 6.89–90 *alius Latio iam partus Achilles, / natus et ipse dea.*

[57] The same explanation would apply, of course, had Vergil written *penitus pereat, modo nunc, genus omne*, "May the whole race perish utterly—only now!" But (1) the phrasing *pereat, penitus modo* responds more directly to *periisse* in 140, and (2) a strong pause at

tense, of sense) one is only too happy to nominate *perosos*. Observe
that the position of the participle is consistent with this theory. In
most cases where a verse has been abridged by haplography, the site
of the omission is revealed by a flaw in the meter, so that the interpolation, when there is an interpolation, is supplied in or around the
original gap.[58] In this case, since the verse will have read smoothly
enough through its first five feet even after the loss of *pereat* (i.e. *ante
satis penitus modo nunc genus omne ...*), an ancient reader would not have
"missed anything" until he reached *genus omne*, and it is there—at the
very end of the verse—that he would have been tempted to supply
"the verb." Confronted by the seemingly docked line *genus omne ∪ - - /
femineum*, the reader will have taken his cue from Ovid (*Met.* 7.744–746):

> insidiosa malo cum coniuge limina fugit (sc. Procris)
> offensaque mei <u>genus omne</u> perosa <u>virorum</u>
> montibus errabat, studiis operata Dianae.

The reader himself need not have been the interpolator. It is enough,
if he simply recorded the "parallel" in the margin, leaving it to a
later copyist to integrate *perosos*.[59] Whether the pertinent manuscript
showed *nunc* or the corruption *non* does not much matter. Both readings, as we have seen, shed at least a ray of sense, and since neither ray
is particularly illuminating, either reading might have provoked the
other after the interpolation by way of "correction."

But might not the debt have worked the other way? Ovid borrows
frequently from Vergil and does so conspicuously elsewhere in this
narrative (*Met.* 7.749 = *Aen.* 4.19 *succumbere culpae*). One may doubt,

---

4½ is apparently unexampled in Vergil, the nearest exception being *G.* 2.153 *nec rapit
immensos orbis per humum neque tanto* (Winbolt 1903:50).

[58] Compare, for instance, *Aen.* 9.782, where the true reading (*pace* Dingel 1997:271)
is *quos alios muros, quaeve ultra moenia habetis?* (P). The combination *EVEV* shrank to *EV*,
leaving the unmetrical *quae ultra*, whereupon someone plugged the hole with *iam*,
i.e. *quae iam ultra moenia habetis* (MR). Housman (1903:lix–lxvi) cites this among many
instances, including three others from the *Aeneid*, where haplography has led to interpolation. Naturally, in cases where the manuscripts fail to preserve the original reading, not
even the most elegant attempt to unwind the process (e.g. Bentley's *Parim*; ⟨Paris⟩ at *Aen.*
10.705) is likely to convince everyone.

[59] For the incorporation of readers' citations within texts, see Tarrant 1987:292–294.

however, whether he would have chosen to imitate a verse he found hard to understand.[60] It is true that the Ovidian passage shares certain vocabulary with our own (7.744 *coniuge*, 748 *peccasse*), but that is not terribly surprising in another treatment of sexual malfeasance. These similarities *might* argue for Ovidian imitation, but they might also explain, in combination with the words *genus omne ... virorum*, why one of Vergil's readers recalled the Ovidian passage in the first place. What matters here is not estimates of general probability, but the particular circumstances.[61] If we start from the assumption that both the logical and the grammatical claims of *perosos* are feeble, it follows that Vergil is unlikely to have written the word. But if that is the case, then the similarity of the two verses makes it highly probable that the participle was inspired by the instance in Ovid.

A more troubling aspect of this construct, perhaps, is that it entails a metrical anomaly, the placement of *nunc* at the start of the fifth foot. Monosyllables in this position are not very common in Vergil, though not so uncommon as they are, say, in Catullus.[62] It tells in favor of *nunc*, however, that it occurs in a predictable context: the majority of instances are found in direct discourse, often with emotional emphasis.[63] Another such monosyllable occurs just a few lines earlier: "I have my own fates, too!" says Turnus (136–137 *sunt et mea contra / fata mihi*).

---

[60] Perhaps, again, because of the obscurity of the Vergilian verse, the correspondence seems to have eluded Ovid's commentators.

[61] For the principle, cf. Housman 1922:78–79.

[62] Norden (1926:447) counts 79 instances in the *Aeneid* where the monosyllable is followed by two or more words. He appears to omit formulations like 2.94 *si qua tulisset* and 8.205 *ne quid inausum*, but includes those where the monosyllable is proclitic (e.g. 6.123 *ab Iove summo*) or followed by a closely cohering disyllable (e.g. 6.30 *tu quoque magnam*, 365 *tu mihi terram*). Note especially 10.34 *nunc tua quisquam*, cf. 5.808 *tunc ego forti*, 6.138 *hunc tegit omnis*. Note also *G.* 2.20 *his genus omne*; cf. Lucr. 5.902 *quam genus omne*; Hor. *Sat.* 1.2.2 *hoc genus omne*. (Vergil has *omne* once more in the sixth foot, *Aen.* 7.514 *protinus omne*.)

[63] The emphasis may be the result of anaphora (e.g. *Aen.* 5.414 *his magnum Alciden contra stetit, his ego suetus*), or polyptoton (10.9 *quae contra vetitum discordia? quis metus aut hos ...?*), or interjection (4.13 *heu, quibus ille ...!*), or negation (11.688 *haud leve patrum*), or some other effect (3.42–43 *non me tibi Troia / externum tulit*). Often there is no emphasis (2.530 *et premit hasta*). The scheme occurs in successive lines when Aeneas meets his disguised mother on the outskirts of Carthage (1.327–328 *haud tibi vultus / ... o, dea certe*), and twice in three lines during one of Juno's angry rants (7.319, 321).

Here the adverb would stand in pointed contrast to *ante* at the beginning of the line. Turnus in fact lands a *series* of hammer blows: "*Let them perish, only utterly, here and now, the cowards.*" It might seem a further flaw that the line is so "malleable," *pereat, penitus,* and *modo nunc* presenting successive anapaestic units. But this feature too can be paralleled. A more extreme example (three anapaestic *words*) occurs later in Turnus' speech, *nunc adeo, melior quoniam pars acta diei* (9.156).[64] Compare also, in particular, the anapaestic cadence of Remulus' gibe *et tunicae manicas et habent redimicula mitrae* (9.616)—"a special sneering rhythm."[65]

Note, finally, that the proposed conjecture has the merit of providing a smooth transition, previously lacking, to Turnus' next point. According to such sense as can be made of the paradosis, the hero first enjoins the Trojans to loathe the race of women and then says without further ado that their fortifications give them a false sense of security (142–144 *quibus haec medii fiducia valli / fossarumque morae, leti discrimina parva, / dant animos*). With the proposed conjecture, Turnus wishes for the complete destruction of the Trojans, a womanish (i.e. cowardly) race, to whom[66] their fortifications give a false sense of security. Although Dingel's attempt to *include* the Trojans in the *genus ... femineum* is unconvincing, he rightly argues that the imputation of cowardice is essential to the logical progression of Turnus' argument: "Andernfalls haben wir es mit einem abrupten gedanklichen Neuansatz zu tun."[67] The new sequence of thought—"the Trojans are sissies, who cower behind their walls"—precisely reflects the impression of the Rutulians at large when, on first reaching the Trojan camp, they find its occupants unwilling to come out and "fight like men" (9.55–57):

> Teucrum mirantur inertia corda,
> non aequo dare se campo, non obvia ferre
> arma viros, sed castra fovere.

---

[64] For successions of anapaestic words, see Norden 1926:219; Clausen 1994:43.

[65] So Highet 1972:258, who adds, "It has ... been pointed out [by Jacobson 1966:156] that the rhythm of this line is modelled on a verse of Lucretius which describes a menstruous woman fainting (6.795): *et manibus nitidum teneris opus effluit ei.*"

[66] For the *ad sensum* construction *genus ... quibus,* cf. *Aen.* 6.580–581 *hic genus antiquum Terrae, Titania pubes, / fulmine deiecti fundo volvuntur in imo.*

[67] Dingel 1997:89.

The noun *viros* is especially pointed here, the more so as it recalls the lofty promise of *arma virumque cano*. David West's translation does a good job of capturing the contempt: "They were men. Why did they huddle in their camp and not meet arms with arms?"[68] Remulus extends the theme later in the book when he implies a link between the Trojans' besieged position and their soft "Phrygian" nature (9.598–599 *non pudet obsidione iterum valloque teneri, / bis capti Phryges, et morti praetendere muros?*). Another invidious variation on *arma virumque* marks the end of his speech (620 *sinite arma viris et cedite ferro*).[69]

The process of corruption sketched in these pages is not simple, but neither, I think, is it implausibly complex. Homoeoarchon led to haplography. The missing syllables were supplied in just the place one would expect to find them. Everything points to *perosos* as the intrusive word. It was probably after the interpolation that the poet's *nunc*, read by Donatus and perhaps also by Servius,[70] was altered to *non*, in a deliberate, if not altogether successful attempt to improve the sense. Nothing in this scheme is unusual except the manner of suppletion—by addition rather than replacement, as if a pearl necklace, having lost one of its complement, were repaired by the addition of a different pearl in a different position. Again, however, that quirk was to be expected given the metrical character of the line. Hardie observes that "the heavy pause after *femineum* lends it misogynistic emphasis."[71] And so it does. But if the *genus ... femineum* are Trojans, this is misogyny of another sort.

Santa Cruz, California

WORKS CITED

Austin, R. G. 1963. *P. Vergili Maronis Aeneidos Liber Quartus*. Oxford.

Barrett, W. S. 1966. *Euripides. Hippolytus*. Oxford.

---

[68] West 2003:188.

[69] See Hardie 1994:82.

[70] For Servius, see n. 16.

[71] Hardie (1994:101) compares 4.569–570 *varium et mutabile semper / femina*.

Brown, P. 1988. *The Body and Society: Men, Women, and Sexual Renunciation in Early Christianity.* New York.

Brundage, J. A. 1987. *Law, Sex, and Christian Society in Medieval Europe.* Chicago.

Clausen, W. 1994. *A Commentary on Virgil, Eclogues.* Oxford.

Conington, J. 1883. *P. Vergili Maronis Opera.* Vol. 3, *Aeneid* 6–12. 3rd ed., rev. H. Nettleship. London.

Conte, G. B. 2009. *P. Vergilius Maro. Aeneis.* Berlin.

Corbeill, A. 1996. *Controlling Laughter: Political Humor in the Late Roman Republic.* Princeton.

Cunliffe, R. J. 1963. *A Lexicon of the Homeric Dialect.* Norman, OK.

Dingel, J. 1997. *Kommentar zum 9. Buch der* Aeneis Vergils. Heidelberg.

Fordyce, C. J. 1977. *P. Vergili Maronis Aeneidos Libri VII–VIII.* Oxford.

Frazel, T. D. 2009. *The Rhetoric of Cicero's* In Verrem. Göttingen.

Georges ("Georgii"), H. 1906. *Tiberi Claudi Donati ... Interpretationes Vergilianae.* 2 vols. Leipzig.

Geymonat, M. 1973. *P. Vergili Maronis Opera.* Turin.

Hainsworth, B. 1993. *The* Iliad: *A Commentary.* Vol. 3, *Books 9–12.* Ed. G. S. Kirk. Cambridge.

Hardie, P. 1994. *Virgil.* Aeneid *Book IX.* Cambridge.

———. 1999. Review of Dingel 1997 (q.v.), "Interpretatio Germanica." *CR,* n.s., 49:385–386.

Henry, J. 1881. *Aeneidea.* Vol. 3, *Books V, VI, VII, VIII, and IX.* Dublin.

Highet, G. 1972. *The Speeches in Vergil's* Aeneid. Princeton.

Hoffmann, E. 1853. Review of two editions of *Virgils Gedichte,* by W. Freund and T. Ladewig. *Zeitschrift für die Österreichischen Gymnasien* 4:871–890.

Housman, A. E. 1903. *M. Manilii Astronomicon Liber Primus.* London.

———. 1922. "The Application of Thought to Textual Criticism." *Proceedings of the Classical Association* 18:67–84 (= 1972. *The Classical Papers.* Vol. 3, 1058–1069. Ed. J. Diggle and F. R. D. Goodyear. Cambridge).

Jacobson, H. 1966. "Nonnulla Lucretiana." *CP* 61:151–157.

Kühner, R., and C. Stegmann. 1976. *Ausführliche Grammatik der Lateinischen Sprache.* Part 2, *Satzlehre.* 5th ed., rev. A. Thierfelder. Hanover.

Madvig, J. N. 1873. *Adversaria Critica.* Vol. 2, *Ad Scriptores Latinos.* Copenhagen.

Markland, J. 1728. *P. Papinii Statii Silvarum Libri Quinque.* London.

Mynors, R. A. B. 1969. *P. Vergili Maronis Opera.* Oxford.

Norden, E. 1926. *P. Vergilius Maro. Aeneis Buch VI.* 3rd ed. Leipzig.

Oakley, S. P. 2005. *A Commentary on Livy: Books VI-X.* Vol. 3, *Book IX.* Oxford.

Page, T. E. 1900. *The* Aeneid *of Virgil.* Vol. 2, *Books VII-XII.* London.

Paratore, E., and L. Canali. 1982. *Virgilio. Eneide.* Vol. 5, *Libri IX-X.* Milan.

Peerlkamp, P. Hofman. 1843. *P. Virgilii Maronis Aeneidos.* Vol. 2, *Libri VII-XII.* Leiden.

Ribbeck, O. 1862. *P. Vergili Maronis Opera.* Vol. 3, *Aeneidos Libri VII-XII.* Leipzig.

Richlin, A. 1983. *The Garden of Priapus: Sexuality and Aggression in Roman Humor.* New Haven, CT.

Tarrant, R. J. 1987. "Toward a Typology of Interpolation in Latin Poetry." *TAPA* 117:281–298.

Wagner, P. 1861. *P. Virgili Maronis Carmina.* 3rd ed. Leipzig.

West, D. 2003. *Virgil. The Aeneid.* London.

Williams, C. A. 1999. *Roman Homosexuality: Ideologies of Masculinity in Classical Antiquity.* Oxford.

Williams, R. D. 1973. *The* Aeneid *of Virgil.* Vol. 2, *Books 7-12.* London.

Winbolt, S. E. 1903. *Latin Hexameter Verse: An Aid to Composition.* London.

HYLAS, HERCULES, AND VALERIUS FLACCUS' METAMORPHOSIS OF THE *AENEID*

MARK HEERINK

I. INTRODUCTION: VALERIUS AND VERGIL

EVER SINCE POST-AUGUSTAN EPIC was condemned as "Silver Latin" in the second half of the nineteenth century, and thus as inferior to the *Aeneid*,[1] the influence of Vergil's epic on the *Argonautica* of Valerius Flaccus has been cast in a negative light. Wilamowitz's harsh characterization of Valerius as a slavish imitator of Vergil is the most famous example of this bias,[2] which proved so pervasive that the few scholars who demonstrated Valerius' originality vis-à-vis Vergil tended to

---

The writing of this article, which is based on a chapter from my PhD thesis (Heerink 2010), was made possible by a postdoctoral VENI grant of the Netherlands Organisation for Scientific Research (NWO). Except when indicated otherwise the translations used (and sometimes slightly adapted) are the following: Celoria 1992 (Ant. Lib.); Race 2008 (Ap. Rhod.); Cornish and Goold 1988 (Cat.); Hill 1985 (Ov. Met.); Heyworth 2007 (Prop.); Gow 1950 (Theoc. Id.); Barich 2009 (Val. Flacc.); Lee 1984 (Verg. Ecl.); Johnson 2009 (Verg. G.); West 1991 (Verg. Aen.).

[1] Although the "Silver Latin" terminology predates the nineteenth century (cf. Hinds 1998:83n66: "The earliest OED entry for 'Silver Age' Latin finds the term already standard in 1736"), it was in this century that all post-Augustan poetry was definitively condemned as "Silver" and thus inferior, for instance in Teuffel's influential study (1870), which describes the development of Roman literature in metaphorical terms by means of Hesiod's myth of the degenerating ages of man (*Op.* 106–201). For earlier, more positive scholarly evaluations of the *Argonautica*, see the list of testimonia in Burmannus 1724. See also Zissos 2006a for literary and artistic receptions of Valerius Flaccus' *Argonautica* (with a brief discussion of the scholarly reception on pages 181–182).

[2] Wilamowitz 1924: vol. 2, 165n2: "Ganz erbärmlich ist ... seine sklavische Abhängigkeit von Vergil."

emphasize that he must have been unaware of it: Valerius had wanted to write like Vergil but failed.[3] In recent years, however, Flavian epic in general and Valerius Flaccus in particular have been rehabilitated. Denis Feeney, Philip Hardie, and Andrew Zissos among others have shown how Valerius self-consciously imitates and emulates his Augustan predecessor.[4] Debra Hershkowitz's 1998 monograph on the *Argonautica* is part of this recent reevaluation of Valerius Flaccus' work. Focusing on the actions of the epic's protagonist Jason, Hershkowitz argues that Valerius wrote a heroic version of Apollonius' un-heroic *Argonautica* by making it resemble Vergil's *Aeneid*.[5] Although Hershkowitz regards Valerius' epic as a positive success, in a way her argument—that Valerius "recuperated" the Hellenistic version of the myth by "Vergilization"— strengthens the bias that was responsible for the negative evaluation of the *Argonautica*, namely that the epic is a (mere) imitation of the *Aeneid*. Although Hershkowitz's theory has been challenged,[6] it still represents the *communis opinio* on Valerius Flaccus' relationship to the *Aeneid*.[7]

In this paper, I will further problematize Hershkowitz's assessment of the *Aeneid* as a straightforward model for the *Argonautica* by a metapoetical re-reading of one of Hershkowitz's primary examples: Valerius' treatment of Hylas and Hercules.[8] Although the Flavian *Argonautica* is obviously influenced by the *Aeneid*, I suggest that the allusions to

---

[3] See e.g. Mehmel 1934:135: "der revoltiert, womöglich ohne es zu wissen, gegen das Klassische Virgils." See Barnes 1995:276–277 for similar examples. For un-Vergilian aspects discerned in the *Argonautica* by scholars, see also Zissos 2004:22; 2008:xxxviii.

[4] Feeney 1991:313–337; Hardie 1993; Zissos 2002; 2004; 2006b; 2009:363–366.

[5] See in particular Hershkowitz 1998:105–198 (= Ch. 3: "Recuperations: Better, stronger, faster"), but see already e.g. Malamud and McGuire 1993, who speak of Valerius "consistently reading Apollonius through a Virgilian lens" (192). See also Stover 2003; 2012.

[6] See e.g. the reaction of Zissos 2002:70: "Despite its obvious appeal, the notion of the Flavian poem as an *Argonautica* striving against all odds to be an *Aeneid* no longer seems to do full justice to Valerius' complex artistry or to the richness and subtlety of his poetic program."

[7] See e.g. Conte 1994a:490: "Whereas Apollonius had made Jason a problematic and ambiguous hero, nearly an anti-hero, Valerius once again places his protagonist on a high epic level"; Stover 2003:124.

[8] Hershkowitz 1998:159–165.

Vergil's epic should not be taken at face value. Thwarting the expectations of his readers, these allusions are instead only the prelude to Valerius' self-conscious challenge to Vergil and his poetic agenda.

II. THE EPIC POTENTIAL OF VALERIUS' HYLAS

The boy Hylas initially seems to fulfill an epic role in Valerius' *Argonautica*. When the Greek heroes assemble at the beginning of the epic to join the Argonautic expedition and Hercules and Hylas are introduced, the boy is described as happily carrying the hero's weapons:

> Protinus Inachiis ultro Tirynthius Argis
> advolat, Arcadio cuius flammata veneno
> tela puer facilesque umeris gaudentibus arcus
> gestat Hylas; velit ille quidem, sed *dextera* nondum
> par *oneri* clavaeque capax.
>
> *Argonautica* 1.107–111

> At once Tirynthian Hercules hurries there
> unprodded, from Inachian Argos' land.
> His arrows tipped with venom's Arcadian fire
> and his bow the youngster Hylas carries,
> an easy load his shoulders gladly bear.
> The club as well he'd hold, but still
> his arm can't bear the weight.

Although he is a boy (*puer*) not able to carry Hercules' club, *nondum* ("not yet") suggests that he will be able someday and will thus become an epic hero like his adoptive father. This suggestion is not present in the parallel passage in Apollonius' *Argonautica*:

> σὺν καί οἱ Ὕλας κίεν, ἐσθλὸς ὀπάων
> πρωθήβης, ἰῶν τε φορεὺς φύλακός τε βιοῖο.
>
> *Argonautica* 1.131–132

> And with him went his noble squire Hylas, in the first-
> bloom of youth, to be the bearer of his arrows and guardian
> of his bow.

Hershkowitz argues that Valerius is here viewing Apollonius' epic through a "Vergilian lens." In fact, she shows that the relationship between Valerius' Hylas and Hercules is modeled on that between Vergil's Ascanius and Aeneas.[9] This is already apparent from the passage quoted above, which alludes to *Aeneid* 2. There, in a similar context, at the start of the epic journey of the Trojans, Ascanius is following Aeneas (compare the italicized words in the two passages):

> haec fatus latos umeros subiectaque colla
> veste super fulvique insternor pelle leonis,
> succedoque *oneri*; *dextrae* se parvus Iulus
> implicuit <u>sequiturque patrem non passibus aequis</u>.
>
> *Aeneid* 2.721–724

> When I had finished speaking, I put on a tawny lion's skin
> as a covering for my neck and the breadth of my shoulders
> and then I bowed down and took up my burden. Little Iulus
> twined his fingers in my right hand and kept up with me
> with his short steps.

Later in the epic, at the beginning of the Hylas episode, the intertextual contact with this Vergilian passage is made even more clear. After Hercules has broken his oar in a rowing contest, the Argo slows down and Tiphys steers it towards the Mysian coast. Hercules then heads for the ash trees to cut one down to make a new oar. As several scholars have noted, Hylas following Hercules resembles Ascanius in the footsteps of Aeneas (as the underlining highlights):[10]

> petit excelsas Tirynthius ornos,
> haeret Hylas lateri <u>passusque moratur iniquos</u>.
>
> *Argonautica* 3.485–486

> The man from Tiryns heads toward towering ash trees;
> Hylas keeps close, slowing his longer stride.

---

[9] Hershkowitz 1998:150–154.

[10] See Langen 1896–1897:253 (on Val. Flacc. *Arg.* 3.486); Garson 1963:261; Hershkowitz 1998:151 for the allusion.

Hylas thus again seems to be presented as a potential epic hero, destined to follow in the footsteps of his heroic father, just like Ascanius in the *Aeneid*. For whereas Aeneas' son is still a child at the beginning of the expedition (*parvus Iulus*), he is "flirting with adulthood" in *Aeneid* 9.[11] After Ascanius has slain the aboriginal Numanus Remulus, for instance, who was mocking the Trojans, he is congratulated by Apollo in terms that suggest that he is becoming a *vir*:

> macte nova virtute, puer, sic itur ad astra,
> dis genite et geniture deos.

Aeneid 9.641–642

> You have become a man, young Iulus, and we salute you!
> This is the way that leads to the stars. You are born of the
> gods and will live to be the father of gods.

Ascanius' development in the *Aeneid* deals not only with maturation, however, but also self-reflexively with epic poetry, which, from Homer onwards, was a distinctly masculine affair.[12] As Alison Keith adds, however, "additional pressure on gender may be felt in Latin epic, given the centrality of *vir-tus* in all its senses to the genre at Rome."[13] Because of this particularly close association of Roman epic with masculinity, it is not surprising that Roman poets often self-consciously define epic in programmatic places by reference to men and their stereotypically epic activity, war.[14] Vergil, for instance, in the programmatic prologue of *Eclogue* 6, speaks of *reges et proelia*, "kings and battles" (6), and Horace, in his *Ars Poetica*, describes epic as dealing with *res gestae regumque*

---

[11] Morgan 2003:75. See also Hardie 1994:15–17 on Ascanius in Verg. *Aen.* 9.

[12] As Morgan 2003:66 expresses it: "Genres are gendered, and the epic genre is emphatically masculine." See also Keith 1999:214 and Hinds 2000 on the masculinity of (in particular Roman) epic.

[13] Keith 1999:214.

[14] See, however, Hinds 2000, who shows that in practice Roman poets do not live up to this narrow definition: "'Unepic' elements, no matter how frequently they feature in actual epics, continue to be regarded as unepic; as if oblivious to elements of vitality and change within the genre (for which he himself may be in part responsible), each new Roman writer reasserts a stereotype of epic whose endurance is as remarkable as is its ultimate incompatibility with the actual plot of any actual epic in the Greek or Latin canon" (223).

ducumque et tristia bella, "deeds of kings and leaders and grim wars" (73). The opening of the *Aeneid* (*arma virumque*) is another example, to which Roman poets often refer in more implicitly programmatic, meta-poetical contexts. At the end of his taunting speech to the Trojans, for instance, in which he calls them effeminate, Numanus Remulus tells the Trojans to "leave arms to men" (*sinite arma viris*, *Aeneid* 9.620). Ascanius, by then attacking and killing him, shows Numanus what epic (and more specifically the *Aeneid*) is all about. The juxtaposition of *virtute* and *puer* in Apollo's words (just quoted) reveals how striking this feat actually is: a *boy* has just won a male-epic fight. In his second address to Ascanius, Apollo reminds him of the fact that he is still only a boy, not an epic warrior, a point emphasized by the juxtaposition of *puer* and *bello*:[15]

> sit satis, Aenide, telis impune Numanum
> oppetiisse tuis. primam hanc tibi magnus Apollo
> concedit laudem et paribus non invidet armis;
> cetera parce, puer, bello.
>
> *Aeneid* 9.653–656

> Let that be enough, son of Aeneas. Numanus has fallen to
> your arms and you are unhurt. Great Apollo has granted
> you this first taste of glory and does not grudge you arrows
> as sure as his own. You must ask for no more, my boy, in
> this war.

The killing of Numanus on the battlefield, however, makes it clear that Ascanius is on the verge of becoming a *vir* and thus an epic hero.

In book 3 of Valerius' *Argonautica*, Hylas is also successful on the battlefield, when he defeats Sages from Cyzicus:

> at diversa Sagen turbantem fallere nervo
> tum primum puer ausus Hylas (spes maxima bellis
> pulcher Hylas, si fata sinant, si prospera Iuno)
> prostravitque virum celeri per pectora telo.
>
> *Argonautica* 3.182–185

---

[15] Hardie 1994:209 (ad loc.).

But elsewhere in the field, where Sages works havoc,
boy Hylas for the first time ventures bold
and cheats him with his bow. (The greatest promise
fair Hylas showed for war, if only fate
allowed it, if only Juno had been kind.)
He sends the man sprawling with swift arrow through chest.

As in the case of Ascanius (*tum primum, Aeneid* 9.590), this is Hylas' first fight on the epic battlefield (*tum primum,* 183), and like Aeneas' son, Hylas seems destined to become an epic *vir*. The connection between the two epic boys is reinforced by the denotation of Hylas as *spes maxima bellis* (183), which recalls *Aeneid* 12.168, where Ascanius is called the "second hope of great Rome" (*magnae spes altera Romae*).[16] But there is an important difference, for although Hylas is involved in a battle of epic proportions, it concerns a perversion of war, as the Argonauts are unwittingly killing their own friends, the hospitable Cyzicans.[17] Valerius here seems to decline to write "essential epic,"[18] heroic-epic poetry in its purest form dealing with men and war, in a Vergilian way.

I will now turn to the Hylas episode proper, arguing that it reinforces the impression created by the Cyzicus episode that the *Argonautica* cannot continue in a Vergilian direction. Despite the fact that the Hylas episode is set as a kind of miniature *Aeneid*, as I will first show, Valerius metapoetically states that he only imitates his Augustan predecessor to a limited extent.

---

[16] These intertextual connections between Hylas and Ascanius have also been documented by Spaltenstein 2004:62–63 (ad loc.), who in addition notes the allusion to Marcellus' premature death as mentioned in *Aen.* 6.882–883 (*heu miserande puer, si qua fata aspera rumpas. / tu Marcellus eris.* "Child of a nation's sorrow, could you but shatter the cruel barrier of fate! You are to be Marcellus.") in line 184 (*si fata sinant, si prospera Iuno*), which announces Hylas' disappearance later in the book.

[17] The battle is wholly described in terms of an "unholy" (*nefas*) civil war (see McGuire 1997:108–113), comparable to e.g. the second half of the *Aeneid*. The war at Cyzicus, however, is completely useless (pace Stover 2012:114) , as it serves no purpose whatsoever, and can be considered a perversion even of civil war, "a veritable Hell on Earth" (Hardie 1993:87). That the war is an extreme case is reinforced by Jupiter, who breaks off the battle (Val. Flacc. *Arg.* 3.249–253), and by Valerius' own question to Clio concerning the war: *cur talia passus / arma, quid hospitiis iunctas concurrere dextras / Iuppiter?* "Why Jupiter permits a war like this, a clash / of guest and host?" (Val. Flacc. *Arg.* 3.16–18).

[18] Hinds 2000. See also n. 14 above.

III. A MINIATURE *AENEID*

Contrary to all previous versions of the Hylas story we have,[19] the events in Valerius' episode are motivated by Juno, who wants to remove the hated Hercules from the Argonautic expedition. Although the goddess is the traditional patron deity of the expedition, as she is in Apollonius' epic,[20] she plays no part in the Hellenistic Hylas episode. The inspiration for Valerius' innovation seems to come from his other primary model, Vergil's *Aeneid*; for with her hatred and persecution of a single hero, Valerius' Juno resembles her Vergilian counterpart.[21] In fact, because of her sympathetic role towards the Argonauts and their quest, Juno's hatred in the Hylas episode is striking, and creates the impression that the episode is an *Aeneid* in miniature. This impression is sustained by allusions to Vergil's epic. Juno's entrance in the Hylas episode, for instance, is accompanied by an allusion to *Aeneid* 7:[22]

illum ubi Juno poli summo de vertice puppem
deseruisse videt, *tempus* rata *diva nocendi*

Argonautica 3.487–488

When Juno from the heaven's zenith sees
that he [sc. Hercules] has left the ship, the goddess deems
the time has come for harm.

---

[19] Ap. Rhod. *Arg.* 1.1153–1362; Theoc. *Id.* 13; Prop. 1.20. If we may believe Antoninus Liberalis (*Met.* 26), Nicander also wrote about Hylas in his *Heteroeumena*, a version that Antoninus summarizes (cf. his heading: ἱστορεῖ Νίκανδρος Ἑτεροιουμένων Β′, "Nicander tells this tale in the second book of his *Metamorphoses*"). See also n. 57 below for Nicander's Hylas.

[20] On Hera's role in Apollonius' *Argonautica*, see e.g. Feeney 1991:62–64, 81–85; for Hera in the earlier tradition, see e.g. Klein 1931:19–27.

[21] Malamud and McGuire 1993:201–202; Hershkowitz 1998:160–163 (pages 160–172 discuss the intertextual contact between Vergil's and Valerius' Juno in the rest of the *Argonautica*). On Valerius' Juno in general, see also Schubert 1991; Monaghan 2005.

[22] Langen 1896–1897:253 (on Val. Flacc. *Arg.* 3.488) already noticed the parallel, on which see also Malamud and McGuire 1993:202, but is curiously omitted by Hershkowitz 1998, when dealing with the intertextual contact between Valerius' Juno and her Vergilian counterpart.

at saeva e speculis *tempus dea* nacta *nocendi*
ardua tecta petit stabuli et de culmine summo
pastorale canit signum cornuque recurvo
Tartaream intendit vocem, qua protinus omne
contremuit nemus et silvae insonuere profundae.

Aeneid 7.511–515

The cruel goddess [sc. Allecto] saw from her vantage point
that this was a moment when harm might be done and,
flying to the top of the farm roof, from the highest gable
she sounded the herdsman's signal with a loud call on the
curved horn, and its voice was the voice of Tartarus. The
trees shivered at the noise and the whole forest rang to its
very depths.

Although it is strictly Allecto who initiates the war in Latium in the
Aeneid, it is of course Juno who has commanded her to do so. Valerius'
allusion thus suggests that Juno's action in the Hylas episode—the
climax of Juno's hatred of Hercules in the *Argonautica*, bringing about
the removal of the great hero from the epic[23]—is comparable to her
inciting the war in Latium, which can be considered the culmination of
her hatred against Aeneas and his Trojans.

This connection with *Aeneid* 7 is reinforced somewhat later. After
Juno has set her plan in motion, she delivers an embittered monologue,
the end of which clearly alludes to a similar monologue in *Aeneid* 7,
right before she orders Allecto to stir things up:[24]

verum animis insiste tuis actumque per omnem
tende, pudor; mox et *Furias Ditemque movebo.*

Argonautica 3.519–520

But keep to your resolve, my shame, through all:
I'll soon stir Furies and the god of Hell.

---

[23] Hershkowitz 1998:160.
[24] See e.g. Garson 1963:266; Adamietz 1976:48–49; Eigler 1988:39–47; Malamud and
McGuire 1993:202; Hershkowitz 1998:161 for the allusions to the *Aeneid* in this speech.

flectere si nequeo superos, *Acheronta movebo.*

Aeneid 7.312

If I cannot prevail upon the gods above, I shall move hell.

Valerius' mention of the Furies almost seems a gloss on Vergil's less specific expression, as it is the Fury Allecto that Vergil's Juno will call from Hades.[25] Picking up the previous allusion to *Aeneid* 7 in line 488, Valerius suggests that Juno will call up Allecto in the *Argonautica* as well. Although no Fury appears in the remainder of the episode, Valerius' Juno herself seems to take the role of Vergil's Allecto. Just as the latter stirs up Ascanius' hounds, so that the boy will hunt the stag and unwittingly start the war in Latium, so too Juno rouses a stag to lure Hylas into hunting it:[26]

> sic ait et celerem frondosa per avia cervum
> suscitat ac iuveni sublimem cornibus offert.
> ille animos tardusque fugae longumque resistens
> sollicitat suadetque pari contendere cursu.
> credit Hylas praedaeque ferox ardore propinquae
> insequitur, simul Alcides hortatibus urget
> prospiciens.

Argonautica 3.545–551

[25] Cf. Spaltenstein 2004:153 (on Val. Flacc. *Arg.* 3.517–520. Although Langen 1896–1897:256 (on Val. Flacc. *Arg.* 3.520) notes the Vergilian parallel, he does not see the allusion to *Aeneid* 7 as part of a nexus, and thus interprets the allusion differently: "Videtur Valerius tangere ultimum duodecim laborum, quo Hercules iussus est Cerberum ex inferis afferre; cfr. etiam Verg. Aen. VII, 312."

[26] On the intertextual contact between Hylas' and Ascanius' hunt, see Koch 1955:135–136; Garson 1963:262; Malamud and McGuire 1993:202; Hershkowitz 1998:152–153. In the passage quoted, the denotation of the stag as *sublimem cornibus*, "with antlers high" (545) alludes to Verg. Aen. 7.483, where Silvia's stag is described as having "mighty antlers" (*cornibus ingens*). Hylas' mood during the hunt (*ferox ardore*, "fierce with desire," 549) seems to be inspired by Verg. Aen. 7.496, where the hunting Ascanius is depicted as *laudis succensus amore*, "fired with love for praise" (see Section IV below for the way that Valerius differs from Vergil here). In the passage immediately following the one quoted here, *quadripes*, "four footed (animal)," which denotes Valerius' stag (552), alludes to Aen. 7.500, the only occurrence of *quadripes* to describe a deer in Vergil. Both animals are moreover far away from their hunters (*procul*, Val. Flacc. *Arg.* 3.553 ~ *procul*, Verg. Aen. 7.493). The intertextual contact between Valerius' *spiracula* (553) and Vergil's *saevi spiracula Ditis* (7.568) is discussed in Section VII below.

She spoke, then quickly through the leafy thicket
flushed a stag and brought it in youth's sight
with antlers high. Its slow escape and long
delays arouse the boy's spirit, convincing him
to keep up with the stag's course. He thinks he can
and, hot and fierce, he tracks his nearby quarry,
while Hercules looks on and shouts support.

In no previous version of the story we know is Hylas depicted as
hunting, and Valerius' innovation again "epicizes" Hylas by associating him with Ascanius. Hunting is the traditional activity to prepare
boys for war,[27] but Ascanius' hunt in *Aeneid* 7 is particularly associated with epic, as his shooting of Silvia's stag sets in motion the war
in Latium and thus starts the "essential epic" that Vergil announced in
his programmatic "proem in the middle"[28] at the beginning of *Aeneid*
7.[29] This transition to epic war in *Aeneid* 7 is emphasized by a contrast
between the pastoral and loving world of Latium and the grim reality
of war to which Latium will turn. This contrast can be read in metapoetical terms of genre transformation, as a bucolic and elegiac world
turns into epic.[30] But what about Valerius' Hylas episode? Does Hylas

---

[27] See Aymard 1951:469–481.

[28] The term is borrowed from Conte 1992 (= 2007:219–231), who discusses the
programmatic force of "proems in the middle" in general and this proem in particular.

[29] Verg. *Aen.* 7.41–45: *tu vatem, tu diva, mone. dicam horrida bella, / dicam acies actosque
animis in funera reges, / Tyrrhenamque manum totamque sub arma coactam / Hesperiam. maior
rerum mihi nascitur ordo, / maius opus moveo.* "Come, goddess, come and instruct your
prophet. I shall speak of fearsome fighting, I shall speak of wars and of kings driven into
the ways of death by their pride of spirit, of a band of fighting men from Etruria and the
whole land of Hesperia under arms. For me this is the birth of a higher order of things.
This is a greater work I now set in motion."

[30] See esp. Putnam 1995:118–123 (= 1998:106–110). Hardie 1998:61 conveniently
summarizes the switch from bucolic to epic: "In the *Eclogues* the tranquil world of the
shepherds is recurrently threatened by violent events in the historical world; the transition in *Aeneid* 7 from the peaceful state that preceded the Trojan arrival to all-out war
is also figured as a generic transition, from pastoral to epic: Allecto's last intervention
(7.475–539) causes Ascanius unwittingly to shoot the pet stag belonging to the royal
herdsman's daughter Silvia ('girl of the woods'); Allecto, the 'plague lurking in the
woods,' 7.505, calls the vengeful farmers to arms with a blast on her trumpet, cruelly
labelled a *pastorale signum* ('herdsmen's signal'), to which nature resounds in a parody of

like Ascanius initiate a metapoetical transformation of the poem in which he features?

IV. HYLAS' ELEGIAC HUNT

While hunting for Juno's stag, Hylas is depicted as the potential epic hero that Ascanius has become in the *Aeneid*. Accordingly, the expectation is raised that Hylas' hunt will also lead to an outbreak of war, turning the *Argonautica* into an essential epic. Unlike Ascanius, however, Hylas does not succeed in shooting the animal; for when the stag jumps over a spring, the exhausted boy gives up, just before being pulled into the water by a nymph called Dryope:

> iamque ex oculis aufertur uterque,
> cum puerum instantem quadripes fessaque minantem
> tela manu procul ad nitidi spiracula fontis
> ducit et intactas levis ipse superfugit undas.
> hoc pueri spes lusa modo est nec tendere certat
> amplius; utque artus et concita pectora sudor
> diluerat, gratos avidus procumbit ad amnes.
>
> *Argonautica* 3.551–557

Now both the stag and the boy move out of sight,
and as the boy pressed on and brandished spear
with weary arm, the stag led him to the opening
of a glistening spring, then lightly sprang across,
not touching water. Hopes are this way thwarted
for the boy, and he no longer fights
to keep on going. Sweat has bathed his limbs
and heated chest, and he eagerly falls to the ground
beside the pleasant stream.

Hylas thus seems to fail as an epic hero, an interpretation that is reinforced by the remark that "the boy's hope is thwarted" (*pueri spes lusa ... est*); for although the words refer to Hylas' hope to shoot the stag, they

---

the pastoral echo (7.514–518)." For the metapoetic transition from elegy to epic in *Aeneid* 7, see Section IV below.

also recall the preceding Cyzicus episode in which Hylas was made to resemble Ascanius in the epic potential that he now fails to realize: *spes maxima bellis* (3.183).[31]

Hylas' hunt seems in retrospect less a narrative-doublet for Ascanius' epic hunt than a metaphorical, erotic hunt, as noted by Martha Malamud and Donald McGuire.[32] At the start of the hunt Hylas is described as *ferox ardore* ("fierce with desire," 549). The erotic connotation of these words suggests that Hylas like Silvia—with whom he is etymologically connected[33]—is involved in a elegiac relationship with the stag. This interpretation is supported by the erotically charged language describing the stag's leap over the pool: the water remains untouched (*intactas ... undas*, 554), the adjective suggesting the virginity of the "beloved."[34] Valerius has in this way rewritten Vergil's characterization of Ascanius during the hunt as *eximiae laudis succensus amore* ("burning with love of the highest glory," *Aeneid* 7.496)—while *succensus* can be used in an erotic context,[35] it is clearly used by Vergil in a martial sense. But there is more. As Michael Putnam has noted, Ascanius' "love" is here contrasted with the relationship between Silvia and her stag as described in the ekphrasis of the animal in *Aeneid* 7.493–502,[36] a passage that is replete with elegiac vocabulary.[37] When

---

[31] See the end of Section II above.

[32] Malamud and McGuire 1993:202–203. They do not, however, contrast Hylas' "erotic hunt" to Ascanius' hunting in *Aeneid* 7, but relate it to the "hunting imagery set up in *Aeneid* 1–4," which "becomes one of the dominant metaphors for the fatal love of Dido" (202).

[33] *Silva* is the Latin equivalent of ὕλη (both can mean "forest," "wood" [*OLD* 1, 2; LSJ I, II], but also metaphorically "(literary) material" [*OLD* 5b; LSJ III.3]), which is an ancient etymology of Hylas: see Barchiesi 2001:189n41 for examples of puns on Hylas' etymology. See Petrain 2000 for an etymological play in Prop. 1.20.6–7 on Hylas and ὕλη through the latter's equivalent *silva*; see Section VI below for an example in Valerius' Hylas episode.

[34] These erotic connotations of *ferox ardore* and *intactas undas* have been noted by Malamud and McGuire 1993:203. For the erotic sense of the verb *tangere*, see also *OLD* 5b: "to touch (in a sexual or erotic sense)."

[35] Horsfall 2000:333 (on Verg. *Aen.* 7.496) adduces Prop. 1.2.15 and 3.19.15 as parallels for the verb *succendere* in an amatory sense.

[36] Putnam 1995:112 (= 1998:101–102). Ovid also seems to have reworked Vergil erotically in *Her.* 15.157: *Pyrrhae succensus amore* ("burning with love for Pyrrha").

[37] Putnam 1995:126–128 (= 1998:113–116).

Ascanius is described hunting the stag immediately after the ekphrasis, the elegiac association of the deer is continued through allusion to the famous simile in *Aeneid* 4.68–73 comparing Dido, struck by "elegiac" love,[38] to a wounded deer (and, by implication, Aeneas to the hunter),[39] albeit with a twist. The difference between the two Vergilian passages is, of course, that the hunting in book 4 is only metaphorical, whereas Ascanius is literally hunting a stag; but another verbal parallel between the two texts reveals that both Aeneas' metaphorical wounding of the elegiac Dido and Ascanius' shooting of Silvia's stag are in fact comparable from a metapoetical point of view. Immediately before the ekphrasis of the stag, Vergil comments on Allecto's rousing of Ascanius'

---

[38] For the influence of Roman love elegy on *Aeneid* 4, see e.g. Hinds 1987:134–135; Cairns 1989:135–150 (Ch. 6: "Dido and the elegiac tradition"); Hardie 1998:61–62; Harrison 2007:208–214. Like the love of Silvia for her stag, however, Dido's love is not typically elegiac. As Stephen Harrison puts it (2007:211): "In elegy it is almost always the tormented male lover who describes himself as feeling the symptoms of love and suffering rejection and abandonment; in the *Aeneid* it is Dido who is depicted as enduring this range of emotions, while Aeneas steadfastly keeps his (genuine) feelings under control ... and suffers insomnia only in the manner of a good leader."

[39] Compare Verg. *Aen.* 7.493–494: *hunc procul errantem rabidae venantis Iuli / commovere canes* ("This is the creature that was roaming far from home when it was startled by the maddened dogs of the young huntsman Iulus") and Verg. *Aen.* 7.498–499: *actaque multo / perque uterum sonitu perque ilia venit harundo* ("The arrow flew with a great hiss and passed straight through the flank into the belly") with Verg. *Aen.* 4.68.73: *uritur infelix Dido totaque vagatur / urbe furens, qualis coniecta cerva sagitta, / quam procul incautam nemora inter Cresia fixit / pastor agens telis liquitque volatile ferrum /nescius; illa fuga silvas saltusque peragrat / Dictaeos; haeret lateri letalis harundo.* "Dido was on fire with love and wandered all over the city in her misery and madness like a wounded doe which a shepherd hunting in the woods of Crete has caught off guard, striking her from long range with steel-tipped shaft; the arrow flies and is left in her body without her knowing it; she runs away over all the wooded slopes of Mount Dicte, and sticking in her side is the arrow that will bring her death." Furthermore, like Dido in the first line of book 4, the stag is wounded (*saucius*, 500), and like the elegiac *questus* of Dido in her soliloquy (*tantos ... questus*, Verg. *Aen.* 4.553), the wounded stag is also complaining (*questu*, 501; see n. 48 below for the elegiac ring of *questus*). One of Dido's complaints, incidentally, that she was not allowed to live her life *more ferae*, "like a wild animal" (Verg. *Aen.* 4.551), further strengthens the contact between Dido and Silvia's stag, a literal "wild animal," which is (like Dido) disturbed and wounded by a Trojan (Putnam 1995:112 [= 1998:101]). For the intertextual contact between Ascanius' hunt in *Aeneid* 7 and the simile in *Aeneid* 4, see also Griffin 1986:180–182; Putnam 1995:111–112 (= 1998:101), to whom my discussion owes much. See Horsfall 2000:321 (on Verg. *Aen.* 7.525–539) for more bibliography.

hounds as "the first cause of suffering" and the beginning of war in Latium (*quae prima laborum / causa fuit belloque animos accendit agrestis,* 7.481–482). This language recalls another famous scene in *Aeneid* 4, the marriage of Aeneas and Dido in the cave, which is commented on by the authorial narrator in similar terms: *ille dies primus leti primusque malorum / causa fuit.* "That day was the first cause of death and the first of disaster" (4.169–70).[40] So the misery and death of Dido (to which this marriage will eventually lead) and the war in Latium are associated, a link described by Putnam as follows: "Had circumstances been otherwise and Aeneas not impinged upon her world, she [sc. Dido] might have continued through life with a type of freedom similar to that which Virgil allots both the Latins and Silvia's stag."[41] In metapoetical terms, this implies that the two poetic, elegiac worlds that oppose the epic mission of the *Aeneid*, that of Dido and that of Silvia and her stag, yield to their opposite—(essential) epic—as represented by two male epic heroes, Aeneas and his son Ascanius.[42] In Valerius' *Argonautica,* however, this poetic transformation is reversed: exploiting the intertextual contact between *Aeneid* 7 and *Aeneid* 4, Hylas' initial Ascanian, epic hunt has turned into an erotic, elegiac hunt.

V. HERCULES AS ELEGIAC LOVER

Hylas is not the only one elegized in Valerius' Hylas episode. Through his abduction the boy becomes the unattainable elegiac beloved of Hercules, who is consequently also transformed, from an epic hero into an elegiac lover. As soon as Hercules notices that Hylas is gone, he is stricken by elegiac *amor:*[43]

> varios hinc excitat aestus
> nube mali percussus amor: quibus haeserit oris,

[40] The translation is mine.

[41] Putnam 1995:112 (= 1998:101).

[42] Cf. Hardie 1998:61–62: "[O]ne way of viewing the situation in *Aeneid* 4 is as the interference of the values of the world of love elegy in the Roman (and epic) mission of Aeneas."

[43] Spaltenstein 2004:166 (ad loc.). Cf. Val. Flacc. *Arg.* 3.736: *urit amor* ("his love burns"); *Arg.* 4.2: *amores* (discussed in Section VIII below).

quis tales impune moras casusve laborve
attulerit?

Argonautica 3.572–575

Then his love stirs a surge of feelings,
assailed by a cloud of trouble: where did he linger,
what brought such long, inordinate delay?
Was it accident, or some task he's doing?

The pallor and madness that Hercules experiences next are also typically elegiac:[44] *tum vero et pallor et amens / cum piceo sudore rigor.* "Truly
did he turn pale then, and a numb frenzy took hold of him, while sweat
pours down, black like pitch" (576–577).[45] Somewhat later, he is even
described as experiencing the typically elegiac *furor*,[46] and is in this
respect compared to a wounded lion:

ille, velut refugi quem contigit improba Mauri
lancea sanguineus vasto leo murmure fertur
frangit et absentem vacuis sub dentibus hostem,
sic furiis accensa gerens Tirynthius ora
fertur et intento decurrit montibus arcu.

Argonautica 3.587–591

[44] For *amens*, see e.g. the programmatic passage in Prop. 1.1.11, where Milanion is
"wandering madly in the dells of mount Parthenius" (*nam modo Partheniis amens errabat
in antris*). For *pallor*, compare what Propertius tells Gallus about Cynthia's effect on the
elegiac lover in 1.5.21: *tum grave servitium nostrae cogere puellae / discere et exclusum quid sit
abire domum; / nec iam pallorem totiens mirabere nostrum, / aut cur sim toto corpore nullus ego.*
"Then you will be forced to learn how hard it is to be a slave of our mistress and what it
is to depart from the house shut out. Nor will you any longer be surprised at my frequent
pallor, or wonder why my whole body is as nothing."
[45] Translation: Mozley 1934.
[46] Cf. Val. Flacc. *Arg.* 4.5: *haeret inops solisque furit Tirynthius oris.* "Tirynthian clings
helpless to a lonely shore / and rages." For the elegiac associations of *furor* ("madness"),
see e.g. Conte 1994b:54: "[T]he ideology of elegy ... associated love and *furor* in a strict
rhetorical bond and, by entrusting erotic passion to the logic of impetuous impulses,
denied it the positivity of a stable satisfaction." Cf. also *furor* at the beginning of
Propertius' oeuvre in 1.1.7: *ei mihi, iam toto furor hic non deficit anno, / cum tamen adversos
cogor habere deos.* "Alas, already a whole year has gone by and still madness has not left
me." Cf. also Conte 1986:109n13: "In Ovid's 'Triumph of Love,' *Amores* 1.2.25ff. ... a mocking
parody of a solemn Roman triumph ... one of the elegiac personifications in Eros' train is,
significantly, called Furor."

The man was like
a bloodied lion whom a shameful spear
thrown by a fleeing Moor has hit, who moves
along with cavernous roar; in empty teeth
it grinds its absent foe. So Tiryns' man,
his face aflame with rage, now moves along.
and runs down hillsides with his bowstring drawn.

Aeneid 4 also comes into play again, for in this context Hercules obviously resembles the lovesick, elegiac Dido compared to a wounded deer. Later in the episode, when it is said that "his love burns" (*urit amor*, 736), Hercules' *amor* again resembles Dido's elegiac passion, for which the fire metaphor is continuously employed.[47] The elegiac nature of Hercules' love is made even more clear when Hylas addresses Hercules in the aftermath of the episode, at the beginning of book 4, and describes his love as *questus* ("complaint"), a word that is often used to denote Roman love elegy, by reference to the genre's supposed origin:[48] *quid, pater, in vanos absumis tempora questus?* "Why do you waste your time, / father, in useless complaint?" (25).

VI. THE BUCOLIC WORLD OF VALERIUS' HYLAS EPISODE

By elegizing Hylas' hunt and turning Hercules in the Hylas episode into an elegiac lover, Valerius inverts Vergil's transformation of Latium into an epic world of war. But Vergil's pre-war Latium was also associated with bucolic poetry, in fact with his own *Eclogues*.[49] Valerius correspondingly inverts Vergil's metapoetical progress in book 7, from the world of the *Eclogues* to the essential-epic world of the *Aeneid*, by staging both the disappearance of Hylas and Hercules' mourning in a bucolic landscape. Already the nymphs who inhabit Mysia evoke a bucolic world, but Valerius seems to associate the world of Mysia specifically with

---

[47] E.g. Verg. *Aen.* 4.68: *uritur infelix Dido.* "Unhappy Dido burns." See n. 38 above for the elegiac nature of Dido's passion.

[48] See e.g. Barchiesi 1993:365: "There is a strong tradition in Roman culture (not, apparently, in Alexandria) connecting the birth of elegy with lament, *querela*, ἒ ἒ λέγειν and the like."

[49] See n. 30 above.

Vergil's *Eclogues*; the landscape Hercules traverses as an elegiac lover is repeatedly referred to as *silvae*,[50] a word that Vergil uses metonymically to denote his own bucolic poetry.[51] Furthermore, the forest (and nature more generally) is personified by Valerius, for when Hercules wanders through the *silva* in his search for Hylas, it is said to be afraid:

> pavet omnis conscia late
> silva, pavet montes, luctu succensus acerbo
> quid struat Alcides tantaque quid apparet ira.
>
> *Argonautica* 3.584–586

> Far and wide whole forest knows what passed
> and trembles, and hilltops tremble: what might he do,
> Alcides, fired by bitter grief? What could
> a wrath so huge devise?

At the beginning of book 4, Valerius' *silvae* again show emotions. After Jupiter has let his son fall asleep, the forests, wearied by Hercules' loud presence, get relief at last:[52]

> tandem fessis pax reddita silvis,
> fluminaque et vacuis auditae montibus aurae.
>
> *Argonautica* 4.20–21

> Peace returns at last to the weary forest,
> and streams and breezes can be heard in empty hills.

Silvae in the *Eclogues* are also commonly personified, as part of an omnipresent "pathetic fallacy," for instance in *Eclogue* 5:[53]

---

[50] Val. Flacc. *Arg.* 3.585, 597, 685, 736; 4.20, 66.

[51] Heyworth 2005:149.

[52] As Murgatroyd 2009:41 suggests, *vacuis* (21) can here also mean "free from distractions" (*OLD* 11) or "free from anxiety" (*OLD* 12b), which would further personify the hills, and by extension the *silvae* as well. Murgatroyd's argument for this sense of *vacuis* here, however, that "'vacant' is not a likely sense as Hercules is still in the area, and so is Hylas ... not to mention animals" is nonsensical: in the first instance the word clearly refers to the absence of Hercules' *screaming*, not his (or, for that matter, anyone else's) presence, the personifying sense being secondary.

[53] On the "pathetic fallacy," i.e. the attribution of human feelings to nature, in Theocritus and Virgil's *Eclogues* in general, see e.g. Dick 1968.

Daphni, tuum Poenos etiam ingemuisse leones
interitum montesque feri silvaeque loquuntur.

Eclogue 5.27–28

The wild hills, Daphnis, and the forests even tell
how Punic lions roared in grief at your destruction.

This personification of nature is one aspect of the harmony that exists in the *Eclogues* between man and a sympathizing, responding landscape—as symbolized by the "pastoral echo"—and that is a precondition for bucolic poetry.[54] Valerius' personified landscape, however, is not at all in harmony with Hercules, who frightens the *silvae*. The archetypal hero Hercules is thus presented as thoroughly out of place in this bucolic world. In fact, he is forced into the role of frustrated elegiac lover in a bucolic landscape with which the hero does not know how to deal.

Hylas, too, is associated not only with elegy (through his "erotic hunt") but also with Vergil's *Eclogues*. When Hercules cries out Hylas' name, he is answered by the woods, *silvae*. The echo at first seems to be merely a natural phenomenon:

rursus Hylan et rursus Hylan per longa reclamat
avia: responsant silvae et vaga certat imago.

Argonautica 3.596–597

---

[54] On the importance of "pastoral echo" in the *Eclogues*, see Desport 1952:63–69; Damon 1961:281–290; Boyle 1977; Hardie 1998:11; Hardie 2002:123–124. For similar expressions of sympathy by a personified bucolic landscape in the *Eclogues*, see e.g. Verg. *Ecl.* 1.38–39: *ipsae te, Tityre, pinus, / ipsi te fontes, ipsa haec arbusta vocabant.* "The very pines, Tityrus, / the very springs, these very orchards called to you!"; Verg. *Ecl.* 10.13–15: *illum etiam lauri, / etiam flevere myricae, / pinifer illum etiam sola sub rupe iacentem / Maenalus, et gelidi fleverunt saxa Lycaei.* "The laurels even, even the tamarisks wept for him / lying beneath a lonely cliff; even Maenalus' / pine-forests wept for him, and cold Lycaeus' rocks." Cf. Verg. *G.* 4.460–463 (nature's reaction to the death of Eurydice): *At chorus aequalis Dryadum clamore supremos / implerunt montes; flerunt Rhodopeiae arces / altaque Pangaea et Rhesi mavortia tellus / atque Getae atque Hebrus et Actias Orithyia.* "The chorus of her companion dryads with wailing rimmed / the mountain's peak, the crags of Rhodope mourned, / and alpen Pangaea, the martial land of Rhesus and the Getae, / the Hebrus mourned, and Orithyia the northwind's Attic bride."

"Hylas," he shouts, "Hylas," over and over again through pathless territory. The forests reply and the wandering echo emulates his cry.[55]

Silva, however, can translate ὕλη—an ancient etymology for Hylas' name. It thus becomes possible to read Hylas as a personified echo responding to Hercules' cries,[56] into which he was in fact transformed by Nicander's nymphs in his lost *Heteroeumena*.[57] This echo motif is reflected both by Theocritus in *Idyll* 13 (58–60) and by Vergil in his sixth *Eclogue* (43–44), in which Hylas also seems to respond as an echo:

τρὶς μὲν Ὕλαν ἄυσεν, ὅσον βαθὺς ἤρυγε λαιμός·
τρὶς δ' ἄρ' ὁ παῖς ὑπάκουσεν, ἀραιὰ δ' ἵκετο φωνά
ἐξ ὕδατος, παρεὼν δὲ μάλα σχεδὸν εἴδετο πόρρω.

Idyll 13.58–60

"Hylas" he [sc. Heracles] shouted thrice with all the power of his deep throat, and thrice the boy replied, but faint came his answering cry from the water, and far off though very near at hand.

The reply of Theocritus' Hylas to Heracles has much in common with an echo: three cries, three replies, and the answer is distant and faint.[58] Furthermore, line 59, describing Hylas' answer, "echoes" Heracles' cry in the previous line on both a textual and a phonic level (τρίς - τρίς, ἄϋσεν - ὑπάκουσεν).[59]

[55] The translation is mine.

[56] Barchiesi 2001:140: "Valerius has his *silvae* repeat the name *Hylas*, a word containing the Greek equivalent to *silva—hulê—*producing a perfect convergence of signifier and signified." See also n. 33 above on the etymological wordplay on Hylas - ὕλη through *silva*.

[57] Nic. fr. 48 Gow-Scholfield (= Ant. Lib. *Met.* 26.4): νύμφαι δὲ δείσασαι τὸν Ἡρακλέα, μὴ αὐτὸν εὕροι κρυπτόμενον παρ' αὐταῖς, μετέβαλον τὸν Ὕλαν καὶ ἐποίησαν ἠχὼ καὶ πρὸς τὴν βοὴν πολλάκις ἀντεφώνησεν Ἡρακλεῖ. "The nymphs, fearing that Heracles might discover that they had hidden the lad among them, changed him into an echo which again and again echoed back the cries of Heracles." See also n. 19 above.

[58] Cf. Hunter 1999:282 (on Theoc. *Id.* 13.58–60): "the experience of deceptive distance suggests the familiar echo effect."

[59] Bonanno 1990:195–196. Furthermore, the postponed metrical position of ὑπάκουσεν in relation to ἄϋσεν creates the fading effect of an echo. Incidentally, the great acoustic

In his miniature version of the Hylas myth in *Eclogue* 6, Vergil concentrates on the echo, which he literally repeats:

> his adiungit, Hylan nautae quo fonte relictum
> clamassent, ut litus "Hyla Hyla" omne sonaret.
>
> *Eclogue* 6.43–44

> [Silenus] adds at what fountain mariners for Hylas lost
> shouted till all the shore re-echoed *Hylas, Hylas.*

Much as in Theocritus' echoing lines, Vergil's echo is imitated in the prosody, as the sequence of the long and the short *a* in *Hylā Hylă* creates the effect of a fading echo.[60]

The cry of Valerius' Hercules, with its double *Hylan*, is a clear allusion to Vergil's repetition *Hyla Hyla*,[61] further marked by Valerius' double *rursus* and *reclamat* in 596.[62] The allusive play is quite sophisticated as the intertextual echo inverts the acoustic one: Vergil's *Hyla Hyla* paradoxically becomes the echo of Hercules' cry *Hylan ... Hylan* in the *Argonautica*.[63] Furthermore, as Alessandro Barchiesi notes on Valerius' passage, "Virgil's presence is supported ... above all by the echo of another acoustic phenomenon from the *Eclogues*."[64] The passage referred to is *Eclogue* 10.8, an instance of the "pastoral echo": *non canimus surdis: respondent omnia silvae.* "Not to the deaf we sing; the forests answer all."[65]

---

distance between Heracles and Hylas seems to be expressed mimetically by the separation of παρεών and πόρρω.

[60] E.g. Barchiesi 2001:188n3. See also Wills 1996:346–347 and Hinds 1998:5–6 for similar, rare reproductions of echoes in Ovid and Vergil. Vergil even seems to react to Theocritus, whose Heracles cried "Hylas" thrice, by mimetically reproducing Theocritus' statement with *Hylan* and the repeated *Hyla Hyla*; morphologically, *Hylan* is distinct from the two vocatives, but not phonetically, because of the subsequent *nautae* (Bonanno 1990:197; Wills 1996:53 with n. 11).

[61] See Hollander 1981:13; Malamud and McGuire 1993:213; Barchiesi 2001:140 for the intertextual contact.

[62] Barchiesi 2001:188n39: "'Once again' expresses both the phonic and intertextual reiteration of the name; *reclamat*, coming after the Virgilian *clamassent*, is a gloss on this process of replicating what has also been said / written." See also Wills 1996:30–31 on "external markers" of allusion.

[63] Barchiesi 2001:140 with n. 39.

[64] Barchiesi 2001:140.

[65] See n. 54 above for the "pastoral echo."

Valerius' etymological wordplay and allusions to Vergil's *Eclogues* in this passage thus suggest that Hylas, transformed into an echo, answers Hercules' cry as Vergil's bucolic *silvae*, the woods that the boy represents in accordance with his name.

VII. DRYOPE AS FURY OF LOVE

While there is a clear evocation of a bucolic world in the Hylas episode, it is the elegiac elements that are most prominent in Valerius' inversion of the genre transformation in *Aeneid* 7. Juno is the main agency responsible for this "elegizing" of the *Aeneid*, but she is helped by the nymph Dryope, who in this respect resembles Juno's Vergilian assistant, the Fury Allecto. This resemblance is strengthened by an allusion to *Aeneid* 7. Valerius' striking *spiracula* ("opening," *OLD* 2) in line 553, describing Dryope's pool, alludes to *Aeneid* 7.568 (*saevi spiracula Ditis*), the only occurrence of the word in Vergil, and in fact one of the few occurrences in Latin poetry.[66] It there denotes Allecto's abode, to which the Fury returns after having performed her duty for Juno. The allusion implies that Juno's words *Furias Ditemque movebo* ("I will stir the Furies and Dis," 3.520)[67] earlier in the Hylas episode refer not only to the action of the goddess herself, who shares characteristics with Allecto, as we have seen, but also to the nymph Dryope, whose dwelling resembles that of Allecto and who, in parallel with Vergil's Fury, is helping Juno on her mission against an epic hero. The difference is that whereas Allecto starts a war, transforming Vergil's elegiac Latium into the grim world of epic, Valerius' "Fury" Dryope does quite the opposite. By means of the abduction she elegizes a potentially epic episode, by turning a potential epic hero, Hylas, and Hercules, the epic hero *par excellence*, into elegiac beloved and elegiac lover, respectively. Dryope does in fact satisfy the etymological definition of a fury by inspiring *furor*, albeit the elegiac kind, and not the madness of epic war.[68] As Ascanius' epic hunt is trans-

---

[66] The word only occurs in Lucretius (6.493), but cf. Enn. *Ann.* 222 (*sulpureas posuit spiramina Naris ad undas*). See Spaltenstein 2004:161 (ad loc.) for a discussion of the meaning of *spiracula* in *Arg.* 3.553.

[67] The translation here is mine.

[68] See n. 46 above for elegiac *furor*.

formed into an erotic one, so is Allecto transformed by Valerius into what can be called a "Fury of love."

So Valerius has elegized the *Aeneid*—or more specifically the "essential epic" into which it turned in book 7—in an episode that is set up as a miniature *Aeneid*, but is in fact an inversion of it. As I will now argue, the episode represents the entire *Argonautica* in this respect, as it prefigures the eventual outcome of the epic.

VIII. LEAVING THE *AENEID* BEHIND

In the epilogue to the Hylas episode at the beginning of book 4 the elegiac transformation of Hercules is commented on by Jupiter. The god is not pleased with the situation and angrily addresses Juno:

> atque ea non oculis divum pater amplius aequis
> sustinuit, natique pios miseratus amores
> Iunonem ardenti trepidam gravis increpat ira.
>
> *Argonautica* 4.1–3

> The Father of gods could stand the sight no more
> unmoved; he pitied his son's devoted love
> and railed at Juno hard, burning with anger
> as she quailed before him.

The word *amores*, which describes Hercules' passion, again seems to refer to love elegy, by reference to Gallus' and Ovid's elegiac *Amores*.[69] But Hercules' elegiac love is called *pius*, which associates the hero

---

[69] Jupiter's depiction of Hercules as "raging on lonely shores" (*solisque furit Tirynthius oris*, Val. Flacc. *Arg.* 4.5) also has elegiac connotations: see n. 46 above for elegiac *furor*, and Sharrock 1990:571 (on Prop. 3.3.23–24: *alter remus aquas alter tibi radat harenas, / tutus eris: medio maxima turba mari est.* "Let one of your oars skim the water, the other the sand: you will be safe; the greatest storm [*and* crowd] is in mid sea.") for the possible elegiac association of the shore: "The high sea which Propertius is to avoid by staying close to the shore is epic poetry. Could it be that the image is quite precise? One line of his poetry (*alter remus*) touches the open sea (epic); the other touches the shore (elegy). One line (the hexameter) is 'epic,' in that it is common to both epic and elegy; the other line (the pentameter) is peculiar to elegy and so is the element which defines the poetry's generic status."

with Vergil's Aeneas, whose defining characteristic is his *pietas*.[70] This Vergilian association accords with the rest of the episode. As we have seen above, for instance, the scene in which Hylas follows Hercules alluded to Ascanius following Aeneas in *Aeneid* 2. Most importantly, the entire episode was determined by Juno, whose action against Hercules resembled that of her Vergilian counterpart against Aeneas. But whereas Jupiter kept control over the epic in the *Aeneid*, Juno gets what she wants in the *Argonautica*. Jupiter's beloved, Aeneas-like Hercules, is removed from the epic and Jupiter's chances of being honored with an *Aeneid* are gone. When the angry Jupiter comments on this situation a few lines after the passage just quoted, his words get a metapoetical charge via an allusion to the first words of the *Aeneid*:

> sic Iuno ducem fovet anxia curis
> Aesonium, sic *arma viro* sociosque ministrat!
>
> *Argonautica* 4.7–8

> So that's how Juno, racked with worry, nurtures
> her captain Jason, that is how she gives him
> the men and arms he needs.

Feeney has paraphrased the metapoetical implications of line 8 as: "So this is your idea of how to run an epic."[71] In the light of my interpretation of Valerius' interactions with the *Aeneid*, however, I propose that Jupiter's metapoetical statement refers specifically to Vergil's epic. Realizing that this poem cannot become an heroic *Aeneid* any more, Jupiter then tells Juno to continue her approach (13–14):[72] *i, Furias*

---

[70] Malamud and McGuire 1993:208 have noted the "Virgilian overtones" of the phrase. Cf. Murgatroyd 2009:34 (on Val. Flacc. *Arg.* 4.2): "VF may be presenting Hercules here as a second Aeneas." See also Galinsky 1972:163 on Hercules in Valerius' Hylas episode in general: "He is the pious son of Jupiter, almost another Aeneas."

[71] Feeney 1991:324. See Hershkowitz 1998:163 (followed by Murgatroyd 2009:37 [on Val. Flacc. *Arg.* 3.7–8]) for another interpretation of the line: "Jupiter indicates that Juno in her Vergilian guise is not behaving in a manner appropriate to her role in this epic." This reading cannot, however, be reconciled with the fact that Juno gets what she wants, and that the epic will / must take a different course in what follows (see below).

[72] Cf. Feeney 1991:324: "Robbing Jason of Hercules means that the gaining of the fleece cannot remain a martial endeavour: now, says Jupiter, Juno will have to fall back on the Furies, and Venus, and Medea."

Veneremque move, dabit impia poenas / virgo. "Go on and rouse the Furies and Venus too. / The wicked girl will have her punishment." Jupiter here ironically alludes to Juno's own words, which immediately preceded and referred to the action she planned against Hercules to remove him from the epic:[73] *mox et Furias Ditemque movebo.* "I'll soon stir Furies and the god of Hell." (3.520). These words, as argued above, alluded to *Aeneid* 7.312 (*Acheronta movebo*), initially creating the expectation that Juno would also start an essential epic in the *Argonautica*. The "Fury" appeared to be Juno herself, however, and her accomplice Dryope was also associated with the Vergilian Allecto. But Valerius, instead of developing from this point an heroic epic in its purest form, allowed Juno and Dryope to elegize it. Jupiter now tells Juno to employ "the Furies and Venus" in the remainder of the epic, clearly referring to the elegiac passion of Medea that Juno and Venus will stir up and that will eventually ensure the success of the epic mission.[74] The god's remark is more or less a hendiadys, since, as Hardie has argued, "for Valerius the workings of Venus, of Juno, and of the Furies are practically indistinguishable."[75] A link thus seems to be created between the elegized *Aeneid* that the Hylas episode has turned into, through the agency of the "Furies of love" Juno and Dryope, and the outcome of the epic, which requires the same kind of elegiac Fury now that Hercules is gone.[76]

---

[73] Hershkowitz 1998:164n219: "4.13 is an ironic echo of Juno's declaration at 3.520." Cf. Murgatroyd 2009:38 (on Val. Flacc. *Arg.* 4.13): "There may also be a barbed echo of Juno's *Furias Ditemque movebo* at 3.520, indicating that the omniscient Jupiter overheard her."

[74] For Medea's elegiac passion, see e.g. Val. Flacc. *Arg.* 7.154; 315, where it is denoted as *furor*, "madness" (cf. n. 46 above); Val. Flacc. *Arg.* 7.12, where Medea is called *demens*, "mad" (as Dido in Verg. *Aen.* 4.78; see n. 87 below for bibliography on the parallels between the love of Dido and that of Medea); Val. Flacc. *Arg.* 7.307, where her love is described as *saevus amor*, "cruel love."

[75] Hardie 1989:6. Cf. Feeney 1991:322–324, esp. e.g. 324n36 on Valerius' Lemnos episode: "It was Venus, assimilated to the condition of a Fury, who was responsible for the Lemnian episode (2.101–106)" and Elm von der Osten 2007, e.g. 179n501: "Außer dem Eingreifen der Göttin Venus bzw. Iuno in der Lemnosepisode und in der Medeahandlung ist auch ein Episode im dritten Buch relevant, in der Iuno die Nymphe Dryope zu beinflussen sucht (3.487ff.)."

[76] Incidentally, this inversion of the role of elegy in the *Argonautica* in comparison with that in the *Aeneid* is also visible in the inversion of the roles that the gods Juno and Venus play in the respective epics: "Venus, like Vergil's Juno, is out for destruction at any cost, while Juno, like Vergil's Venus, wants to protect her hero." (Hershkowitz 1998:170).

Juno also makes the importance of Medea quite clear later in the epic, for when the *Argonautica* has turned into a full-scale Iliadic, essential-epic battle between Aeetes, helped by the Argonauts, and his brother Perses in book 6, Juno sees that this is not the way for this epic to succeed:[77]

> talia certatim Minyae sparsique Cytaei
> funera miscebant campis Scythiamque premebant.
> cum Iuno Aesonidae non hanc ad vellera cernens
> esse viam nec sic reditus regina parandos,
> extremam molitur opem ...
> . . . .
> sola animo Medea subit, mens omnis in una
> virgine, nocturnis qua nulla potentior aris.
>
> *Argonautica* 6.427–431, 439–440

> Such deaths the Minyae dealt on field of battle;
> vying with the scattered men of Cytaeae,
> they overwhelmed Scythia. Juno saw
> that this was not the way to get the Fleece
> for Jason, or arrange his coming home,
> and she contrives a last resort ...
> . . . .
> Medea only comes to mind; this girl
> alone gets full attention, potent more
> than any at the altars of the night.

In fact, Juno elegizes this most epic, most Homeric, moment in the poem—a moment that invites further comparison with the second half of the *Aeneid*[78]—in a move that recalls her interference in the Hylas

---

[77] Cf. Feeney 1991:326 on this passage: "The confrontation between the irrelevant grandiosity of martial epic and the present needs of this poem could not be more starkly engineered." Cf. also Monaghan 2005:15–16. For the influence of the *Iliad* on the battles of *Argonautica* 6, see e.g. Fuà 1988; Smolenaars 1991.

[78] E.g. Baier 2001:11: "Die Anführung von Truppenkatalogen sowie die Schilderung von Schlachtszenen ist zum einen als Reminiszenz an die *Ilias* gestaltet, zum anderen als Wiederaufnahme des Krieges zwischen Trojanern und Rutulern in der *Aeneis*." See Baier 2001:65–68 and Wijsman 2000:5–8, 12–13 for a more detailed discussion of the parallels.

episode. As Feeney observes: "The poem's great set-piece battle book is undermined, to become only an occasion for the girl to fall in love with her future husband; Jason's greatest moment of heroic action is engineered by Juno in order to impress Medea (6.600–620)."[79]

This course of events is already announced by Valerius' programmatic second proem, in book 5 of the *Argonautica* (217–224). The passage is clearly modeled on Vergil's "proem in the middle" in *Aeneid* 7 (37–45),[80] which initiates the second half of the epic. Similarly, Valerius invokes the Muse to start the second half of his *Argonautica*, which will be markedly different from the first:[81]

> incipe nunc cantus alios, dea, visaque vobis
> Thessalici da bella ducis. non mens mihi, non haec
> ora satis. ventum ad furias infandaque natae
> foedera et horrenda trepidam sub virgine puppem;
> impia monstriferis surgunt iam proelia campis.
> ante dolos, ante infidi tamen exsequar astus
> Soligenae falli meriti meritique relinqui,
> inde canens.
>
> Argonautica 5.217–224

> And now, goddess, begin another song,
> of Thessaly's captain tell the wars you witnessed.
> My heart and voice have not the strength for this.
> I come to mad passion and a pact past telling
> of a daughter, a maiden to be dreaded,
> who caused the ship to shake beneath her.
> A sacrilegious war now looms on plains

---

[79] Feeney 1991:326. Cf. Hershkowitz 1998:123–125; Lovatt 2006; Elm von der Osten 2007:68–73 for the way the typically epic teichoscopy is transformed by Valerius.

[80] See also the end of Section III with n. 29 above for Vergil's second proem. For the parallels between the two proems, see e.g. Hershkowitz 1998:7–10 and Spaltenstein 2004: 442–443 (ad loc.).

[81] With most scholars I agree that the intended length of Valerius' epic was eight books, for which this proem in book 5 is the main argument, as it parallels the placement of the proems of both Vergil and Valerius' other model, Apollonius (Ap. Rhod. *Arg.* 3.1–4), at the beginning of the second half of their respective epics (see esp. Schetter 1959 for this theory).

that bring forth monsters; still I must first
recount the lies and first the trickery
of Sol's treacherous child, himself to be
justly deceived and justly left behind;
from there I tell my story.

Valerius will sing "another song" (*cantus alios*), and when he immediately mentions wars, *bella*, as his subject,[82] one gets the impression
that the *Argonautica* will indeed turn into the "essential epic" of
Aeneid 7–12, announced by Vergil in the proem as a *maius opus* (*Aen.*
7.45). This apparent parallelism is reinforced by Valerius' mention of
furias, as the epic war in Latium was of course motivated by the Fury
Allecto.[83] Valerius states, however, that he is not able to deal with the
topic (*non mens mihi, non haec ora satis*),[84] and accordingly changes the
subject (*ventum ad*).[85] The subject of the second half of his epic, which is
introduced by means of a rising tricolon (*furias - infanda natae foedera -
horrenda trepidam sub virgine puppem*) will be Medea.[86] So *furias* refers
to Medea's passion for Jason, with which Valerius will indeed deal
extensively, in particular in book 7. Valerius thus erotically redefines
Vergil's Fury and programmatically rewrites the proem of *Aeneid* 7. In
this context, the striking plural of *furias* triggers an allusion to Juno's
announced elegiac rewriting of *Aeneid* 7 in the Hylas episode (*mox et
Furias Ditemque movebo*, *Arg.* 3.520) and Jupiter's metapoetical reaction
(*i, Furias Veneremque move*, *Arg.* 4.13), as discussed above. Here, in the
proem to the second half of his epic, Valerius states that the elegiac
rewriting of the second half of the *Aeneid* will now start, and the topic
switch *ventum ad furias* can be read metapoetically: "At last I have come
to the 'furies' announced earlier." This interpretation is reinforced by
an allusion to an intertext that played an important role in Valerius'

---

[82] These "wars" refer to the extensive battle narrative in book 6 (Wijsman 1996:125 [ad
loc.]), but perhaps to Jason's trials in book 7 as well.

[83] Cf. Hershkowitz 1998:10.

[84] See Wijsman 1996:125–126 (ad loc.) for the way Valerius recasts the "many mouths"
topos here (on which see esp. Hinds 1998:35–46).

[85] Spaltenstein 2004:443 (ad loc.), referring to *OLD* s.v. *venio* 8a.

[86] Cf. Wijsman 1996:124 (on Val. Flacc. *Arg.* 5.217–224): "The rising tricolon ... seems to
summarize the whole rest of the story of Medea."

inversion of Vergil's *Aeneid* in the Hylas episode. In book 4 of the *Aeneid*, Aeneas tells Dido that he never promised to marry her (339-340): *nec coniugis umquam / praetendi taedas aut haec in foedera veni*. "Nor did I ever offer you marriage or enter into that contract with you." Through this allusion, Medea and her elegiac passion are associated with Dido, as a prelude to their intertextual relationship in the remainder of the epic.[87] But whereas Aeneas, when he utters these words, is about to leave Dido behind in pursuit of his epic goal, Medea and her love for Jason are on the verge of dominating the remainder of the *Argonautica*.

So the second half of the *Argonautica* makes clear what the Hylas episode foreshadowed, i.e. that Valerius' epic will not be an *Aeneid*. The Vergilian epic contains elegiac elements that it must leave behind (Dido, Silvia and her stag), as they stand in the way of the epic mission. But contrary to Dido's passion in the *Aeneid* Medea's elegiac passion is essential for Valerius' epic to succeed. The *Argonautica* can thus be seen as an elegized epic and, to a certain extent, an anti-*Aeneid*, in a sense comparable to Ovid's *Metamorphoses*. In fact, as I will argue in the next and final sections, Valerius aligns himself with the poetical agenda of Ovid's "elegiac epic" by alluding to the Hermaphroditus episode in both the Hylas episode and in book 5, where Jason and Medea meet for the first time.

IX. HYLAS AND HERMAPHRODITUS

When the nymph Dryope abducts Hylas they seem to merge and become one, just as Salmacis and Hermaphroditus do in book 4 of the *Metamorphoses*, as Malamud and McGuire have shown through an analysis of several similarities between the two episodes.[88] The setting of both is a pool with very clear water; Salmacis and Dryope are both nymphs and hunters and they both fall in love with and abduct a beautiful boy; when Salmacis sees Hermaphroditus, her eyes shine like the sun reflected in a mirror (*Met.* 4.346-349), a comparison that finds a

---

[87] On Medea and Dido in the *Argonautica*, see e.g. Hershkowitz 1998:99–100 (with 99n42 for further bibliography).

[88] Malamud and McGuire 1993:205–208. The correspondences discussed below are derived from this article, where they are treated in greater detail.

parallel in Valerius' Hylas episode, where the gleam that the boy sheds on the pool is compared with the sun or the moon shining on the water (*Arg.* 3.558–559). Moreover, as Hylas sheds a gleam on the water (*Arg.* 3.560), so Hermaphroditus gleams while swimming in the pool just before the nymph rapes him (*Met.* 4.352–355). Finally, the blush of Hermaphroditus earlier in the story, when Salmacis asks him to marry her, resembles the appearance of the moon in eclipse (*Met.* 329–333), much as Valerius likens Hylas' gleam on the water to the shining of the moon (*Arg.* 3.558–560).

There are also interesting parallels between Ovid's episode and Propertius' Hylas poem 1.20, which suggests that Valerius is "window-alluding" to Propertius through Ovid.[89] When Propertius' Hylas arrives at the spring, he forgets his duty and starts picking flowers:

> quae modo *decerpens tenero* pueriliter *ungui*
> proposito *florem* praetulit officio;
> et modo formosis incumbens nescius undis
> errorem blandis tardat imaginibus.

Prop. 1.20.39–42

> Now childishly picking these with youthful nail, he put flowers ahead of his intended task; and now leaning unawares over the fair water he delays his wandering with the charming images.

The significance of this act is underlined by an allusion to Catullus' wedding poem 62:

> ut *flos* in saeptis secretus nascitur hortis
> . . . .
> multi illum pueri, multae optavere puellae:
> idem cum *tenui carptus* defloruit *ungui*,
> nulli illum pueri, nullae optavere puellae:
> sic virgo, dum intacta manet, dum cara suis est.

Cat. 62.39, 42–45

---

[89] Cf. Malamud and McGuire 1993:206: "Like Hylas in Propertius' poem, Salmacis plucks flowers by the side of her pool."

> As a flower springs up secretly in a fenced garden ... many
> boys, many girls desire it; when the same flower fades,
> plucked by a delicate nail, no boys, no girls desire it: so a
> maiden, while she remains untouched, the while is she
> dear to her own.

"The comparison of the bride to a flower, ready for defloration, is a conventional epithalamial image,"[90] and we can anticipate that Hylas will soon lose his virginity. In the *Metamorphoses* it is Salmacis who is picking flowers, which there prefigures the loss of virginity of Hermaphroditus.[91]

X. ELEGIZING HERMAPHRODITUS

Valerius' Dryope obviously resembles Ovid's Salmacis in that she deflowers a boy. From a metapoetical point of view, as I argued above, Dryope's action elegized Hylas and the *Argonautica* in general, prefiguring the way the epic would go. Interestingly, the nymph also resembles her Ovidian counterpart in this respect, since she also appears to elegize the potential epic hero Hermaphroditus. This metapoetical dimension of Ovid's episode is related to a play on gender. Epic poetry is, particularly in Roman times, self-consciously characterized as a distinctly masculine affair, dealing with masculine activities such as warfare.[92] Like Hylas at the beginning of Valerius' Hylas episode, the young Hermaphroditus is initially depicted as an epic hero, resembling Aeneas and, in particular, Odysseus, as Alison Keith has shown:[93]

> Mercurio puerum diva Cythereide natum
> Naides Idaeis enutrivere sub antris,
> cuius erat facies in qua materque paterque
> cognosci possent; nomen quoque traxit ab illis.
> is tria cum primum fecit quinquennia, montes
> deseruit patrios Idaque altrice relicta

---

[90] Hardie 2002:156.
[91] Segal 1969:34–35.
[92] See also Section II above.
[93] Keith 1999:216–217. Incidentally, in this context, *labor* ("toil") in line 295 also evokes epic.

ignotis errare locis, ignota videre
flumina gaudebat, studio minuente laborem.

Met. 4.288–295

There was a boy born to Mercury and the goddess of
Cythera and cared for by the Naiads in the caves of Ida;
his was a face in which both mother and father could be
recognized; and he took his name from them. As soon
as he had lived three times five years, he left his father's
mountains and abandoned Ida where he had been brought
up and began to enjoy wandering in unfamiliar places and
seeing unfamiliar rivers with a zeal that made light of toil.

That Hermaphroditus is nursed by nymphs on Mt. Ida recalls Venus'
wish to have her son Aeneas raised there (*H. Hom.* 5.256–258), and just
like Aeneas Hermaphroditus sets out on a journey. But the boy's wander-
ings (*errare*, 294) are even more reminiscent of those of Odysseus, who,
returning from Troy, sees the cities of many men (*Od.* 1.3).

When Hermaphroditus arrives at Salmacis' spring, the allusions
continue as the scene evokes several arrival scenes from the *Odyssey*
and *Aeneid*. As Keith observes:

Until the moment when Salmacis sees Hermaphroditus ...
the Ovidian narrative proceeds on a gendered narrative
trajectory that distinguishes the male epic hero from the
feminized site of his labours: Hermaphroditus, a mobile
male hero (like Odysseus or Aeneas) arrives in the course
of his voyage of (self-)discovery at the home of Salmacis,
an immobile female obstacle (like Nausicaa or Dido).[94]

When Salmacis addresses the beautiful boy, her words (320–328)
recall those of Odysseus to Nausicaa in *Odyssey* 6.149–159, but it is
Salmacis who takes Odysseus' role in a complete reversal of gender
roles.[95] The eventual result of the episode is that the two characters

---

[94] Keith 1999:217.
[95] Keith 1999:218. Cf. Nugent 1990:175–176 on the intertextual contact with *Od.* 6.149–
159.

merge and the potentially epic *vir* Hermaphroditus ends up as a *semivir*, "half-man," his limbs "weakened." In accordance with the boy's wish the spring will have the power to weaken men from that moment on:

> ergo ubi se liquidas, quo vir descenderat, undas
> semimarem fecisse videt mollitaque in illis
> membra, manus tendens, sed iam non voce virili
> Hermaphroditus ait: "nato date munera vestro,
> et pater et genetrix, amborum nomen habenti:
> quisquis in hos fontes vir venerit, exeat inde
> semivir et tactis subito mollescat in undis."

> *Met.* 4.380–386

And so, when he saw that the transparent waters, to which he had gone down a man, had made him a half-male, and that his limbs had been made soft in them, Hermaphroditus stretched out his hands and said, but no longer with a man's voice, "Grant your son a favour, oh father and mother too, for my name comes from both of you: whoever comes into this spring a man, let him come out from there a half-man, softened immediately he touches the waters."

This "feminization" of Hermaphroditus also clearly has a metapoetical dimension, as it is associated with Roman love elegy. Whereas the other nymphs are involved in the male activity of hunting, the epic association of which is enhanced by the emphatic use of the adjective *durus*,[96] Salmacis herself is depicted as very feminine. In fact, she is described as a society lady from Roman love elegy, bathing, combing her hair and looking in the mirror (310–315), in a passage influenced by Ovid's *Ars Amatoria*.[97] The terminology that is strikingly often applied to both Salmacis' feminizing spring—with which the eponymous nymph can

---

[96] Ov. *Met.* 4.307, 309: *duris venatibus* ("strenuous hunt"). For the elegiac poets' association of *durus* with epic and the contrasting association of *mollis* with their own elegiac poetry, see e.g. Baker 2000:102 (on Prop. 1.7.19).

[97] Jouteur 2001:273; Barchiesi and Rosati 2007:288 (on Ov. *Met.* 4.310–315).

be identified[98]—and her / the spring's feminizing action, i.e. *mollire* ("to soften," "to make effeminate") and its cognates, also refer to love elegy, where the word is used metapoetically to denote the genre.[99] When Salmacis is said to soften / feminize Hermaphroditus (*Salmacis ... remolliat*, 286; *mollita ... / membra*, 381–382; *mollescat*, 386), the nymph can thus be seen metapoetically to elegize the epic Hermaphroditus.[100] This interpretation is reinforced by the union of the boy with the nymph, which seems a perversion of the elegiac ideal of lover and beloved to become one.[101]

The phasing of this merging—*mixta duorum / corpora iunguntur.* "Their two bodies, joined together as it were, were merged in one" (373–374)—recalls the proem of the *Metamorphoses*, where *corpus* clearly has a metapoetical meaning (*Met.* 1.1–2):[102] *in nova fert animus mutatas dicere formas / corpora.* "My spirit moves me to tell of shapes changed into strange bodies." As Stephen Harrison conveniently summarizes the programmatic meaning of the prologue:

> Metamorphosis is the theme of the poem, both in terms of its formal content, and in terms of its generic variety. Genres appear and disappear and are transformed into each other through the long course of the poem, following its explicit programme (1.1–2): literary *forms* are transformed into new *bodies* of poetic work.[103]

---

[98] See Keith 1999:217–218 for the ways in which Salmacis "quite literally embodies the landscape through which Hermaphroditus travels."

[99] See n. 97 above. Cf. Jouteur 2001:272.

[100] Hermaphroditus' elegizing perhaps already starts when he swims in Salmacis' spring, for his alternating strokes (*alternaque bracchia ducens*, Ov. *Met.* 4.353; also quoted above) bring to mind the technical term for the elegiac couplet, *alternus versus*, to which elegiac poets often allude. In Prop. 1.11, for instance, Cynthia is envisaged swimming at Baiae "with an elegiac stroke, parting the water with alternating hand (*alternae ... manu* 1.11.12)" (McNamee 1993:225). Cf. n. 69 above.

[101] Robinson 1999:221–222.

[102] See esp. Farrell 1999 and Theodorakopoulos 1999 for the metapoetical meaning of *corpus* here and throughout the *Metamorphoses*.

[103] Harrison 2002:89. Cf. Keith 2002:238.

Two "poetic bodies," one epic and one elegiac, are thus merged in Ovid's Salmacis and Hermaphroditus episode, and the result is a (poetic) body that is neither male/epic nor female/elegiac:[104]

> nec duo sunt sed forma duplex, nec femina dici
> nec puer ut possit, neutrumque et utrumque videntur.
>
> *Met.* 4.378–379

> They were not two, but they had a dual form that could
> be said to be neither woman nor boy, they seemed to be
> neither and both.

On the other hand, although Salmacis has feminized/elegized the boy, he is still a man—albeit just a half-man (*semivir*)—who keeps his male name Hermaphroditus and addresses himself as a male (*nato*, 383). Metapoetically, this implies that although the epic Hermaphroditus is elegized, he still remains epic up to a point.

This paradoxical situation recalls the generic status of Ovid's *Metamorphoses* in general, which is often denoted as an "elegiac epic." While Ovid's pose *vis-à-vis* the epic tradition evokes other genres that his epic incorporates or into which it can transform, such as tragedy and bucolic,[105] it is mainly elegiac poetry that works against the epic nature of the poem.[106] In light of the strong opposition set up by Augustan poets between elegy (as dealing with women and love) and traditional epic (as dealing with men and war), and in light of Ovid's own past as a versatile elegist, this is hardly surprising.

Ovid's elegizing of epic in the *Metamorphoses* can also be seen in light of the *Aeneid*. As scholars have extensively shown in recent decades, Ovid's poem "is both a challenge as well as a response to the

---

[104] Jouteur 2001:280.

[105] E.g. Harrison 2002:88: "[T]he epicization of Euripides' *Bacchae* in 3.511–733 and of his *Hecuba* in 13.399–733 are only two of the most notable examples." See e.g. Farrell 1992 and Barchiesi 2006 for bucolic influences in Ov. *Met.* 13.235–268 (Polyphemus). See Hinds 2000:221–223 for an overview of the various approaches with regard to the generic status of the *Metamorphoses*.

[106] As, incidentally, was the case in Valerius' Hylas episode. For elegiac influences in the entire *Metamorphoses*, see e.g. Tränkle 1963; Knox 1986; Hinds 1987; Harrison 2002:87–89; Keith 2002:245–258.

Aeneid,"[107] and the elegized nature of the *Metamorphoses*, as emblematized by Salmacis and Hermaphroditus, who evokes Aeneas, can be seen as part of this reaction to the *Aeneid*. In fact, Hermaphroditus, before he was elegized by Salmacis, resembled Aeneas.

XI. JASON AND MEDEA

When Valerius' Dryope rapes Hylas—as Salmacis rapes Hermaphroditus—and when the two merge—as the Ovidian characters do—Valerius imports the metapoetical dimension of the Ovidian episode and of the entire work it represents. Valerius' metamorphosis of the *Aeneid*—his elegizing of the potential Vergilian hero Hylas and the Aeneas-like Hercules—can thus be seen as an Ovidian move. Like Ovid's story of Hermaphroditus, however, the Hylas episode has more than local significance, as I argued above, in that it prefigures the way the *Argonautica* will develop, i.e. that it will be an elegized *Aeneid*, for which Medea's elegiac passion is of crucial importance. This broader significance is reinforced by Valerius' use of this same Ovidian intertext at the crucial moment when Jason and Medea first meet (*Arg.* 5.378–384).

The initial encounter of Jason and Medea obviously evokes the first meeting between Aeneas and Dido in *Aeneid* 1.[108] As Tim Stover expresses the implications of the intertextual contact: "Valerius thus sets the stage for the important meeting between Jason and Medea by alluding to the moment when Vergil's epic and its hero are confronted and threatened by amatory themes."[109] Contrary to what happens in *Aeneid* 4, however, where Aeneas leaves Dido as well as her elegiac associations behind,

---

[107]Papaioannou 2005:1. Cf. Hardie 1991:47; 2005:91. See also e.g. Hardie 1990; Baldo 1995; Smith 1997 on the *Metamorphoses* and the *Aeneid* in general. For Ovid's most obvious challenge of the *Aeneid*, his "little *Aeneid*" (Ov. *Met.* 13.623–14.582), see e.g. Papaioannou 2005, with pp. 3–16 for a discussion of earlier work.

[108]Compare, for instance, Val. Flacc. *Arg.* 5.376–377 (*haeret in una / defixus*), where Jason looks at Medea for the first time, with Verg. *Aen.* 1.495 (*obtutuque haeret defixus in uno*), in the context of (or rather just before) the first meeting between Dido and Aeneas (when Jason is looking at the pictures in Juno's temple). See also Stover 2003:126 for this parallel. Of course, Odysseus's encounter with Nausicaa in *Od.* 6 is an intertext for both Virgil and Valerius. I here focus, however, on the striking verbal parallels between *Arg.* 5 and *Aen.* 1.

[109]Stover 2003:126.

Medea (and Juno) will "elegize" Jason and the epic by eventually taking control. So Medea resembles her prefiguration Dryope in the Hylas episode, as was made explicit by Jupiter in his address to Juno at the beginning of book 4. The process of Jason's "elegization" already starts just before his meeting with Medea, when Juno beautifies the hero and makes him surpass his fellow Argonauts in looks (*egregio supereminet ore*, 5.367). The rare verb used here triggers an allusion to *Aeneid* 1, where Dido is compared to Diana, who is said to stand out above all goddesses (*deas supereminet omnis*, 1.501).[110] Quite surprisingly Valerius has used the verb for Jason, not for Medea, whose model is Dido and whom Jason will compare with Diana in his first address to her a few lines later (see below). So Jason is here playing the role of Vergil's elegiac Dido, and as a result he is elegized, like Hylas and Hercules earlier in the epic.

As in the Hylas episode, this elegization has Ovidian overtones. First of all, the setting of the encounter between Jason and Medea—a seemingly peaceful landscape—already primed the reader for this intertext.[111] This is reinforced by the simile (343–349) comparing Medea to Proserpina, who is about to be raped by Pluto and whose story Ovid tells in book 5 of the *Metamorphoses* (as well as in *Fasti* 4).[112] Most striking, however, are the allusions to Ovid's Salmacis and Hermaphroditus episode that accompany the inversion of Vergil's *Aeneid* when Jason addresses Medea for the first time:

> "*si* dea, *si* magni decus huc ades" inquit "Olympi,
> has ego *credo* faces, haec virginis ora Dianae,
> teque renodatam pharetris ac pace fruentem
> ad sua Caucaseae producunt flumina Nymphae."

[110] See Stover 2003:129–131 for this allusion. Incidentally, as Wijsman notes (1996:184 [ad loc.]), Valerius' clause also alludes to Verg. *Aen.* 4.150: *tantum egregio decus enitet ore*, where Aeneas' beauty is compared to that of Diana's brother, Apollo.

[111] As Stover (2003:127) has it: "[F]or the post-Ovidian reader the landscape also recalls the motif of the peaceful pastoral retreat, the context in which acts of sexual violence often occur in the *Metamorphoses*."

[112] Stover 2003:127. In the context of these Ovidian allusions, Valerius' use of the verb *supereminet* in *Arg.* 5.367 (see above) may also echo the only occurrence of the verb in Ovid's *Metamorphoses*, in the Actaeon episode (*Met.* 3.182; itself alluding to *Aen.* 1.501, Valerius' main model), where it is used to describe the way Diana towers over her nymphs (see Stover 2003:130–131).

si domus in terris atque hinc tibi gentis origo,
felix prole parens, *olimque beatior ille*,
qui tulerit *longis* et te sibi iunxerit annis.

Arg. 5.378–384

If you're a goddess, jewel of great Olympus
who come here, these are the torches, I believe,
and face of the maid Diana, and these the nymphs
of Caucasus who bring you to their streams
with your arrow sheath untied, enjoying leisure.
If you call earth your home and your family's birth
is here, then blessed is your father in his child,
and happier yet that man who will one day
win you and be your mate throughout long years.

This speech is obviously modeled on Odysseus's address to Nausicaa in *Odyssey* 6.149–185,[113] but the verbal parallels with Salmacis' first words to Hermaphroditus detected by Stover establish the Ovidian episode as Valerius' main intertext.[114]

puer o dignissime *credi*
esse deus, seu tu deus es, potes esse Cupido,
sive es mortalis, qui te genuere, beati
et frater *felix*, et fortunata profecto,
si qua tibi soror est, et quae dedit ubera nutrix.
sed *longe* cunctis *longeque beatior illa*,
si qua tibi sponsa est, si quam dignabere taeda.

Met. 4.320–326

Oh boy, most worthy to be thought a god or, if you are a
god, you could be Cupid, but if you are a mortal, blest are
those who gave you birth, your brother is a lucky man and,
if you have a sister, she is fortunate too and so is the nurse

---

[113] See e.g. Wijsman 1996:189–190 (ad loc.); Spaltenstein 2004:485–486 (ad loc.).

[114] See Stover 2003:128–129 for this allusion (the emphasis is both passages is his). Cf. Spaltenstein 2004:486 (ad loc.). Of course, the Ovidian passage itself is also modeled on *Odyssey* 6 (see Section X above).

who gave the breast to you. But far, far more blest than all of them is that girl, if there is one, that is engaged to you, if you think that there is any that deserves the wedding torch.

Jason is thus again cast in a female role and, as Stover observes, the Ovidian intertext creates a tension in Valerius' epic: "Will Jason's confrontation with Medea be as unmanning for him as a dip in the emasculating waters of Salmacis' spring?"[115] As I have argued above, however, Ovid's story was not just about gender; the emasculation of Hermaphroditus could be read in elegizing terms as well. As in the Hylas episode, Valerius imports the metapoetical dimension of Ovid's episode, again at a crucial junction in the epic, in which Medea enters the scene and Valerius starts to elegize Jason. As was already predicted when Hercules left the stage, the *Argonautica* is now fully becoming an elegiac epic.

UNIVERSITY OF AMSTERDAM AND VU UNIVERSITY AMSTERDAM

WORKS CITED

Adamietz, J. 1976. *Zur Komposition der Argonautica des Valerius Flaccus.* Munich.

Aymard, J. 1951. *Essai sur les chasses romaines, des origines à la fin du siècle des Antonins: Cynegetica.* Rome.

Baier, T. 2001. *Valerius Flaccus, Argonautica, Buch VI: Einleitung und Kommentar.* Munich.

Baker, R. J. 2000. *Propertius I.* 2nd ed. Warminster.

Baldo, G. 1995. *Dall'Eneide alle Metamorfosi: Il codice epico di Ovidio.* Padua.

Barchiesi, A. 1993. "Future Reflexive: Two Modes of Allusion and Ovid's *Heroides.*" *HSCP* 95:333–365 (= Barchiesi 2001:105–127).

———. 2001. *Speaking Volumes: Narrative and Intertext in Ovid and Other Latin Poets.* London.

[115] Stover 2003:132.

——. 2006. "Music for Monsters: Ovid's *Metamorphoses*, Bucolic Evolution, and Bucolic Criticism." In *Brill's Companion to Greek and Latin Pastoral*, ed. M. Fantuzzi and T. D. Papanghelis, 403–426. Leiden.

Barchiesi, A., and G. Rosati 2007. *Ovidio, Metamorfosi.* Vol. 2, libri III–IV. Milan.

Barich, M. 2009. *Valerius Flaccus: Argonautica.* Gambier, OH.

Barnes, W. R. 1995. "Virgil: The Literary Impact." In *A Companion to the Study of Virgil*, ed. N. Horsfall, 257–292. Leiden.

Bonanno, M. G. 1990. *L'allusione necessaria: Ricerche intertestuali sulla poesia greca e latina.* Rome.

Boyle, A. J. 1977. "Virgil's Pastoral Echo." *Ramus* 6:121–131.

Burmannus, P. 1724. *C. Valerii Flacci Setini Balbi Argonauticon libri octo.* Leiden.

Cairns, F. 1989. *Virgil's Augustan Epic.* Cambridge.

Celoria, F. 1992. *The Metamorphoses of Antoninus Liberalis.* London.

Conte, G. B. 1986. *The Rhetoric of Imitation: Genre and Poetic Memory in Virgil and Other Latin Poets.* Ithaca, NY.

——. 1992. "Proems in the Middle." *Yale Classical Studies* 29:147–159.

——. 1994a. *Latin Literature: A History.* Baltimore.

——. 1994b. *Genres and Readers: Lucretius, Love Elegy, Pliny's Encyclopedia.* Baltimore.

——. 2007. *The Poetry of Pathos: Studies in Virgilian Epic.* Ed. S. J. Harrison. Oxford.

Damon, P. 1961. *Modes of Analogy in Ancient and Medieval Verse.* Berkeley.

Desport, M. 1952. *L'incantation virgilienne: Virgile et Orphée.* Bordeaux.

Dick, B. F. 1968. "Ancient pastoral and the pathetic fallacy." *Comparative Literature* 20:27–44.

Eigler, U. 1988. *Monologische Redeformen bei Valerius Flaccus.* Frankfurt.

Elm von der Osten, D. 2007. *Liebe als Wahnsinn: Die Konzeption der Göttin Venus in den Argonautica des Valerius Flaccus.* Stuttgart.

Farrell, J. 1992. "Dialogue of Genres in Ovid's 'Lovesong of Polyphemus' (*Metamorphoses* 13.719–897)." *AJP* 113:235–268.

——. 1999. "The Ovidian *Corpus*: Poetic Body and Poetic Text." In Hardie, Barchiesi, and Hinds 1999, 307–338.

Feeney, D. C. 1991. *The Gods in Epic: Poets and Critics of the Classical Tradition.* Oxford.

Fuà, O. 1988. "La presenza di Omero in Valerio Flacco." *Atti della Accademia delle scienze di Torino 2, classe di scienze morali, storiche e filologiche* 122:23–53.

Galinsky, G. K. 1972. *The Herakles Theme: The Adaptations of the Hero in Literature from Homer to the Twentieth Century.* Oxford.

Garson, R. W. 1963. "The Hylas Episode in Valerius Flaccus' *Argonautica.*" *CQ,* n.s., 13:260–267.

Gow, A. S. F. 1950. *Theocritus.* 2 vols. Cambridge.

Griffin, J. 1986. *Latin Poets and Roman Life.* Chapel Hill, NC.

Hardie, P. R. 1989. "Flavian Epicists on Virgil's Epic Technique." *Ramus* 18:3–20.

———. 1991. "The Janus Episode in Ovid's *Fasti.*" *MD* 26:47–64.

———. 1993. *The Epic Successors of Virgil: A Study in the Dynamics of a Tradition.* Cambridge.

———. 1994. *Virgil. Aeneid IX.* Cambridge.

———. 1998. *Virgil.* Oxford.

———. 2002. *Ovid's Poetics of Illusion.* Cambridge.

———. 2005. "Narrative Epic." In Harrison 2005, 83–100.

Hardie, P. R., A. Barchiesi, and S. Hinds, eds. 1999. *Ovidian Transformations: Essays on the Metamorphoses and its Reception.* Cambridge.

Harrison, S. J. 2002. "Ovid and Genre: Evolutions of an Elegist." In *The Cambridge Companion to Ovid,* ed. P. R. Hardie, 79–94. Cambridge.

———, ed. 2005. *A Companion to Latin Literature.* Oxford.

———. 2007. *Generic Enrichment in Vergil and Horace.* Oxford.

Heerink, M. A. J. 2007. "Going a Step Further: Valerius Flaccus' Metapoetical Reading of Propertius 1.20." *CQ,* n.s., 57:606–620.

———. 2010. *Echoing Hylas: Metapoetics in Hellenistic and Roman Poetry.* PhD diss., Leiden University.

Hershkowitz, D. 1998. *Valerius Flaccus' Argonautica: Abbreviated Voyages in Silver Latin Epic.* Oxford.

Heyworth, S. J. 2005. "Pastoral." In Harrison 2005, 148–158.

———. 2007. *Cynthia: A Companion to the Text of Propertius.* Oxford.

Hinds, S. E. 1987. *The Metamorphosis of Persephone: Ovid and the Self-Conscious Muse.* Cambridge.

———. 1992. "*Arma* in Ovid's *Fasti.*" *Arethusa* 25:81–153.

———. 1998. *Allusion and Intertext: Dynamics of Appropriation in Roman Poetry*. Cambridge.

———. 2000. "Essential Epic: Genre and Gender from Macer to Statius." In *Matrices of Genre: Authors, Canons, and Society*, ed. M. Depew and D. Obbink, 221–244, 302–304. Cambridge, MA.

Hollander, J. 1981. *The Figure of Echo: A Mode of Allusion in Milton and After.* Berkeley.

Horsfall, N. 2000. *Virgil, Aeneid 7: A Commentary*. Leiden.

Hunter, R. L. 1999. *Theocritus: A Selection*. Cambridge.

Johnson, K. 2009. *Virgil's Georgics: A Poem of the Land*. London.

Jouteur, I. 2001. *Jeux de genre dans les Métamorphoses d'Ovide*. Leuven.

Keith, A. M. 1999. "Versions of Masculinity in Ovid's *Metamorphoses*." In Hardie, Barchiesi, and Hinds 1999, 214–239.

———. 2002. "Sources and Genres in Ovid's *Metamorphoses* 1–5." In *Brill's Companion to Ovid*, ed. B. W. Boyd, 235–269. Leiden.

Klein, L. 1931. "Die Göttertechnik in den *Argonautika* des Apollonius Rhodius." *Philologus* 86:18–51; 215–257.

Knox, P. E. 1986. *Ovid's Metamorphoses and the Traditions of Augustan Poetry*. Cambridge.

Koch, H. H. 1955. *Die Hylasgeschichte bei Apollonios Rhodios (Arg. I 1153 ff.), Theokrit (Eidyllion XIII), Properz (Elegie I 20), Valerius Flaccus (Arg. III 459ff.)*. PhD diss., Kiel University.

Korn, M. 1989. *Valerius Flaccus, Argonautica 4.1–343. Ein Kommentar.* Hildesheim.

Korn, M., and H. J. Tschiedel, eds. 1991, *Ratis omnia vincet: Untersuchungen zu den Argonautica des Valerius Flaccus*. Hildesheim.

Labate, M. 1993. "Storie di instabilità: L' episodio di Ermafrodito nelle *Metamorfosi* di Ovidio." *MD* 30: 49–62.

Langen, P. 1896–1897. *C. Valeri Flacci Setini Balbi Argonauticon libri octo*. Berlin.

Lee, G. 1984. *Virgil: The Eclogues*. London.

Lovatt, H. 2006. "The Female Gaze in Flavian Epic: Looking out from the Walls in Valerius Flaccus and Statius." In Nauta, van Dam, and Smolenaars 2006, 59–78.

McGuire, D. T. 1997. *Acts of Silence: Civil War, Tyranny, and Suicide in the Flavian Epics*. Hildesheim.

McNamee, K. 1993. "Propertius, Poetry, and Love." In *Woman's Power, Man's Game: Essays on Classical Antiquity in Honor of Joy K. King*, ed. M. DeForest, 215–241. Wauconda, IL.

Malamud, M. A., and D. T. McGuire 1993. "Flavian Variant: Myth; Valerius' *Argonautica*." In *Roman Epic*, ed. A. J. Boyle, 192–217. London.

Mehmel, F. 1934. *Valerius Flaccus*. PhD diss., University of Hamburg.

Monaghan, M. E. 2005. "Juno and the Poet in Valerius' *Argonautica*." In *Roman and Greek Imperial Epic*, ed. M. Paschalis, 9–27. Herakleion.

Morgan, L. 2003. "Child's Play: Ovid and his Critics." *JRS* 93:66–91.

Mozley, J. H. 1934. *Valerius Flaccus: Argonautica*. Cambridge, MA.

Murgatroyd, P. 2009. *A Commentary on Book 4 of Valerius Flaccus' Argonautica*. Leiden.

Nauta, R. R., H.- J. van Dam, and J. J. L. Smolenaars, eds. 2006. *Flavian Poetry*. Leiden.

Nugent, S. G. 1990. "This Sex Which is Not One: De-constructing Ovid's Hermaphroditus." *Differences* 2.1:160–185.

Papaioannou, S. 2005. *Epic Succession and Dissension: Ovid, Metamorphoses 13.623–14.582, and the Reinvention of the Aeneid*. Berlin.

Petrain, D. 2000. "Hylas and *Silva*: Etymological Wordplay in Propertius 1.20." *HSCP* 100:409–421.

Putnam, M. C. J. 1995. "Silvia's Stag and Virgilian Ekphrasis." *Materiali e discussioni per l'analisi dei testi classici* 34:107–133.

———. 1998. *Virgil's Epic Designs: Ekphrasis in the Aeneid*. New Haven, CT.

Race, W. H. 2008. *Apollonius Rhodius' Argonautica*. Cambridge, MA.

Robinson, M. 1999. "Salmacis and Hermaphroditus: When Two Become One (Ovid, *Met.* 4.285–388)." *CQ*, n.s., 49:212–223.

Schetter, W. 1959. "Die Buchzahl der *Argonautica* des Valerius Flaccus." *Philologus* 103:297–308.

Schubert, W. 1991. "*Socia Iuno*: Zur Gestalt der Götterkonigin in den *Argonautica* des Valerius Flaccus." In Korn and Tschiedel 1991, 121–37.

Segal, C. P. 1969. *Landscape in Ovid's Metamorphoses: A Study in the Transformations of a Literary Symbol*. Wiesbaden.

Sharrock, A. 1990. "*Alternae voces* – Again." *CQ*, n.s., 40:570–571.

Smith, R. A. 1997. *Poetic Allusion and Poetic Embrace in Ovid and Virgil*. Ann Arbor, MI.

Smolenaars, J. J. L. 1991. "Quellen und Rezeption: Die Verarbeitung homerischer Motive bei Valerius Flaccus und Statius." In Korn and Tschiedel 1991, 181–196.

Spaltenstein, F. 2004. *Commentaire des Argonautica de Valérius Flaccus (livres 3, 4 et 5)*. Brussels.

Stover, T. 2003. "Confronting Medea: Genre, Gender, and Allusion in the *Argonautica* of Valerius Flaccus." *CP* 98:123–147.

———. 2012. *Epic and Empire in Vespasianic Rome: A New Reading of Valerius Flaccus' Argonautica*, Oxford.

Teuffel, W. S. 1870. *Geschichte der Römischen Literatur*. Leipzig.

Theodorakopoulos, E. 1999. "Closure and Transformation in Ovid's *Metamorphoses.*" In Hardie, Barchiesi, and Hinds 1999, 142–161.

Tränkle, H. 1963. "Elegisches in Ovids *Metamorphosen.*" *Hermes* 91:459–476.

West, D. 1991. *Virgil: The Aeneid*. London.

Wijsman, H. J. W. 1996. *Valerius Flaccus, Argonautica, Book V: A Commentary*. Leiden.

———. 2000. *Valerius Flaccus, Argonautica, Book VI: A Commentary*. Leiden.

Wilamowitz-Moellendorff, U. von. 1924. *Hellenistische Dichtung*. 2 vols. Berlin.

Wills, J. 1996. *Repetition in Latin Poetry: Figures of Allusion*. Oxford.

Zissos, A. 2002. "Reading Models and the Homeric Program in Valerius Flaccus's *Argonautica.*" *Helios* 29:69–96.

———. 2004. "*L'ironia allusiva*: Lucan's *Bellum Civile* and the *Argonautica* of Valerius Flaccus." In *Lucano e la tradizione dell'epica latina*, ed. P. Esposito and E. M. Ariemma, 21–38. Naples.

———. 2006a. "Reception of Valerius Flaccus' *Argonautica.*" *International Journal of the Classical Tradition* 13:165–185.

———. 2006b. "Sailing and Sea-storm in Valerius Flaccus (*Argonautica* 1.574–642): The Rhetoric of Inundation." In Nauta, van Dam, and Smolenaars 2006, 79–95.

———. 2008. *Valerius Flaccus' Argonautica, Book 1: A Commentary*. Oxford.

PLINY THE YOUNGER ON HIS VERSE AND MARTIAL'S NON-RECOGNITION OF PLINY AS A POET

LOWELL EDMUNDS

sic forensibus ministeriis exercitati frequenter ad carminis tranquillitatem
tamquam ad portum feliciorem refugerunt, credentes facilius poema
extrui posse quam controversiam sententiolis vibrantibus pictam.[1]

Eumolpus

PLINY GIVES HIS AUTOBIOGRAPHY as poet in *Epistle* 7.4 and offers a two-part apology for his composition of light verse. This activity, he says, is a diversion appropriate to the orator and justified by distinguished precedents; it can also, no matter what its levity, bring fame. Pliny elaborates on the two parts of this apology in other letters. The more Pliny insists on his lack of seriousness as a poet, however, the more the two parts come to seem self-contradictory. If verse composition is really only a diversion from graver pursuits, then why the publication of *libelli*, and why the pursuit of *gloria* as a poet (*Ep.* 9.25.2)? Given this ambition, and given the probability that Pliny's career as poet was already underway at the time of the epigram addressed to him by Martial (10.20[19]), it is odd that Martial seems to be unaware of him as a poet. It is also odd that Pliny, in the letter in which he refers to this epigram (3.21), gives no sign that he expected Martial to be aware of him in this role. While in that letter Pliny shows his customary self-confidence about his own aspirations, he slyly raises the ques-

---

[1] Petr. *Sat.* 118.2 M. "Thus, vexed by their duties in the law-courts they often flee to the calm of poetry, as if to a happier port, believing that a poem can be constructed more easily than a case colored with scintillating bons mots."

tion of Martial's immortality.[2] In this way, he prompts, willy-nilly, a comparison of his own poetic career, based on senatorial precedents and centered in an elite group, with that of the arriviste from Bilbilis, the poet of the *populus*.

I. THE AUTOBIOGRAPHY OF A POET

The senator Pontius Allifanus has asked, in reaction to the publication of Pliny's first book of poems, how a serious (*severus*) man like him could write hendecasyllabics.[3] Pliny answers by giving his autobiography as poet, in two parts (*Ep.* 7.4).[4] First, he explains that he was never a stranger to poetry. When he was fourteen he wrote a tragedy. In his early twenties, returning from his military tribunate in Syria, he was becalmed on the island of Icaria (modern Nicaria), and he composed some elegiac verses about the island and the sea (about 81 CE). He sometimes tried heroic verse, too. (He seems to mean that he tried epic.) Then, apparently at the beginning of his public career, he stopped writing verses.[5] Turning to the particular question of the hendecasyllabics, which he has written for the first time, he proceeds to explain how they came about—how he became a poet again. One day in his house at Laurentum (modern Tor Paterno, south of Ostia), he was listening to the reading of some books of Asinius Gallus that compared his father, Asinius Pollio, and Cicero. Asinius Gallus quoted an epigram (*epigramma*) by the latter addressed to Tiro. At midday, planning to take a nap (it was summer, he adds), Pliny could not fall asleep. Lying

---

[2] Hoffer 1999:1: "The leading trait in Pliny's epistolary self-portrait is his confidence." Cf. Mayer 2003:227: "He seems to trumpet his own achievements too much for our taste" (with later qualification and with citation of Gibson 2003, on Pliny's various ways of mitigating his self-praise).

[3] On the conflicting values of literary leisure and the life of politics, see the exegesis of *Ep.* 1.9 by Hoffer 1999:111–118; on the pervasive conflict in Pliny between *negotium* and *otium* in his account of his life, see Bütler 1970: ch. 4. Leach 2003:162 wryly observes: "Pliny's investment schedule for *otium* aims toward the procurement of further *negotium* with a single-mindedness that many persons would not consider to resemble leisure at all."

[4] Some of the information in my summary has come from the commentary on *Ep.* 7.4 in Sherwin-White 1966. For the publication of Pliny's first book, cf. *Ep.* 4.14; 5.3, 10.

[5] Sherwin-White 1966:289; n.b. *Ep.* 7.4.5: *post longam desuetudinem*.

awake, he began to reflect that the greatest orators had entertained themselves with this kind of pursuit, i.e., the writing of epigrams, and considered it praiseworthy (*coepi reputare maximos oratores hoc studii genus et in oblectationibus habuisse et in laude posuisse*, 4). He immediately composed some hexameters. At this point, Pliny has answered Pontius.

Pliny implicitly and perhaps with wry humor gives himself another kind of authority, too, in his evocation of a great precedent. The circumstances (season, time of day, countryside) and the experience (inspiration) in Laurentum correspond almost exactly to those described in Plato's *Phaedrus*.[6] At midday in the summer (229a5–6; 242a3–5), Socrates and Phaedrus recline in a *locus amoenus* on the bank of the river Ilisos (230b2–c5). Here Socrates is inspired to give a completely uncharacteristic speech—a flow of eloquence. Pausing in the middle of it, he says that he has undergone a "divine experience" (238c5–6). This is "a divine place," so that, says Socrates, Phaedrus should not be surprised if perhaps Socrates is possessed by the nymphs as he continues his speech (238c9–d2). Only the nymphs are missing in Pliny's replay of Socrates' inspiration. Pliny's inspiration was the epigram of Cicero quoted by Asinius Gallus, and Pliny was presumably reclining on a bed, indoors.[7]

He quotes thirteen of the hexameters, which may or may not constitute a complete poem. They include a development of his thought concerning great men's indulgence in light verse:

> lascivum inveni lusum Ciceronis et illo
> spectandum ingenio, quo seria condidit et quo
> humanis salibus multo varioque lepore[8]
> magnorum ostendit mentes gaudere virorum.

---

[6] Hass 1998:142 includes Pl. *Phdr.* in her inventory. She does not cite Pliny.

[7] Another resonance is explored by Gibson and Morello 2012:94–95, 99–100: "Pliny seizes upon an ... erotic epigram quoted in Asinius' work, and then casts the next part of the story in the language of erotic poetry. Instead of an Ovidian afternoon with a girl while sleep eludes him [Ov. *Am.* 1.5.1–2, cited by the authors at this point], Pliny expresses poetic eroticism by constructing a kind of 'meeting with a mentor' [i.e. Cicero] moment (in the style of Callimachus' dream of Hesiod, for example)."

[8] For the collocation of *sal* and *lepos*, cf. Cat. 16.7; Mart. 3.20.9.

> I found a wanton trifle of Cicero, admirable both for the
> talent with which he composed serious works and for that
> with which he showed that the minds of great men delight
> in human witticisms and abundant and varied charm.
>
> 3 = Courtney 1.3–6 (p. 368)[9]

From hexameters, he went on to elegiac couplets.[10] Returning to Rome,
he read his verse to his friends, who approved. Then he tried other
meters. Finally, he decided to publish the separate book of hendecasyllabics that prompted Pontius' question. The lapse of time from the
Laurentine inspiration to the book (referred to for the first time in
Ep. 4.14, i.e., in 104–105 CE), the traversal of the three stages outlined
above, seems not to have been great.[11]

II. THE APOLOGY

Pliny's autobiography as poet begins and ends as an apology.[12] His main
defense in *Ep.* 7.4 is that his verse composition started as a diversion,
which he could justify by the precedent of Cicero. He is careful to point
out that he continued this activity when he had leisure, and especially
when he was traveling (8). Referring in the lines of his poem quoted
above to a *lusus* of Cicero, Pliny means not simply a piece of light verse
but light verse as the product of non-serious activity. After the publication of his book, however, which is justified in the first place *exemplo
multorum*, Pliny can offer another kind of apology: its success (9–10).[13] It
is read, it is copied, it is even sung, and even Greeks, who have learned

---

[9] The interpretation and some of the translation are owing to Peter White.

[10] Thus reversing the sequence (elegiac couplets–hexameters) of his youthful versification. In Quintilian's survey of poets who may be read by the future orator, which is
analytical and hierarchical, elegiac poets follow epic poets (*Inst.* 10.1.53–58 [Greek];
10.1.85–93 [Roman]).

[11] On this and other dates for Pliny's letters, see the Appendix.

[12] For a detailed survey of Pliny's apologetic strategy in this and other Epistles, see
Roller 1998:281–289.

[13] *Postremo placuit exemplo multorum unum separatim hendecasyllaborum volumen absol-
vere* (7.4.8). If, as one suspects, "example of many others" refers to the publication of
a separate volume and not to a separate volume of hendecasyllabics in particular, it is
unclear why Pliny restricts himself to this one meter.

Latin because of this book, are setting it to music for public and private performance (7.4.9).[14] Pliny evokes a hubbub. But how many copies were made, how many readers did he have outside his circle, and how many Greeks learned Latin on his account? Pliny could hardly say, as Martial could (1.1.2; cf. 5.13.4), that he was *toto notus in orbe*.[15] In his mind, his success has a smaller basis, as will be seen.

Pliny is prepared to restate the two main points of his apology for light verse as general rules. Advising a young friend on how to train for oratory during his holiday (*Ep.* 7.9.9–14), Pliny first prescribes exercises in translation and composition, and then he comes to poetry. It is permitted (*fas est*), he says, to find relaxation in composing verse, which must be clever (adj. *argutus*) and short (adj. *brevis*), because you do not have the leisure for something long. Now come the two apologetic points again, in reverse order. First, even if they are called trifles (*lusūs*) (9–10; cf. *Ep.* 7.4.9–10), these poems can sometimes attain a greater fame (*gloria*) than serious works. After breaking into verse to illustrate his point (11 = Courtney 2 [p. 368]), Pliny continues with his second point, the one that comes first in *Ep.* 7.4. The greatest orators, indeed the greatest men, he says, combined their professional training with this kind of amusement (*sic se aut exercebant aut delectabant, immo delectabant exercebantque*, 12). For these trifles (he now uses *opuscula*) both stimulate and relax the mind. "They take in our loves, our hatreds, our anger, our pity, our urbanity, in short everything you find in life and even in politics and law" (*Recipiunt enim amores odia iras misericordiam urbanitatem, omnia denique quae in vita atque etiam in foro causisque versatur*, 13). Although Pliny speaks of the themes of light verse, his point is the salutary effect of composition on the great orator. (In passing, one could say that Pliny thus resolves the conflict between poetry and oratory that remains unresolved at the end of Tacitus' contemporary *Dialogus de oratoribus*.[16])

---

[14] On *nunc cithara nunc lyra personatur*, see Sherwin-White 1966:406.

[15] Martial is read in Vienna (Vienne on the Rhone) (7.88); by centurions on the lower Danube (*in Geticis ... pruinis*, 11.3.3); and in Britain (11.3.5). Many a stranger takes Martial's poems with him when he returns to his own country (8.3.7–8).

[16] See Johnson 2010:63–73 (ch. 4: "Pliny, Tacitus, and the *Dialogus de oratoribus*"), esp. 71–73. The comment of Mayer 2001:18 suggests a subtle resolution of the conflict: "[T]he

He is thus reiterating the position that he took when he first mentioned his book of hendecasyllabics (*Ep.* 4.14).[17] At that time, sending a
copy of the book to a friend, he said:

> Accipies cum hac epistula hendecasyllabos nostros, quibus
> nos in vehiculo in balineo inter cenam oblectamus otium
> temporis. His iocamur ludimus amamus dolemus querimur
> irascimur ...
>
> You will receive with this letter my hendecasyllabics, with
> which, on a trip or at my bath or during dinner, I beguile
> my leisure-time. In these we joke, we play, we love, we feel
> pain, we complain, we are annoyed ...

4.14.2–3

His poems are, in the first place, a pastime. "On a trip" has been heard
once before, in the autobiography of the senatorial poet (*si quid otii,
ac maxime in itinere, Ep.* 7.4.8), and one will hear of composition in the
country, "when I had nothing better to do" (*Ep.* 9.10.2).[18] Pliny, then, in
the passage just quoted from *Ep.* 4, states the themes of the poems, or
what we would call their "subjects," in performative terms—not jokes
but joking, not trifles but trifling, not love poems but loving, etc.[19]

It might be objected that Pliny's *iocamur* etc. are a matter of *causa
pro effectu*, that he is really in *Ep.* 4.14 talking about the effects of his
joking, etc., i.e., the subjects of his poems. But in another letter (5.3),

---

figure of Maternus, the tragic poet whose subject matter is drawn from the Roman past,
is clearly a type for the historian," i.e., poetry as historical is a licit pursuit and history
succeeds oratory. For the chronology of Tac. *Dial.* and relevant letters of Pliny (esp. 1.6;
9.10), see Murgia 1985:172 (the conclusion of a lengthy demonstration). Mayer 2001:24
distinguishes between the date of publication of *Dial.*, on the one hand, and the date at
which Pliny came to know it, which, from his hearing it at a recitation or receiving a
version from Tacitus, could have been earlier.

[17] To Plinius Paternus. On this otherwise unknown person, to whom three letters are
addressed, see Sherwin-White 1966:135, who concludes: "He evidently belongs to the
same circle of society at Comum as Caninius and Calvisius Rufus."

[18] For Book 7 as a rich source of letters on *otium*, see Gibson and Morello 2012:169–199
(ch. 6: "Otium: How to Manage Leisure").

[19] "Subjects": Sherwin-White 1966:290 on *Ep.* 4.14.2–3.

where once again he has to apologize for his verse, or rather for composing it and then reading it in public, he says defiantly:

> facio non numquam versiculos severos parum, facio; nam et comoedias audio et specto mimos et lyricos lego et Sotadicos intellego; aliquando praeterea rideo iocor ludo, utque omnia innoxiae remissionis genera breviter amplectar, homo sum.[20]

> I often write verse that is quite unserious, yes, I do. For that matter, I listen to comedies and I watch mimes and I read lyric poetry and I appreciate Sotadics. Further, I sometimes laugh, joke, have fun, and, to sum up all kinds of innocent relaxation in a word, I am human.

5.3.2

Writing light verse is here justified as equivalent to listening to comedies, etc. and laughing and joking, etc. It is justified, in short, as a certain kind of activity.

Pliny continues in *Ep.* 5.3, not unexpectedly, with the other argument, the one from precedent, and lists sixteen worthies, beginning with Cicero, who composed light verse (5).[21] He goes on to mention Augustus, Tiberius, and Nerva, and also, in praeteritio, Nero, as versifiers. Finally, he cites Vergil, Cornelius Nepos, Accius, and Ennius.[22] The last-named, Pliny says, were not senators (and thus cannot serve as precedents for versification by a senator like me) but "moral virtue is not a matter of class distinction" (*sanctitas morum non distat ordinibus,*

---

[20] *Sotadicos* is Catanaeus' generally accepted emendation of *Socraticos*. Pliny alludes to Ter. *Haut.* 77 again at *Ep.* 7.4.2. See Marchesi 2008:80–81.

[21] The sum of sixteen includes the two Torquati indicated by *immo Torquatos*. Sherwin-White 1966:317 gives a list of references to sources for the versification of these worthies.

[22] Cornelius Nepos is not otherwise known to have written verse. Sherwin-White 1966:318 believes that passages in the plays of Accius and Ennius are meant. For Ennius there exists a body of minor literature, i.e., literature that we call minor, as in the title of Russo 2007, which refers to *Praecepta, Protrepticus, Saturae, Scipio,* and *Sota*. Of these works, Pliny might perhaps have had the last in mind but not satire. Pliny's contemporary Martial, in a ranking of genres (12.94), puts satire in about the middle, below epic, tragedy, and lyric and above elegy, iambic, epigram, and fable. Ennius also, however, wrote epigrams (Courtney 43–46 [pp. 39–43]).

6).[23] Pliny's need, as a senator, for self-justification as poet dogs him to the end.

Likewise in the exemplary daily regimen of Vestricius Spurinna, set out in *Ep.* 3.1, verse composition is an activity, following his carriage ride and short walk. It forms part of the mid-day wind-down from the morning's more serious pursuits.[24] In this letter, as in his arguments in defense of his own verse composition, Pliny in effect provides the rationale for a pastime that was not unusual in his circle (and was sanctioned by Quintilian [*Ne carmine quidem ludere contrarium fuerit, Inst.* 10.5.15, where note that the activity is emphasized]).[25] This rationale serves in turn as part of the Epistles' larger project (as it is now understood) of configuring (not simply recording) a particular community and its values.[26]

III. VERSE IN AND BEYOND SOCIAL LIFE

Pliny's letters about his own verse tend to emphasize two things: composition or the activity of versification itself; and publication in the form of a *libellus*. The intervening stage, however, in which poems have social currency of various kinds, is not missing.[27] The social life of Pliny's circle includes recitation to one's friends (7.4.7, of the results of the Laurentine inspiration; 9.34, on his doubts about himself as a reader of his verse) and attending recitations, which can be a way to cultivate the powerful, as the case of a certain Julius Naso (otherwise unknown)

[23] This passage is the sole evidence adduced by Gamberini 1983:116 for his claim that class difference has nothing to do with Pliny's "lukewarm" attitude toward Martial.

[24] On this letter, see Johnson 2010:36–39. "Literary pursuits are a central component of Spurinna's regimen, but ... are not ends in themselves. Rather, it is their incorporation into his other activities that makes him a model of cultured existence" (37).

[25] For an overview of the poets in Pliny's literary circle, see Gamberini 1983:92–93; for the circle of all literary friends, White 1975:299–300.

[26] Fantham 1996:201; Fitzgerald 2007:23 ("virtual society"); Johnson 2010:35 and the bibliographical survey in n. 11. The "Letters and communities project" of Durham University concluded with a conference on 14–16 July 2011, "Configuring Communities: The Socio-Political Dimensions of Ancient Epistolography." See http://www.dur.ac.uk/mediterranean.centre/letters/.

[27] On the three-stage process of publication, see Edmunds 2010:68–72. On Pliny in particular, see Murgia 1985:200.

shows. A young man who is standing for election (probably to the quaestorship), he has done everything, Pliny says, he should have done. In particular, he has cultivated friends, like Pliny, whose recitations he has attended, and he has shown an interest in Pliny's poems as they come forth (*nascentibus opusculis meis interest*, 6.6.6). Pliny of course attended recitations himself. He reports on hearing Q. Gellius Sentius Augurinus, who went on for three days (as did Pliny himself when he read aloud the *Panegyricus*, *Ep.* 3.18). Ostensibly Pliny's purpose is to commend Sentius as poet to his addressee, but his estimate, as he admits, is perhaps influenced by the fact that Sentius read a poem that took for its subject the fact that Pliny sometimes "sports in verses" (*ego interdum versibus ludo*, 4.27.3, where note again the emphasis on versification as an activity). Pliny quotes the poem in question (4.27.4 = Courtney, pages 365–366). Pliny also can pay a friend a compliment by translating his Greek verses into Latin, as he did in the case of Arrius Antoninus (*Ep.* 4.18). He can propose a subject for a poem to a friend, as he proposes the story of a friendly dolphin to Caninius Rufus (9.33), who had been contemplating an epic on the Dacian Wars of Trajan (*Ep.* 8.4). Arrius Antoninus, it can be added, was a friend of Vestricius Spurinna (Sherwin-White 1966:267) and with both of these Sentius Augurinus was on close terms (*Ep.* 4.27.5; see also below on Sentius). They were all, like Pliny, poet senators.

Pliny's stance toward poetry leaves a sense of self-contradiction. If the activity of composition is primary, then the publication of one's book of poems ought not to matter except as a token of friendship that moves in the same circles in which one's individual poems come to life. But gathered in the material form of the *libellus* the poems take on a new life. Even if the poems are only in minor genres, even if they are called trifles (*lusūs*), they can, as we have heard, sometimes attain a greater fame than serious works.[28] Pliny delighted in the success (as he describes it) of his first book (*Ep.* 7.4.9–10), and he went on to publish

---

[28] Not that there could not also be an immediate, practical reason for publishing a book. It was a way to attach your name to your poems and to thwart plagiarism. Cf. Pliny's advice on this matter to Octavius Rufus (*Ep.* 2.10.3). Plagiarism was, however, easy, a matter of changing the name on the *titulus* of the roll or of reciting someone else's poems as one's own. Thus it was something to be feared and, when detected, to be chal-

a second (8.21).[29] He announces the work with the same apologies as before, and explains that he read it aloud to friends over two days, in order to make last-minute corrections.[30] His aspirations now clearly go far beyond his immediate circle.[31] Writing to the consular legate Pomponius Mamilianus, who has already read his book (probably the second one) in camp and has encouraged him to continue writing verse, Pliny says: "I am beginning to seek from this kind of pursuit not only entertainment (*oblectationem*) but even honor (*gloriam*)" (9.25.2).[32]

---

lenged, as by Martial (1.29, 38, 52, 66, 72). Cf. Vitr. 7 *praef*. 10: *Ego vero, Caesar, neque alienis indicibus mutatis interposito nomine meo id profero corpus.*

[29] Sherwin-White 1966:473. Pliny's reference to *novos versiculos* is sometimes taken to indicate a third book (9.16.2). Sherwin-White 1966:501 thinks not. Sherwin-White 1966:507 on 9.25: "Mamilianus has now received the promised volume of verses," i.e. the second volume. On the character of the *novi versiculi*, whether or not they constituted a *libellus*, see Gamberini 1983:90–91. For the question of the genres and subject-matter of Pliny's poems and the number of books of poems he published, see Aubrion 1989:312.

[30] Note that the desire to publish the book precedes and is the reason for the recitation (8.21.6). The book does not come into existence after the recitation, simply as a record of his friends' corrections introduced into the social process of literary display. Cf. Gamberini 1983:98–99: "The invited guest was expected to attend not for the sake of his own entertainment but to participate in the creation of the work itself." On *Ep.* 8.21 and what it shows about Pliny's expectations of his audience, see Johnson 2010:43–45 (for a reasoned bibliography on recitation and Pliny, see 42n24). Note that as the recitation is about to begin Pliny is called away to appear in court (3). *Negotium* supervenes. Cf. Bütler 1970:53–54. Gurd 2012: ch. 5 ("Pliny the Younger: Genetic and General Publics") emphasizes the general, anonymous readership that Pliny expects, beyond the "genetic" readership consisting of friends who participate in revision of his work.

[31] Like his aspirations for his letters. At around the same time as *Ep.* 8.21 (in or after July 107 CE: Sherwin-White 1966:473), Pliny has learned that his books (*libelli*, plural, i.e., copies of a book) are on sale in Lugdunum (Lyon). "I did not think that there were booksellers in Lugdunum ... I am delighted that they keep abroad the favor they have accumulated in Rome" (9.11.2; for the publication date of the book [106–108 CE], see Sherwin-White 1966:39–41). Sherwin-White 1966:490: "Pliny's surprise contrasts with his own suggestion that Octavius Rufus' verses will be read as far as the bounds of the Latin tongue, II.10.2." Some readers of this letter will doubt the genuineness of Pliny's modesty. Fantham 1996:211 takes Pliny to be referring to books of his letters.

[32] Note that *oblectatio* and *gloria* correspond to the two parts of the apology discussed in Section II. Surely Pliny is here acknowledging Manilius' compliment, and the letter is brief, elegant, and ceremonious. But if Pliny was serious about *gloria* in his advice to a young friend concerning verse composition (7.9.9–10, paraphrased above in Section II), why would he be unserious now concerning his own verse? The skepticism of Gamberini 1983:101–103 seems to me unwarranted. The fact that "When all was said and done, he had to found his claim to *gloria* upon his oratory" (Mayer 2003:229) does not mean (and

Although Pliny often seems to be dismissive of his verse, he is never anything but serious about *gloria*.[33]

IV. PLINY AND MARTIAL

Pliny was a prominent figure in Rome, successful in the senatorial career, consul, holder of various high-level administrative posts, and distinguished lawyer. When he speaks about poetry, one tends to surmise that he speaks from the center of Roman literary life. In fact, his letters on poetry, on his own and others', show that there was no center. Comparing the acquaintances of Pliny and Martial, Peter White found that the two had few mutual friends. His finding was the same for Statius and Martial.[34] As for Pliny and Statius, curiously they had no friends in common. Each of the three lived in his own sphere. "We have to do with three separate groups (or aggregates), not with a literary circle in the Augustan sense."[35]

It is against this background that one can set the relationship of Martial and Pliny as Pliny presents it in *Ep.* 3.21. Pliny wrote this letter on the occasion of Martial's death (the exact year of which is unknown; the Epistles of the third Book are dated September 100–103 CE). He says that he gave Martial a viaticum when Martial left Rome a few years earlier (98 CE). He did so in gratitude for a poem that Martial wrote about him (i.e. 10.20[19]), and he quotes the last ten of its twenty-one lines. Martial published the poem in his tenth Book (first edition 95 CE, second edition 98–99 CE), thus not long, whichever the edition, before Pliny responded with the viaticum. In the period in which this

---

Mayer is not, in the context, saying that it means) that Pliny did not also hope for *gloria* from his verse. The irony is that of his speeches only the *Panegyricus* survives and of his verse only the few fragments in Courtney 2003.

[33] In her pages on *gloria* (13–22) Guillemin 1929 does not discuss or cite *Ep.* 9.25. As for Pliny's attitude toward his verse, Marchesi 2008:78–88 reads *Ep.* 7.4 as "an enjoyable virtuoso piece on the inessential nature of poetry." She says: "Although not immune to flattery when it comes to his poetry (*Ep.* 3.21 and 4.27) Pliny is always careful to understate the admittedly numerous instances of self-praise he records in his letters" (79). Cf. Gibson 2003 (cited above, note 2).

[34] Fantham 1996:177–179 points out that for a few patrons Martial and Statius were in competition.

[35] White 1975:300.

exchange of gift for poem took place, Martial was reaching the end of his career. Where was Pliny in his career as poet? Far enough along, it is presupposed here—as it has been by others scholars, whose views will be discussed—for Martial to have known that Pliny was a poet. The chronological question is gone into in greater detail in the Appendix.

In that epigram, sending Pliny a book of poems, Martial praises Pliny as an orator whom future ages will recognize as equal to Cicero, but he makes no mention of Pliny as poet, and Pliny shows not the least sign of taking umbrage. Pliny appears not to have expected Martial to refer to him as a poet. White's findings provide an explanation for Pliny's unconcern. As poets, Pliny and Martial moved in different circles. Pliny could expect Martial to know him as an orator and public figure; he did not expect Martial to know him or to recognize him as a poet, even if in his view he and Martial were writing in the same genre.[36] Their writing of poetry is simply a surd element in the *amicitia* to which Pliny refers in the letter discussed here.[37] If Martial had been alive and in Rome at the time (105–116 CE), he would not have been invited to Pliny's house to hear the readings to which Pliny refers (*Ep.* 5.3.7–11). Pliny's friend Sentius, on the other hand, a man of Pliny's own rank, of course knows Pliny as a poet and even writes a poem about him as a poet, something that the prolific Martial never did in the books that have come down to

---

[36] Citroni 2004:191 calls attention to Pliny's use of *versiculi* of Martial, the same word that Pliny uses of his own verse.

[37] White 1978:84, referring to "peculiarities of perspective" in the Epistle (i.e. how little Pliny says about Martial as a poet and the dissociation of the viaticum from the promotion of Martial's career as poet), says that they "disappear as soon as we discard modern preconceptions about literary patronage, and interpret the letter about Martial in terms of *amicitia*. We do not perceive Martial as a prominent public figure because he is being described as another individual gathered into the web of personal services and obligations. The public figure presented to us in fact is not Martial but Pliny." On *amicus* and *amicitia*, see White 1978:80–82. Nauta 2002:37–39, on the other hand, discusses Pliny *Ep.* 3.21 as a model of patronage. He remarks on the matter of *amicitia*, however: "whether there had been more to the *amicitia* than the exchange recorded in the letter is not clear." It is not clear, I would say, that we have good reason to understand the relation behind *Ep.* 3.21 and Martial 10.20(19) in terms of patronage. It is, of course, the case that 10.20(19) falls into a category of epigrams composed to accompany collections of his verse (Nauta 2002:79–80).

us.[38] Another senatorial patron, Arruntius Stella, who saw himself as a poet, was praised as such by Martial.[39]

V. SUPPOSED RECOGNITION OF PLINY AS A POET IN MARTIAL 10.20[19]

Despite Martial's silence on the matter and despite his references to Pliny as an orator in the poem under discussion (3, 12), some have seen implicit recognition of Pliny as a poet in lines 4–11:[40]

> i perfer: brevis est labor peractae
> altum vincere tramitem Suburae.
> illic Orphea protinus videbis
> udi vertice lubricum theatri
> mirantisque feras avemque regem,
> raptum quae Phryga pertulit Tonanti;
> illic parva tui domus Pedonis
> caelata est aquilae minore pinna.[41]

8 regem *Shackleton Bailey* : regis *codd., edd.* : regi *Heinsius et Gronovius*

---

[38] If the Secundus in Martial 5.80, who is implicitly a poet (or is at least expected to be able to polish the poems of Martial), is Pliny, then Martial has at least recognized him as a poet and at a fairly early stage of Pliny's revived interest in verse composition. (Citroni 1989:221–222 dates Book 5 to the Saturnalia of 89 CE.) But is it Pliny? Howell 1995:162 thinks not. Nauta 2005:218–219 reaches a *non liquet* (he points out that Secundus is one of the commonest Roman cognomina).

[39] More than a third of the poems to him refer to his poetry (White 1975:267–272, 291).

[40] The purpose of this section is to analyze the lines in Martial 10.20(19) that supposedly recognize Pliny as a poet, not to interpret the poem as a whole. In this section, as in others, I have cited some other epigrams of Martial, but as few as possible. For each epigram that one cites one can always cite ten others. It is rarely necessary to do so. The commentaries on the individual books of Martial, the search engines for the PHI database, articles and books on the relevant theme (for which see the bibliography of Lorenz [2003; 2006]), and the "Index of Topics" in Shackleton Bailey (1993: vol. 3, 327–336) lead the scholar along the desired path.

[41] The text is that of Shackleton Bailey 1990. Shackleton Bailey 1978 gives the argument for the emendation. *Rex* by itself will not mean "king of the gods." The emendation of *regis* to *regi* produces the unparalleled "thundering king." Neither the juxtaposition of fem. (*avis*) and masc. (*rex*) nor the adj. use of *rex* is an objection. Shackleton Bailey 1980 adds Mart. 5.55.1 (*volucrum regina*, of the eagle).

> Go take [my book]. Brief is the toil, once you have crossed
> Subura, to overcome the steep path [i.e., up the Esquiline].
> There you will immediately see a slippery Orpheus rising
> above his wet theater and marveling beasts and the royal
> bird [i.e., the eagle] that bore away the Phrygian boy and
> carried him to the Thunderer. There the small house of
> your Pedo has the relief of the wing of a lesser eagle.

Martial has thus provided an itinerary and two landmarks for Thalia, a fountain (the "theater" in line 7) and a house with a relief. Greg Woolf has written: "Landmarks are appropriately chosen—a fountain depicting Orpheus for the poetic senator, and a statue of Ganymede riding the eagle of Zeus for the emperor's friend. Finally the home of an Augustan epigrammatist perhaps alludes to Martial?"[42]

To dispose of these views will not take long. To advance a positive account of the two figures in the fountain, Orpheus and the eagle, will take longer. Martial's description, in the first place part of a verse "map," will prove to be also Ovidian—a miniature Ovidian ecphrasis of a known type of fountain acroterium. The archaeological evidence for this type and the topography of the fountain, hitherto left out of interpretation of the epigram, will have to be brought in. As for Pedo, he is one of the great exponents of the epigram and Martial looks to him as a forebear (see the section on Catullus below). Mention of him might make a reader expect reference to Pliny himself as epigrammatist. As already said, this expectation is not met.

In order to discuss Woolf's suggestions and thus inevitably to enter the question of Martial's tone and strategy in this epigram, some hermeneutic rules of the road would be desirable. First of all, one must distinguish between Pliny's reading and other possible readings. Pliny took the poem as an expression of *amicitia* and repaid Martial with a gift of cash. Pliny mourns Martial's death as the death of one of his dearest friends (perhaps suggesting that Martial was not in fact one of his dearest friends, but that is another matter—he did, after all, write the

---

[42] Woolf 2003:211. Henderson 2002:52 takes Martial's ecphrasis as frankly scoptic: "Why the statuary? For the smears latent in their myths …?"

letter). *Dedit enim mihi quantum maximum potuit, daturus amplius si potuisset* ("For he gave me the most he could, and would have given more if he had been able," 6). A correlate of this first rule is that Martial's epigram was trying to please Pliny. If Martial was also in some way uncomplimentary to, or distanced himself from, Pliny, it must be that Pliny did not perceive, or chose to ignore, it.[43] Nothing obliged him to write the letter if he felt himself injured or, perhaps more importantly, if he thought that others perceived him as the object of some malice on Martial's part. Second, the context of Pliny's reading of the epigram, a fortiori of the lines quoted above, is unknown and largely unknowable. Pliny had undoubtedly read other epigrams by Martial. How many it is impossible to say. (We know at least that he did not have the modern reader's advantage of a compact printed edition of the complete oeuvre of Martial.) Even if we knew, there would remain the question of how he read them. Only a very general framework can be inferred. While Pliny is well aware of Martial's acerbic wit (*plurimum ... salis ... et fellis*) he also takes him to be just as capable of sincerity (*nec candoris minus,* 1).[44] Further, an epigram, and this epigram in particular, might convey *gloria et laus et aeternitas* (6). Especially in the current state of scholarship on Martial, it is necessary to remind oneself of an ancient reader's, and an intelligent one's, apparently simplistic way of reading Martial.

Today's reader thinks immediately of "the city as text" and the device found in other epigrams by which Martial sends his book to someone by a certain route (1.70, 3.5) or gives directions for finding his

---

[43] Nauta 2005:218–219: "[B]ehauptet Martial immer wieder, daß seine Dichtung denjenigen, die darin lobend erwähnt werden, ewigen Ruhm verschafft," with qualifications. One of the examples he discusses is Martial 10.20(19). The theme of Nauta's article, however, is Martial's rather free, joking relation with his addressees of senatorial rank.

[44] For discussion of the sense of *candor* here, see Lefèvre 2009:157n186. Pliny's allusion to Mart. 7.25 (where note the opposition between *sal* and *fel,* on the one hand, and *candidus,* on the other), for which Henderson 2002:48–49 cites Mayor 1889:259 and Post 1908 ad loc., ought to be a compliment to Martial, in the spirit of candor that Pliny finds not lacking in Martial. Henderson attempts to see the allusion as Pliny trying to play (the mocking) Martial. It seems to me inconsistent with the rest of the letter. For other allusions, via the quotation of Martial, by Pliny to his own *Ep.* 1.5, to other of his Epistles, and further to epigrams of Martial evoked by these other Epistles, see Marchesi 2013.

books at booksellers (1.2; cf. 1.3.1, 1.117).[45] The itinerary is, in short, a poetic device in Martial. It has a well-known precedent in *Tristia* 3.1, one that Martial surely remembered.[46] The exiled Ovid has sent a book of poems to Rome. Where should the book go in the city? An unnamed person serves as a guide. "This is Caesar's forum," and so forth (26–32). One does not know if Pliny had read and remembered these epigrams or if he remembered Ovid's pedestrian book. Even if he did and even if he was aware of the particular device, Orpheus might still, of course, have had for him the particular connotation that Woolf proposes— "Orpheus for the poetic senator."

But was Orpheus a *poet*? The Orpheus of the fountain on the Esquiline is the singer who has the power to enchant all of nature, the Sirens (when he accompanies the Argonauts), and even the powers of the underworld (when he goes there to recover Eurydice). Only secondarily did Orpheus become the poet to whom were attributed various eschatological and theogonical texts and a corpus of hymns— all functional in cult and ritual, especially initiation rites.[47] As for the Roman Orpheus, including the one on the Esquiline, he is the singer and wielder of the plectrum. Woods, rivers, and the winds are calmed and attracted by his playing (Sen. *Med.* 625–629). When Proteus tells the story of Orpheus' descent into the underworld (Verg. *G.* 4.453–527), he expatiates on the power of his song (471–484, beginning *at cantu commotae ... / umbrae ... tenues*, "but startled by his song thin shades ...").[48]

---

[45] Cf. Coleman 2006:18–19 on *Spect.* 2: "A poem celebrating a building or, as here, a complex of buildings, also affords an opportunity for a *tour de force* whereby a 'map' is supplied in verse. This feat is most commonly performed in the context of poems issuing invitations or otherwise supplying directions for finding the way." For bibliography on the "city as text" in Roman poets, see Roman 2010:88nn2–3. For Martial in particular, see Lorenz 2003:241–244 (with overview); 2006:117–118. For this area of research Lorenz calls attention to the importance of Rodríguez Almeida, who will be cited several times below.

[46] For the tissue of Ovidian reminiscences at the beginning of Martial 1.70, one of his itinerary poems, see Howell 1980:266 on line 1. For the larger picture of Martial's poetic "repatriation" of the exiled Ovid (including brief discussion of *Trist.* 3.1), see Fitzgerald 2007:186–190.

[47] On the relation of these two Orpheuses, see Calame 2010.

[48] Vergil's Orpheus is mainly a singer. See the survey in Heurgon 1987.

The Latin poet who presents Orpheus as a poet is Ovid (*Met.* 10.1–11.84). In Book 10 of the *Metamorphoses*, an Orpheus who has turned to pederasty after three years of grief for Eurydice (78–85) announces as his themes the love of gods for boys and girls maddened by illicit passions (152–154) and proceeds to develop them at length.[49] It is Orpheus as poet, but it is also the other Orpheus, whose singing enchants nature. Indeed Ovid provides a catalog of the trees attracted by Orpheus' song (86–142), and the audience to which Orpheus delivers his performance is the usual one:[50]

> Tale nemus uates attraxerat inque ferarum
> concilio medius turbae volucrumque sedebat.[51]

> Such was the grove that the bard had drawn to him and he
> was sitting in an assembly of wild beasts and birds, in the
> middle of the crowd.

Whether or not the designer of the fountain took any particular Orpheus as his model, Martial's description of the fountain seems to look to Ovid.[52] His three-line picture changes Ovid's striking metaphor *concilium* to *theatrum* (6–8).[53] Ovid himself might have inspired the change. Concluding the story of Orpheus with his death, he tells that the first victims of the Ciconian women's stones were the birds and animals who had been enchanted by Orpheus' singing:

---

[49] After a kind of *recusatio* (149–151). His long performance does not exactly follow this program but that is another matter (155–707). For Orpheus as pederast and apostle of pederasty to the Thracians, see Bömer 1980:37 on line 83.

[50] As Bömer 1980:60 on line 143 *ferae* says: "Orpheus und die Tiere; zur Zeit Ovids ein Topos." He gives a list of antecedents, starting with Simonides.

[51] 10.143–144. The text of this and of subsequent quotations from *Met.* is that of Tarrant 2004. Ovid's conclusion of the Orpheus episode begins: *Carmine dum tali silvas animosque ferarum / Threicius vates et saxa sequentia ducit* (11.1–2).

[52] Henderson 2002:52–53, takes Mart. 10.20(19).6–9 as "a wicked parody of Ovid's mighty epic extravaganza on Orpheus." He adds: "Ovid's 'Orpheus' is itself a mighty epic ... send-up, of the arch-poet's performance in *his* magicked-up auditorium" (his ellipsis and emphasis). He discusses Ov. *Met.* 10.143–144, 155–158; 11.1–2, 4–5, 20–22, but not 11.25–28. One of the three parts of Hinds 2007 is "Martial's *Metamorphoses*" (136–154). His discussion provides what might be called strong circumstantial evidence for the reading of the Orpheus fountain in Mart. 10.20(19) in terms of Ovidian allusion.

[53] On *concilium*, see Bömer 1980:60 on line 143.

ac primum attonitas etiamnum voce canentis
innumeras uolucres anguesque agmenque ferarum
Maenades Orphei titulum rapuere theatri;[54]

And first of all the Maenads dispatched countless birds and
snakes and the column of beasts—his fame and his public—
even still entranced by the voice of the singer.[55]

Ovid himself, after calling Orpheus' audience a *concilium*, calls it a
theatrum, and says, in effect, that it is this particular public, i.e., the
beasts and birds, that is Orpheus' claim to fame. Ovid indeed repeats
the word *theatrum* in his description of the death of Orpheus:

structoque utrimque theatro
ceu matutina cervus periturus harena
praeda canum est,[56]

Like a stag in a theater built round about, to die in the
arena at the forenoon performance, the prey of dogs ...

Here *structo ... utrimque theatro* is a playful periphrasis of *amphitheatrum*.
It is worth calling attention to this second instance of *theatrum* because
this time Martial's uptake of the image, in *Liber Spectaculorum* (80 CE), is
beyond doubt.[57] At the time of Book 10 of the Epigrams (to repeat, first
edition 95 CE, second 98 CE), Martial had not forgotten Ovid's Orpheus.

---

[54] 11.20–22. Note that it is a matter of Orpheus the singer. Cf. 11.44–48: all of nature
mourns his death.

[55] Following Bömer 1980:244 on line 20: take *theatrum* as meaning "public" and the
gen. as defining gen.; take *titulus* as meaning "fame." Thus lit., "the fame of his public," in
apposition with *volucres*, etc. One could say that the audience of beasts and birds was his
"claim to fame."

[56] *Met.* 11.25–28.

[57] *Spect.* 24(21).1–2: *Quidquid in Orpheo Rhodope spectasse theatro / dicitur, exhibuit, Caesar,
harena tibi* ("Whatever [Mt.] Rhodope is said to have beheld in the theater of Orpheus,
Caesar, the arena displayed to you"). For details and discussion, see Coleman 2006:176.
On Mt. Rhodope and Orpheus, see Verg. *Ecl.* 30. Note, on the question of Orpheus as poet,
her comment: "Martial treats Orpheus as a stage-performer: his 'act' consisted of hypno-
tizing with this music the flora, fauna, and inanimate elements in his environment, and
his 'audience' comprised the surrounding topographical features (here represented
by the most prominent, Mt. Rhodope)." For the relation of *Spect.* 24 to Ovid, see Hinds

On the question of whether or not Pliny or anyone else would have thought of Orpheus in his fountain as a poet, archaeology has the final word. The Severan Marble Plan (*Forma Urbis Romae* or *FUR*) shows a complex of a larger central basin (5–6 meters in diameter) and two smaller flanking ones (2.5–3 meters).[58] These basins have been identified as the fountain to which Martial refers.[59] (In topographical parlance it is the Lacus Orphei.) It was in or near the Piazza di S. Martino ai Monti, and the two medieval churches in this district, of S. Martino ai Monti (after the sixth century also known as the church of SS. Silvestro e Martino ai Monti) and of S. Lucia in Selci, were called "in Orphea."[60] The Orpheus of the fountain, Charles Picard argued, was an acroterium. Thus Martial says *udi vertice theatri*.[61] There are examples of several such fountain acroteria: one at Byblos (Lebanon) and the remains of three in museums (Athens, Istanbul, Sabratha [Libya]). The one at Byblos has been reconstructed. They are all made in the same way, of open-work relief; i.e. they are free-standing but not three-dimensionally conceived. Three trees grow from the plinth, against one of which Orpheus is leaning as he charms the animals. The branches of the trees intertwine around and above him and the animals crouch in the branches of trees. The elevation of the fountain at Byblos published by Jean Lauffray shows a roof, which is where the

---

2007:148–151. (To one's surprise Calpurnius' *Eclogues* turn out to be equally or more important to Martial's conception.)

[58] Rodríguez Almeida 1981: vol. 2, pl. 7; Lanciani 1990: pl. 24. One begs to differ with Henderson 2002:199n19: "n.b.: the Martial locus provides *all* our data on the lacus" (his emphasis). Overviews: Coarelli 1996; Thein 2002 (or see "Digital Augustan Rome" 330 at http://digitalaugustanrome.org/).

[59] For a brief history of the discovery of the relative fragments, see Rodríguez Almeida 1987:415. As for the denial by Fridh 1990 that Martial's fountain has anything to do with the Lacus Orphei on the *FUR*, I share the opinion of Grüner 1993:45n28.

[60] So says Coarelli 1996 but I find "in Orphea" attached only to the church of S. Lucia. Chiesa dei SS. Silvestro e Martino ai Monti: for photographs and brief comment, see http://www.romeartlover.it/Vasi124a.htm#Today; for history, see http://romanchurches.wikia.com/wiki/San_Martino_ai_Monti. Chiesa e Monastero di S. Lucia in Selci: for photographs and brief comment, see http://www.romeartlover.it/Vasi143.htm. Coarelli does, however, cite medieval sources for *Orfienses* as the name of the inhabitants of this quarter and for the phrase *domus in regione Orfea intra urbem*.

[61] Picard 1948:84: "Il est evident que *udi vertice theatri* ... désigne l'*acrotère* faîtier du Nymphée."

acroterium would have stood.[62] The Orpheus of the fountain on the Esquiline could not have stood on a roof, beyond the reach of the water from the fountain. He and his audience of animals would not have been wet, as Martial says that they were. The acroterium of the Esquiline fountain would have stood on or have been affixed to a wall forming the backdrop of the fountain and serving as the implicit *scaenae frons* in Martial's "theater." (Compare the fresco in the "House of Orpheus," in which a central Orpheus sits with his lyre, distinctly *in vertice*, the animals beside and below him.[63]) One can imagine sculptures of birds and animals also in the basins and in niches of the walls such as are shown in the Byblos elevation.[64] It is Orpheus' usual audience, which he charms with singing. The animals' and birds' grasp of the semantic value of whatever he was singing does not seem to be entailed. The eagle referred to by Martial was one of the birds in the trees.[65] (There is no reason to think that Ganymede was also represented. Martial's relative clause [9] does not look ecphrastic.)

---

[62] Lauffray 1940: pl. 2.

[63] Photograph: www.pompeiiinpictures.com/pompeiiinpictures/r6/6%2014%2020. htm.

[64] Cf. Picard 1948:84.

[65] It is impossible to reconcile the conclusions of Picard with those of Rodríguez Almeida 1981: vol. 1, 88. The latter believes that the "lesser wing" is (1) a part of the very eagle in the fountain sculpture and (2) that it was touching the building in which Pedo lived. Because the eagle would have been located high up in the fountain, Pedo must have been living on an upper floor of the building. "Da notare ... che la casa di Pedone, da quanto si legge nel passo di Marziale, doveva essere un piano superiore, da situare nell' isolato che vediamo dietro la fontana. Infatti, se un'ala dell'aquila *caelat domum* ..., è evidente che, nell'insieme figurativo della fontana, il ratto di Ganimede figurava nelle parti alte. Solo una finestra o balcone poteva essere toccata dal gruppo scultoreo, o servirsene come di una decorazione" (second ellipsis is his). This strange idea is repeated in Rodríguez Almeida 1995a. (Rodríguez Almeida does not cite Picard.)

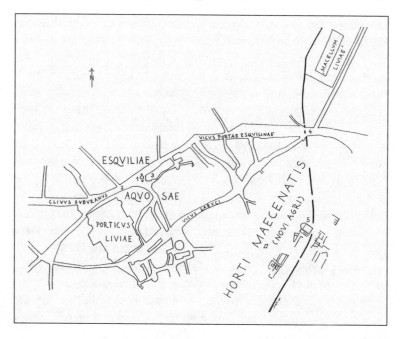

Fig. 1. Esquiliae Aquosae (Prop. 4.8.1). 1. Lacus Orphei. 2. Trames peractae Suburrae (Mart. 10.20[19].4–5; cf. 5.22.5). 3. House of Pedo (Mart. 10.20[19].10). 4. Porta Esquilina. 5. Auditorium of Maecenas.[66]

What does the eagle in Martial's poem communicate to Pliny? Woolf suggested "a statue of Ganymede riding the eagle of Zeus for the emperor's friend," later adding "the Ganymede statue reminding the reader of the homoerotic revels celebrated by other epigrams in the collection (and by Trajan?)," as an example, along with the drunken Muse, of Martial's distancing himself from Pliny, of "a collusion between author and reader."[67] However great the distance, the fact remains, to apply the

---

[66] From Grüner 1993:41, who followed Häuber 1990, map 3. My caption expands Grüner's somewhat. In Edmunds 2009:126n6 I said: "It is not clear why at *Sat.* 2.6.32–33 Hor. says *atras / ... Esquilias.*" Grüner 1993:44 plausibly suggests that, as *Esquiliae aquosae* refers to a part of the Esquiline, not to the whole, so *atrae Esquiliae* refers only to a part, i.e., the potter's field over which Maecenas would build his gardens.

[67] Woolf 2003:212.

correlate of the first rule proposed above, that Martial's instructions to Thalia ought to be in the first instance complimentary to Pliny. How an allusion to the pederastic emperor or a reminder of homoerotic revels in other epigrams would be complimentary to Pliny is unclear. Woolf further believes that Pliny's partial quotation of the epigram, omitting the landmarks, is Pliny's "answering distancing,"[68] But for such distancing on Pliny's part to be noticeable, there must be some reader who has read both the epigram in its entirety and Pliny's letter. The reader who has read both will wonder why, if Pliny wanted to distance himself from Martial, he also desired to give him a gift in return for the poem and, further, to write a letter on the death of Martial. If it was good to suppress the first half of the epigram, it was better to suppress the whole epigram and not to publish the letter, especially when Pliny has high hopes for his immortality and doubts about Martial's.[69]

Earlier I suggested that Martial's description of the fountain looks to Ovid's myth of Orpheus and Eurydice in *Metamorphoses* 10–11. The acroterium also may come from the same passage. Ovid's Orpheus, the convert to pederasty, takes as one of his themes the love of gods for boys and one of his examples is Jupiter and Ganymede.

> Rex superum Phrygii quondam Ganymedis amore
> arsit, et inuentum est aliquid quod Iuppiter esse,
> quam quod erat mallet. nulla tamen alite verti
> dignatur, nisi quae posset sua fulmina ferre.
> nec mora, percusso mendacibus aere pennis
> abripit Iliaden; qui nunc quoque pocula miscet
> inuitaque Ioui nectar Iunone ministrat.[70]

> Once upon a time the king of the gods burned with love
> for the Phrygian Ganymede, and something was found that

---

[68] Woolf 2003:212n17. For a sensible critique of an earlier "distancing" reading of Pliny *Ep.* 3.21, see Pitcher 1999 on Santoro L'Hoir 1992:154–159.

[69] For this point, it makes no difference whether the letter was a fiction or a real letter edited for publication. The relevant consideration is that Pliny published it. For the "question liminaire" of the fictionality or reality of the letters, see the discussion and bibliographical indications of Aubrion 1989:315–316.

[70] *Met.* 10.155–161.

Jupiter would rather be than what he was (i.e., an eagle). Nevertheless he did not see fit to be turned into any bird except the one that could bear his lightning. He did not delay. Beating the air with his deceptive wings, he snatches away the Trojan. Now also he mixes cups and serves nectar, with Juno all unwilling.

In Orpheus' version, which is Hellenistic, Jupiter himself, the *rex superum* (155), takes the form of an eagle.[71] In Martial, the roles of Jupiter and raptor are still separate; only the title *rex* has been shifted to the eagle.[72] But the association of the eagle with Zeus as the source of lightning in Ovid (157–158) persists in Martial, whose gloss on "royal bird" includes "Thunderer" (8–9).

The acroterium might, then, also recall Ovid. Martial calls attention to it not to make a comment on Trajan or on contemporary Roman homoeroticism but in order to allude once again to Ovid and thus to complete a miniature ecphrasis that wittily pictures the Orpheus of the fountain as Ovid's Orpheus. (Pliny's summary of the first eleven lines of the poem, which include the lines under discussion [6–9], gives no indication of what he thought: *Adloquitur Musam, mandat ut domum meam Esquilis quaerat, adeat reverenter.* "He addresses the Muse, he bids her to seek out my house on the Esquiline, and to approach it with respect," 5.) There is also the fact that the eagle of the acroterium is brought into relation with a smaller eagle incised in relief on the house of Pedo (10–11). The ratio of their sizes is not functional in the itinerary. Either bird by itself, larger or smaller, would provide a landmark. The comparison of the two belongs, like the Ovidian allusions, not to the itinerary as such but to the cleverness of Martial's directions. The itinerary as such is lacking, after all, Thalia's starting-point, presumably Martial's house on the Quirinal, and her end-point, Pliny's house.[73] It is not,

---

[71] Bömer 1980:64.

[72] On Shackleton Bailey's emendation in 10.20(19).8, see n. 41 above.

[73] For Martial's house, see Rodríguez Almeida 1995c. Roman 2010:106n83: "It is significant that Martial does not describe or laud Pliny's house," citing Henderson 2002:52. If this omission is significant, then, by parity of reasoning, the omission of reference to Martial's humble dwelling is also significant, and the question then becomes one of the symmetrical omissions framing the brief ecphrasis, the very brevity of which ought to be

then, a matter of some allegorical significance that Martial is trying to impart to objects in the fountain or to a figure incised on a building. A monumental fountain, a complex organization of statues and architectural features like the acroterium, came with a coded message, not only with aesthetic pleasure and utilitarian benefit.[74] In order fully to understand Martial's Ovidian picture, one would have to know in the first place who built the fountain and what its message was. The Lacus Orphei, it has been suggested, was part of Augustus' reorganization of the Anio Vetus in 11 BCE. This aqueduct had a catch-basin inside the Porta Esquilina (see Fig. 1), and the fountain, whatever else it stood for, was in the nature of a celebration of the renewed water supply.[75] If, then, the fountain belongs in the long list of Augustan building projects, one can be sure that the message, whatever it was, had nothing to do with pederastic revels. As for Ovid, it was not one of the dozens of Augustan monuments which he referred to or described, whether for "erotic catachresis," in his amatory poems, or with nostalgia, in the poems of his exile.[76] One could speculate that Martial, with his Ovidian redescription of Orpheus, is giving Ovid the final word on Augustus' fountain.

The house of Pedo, the second of the two landmarks given Thalia by Martial, is not the house in which Pliny lives.[77] Someone who owns

---

the starting-point of interpretation of the tipsy Thalia's lurching course up the *trames*, past the fountain and Pedo's building, and on to Pliny's house. Cf. Watson 2006:292–296 on the ethos of Martial's hendecasyllabics. She singles out speed as one of three main characteristics, the other two being wit and informality.

[74] As Longfellow 2011 shows for the monumental fountain in cities in various parts of the Roman empire.

[75] Rodríguez Almeida 1983. Longfellow 2011:22–23 takes up his suggestion.

[76] Surveyed by Boyle 2003. The quoted phrase is his (20).

[77] Rodríguez Almeida 1987:420 summarizes his views: Pedo lived in an apartment building directly behind the fountain. Passing the fountain and that building on her left, Thalia arrives immediately at the imposing house of Pliny, which Rodríguez Almeida locates on one of the fragments of the *FUR* (from a Renaissance plan) and is able to describe in some detail. (See his Fig. 1 [not satisfactorily reproducible and thus not reproduced here].) Cf. Rodríguez Almeida 1995b. Cf. Lanciani 1990: pl. 23. In my Fig. 1, the house of Pedo is 3. Rodríguez-Almeida 1987:421–423: "subito dopo (the house of Pedo), quasi attaccata (to the house of Pedo, i.e., to the building in which Pedo lived), ma diversa in splendore, come corrispondeva al personaggio, v'era anche la (*magna*) *domus Plinii*

as many estates as Pliny will not be living in a *parva domus* in Rome.[78] Martial calls Pedo Thalia's ("your Pedo," [10]) because she is the Muse of the epigram and Pedo is one of the great exponents of the genre, one to whom, along with Catullus and Marsus, Martial refers as a forebear.[79] Even if Pliny had not read the epigrams in which Martial defines his poetic lineage, he knew who Albinovanus Pedo was and that he had written epigrams. Pliny could not have missed the point of "your Pedo." It is all the more striking, then, that Martial does not even allude to Pliny as an epigrammatist. Further, Pedo's house was not the only house of a poet on the Esquiline. The house of Propertius was nearby.[80] So was the house of Horace.[81] The house of Vergil was in the area (Donat. *Vit. Verg.* 6: *iuxta hortos Maecenatianos*).[82] Someone much less witty than Martial could easily have found a way to suggest that Pliny was appropriately domiciled in a poets' quarter. In sum, the references to Orpheus and Pedo do not constitute an indication that Martial is obliquely praising Pliny's poetry.

Secundi." (Rodríguez Almeida 2003, despite the title of this work, does not discuss Mart. 10.20[19].)

[78] The descriptions of the Laurentine (2.17) and the Tifernum (5.6) villas are a famous pair. He proposes to build a temple in Tifernum and writes to Trajan asking for, *inter alia*, permission to include a statue of him (10.8). He considers buying the estate next to his at Lake Como (3.19). (For his finances see the last section of this letter.) He refers indeed to several villas at Lake Como (*plures meae villae*, 9.7.2). To Corellia, his mother's dearest friend, he offered to sell any one of the Lake Como villas that she liked (7.11.5).

[79] 5.5. See on Martial and Catullus below. Because Martial speaks of Pedo as Thalia's, it seems certain, *pace* Niehl 2004:103, that Martial is referring to Albinovanus Pedo.

[80] As Grüner 1993 has argued with reference to Prop. 4.8.1–2. Cf. Prop. 3.23.23–24. In this connection, the suggestion of Grüner 1993:44–45 that Prop. 4.8.58 (*vicinas ... aquas*) refers to the Lacus Orphei should be taken into account.

[81] See Rodríguez Almeida 1987:416–420. He combines Juv. 1.12–14 (Fronto's house) with schol. ad loc. (*in Horatiana domo, ubi poetae recitabant*). If this Fronto is the orator and consul of 96 CE, then a further combination becomes possible: Fronto *Ep.* 1.89.5 (*plane multum mihi facetiarum contulit istic Horatius Flaccus, memorabilis poeta mihique propter Maecenatem ac Maecenatianos hortos meos non alienus*). He combines Hor. *Epist.* 2.2.65–76 with Mart. 5.22.5–8 to argue that the house was very close to the Lacus Orphei and the steep ascent of the *trames* (cf. Fig. 1.2), still observable today at the eastern end of the Via in Selci.

[82] Rodríguez Almeida 1987:417, suggesting the Oppian Hill, i.e., the southern spur of the Esquiline.

VI. IMMORTALITY

To return to Epistle 3.21, Pliny curiously raises the question of Martial's immortality. Having said that Martial's poem confers fame, praise, and eternity (*gloria et laus et aeternitas*, 6) on him, he imagines an objection from the addressee of his letter: But the verses that Martial wrote will not be immortal. Pliny answers, and these are the last words of the letter: "perhaps not, but he wrote them as if they would be" (*ille tamen scripsit tamquam essent futura*, 6). What is Pliny's premise? It might be that he assumes that all poets hope that their work will be immortal. It might be that he remembers lines like 7.44.7–8 and 12.11.7, in which Martial says that a name committed to verse by him will live forever, or epigrams in which similar large claims are made (1.61; 7.84; 8.3.4–8; 8.73.4 [*victura ... carmina* are a hope]). It cannot be that he "means to cast doubt on Martial's motives as a writer."[83] To do so, i.e., to raise the question of Martial's attitude toward him in particular or toward the writing of epigrams in general, would be to make his own reciprocal gift to Martial, the viaticum, seem foolish and the publication of the letter even more foolish. The first of the hermeneutic rules stated above applies here. The distinction between Martial's "commitment to his work's autonomous validity" and "an ephemeral use in furnishing a necessary ingredient between poet and patron" does not apply to the epigram sent by Martial to Pliny.[84] Indeed the ephemeral use is impossible without the presumption of commitment. Whatever someone other than Pliny, then or now, may know about Martial's real intentions, Pliny must be assumed to assume that the poem composed for him by Martial was intended to be immortal. The second hermeneutic rule applies.

Pliny at the end of his letter combines a noble-sounding generosity toward Martial with reservation about his chances for immortality.[85] Is

---

[83] Roman 2001:117 briefly discusses *Ep.* 3.21 in the context of a larger deliberation on self-denigration, which he says is "the central, hermeneutic problem posed by Martial's conception of literary activity" (113).

[84] Roman 2001:117

[85] Guillemin 1927–1948:1.143: "Le ton de Pline en parlant de lui, bien qu'affecteux, est légèrment protecteur. On y perçoit nettement la différence du rang social." Marchesi 2008:65: "a rather (perhaps deceptively) condescending tone."

it possible that Pliny has in the back of his mind a comparison between himself as poet and Martial? The honor (*gloriam*, 9.25.2) that Pliny has begun to seek as a poet would entail the hope of immortality.[86] Sallust said in the prooemium to the *Bellum Catilinae*, stressing the *animus* as the distinguishing human characteristic: *quo mihi rectius videtur ingeni quam virium opibus gloriam quaerere, et, quoniam vita ipsa qua fruimur brevis est, memoriam nostri quam maxume longam efficere* (1.3). ("So much the righter does it seem to me to seek honor with the resources of the intellect than of strength and because the life we enjoy is brief to render the memory of ourselves as long as possible.")[87] Sallust's *gloriam quaerere* and Pliny's *gloriam petere* have the same sense and the goal is the same in both cases. In a letter prompted by the death of Silius Italicus, often discussed in connection with the one on the death of Martial, Pliny speaks explicitly of leaving literary works (*studia*, as opposed to *facta*) as memorials of one's life (*Ep.* 3.7.14).[88] The word *studia* here could take in Pliny's orations, his verse, and also the aspirations of his friend, Caninius Rufus, as a poet.[89] Pliny and Caninius Rufus spur each other on to the love of immortality (*ad amorem immortalitatis*, 15). (A subject for a poem proposed by Pliny to Caninius was mentioned above.) Such were the terms in which, with Horatian resonance (*C.* 3.30), he encouraged Octavius Rufus to publish his verse: "Keep your mortality before your

---

[86] Hershkowitz 1995:177 on *Ep.* 9.25.2: Pliny is "ironic, nevertheless there is a sense that something genuine underlies this remark." Hershkowitz substantiates her finding of irony with reference to self-depreciating remarks that Pliny makes at the end of the letter. These remarks are conventional. Cf. *nugae* and *ineptiae* (4.14.8); *lusūs* and *ineptiae* (9.25.1); *versiculi*: 4.27.4 (Sentius Augurinus uses of Pliny); 5.3.2; 9.16.2. Roller 1998:300, citing Hershkowitz: "It does not seem to me that Pliny is being 'ironic' or 'off-handed' ... in his claim to seek *gloria* from his polymetric poems."

[87] One could say that immortality begins in *gloria*: cf. Cic. *Tusc.* 110. Bütler 1970:22: "Weg zum Ziel der *immortalitas* ist die *gloria*." This sentence comes from Bütler's second chapter, "Das Ringen um Unsterblichkeit und Ruhm" (21–27). Cf. Trisoglio 1972:176–181; Mayer 2001:9–12, apropos of Tac. *Dial.* but with discussion of fame in Pliny.

[88] On the letter, see Lefèvre 1989:118–123. *Studia* in Pliny means primarily oratory, as one might expect, but as in *Ep.* 7.9 verse composition is included: see Bütler 1970:29–30, 38 in his chapter "*studia.*" Ludolph 1997:78–79: in Pliny's view both Silius Italicus and Martial were his rivals for literary fame.

[89] See Gamberini 1983:96–97 for an argument that the *studia* to which Pliny exhorts Caninius Rufus in *Ep.* 1.3.3 are verse composition.

eyes. You can free yourself from it with this single memorial" (*Habe ante oculos mortalitatem, a qua adserere te hoc uno monimento potes, Ep.* 2.10.4).

If Pliny has this hope for himself as a poet, then he must have imagined that success in his own circle was a sufficient beginning.[90] Probably he was aware of the *fama* on which Martial prided himself, a *fama* that, according to Martial, gives him in his own lifetime what other poets received only *post cineres* (1.5.6). If so, Pliny did not think that Martial's kind of *fama* was the same as *gloria* or was a path to *gloria*. Whereas Martial sends his twelfth Book, by way of Stella, to the people (*populus*), the patriciate, and the knights (12.2.15), the readings to which Pliny refers in the letter cited above admitted only his friends, i.e., the elite. He was not, he explains, inviting the *populus* into an auditorium.[91] Pliny's hopes for his fame are tied to the circle within which and for which his verse is composed.

VII. CATULLUS

Comparison of Pliny and Martial becomes less speculative when one turns to their different relations to the great forebear of epigram in Latin, Catullus.[92] As one prominent in Roman political and forensic life, Pliny always had to respect the distinction between duty and the permissible pleasures of *otium*. For him, the neotericism of his Catullus, even if Catullus is his model, could not include its subversive side; it had to be acceptable in the vastly changed political climate of the first

---

[90] See Johnson 2010:53–56 on the crucial importance of his literary circle, reached primarily for the most part through recitation, to Pliny's hopes for the success of his verse.

[91] *Ep.* 5.3.11, on which see Sherwin-White 1966:318.

[92] Citroni 2004:181–186 finds a series of similarities, beginning with their relation to Callimachus and Catullus as archetypes of the genre. (In this respect the differences are, as I argue, more important than the similarities.) He then discusses two main differences between Pliny and Martial: for the former, minor poetry is "(1) un domaine quasiment sans liens quant au choix métrique et, (2) en meme temps, largement libre quant au choix de la dénomination du genre." (I have tried to suggest a strategic reason on Pliny's part for his comments on nomenclature.) For Martial, "(1) la variété métrique est ... rigidement contrôlée et (2) la dénomination du genre est rigoureusement univoque." (The numbers are mine.) For Martial's meters, see n. 103 below. For Citroni's relation to Puelma 1997 (a longer version of Puelma 1996), see Citroni 2004:178n2.

century CE.[93] Pliny refers to Catullus for the first time in his Epistles apropos of Pompeius Saturninus: *facit versus quales Catullus meus aut Calvus, re vera quales Catullus aut Calvus* ("he writes verses like those of my favorite Catullus or Calvus, exactly like theirs," 1.16.5), and specifies the qualities of these poets that he finds and prizes in Saturninus: *lepor, dulcedo, amaritudo, amor* ("charm, sweetness, bitterness, passion," 1.16.5), with some harsher verses inserted in the soft, smooth ones (*mollibus levibusque duriusculos quosdam*, 1.16.5). It is thus "my Catullus" in more than one sense. It is a Catullus delimited in such a way as to be a suitable favorite for a man like Pliny. The pairing of Catullus and Calvus returns, not, one suspects, by chance, in the poem in honor of Pliny by Sentius Augurinus referred to above (4.27.4 = Courtney, pages 365–366):

> Canto carmina uersibus minutis,
> his olim quibus et meus Catullus
> et Caluus ueteresque. Sed quid ad me?
> Unus Plinius est mihi priores.

> I sing songs in miniature verse-forms, in those that once my Catullus and Calvus and the old-timers used. But what do I care about them? Pliny alone is worth all who came before.

(Pliny's quotation of the poem goes on for four more lines.) In Pliny's only other reference to Catullus, he is introducing some lines by this poet, and Calvus is naturally omitted (4.14.5). The lines are the famous ones in which Catullus distinguishes between his own chastity and that of his verses, which will have wit and charm on the condition that they are on the soft side and not completely shamefast (16.5–8).

---

[93] Roller 1998:278: "Catullan poetry must present formidable ideological difficulties for someone with Pliny's commitments." He proceeds to show how Pliny suppressed the radical side of Catullus and narrowed Catullus as model to the "producer of polymetric poetry and jokes, activities that for Pliny are safely restricted within the devalorized zone of otium" (289; for another formulation of Pliny's strategy: 299). Marchesi 2008 has formulated somewhat differently the manner in which Pliny depoliticized his Catullan model (62–71; also 71–78 on *Ep.* 4.14). "Catullus is not a model of the distinctive integration of light poetry and serious life that Pliny deems suitable only for himself and his aristocratic friends" (76).

Martial defends himself by this Catullan rule, as Pliny calls it (*lex*, 4.14.5), in the preface to his first Book, where Catullus forms a group with Pedo, Marsus, and Gaetulicus.[94] He refers to Catullus again nineteen times in his epigrams, three times along with other poets. It is useful to compare these references with Pliny's pairing of Catullus and Calvus. Schematically:

		C	M	P	G
1 *pr.* 4		✓	✓	✓	✓
2.71	ec	✓	✓		
5.5	ec	✓	✓	✓	
7.99	ec	✓	✓		

Fig. 2. C = Catullus; M = Marsus = Domitius Marsus (Courtney, pages 300–305); P = Pedo = Albinovanus Pedo (Courtney, pages 315–319); G = Gaetulicus = Cn. Cornelius Lentulus Gaetulicus (Courtney, pages 345–346); ec = elegiac couplets.

Whenever, then, Martial mentions Catullus along with another poet or with other poets, Marsus is mentioned. Marsus also appears in the Epigrams as one of the poets made rich by Maecenas (8.55[56].21–24), once paired with Pedo (2.77), and twice by himself (4.29; 7.29). Pliny never mentions Marsus nor does he mention Pedo or Gaetulicus. To sum up, in the nexus Catullus + x as it appears in Pliny and Martial, the main differentiae for x are, so to speak, systematic: in Martial, Marsus and Pedo; in Pliny, Calvus.

Martial goes so far as to contrast Catullus with Calvus. The *Apophoreta* (Book 14), a series of distichs to accompany books as Saturnalia gifts (183–196), concludes with one for Catullus and one for Calvus. In

---

[94] 1 *praef.* 4. *Lasciuam uerborum ueritatem, id est epigrammaton linguam, excusarem, si meum esset exemplum: sic scribit Catullus, sic Marsus, sic Pedo, sic Gaetulicus, sic quicumque perlegitur.*

the pattern of alternation between gift for a rich man and gift for a poor man (14.1.5), the former receives a Catullus (14.195), the latter a Calvus (14.196).[95] As for Calvus, the papyrus on which his book is written would be better off in the river in which it grew. Martial had no liking for obscure erudite poetry like his.[96] After one has said everything that can and must be said about the similarities of Martial to Catullus, and especially about Martial's choices in the area of meter, the fact remains that the Catullan Martial was not a neoteric Martial, that Martial was less Catullan than Catullus.[97] Martial associates Catullus especially with Marsus, whose satirical epigrams Martial would have regarded as precedents for his own. Martial thus delimits his own Catullus, as part of a new conception of epigram. The activities in which Pliny includes the writing of verse, with the justification *homo sum*, have become in Martial his actual subject-matter—*hominem pagina nostra sapit* (10.4.10). While Pliny still thinks of readership in Augustan terms, Martial sees himself as writing for what we would call the general reader.[98]

---

[95] Each distich has a lemma. The lemmata serve as a kind of index (14.2.3–4). Pointing to the apparent lack of fit between lemma and distich in 14.196, Leary 2001:262 proposes a lacuna. (The lemma goes with a missing distich, etc.) He also discusses Hermann's suggestion, arising from mss. variants in the lemma (*calidae* Q : *caldae* γ), that the reference is not to Calvus but to the poet L. Iulius Calidus (known by name only; not in Courtney 1993). Lorenz 2002:103n213 has dealt brusquely but I think justly with this idea. Lorenz's discussion of the relation between 14.196 and Cat. 14 (Catullus returns to Calvus an anthology of inferior poets which Calvus has sent as a Saturnalia gift) seems germane and increases the likelihood that Calvus is correct in the lemma to 14.196.

[96] Cf. on Cinna, 10.21 and on Callimachus, 4.23 and 10.4.

[97] See Mattiacci 2007 for Martial's critical relation to Catullus. Her theme: "il 'catulliano' Marziale non è un Marziale 'neoterico'" (177). At 178n3 she lists the most important of the numerous studies of Martial and Catullus. See also the fuller bibliography of Lorenz 2003:253–255 with Lorenz's overview ad loc. (My purpose in this short section on the relation of Pliny and of Martial to Catullus is not to enter into the nuances of each of these relations, thus not, for example, to explore a finely spun distinction like that of Roman 2001:120n24: "That Martial allied himself with Catullus is, of course, quite true, but rather than interpreting this advertisement of literary inheritance as a sign that Martial saw Catullus as a writer of epigrams, it is more in the spirit of Martial's own language to read it as proclaiming that Martial is Catullus' heir in the domain of playful, nugatory, first-person poetry at Rome." Cf. Roller 1998, quoted in n. 93 above, on *Pliny's* relation to Catullus.)

[98] With all the uncertainties that an audience so conceived entails: cf. Fitzgerald 2007:23–24; ch. 5 ("The Society of the Book").

VIII. NOMENCLATURE

These comparisons of Pliny and Martial move toward a conclusion with some observations on the nomenclature of light verse. Pliny called his first book "Hendecasyllabics," which has a self-evident plausibility, because it consisted of poems in this meter (*Ep.* 4.14.8). His second book consisted of poems in various meters (8.21.4). He seems to be open-minded as regards the name of the genre in which he is working. As for his first book, he says that the title refers to the meter only. He is unconcerned about the title: *Proinde, sive epigrammata sive idyllia sive eclogas sive, ut multi, poematia seu quod aliud vocare malueris, licebit voces; ego tantum hendecasyllabos praesto* (4.14.9). "Please call them as you wish, either epigrams or idylls, or eclogues, or, as many do, little poems or anything else you prefer to call them. I am offering only 'hendecasyllables.'" ("Little poems" (*poematia*) is what Sentius Augurinus chose to call his poems [4.27.1].)[99] It would not have taken a very extensive awareness of Martial on Pliny's part to be aware that Martial had made *epigramma* into a technical term for the genre in which he was writing, a genre that Martial saw himself as transvaluing.[100] Pliny never uses *epigramma* of his own verse; he uses it only of Cicero (7.4.3) and of someone's Greek epigrams (4.3.3). With "Please call them as you wish" Pliny seems to be protesting too much. If he was in fact aware of Martial's appropriation of the term *epigramma*, then he was avoiding comparison.[101]

---

[99] For a detailed survey of terms for poetry and poetic forms in Pliny, see Roller 1998:267–273; 300–302.

[100] For the genre of epigram as received by Martial, see Fitzgerald 2007:25–33 ("Excursus: Epigram at Rome"). Citroni 2004:178 asks where the concept of the epigram which one finds in Martial came from. He rules out Greek epigram as the answer (179–180). As evidence for his investigation, he puts aside the *Catalepton*, the *Priapea*, and the epigrams in the *Anthologia Latina* that might seem relevant: they are all "receuils au caractère particulier et de paternité incertaine ou inconnue et difficilement datable" (180). (Cf., however, Reeve 1985:176: In the *Anthologia Latina*, "nothing of 236–237 + 396–479 has ever been proved later than Nero.")

[101] Statius, on the other hand, when he uses *epigramma* in *Silv.* 2 *praef.* 16 (the only occurrence of this word in *Silv.*) to depreciate three of his poems (2.3–4, and, linked to these two by *eandem ... facilitatem* [17], 2.5), has been suspected by D. W. T. Vessey of a hit at Martial. So Van Dam 1984:59 reports. (Van Dam's reference to Vessey is incorrect and I do not have the correct one.) If Vessey is right, there is an irony of which Statius seems to

IX. CONCLUSION

Pliny's autobiography as a poet (*Ep.* 7.4), taken with various comments on his verse composition, have served as background to his letter on the death of Martial (3.21). In that letter he did not speak of himself as a poet, as he did in the letter on the death of Silius Italicus (3.7). Nor, in raising the question of Martial's immortality, did he raise the question of his own, as he did in the letter just cited. In short, Pliny did not deign to compare himself as poet with Martial. The reader of the letter on Martial, however, especially if he or she has read the autobiography as poet and the other letters on Pliny as poet, inevitably makes the comparison, as Pliny perhaps, with his abundant self-confidence, would have wished.[102] He was secure in his own elite-centered notion of literary activity and fame.

As for the epigram of Martial that Pliny quotes (10.20[19]), again a comparison is implicit. The oppositions that organize the epigram, in particular, work and relaxation, oratory and light verse, are precisely the ones that govern Pliny's activities as poet in his account of himself. If one is determined to find in Martial's epigram recognition of Pliny as poet, one will have to find it in Martial's mirroring of the terms of Pliny's own apology for writing epigrams. Martial's use of hendecasyllabics, the meter of Pliny's first *libellus* but not a statistical favorite in Martial, might be another kind of recognition.[103] In the end, however, as Roland Mayer points out, "The part of Martial's epigram that Pliny quotes (the last ten lines) relates to his oratory: how it rivals Cicero's and will appeal to *saecula posterique* ('future generations'). This is just what Pliny hankered after and the letter keeps before us Pliny as successful orator in the great tradition."[104]

---

be unaware: he is using a mode, namely the prose letter as the introduction to a book of poems, which was originated by Martial. See Van Dam 1984:52.

[102] Syme 1958:97 notes Pliny's implicit claim for the immortality of his letters.

[103] The distribution of meters in Martial: elegiac distichs (79%); hendecasyllabics (15%); choliambics (5%); other (1%) (Sullivan 1991:227n22; Citroni 2004:198–200). For the ethos of the meters, see Watson 2006.

[104] Mayer 2003:232–233. See the portrait of Pliny as a literary man by Fantham 1996:200–211. She says: "The oratory of Senate and law court was in Pliny's eyes the real source of his dignity" (204).

Pliny's letter on Martial is often discussed under the heading of patronage. The viaticum, however, sounds like a nonce gift, and the *amicitia* to which Pliny refers may not have been deep. White's findings suggest that Pliny and Martial moved in different circles. The distance between the two which some have seen as subtle antagonism may, then, be nothing but a given in a relationship that Martial could not represent as closer than it was. Comparison with the epigram by Sentius, partly quoted above, shows that Martial, without speaking of Pliny as a poet, knew what Pliny would like to hear. Martial uses the same basic opposition found in Sentius (where it is in terms of *forum* vs. *amor*, 5–6). Martial uses the same *Catones* (7) in the same "even Cato's [i.e. plural of Cato] will unbend" rhetoric.[105]

To tie the interpretation of Martial's epigram to its first recipient and to that recipient's response, in the form of a gift, might seem to be a return to the kind of interpretation that Don Fowler warned against in an article published in 1995.[106] His article, framed as a critique of one by White that argued that Martial's epigrams circulated in small assortments before they were published as *libelli*, opposed the textuality of the epigrams to their use as a "a source for social history" (35) or as "a log of 'real' social relations" (51).[107] In other words, Fowler opposed the textuality of the text to its instrumentality in social exchange. It was in particular the *libellus* that gave the epigram this character. "The constant reference to the book in Martial should be an invitation to treat his poems as more than a source for social history, and to allow the interplay of possible readers to produce its myriad and complex effects" (36).

No one would doubt that in the larger context of the *libellus* the individual epigram acquires significance that it does not have in isolation. Much research on Martial, especially on sequences of epigrams in various *libelli*, has now abundantly proven Fowler's point. As for Pliny as a reader of Martial, however, one will always remain in ignorance of the context in which he read the epigram to which he refers in *Ep.* 3.21.

---

[105]For the interpretation of line 7, see Courtney 1993:366. For the basic opposition in Martial, see Marchesi 2008:64–68.

[106]Fowler 1995. I have put the page numbers in Fowler's article to which I refer in parentheses in the text.

[107]White 1974. White 1996 replies to Fowler 1995.

One does not know how many other epigrams of Martial he had read. Nor does one know how he read the epigrams that he did read. Would he have noticed in Sentius' epigram the allusions to Martial that the modern scholar notices?[108] His generalizations at the beginning of the letter show that he had read a certain number of Martial's epigrams. They also show that he believed that Martial was capable of sincerity, and the rest of his letter presupposes that he took the epigram we know as 10.20(19) to be sincere.

As for possible readings of individual epigrams by the "possible readers" to whom Fowler refers, again a hundred flowers have bloomed. The question remains of how to read 10.20(19) as an epigram sent to Pliny. Scholars cited in this article have read it as antagonistic. The objection to this interpretation that I have offered is that it makes Pliny's letter seem foolish—Pliny simply missed the venom that we now perceive. Perhaps it is now a possible reading. Perhaps it was then, too, for readers other than Pliny. One can be fairly certain that it was not possible for Pliny, simply because it makes no sense in the context of the primary communication of the epigram (unless one is going to argue, as John Henderson did, that Pliny perceived it and surreptitiously countered it in *Ep.* 3.21). With the notion of primary communication, one returns to White's view of publication. One also returns to the epistemological reflections that appeared at the end of his reply to Fowler.[109] To restate some implications less politely than White would have done, if all possible readings are always possible, then interpretation is adrift in a *mare magnum* in which no bearings can be taken.

Nevertheless, Fowler's emphasis on Martial's epigrams as texts for reading and re-reading, affirmed as such in the epigrams themselves, is worth bearing in mind. The present article, even if, in terms of Fowler's binarism, it has often affirmed social history against textuality, is in the end another moment in the history of reading. The discussions of Martial 10.20(19) and of Pliny *Ep.* 3.21 offered here are readings that have focused on silences, Martial's on Pliny as poet, Pliny's on himself as poet (again compare his letter on the death of Silius Italicus). The

---

[108] Courtney 1993:365.
[109] White 1996:412.

purpose of these readings was to argue not from but about these silences. It seemed, to turn again and for the last time toward the other side of the binarism, that they could not be understood outside social history; and topography also helped.

APPENDIX

The preceding discussion has presupposed that Pliny was already composing verse at the time of *Ep.* 3.21 and that Martial would have known of it. Sherwin-White, however, in his discussion of the date of Book 4 (book-date 104–105 CE), speaks of Pliny's "new hobby of versification" and observes that it is never mentioned in Books 1–3. "This new pursuit was evidently taken up *after the date of the letters in (Book) III*" (1966:33; my emphasis).

These remarks of Sherwin-White on Pliny's verse composition (and other related remarks to be discussed below) rest on a particular view of the dates and organization of the Books of Pliny's Epistles, a view that arose, paradoxically, in opposition to what Pliny himself said in the dedicatory Epistle with which Book 1 begins: *Collegi non servato temporis ordine—neque enim historiam componebam—sed ut quaeque in manus venerat.* What might be considered the common-sense reading of this statement was in Sherwin-White's words "rudely reversed" by Theodor Mommsen, who "constructed the theory of 'book-dates'—that the letters in each book all belong to the date of the period of the dateable letters, none earlier, none later" (1966:20, with discussion of subsequent debate and with bibliography, 21–23). Further, the book-dates thus determined are in chronological order. Book-date in this sense refers to "the period covered by the datable contemporary events described in the component letters of each book" (1966:22), not to date of compilation or of publication (for a survey of the questions see Aubrion 1989:316–323; for a summary of Bodel (forthcoming) on dates of publication, see Marchesi 2008:12 note 1; for linear chronology of letters on the same subject and of letters in each successive book, see Gibson 2012:67–69).

Sherwin-White went beyond Mommsen's theory, however, in assuming, in the matter of verse composition, that the date of first mention in the Epistles corresponds to the date of first occurrence in

Pliny's life. He therefore relied on the argumentum ex silentio referred to above (the hobby is never mentioned in Books 1–3 and therefore it is new at the time of Book 4). To reply to Sherwin-White on the particular matter at hand it is not necessary to go into the question of Mommsen's book-dates (confirmed by Syme 1958: vol. 2, 660–64 and Syme 1985:176 ["In general, his scheme stands the test ..."], challenged by Murgia 1985:191–202) or of others' book-dates. It is only necessary to loosen the bond between the date of composition of individual letters, on the one hand, and book-date, on the other, as can be done in the cases of some of Pliny's letters on his verse.

Ep. 7.4 (book-date 107 CE), in which Pliny gives his autobiography as a poet, is a good starting-point. In summary, by section, with two dates as in Sherwin-White's commentary:

2 Pliny refers to his writing a tragedy when he was fourteen years-old (about 76 CE).

3 When he was returning from military service (81 CE), becalmed on the island of Icaria, he composed elegiac verses.

3 He also tried hexameters. (From this point on in the letter there are no indications of date.)

3 He has tried hendecasyllabics now for the first time (*nunc primum*, on which see below).

3–4 He had the experience in his Laurentine villa described above and *post longam desuetudinem* began to write verse (he quotes some hexameters).

7 Next he wrote elegiac verse.

7 Returning to Rome he read his verse to his friends.

8 He then tried composition in several meters when he had leisure to do so.

8 Finally he decided to complete the separate book of hendeca-syllabics (cf. 3).

9 They are avidly received.

Scholars before Sherwin-White took this letter to be contemporary with Pliny's first reference to his book, in *Ep.* 4.14 (book-date 104–105 CE), two or three years earlier than the book-date of Book 7 (e.g. Schultz 1899:31). Sherwin-White, on *expertus sum me aliquando et heroo, hendecasyllabis nunc primum*, said: "It is very forced to take this to mean 'I have just finished my first efforts', as do Peter [1872:703] and the rest [Schultz 1899:31–32; Prete 1948:90]. Pliny quite naturally says 'this is my first effort in this line'. Besides, ss. 8–9 make it plain that the book was published and in circulation." His point is not obvious. The sentence in question is part of an answer to Pontius' question why a serious person like Pliny wrote hendecasyllabics (1). Pliny's answer twice contrasts this kind of verse with more serious genres, first in sections 2–3, then in sections 3–9. Each of these contrasts is also between periods of time, earlier and now. (Note the change to the present tense that begins with *paenitet* at section 8.) Indeed, the temporal contrast is built into the sentence in question. *Nunc primum* puts the activity (as distinguished from its product, as in Sherwin-White's substantivizing of the adverbial expression) in the perspective of the here and now. No one would doubt that Pliny's description of the success of his book (8–9) also refers to the here and now. The book has indeed been published, as Sherwin-White observes. But what has been the lapse of time between its publication and its reception as described by Pliny? Has this enthusiasm been raging since 104–105 CE (the book-date of the letter in which publication is first mentioned), i.e., for as long as three years? The success Pliny describes would plausibly be taken as belonging to the same perspective as *nunc primum*.

The conclusion to be drawn concerning the coordination of book-date and letter date is negative. If the date of the composition of *Ep.* 7.4 is moved back in time from the book-date, there still remains the big chronological question, viz., what is the relation of the letter on the death of Martial (3.21) to Pliny's verse composition? One of the details concerning Pliny's return to Rome as a newly inspired poet is relevant to this question of relative chronology. He says that he read his verse to his friends (7.4.7).

This detail can be combined with a reference to readings in another letter, 4.19, which concerns his wife Calpurnia.

Qua illa sollicitudine cum videor acturus, quanto cum egi
gaudio afficitur! Disponit qui nuntient sibi quem assensum
quos clamores excitarim, quem eventum iudicii tulerim.
Eadem, si quando recito, in proximo discreta velo sedet,
laudesque nostras avidissimis auribus excipit. Versus
quidem meos cantat.

3–4

How concerned she is when she sees that I am going into
court, how joyful she is when I have finished! She has those
who report to her the applause, the shouts of approval that
I have stirred up, the decision that I obtain in the case. She
also, whenever I give a reading, sits nearby concealed by a
curtain, and takes in with most eager ears the praise that I
receive. She even sings my verses.

The readings referred to here are readings of verse (and so I think the
reference of Sherwin-White 1966:296 to his comment on *Ep.* 2.19.1 on
the recitation of speeches is irrelevant). These readings would be the
same as the ones following the Laurentine inspiration (*Ep.* 7.4.7), unless
one posits two distinct phases of verse-recitation. The date of the letter
about Calpurnia is thus of great interest. While the book-date of Book 4
is 104–105 CE, Otto dated the marriage to 97 CE (1919:36n1, 40) and this
letter to 99–100 CE (discussion by Sherwin-White 1966:33). Sherwin-
White himself says the marriage took place not more than a year before
this letter (1966:264; 296). Otto's dating of the letter would put Pliny's
verse-composition close in time to Martial's publication of Book 10
(first edition 95 CE, second edition 98–99 CE), which includes the poem
for Pliny. This possibility is further explored below.

 Sherwin-White's main argument for the coincidence of book-date
and autobiographical date in the case of *Ep.* 4.19 takes the general
form that I have already described. Nowhere in Books 1–3, he says,
does Pliny mention the marriage to Calpurnia, whereas he mentions it
frequently in Books 4–8. Further, "[t]hese references to the marriage ...
tie up in Epp. [4.]13.1 and [4.]19.4 with mention of Pliny's new hobby
of verse-writing, which is entirely absent from I–III" (264). In short,

Sherwin-White links two arguments from silence, presented as mutually corroborating, one about verse-composition, the other about the marriage. Indeed there is a third such argument, concerning visits to Comum, to which I shall return.

Sherwin-White was a close observer of pairs and larger sets of topics occurring in letters within a single book, and he uses his observations in the kind of argument just observed. He puts six letters in Book 4 referring to Pliny's verse composition in a chart along with three other topics (1966:33). (Of the six letters, two [4.3 and 4.18] have nothing to do with Pliny's aspirations as a poet in his own language. The others are 4.13, 14, 19, 27.) Sherwin-White's observations can be used to support a different kind of argument, based on premises concerning the composition of the Epistles different from his, but his own argument needs further comment. As I have pointed out, he holds not only that all the letters in each book belong to the date of the period of the dateable letters in that book but also that, as concerns the life of Pliny, first mention corresponds to first occurrence. Two of the letters in Book 4 concerning Pliny's verse composition go against this view and Sherwin-White's own form of argument can be used against him. One is the letter about Calpurnia just discussed (4.19). It is addressed to Calpurnia Hispulla, his wife's aunt, who is living at Comum with her father. When Pliny introduces his wife's enthusiasm for his verse, he says: *Eadem, si quando recito* ... Pliny does not have to begin by explaining that he composes verse and gives readings. He assumes that Calpurnia Hispulla already knows. Likewise, in writing to Cornelius Tacitus, he can refer to an *opusculum* on which he is working (4.13.2), meaning the book of hendecasyllabics, without any explanation at all. He assumes either that Tacitus already knows of the *opusculum* or at least that Tacitus knows that Pliny composes verses. Both of these letters, then, even if they were composed and sent (in whatever their original, unedited form was) in the period 104–105 CE (the book-date of Book 4), presuppose that in the life of Pliny verse composition started earlier. (How much earlier is a separate question.) The argument that I have used is like one that Sherwin-White uses, i.e., from silence. It can be expressed as a modus tollens: If Calpurnia Hispulla (or Tacitus) had been ignorant of Pliny's verse composition, Pliny would have had to explain. He did not explain. Therefore she (or Tacitus) was not ignorant of it, i.e., it was already going on.

One could continue in this vein for a long time, rehearsing the controversies already indicated and several others and finding new ways to challenge this or that letter-date. It is of much greater interest, and also of greater utility to the limited goal of this Appendix, to consider Sherwin-White's working hypothesis itself. Useful terms and concepts come from Ilaria Marchesi's study of literary allusion in Pliny's letters (2008). She distinguishes three scholarly approaches to the organization of the letters. The oldest of the three, which takes the letters as documents of the author's life and times, she refers to as the "heteronomous hypothesis." On this hypothesis, the chronology of events determines the sequence of letters, which are taken as primarily documentary in nature. This approach was followed (not replaced) by study of the letters as the author's self-fashioning. (For the recent interest in what might be called "group-fashioning," see my note 26.) Her own approach, taking the collection of letters as a literary artifact in its own right, and showing pervasive intertextuality with major Roman poets and prose writers, begins from the "autonomous hypothesis" (2008:ix). She demonstrates, in support of her hypothesis, a large component of intertextuality with poets, especially Vergil, Catullus, Horace, and Ovid, and other prose writers, notably Tacitus. In the longer view, the approaches well described by Marchesi belong to a cycle of Plinian scholarship in which heteronomous and autonomous hypotheses alternate. Mommsen's strict chronology was soon challenged by other scholars who asserted aesthetic and other kinds of organization of the Epistles (see the extensive critique of Mommsen by Peter 1901, although still within the "heteronomous hypothesis"; for an overview of the cycle, a half-century later, see Prete 1948:91–93).

Sherwin-White is of course one of the main exponents of the "heteronomous hypothesis." To return now to his pattern of three interlocking silences, the pattern that includes the first letters on verse-composition, one asks which of the two competing hypotheses defined by Marchesi will best explain them. First, Sherwin-White's fullest statement of the pattern:

These references to the marriage and to Comum tie up in Epp. [4.]13.1 and [4.]19.4 with mention of Pliny's new hobby of verse-writing, which is entirely absent from I–III. This is decisively in favor of the book-date [for Book 4, 104–105 CE]. It is hard to believe that Pliny kept silent about his verses for three whole books. [I.e., he had not written verses at the time of Books 1–3.] Otto [1919:34–37, 84n2] was rightly surprised that Pliny, freed from public duties since November 100 [when his consulate ended], should not mention a visit to Comum until 104 [i.e. not until Book 4.1, which Otto 1919:36 dates to 100]. The solution lies in the nature of the collection. Book III, covering the longest span of any book, mentions the *secessus* [plural] of Pliny in Epp. [*sic*] 1, 4, 6, 10, 15. That sufficed. Pliny may have visited Comum and married Calpurnia at the earliest possible moment for legal reasons, without writing a literary letter about her until she was old enough to be of interest.

1966:264, note on *Ep.* 4.1; cf. 33

One senses that here the "heteronomous hypothesis" is put under stress by the phenomena that it is trying to account for. Sherwin-White clearly regards Pliny's failure to mention his verse-composition in Books 1–3 as his strongest argument from silence (cf. 1966:33, cited at the outset of this Appendix). But with the two items that form the larger pattern the argument ceases to work. The reasonableness of Otto's expectation of earlier mention of Comum is conceded and then weakly explained as unnecessary because several other *secessūs* were mentioned. In the end, Sherwin-White grants that both a visit to Comum and the marriage might have occurred earlier than the book-date of their first mention. It follows that the verse-composition might have started earlier, too. Sherwin-White was not wrong about the pattern, but the pattern would, almost by his own admission, be more reasonably explained on the "autonomous hypothesis."

Pliny has grouped letters on certain subjects in the interest of thematic and other kinds of organization. It is unlikely that someone who put such effort into the editing of individual letters would have published them in random order. (Cf. Schultz 1951:448: "Ein jeder Brief bildet ein sorgfällig überdachtes, in sich abgeschlossenes, kleines Kunstwerk.") *Ut quaeque in manus venerat* is the part of Pliny's programmatic statement, quoted above, that it is not to be taken seriously. At the same time, one could say that Pliny seeks to give the impression of randomness by the organizing principle of *varietas* described by Hermann Peter. Having said that Pliny gave himself the task of forming each letter into a "kleines Ganzes," he continued: "Daher zerschlägt er nicht nur die Behandlung eines und desselben Dinges oder eng zusammenhängender, wenn sie sich zu lang auszudehnen droht, ja er hat sogar ... zwischen diese Teile fremdes eingeschoben und das Interesse des Lesers auf etwas anderes gelenkt" (1901:110–111; cf. Prete 1948:90). Peter gives several lists of "aesthetic groups" (109) the items of which are distributed over two or more books.

If, then, Cornelia's enthusiasm for her husband's verse is, as Otto thought, as early as 100–101 CE and if the recitations to which *Ep.* 4.19 refers were the same as the ones that Pliny says that he gave on his return from Rome after the Laurentine revelation, one has come close to the date of Martial's Book 10 (first edition 95 CE, second 98). Perhaps one can come still closer. In *Ep.* 1.13 (dated by Sherwin-White to April 97 CE) Pliny begins by noticing a new crop of talented poets. In April hardly a day has passed without a recitation. (He uses the word *studia* for this activity.) Pliny's concern in the rest of the letter is the sorry state of this social institution, by which, unlike Marcus Aper (Tac. *Dial.* 9), not to mention Persius earlier and Juvenal later, Pliny set much store. He contrasts his own dutiful attendance with others' shameful derelictions. He has stayed on in town longer than he expected. Now he can seek a *secessus* and write something (*scribere aliquid*) himself, which he will not read to friends, lest it seem that he attended their recitations in order to put them under obligation. The something that Pliny intends to write is in this context naturally taken (*pace* Sherwin-White) to be verse. Pliny did, of course, give recitations of his verse, as we know from *Epp.* 4.19 (the letter from which this discussion started), 5.3.7–11, 8.21.4–5, and 9.34. Should one conclude that Pliny did not in fact begin to give recitations until some time after *Ep.* 1.13 and that the ones referred to in *Ep.* 4.19 are, à la Sherwin-White, the first? The answer depends on the hypothesis of one's reading. If one reads *Ep.* 1.13 as a document of Pliny's life and times, one learns only that he attended recitations; that he intended to write something himself, but not, on principle, to recite it. Continuing in this historicizing vein, one would say that he later sacrificed the principle and gave recitations. If, however, one reads this letter as a reflection on the institution of the recitation, a different conclusion is reached. This letter is one of several in which Pliny gives, implicitly or explicitly, norms for recitation (of speeches [3.18.3–9; 7.17] or verse [5.3.7–11, 5.12]), which, as Matthew Roller has said, Pliny saw as "a new arena of aristocratic competition" (1998:289–298). (John Bodel has pointed out to me that 3.15.2–5, where Sherwin-White 1966:33 thinks that Pliny might have mentioned his own versifying, is likewise easily read as a general comment on recitation, from which Pliny gets an overall impression [*de universitate*], as against his scrutiny of individual sections [*de partibus*] in reading.) Pliny's norms for this institution are part of his larger configuration of his community (on which see Johnson 2010:42–56; cf. my note 26). The principle that Pliny enunciates at the end of *Ep.* 1.13 can be interpreted in this broader context (... *ne videar, quorum recitationibus adfui, non auditor fuisse sed creditor. Nam ut in ceteris rebus ita in audiendi officio perit gratia si reposcatur*). In the first place, the thought is hardly new with Pliny. Pericles states a version of it in the Funeral Oration (Thuc. 2.40.5). Cicero's statement of this principle has the ring of a commonplace (*Grave est enim homini pudenti petere aliquid magnum ab eo de quo se bene meritum putet, ne id quod petat exigere magis quam rogare et in mercedis potius quam benefici loco numerare videatur, Fam.* 2.6.1). Seneca analyzes the proposition that repayment of a benefit should never be sought (*Ben.* 5.6–7; cf. Sen. *Ep.* 81.19: *recte facti fecisse merces est*, and various similar statements in this letter). The principle that Pliny states in terms of his own intention at a particular moment is one that, implicitly, should always govern the institution of the recitation. It should not be reduced, as it now is, to a formality, like other obligations in the daily round of members of Pliny's social class, still less to something like a business transaction.

Eckard Lefèvre's reading of another of Pliny's letters on the recitation is instructive (2009:167–168). In *Ep.* 9.34, Pliny asks Suetonius for advice. Pliny intends to read his verse to a group of friends. Should he, who has been told that he reads badly, give the reading himself or should he use one of his freedmen? He does not know what he would do when the freedman was reading—sit immobile and silent or, as some do, follow the reading *murmure oculis manu*. But he is no better at this kind of enactment (which he calls *saltare*, lit. "dancing") than he is at reading. Lefèvre argues that Pliny's concerns about himself and the freedman (who, Pliny says, will not read well, even if better than Pliny) are not seriously meant. Pliny's real concern is the behavior of poets when someone else is reading their work aloud—the behavior of others, that is, not his own. The exaggeration *saltare*, suggesting performance by a mime (he cites Benz 2000), is a satirical description of what these others do. It is not something that Pliny seriously imagines himself doing. In short, Pliny is not really asking Suetonius for advice. He is commenting on a particular aspect of contemporary recitation.

To return to *Ep.* 1.13, in this letter, too, Pliny speaks of others by speaking about himself, by making himself, in effect, an example. When he says *aliquid, quod non recitem, ne videar*, etc., he is saying "something, but not to recite, lest I be perceived by my friends, whose recitations I have attended, as calling in, by inviting them, the repayment of a debt." On the "autonomous hypothesis," then, *Ep.* 1.13 is about the proper use of the institution of the recitation. Nothing that Pliny says rules out some future reading by him, which could have taken place before 100–101 CE, the date assigned by Otto to the letter about Calpurnia (*Ep.* 4.19). It is worth recalling Syme's suggestion that *Ep.* 1.13.6 indicates that Pliny holds no office in 97 CE (Syme 1958: vol. 2, 658). On the other hand, even when Pliny was in office, as he usually was, nothing prevented a vacation, as the various references to *secessūs* show (for Pliny's cursus: Syme 1958: vol. 1, 75–85; Syme 1958: vol. 2, 652–653; 656–659; now Birley 2000:5–17). The Laurentine villa was not far away.

This appendix has sought to replace Sherwin-White's severe Mommsenian reading of various Epistles with a literary-critical one, i.e., one that assumes the primacy of thematic and aesthetic kinds of organization. The goal of this approach, somewhat paradoxically, was to decide a chronological question, namely, the relation of *Ep.* 3.21 to Martial 10.20(19). As in the article preceding this appendix, historical and literary concerns were inseparable. Whereas, however, in the article the historical—as the primary communication of the epigram and its reception by Pliny—served as a control on Fowlerian openness of reading, in this appendix, interpretation (assuming the kinds of organization just mentioned) has opposed a too strict historical-documentary conception of the *Epistles*. Still, historical and literary interpretation are here in the same circle; one has tried to move around and stay within this circle. As Fowler's binarism was earlier resisted, so the opposition of the two hypotheses, heteronomous and autonomous, was not wholly accepted, even if much more came from one than from the other.[110]

RUTGERS, THE STATE UNIVERSITY OF NEW JERSEY

WORKS CITED

Aubrion, Étienne. 1989. "La Correspondance de Pline le Jeune: Problèmes et orientations actuelles de la recherche." In *Aufstieg und Niedergang der Römischen Welt*, ed. Wolfgang Haase, part 2 (Principat), vol. 33.1. Berlin.

Benz, Lore. 2000. "Pantomimos." In *Der Neue Pauly: Enzyklopädie der Antike*, ed. Hubert Cancik and Helmuth Schneider, vol. 9, 274–276. Stuttgart.

Birley, Anthony R. 2000. *Onomasticon to the Younger Pliny: Letters and Panegyric*. Munich.

Bodel, John. Forthcoming. "The Publication of Pliny's Letters." In *Pliny the Book-Maker: Betting on Posterity in the Epistles*, ed. Ilaria Marchesi. Oxford.

Bömer, Franz. 1980. *P. Ovidius Naso. Metamorphosen. Buch [sic] X–XI*. Heidelberg.

[110] First thanks go to Peter White, whose critical reading caused me to clarify the structure and the direction of the argument. I am grateful also to Ilaria Marchesi, Kristen Baxter, John Bodel, and the reader for *Harvard Studies in Classical Philology* for corrections and useful suggestions.

Boyle, A. J. 2003. *Ovid and the Monuments: A Poet's Rome*. *Ramus* Monographs 4. Bendigo, Vic., Australia.

Bütler, Hans-Peter. 1970. *Die geistige Welt des jüngeren Plinius: Studien zur Thematik seiner Briefe*. Bibliothek der klassischen Altertumswissenschaften. Neue Folge, Reihe 2, Bd. 38. Heidelberg.

Calame, Claude. 2010. "The Authority of Orpheus, Poet and Bard: Between Tradition and Written Practice." In *Allusion, Authority, and Truth: Critical Perspectives on Greek Poetic and Rhetorical Praxis*, ed. Phillip Mitsis and Christos Tsagalis, 13–35. Trends in Classics Suppl. vol. 7.

Citroni, Mario. 1989. "Marziale e la letturatura per i Saturnali (poetica dell'intrattenimento e cronologia della pubblicazione dei libri)." *ICS* 14:201–226.

———. 2004. "Martial, Pline le Jeune et l'identité du genre de l'épigramme latine." *Dictynna: Revue de poétique latine* 1:175–203.

Coarelli, Filippo. 1996. "Lacus Orphei." In *Lexicon topographicum urbis Romae*, ed. Eva Margareta Steinby, vol. 3, 171. Rome.

Coleman, Kathleen M., ed. 2006. *M. Valerii Martialis Liber spectaculorum*. Oxford.

Courtney, Edward., ed. 1993. *The Fragmentary Latin Poets*. Oxford.

Edmunds, Lowell. 2009. "Horace's Priapus: A Life on the Esquiline (*Sat.* 1.8)." *CQ*, n.s., 59:125–131.

———. 2010. "Toward a Minor Roman Poetry." *Poetica* 42:29–80.

Fantham, Elaine. 1996. *Roman Literary Culture: From Cicero to Apuleius*. Baltimore.

Fitzgerald, William. 2007. *Martial: The World of the Epigram*. Chicago.

Fowler, Don. 1995. "Martial and the Book." *Ramus* 24:31–58.

Fridh, Åke. 1990. "Esquiliae, Fagutal, and Subura Once Again." *Eranos* 88:139–161.

Friedlaender, Ludwig. 1886. *M. Valerii Martialis Epigrammaton libri*. 2 vols. Leipzig.

Gamberini, Federico. 1983. *Stylistic Theory and Practice in the Younger Pliny*. Altertumswissenschaftliche Texte und Studien 11. Hildesheim.

Gibson, Roy K. 2003. "Pliny and the Art of (In)offensive Self-Praise." *Arethusa* 36:235–254.

———. 2012. "On the Nature of Ancient Letter Collections." *JRS* 102:56–78.

Gibson, Roy K., and Ruth Morello. 2012. *Reading the Letters of Pliny the Younger: An Introduction*. Cambridge.

Grüner, Andreas. 1993. "Zur Topographie des Esquilin in der frühen Kaiserzeit: Das Haus des Properz; Versuch einer Lokalisierung." *Boreas: Münstersche Beiträge zur Archäologie* 16:39–55.

Guillemin, Anne-Marie, ed. 1927–1948. *Pline le Jeune. Lettres.* 4 vols. Vol. 4 (Book 10 and *Pan.*) by Marcel Durry. Paris.

———. 1929. *Pline et la vie littéraire de son temps*. Paris.

Gurd, Sean. 2012. *Work in Progress: Literary Revision as Social Performance in Ancient Rome*. Oxford.

Hass, Petra. 1998. *Der locus amoenus in der antiken Literatur: Zu Theorie und Geschichte eines literarischen Motivs*. Bamberg.

Häuber, Chrystina. 1990. "Zur Topographie der Horti Maecenatis und der Horti Lamiani auf dem Esquilin in Rom." *Kölner Jahrb. Vor- u. Frühgesch.* 23:11–107, with four loose-leaf maps by Helga Stöcker at the end of the vol.

Henderson, John. 2001. "On Pliny on Martial on Anon ... (*Epistles* 3.21 / *Epigrams* 10.19)." *Ramus* 30:56–87.

———. 2002. *Pliny's Statues: The Letters, Self-Portraiture, and Classical Art*. Exeter.

Hershkowitz, Debra. 1995. "Pliny the Poet." *G&R* 42:168–181.

Heurgon, Jacques. 1987. "Orfeo." In *Enciclopedia Virgiliana*, vol. 3.882–884. Rome.

Hinds, Stephen. 2007. "Martial's Ovid/Ovid's Martial." *JRS* 97:113–154.

Hoffer, Stanley E. 1999. *The Anxieties of Pliny the Younger*. American Classical Studies 43. Atlanta, GA.

Howell, Peter. 1980. *A Commentary on Book One of the Epigrams of Martial*. London.

———. 1995. *Martial. Epigrams Book V*. Warminster.

Johnson, William A. 2010. *Readers and Reading Culture in the High Roman Empire: A Study of Elite Communities*. New York.

Lanciani, Rodolfo. 1990. *Forma Vrbis Romae*. Rome.

Lauffray, Jean. 1940. "Une fouille au pied de l'acropole de Byblos." *Bulletin du Musée de Beyrouth* 4:7–36.

Leach, Eleanor. 2003. "*Otium* as *Luxuria*: Economy of Status in the Younger Pliny's *Letters.*" *Arethusa* 36:147–165.

Leary, T. J. 2001. *Martial XIII: The Xenia; Text with Introduction and Commentary.* London.

Lefèvre, Eckard. 1989. "Plinius-Studien V: Vom Römertum zum Ästhetizismus; Die Würdingungen des älteren Plinius (3,5), Silius Italicus (3,7) und Martial (3,21)." *Gymnasium* 96:113–128.

———. 2009. *Vom Römertum zum Ästhetizismus: Studien zu den Briefen des jüngeren Plinius.* Beiträge zur Altertumskunde 269. Berlin.

Longfellow, Brenda. 2011. *Roman Imperialism and Civic Patronage: Form, Meaning, and Ideology in Monumental Fountain Complexes.* Cambridge.

Lorenz, Sven. 2002. *Erotik und Panegyrik: Martials epigrammatische Kaiser.* Classica Monacensia 23. Tübingen.

———. 2003. "Martial 1970–2003." Part 1. *Lustrum* 45:167–277.

———. 2006. "Martial 1970–2003." Part 2. *Lustrum* 48:109–223; 233–47.

Ludolph, Matthias. 1997. *Epistolographie und Selbstdarstellung: Untersuchungen zu den "Paradebriefen" Plinius des Jüngeren.* Tübingen.

Marchesi, Ilaria. 2008. *The Art of Pliny's Letters: A Poetics of Allusion in the Private Correspondence.* Cambridge.

———. 2013. "Silenced Intertext: Pliny on Martial on Pliny (on Regulus)." *AJP* 134:101–118.

Mattiacci, Silvia. 2007. "Marziale e il neoterismo." In *Dialogando con il passato: Permanenze e innovazioni nella cultura latina di età flavia,* ed. Alessia Bonadeo and Elisa Romano, 177–206. Florence.

Mayer, Roland. 2001. *Tacitus. Dialogus de oratoribus.* Cambridge.

———. 2003. "Pliny and *Gloria Dicendi.*" *Arethusa* 36.2:227–234.

Mayor, John E. B., ed. 1889. *Pliny's Letters, Book III.* New York.

Murgia, C. E. 1985. "Pliny's Letters and the *Dialogus.*" *HSCP* 89:171–206.

Nauta, Ruurd R. 2002. *Poetry for Patrons: Literary Communication in the Age of Domitian.* Mnemosyne Supplement 206. Leiden.

———. 2005. "Die mächtigen Freunde des Spötters: Martial und seine Patrone." In *Senatores populi Romani: Realität und mediale Präsentation einer Führungsschicht; Kolloquium der Prosopographia Imperii Romani vom 11.-13. Juni 2004,* ed. Werner Eck and Matthäus Heil, 213–228. Heidelberger althistorische Beiträge und epigraphische Studien 40. Stuttgart.

Niehl, Rüdiger. 2004. "Die betrunkene Muse in der Großstadt." In *Epigrammaton liber decimus: Das zehnte Epigrammbuch; Text, Übersetzung, Interpretationen*, ed. Gregor Damschen and Andreas Heil, 101–104. Studien zur klassischen Philologie 148. Frankfurt am Main.

Otto, Walter. 1919. *Zur Lebensgeschichte des jüngeren Plinius. Sitzungsberichte der Bayerischen Akademie der Wissenschaften.* Philosophisch-philologische u. historische Klasse Abt. 10.

Peter, Carl. 1872. "Plinius der Jüngere." *Philologus* 32:698–710.

Peter, Hermann. 1901. *Der Brief in der römischen Litteratur.* Leipzig.

Picard, Charles. 1948. "Lacus Orphei (ad Martial, Epigr. libr. X,20)." *Revue des études latines* 25:80–85.

Pitcher, R. A. 1999. "The Hole in the Hypothesis: Pliny and Martial Reconsidered." *Mnemosyne* 52:554–561.

Post, Edwin. 1908. *Selected Epigrams of Martial.* Boston.

Prete, Sesto. 1948. "Gli endecasillabi di Plinio il Giovane." *Aevum* 22:333–336.

Puelma, Mario. 1996. "'Ἐπίγραμμα – *epigramma*: Aspekte einer Wortgeschichte." *Museum Helveticum* 53:123–139.

———. 1997. "Epigramma: osservazioni sulla storia di un termine Greco-latino." *Maia* 49:189–213.

Reeve, M. D. 1985. Rev. of Shackleton Bailey 1982. *Phoenix* 39:174–180.

Rodríguez Almeida, Emilio. 1981. *Forma urbis marmoreal: Aggiornamento generale 1980.* 2 vols. Rome.

———. 1983. "I confine interni della 'regio V' Esquiliae nella 'Forma Urbis marmorea.'" In *L'archeologia in Roma capitale tra sterro e scavo*, ed. Giuseppina Pisani Sartorio and Lorenzo Quilici, 106–115. Venice.

———. 1987. "Qualche osservazione sulle Esquiliae patrizie e il Lacus Orphei." In *L'urbs: Espace urbain et histoire (Ier siècle av. J.-C.-IIIe siècle ap. J.-C.); Actes du colloque international organisé par la Centre national de la recherche scientifique et l'École française de Rome (Rome, 8–12 May 1985)*, no ed., 415–428. Paris.

———. 1995a. "Domus: Albinovanus Pedo." In Steinby 1995, 27–28.

———. 1995b. "Domus: C. Plinius Caecilius Secundus." In Steinby 1995, 158–159.

———. 1995c. "Domus: M. Valerius Martialis." In Steinby 1995, 208–209.

———. 2003. *Terrarum dea gentiumque: Marziale e Roma; Un poeta e la sua città*. Rome.

Roller, Matthew. 1998. "Pliny's Catullus: The Politics of Literary Appropriation." *TAPA* 128:265–304.

Roman, Luke. 2001. "The Representation of Literary Materiality in Martial's Epigrams." *JRS* 91:113–145.

———. 2010. "Martial and the City of Rome." *JRS* 100:88–117.

Russo, Alessandro. 2007. *Ennio. Le opere minori*. Pisa.

Santoro L'Hoir, Francesca. 1992. *The Rhetoric of Gender Terms: "Man," "Woman," and the Portrayal of Character in Latin Prose*. Mnemosyne Suppl. 120. Leiden.

Schultz, Maximilian. 1899. *De Plinii epistulis quaestiones chronologicae*. Diss. Friedrich Wilhelm (now Humboldt) University. Berlin.

Shackleton Bailey, D. R. 1978. "Corrections and Explanations of Martial." *CP* 73:273–296.

———. 1980. "Martial 2.91 and 10.20." *CP* 75:69–70.

———, ed. 1990. *M. Valerii Martialis Epigrammata*. Stuttgart.

———. 1993. *Martial. Epigrams*. Loeb Classical Library. 3 vols. Cambridge, MA.

Sherwin-White, Adrian N., ed. 1966. *The Letters of Pliny*. Oxford.

Steinby, Eva Margareta, ed. 1995. *Lexicon topographicum urbis Romae*. Vol. 2. Rome.

Sullivan, J. P. 1991. *Martial: The Unexpected Classic; A Literary and Historical Study*. Cambridge.

Syme, Ronald. 1958. *Tacitus*. 2 vols. Oxford.

———. 1985. "The Dating of Pliny's Latest Letters." *CQ*, n.s., 35:176–185.

Tarrant, R. J., ed. 2004. *P. Ovidi Nasonis Metamorphoses*. Oxford.

Thein, Alexander G. 2002. "Lacus Orphei." In *Mapping Augustan Rome*. Directed by Lothar Haselberger, with David Gilman Romano; ed. by Elisha Ann Dumser. *Journal of Roman Archaeology* Suppl. 50. Portsmouth, RI.

Trisoglio, Francesco. 1972. *La personalità di Plinio il Giovane nei suoi rapporti con la politica, la società e la letteratura*. Memoria dell'Accademia delle Scienze di Torino. Classe di scienze morali, storiche e filologiche, 4th series, 25. Turin.

Van Dam, Harm-Jan, ed. 1984. *P. Papinius Statius. Silvae. Book II*. Leiden.

Watson, Patricia. 2006. "Contextualising Martial's Metres." In *Flavian Poetry*, ed. Ruurd R. Nauta, Harm-Jan van Dam, and Johannes J. L. Smolenaars, 285–298. Mnemosyne Suppl. 270. Leiden.

White, Peter. 1974. "The Presentation and Dedication of the *Silvae* and the Epigrams." *JRS* 64:40–61.

———. 1975. "The Friends of Martial, Statius, and Pliny and the Dispersal of Patronage." *HSCP* 79:265–300.

———. 1978. "*Amicitia* and the Profession of Poetry in Early Imperial Rome." *JRS* 68:74–92.

———. 1996. "Martial and Pre-Publication Texts." Échos du monde classique / *Classical Views* 40 = n.s. 15:397–412.

Woolf, Greg. 2003. "The City of Letters." In *Rome the Cosmopolis*, ed. Catharine Edwards and Greg Woolf, 203–221. Cambridge.

CAESAR'S ONE FATAL WOUND

SUETONIUS *DIVUS IULIUS* 82.3

ELEANOR COWAN

> *nec in tot uulneribus, ut Antistius medicus existimabat, letale ullum repertum est, nisi quod secundo loco in pectore acceperat.*
>
> And among so many wounds no fatal one was found, in the judgment of Antistius medicus, except that which he had received second in the breast.

A T THE END of his description of Caesar's murder, Suetonius reports that, in the view of Antistius *medicus*, only one of the many wounds that the Dictator suffered was fatal. This curious and hitherto overlooked detail deserves attention.[1] The argument that follows has three parts. The first collects the surviving ancient evidence for the number, order, and locations of the wounds that Caesar received. In this section, I demonstrate that Suetonius' description of the order or location of the wound (*secundo loco in pectore acceperat*) and his statement that Antistius asserted that only one wound was fatal do not correspond to any other surviving account. The second, and most substantial, part of my article then explores the possible historical context(s) that may have given rise to Antistius' statement. In this section, I argue that the claim that only one wound was fatal represented a pro-Caesarian response to the rhetoric of tyrant-slaying adopted by Caesar's assassins. The third section considers the passage in its Suetonian context and asks why Suetonius may have included this unique detail in his narrative.

---

[1] Studies by Brutscher 1958:114–136; Gugel 1970:5–22; and Lambrecht 1984:63–78 omit treatment of this detail.

I

There are six main surviving accounts that give a narrative of the assassination itself (Nicolaus of Damascus, *FGrH* 90.130.88–90; Plutarch *Caes.* 66.3–7; *Brut.* 17.1–4; Appian *B. Civ.* 2.117; Dio 44.19; and Suetonius *Iul.* 82.1–3), all of which must have drawn on a myriad of contemporary accounts and all of which, while they share many points of detail, differ from one another.[2] All but Dio's account include the information that, when Caesar entered, Tillius Cimber snatched his toga while supplicating on behalf of his exiled brother. The accounts of the Caesar's wounds follow. In Nicolaus' version, Servilius Casca struck first at his shoulder, above the collarbone (κατὰ τὸν ἀριστερὸν ὦμον ... μικρὸν ὑπὲρ τὴν κλεῖν). Casca called upon his brother's aid and this man struck Caesar in the side (κατὰ τῆς πλευρᾶς). Just before this, however, Cassius had struck at Caesar's face (εἰς τὸ πρόσωπον) and Decimus Brutus struck him in the flanks (ὑπὸ ταῖς λαγόσι). Nicolaus lists two further attempts on Caesar's person that went astray: Cassius Longinus intended another blow, but missed and caught M. Brutus in the hand, while Minucius' blow, intended for Caesar, struck Rubrius in the thigh. Caesar collapsed but the conspirators continued to strike and he died under their blows, having received thirty-five wounds. Similarly, in Plutarch's account (*Caes.* 66.3–7), the first blow, in the neck, was struck by Casca. Plutarch also agrees with Nicolaus in specifying that this blow was not fatal since Casca was too confused and overcome by the occasion. His Caesar confronted his assassins and, like a wild beast (ὥσπερ θηρίον), was driven around the circle with blows aimed at face and eyes. Plutarch has him cry out—once to Casca ("μιαρώτατε Κάσκα, τί ποιεῖς;") and also more generally as he confronted his attackers. He continued to resist the attack until he noticed Brutus also drawing his dagger. Brutus gave him one blow "in the groin" (εἰς τὸν βουβῶνα). When he saw Brutus, Caesar drew his toga over his head and sank down. He lay "quivering from a multitude of wounds" (περισπαίροντος ὑπὸ πλήθους

---

[2]   The various ancient accounts, their similarities and differences, have recently been summarized and discussed in Woolf 2007:8–18, who notes that while "the main lines of the story are not at issue," the surviving accounts offer a plethora of differences in substance and emphasis.

τραυμάτων), the number of which was twenty-three. The account in Plutarch's life of Brutus (17.1–4) also has Casca strike the first blow. Appian's Caesar is similarly depicted as reacting like a wild beast at bay.[3] In his account, Casca struck the first blow, aiming at Caesar's throat but hitting his breast. The second blow, in the side, was delivered by an unnamed assassin (τὸ πλευρὸν ἕτερος ... διελαύνει ξιφιδίῳ), the third by Cassius who struck Caesar in the face (ἐς τὸ πρόσωπον ἔπληξε). The final assailants to be named are Brutus and Bucolianus; the former stabbed Caesar "in the thigh" (ἐς τὸν μηρόν) and the latter, "in the back" (ἐς τὸ μετάφρενον). Appian agrees that Caesar died of twenty-three wounds. Dio gives a brief and anonymized account (44.19.4–5):

ἐπεί τε ὁ καιρὸς ἐλάμβανε, προσῆλθέ τις αὐτῷ ὡς καὶ χάριν τινὰ γιγνώσκων, καὶ τὸ ἱμάτιον αὐτοῦ ἀπὸ τοῦ ὤμου καθείλκυσεν, σημεῖόν τι τοῦτο κατὰ τὸ συγκείμενον τοῖς συνωμόταις αἴρων· κἀκ τούτου προσπεσόντες αὐτῷ ἐκεῖνοι πολλαχόθεν ἅμα κατέτρωσαν αὐτόν, ὥσθ' ὑπὸ τοῦ πλήθους αὐτῶν μήτ' εἰπεῖν μήτε πρᾶξαί τι τὸν Καίσαρα δυνηθῆναι, ἀλλὰ συγκαλυψάμενον σφαγῆναι πολλοῖς τραύμασι.

And when the right moment came, one of them approached him, as if to express his thanks for some favour or other, and pulled his toga from his shoulder, thus giving the signal that had been agreed upon by the conspirators. Thereupon they attacked him from many sides at once and wounded him to death, so that by reason of their numbers Caesar was unable to say or do anything, but veiling his face, was slain with many wounds.[4]

While each of these accounts preserves a variety of details about the order in which the assassins attacked and the places where their blows fell, none gives us the combination set out in Suetonius: a second blow in the breast.[5] In Suetonius' account, as in others, Tillius Cimber, pretending

---

[3] Dunkle 1971:14 notes that acting like a wild beast is a characteristic of tyrants.
[4] Trans. Cary (Loeb edition).
[5] I note that this is the case on either reading of *nisi quod secundo loco in pectore acceperat*: a second blow that happened to be delivered to the chest or a second chest wound.

to have a question, caught hold of Caesar. Caesar then cried out ("*ista quidem uis est!*") and, in retaliation to a first blow from Casca, ran his arm though with his stylus. Suetonius' Caesar did not continue to resist his attackers. After trying unsuccessfully to rise from his seat and perceiving the number of his attackers, he drew his toga over his head and down to his feet so as to fall decently. Like Dio, Suetonius only reports the story of Caesar's speaking to Brutus as an addendum to his own account in which Caesar was stabbed twenty-three times without uttering a word (*atque ita tribus et uiginti plagis confossus est uno modo ad primum ictum gemitu sine uoce edito*).[6] Like Nicolaus, Suetonius has Caesar deserted by friends and enemies alike and then carried home by three slaves on a litter. It is at this point that he records that only one of the wounds was fatal.

Why include this curious detail? It is, of course, conceivable that in the frenzy of the attack only one wound did in reality prove to be deep enough to be fatal and that this was duly reported by Antistius as Suetonius claims. We might speculate, therefore, that Suetonius has reported a matter of fact that was somehow unknown to, or ignored by, other surviving authors. Such speculation does not get us very far, however, and it leaves more important questions unanswered: what do the existence and inclusion of such a story tell us about ancient responses to Caesar's murder and, in particular, about Suetonius' treatment of it?

II

II.1 The Rhetoric of Tyrannicide at Rome

Caesar's murder was immediately controversial. His status as "tyrant" and, consequently, the legitimacy of the actions taken against him were the subject of an ongoing debate; the rhetoric of the different stances taken in this debate looked back to a longer discussion of tyrannicide at Rome[7] (and, of course, in Greece). The rhetoric of Roman tyrannicide, particularly as it developed in the late Republic and after Caesar's murder, castigated certain individuals for seeking *regnum* and cast them as threats to the *libertas* of the *populus Romanus* and the workings of

---

[6] Suet. *Iul.* 82.2

[7] On the Roman discussion of tyrannicide, see Lintott 1999:54–56; Woolf 2007:72–88.

the democracy at Rome. This rhetoric was frequently deployed against politicians who could be presented (in Livy or by Cicero for instance[8]) as *populares* and the final action taken against those deemed "tyrants," though the act itself took different forms, was envisaged as an expression of the will or judgment of the state—or at least of all those "good men" who mattered. In each instance, justification for political assassination derived from the assertion that some large collective (the whole of the *populus Romanus* or all the senate or all the *boni*) recognized the legitimacy of the allegation of tyranny. The two versions of the death of Sp. Cassius (Livy. 2.41.2, a private trial and a public one) are a case in point. Although different versions of his trial and death are offered in Livy's narrative, both are preceded by an account of how he came to be suspected by the patricians of infringing *libertas* and by the plebeians of aiming at monarchy. Likewise, the versions of the death of Tiberius Gracchus known to Appian (*B. Civ.* 1.16) and Plutarch (*Ti. Gracch.* 19.4) drew attention to the fact that Scipio Nasica saw himself as the representative of a collective. The mythical death of Romulus and the historical death of Saturninus and his supporters illustrate the way in which this collective will could be translated into collective action. Romulus, whose murder is specifically invoked in Appian's account of Caesar's murder and is implicit in others, was, according to one version of the story,[9] butchered by the senate after it was alleged that he had become tyrannical, each senator carrying away and burying a small piece of his corpse. In similar fashion, Saturninus' "stoning" with roof tiles demonstrates another means of effecting a "collective" method of execution.[10]

---

[8] On which, see Seager 1972:328–338; 1977:377–90.

[9] Romulus: Cic. *Rep.* 2.20; Dion. 1.56.3; Val. Max. 5.3.1; Plut. *Rom.* 27.6; App. *B. Civ.* 2.114.476. These references are discussed by Weinstock 1971:347. Bob Cowan reminds me that this tradition may have originated in the anti-Sullan history of Licinius Macer, on which see Classen 1962:184.

[10] Saturninus: App. *B. Civ.* 1.32. Nippel 1995:43–44: "The claim of legitimacy which underlay ritualized collective killings could also be expressed by the *modus operandi* chosen. In Greek and Jewish culture this was especially the case with stoning, which might on the one hand be the collective execution of legal punishment, and on the other hand be the result of action that though spontaneous was understood to be the immediate execution of justice, the public and communal punishing of manifest crime." Nippel further notes that stoning was not a Roman civilian tradition but could be found in the *fustrarium* (Polyb. 6.37–8; Livy 5.6.14; Cic. *Phil.* 3.14) and in "the stoning by muti-

II.2 Collectively Killing Caesar

Enormous symbolic capital was invested in the idea that Caesar was assassinated by a multitude and not by any one individual. Cicero quickly began to build on the idea of a collective murder that expressed the will of the good men: his language of "us" and "our" in the letters and *Philippics* emphasizes this collectivity.[11] Nicolaus[12] believed that no other conspiracy had ever attracted so many men, and Appian suggested that one of the reasons that the conspirators selected the *curia* for their act was that they thought that other senators, not originally privy to the plot, would join them as soon as they saw what was happening. Even the *Lex Pedia*, formulated by Caesar's defenders and attributed to the influence of Octavian, seems specifically to have responded to the rhetoric of a collective tyrant-slaying by extending punishment to those associated with the murder. At the same time, against the backdrop of collective action, individuals also had a vested interest in promoting the account of their own participation.[13] It is easy to imagine that from the very beginning, and perhaps even after the publication of the *Lex Pedia*, individuals would be eager to valorize or justify their participation.[14] Thus, within the narrative of collective action, are preserved the stories of individuals: Brutus, Cassius, Tillius

---

nous soldiers of officials," and that the usual Roman expression of collective killing was *manibus discerpere*: the victim was torn to pieces by the crowd.

[11] Cic. *Att.* 14.1, 4, 10, 11, 15, 16 and passim, and *Philippics* passim.

[12] Nic. Dam. *FGrH* 90.130.59 and App. *B. Civ.* 2.114.

[13] App. *B. Civ.* 2.119 lists the names of men who joined the Liberators after the deed, eager to share their glory. Cf. Suet. *Vitellius* 10 and Plut. *Galba* 27.5–9, which both record numbers of individuals wishing to claim rewards for involvement in the murder of Galba. Plutarch, drawing on the Greek tradition of tyrannicide, here quotes Archilochus (Gerber 1999:101): "a thousand of us are the slayers of the seven who fell dead, overtaken by us in pursuit" (Loeb edition).

[14] It is interesting to think about the context in which individuals might have been eager to assert their participation after the event (App. *B. Civ.* 2.119). Did their assertion precede the publication of the *Lex Pedia* or did some defiant individuals (or their families) have vested interests in asserting their involvement despite the possibility of punishment? A rhetoric that sought to force individuals to declare their support of the Liberators seems quickly to have developed and surely lies behind the *Lex Pedia*'s insistence on punishing associates. I am grateful to Kathryn Welch for reminding me of the importance of the *Lex Pedia*.

Cimber, Trebonius, Casca, and others whose accounts of blows given or wounds received were woven into the developing narratives.[15] Of course, despite the apparent rhetorical necessity for collective *support* of an assassination, not all tyrants had to be killed by collective action and there were well-known examples, such as the assassination of Sp. Maelius by Servilius Ahala, in which individuals acted on behalf of the will of a wider group.[16] Likewise, there existed at least one version[17] of the death of Tiberius Gracchus in which, during a general skirmish, he was hit by a piece of a bench—a version that makes an anonymous individual responsible for his actual death.

During the 50s, Cicero had already begun to pursue the idea that individuals could take responsibility for killing tyrants and, after the murder, he was quick to assert his opinion that it was in fact the duty of each individual to take such action.[18] But, in the narrative accounts of Caesar's murder that survive, individuals and their stories are never allowed to detract from the overall picture of collective tyrannicide. The careful way in which three of these narratives treat Casca's initial blow is worth noting in this context. Nicolaus, Plutarch, and Appian all record that Casca aimed for Caesar's throat but was not able to deliver the blow he had intended. Appian states that he "who was standing over Caesar's head, first drove his dagger at his throat, but swerved and wounded him in the breast" (trans. White; ἐφεστὼς ὑπὲρ κεφαλῆς ἐπὶ τὴν σφαγὴν τὸ ξίφος ἤρεισε πρῶτος, παρολισθὼν δὲ ἐνέτεμε τὸ στῆθος), but both Nicolaus and Plutarch are more explicit. They attribute Casca's

---

[15] Dio's assertion that he will not give lists of names of participants, which implies that he could do so if he so wished, is in keeping with his largely anonymized account of Caesar's murder. At 44.14.3–4, ἐγὼ δὲ τὰ μὲν τῶν ἄλλων ὀνόματα οὐδὲν δέομαι καταλέγειν, ἵνα μὴ καὶ δι' ὄχλου γένωμαι, τὸν δὲ δὴ Τρεβώνιον τόν τε Βροῦτον τὸν Δέκιμον, ὃν καὶ Ἰούνιον Ἀλβῖνόν τε ἐπεκάλουν, οὐ δύναμαι παραλιπεῖν. πλεῖστα γὰρ καὶ οὗτοι εὐεργετηθέντες ὑπὸ τοῦ Καίσαρος, καὶ ὅ γε Δέκιμος καὶ ὕπατος ἐς τὸ δεύτερον ἔτος ἀποδεδειγμένος καὶ τῇ Γαλατίᾳ τῇ πλησιοχώρῳ προστεταγμένος, ἐπεβούλευσαν αὐτῷ.

[16] Livy 4.14. Although he continued to have his own supporters, the senate had been convinced that Maelius was plotting *regnum* and appointed a Dictator to defend the state. Maelius' execution was justified *ex post facto* on the grounds that he had refused to obey the summons of the newly-appointed Dictator.

[17] Vell. Pat. 2.3.2–3.

[18] Cic. *Rep.* 2.46, 3.43; *Dom.* 91; *Att.* 2.24.3; *Vat.* 26; *Sest.* 132; *Phil.* 2.117, 13.2; *Off.* 1.76. Many of these passages are discussed in Woolf 2007 and Lintott 1999.

failure to strike as he had intended to nervousness and being overcome by the occasion: "he had aimed for it [the collar-bone] but had
been unable to hit it because of his nervousness" (trans. Bellemore alt;
εὐθύνων ἐπ' αὐτὴν, ταραττόμενος δὲ οὐκ ἠδυνήθη, Nic. Dam. 130.89);
"It was Casca who gave him the first blow with his dagger, in the neck,
not a mortal wound, nor even a deep one, for which he was too much
confused, as was natural at the beginning of a deed of great daring"
(trans. Perrin; πρῶτος δὲ Κάσκας ξίφει παίει παρὰ τὸν αὐχένα πληγὴν
οὐ θανατηφόρον οὐδὲ βαθεῖαν, ἀλλ' ὡς εἰκὸς ἐν ἀρχῇ τολμήματος
μεγάλου ταραχθείς, Plut. *Caes.* 66.7). Whether or not it was Casca's original intention to strike a fatal blow—and however his personal story
was subsequently played out in contemporary attempts to describe or
justify his actions—what quickly became important in the developing
tradition of these narratives was not that he struck first but that he did
not inflict a decisive blow. It is his *failure* to strike a fatal wound that is
symbolically important in all three of these narratives. Nicolaus, who
records the highest number of wounds, sets out the symbolic importance of this collective action clearly (130.90):

> Πίπτει δὲ ὑπὸ πλήθους τραυμάτων πρὸ τοῦ Πομπηίου
> ἀνδριάντος. Καὶ οὐδεὶς ἔτι λοιπὸν ἦν ὃς οὐχὶ νεκρὸν
> κείμενον ἔπαιεν, ὅπως ἂν καὶ αὐτὸς δοκοίη τοῦ ἔργου
> συνῆφθαι εἰς ὃ ε΄ καὶ λ΄ λαβὼν τραύματα ἀπέπνευσεν.

> He fell struck through by many wounds in front of
> Pompey's statue, and there was not one of the conspira-
> tors still left who did not strike the body as it lay there, so
> that each man would seem to have taken part in the crime,
> until he had died, having received thirty-five wounds.[19]

In these accounts, therefore, the story of Caesar's assassination is
fundamentally the story of shared initiative and shared action. From
joint-figureheads of the plot (Brutus and Cassius), to the orchestration
of Caesar's reception, to the final struggle itself, no single individual is
marked out as Caesar's murderer. The numbers of men involved in the

---

[19] Trans. Bellemore 1984.

conspiracy, their eagerness to all participate in the act, even the choice of the *curia* itself were all intended to present the assassination as a public and collective act.[20]

By suggesting that only one wound had in fact been fatal, Antistius' diagnosis, as reported by Suetonius, laid what was intended as a *collective* act in the struggle against a tyrant firmly at the door of an unnamed *individual*. In this way, the assertion that only one of Caesar's wounds was fatal recast what could be represented as collective action in defense of the *res publica* and carried out, as it were, by the state, as instead the act of one individual against another. Such a "take" on the assassination had enormous political and rhetorical potential.

II.3 Responding to Caesar's Murder

It is not hard to imagine the kind of version or versions of Caesar's assassination that might have circulated among Caesar's supporters both at the time and in later traditions. The central allegation that they sought to refute was the accusation that Caesar was a tyrant. This allegation could be addressed in two main ways: by presenting Caesar's achievements and ambitions in a wholly different and positive light[21] and/or by attacking the idea that the conspirators were genuinely motivated by their shared belief that Caesar was a tyrant. Nicolaus, writing for a generation who had lived though and perhaps even witnessed the events surrounding Caesar's assassination, already knew of a tradition that emphasized the extent to which the conspirators were motivated by personal animosities and jealousies towards Caesar. He states categorically that the motive proclaimed by the Liberators (the liberation of the state from tyranny) was a façade and one adopted

---

[20] Nippel 1995:44: "Making public the events within the *curia* (by analogy with the Romulus case), an open acceptance of responsibility for it, was supposed to guarantee that the actions of Caesar's murderers would be understood to be in the public interest ... but this proved to be a miscalculation."

[21] Evidence for the kinds of positive things Caesar's supporters were saying may be found in Cicero's letters. He complained to Cassius that Antony had set up a statue on the rostra with the inscription "To Father and Benefactor" (*Fam.* 12.3) and complained to Atticus that he had heard Caesar called a very great man and an illustrious Roman in a public speech (*Att.* 14.11.1, 15.20.2).

by only some of the conspirators. He claims that all of the conspirators were former enemies of Caesar and "Pompeians" and gives various reasons for their participation: hope that they would be the leading men in the state instead of Caesar; anger about the sufferings endured in the civil war. More reasons are hinted at. Some, for instance, joined because of the standing of the men already involved, while Caesar's friends were disenchanted because they saw him pardon and advance the careers of former enemies.[22]

But the conspirators' actions might also be attacked on other grounds by, for instance, calling into question not just the motive for their action, but also their use of force: an echo of this rhetoric might, for example, be found in Suetonius' claim that Caesar cried out "*ista quidem uis est!*", a cry that invoked *uis* legislation (possibly Caesar's own interest in *uis* legistation[23]) and drew attention to the conspirators' illegal recourse to violence. Amongst these various attempts to counter the central claims of the conspirators, a story such as that reported in Suetonius added an important, though sophistic, twist. Antistius' statement is made to look like exclusive, special information that emanates from the house of the murdered Dictator himself. His claim that only one wound was, in fact, fatal seemed to undermine the very *effectiveness* of the conspirators' collective action. That is, rather than attacking the *basis* of their collectivity (their motives), such a story attacked the achievement itself: the conspirators failed to act as an expression of collective will because they did not, in the event, *all* kill Caesar.

III

Antistius' statement may, therefore, have formed part of a response, formulated at the time or in the later traditions, to the claims of the so-called Liberators. Suetonius' inclusion of the story nevertheless also

---

[22] Nic. Dam. *FGrH* 90.130.59–63.

[23] On *leges Iuliae de ui*, see Cloud 1987:82–85; and Lintott 1999:22–23, 29. Both Cloud and Lintott suggest that the actual Julian legislation is Augustan rather than Caesarian. Gugel 1970:16 sees Caesar's exclamation as the pinnacle towards which the account of his murder has been building.

deserves attention.[24] Suetonius' account of Caesar's murder falls into four main parts: the growing dissatisfaction with Caesar's behavior, the initial planning, the ill-omens and delays that Caesar ignored, and the assassination itself.[25] Readers of the biography knew the end of Caesar's story. Each new telling needed to establish itself in competition with others by, for example, the erudition of its narrative, the inclusion of new information, or by manipulating the readers' responses to the story.[26] Antistius' reported statement thrust to the fore elements of contingency and chance in the murder. The success of the whole assassination attempt is made to turn on a single blow and the reader cannot help asking whether, but for this one blow, Caesar might have survived? Suetonius' inclusion of this detail at the end of his account of the murder itself thus has the effect of destabilizing the antici-pated end of the preceding narrative. It recalls and revives the tension created by the list of evil omens and delays that prefaces the narrative of the murder itself. The assassination narrative is, therefore, framed by a series of anxiety-provoking "what if" scenarios that defamiliarize a familiar story.[27] If Suetonius' information about Antistius was also new or at least not well known, then this too added frisson and fresh-ness to a well-known story.[28]

[24] On Suetonius' collection and treatment of his material, see Wallace-Hadrill 1983:15, 62–66; Gascou 1984:168–172, 458–466; and Hurley 2001:4–9.

[25] On Suetonius' treatment of Caesar's murder, see Brutscher 1958:134–136; Gugel 1970:5–22; Müller 1972:102; and Lambrecht 1984:66–78.

[26] Cicero's early retelling of the murder in *Div.* 2.9.22–23 illustrates the way in which Caesar's murder was, already, a narrative that could be played around with in order to provoke different questions or elicit different responses from a reader. Cicero's assertion that it was better (for Caesar) that he did not know how his life would end asks the reader to engage with an elaborate "what if" scenario in which she is supposed to imagine the effect on Caesar of knowing this information. Wallace-Hadrill's (1983:17) comments on Suet. *Aug.* 19.1–2 are perhaps equally relevant here: "These details are of no historical consequence. Why else did Suetonius give them ... except that ... they were absent from the standard history books?"

[27] On the drama of the narrative engendered by "retarding moments," see Gugel 1970:16 and 21; cf. Pagán's analyses of the ways in which Appian engenders tension into his account of the murder (Pagán 2004:113–119; 2006:193–218).

[28] Paul Roche has observed to me that the inclusion of the detail *medicus* may in fact do more than function to set out Antistius' expert credentials when judging the nature of the wound: it may also indicate that this was a new character in the familiar story,

In addition to his desire to retell the story in a captivating and exciting way, Suetonius also appears to have had an interest in recording alternative versions of, or variations on, the murders of *principes*.[29] In addition to the suggestion that only one of Caesar's wounds was in fact fatal, he preserves two versions of the murders of Gaius (*Gaius* 58–60) and gives two accounts, told with different levels of detail, of the murder of Galba (*Galba* 19–20). The relationship between the *Divus Iulius* and the *Gaius* is especially interesting in this respect. The assassination of Gaius, the first *princeps* of the Julio-Claudian dynasty established by Caesar to have been assassinated, shared several similarities with that of Caesar: both murders were associated in many ancient accounts with failed attempts to restore *libertas*; both were concerned with the elimination, though a representative figurehead, of a dynastic autocracy (Suetonius' life of Gaius concludes [60] by stating that some people wished to do away entirely with the memory of the Caesars); Suetonius' himself notes that both were assassinated by men named "Cassius."[30] Suetonius' *narrative* of Gaius' murder also shares superficially similar characteristics of detail and construction with that of Caesar. The narrative of both murders begins with an account of widespread conspiracies, both deaths are presaged by lists of bad omens and both accounts deploy similar delaying-tactics in order to introduce tension into well-known stories: Gaius nearly did not go down to his lunch because of a stomach upset; on his way, he stopped to watch some boys from Asia rehearsing for a performance and would have had the performance delivered immediately, had not one of the boys been unwell. The second version of the conspiracy that Suetonius offers, in which Sabinus' attack was the signal for others to strike and in which Gaius died as the result of thirty wounds, seems directly to evoke or

---

one who was unfamiliar to Suetonius' readers and who therefore needed to be introduced with his explanatory epithet.

[29] Wallace-Hadrill 1983:11: "the death narrative, for instance, is a familiar feature of biography and by Suetonius' day there had spawned the fashionable sub-genre of 'Deaths of Famous Men.'" Suetonius' account of the murder of Gaius has recently been re-examined by Scherberich (1999).

[30] Hurley (1993:xv) notes, "a comparison between Gaius and his ancestor of the same name, the Dictator Gaius Julius Caesar, was unavoidable ... but it was the ancient tradition, not Suetonius, that first made the connection between the two."

recall the description of Casca's initial action, followed by the general mêlée.

Caesar's assassination is also explicitly recalled in two places in the *Gaius*. First, in the list of omens that precedes the account of Gaius' death (57.2): the Capitol at Capua and, in Rome, the *cella Palatini atriensis* were struck by lightning on the Ides of March. These events were taken as signs: *nec defuerunt qui coniectarent altero ostento periculum a custodibus domino portendi, altero caedem rursus insignem, qualis eodem die facta quondam fuisset.* His murder is then deliberately, though less explicitly, recalled again at the very end of the biography: after Gaius Caesar's murder, Suetonius states, "men further observed and commented on the fact that all the Caesars whose forename was Gaius perished by the sword, beginning with the one who was slain in the time of Cinna" (*obseruatum autem notatumque est in primis Caesares omnes, quibus Gai praenomen fuerit, ferro perisse, iam inde ab eo, qui Cinnanis temporibus sit occisus*).[31] Julius Caesar's assassination is thus firmly located on a continuum from past to present, linking together the Republican example of his ancestor and his Imperial descendant. The neatness of the link was apparently not undermined by the fact that Julius Caesar's father died a natural death and Gaius' own brother, also called Gaius, died as a young child (7, 8.2).

But there are important differences between Suetonius' narratives of the two murders as well. In contrast to Josephus, who gives the fullest account of the motives of the conspirators lead by Chaerea against Gaius, Suetonius' version focuses exclusively on private motivations for the plot: he gives as the only reason for Chaerea's participation the fact that he was routinely humiliated by Gaius.[32] Moreover, where Josephus attributes to the conspirators the desire to rid the state of tyranny, Suetonius (60) implies a difference between the aims of the conspirators (who had not agreed about succession [*neque coniurati cuiquam imperium destinauerunt*]) on the one hand and, on

---

[31] Suet. *Gaius* 60. The translation is taken from the Rolfe's Loeb edition.

[32] Josephus' treatment of the conspiracy to murder Gaius is given extensive treatment in Pagán 2004:93–108. She observes (100) the ideological content of the narrative of the conspiracy in Josephus' account: "These details recall the deaths of Brutus and Cassius ... Indeed the conspiracy of Brutus and Cassius looms large in Josephus' imagination."

the other hand, the senate (who wanted to restore *libertas*) and those
who wished for the Caesars to be removed altogether, thus explicitly
distancing the conspiracy from these "grand causes."[33] Suetonius also
notes (56) that the conspiracy against Gaius involved freedmen and
the praetorian guard, those characteristic emblems of the rise of the
court and the shift of power away from the public sphere. The differences between the narratives of the murders of Caesar and Gaius thus
serve, in Suetonius work, to allow him to explore the extent to which
assassination in the principate had changed from assassination as an
expression of the collective desire to rid the state of tyranny to the
expression of dissatisfaction with the current *princeps*, private animosities, and struggles within the court. Suetonius' inclusion of Antistius'
little remark about Caesar's single wound, a story that specifically
denies the effectiveness of collective tyrannicide and focuses on the act
of an individual, seems thus to foreshadow the skepticism about grand
causes manifest in his account of the murder of Gaius.[34]

Caesar's murder had a profound and lasting impact on ancient
and modern thinking about tyrannicide. The questions that his assassination posed concerning the ethics of political murder continue to
fascinate us.[35] Details of his murder, unlike that of almost any other
victim of collective violence in antiquity, are abundant. We have a
comparative wealth of information about the plans for his assassination, the events of the day, and the people involved. His murder is
also one of the few instances of an imperial murder in which we can

---

[33] Josephus' account of the conspiracy and murder of Gaius (*AJ* 19.14–73, 105–111, 175)
claims that there were three main conspiracies. Josephus notes Chaerea's humiliation by
Gaius (19, 28–30) but also claims that the conspiracies were prompted by resistance to
tyranny (17–18). He depicts Chaerea's forced torture of potential co-conspirators as a key
moment in his assumption of the leadership of the conspiracy. At this point, Chaerea's
motives are re-stated: Gaius, not his tribunes, should be held responsible for the horrors
of his regime (38–39); he and the other conspirators want to execute a tyrant (64) and
Chaerea desires a rule of law (72–73). Cf. Sherberich 1999.

[34] Suetonius' account of the murder of Domitian (*Dom.* 14–17, 23), the court murder
par excellence, then functions, both in terms of the narrative itself and its place at the end
of the *Caesars*, as a logical extension of this foreshadowing. I am grateful to Paul Roche for
suggesting that I look at Domitian.

[35] Further discussion of the impact of Caesar's murder on subsequent writers and
thinkers may be found in Wyke 2006 and Woolf 2007.

glimpse not only the plethora of motives held by the assassins, but also the various *responses* to which his assassination gave rise. In this article, I have been concerned to demonstrate that Suetonius' unique little story gives us a glimpse of another of these responses to the murder of Caesar, while also telling us something about Suetonius' own crafting of his narrative, his interests, and concerns.

UNIVERSITY OF SYDNEY

WORKS CITED

Bellemore J. 1984. *Nicolaus of Damascus. Life of Augustus.* Bristol.

Brutscher, C. 1958. *Analysen zu Sueton Divus Julius und der Parallelüberlieferung.* Bern.

Classen, C. J. 1962. "Romulus in der römischen Republik." *Philologus* 106:174–204.

Cloud, J. D. 1987. "Augustan Authorship of the *lex Iulia de vi publica* (*Digest* 46.6)." *Liverpool Classical Monthly* 12

Dunkle, J. R. 1971. "The Rhetorical Tyrant in Roman Historiography: Sallust, Livy and Tacitus." *CW* 65:12–20.

Gascou, J. 1984. *Suétone historien.* Rome.

Gugel, H. 1970. "Caesars Tod (Sueton. *Div. Iul.* 81.4–82.3). Aspekte zur Darstellungskunst und zum Caesarbild Suetons." *Gymnasium* 77:5–22.

Hurley, D. W. 1993. *An Historical and Historiographical Commentary on Suetonius' Life of C. Caligula.* Atlanta.

———. 2001. *Suetonius. Divus Claudius.* Cambridge.

Lambrecht, U. 1984. *Herrscherbild und Principatsidee in Suetons Kaiserbiographien: Untersuchungen zur Caesar- und zur Augustus-Vita.* Bonn.

Lintott, A. 1999. *Violence in Republican Rome.* 2nd ed. Oxford.

Müller, W. 1972. "Sueton und seine Zitierweise im 'Divus Iulius.'" *Symbolae Osloenses* 47:95–108.

Nippel, W. 1995. *Public Order in Ancient Rome.* Cambridge.

Pagán, V. 2004. *Conspiracy Narratives in Roman History.* Austin.

———. 2006. "Shadows and Assassinations: Forms of Time in Tacitus and Appian." *Arethusa* 39:193–218.

Scherberich, K. 1999. "Sueton und Josephus über die Ermordung des Caligula." *Rheinisches Museum* 142 (1):74–83.

Seager, R. 1972. "Cicero and the Word *Popularis*." *CQ*, n.s, 22:328–338.

———. 1977. "'Populares' in Livy and the Livian Tradition." *CQ*, n.s, 27:377–390.

Wallace-Hadrill, A. 1983. *Suetonius.* Bristol.

Weinstock, S. 1971. *Divus Iulius.* Oxford.

Woolf, G. 2007. *Et Tu Brute? A Short History of Political Murder.* Cambridge, MA.

Wyke, M. ed. 2006. *Julius Caesar in Western Culture.* Oxford.

CLASSICAL SOPHISM AND PHILOSOPHY IN PSEUDO-PLUTARCH *ON THE TRAINING OF CHILDREN*

GRAEME BOURKE

THE TREATISE *ON THE TRAINING OF CHILDREN* appears first in the traditional order of the collection of works once entirely ascribed to
Plutarch and known as the *Moralia* (Plut. *Mor.* 1A–14C).[1] The opening
sentence indicates the subject matter and tone of the piece:

> Τί τις ἂν ἔχοι εἰπεῖν περὶ τῆς τῶν ἐλευθέρων παίδων
> ἀγωγῆς καὶ τίνι χρώμενοι σπουδαῖοι τοὺς τρόπους ἂν
> ἀποβαῖεν, φέρε σκεψώμεθα.[2]

> Well, let us consider what one could say about the training
> of free children and what should be provided so that they
> turn out conscientious in manner.

1A

Scholars often render the title in English as *On the Education of Children*,[3]
but the Greek περὶ παίδων ἀγωγῆς indicates that the entire ἀγωγή,
the 'rearing' or 'training' of children, is meant.[4] The treatise, indeed,
consists largely of advice to fathers about the development of their

I wish to thank G. R. Stanton and K. McQueen of the University of New England,
Australia, who read earlier drafts of this paper, and to acknowledge the generous assistance of G. H. R. Horsley, of the same university. This research has been facilitated by a
grant from the School of Education at UNE. I am, in addition, thankful for the helpful
suggestions offered by the anonymous readers for *HSCP*.

[1] Sirinelli 1987:3.

[2] The text of Plutarch *Moralia* followed here is that of Bernardakis and Ingenkamp,
2008. All translations are my own.

[3] Babbitt 1949:5; Joyal et al. 2009:87.

[4] Marrou 1956:221 refers to τῶν παίδων ἀγωγή as "the training of the child." Cf.
Bloomer 2006:72.

sons, from conception to marriage, and little is said about any actual pedagogy.[5] As the only ancient Greek treatise concerning education that has come down to us in its entirety, nevertheless, it is as much now as when Berry's dedicated discussion was published in 1958 worthy of more attention than it has received.[6] It was so influential from the early Renaissance until the nineteenth century that it is reasonable to conclude that it was largely responsible for the transmission of the Classical educational tradition to the West.[7] Aside from the direct value of the study of this treatise for advancing our understanding of ancient educational theory, it also has the potential to illuminate the relationship between Classical Greek thought and that of the Early Roman Imperial period.

Plutarch, who wrote from the late first to the early second centuries AD, is unlikely to have composed the treatise. It does seem to belong, however, to some time between the late first and early third centuries AD, and thus, like Plutarch's genuine work, to the period of the Second Sophistic.[8] While, as made clear below, the author derived many of the ideas that he promotes from philosophers in the broadly Socratic tradition, the question of what he might owe to the sophists of Classical times has attracted only passing mention. This paper, after first outlining the case for Socratic influence, seeks to establish the degree to which Classical sophistic thought is reflected in the treatise.

I. PSEUDO-PLUTARCH AND SOCRATIC PHILOSOPHY

We can gain a preliminary impression of the sources of Pseudo-Plutarch's ideas from a survey of the twenty-three literary and intellectual figures he mentions. Seven of these—Homer, Hesiod, Phokylides of Miletos, Euripides, Aristophanes, Eurydike of Hirra, and Sotades—are poets (3F, 6B, 9E–F, 10A, 10C, 11B, 11F, 14B). Twelve are philosophers. Pythagoras is mentioned twice, and both the pre-Socratic Demokritos

---

[5] Marrou 1956:147; Sirinelli 1987:13; Bloomer 2006:72.

[6] Berry 1958:387. Bloomer 2006 and Bourke 2013 appear to be the only dedicated pieces published since that time.

[7] Bourke 2013:1174–1175; cf. Babbitt 1949:xxviii; Sirinelli 1987:3–6.

[8] Marrou 1956:147n14; Berry 1958:387; Sirinelli 1987:24–26.

of Abdera and the Pythagorian Arkhytas of Taras once each (2C, 9F, 10D, 12D–F). Socrates is mentioned on four occasions, Plato on no less than eight, and Aristippos of Kyrene, Xenophon, and Kebes, also disciples of Socrates, once (2C, 3F, 4F, 6A, 8B, 8D, 10C, 10D, 11D, 11E, 11F).[9] The Cynic philosophers, too, are well represented: Diogenes, whose teacher was Antisthenes, also a disciple of Socrates, is quoted twice, and both Diogenes' own disciple Krates, who taught Zeno, the founder of the Stoic school, and Bion once each. We also hear of the cynicizing Socratic philosopher Stilpon of Megara, another of Zeno's teachers (2A, 4E, 5C, 5F–6A, 7D).[10] In addition to these, two rhetors, Aiskhines and Demosthenes, are named (6D–E, 11E), and two sophists, Gorgias and Theokritos of Khios (6A, 11A–C). The four references to rhetors and sophists combined, it is clear, are heavily outweighed by the twenty-four to philosophers, twenty of which are to Socrates or those descended in a direct line of teacher–pupil relationships from him.

The extent to which the treatise is indebted to Socrates and his successors, however, is more fully revealed by the close examinations of the text undertaken by two scholars. Dyroff, claiming that the original source of the treatise is a lost work of Khrysippos, the "second founder" of the Stoic school, identifies terminological parallels with Stoic texts.[11] Berry, nevertheless, is skeptical about the influence of Khrysippos, concluding that "apart from the terminology ... the only important element in the treatise which may well be Stoic is the extremely limited emphasis laid on service to the state."[12] He finds instead ample evidence of the ubiquitous influence, whether direct or mediated through later works, of Plato, Aristotle, and in particular Xenophon.[13] In Berry's view, "all the aspects of 'philosophy' go back beyond Stoicism to the Socratic school."[14] Even if Dyroff is correct in identifying a Stoic work as the substantial source of the Pseudo-Plutarchian treatise, that work itself is likely to have drawn heavily upon the early Socratics, since the ethical

[9] Cf. Sirinelli 1987:16.
[10] Sedley 2003:9–11.
[11] Dyroff 1897:238–94; cf. Quint. 1.11.17.
[12] Berry 1958:388; cf. Plut. Mor. 7F–8A.
[13] Berry 1958:390–8; cf. Sirinelli 1987:21–22, 28–29.
[14] Berry 1958:389, cf. 397.

system of the Stoa, which by the Hellenistic period had become the most influential of the Socratic schools and remained so during the first two centuries AD, was "thoroughly Socratic in inspiration."[15] Whatever Pseudo-Plutarch's direct sources, it seems, the influence of what we might call a broadly Socratic tradition upon his work is undeniable. While Pseudo-Plutarch only ever cites these philosophers approvingly, he never uses the Classical and Hellenistic sophists as positive exemplars. Gorgias, the only Classical sophist whose name appears in the treatise,[16] is mentioned only in the context of a question he asks of Socrates:

οὗτος ἐρωτήσαντος αὐτόν μοι δοκεῖ Γοργίου εἰ ἔχοι περὶ τοῦ μεγάλου βασιλέως ὑπόληψιν καὶ εἰ νομίζοι τοῦτον εὐδαίμονα εἶναι, "οὐκ οἶδ'" ἔφησε "πῶς ἀρετῆς καὶ παιδείας ἔχει", ὡς τῆς εὐδαιμονίας ἐν τούτοις, οὐκ ἐν τοῖς τυχηροῖς ἀγαθοῖς κειμένης.

When someone asked [Socrates]—I think it was Gorgias— if he had a notion about the Great King [of Persia] and if he thought that this man was happy, he replied, "I do not know how he is placed for excellence and education," believing that happiness lies in these, not in the goods acquired by chance. [17]

6A

After relating how the loose tongue of the sophist Theokritos had made him the enemy of Alexander, Pseudo-Plutarch reports that:

Ἀντίγονον δὲ τὸν βασιλέα τῶν Μακεδόνων ἑτερόφθαλμον ὄντα τὴν πήρωσιν προφέρων εἰς οὐ μετρίαν ὀργὴν κατέστησε. τὸν γὰρ ἀρχιμάγειρον Εὐτροπίωνα γεγενημένον ἐν τάξει πέμψας παραγενέσθαι πρὸς αὐτὸν ἠξίου καὶ λόγον δοῦναι καὶ λαβεῖν. ταῦτα δ' ἀπαγγέλλοντος ἐκείνου πρὸς

---

[15] Sedley 2003:11; cf. Gill 2003:33.
[16] Harrison 1964:183–192 compellingly defends the view that Gorgias should continue to be counted among the sophists.
[17] The question, in fact, comes from Polos, Gorgias' disciple and a teacher of rhetoric: Pl. *Grg.* 462C, 470E; Philostr. *VS* 497; cf. Grote 1907:344.

αὐτὸν καὶ πολλάκις προσιόντος "εὖ οἶδ'" ἔφησεν "ὅτι ὠμόν
με θέλεις τῷ Κύκλωπι παραθεῖναι", ὀνειδίζων τὸν μὲν ὅτι
πηρός, τὸν δ' ὅτι μάγειρος ἦν. κἀκεῖνος "τοιγαροῦν" εἰπών
"τὴν κεφαλὴν οὐχ ἕξεις ἀλλὰ τῆς ἀθυροστομίας ταύτης καὶ
μανίας δώσεις δίκην", ἀπήγγειλε τὰ εἰρημένα τῷ βασιλεῖ, ὁ
δὲ πέμψας ἀνεῖλε τὸν Θεόκριτον.

Antigonos, the king of the Makedonians, too, who was
disabled in one eye, Theokritos brought to immoderate
anger by bringing up his disability. Sending the chief cook
Eutropion, who had served in the ranks, Antigonos asked
Theokritos to come to him and engage in discourse. When
Eutropion had brought this message to him and often kept
coming around, Theokritos said, "I know well that you wish
to serve me up raw to the Cyclops," abusing the one for his
defect and the other for being a cook. Eutropion replied,
"Well, in that case, you will not have your head, and you
will pay the penalty for both not being able to keep your
mouth shut, and your madness." He then reported what
had been said to the king, who sent someone to do away
with Theokritos.

11B–C

Of only two sophists to whom our author directly refers, one thus
appears as the perhaps naïve interrogator of Socrates, while the other
exemplifies untimely outspokenness. It may be just coincidental that
the only sophists mentioned appear in a negative light, but it remains
significant that Pseudo-Plutarch does not make any positive statements
about these sophists, and we can safely conclude that, while holding
out philosophers in the Socratic tradition and their words as worthy of
high esteem, he expresses no admiration for either the Classical sophists or their beliefs.

II. THE DOCTRINES OF CLASSICAL SOPHISM

Considering our author's hesitation, despite an evident admiration for
the Classical past, to acknowledge a debt to the so-called "sophists" of

that era, we might well wonder whether any elements of the thought of this writer from the period of the Second Sophistic originated with them. A straightforward means of addressing this question might be first to establish the main features of the doctrine of the Classical sophists and then to examine the treatise for signs of those features. Scholars, however, are in disagreement about the character of Classical sophism, some doubting that the sophists shared any doctrinal beliefs at all. While it is not possible to support a stance on this much-debated question in the present paper, it would be hasty to proceed, nevertheless, without at least setting my views in the context of the on-going debate.

Since Schiappa presents a systematic survey of earlier scholarship on sophism, it is convenient to begin with his book on Protagoras, published in 1991. "So powerful," Schiappa points out, "was the combined indictment by Plato and Aristotle that their judgments concerning the Sophists remained the standard view in most modern histories of ancient Greece." While Hegel restored the philosophical significance of the sophists, he believed that they were "rightfully opposed and defeated by Plato." Grote, however, "rejected the traditional assessment and offered a case for considering the Sophists a positive force in Greek culture and philosophy." In defending the sophists, Grote characterized them as traditional teachers of rhetoric, observing that they "shared few if any common doctrines." Most modern scholars, Schiappa points out, accept Grote's general position, rejecting Platonic condemnation and avoiding, in Kerferd's words, a "premature schematisation of the history of thought." Schiappa sympathizes with Grote's defense of the Classical sophists, which he says suggests that "the Platonic and Hegelian interpretive frameworks missed their significance by assuming more doctrinal commonality than the Sophists actually shared."[18]

---

[18] Schiappa 1991:7–12; cf. Kerferd 1981:13. More recently, Tell 2011, highlighting the competitive aspects of a Greek wisdom tradition that began with the Seven Sages in the Archaic period, has implied that Plato's negative portrayal of the sophists was merely a manifestation of such competitive behavior.

Grote's restoration of the reputation of the sophists is entirely warranted. Their rehabilitation does not depend, however, upon the assumption that there was no doctrinal basis to their movement, and may instead be enhanced by the opposite conclusion. It seems, in fact, that the hostility displayed by Plato towards these rival intellectuals stemmed to a large extent from the significant differences in outlook that are apparent in the surviving sources, and that a deep chasm divided the thought of the sophists from that of Socrates and his followers. De Romilly, whose work on the sophists was published in French three years before Schiappa's and in English one year afterwards, successfully reconciles apparent, but not actual, contradictions in the record of the beliefs of the Classical sophists and thus reveals the development during the fifth century BC of a consistently relativist and humanistic school of thought.[19] In her view, a fragment preserved from Protagoras' treatise *On Truth*, the famous "man-measure" statement discussed below, "sounds the keynote to the Sophists' thought and dictates all the rest."[20] Sophistic relativism, de Romilly explains, "swept aside the very concept of objective truth."[21] This relativism is, of course, the antithesis of the belief in universal, metaphysical truths cherished by Socrates and his followers.[22] On the basis of such a dichotomy, it is possible to identify signs of a specific set of interrelated ideas that were promoted by several of the sophists and which appear to distinguish their thought from that of the Socratic philosophers of their era.

One idea found in the surviving record of the thought of the Classical sophists is the contrast between φύσις, 'nature,' on the one hand, and νόμος, which in this context may be called 'convention,'

[19] De Romilly 1992:162–188.

[20] De Romilly 1992:97–98, 177; cf. Protagoras *On Truth* fr. 1 (Diels and Kranz 1952).

[21] De Romilly 1992:98.

[22] De Romilly 1992:234–236. Even Schiappa 1991:13, in justifying his decision to focus upon Protagoras alone, declares that "his human-measure tenet was at the heart of the sophistic move to democratize *aretê* and knowledge." In Kerferd 1981, too, for whom the sophists gave intellectual expression to profound social and political changes that took place in the Greek world of the second half of the fifth century BC, we find a comprehensive and consistent range of sophistic thought that can be linked to the relativism of Protagoras.

on the other. Protagoras, for example, held that if civilized society is to exist, νόμος is a necessary modification of φύσις.[23] Social, judicial, and political structures, in other words, were prerequisites for human cultural development, which owed its existence to the establishment of these accepted conventions, rather than to any innate qualities that may have been received as a gift of nature.[24] Protagoras, in accord with his preference for νόμος over φύσις, with his belief, in other words, that convention rather than nature determined human behavior, concluded that there was no such thing as objectively right or wrong conduct. This conclusion is encapsulated in the statement that "a person is the measure of all things," by means of which he proclaimed the relativity of human values.[25] Protagoras disputed the existence as such of metaphysical truths and, unlike Plato, believed that our values were based upon νόμος rather than φύσις.[26] This may seem to some to be too strong a claim of opposition between the thought of Protagoras and that of the philosophers, but Plato's Socrates twice makes it abundantly clear that he is opposed to Protagoras' view on this question,[27] and in the Laws the "Athenian," directly contradicting Protagoras, makes God rather than man the measure of all things.[28] It is not that the sophists were unconcerned with the search for "goodness" and "truth," but that their truth was the relativist's one, that there is no transcendental truth. Instead, human utility determined value.[29] The relativism of the sophists led them to question the basis in nature of such institutions as the family,

[23] Pl. Prt. 320C–328D; Dillon and Gergel 2003:xv–xvi. Cf. Kerferd 1981:111–130; Joyal et al. 2009:61. Contra Schiappa 1991:130.

[24] De Romilly 1992:29–36.

[25] Protagoras On Truth fr. 1 (Diels and Kranz 1952). The complete quotation from Protagoras: πάντων χρημάτων μέτρον ἐστὶν ἄνθρωπος, τῶν μὲν ὄντων ὡς ἔστιν, τῶν δὲ οὐκ ὄντων ὡς οὐκ ἔστιν. Cf. Diog. Laert. 9.51: πάντων χρημάτων μέτρον ἄνθρωπος, τῶν μὲν ὄντων ὡς ἔστιν, τῶν δὲ οὐκ ὄντων ὡς οὐκ ἔστιν (Long 1964:464). Kennedy 1963:13 and 1989b:82–84; Beck 1964:148; de Romilly 1992:84–85.

[26] Beck 1964:150, cf. 147–187; Lawton and Gordon 2002:14; Dillon and Gergel 2003:xvi–xvii. Sophistic relativism: Kerferd 1981:47–110; Schiappa 1991:117–133; de Romilly 1992:93–103.

[27] Pl. Cra. 385E–386D; Tht. 152A–C.

[28] Pl. Leg. 716C (Burnet 1907): ὁ δὴ Θεὸς ἡμῖν πάντων χρημάτων μέτρον ἂν εἴη μάλιστα, καὶ πολὺ μᾶλλον ἤ πού τις, ὥς φασιν, ἄνθρωπος.

[29] De Romilly 1992:186, 189–196, 199.

private property, slavery, and the subordinate status of women, and to place under scrutiny the commonly held belief in a polarity between Greeks and barbarians.[30] Protagoras, too, in his treatise *On the Gods*, declared that he could not say whether or not they existed.[31] While this statement need not signify that he took an agnostic, let alone an atheistic, position, it must at least have "served as an introduction to a different approach to religion."[32]

The originality of the sophists in the field of education, a major concern of the treatise under investigation, lay in their advocacy of a view that further reflects their preference for νόμος over φύσις, the belief that ἀρετή was not the exclusive preserve of those who had inherited the requisite nature, but could be taught to anyone.[33] As Jaeger points out, the ἀρετή that the sophists taught was an excellence in "intellectual power and oratorical ability" rather than in "virtue," a common translation, and was thus an acquired set of skills rather than an innate moral quality.[34]

Four interrelated, innovative features, we are able to conclude, may be present to some degree in a work that reflects Classical sophistic rather than Socratic thinking:

1. νόμος is considered dominant over φύσις in determining human behavior.

2. Human values are seen as relative rather than absolute.

---

[30] Antiph. *On Truth* fr. 44(b), II–III (Pendrick 2002). Kerferd 1981:153–162; Dillon and Gergel 2003:xvii; Joyal et al. 2009:60–61.

[31] Diog. Laert. 9.51; Philostr. *VS* 1.494. Cf. Kerferd 1981:163–169; de Romilly 1992:103–111; Dillon and Gergel 2003:xvii; Joyal et al. 2009:61. Grote 1907:329 sees this passage as a mere explanation of "why he said nothing about the gods, in a treatise where the reader would expect to find much upon the subject." The fact that he does say so little here, however, is significant in itself.

[32] Schiappa 1991:148.

[33] Pl. *Hp. mai.* 283C; *Meno* 91B, 95B–C; *Prt.* 349A; *Soph.* 223A. Cf. Jaeger 1954:286–288, 291–292, 307–308, 311; Harrison 1964:188 and n. 28; Kerferd 1981:131–138; de Romilly 1992:30–55. Harrison 1964:188–190 convincingly rejects the suggestion that Gorgias was an exception in this regard. Cf. Pl. *Grg.* 519E–520A; *Meno* 95B–C.

[34] Jaeger 1954:291. Kerferd 1981:131 provides a broader definition: "In general terms, the virtue denoted by *aretē* comprised all those qualities in a man which made for success in Greek society." Cf. Plut. *Mor.* 24D; Russell 1989:303.

3. The basis in nature of social, religious, and political institutions is questioned.

4. It is maintained that ἀρετή might be taught to anyone.

Pseudo-Plutarch has much to say about φύσις, employing the term on a total of twenty-two occasions (2A–3B, 4C, 10B, 12C–D), but mentions νόμος in only one passage (7E). It would be simplistic to conclude from this observation that he sides with the Socratics rather than the Classical sophists on the question of the relative importance of these elements, since all kinds of τέχνη, including rhetoric, might be said to require a certain kind of natural ability. We would need, however, to hear much more about the role of νόμος to be able to justify aligning Pseudo-Plutarch with the Classical sophists in regard to the first of the four features of sophistic thought enumerated above.

Of the second of the four features, the "potentially subversive" relativity of human values,[35] there is no sign in the treatise, and when it comes to the third feature, the questioning of human institutions, it is abundantly clear that the author is instead intent upon positioning himself as an ardent advocate of tradition. In the second sentence, for example, marriage to a socially respectable partner is encouraged:

τοῖς τοίνυν ἐπιθυμοῦσιν ἐνδόξων τέκνων γενέσθαι πατράσιν ὑποθείμην ἂν ἔγωγε μὴ ταῖς τυχούσαις γυναιξὶ συνοικεῖν, λέγω δ' οἷον ἑταίραις ἢ παλλακαῖς· τοῖς γὰρ μητρόθεν ἢ πατρόθεν δυσγενέσιν ἀνεξάλειπτα παρακολουθεῖ τὰ τῆς δυσγενείας ὀνείδη παρὰ πάντα τὸν βίον καὶ πρόχειρα τοῖς ἐλέγχειν καὶ λοιδορεῖσθαι βουλομένοις.

I myself would enjoin those who desire to become the fathers of children held in high esteem not to live together with women randomly, and I mean, for example, whores or mistresses; for the reproaches of low birth are indelible, and follow closely for their entire lives those who are not well-born on either their mother's or their father's side,

---

[35] Anderson 1993:13.

and are readily available to those who want to disgrace and abuse them.

1A–B

Near the end of the treatise, when advice is given about the problem of uncontrollable youth, a final solution is suggested:

Πειρατέον δὲ τοὺς τῶν ἡδονῶν ἥττους καὶ πρὸς τὰς ἐπιτιμήσεις δυσηκόους γάμῳ καταζεῦξαι, δεσμὸς γὰρ οὗτος τῆς νεότητος ἀσφαλέστατος.

You must attempt to yoke in marriage those who give in to pleasures and are deaf to criticism, for this is the most secure bond of a youthful spirit.[36]

13F

Nor is the traditional distinction between Greeks and barbarians questioned. The slave boys who will be brought up with one's children should be Ἑλληνικὰ καὶ περίτρανα λαλεῖν, ἵνα μὴ συναναχρωννύμενοι βαρβάροις, "Greek and speak very distinctly, in order that they are not contaminated by barbarians," and the supervisors to whom the boys are allocated, it is urged, must not be "barbarians" (4A). The list of desired educational outcomes presented in a further passage should suffice to illustrate the traditional tone of the work:

τῶν δὲ τῆς ψυχῆς ἀρρωστημάτων καὶ παθῶν ἡ φιλοσοφία μόνη φάρμακόν ἐστι. διὰ γὰρ ταύτην ἔστι καὶ μετὰ ταύτης γνῶναι τί τὸ καλὸν τί τὸ αἰσχρόν, τί τὸ δίκαιον τί τὸ ἄδικον, τί τὸ συλλήβδην αἱρετόν ἢ φευκτόν· πῶς θεοῖς πῶς γονεῦσι πῶς πρεσβυτέροις πῶς νόμοις πῶς ἀλλοτρίοις πῶς ἄρχουσι πῶς φίλοις πῶς γυναιξὶ πῶς τέκνοις πῶς οἰκέταις χρηστέον ἐστί· ὅτι δεῖ θεοὺς μὲν σέβεσθαι, γονέας δὲ τιμᾶν, πρεσβυτέρους αἰδεῖσθαι, νόμοις πειθαρχεῖν, *** ἄρχουσιν

---

[36] Sedley 2003:10 observes that the inspiration for such statements may come in part from Stoicism, which, unlike Cynicism, could "underpin a thoroughly conventional set of social and personal choices." It may also be maintained, however, as pointed out by Bolgar 1969:45, that "the rhetorical discipline ... was admirably suited for the task of transmitting a traditional culture."

ὑπείκειν, φίλους ἀγαπᾶν, πρὸς γυναῖκας σωφρονεῖν, τέκνων στερκτικοὺς εἶναι, δούλους μὴ περιυβρίζειν·

For illnesses and troubles of the soul, philosophy alone is the medicine. For by means of this and with this it is possible to come to know what is good and what is shameful, what is just and what is unjust, what, in short, is to be chosen or avoided; how one must treat the gods, how one's parents, how one's elders, how the laws, how strangers, how magistrates, how friends, how wives, how children and how house-slaves; that it is necessary to revere the gods, to honor one's parents, to respect one's elders, to obey the laws, to give way to magistrates, to love one's friends, to behave moderately towards women, to be affectionate with one's children, and not to insult one's slaves gratuitously.

7D–E

There is no sign in the treatise that Pseudo-Plutarch sided with the Classical sophists on the first three of the four features of their thought listed above: he has little to say about νόμος; is no relativist; and is clearly an advocate of traditional values, the inculcation of which, in fact, appears to be the central aim of the curriculum that he advocates.[37] In the passage just quoted, nevertheless, we may discern an assumption that ethical behavior could be learned. This leads us to a more extensive discussion of his position on the fourth feature, the belief that ἀρετή could be taught to anyone.

III. THE EDUCATIONAL "TRIAD"

In a passage that constitutes the most comprehensive statement of his educational philosophy (2A), Pseudo-Plutarch names three elements, φύσις, λόγος, and ἔθος, that he says must be brought together in order to achieve the aims of the training that he recommends:

[37] Bourke 2013:1174–1186.

1. φύσις ('nature').

2. λόγος ('discourse'), also called μάθησις ('learning').

3. ἔθος ('habit'), also called ἄσκησις ('exercise'), and referred to as μελέτη ('care').

The fundamental position occupied by this "triad" in the Pseudo-Plutarchian ἀγωγή raises again the problem of what constitutes sophistic rather than Socratic thought, since, despite its insistence that the possession of the right kind of φύσις is essential to the achievement of ἀρετή, scholars have associated it with the sophists rather than the Socratics. The question of the origin of the educational triad lies at the heart of the issue addressed by this paper: if it were to turn out to be of sophistic provenance, on the one hand, we would be obliged to acknowledge that the author of the treatise owed a considerable debt to Classical sophism; if it were to be identified as entirely Socratic in origin, on the other, little evidence would remain of sophistic influence.

Jaeger, citing passages from both the works of Isokrates and Xenophon's *Memorabilia*, asserts that "three factors ... according to the pedagogical theories of the sophists, are the foundation of education."[38] In support of such an assertion, Jaeger elsewhere acknowledges the contributions of Aristotle and Isokrates, among others, and offers a fragment of Protagoras.[39] In his discussion of the treatise under examination in this paper, furthermore, he claims that the "educational trinity" advocated by Pseudo-Plutarch "is otherwise known to be sophistic in origin."[40] Let us then, beginning with Aristotle's *Politics*, work back through the relevant works of Isokrates, Xenophon's *Memorabilia*, and the record of Protagoras' thought, in order to uncover the roots of the triad and determine when and by whom it was first formulated as a consistent educational scheme.

In two separate passages of the *Politics*, Aristotle sets out precisely the same triad of elements, φύσις, λόγος, and ἔθος, found in our

---

[38] Jaeger 1947:63 and nn. 66–70 (the three elements are translated 'talent', 'study', and 'practice'). Isoc. *C. soph.* 1, 8, 14, 15; Xen. *Mem.* 4.1. Cf. Berry 1958:392.

[39] Jaeger 1954:306 and n. 55.

[40] Jaeger 1954:312–313.

treatise.[41] In the first of these passages, moreover, the objectives of the recommended education are that the students should become ἀγαθοί ('good') and σπουδαῖοι ('conscientious'), while in the second ἀρετή is the aim. Together, these passages display a close terminological parallel with that in which Pseudo-Plutarch expounds the triad (2A). As Berry points out, however, "Dyroff is incorrect in calling the triad Aristotelian even if it does occur in the _Politics_,"[42] and we turn now to the sophist Isokrates, who wrote before Aristotle completed the only work in which he mentions the triad, the _Politics_.

In _Against the Sophists_,[43] Isokrates argues that "ability in both discourse (λόγος) and all other activities appears in those who have a good natural disposition (εὐφυής), and are practiced in experiences (ἐμπειρία)." Education (παίδευσις), despite its advantages, he claims, cannot turn those without the right φύσις into good debaters or composers of λόγοι. The ability to compose elaborate λόγοι, Isokrates continues, requires both attention (ἐπιμελεία) and the right kind of ψυχή, for which the student must have the requisite φύσις, learn the different kinds of λόγοι, and practice their uses. For success, all three elements must be present.[44] In the _Antidosis_, composed near the end of his long career, furthermore, Isokrates sets out the demands that he makes of his students: they must be well endowed from birth (φύω καλῶς) for what they choose to do; they must be taught (παιδεύω) successfully; and they must become practiced in the use and exercise (ἐμπειρία) of what they have learned.[45]

Isokrates thus mentions φύσις and some of its cognates, some cognates of both παιδεία and μελέτη, and λόγος. While his terminology is not a precise match for that of the triad advocated by Pseudo-Plutarch, the passages cited above constitute a consistent scheme based upon three elements that are conceptually equivalent to those

[41] Arist. _Pol._ 1332a.39–40, 1334b.7–8.
[42] Berry 1958:392.
[43] Despite his criticism of certain tendencies in sophism (_C. soph._ 1–20; _Antid._ 2–4, 221; _Panath._ 18), Isokrates counted himself as a sophist, and Philostratos includes him among them: _C. soph._ 11, 14; _Antid._ 197–198, 220; Philostr. _VS_ 1.503.
[44] Isoc. _C. soph._ 14–18.
[45] Isoc. _Antid._ 186–88.

found in the treatise under examination: φύσις, παίδευσις ('education'), which Isokrates makes clear consists of learning the different kinds of λόγος, and ἐμπειρία ('experience'), which he also calls ἐπιμέλεια, close in meaning to μελέτη, one of Pseudo-Plutarch's alternative names for ἔθος.[46] While it is only in Aristotle's *Politics* that we first see our author's primary names for the elements, φύσις, λόγος, and ἔθος, presented as a triad by means of which men become good and conscientious, it is clear that the relevant concepts had already been organized into a consistent scheme in the school of the sophist Isokrates.

We now turn to the passages of Xenophon's *Memorabilia* in which Berry finds evidence of a Socratic origin for the triad.[47] In one of these passages, Socrates uses ἐπιμελέομαι when referring to the duties of a cavalry commander; denotes "what we have learned" with a perfect of μανθάνω; and observes that we learn through λόγοι.[48] In three passages, although mainly using μελετάω and ἐπιμελέομαι rather than nouns, Socrates applauds the potential of μελέτη and the similar ἐπιμελεία for improving upon φύσις and leading to ἀρετή.[49] In one passage, again using verbal cognates, he focuses upon the capacity of παιδεία and μάθησις, clearly meant as synonyms here, for building upon the φύσις of even the best students.[50] In none of these passages of the *Memorabilia*, however, does Socrates mention terms from the second and third elements of Pseudo-Plutarch's triad together. In two further passages, nevertheless, he uses μάθησις and μελέτη as a pair, proclaiming that they have the ability to increase all kinds of excellence and lead any nature towards manliness (ἀνδρεία).[51] Xenophon's Socrates, who certainly believed in the importance of having the right φύσις, thus shows that he also accepted the efficacy of both μάθησις and μελέτη, which appear in our author's triad as alternate names for the second and third elements, λόγος and ἔθος.

[46] Isoc. *C. soph.* 10, 14, 15, 17, 18; *Antid.* 186–188.
[47] Berry 1958:392.
[48] Xen. *Mem.* 3.3.11.
[49] Xen. *Mem.* 1.6.7, 1.6.15, 2.1.20.
[50] Xen. *Mem.* 4.1.2–4.
[51] Xen. *Mem.* 2.6.39, 3.9.2.

It is significant, however, that Socrates as portrayed by Xenophon does not, with Isokrates, Aristotle, and Pseudo-Plutarch, specify that λόγος itself, which appears to indicate discourse preserved from the past, is the object of μάθησις.[52] Nor does he present the three elements as necessary and sufficient conditions for the achievement of the desired outcomes. While in the *Memorabilia* nature, learning, and care together contribute towards the achievement of desirable goals, we thus find in that text neither of two important features that are evident, despite some terminological variation, in Isokrates: a precise conceptual parallel with the relevant passages of Aristotle and Pseudo-Plutarch; and the schematic formulation of a triad composed of inter-dependent elements. This places in doubt the veracity of Berry's claim that Xenophon mentions the triad and leaves us with no convincing evidence that it originated with either that author or Socrates himself.

Protagoras, in a fragment from his *Great Logos*, remarks that "teaching (διδασκαλία) requires nature (φύσις) and exercise (ἄσκησις)."[53] Here we see what looks like a consistent scheme in which the first and third elements of the triad as it appears in our treatise, φύσις and ἄσκησις, the latter of which Pseudo-Plutarch makes an equivalent of ἔθος (2A), are present. It is possible, too, that Protagoras intends the qualities he says are necessary for teaching to be present in the students rather than the teachers, in which case διδασκαλία in this passage would function like μάθησις and thus provide the missing second element of the triad. Even though λόγοι are not explicitly mentioned, furthermore, when dealing with the statement of a teacher of rhetoric such as Protagoras we can assume that διδασκαλία is largely concerned with λόγος ('discourse'). It might thus appear that the three elements of the triad are found in Protagoras: φύσις, λόγος by impli-cation as the subject-matter of teaching and learning, and ἔθος in the form of an alternative name used by Pseudo-Plutarch, ἄσκησις. We cannot, however, be sufficiently assured that Protagoras actually does

---

[52] At *Mem.* 3.3.11, Socrates says that we learn through *logoi*, but appears to mean simply that words are a means of transferring knowledge.

[53] Protagoras *Great Logos* fr. 3 (Diels and Kranz 1952): φύσεως καὶ ἀσκήσεως διδασκαλία δεῖται. Jaeger 1954:306n55; cf. Freeman 1948:126 ("Teaching needs endowment and prac-tice"); de Romilly 1992:50.

use the term διδασκαλία here, as both Jaeger and de Romilly appear to assume,[54] to indicate μάθησις. He presents διδασκαλία not as one of the three elements necessary for the achievement of ἀρετή, but as an outcome of φύσις and ἄσκησις, so these last two terms may indicate qualities required of the teacher rather than of the student. Protagoras, in fact, seems to be expressing an idea quite distinct from that indicated by the triad found in Pseudo-Plutarch: that a teacher must have the right kind of nature for the occupation and learn how to teach through practice.[55] And there is a further difficulty.

Certain passages of the Platonic *Protagoras* have been construed to suggest that its namesake adhered to the triad found in the work of Isokrates, Aristotle, and Pseudo-Plutarch.[56] At 323C–D, however, Protagoras argues that ἀρετή is taught and acquired rather than natural or spontaneous. While people do not blame those afflicted with disabilities, the sophist points out, since they know that these come from nature and fortune, they behave differently when it comes to the good qualities that they believe are acquired by ἐπιμέλεια, ἄσκησις, and διδαχή ('teaching'). At 327B, similarly, justice and custom are qualities to be taught. The passages that have been cited as evidence that the triad should be ascribed to Protagoras, in other words, constitute instead an integral component of his argument that a person's φύσις plays little part in the acquisition of ἀρετή. His words stand in pronounced contradiction to the belief, enshrined in the triad, that the right kind of φύσις is an essential precondition for the achievement of ἀρετή.

Even though Protagoras may have discussed some of the concepts of which the triad is constituted, we thus cannot make him its ultimate source. Xenophon's Socrates, too, although he appears to have made a contribution to the development of the elements of the triad, does not specify that λόγος is one of these elements nor state that the three elements that he mentions are the essential components of

[55] The term μάθησις, it is true, appears in the fragment under discussion, but only as part of a separate statement, not even necessarily drawn from the same passage, that "learning must begin in youth": ἀπὸ νεότητος δὲ ἀρξαμένους δεῖ μανθάνειν.

[56] Pl. *Prt.* 323C–D, 377B; Tarrant 2000:113; de Romilly 1992:50 and n. 10.

an integrated educational strategy. The triad, it seems reasonable to conclude, first appears as a conceptually complete schema of mutually dependent elements in the writings of Isokrates.

IV. SOPHISTIC INFLUENCES ON PSEUDO-PLUTARCH

In the *Phaidros*, composed around 370 BC, Plato, most likely using hindsight, has Socrates see a disposition towards philosophy in the mind of the young Isokrates.[57] This passage suggests that, in Plato's view, the thought of the fourth-century sophist had some affinities with that of Socrates. Does Isokrates' formulation of the triad entail, however, that he turned his back upon a central creed of the fifth-century BC sophists and was prepared to accept the apparently traditional and Socratic assumption that the kind of nature that could only be acquired through descent from the gods and heroes, that is, an aristocratic origin, was an essential element in the achievement of ἀρετή?

Jaeger claims that the triad "abandons the aristocratic idea that character and morality can be inherited by blood, but not acquired."[58] An acknowledgment of the need for λόγος and ἔθος, however, does not necessarily imply that the pupil's φύσις is of no consequence: the triad requires training and practice *in addition* to the right kind of nature. So long as this nature is assumed to depend upon the student's parentage, "the aristocratic idea" remains in force. The triad that is advocated by Pseudo-Plutarch and which appears originally to have been formulated by Isokrates, because it insists upon the indispensability of φύσις, might thus appear inconsistent with the belief of the fifth-century sophists that ἀρετή could be taught to anyone.

It seems, however, that Isokrates developed a more socially inclusive understanding of the term φύσις. This may already have been achieved by the time, probably in 388 BC, when he established the school at Athens from which his work stems,[59] although it is equally possible that it evolved throughout the life of the school and reached its fulfillment only towards the end of Isokrates' career, when he wrote

---

[57] Pl. *Phdr.* 279B; de Romilly 1992:43.
[58] Jaeger 1954:306.
[59] Usher 1999:296.

the *Antidosis*. A closer look at the passage from that work cited above reveals that Isokrates was quite particular about the kind of φύσις that each of his prospective students must possess:

λέγομεν γὰρ ὡς δεῖ τοὺς μέλλοντας διοίσειν ἢ περὶ τοὺς
λόγους ἢ περὶ τὰς πράξεις ἢ περὶ τὰς ἄλλας ἐργασίας
πρῶτον μὲν πρὸς τοῦτο πεφυκέναι καλῶς, πρὸς ὅπερ ἂν
προῃρημένοι τυγχάνωσιν.

For we say that those who are about to excel in discourse,
in public office, or in other deeds must first be well born
for that which they may happen to choose.[60]

Here we find that the students are required to have a natural aptitude for a particular kind of endeavor, which is quite a different thing from saying, as Socrates and his followers appear to do, that some natures are suitable for education and others are not. The emphasis is on the potential of the individual, rather than on the assumed overall superiority of a particular category of citizen. Isokrates, in a sense, democratizes the concept of φύσις. He thus obviates a necessity keenly felt by the fifth-century sophists, who wanted to make their teaching available to anyone who could afford it, "well-fathered" or not. Isokrates' stipulation that a student must have a natural aptitude for a specific pursuit removed the need for him to join his sophistic predecessors in denying that the possession of the right kind of nature was an essential element in the achievement of excellence.

In one passage, the author of our treatise appears to follow the early Classical sophistic line on the question of whether or not the right kind of nature is essential for achieving ἀρετή. Here he seems to contradict not only a fundamental Socratic position, but also, in fact, the triad that he has himself prescribed.[61] He issues the following warning:

εἰ δέ τις οἴεται τοὺς οὐκ εὖ πεφυκότας μαθήσεως καὶ
μελέτης τυχόντας ὀρθῆς πρὸς ἀρετὴν οὐκ ἂν τὴν τῆς

---

[60] Isoc. *Antid.* 187 (Mathieu 1960), cf. 186, 188.
[61] Cf. Albini 1997:59.

φύσεως ἐλάττωσιν εἰς τοὐνδεχόμενον ἀναδραμεῖν, ἴστω πολλοῦ, μᾶλλον δὲ τοῦ παντὸς διαμαρτάνων.

If anyone thinks, however, that those who have not been well born, upon encountering learning and practice of the right kind, would not in progressing towards excellence make amends for the diminution of their nature in every possible way, let him know that he is considerably, or rather completely, going astray.

2C

It is possible, however, to resolve the apparent contradiction in the position held by our author by concluding that he is suggesting here that intellectual disadvantage, rather than a lack of *eugeneia*, can be overcome. As in Isokrates *Antidodis*, the right kind of nature might thus be seen as a characteristic of the single individual rather than of a category of citizen.

The "real" Plutarch, to whose intellectual circle our author no doubt belonged,[62] also appears to have been in accord with Isokrates' view of φύσις as peculiar to the individual. In a work included among the *Moralia*, for example, Plutarch makes it clear that even though each student possesses a distinct nature, some being naturally attracted to thought and reason, while others are impetuous and lively, or rough and hot-tempered, all may attain ἀρετή.[63] Deficiencies in one's φύσις can be overcome, and this, in fact, is the recurrent theme of another of Plutarch's works.[64] Even an inherited stain on one's character can be wiped out through ἔθος, δόγμα, and νόμος.[65] As Albini demonstrates, furthermore, in the *Lives*, "λόγος and ἔθος offer the tools to control one's natural dispositions."[66] In a work dedicated to the question of whether or not ἀρετή can be taught, finally, Plutarch argues that it not only can be, but must be.[67] In the intellectual world of Pseudo-Plutarch,

---

[62] Marrou 1956:147n14; Berry 1958:387; Sirinelli 1987:24–26; Albini 1997, 59, 63.
[63] Plut. *Quomodo adul.* 15A, 15B, 31B.
[64] Plut. *Quomodo adul.* 15B, 31B; *De recta ratione audiendi* 38D, 40F, 46E.
[65] Plut. *De sera* 562B; cf. Albini 1997:60–61.
[66] Albini 1997:65.
[67] Plut. *An virtus doceri possit* 439A–440C.

the Isokratic conception of φύσις appears to have been highly influential.

In an anecdote offered by Pseudo-Plutarch in support of his stated belief that those with a lesser nature can still rise to excellence, the legendary Spartan reformer Lykourgos demonstrates that training can make all the difference between two puppies from the same litter (3A–B). Here, our author does not overtly dismiss birth as an element in an individual's ability to achieve ἀρετή, since we could still conclude that puppies from the wrong litter altogether would have been untrainable under any circumstances. Comparison with a passage of the *Memorabilia* that may be a source for this analogy, where Xenophon's Socrates explains that both colts and puppies can benefit from training, however, suggests otherwise. In this passage, it is clear that the philosopher is referring to naturally suited (εὐφυής) animals alone. For Socrates, inherited characteristics, despite depending upon training to reach their potential, remain an essential factor.[68] Our author, by way of contrast, appears to have made a conscious decision not to insist upon this element. His omission of φύσις from this passage, indeed, has prompted one scholar to conclude that "the author has little interest in birth: growth is his main concern."[69] While Pseudo-Plutarch may thus be guilty of a certain degree of equivocation on the matter of the nature of "nature," the apparent contradictions in his work serve to suggest that his educational philosophy was a product of sophistic as well as Socratic influence.

In Isokrates' pedagogy, the three elements that must be present in students discussed above do not constitute the only factors essential for their success. In addition, the διδάσκαλος must teach accurately and comprehensively, on the one hand, and, on the other, set such a good example of rhetoric that the speech of the students who are able to imitate (μιμέομαι) him will become more brilliant and graceful than

---

[68] Xen. *Mem.* 4.1.3–4. Berry 1958:393 implies that in this passage Xenophon's Socrates says that the ungifted man can be improved, but this does not appear in the text, and despite Berry's claim we find in the *Memorabilia* a consistent emphasis on improving those who already possess the requisite nature: Xen. *Mem.* 1.6.13.

[69] Bloomer 2006:87.

that of others.[70] As Too explains, Isokrates' literary prose "provides the *tupos* for imitation."[71] This kind of μίμησις, however, is not found in the treatise under discussion. In the only passage in which Pseudo-Plutarch discusses the matter of students imitating their teachers (4C), it is the general demeanor of the latter rather than their literary prose that provides the model. Similar statements about the value of μίμησις of the teacher can be found in passages from Plato and Xenophon: the sons of the richest men, Plato informs us, imitated Socrates, and, according to Xenophon, Socrates, though unintentionally, made his disciples hope that through imitating him they could achieve excellence.[72] Pseudo-Plutarch's warning to fathers to engage teachers who will provide good models for their sons' behavior thus offers no evidence of a peculiarly sophistic influence upon his work.

Our author, on the other hand, does regularly encourage the young to imitate or model themselves upon the great philosophers of the past (10D, 10E, 11E–F, 12C, 14A–B), a variety of μίμησις that appears to find a precise parallel in the works of neither Plato nor Xenophon. While in several passages of Plato and in Xenophon's *Agesilaos*, it is true, we find advice to imitate great men, this is not directed towards the young.[73] These writers, moreover, often see μίμησις in negative terms,[74] their criticisms of it sometimes appear aimed at the sophists in particular, and we might even infer from certain passages that Plato viewed it as a sophistic pedagogy.[75] While Plato's Socrates sees dangers in the mimetic response of the young to the figures portrayed in poetry,[76] furthermore, the same author's Protagoras proclaims that there is much to be gained from encouraging the young to imitate (μιμέομαι) the good men of the past through reading and memorizing poetry that

---

[70] Isoc. *C. soph.* 17–18; cf. Too 1995:185.

[71] Too, 1995:186, cf. 187–190.

[72] Pl. *Ap.* 23C; Xen. *Mem.* 1.2.3.

[73] Pl. *Menex.* 236E; *Resp.* 3.395C, 396C, 398B, 399A, 6.491A, 7.539C; Xen. *Ages.* 10.2.

[74] Pl. *Criti.* 107B; *Epin.* 975D; *Grg.* 511A; *Phdr.* 264E; *Phlb.* 13D, 40C; *Resp.* 7.539B; Xen. *Ages.* 9.5; *Mem.* 4.2.40.

[75] Pl. *Euthydemus* 288B, 301B, 303E; *Hp. mi.* 37E; *Soph.* 235A, 267A–268D.

[76] Pl. *Resp.* 3.392A–398B, 10.595C–608B, though this is qualified to some extent at 10.607A, and the door is left open for poetry to be redeemed: 607D–608A.

praises them.[77] Isokrates, too, specifically identifies the imitation of the good men of the past as a means of becoming educated: "those who reach out for splendour and contend for *paideia*," he states forthrightly, "should be imitators of the virtuous and not of the mean."[78]

Pseudo-Plutarch's encouragement of the young to imitate and model themselves upon the great philosophers of the past, like his conception of φύσις as a quality peculiar to the individual, thus appears to owe much to the Classical sophists. In the light of this observation, even our author's frequent references to philosophers in the broadly Socratic tradition, outlined at the beginning of this paper, appear characteristically sophistic.

V. CONCLUSION

Previous scholarship has demonstrated that the treatise *On the Training of Children* owes a profound debt to Socrates and his Classical followers, especially Xenophon, and perhaps also to the broadly Socratic philosophers of the Hellenistic period. The primary terminology of the educational "triad" of φύσις, λόγος, and ἔθος, the salient feature of Pseudo-Plutarch's educational philosophy, is first found in Aristotle's *Politics*, and some of its roots can be discerned in the teaching of Xenophon's Socrates. The triad seems, moreover, to contradict a central doctrine of the sophists of the fifth century BC. It can, nevertheless, be said to be sophistic in origin in that it appears first to have been conceptually formulated by Isokrates. In two additional passages, furthermore, our author seems to adopt the Isokratic understanding of the term φύσις, and in regard to μίμησις he appears to follow a generally sophistic pedagogy that can be traced back to Isokrates and Protagoras.

---

[77] Pl. *Prt.* 325E–326A; Hunter and Russell 2011:3. Plato's Protagoras also indicates (325E) that poetry contains many admonitions (νουθετήσεις) useful to the young, instances of which we find scattered throughout Pseudo-Plutarch's treatise: 1B, 1C, 3F, 6B, 9E–F, 10A–B, 11F, 14B–C. Plutarch takes a qualified stand in favor of poetry as a source of model behavior: *Quomodo adul.* 17F–18F, 28E–30C; cf. Hunter and Russell 2011:2–17.

[78] Isoc. *Demonicus* 2 (Mathieu and Brémond 1956): τοὺς δόξης ὀρεγομένους καὶ παιδείας ἀντιποιουμένους τῶν σπουδαίων ἀλλὰ μὴ τῶν φαύλων εἶναι μιμητάς.

Pseudo-Plutarch defers emphatically and consistently to philosophers in the Socratic tradition, but has nothing of a positive nature to say about the sophists or their beliefs. There is, nevertheless, clear evidence of the influence of sophistic thinking upon his educational philosophy. Despite the striking, abundantly acknowledged presence of Socratic inspiration, in regard to one of its fundamental concerns, the education of children, the ideas promoted in the treatise are likely to have originated to an appreciable extent with Classical sophism.

UNIVERSITY OF NEW ENGLAND (AUSTRALIA)

WORKS CITED

Albini, F. 1997. "Family and the Formation of Character: Aspects of Plutarch's Thought." In *Plutarch and His Intellectual World: Essays on Plutarch*, ed. J. Mossman, 59–71. London.

Anderson, G. 1993. *The Second Sophistic: A Cultural Phenomenon in the Roman Empire.* London.

Babbitt, F. C., ed. 1949. *Plutarch's Moralia.* Vol. 1. London.

Beck, F. A. G. 1964. *Greek Education 450–350 BC.* London.

Bernardakis, P. D., and H. G. Ingenkamp. 2008. *Plutarchi Chaeronensis Moralia, recognovit Gregorius N. Bernardakis. Editionem Maiorem.* Vol. 1. Athens.

Berry, E. G. 1958. "The *de Liberis Educandis* of Pseudo-Plutarch." *HSCP* 63:387–399.

Bloomer, W. M. 2006. "The Technology of Child Production: Eugenics and Eulogics in the *de Liberis Educandis." Arethusa* 39:71–99.

Bolgar, R. R. 1969. "The Training of Elites in Greek Education." In *Governing Elites: Studies in Training and Selection*, ed. R. Wilkinson, 23–49. New York.

Bourke, G. F. 2013. "How to Create the Ideal Son: The Unhidden Curriculum in Pseudo-Plutarch *On the Training of Children." Educational Philosophy and Theory* 46:1174–1186.

Burnet, J. 1907. *Platonis Opera.* Vol. 5. Oxford.

De Romilly, J. 1992. *The Great Sophists in Periclean Athens.* Trans. J. Lloyd. Oxford.

Diels, H., and W. Kranz. 1952. *Die Fragmente der Vorsokratiker.* Vol. 2. Berlin.

Dillon, J., and T. Gergel. 2003. *The Greek Sophists.* London.

Dyroff, A. 1897. *Die Ethik der alten Stoa.* Berlin.

Freeman, K. 1948. *Ancilla to the Pre-Socratic Philosophers.* Oxford.

Gill, C. 2003. "The School in the Roman Imperial Period." In Inwood 2003, 33–58.

Grote, G. 1907. *A History of Greece.* Vol. 8. London.

Harrison, E. L. 1964. "Was Gorgias a Sophist?" *Phoenix* 18:183–192.

Hunter, R., and D. Russell. 2011. *Plutarch: How to Study Poetry.* Cambridge.

Inwood, B., ed. 2003. *The Cambridge Companion to the Stoics.* Cambridge.

Jaeger, W. W. 1947. *Paideia: The Ideals of Greek Culture.* Vol. 3. Trans. G. Highet. Oxford.

———. 1954. *Paideia: The Ideals of Greek Culture.* Vol. 1. Trans. G. Highet. Oxford.

Joyal, M., I. McDougall, and J. C. Yardley. 2009. *Greek and Roman Education: A Sourcebook.* London.

Kennedy, G. A. 1963. *The Art of Persuasion in Greece.* London.

———, ed. 1989a. *The Cambridge History of Literary Criticism.* Vol. 1. Cambridge.

———. 1989b. "Language and Meaning in Archaic and Classical Greece." In Kennedy 1989a, 78–91.

Kerferd, G. B. 1981. *The Sophistic Movement.* Cambridge.

Lawton, D., and P. Gordon. 2002. *A History of Western Educational Ideas.* London.

Long, H. S. 1964. *Diogenis Laertii Vitae Philosophorum.* Vol 2. Oxford.

Mathieu, G. 1960. *Isocrate Discours.* Vol. 3. Paris.

Mathieu, G., and É. Brémond. 1956. *Isocrate Discours.* Vol. 1. Paris.

Marrou, H. I. 1956. *A History of Education in Antiquity.* Trans. G. Lamb. London.

Pendrick, G. 2002. *Antiphon the Sophist: The Fragments.* Cambridge.

Russell, D. A. 1989. "Greek Criticism of the Empire." In Kennedy 1989a, 297–329.

Schiappa, E. 1991. *Protagoras and* logos: *A Study in Greek Philosophy and Rhetoric.* Columbia, SC.

Sedley, D. N. 2003. "The School, from Zeno to Arius Didymus." In Inwood
    2003, 7–32.

Sirinelli, J. 1987. "De l'Éducation des Enfants." In *Plutarque Oeuvres,
    Morales.* Vol. 1.1., ed. R. Flacelière, J. Irigoin, J. Sirinelli, and
    A. Philipson, 1–63. Paris.

Tarrant, H. 2000. *Plato's First Interpreters.* London.

Tell, H. 2011. *Plato's Counterfeit Sophists.* Washington.

Too, Y. L. 1995. *The Rhetoric of Identity in Isocrates: Text, Power, Pedagogy.*
    Cambridge.

Usher, S. 1999. *Greek Oratory: Tradition and Originality.* Oxford.

VERSE QUOTATIONS FROM FESTUS

JARRETT T. WELSH

O NE OF THE MORE IMPORTANT SOURCES preserving fragments of early Latin literature and drama is Festus' epitome of Verrius Flaccus' *De significatu uerborum*.[1] Since 1903 students of Ennius have known that Verrius, and by extension Festus, tended to quote complete metrical units from both the *Annales* and the scripts of Ennian tragedy, without regard for whether the resulting quotation gave complete sense.[2] The qualification "tended to" is important, since Vahlen himself accepted as authentically Verrian a few instances where Festus preserves incomplete Ennian verses.[3] Taking up Vahlen's observations, Rychlewska (1948–1949) demonstrated that the same tendency was observable in Verrius' citations of hexameter poetry more generally; she further argued that the metrically incomplete quotations were to be attributed either to the methods of the scholarly sources

References to Festus are given from Lindsay 1913, to Nonius from Lindsay 1903. References to *Gramm.* are to the volumes of Keil 1857–1880. All references are to the initial line of an entry, not to the specific line where a fragment or feature occurs. The fragments of republican drama are cited from Ribbeck 1897–1898; Ennius' *Annales* from Skutsch 1985; Lucilius from Marx 1904–1905; Plautus from Lindsay 1904–1905, except that I use Questa 1995 for the cantica. I am grateful to Alison Keith and to the journal's anonymous reader for their helpful comments. This research was supported by the Social Sciences and Humanities Research Council of Canada.

[1] Most students of the lexicon assume that Festus did little more than abbreviate Verrius' work. Moscadi (1979) attributed a greater degree of independence to Festus.

[2] Vahlen 1903:lxvii–lxxi. Behind Vahlen's argument lies Reitzenstein's (1887:108–110) demonstration that Festus' quotations of Plautus and Ennius occur in the same order as in the texts of those authors, suggesting that Verrius had excerpted their works at first hand.

[3] Vahlen (1903:lxvii) ascribed seven quotations of incomplete verses to a desire to provide complete units of sense without regard for meter. There is room for doubt about this explanation, since six of those quotations belong to exceptions discussed in Section I.2 below.

that Verrius sometimes used or, perhaps just once, to Festus' process of abridgement.[4] Although some modifications to Rychlewska's analysis will be offered in this paper, her descriptions of Verrius' methods and of the sources of his non-conforming quotations seem to be essentially correct, as concerns the hexameter citations.[5]

No comparable examination of the quotations of scenic verse that survive in the text of Festus has been produced. Many students of republican drama have nevertheless assumed, following Vahlen's remarks about Ennian tragedy and Strzelecki's (1932) demonstration of Verrius' regular use of copies of republican literature at first hand, that the same methods are at work in the dramatic quotations.[6] Several partial or preliminary investigations of the citations of individual authors have suggested that those assumptions are not misguided.[7] The lack of a systematic study of these quotations is nevertheless problematic, since complete information about the methods of Verrius and Festus would offer important guidance for editors of fragments preserved in this text. Furthermore, no attempt has been made to examine the metrically incomplete quotations as a group, to determine what information they might collectively reveal that remains obscure in isolation. In the absence of that guidance editors have sometimes adopted unmethodical decisions about the text or metrical setting of fragments preserved by Festus.

---

[4] Rychlewska 1948–1949:197. Her usage does not permit certainty about whether she meant that Festus or Verrius was responsible for the shape of the citation of Lucilius 1138–1142.

[5] In this paper I do not take account of the arguments put forward at Glinister 2007:13–19 and North 2007 about the origins of Verrius' quotations. The purpose of each paper is different from my own, but the arguments there advanced seem to be founded on uncertain assumptions about Verrius' role as mediator of excerpted quotations, rather than first-hand excerpter of republican literature, which the studies of Reitzenstein (1887), Strzelecki (1932), and Rychlewska (1948–1949) preclude. Jocelyn's (1991) observations on quotations of Plautus' *Pseudolus* are rich with relevant information.

[6] See, e.g., Jocelyn 1969:330; Schierl 2006:46, 222. Not all editors take account of these methods.

[7] See De Nonno 1990:610–611; Pieroni 2004:29. Related is the question of Festus' quotations of Saturnians, for which see Strzelecki 1964:x. For further discussion of the quotations of Naevius, see n. 132 below. The undamaged quotations from Livius' *Odysseia* seem to consist of complete Saturnians.

In this paper I examine Festus' quotations of hexameter and scenic poetry, with three principal aims in view. The first is to demonstrate that, as has long been assumed, Verrius employed the same methods of metrical citation for both hexameter and scenic verse. To corroborate that demonstration I also consider the metrically incomplete quotations, for only by explaining the aberrations can one be confident that the description of Verrius' methods has evidentiary value for the setting of fragments preserved by Festus. My second aim is therefore to confirm, extend, or correct the groups of non-conforming quotations that Rychlewska described. Examining Festus' quotations collectively suggests some modifications to her analysis, which in turn will justify some metrically incomplete quotations that may be accepted without further modification. On that foundation I shall argue that Verrius' own quotations of republican poetry are given in complete metrical units with such unflinching regularity that it is unmethodical to set a fragment as an incomplete verse or verses, unless it can be shown to belong to a circumscribed group of exceptions. Although non-conforming quotations need cause no consternation, it is incumbent on an editor to justify such peculiarities. The argument about the predictability of the metrical form of Verrius' quotations leads to my third aim, which is to renew scrutiny of some metrically incomplete quotations of early Latin verse where, I argue, no exception can be justified.

The damaged codex Farnesianus (**F**) that preserves the text of Festus presents several obstacles to such a study, and some evidence must necessarily be excluded from consideration. I have excluded quotations which have lost some text in the charred portions of **F**, even where external evidence provides plausible supplements, since those supplements are sometimes uncertain. Paulus' epitome of Festus is also set aside as a regular source of evidence, since his methods include abbreviating quotations in the text of Festus.[8] I also set aside quotations preserved only in the fifteenth-century apographs, upon which we rely for the three quaternions of **F** that have been lost since the manuscript resurfaced; the apographs sometimes omit unintelligible material and

---

[8] Strzelecki 1932:3–23.

do not always accurately signal lacunae in their text.[9] Such restrictions are somewhat hyperskeptical, but they are essential in order to limit distortion of this analysis.[10] The lexicon's occasional one- or two-word quotations, perhaps more accurately described as testimonia, are likewise excluded from the present study, since they are obviously distinct from Verrius' typical methods of quoting illustrative citations of verse. Finally, a further 13 quotations have been set aside as being too corrupt to admit of secure conclusions, although most seem to support the present argument.[11]

In Section I of this paper I survey Verrius' methods of quoting verse (I.1) before taking up the groups of non-conforming quotations that can be assigned with some probability either to Verrius' sources (I.2) or to Festus' process of epitomization (I.3). Section II offers discussions of 15 fragments that require emendation or explanation, inasmuch as they seem to have been excerpted by Verrius himself but do not conform to his methods, and seem not to be justified by any pattern of abbreviation recognizable as the work of Festus. In Section III I offer conclusions and identify the remaining quotations that do not yield to easy explanation, where more investigation is warranted. Three appendices treat of some problems raised by quotations of Vergil, quotations of Ennius, and the testimonia-style of citation.

I. THE METHODS AND SOURCES OF THE LEXICON

I.1. Metrical Citation

Latin lexicographers in antiquity tended to give their illustrative quotations of poetry either in units of sense or in units of meter.

---

[9] Lindsay 1913:iv, xvii–xviii; Mariotti 1971.

[10] Occasionally I introduce illustrative material from these sources to corroborate a pattern in the undamaged portions of **F**; its origin is always signaled and that material never enters the fundamental reckoning that supports this paper's arguments.

[11] These are the quotations at Festus p. 182.12 (Livius *com.* 3), 238.20 (Naevius *com.* 116), 238.23 (Pacuvius 317 and 249), 306.12 (Novius 88), 318.32 (Naevius *com.* 126–127), 320.24 (Accius 262–263), 322.11 (Trag. inc. 83), 334.8 (Naevius *praet.* 5–6 and Accius 92), 342.13 (Pacuvius 333–334), 350.26 (Afranius 288), and 444.32 (Plautus *fr.* 47). Some of these Lindsay, naturally, did not obelize in his edition of Festus.

Aiming for completeness of sense generally meant that meter was neglected, whereas metrically complete quotations often leave their sense incomplete or obscure. Those habits are complicated by the fact that, in early Latin verse, units of sense and units of meter frequently coincide. That tendency makes it difficult to determine, from isolated examples, whether a quotation of early poetry is given specifically as a complete verse, or rather as a complete unit of sense. For example, the quotation from Ennius' *Cresphontes* (*trag.* 120; ia[8]) at Festus p. 312.7, *ducit me uxorem liberorum sibi quaesendum gratia*, is complete in terms of both meter and sense, and in isolation it would be impossible to describe a lexicographer's methods from it. To control for that tendency of republican poetry it is necessary to show not only that most of Verrius' quotations consist of complete verses, but more specifically that he quoted complete verses even though that method sometimes meant that a quotation did not give complete sense.

The extant portions of **F** present 147 undamaged quotations of scenic verse and 76 undamaged quotations of hexameter verse.[12] 108 quotations of scenic verse (73.5%) and 61 of hexameters (80%) can be scanned as complete verses either as transmitted or with slight, obviously correct interventions. Those high percentages of metrically complete quotations themselves suggest, but do not prove, that the traditional explanation of Verrius' methods holds true for all his quotations of republican poetry.[13] Two significant patterns in the metrically complete quotations corroborate that view. The first pattern is represented by quotations that give incomplete sense; the second, by

[12] These tallies exclude all material set aside in the introduction to this paper. Taking into account material preserved in the apographs and the damaged portions of **F**, I count 355 identifiable quotations of scenic verse and 160 of hexameter poetry.

[13] Some comparative data from Nonius will be useful. Approximately 80% of unemended quotations taken from his sources 26, 27, and 28 (which gave quotations with attention to the completeness of both meter and sense) consist of at least one complete verse. Accounting for exceptions brings the total to over 95% of quotations that accord with those methods; for these statistics, see Welsh 2012:833, 843. Preliminary examinations of Nonius' own excerptions from complete texts (guided by sense, rather than meter, at least in the case of early Latin literature) and of quotations taken from secondary sources that quoted units of sense (e.g. the sources "Gloss. i" and "Gloss. v") suggest that normally 55–65% of quotations made by this method consist of complete verses; see Welsh 2012:836n36 and 2013:267n52.

quotations that include words that are superfluous or irrelevant to the lexical feature being illustrated. Adhering, in other words, to a metrical principle meant that Verrius sometimes quoted too little, and sometimes too much.

Since these patterns have long been recognized in Verrius' quotations of hexameter poetry, here I emphasize the quotations of scenic verse to demonstrate the consistency of Verrius' methods in diverse meters, giving only selected examples of each phenomenon. First, the quotations that are obscure or give incomplete sense:

p. 312.7 (Ennius *trag.* 97; tr⁷)
liberum quaesendum causa familiae matrem tuae

p. 426.5 (Afranius 15; ia⁶)
quis tam sagaci corde atque ingenio unico

p. 439.10 (Ennius *trag.* 338; ia⁶)
*Salmacida spolia sine sudore et sanguine*¹⁴

p. 452.22 (Afranius 240; ia⁶)
orbus uirili sexu adoptauit sibi

p. 484.25 (Pacuvius 37; ia⁶)
*feroci ingenio toruus praegrandi gradu*¹⁵

In these examples a complete verse is quoted but its precise meaning is left partially obscure because the words that completed the thought have been omitted. A lexicographer concerned exclusively with sense (who only incidentally quoted complete verses where sense and meter coincided) would have extended the citation of Ennius *trag.* 97 to include the verb that governed *matrem*, or, in the case of Afranius 15, would either have omitted at least *quis* from the quotation (producing an incomplete verse), or would have quoted additional words to make its sense clearer. Similar arguments about the missing elements of syntax could be advanced about the other quotations in that list.

---

¹⁴ sudore et sanguine *Cic.* (*Off.* 1.61) : sanguine et sudore F. Since Festus' text will not scan as iambo-trochaic verse it is reasonable to assume that these words have been transposed either in transmission (but cf. n. 87, below) or by Festus himself.
¹⁵ praegrandi *Augustinus* : praegnandi F. The conjecture is assuredly correct.

The second pattern is observed in quotations containing material that is superfluous or irrelevant to the point of the entry. Although these quotations usually contain a complete utterance that illustrates the target-word, they also contain some tangential material, under-lined below, that adds little or nothing of relevance:

p. 166.32 (Ennius *Ann.* 238; da[6])
  alter nare cupit, <u>*alter pugnare paratust*</u>

p. 168.15 (Plautus *Stich.* 352; tr[7])
  ecquis huc effert nassiternam cum aqua. :: <u>*sine suffragio*</u>[16]

p. 218.2 (Ennius *trag.* 330; ia[6])
  <u>*Hector,*</u> *qui haud cessat obsidionem obducere*[17]

p. 320.24 (Accius 437–438; tr[7])
  <u>*constit[u]it, cognouit, sensit,*</u> *conlocat sese in locum*
  celsum; hinc manibus rapere roudus saxeum grande[m] et graue[m]

This phenomenon suggests that Verrius did not excerpt his quotations as complete units of sense; that method would have permitted omitting the tangential material. Instead, as is certain in the first two examples and can be presumed in the latter two, Verrius quoted complete verses, although that method meant including superfluous or irrelevant words.

From these patterns of quotation and from the high proportion of metrically complete verses occurring in **F**, it is reasonable to assume that Verrius' method of metrical citation applies in the case of all early poetry. To demonstrate the correctness of that assumption it is

---

[16] Similar quotations of complete verses of Plautus containing a change of speaker occur at Festus p. 172.16 (*Cas.* 646/647), 310.28 (*Pseud.* 257), and 312.14 (*Curc.* 110); cf. p. 214.26 (apogr.), quoting Plautus *Stich.* 91. It has sometimes been suggested (Jocelyn 1991:572; Pieroni 2004:29n113), since changes of speaker are not indicated in the lexi-con's quotations, that Verrius' copy of Plautus marked speaking parts faintly or not at all. However, since Verrius seems not to have aimed at complete intelligibility of every word he quoted, recording changes of speaker would have been somewhat superfluous; it therefore does not seem safe to assume that his copy of Plautus necessarily did not provide him with that information.

[17] This quotation is preserved only in the apographs. However it seems to illustrate the pattern more securely than the similar instance in **F** (p. 482.3), where *Aiax* in Ennius *trag.* 18 is corrupt.

necessary to examine the metrically incomplete quotations; from this investigation it will emerge that those non-conforming quotations were not excerpted by Verrius in that form, but rather were taken over from certain scholarly sources on which he sometimes relied, or were abbreviated by Festus in the process of writing his epitome.

I.2. Aberrant Quotations Transcribed by Verrius

The text of Festus contains a small number of metrically incomplete quotations of republican poetry. Nearly all of them seem likely to descend from Verrius' lexicon but unlikely to have been excerpted in that form by him. Instead they probably derive from lexicographical or more generally scholarly sources whose methods were not identical to Verrius' own. Some of these groups of non-conforming quotations were described by Rychlewska (1948–1949:193–197), but it is necessary to extend those groups, to redefine them in certain instances, and to add some further groups of exceptions that the hexameter citations alone could not reveal.

Rychlewska (1948–1949:194, 196) identified, as Verrius' sources for some of the metrically incomplete quotations, Sinnius Capito's writings on proverbs[18] and the work of an unidentified writer who collected geographical lore from republican poetry.[19] This group can be expanded to include Verrius' use of the works of Artorius.[20] These groups of irregular quotations are clearly identifiable either from the names of scholars attached to them or from the singularity of their interests. Since their interests have been preserved with such fidelity as to still be recognizable, it seems reasonable to assume that their methods have also been preserved intact.

---

[18] For metrically incomplete or otherwise deficient quotations given in connection with proverbs, see Festus p. 174.34, 406.30, 512.15 (apogr.). Rychlewska (1948–1949:194) identified this group of exceptions with some assistance from Sinnius' more general lexicographical material (at Festus p. 458.11) but did not explore that material as a source of irregular quotations; relevant passages occur at Festus p. 158.27 and 482.7. It is clear that Sinnius quoted units of sense without regard for meter.

[19] The passages identified by Rychlewska (1948–1949:196) seem secure; the only possible addition I have noted is p. 494.7 (apogr.), but see also below, n. 39.

[20] Festus p. 482.7 (Accius 387), 500.28 (apogr.) (Afranius 281 only).

Other incomplete quotations can be attributed to Verrius' use of lexicographical works whose authors are not identified by name and whose specific interests cannot now be traced or isolated. Although it would be easy to attribute irregular quotations to Verrius' use of such sources, there is a danger of concealing real difficulties under vague appeals to that solution. Such attributions therefore must not be made or accepted lightly, but sometimes Verrius' reliance on a lexicographical source seems undeniable. At Festus p. 166.11, for example, the entry *naucum* is illustrated with five quotations. Three are metrically incomplete, intelligible utterances; the other two, although metrically complete, also present complete units of sense. Six competing definitions of *naucum* are combined in that entry, and in view of the cluster of metrically incomplete quotations and the diversity of lexicographical sources named, the conclusion that Verrius took at least some of this material from earlier sources seems inescapable. Similar conclusions seem to be required for the mangled entry *oculissimum* (p. 188.3), which is convicted as at least partly alien to Verrius' methods by the two metrically incomplete quotations from Plautus' *Curculio*; suggestive, rather than probative, are the unusual arrangement of quotations that violates Verrius' habit of quoting the scripts of Plautus in alphabetical order[21] and the use of *alibi*, which in its rare appearances in this lexicon introduces incomplete quotations as often as not.[22] These peculiarities suggest some ways of identifying similar entries that contain tralatitious material.[23]

Some incomplete quotations can plausibly be attributed to earlier scholarly sources because they derive from poetic works that seem

---

[21] That is, if *oculatum Ar⟨gum⟩* is rightly thought to refer to Plautus *Aul.* 555 *quos si Argus seruet, qui oculeus totus fuit.* It is possible that that information came from a marginal note in Verrius' copy of *Pseud.* (and see below for another instance of an annotation in the copy of *Pseud.*) or a commentary, which would restore much order to the entry, but since other irregularities are present in the entry the question must be left open; see Jocelyn 1991:579.

[22] With this passage see Festus p. 308.22 and the apparently originally complete (but now damaged) quotations introduced at p. 354.12 and 362.19. If the restoration of *alibi* before a short snippet of Ennius in the entry at p. 186.31 is incorrect it is hard to see what else could fit the available space.

[23] Cf. Festus p. 192.1, 444.23, and perhaps 490.22. From the apographs note p. 208.29 with 214.13 (*obstinato* and *obstinet*; by itself the latter does not provide enough evidence, but the conjunction of the two is significant) and 500.9. See, further, Appendix 2.

not to have been known to Verrius at first hand. The two quotations of Turpilius' *Demetrius* (Festus p. 158.27 and 478.12) provide a clearcut example of the pattern. That dramatist is never otherwise quoted in Festus. The first quotation is given together with Sinnius Capito's doctrine about the meaning of *nec*, while the second seems, although mangled in **F**, to be given with an incomplete quotation of Ennius. From that clustering of irregularities it seems certain that Verrius did not excerpt a copy of Turpilius' *Demetrius*. Two other scripts present comparable situations. Festus' two quotations of Afranius' *Emancipatus* are metrically incomplete. The first quotation, at Festus p. 196.9, is given with a paraphrase of Terence *Hec.* 9–10 that has been cast as an approximation of an iambic senarius; since neither paraphrase nor metrically incomplete quotation belongs to Verrius' normal methods there is reason to think that neither quotation came to Verrius directly from a complete script.[24] The second quotation occurs in an entry (*remeare*, Festus p. 344.11) that shows signs of lexicographical origins that have since been muddled, inasmuch as Afranius' words are introduced as an illustration of *commeatus* even though the fragment does not contain that word.[25] It is therefore probable that Verrius did not know the *Emancipatus* at first hand. Similarly, Festus (p. 352.1 and 416.31) preserves two metrically incomplete quotations of Caecilius' *Carine*. The fourteen intact quotations of Caecilius' other scripts in **F** (and three in the apographs) are metrically complete. Although neither entry contains clear signs of lexicographical origins, the irregularity of these quotations, taken alongside Turpilius' *Demetrius* and Afranius' *Emancipatus*, suggests that the *Carine*, too, was not known to Verrius at first hand.[26]

---

[24] In Afranius 92 Ribbeck (1898:208) restored *sic est orator, si quid oretur, tulit* from **F**'s *sic est orator, si quod oritur tale* (Ribbeck's *quid* was prompted by the text of Müller 1880, which gives *si qui oritur*; however Thewrewk de Ponor's [1893] photographs clearly show *quod*). Although the conjectures make good sense the present suggestion about the origin of this quotation and the clear paraphrase of Terence *Hec.* 9–10 require that the fragment be obelized.

[25] Festus p. 344.11 REMEARE, *redire: ut commeare, ultro citro ire. unde commeatus dari dicitur, id est tempus, quo ire, redire qui possit;* ut *Afranius* etc.

[26] For comparable arguments about irregular quotations taken from a small group of dramatic scripts in Nonius' sources 26, 27, and 28, see Welsh 2012:842.

We can occasionally see Verrius transcribing marginal annotations from his texts or, by a similar process, from notes in a commentary.[27] As is to be expected, the quotations found in those annotations need not conform to his own methods.[28] At Festus p. 182.12, for example, the partial quotation of Plautus *Pseud.* 592 probably came from a note on *Pseud.* 964, which Verrius quotes in its entirety. The relative arrangement of the quotations, with *Pseud.* 592 following *Pseud.* 964, is abnormal, since Verrius' sequential quotations from an author or script regularly mirror their order in the complete text; it suggests that *Pseud.* 592 was not, in this form, excerpted by Verrius himself.

I.3. Quotations Abbreviated by (?)Festus

The preceding section examined metrically incomplete quotations that Verrius probably took over from earlier scholarly sources, to which he could not apply his usual method of excerption. In other cases it seems likely that complete verses excerpted by Verrius have been shortened in Festus' epitome. Abbreviation of Verrius' quotations seems to have been a rare practice of limited scope, and it should not be invoked to justify any metrically incomplete quotation, for the secure instances of it are few in number and occur in highly restricted circumstances. I examine three patterns here: "inserted" quotations; quotations shortened in connection with a refutation of Verrius' claims; and quotations belonging to what I shall call the "*ruri* type," after a quotation of Terence *Phorm.* 363–364.

In his analysis of the methods of composition evident in Nonius Marcellus' *De compendiosa doctrina*, Lindsay suggested that some irregularities in that text were to be attributed to what he called "inserted quotations." These quotations occur in an order contrary to Nonius' usual methods; they may also seem suspicious because of peculiarities of phrasing or content. Lindsay suggested that, at least when the

---

[27] See Jocelyn 1991:571, 579, with further references.

[28] However, Rychlewska's (1948–1949:194–195) argument that the quotations of Ennius at Festus p. 364.1 were taken from marginal annotations in Verrius' copy of Cato cannot, I think, be accepted. An alternative explanation is advanced in the next sub-section.

suspicious quotation occurs elsewhere in Nonius' work, the irregularity could be attributed to later readers, who copied material found elsewhere in the dictionary at points where Nonius never intended it to stand.[29] This model, in which readers expanded a lexicographical text while not being bound by either its methods or its design, suggests a way of understanding a group of irregular quotations in Festus. For sometimes a citation that violates Verrius' methods of quoting complete verses also occurs elsewhere, and in fuller form, in the text of Festus. I make no claim about the origin of these "inserted quotations," and would suggest only that the individual responsible for them did not feel bound to retain Verrius' original methods.[30]

Examples of possible "inserted quotations" occur a few times in the extant text of Festus, although to demonstrate the pattern it will be necessary to admit evidence from the apographs. A clear, if perhaps uncertain, example occurs in the two entries illustrating *pedum*:

p. 230.30 (apogr.):

PEDVM baculi genus incuruum, ut Virgilius in Bucolicis cum ait (5.88):

at tu sume pedum, quod me cum saepe rogaret

p. 292.7:

PEDVM est quidem baculum incuruum, quo pastores utuntur ad conprehendendas oues, aut capras, a pedibus. Cuius meminit etiam Vergilius in Bucolicis, cum ait:

at tu sume pedum.

The apparent existence of the fuller version of the quotation provides a way to explain the shorter, metrically incomplete quotation occurring

---

[29] See Lindsay 1901:6–7; for specific examples, see the notes to Lindsay's lists of lemmata (e.g. 1901:11no).

[30] Festus is the obvious candidate, for he was happy to correct and improve Verrius' dictionary even as he tried to reduce its scale. It would perhaps be easiest to think, as we do in the case of Nonius, of a text augmented by later, post-Festan readers, but the paucity of such quotations and the absence of securely identifiable but unadvertised interpolations do not support this argument. In view of the apparently unfinished state of Verrius' work (see Reitzenstein 1887:80), it would be more daring to suggest that Verrius himself, in the process of revision, added new entries from other parts of the dictionary, but did not feel compelled to maintain the methods he had himself employed earlier.

in the second entry. However, since this quotation presents a number of further difficulties, it is perhaps best to take it as a possible, but not certain, demonstration of this feature.[31]

Rather more extensive is the evidence from entries reporting Verrius' doctrine about nominal gender. The crucial entry containing short snippets of verse occurs at Festus p. 364.1:

> "RECTO FRONTE ceteros sequi si norit." Cato in dissertatione consulatus. Antiquae id consuetudinis fuit, ut cum ait Ennius quoque (*Ann.* 166) "a stirpe supremo" et (*Ann.* 60) "Ilia dia nepos" et (*Ann.* 65) "lupus feta" et (*trag.* 387) "nulla metus." Etiam in commentariis sacrorum pontificalium frequenter est hic ouis, et haec agnus, ac porcus. Quae non ut uitia, sed ut antiquam consuetudinem testantia, debemus accipere.

Vahlen (1903:lxvii) claimed that Verrius, in the four short Ennian quotations, had abandoned his usual practices in favor of giving complete sense without regard for meter. Rychlewska (1948–1949:194–195) suggested that the Ennian phrases descended from marginal notes on the text of Cato. Although neither explanation is impossible, they are uneconomical. The pattern of inserted quotations, in which the original instance of the quotation is complete and any "inserted" occurrence may, contrary to Verrius' usual methods, be given in incomplete form, seems to account for this entry more precisely. Material occurring elsewhere in Festus and Paulus demonstrates or at least suggests that fuller quotations of these verses were to be found elsewhere in the lexicon:

Festus p. 412.13:

> *nomine Pyrrh⟨us, uti memorant⟩ a stirpe supremo*[32]

Paulus p. 65.20:

> ⟨DIVM, quod sub caelo est extra tectum, ab Ioue dicebatur, et Dialis flamen, et dius heroum aliquis a Ioue genus ducens.⟩

---

[31] See Appendix 1 for discussion of the Vergilian quotations.

[32] The letters lost due to damage in **F** may be restored from the version of Ennius *Ann.* 166 given at Nonius p. 226.29; the meter and spacing of what survives in **F** guarantees that the complete verse was quoted here.

Paulus p. 6.7:

(AGNVS ex Graeco ἀμνός deducitur, quod nomen apud maiores communis erat generis, sicut et lupus, quod uenit ex Graeco λύκος.)

Paulus p. 110.16:

uiuam an moriar, <u>*nulla*</u> *in me est* <u>*metus*</u>[33]

The evidence is clearest in the case of *stirps* and *metus*, for which more complete versions of the Ennian quotations survive elsewhere in the lexicon. About *dia nepos* and *lupus feta* there is a little more room for doubt.[34] Other entries discussing nominal gender show a similar tendency of alluding to other examples.[35] It seems easiest, therefore, to think that someone inserted the short snippets from elsewhere in the lexicon into the entry at p. 364.1 but did not feel compelled to retain the complete quotations.[36]

The second pattern is the abbreviation of quotations in connection with a refutation of Verrius. Festus described his own procedure in epitomizing Verrius' lexicon as omitting material that seemed to him to be of no contemporary value or to rely on no good *auctoritas*; we do not know whether he ever fulfilled his promise to collect, in a separate work entitled *Priscorum uerborum cum exemplis libri*, the material on which he disagreed with Verrius.[37] In any case the extant text of Festus' epitome presents many instances in which Verrius' opinions are

---

[33] This fragment is metrically incomplete, lacking at least three metrical elements at its head (if originally an iambic senarius). For Paulus' practice of abbreviating quotations by omitting "extraneous" material at their head, see Strzelecki 1932:19–20.

[34] For the relevance of Paulus' *dius heroum aliquis a Ioue genus ducens* to Ennius, see Skutsch 1985:210–211. The indication that *lupus* was also a common-gender noun suggests the possibility that *Ann.* 65 was quoted in that entry.

[35] Paulus p. 53.1; Festus p. 136.11 (apogr.), 446.9, 462.16.

[36] A further example is the quotation of Ennius *Ann.* 128–129 that occurs at Festus p. 124.19 ("inserted," and partial) and 312.7 (complete); but the apographs' text of the first entry is so problematic that it seems futile to transcribe the texts here.

[37] See Festus p. 242.30–244.1: ... *cum propositum habeam ex tanto librorum eius numero intermortua iam et sepulta uerba atque ipso saepe confitente nullius usus aut auctoritatis praeterire, et reliqua quam breuissime redigere in libros admodum paucos. Ea autem, de quibus dissentio, et aperte et breuiter, ut sciero, scribta in [h]is libris meis inuenientur, ⟨qui⟩ inscribuntur* "*Priscorum uerborum cum exemplis.*"

corrected or called into question.[38] When Festus disagrees with Verrius and reports the latter's opinion with its illustrative quotation, he sometimes seems to have shortened the quotation.[39] Where no quotation now survives, it is of course impossible to know whether Festus has omitted an original example.

This pattern can best be demonstrated by bringing together evidence from both **F** itself and the apographs. At least four examples can still be identified:

(1) Festus (apogr.) p. 218.12: OSCOS quos dicimus, ait Verrius, Opscos antea dictos, teste Ennio, cum dicat (*Ann.* 291):

⟨ – ◡◡ – ◡◡ – ⟩ *de muris rem gerit Opscus.*

Adicit etiam, quod stupra inconcessae libidinis obscena dicantur, ab eius gentis consuetudine inducta. Quod uerum esse non satis adducor, cum apud antiquos omnis fere obscena dicta sint, quae mali ominis habebantur, ut illa Virgilii testimonio sunt, ut superiorum auctorum exempla referre non sit necesse, cum ait Harpyias (~ *Aen.* 3.241) "obscenas uolucres"[40] et (*Aen.* 3.367) "obscenamque famem."[41]

---

[38] Sometimes Festus' exasperation with his predecessor is palpable even when he does not entirely disagree with Verrius' argument; see, e.g., p. 222.6, 228.10, 436.31, 460.13, 460.24.

[39] Skutsch (1985:35) suggested that Festus, in reporting Verrius' views, had shortened quotations of *Ann.* 291 and *Ann.* 220. In the first instance, Festus disagrees with Verrius, and I adopt this explanation below. In the second, Festus seems not to dissent; there Skutsch's explanation raises more problems than it solves. Therefore I would restrict this permissible exception to the instances where Festus expressly disagrees with his predecessor. The citation of *Ann.* 220 will have to be explained in another way; for possibilities, see n. 19 and Appendix 3.

[40] My punctuation differs from Lindsay's, since making *Harpyias* part of the quotation of *Aen.* 3.241 from *Harpyiae* (3.226) is difficult; Festus seems rather to be describing its context. The same usage occurs at Festus p. 378.3 (my punctuation) *idem in Neruolaria uinum ait "sublestissimum."* There some material may have been omitted between *uinum* and *sublestissimum,* or *uinum* may not be the authentic form that occurred in the script.

[41] On quotations of Vergil, see Appendix 1. For Verrius' view about *Obscus,* see Festus p. 204.24.

(2) Festus p. 292.7: PEDVM ... Sed in eo uersu, qui est in
Iphigenia Enni (*trag.* 181–182 = 193–194 Jocelyn)

> *procede gradum proferre pedum*
> *nitere cessas* ⟨. . .⟩

id ipsum baculum significari cum ait Verrius, mirari satis
non possum, cum sit ordo talis, et per eum significatio
aperta: gradum proferre pedum cessas nitere.[42]

(3) Festus p. 378.21: SCVRRAE uocabulum Verrius ineptis-
sime aut ex Graeco tractum ait, quod est σκυρθάζειν, aut a
sequendo, cui magis adsentitur; quod et tenuioris fortunae
homines, et ceteri alioqui, qui honoris gratia prose-
querentur quempiam, non antecedere, sed sequi sint soliti;
quia uidelicet dicat Lucilius (1138–1142):

> ⟨– ◡◡ – ◡◡ –⟩ *Cornelius Publius noster*
> *Scipiadas* †dicto tempus quae intorquet in ipsum
> oti et delici⟨i⟩s luci effictae† *atque cinaedo, et*
> *sectatori adeo ipse suo, quo rectius dicas,*
> *ibat forte domum: sequimur multi atque frequentes.*[43]

cum secutos uideri uelit, ob eorum iurgia, non ob
adsuetum officium.

(4) Festus (apogr.) p. 500.28: TENTIPELLIVM Artorius putat
esse calciamentum ferratum, quo pelles extenduntur ...
Titinium autem Verrius existimare id medicamentum esse,
quo rugae extendantur, cum dicat (173–174):

> ⟨× – × – × – ×⟩ *tentipellium*
> *inducitur, rugae in ore extenduntur* ⟨◡ –⟩

---

[42] Presenting a slight variation on Verrius' opinion, Schol. Veron., Verg. *Ecl.* 5.88, omits *procede* at the head of the quotation but preserves *o fide* where Festus' quotation breaks off. Jocelyn scanned the integrated fragment as an anapaestic dimeter and a paroemiac. Verrius' methods would have been maintained if he originally quoted all eight words of the fragment, which Festus and the scholiast shortened in two different fashions. On the significance of the description of this quotation as a *uersus*, see below, Section II.5.

[43] The corruption in the interior of this fragment (I give Lindsay's text) does not affect the immediate argument, for the metrical setting of *Cornelius Publius noster* | *Scipiadas* seems secure. Rychlewska (1948–1949:197) thought that here Festus quoted by sense, and not by meter.

cum ille τροπικῶς dixerit.[44]

In each instance Verrius' opinion is reported together with a metrically incomplete quotation that supported or prompted it, followed by Festus' correction or modification of Verrius' views. The phenomena are not likely to be unrelated. Festus seems to have stripped Verrius' quotation of extraneous material, converting a quotation given in complete metrical units to a quotation where completeness of sense was the principal concern.[45]

The logic of the third type of quotation apparently abbreviated by Festus (the "*ruri* type") is more difficult to describe. At p. 356.35 Festus presents a quotation from Terence's *Phormio* to illustrate that one correctly says *ruri*, and not *rure*. Comparison of this entry,

> RVRI esse, non rure dicendum, testis est Terentius in Phormione, cum ait: *ruri se continebat, ibi agrum de nostro patre,*

with the corresponding passage in the script of the *Phormio* (363–365) reveals a neglected pattern of quotation in Festus' epitome (words quoted by Festus are underlined):

> pauper, quoi opera uita erat, <u>ruri</u> fere
> <u>se continebat; ibi agrum de nostro patre</u>
> 365 colendum habebat. saepe interea mihi senex ...

Two significant points emerge from this example. First, Verrius' normal method of quoting a complete metrical unit without regard for completeness of sense has been observed in the full quotation of *Phorm.* 364 without its continuation in *Phorm.* 365, where *colendum habebat* completes the sense and syntax of *agrum*. Second, only the immediately relevant word *ruri* has been quoted from *Phorm.* 363; whether Verrius himself gave the quotation in this form or, more plausibly, Festus

---

[44] Jocelyn (1991:577) points to the use of Greek adverbs as one of Festus' affectations, adding to this example the use of ἀπιθάνως (p. 460.13) and περιφραστικῶς (p. 460.24).

[45] Another example of this pattern is discussed in Section II.13 below. For more abundant evidence illustrating the process of converting quotations from one method to the other in Macrobius, see Jocelyn 1964:289–290.

stripped the citation of the extraneous words in *Phorm.* 363 cannot now be known with certainty. This pattern sheds light on some quotations that violate the known methods of Verrius and have otherwise defied explanation. In the quotation of the *Phormio* and in the two examples presented here a relevant word or phrase is preserved together with at least one adjacent and complete metrical unit. Therefore secure instances of the pattern can necessarily only be identified when the relevant word or phrase comes at the beginning or end of the quotation.

At p. 344.15, Festus preserves a quotation of Afranius' *Proditus* to illustrate the word *remeligo*. Ribbeck set the fragment as an acephalous trochaic septenarius (Afranius 277):

⟨ - ⟩ Rĕmĕḷigo a Lărĭbŭs ṃissă ṣum hunc quae çursum
çŏhĭb⟨ĕạm⟩.[46]

This fragment is similar to the quotation of Terence *Phorm.* 363–364. For it may be imagined that, if the script of the *Phormio* had not survived intact, editors would have set that quotation, too, as an acephalous trochaic septenarius: ⟨ - ⟩ *ruri se continebat; ibi agrum de nostro patre*. In each instance, the target-word leads a quotation that seems metrically incomplete, but more significantly each target-word stands in front of what may be scanned as a complete verse. For just as *Phorm.* 364 is properly a complete iambic senarius, so too may Afranius' words be set instead as iambic senarii:

... Rĕmĕligo ...
a Lărĭbŭs ṃissă ṣum †hanc† quae çursum çŏhĭb⟨ĕạm⟩.[47]

I leave *Remeligo* metrically untethered, since it could be set at several positions in a senarius. This arrangement of the text can be justified by comparison with Festus' quotation of the *Phormio*, even if it suggests

---

[46] hunc *Ribbeck* : hanc *F* : huc *Stephanus. hunc* is first printed at Ribbeck 1855:169. In **F** the text after *cohib-* has been lost; Stephanus (1564:56) first suggested *cohibeam*.

[47] Havet (1914:12–14) suggested a similar text but presumed that the gap after *Remeligo* was caused when a line of text was lost in the manuscript tradition. Phillimore's (1915:188–189) attempts to fill Havet's lacuna only confuse matters, although *ego* is not implausible.

a slight deviation from Verrius' normal methods. Further support for this setting comes from the fact that it produces the iambic senarii that have long been sought for this quotation. C. O. Müller observed that Remeligo, "Delay" herself, most probably spoke these words, and it has long been noted that such a speech ought to come from a prologue in senarii. Despite the fact that the end of the quotation has been damaged in **F**, this solution seems more reasonable than do the attempts to extend the fragment to produce an iambic octonarius.[48]

A comparable example seems to occur where the metrically isolated word reinforces the entry's definition but is not itself the target-word. At p. 124.2, the apographs preserve a quotation from Afranius' *Virgo* to illustrate the use of *molucrum* to indicate a *tumor uentris, qui etiam uirginibus* ⟨*incidere*⟩ *solet*. Ribbeck set the Afranian fragment as iambic senarii, the first of which is incomplete (Afranius 336–338):

⟨ × – × – × – × ⟩ ferme u̯irgĭṇi
iam c̨rescĭṭ ŭtĕrus ṭam quam grăŭĭdae mŭlĭĕṛi. ::
mŏlŭc̨rum uŏc̨atur, ṭransit ṣĭnĕ dŏḷorĭḅus.

That text is not impossible, although it does present an aberration from the usual method of quoting complete metrical units. *ferme* is difficult to explain, which raises the possibility that some words have been omitted; since Afranius' *uirgini* supports Festus' definition of *molucrum*, it is perhaps better to be agnostic about the metrical position of these two words in the senarius, since one could, in keeping with the pattern here observed, also restore that text as:

⟨ × – × ⟩ ferme u̯irgĭṇi ⟨ × – ◡ – ⟩
iam c̨rescĭṭ ŭtĕrus ṭam quam grăŭĭdae mŭlĭĕṛi. ::
mŏlŭc̨rum uŏc̨atur, ṭransit ṣĭnĕ dŏḷorĭḅus.

---

[48] For the desired senarii, see Müller 1880:276–277; more explicitly, Fabia 1894:141–142; Beare 1940:47; and Daviault 1981:212. For attempts to produce an octonarius, see Bothe 1824:185; Neukirch 1833:243; and Roeper 1854:273. Proponents of the latter view have never adequately explained how Remeligo, as a comic personage, could recite a trochaic septenarius or iambic octonarius within the established conventions of the second-century stage.

Just as *Remeligo* in the fragment of Afranius' *Proditus* may be set in a number of positions in its verse, so too here should it be left open where *ferme uirgini* belongs in its verse.[49]

The rationale for this pattern of quotation is difficult to explain, although it is guaranteed by the example from Terence's *Phormio*. In view of the doubts that even Strzelecki (1932:82n1) had about Verrius' first-hand excerptions of Terence, it remains possible that these quotations were taken by Verrius from a secondary source that employed methods that were related, but not identical, to his own.[50] But since this pattern is as precisely delimited as the other two discussed in this section, it is possible that Festus occasionally omitted some superfluous material from a long quotation, preserving at least one complete verse together with the target-word or with material relevant for the definition. The justification of this pattern must remain an open question.

It will be obvious from these examples, from two further examples conjecturally restored in Sections II.10 and II.11 below, and from the fact that Rychlewska did not describe this pattern that it seems only to be found in quotations of scenic verse. Its absence from the citations of hexameter poetry requires some explanation, although that absence seems legitimate. There are few examples of each type of exception, and it is of course possible that **F** simply does not preserve examples of this pattern in hexameter verse that were to be found elsewhere in Festus. But given that scenic verse is quoted about twice as often as hexameter poetry in **F**, and given that the intact quotations of scenic verse are three times more likely to run for longer than one verse than are the quotations of hexameter poetry,[51] Festus simply would have been presented with fewer instances where shortening a hexameter quotation was either necessary or desirable.

[49] One could also set the text so that the first syllable of *ferme* occupies a B position, presuming elision of the final syllable of *uirgini*. The apographs could also have omitted some portion of illegible text; the position of *ferme uirgini* would be similarly uncertain.

[50] Similarities emerge in the style of quoting by meter rather than sense (noting *ibi agrum de nostro patre* and the superfluous *transit sine doloribus* in the quotation from Afranius' *Virgo*).

[51] **F** has 21 undamaged quotations of scenic verse that are longer than one verse against 6 comparable hexameter citations.

I.4. Preliminary Conclusions

The method of metrical citation that has long been attributed to Verrius' own excerptions of republican poetry is abundantly in evidence in what remains of Festus' epitome. The metrically incomplete quotations are quite few in number; the exceptional patterns and sources discussed in this section each have contributed just a handful of anomalies. Nevertheless these patterns lend invaluable support to the description of the methods of Verrius and Festus. The exceptions described account for 23 of the 39 incomplete quotations of scenic verse, and 7 of the 15 of hexameter poetry. Additional incomplete quotations will be explained or corrected in the next section of this paper, further reducing the number of irregular citations.

The implications for the textual criticism of fragments preserved by Festus are clear. An editor of these fragments must normally presume that any particular quotation was set down by Verrius, and was preserved by Festus, as a complete metrical unit. When an exception can be justified by appealing to one of the patterns established above, there are grounds to set a fragment such that it is metrically incomplete. When no exception can be justified, however, it is unmethodical to set a fragment as an incomplete verse, and an alternative scansion or a conjecture must be adopted or at least desiderated.

II. CONJECTURES, CORRECTIONS, AND REVERSIONS

In this section I examine fifteen fragments (twelve of scenic verse and one of hexameters from **F**, with two further quotations from the apographs) that appear to come from Verrius' own excerptions of poetry, but offend against his usual methods. My aim is to offer new conjectures or settings to restore metrically complete verses, in keeping with the principle just articulated, or to demonstrate how an irregular quotation may be corrected or justified from the patterns discussed in the preceding section. In a few instances my suggestions are necessarily tentative, owing to the state of our evidence, and are offered to call attention to some neglected problems in the fragments of early Latin verse.

II.1. Ennius *trag.* 2–3 (= 3–4 Jocelyn)

This fragment, taken from Ennius' *Achilles*, must be patched up from the versions of it preserved in Festus (p. 394.33) and Gellius (*NA* 4.17.13–15).[52] It was printed by Ribbeck, Vahlen, Jocelyn, and Manuwald[53] as trochaic septenarii:

⟨ - × - × - ⟩ pĕṛ ĕgŏ dĕụm subḷimas ṣubĭçes
ụmĭḍas, unḍe ŏrĭtūṛ imber ṣŏnĭtu ṣaeuo et ṣpirĭṭu.

sublimas] *om. F* sonitu saeuo et *Gell.* : sonitus aeuo *F* spiritu *F* : strepitu *Gell.*

Bothe had set the text instead as two complete iambic senarii divided after *umidas*.[54] The competing scansions arise from different metrical treatments of *subices* as either *sūb(i)ĭces* or *sŭbĭces*;[55] the modern preference for the former, and the septenarii it requires, descends from Lachmann's tart remarks about what Gellius has to say about the fragment.[56] Whether Lachmann was correct remains to be determined.

Festus' definition (*SVBICES Ennius in Achille pro subiectis posuit cum dixit nubes*) treats *subices* as an alternative for *subiecti*. Nothing in Festus' entry suggests that Verrius' traditional method of metrical citation was in this instance abandoned or that Festus abbreviated the quotation he found in Verrius. The incomplete trochaic septenarii that Lachmann demanded therefore seem suspect. Without justification for such an exceptional manner of quotation in the text of Festus, the editor's preference should be for setting this fragment as complete iambic senarii.

---

[52] Nonius (p. 169.1) transcribed a partial version of the quotation from Gellius; see Lindsay 1901:55, Strzelecki 1959. In that process he slightly muddled Gellius' interpretation. Since his evidence has no independent value and offers no better version of Gellius' text, it may be set aside in the present discussion.

[53] For discussion and doubts, see Vahlen 1903:lxx–lxxi, Jocelyn 1969:169, Manuwald 2012:35–37.

[54] Bothe 1823:30. Warmington (1935:224) returned to the same scansion.

[55] For *sŭbĭces*, cf. the references assembled by Jocelyn 1969:169n1.

[56] First at Lachmann 1850:152 *ad* Lucr. 3.227: "sed hac longiore littera [*scil.* "j," which Lachmann meant to be understood as the consonantal and vocalic "ii"] si usi essent editores [...] uersus Ennii hoc modo disposuissent, *per ego deum sublimas subjces | Umidas, unde oritur imber sonitu saeuo et spiritu*; quos illi turpi errore, quasi Gellii disputationem non legissent, fecerunt iambicos trimetros."

The question is therefore whether Gellius' testimony justifies thinking that Verrius' customary methods were here ignored. In *NA* 4.17 Gellius offers a general discussion of the natural and metrical quantity of verbal prefixes in words such as *obicere, subicere, conicere,* and the like. His argument is that such prefixes, containing naturally short vowels, ought so to be pronounced—despite a certain tendency in contemporary pronunciation (*'obiciebat' o littera producta multos legere audio*)—and are only rendered heavy by position in a form like *confecit*. Inference from the etymology of a form like *obicere* (⟩ *ob* + *iacere*) permits Gellius to explain *obiciebat* in Lucilius 394, *conicere* in Lucilius 411, *subicit* in Lucilius 509, and *conice* in Plautus *Epid.* 194 as scanning with their initial syllables rendered heavy by position.[57] From this material Gellius turns to *obicibus* (Verg. *G.* 2.480), which, he suggests, ought to be pronounced with a short *o*, but be treated as metrically heavy (i.e. *ob(i)ices*), as the careful speaker Sulpicius Apollinaris was observed to do.

The quotation of Ennius' *Achilles* follows this pronouncement about *obices*. The discussion of Ennius' *subices*, however, is qualitatively different from the material that precedes it (*NA* 4.17.13–15):

> Congruens igitur est, ut 'subices' etiam, quod proinde ut 'obices' compositum est, 'u' littera breui dici oporteat. Ennius in tragoedia, quae *Achilles* inscribitur, 'subices' pro aere alto ponit, qui caelo subiectus est, in his uersibus: 'per ego deum sublimas subices humidas, unde oritur imber sonitu saeuo et strepitu;'[58] plerosque omnes tamen legere audias 'u' littera producta. Id ipsum autem uerbum M. Cato sub alia praepositione dicit in oratione, quam *de consulatu suo* habuit: 'ita nos (ς : hos *VPR*)' inquit, 'fert uentus ad primorem Pyrenaeum, quo proicit in altum.' Et Pacuuius item in *Chryse*: 'Id⟨ae⟩ (*Vossius* : id *VPR*) promunturium, cuius lingua in altum proicit.'

---

[57] Cf. Servius, Verg. *Aen.* 4.549.

[58] I retain, as what Gellius probably wrote (albeit in error), the reading *strepitu* of **VPR** instead of accepting, from Festus, the *spiritu* that Ennius assuredly wrote.

It is therefore consistent that *subices*, too, which is formed
exactly like *obices*, should be pronounced with a short "u".
Ennius, in the tragedy entitled *Achilles*, uses *subices* for the
upper air, which is below the heavens, in these verses: "I
by the lofty, humid under-realms of the gods, where rain
arises with a savage shriek and sound." Nevertheless you
hear almost everyone read [the word] with the letter *u*
long. But Cato uses that same word with another prepo-
sition, in the speech he gave *On his own consulship*: he said
"Thus the wind brings us to the foothills of the Pyrenees,
where the range extends into the sea." And likewise
Pacuvius in the *Chryses*: "The promontory of Ida, whose
tongue extends into the sea."

From Sulpicius' pronunciation Gellius makes an inference (*congruens
igitur est*) about the text of Ennius, in whose *subices*, Gellius observes,
the *u* in *sub-* is naturally short and ought so to be pronounced. The
metrical treatment of the word is at best ancillary, if not even irrelevant, to Gellius' concern for correct pronunciation, which, as the
discussion of *obices* showed, has nothing to do with metrical quantity. There is, furthermore, nothing to indicate that Gellius has seen
or heard comparable evidence enjoining the scansion *sūb(i)ĭces*. The
only piece of evidence that points even slightly in that direction is the
comment about the pronunciation of the word with a long *u*. If honest,
this comment is suggestive only of the pronunciation of Gellius'
contemporaries and has little evidentiary value for the metrical setting
of Ennius' words; for it should be asked whether that pronunciation
would have been derived simply from the treatment of *obices* in epic
verse, and not from Ennius' dramatic meters.

More damning evidence comes from Gellius' own introduction
to this fragment, which suggests that it came to him from a lexicographical text sharing some affinity with Festus, to judge from their
etymology of *subices* (Festus' *pro subiectis*, Gellius' *qui caelo subiectus
est*).[59] That introduction shows no more concern for the scansion of

---

[59] It would be reasonable to ask whether the source of that affinity is not in each
instance the text of Verrius itself, perhaps with an intermediary in the case of Gellius.

subices than does Festus himself. The quotations of Catonian prose and Pacuvian verse that follow demonstrate clearly that this material has nothing to do with the metrical disquisition with which *NA* 4.17 begins. Both quotations are made to illustrate the sense, rather than the quantities, of *proicit*.[60] There is thus no justification for thinking that Gellius took the Ennian quotation from a source commenting on the natural or metrical quantity of *subices*. He seems rather to have spliced a discussion of vowel quantities together with diverse materials from one or two lexicographical sources concerned with the meaning, and not the prosody, of *subices* and *proicit*.[61]

On that argument about the composition of *NA* 4.17, Gellius' discussion does not require that Ennius' *subices* be scanned as a cretic at the beginning of a trochaic septenarius. Rejecting Lachmann's claim does not exclude the trochaic scansion of this fragment; rather, it leaves open the question of whether it is to be set as trochaic septenarii or as iambic senarii. Verrius' customary methods therefore acquire renewed significance in this context, as the sole evidence for the meter of this quotation. With no indication of irregularity in those methods, the only rational editorial decision is to revert to the complete iambic senarii preferred by Bothe and Warmington:

> pĕṛ ĕgŏ dĕụm subḷimas ṣŭbĭceṣ umĭḏas
> unḍe ŏrĭtŭṛ imber ṣŏnĭtu ṣaeuo et ṣpirĭṭu.

II.2. Com. inc. 64

The illustration of four kinds of *metonymia* at Festus p. 138.13 gives two metrically complete quotations of Ennius' *Annales*, a short snippet of text taken apparently from colloquial patterns of speech, and an unattributed verse of an unnamed, and presumably comic, dramatist. The scenic fragment, adduced to demonstrate how *ab inferiore* (scil.

---

[60] Gellius discusses the variable quantity of *pro-* in *NA* 2.17.3–6 without reference to *proicere*.

[61] Structurally similar chapters, in which certain lexicographical materials are spliced to leading discussions by variously strong or weak connections, occur at Gellius *NA* 3.9, 9.1, 10.3, 13.11, 13.22, and 20.5. There the grafts are admittedly more obvious than in *NA* 4.17, but the basic pattern of composition seems to be the same.

re significatur) superior, was set by Ribbeck as an acephalous trochaic septenarius:

⟨ – ⟩ persuasiṭ ănĭmo ụinum, ḍeus qui ṃulto est ṃaxĭṃus.

Elsewhere certain obviously interrelated discussions of *metonymia* (which commonly define six varieties of the trope, against Festus' four) adduce a similar verse of Plautus to illustrate the use of *uinum* to mean the god Liber (*fr.* 159): *uinum precemur, nam hic deus praesens adest.*[62] The absence of Com. inc. 64 from other ancient discussions of the trope and the different schematization evident in them suggest that this entry was compiled from Verrius' own excerptions. Since the thought expressed in Com. inc. 64 is complete and well-paralleled elsewhere in comic verse, it seems unlikely that anything significant has been lost from the fragment.[63] That consideration must guide any restoration of this verse.

A small group of non-conforming quotations of Ennius' *Annales* in Festus similarly lack an initial monosyllable, but comparably deficient quotations are not to be found in citations either of other hexameter poetry or of scenic verse; the quotations of scenic verse that seem to fit this pattern can all be securely corrected or explained, and there is no reason to think that omission of a monosyllable at verse-head was ever a regular practice of either Festus or Verrius.[64] Emendation is therefore quite necessary.

Spengel (1834:710) observed, without reference to the methods of the lexicon, that by bracketing *animo* the text could be set as a complete iambic senarius. Although true, that solution is perhaps too invasive, since *animo* would be a bold interpolation. It is more plausible that a word has been lost in transmission. As in other metrically deficient

---

[62] See Diomedes *Gramm.* I 458.13; Donatus *Gramm.* IV 400.7; Servius, Verg. *Aen.* 1.724; Pompeius *Gramm.* V 307.1; Isidore *Etym.* 1.37.8–10. Our sources for this fragment are divided between the readings *precemur* and *precamur*.

[63] For the thought more generally, cf. Terence *Ad.* 470 *persuasit nox amor uinum adulescentia*; Donatus, Ter. *Ad.* 470.1–2 compares Plautus *Bacch.* 87–88 and rightly explains *persuasit* with the force of *impulit*, for which cf. Plautus *Aul.* 794–795 *ego me iniuriam fecisse filiae fateor tuae,* | *Cereris uigiliis per uinum atque impulsu adulescentiae.* More broadly, cf. Plautus *Aul.* 749–751, *Cist.* 158–159; Terence *Hec.* 822–823.

[64] See Appendix 2.

quotations of scenic verse, the lost element could be set at positions in the verse other than the first. I would therefore suggest restoring:

persuasit ănĭmo ⟨meo⟩ ụinum, ḍeus qui ṃulto est ṃaxĭṃus.

The omission of *meo* can perhaps most easily be attributed to haplography. In any case Ribbeck's (1873:122) ⟨*ita*⟩ *persuasit*, with *ita* having been omitted after the *ut* that introduces the quotation, still deserves mention.

II.3. Plautus *Bacch.* fr. iv (= fr. i De Melo)

Two sources provide contextual information that bears upon the setting and text of this fragment, which derives from the lacuna at the beginning of the *Bacchides*. The first of these sources is Festus' entry itself, which illustrates the word *nassiterna*, an open water vessel with handles, at p. 168.15:

> NASSITERNA est genus uasi aquari ansati et patentis, quale est quo equi perfundi solent. Plautus in Bacchidibus:
> > *ecquis euocat*
> > *cum nassiterna et cum aqua istum impurissimum?*
> et in Neruolaria[65] (*Stich.* 352):
> > *ecquis huc effert nassiternam cum aqua sine suffragio*
>
> ecquis[1] *Ursinus* : haec quis F

The quotation of *Stich.* 352 is given in a form characteristic of Verrius, in which a complete trochaic septenarius is quoted without regard for boundaries of sense; *sine suffragio* belongs to a different speaker and depends grammatically on what follows in *Stich.* 353. The apparent non-conformity of the fragment from the *Bacchides*, which editors set as iambic senarii (as above), is therefore suspicious.

Any restoration of this fragment must also find a suitable home for it within the fragmentary beginning of the *Bacchides*, the second source of contextual information relevant to this fragment. The lost scenes and the available evidence for them have often been discussed, taking

---

[65] Here and at p. 214.26 quotations of the *Stichus* are recorded against the title *Neruolaria*.

into account the metrical sequences with which Plautus typically begins a play, the content and meter of the extant fragments, the information about the plot that these scenes can reasonably be expected to have conveyed, and the order of speakers suggested by the alphabetic notation that survives in part in MS B.[66] I do not propose here to offer a new reconstruction of the beginning of the play. I take as correct the view that the play began with a scene involving the Athenian Bacchis and a member of her household staff before the arrival of Pistoclerus, who then delivers a delayed prologue; that his speech was followed by a canticum performed by Samian Bacchis, the soldier's slave, and Pistoclerus; and that a recitative scene between the two Bacchises and Pistoclerus followed thereupon, the latter part of which survives in the manuscripts (*Bacch.* 35–108).

Although such a reconstruction seems in outline to be essentially correct, at least two neglected problems remain to be explored. These are the possibility that *Bacchides* began with an "atypical" metrical sequence, and the question of whether our sources for the play's fragments give a reliable view of their original meter. Those two issues, taken together with Verrius' usual methods of citation, will suggest a slight modification to the traditional setting of fr. IV and to the accepted reconstruction of the beginning of the play.

Fourteen Plautine scripts begin with a metrical sequence of iambic senarii followed by a canticum and then a passage in recitative verse. That progression has long been taken as typical and used, with some circumspection, as a means to arrange the fragments of the *Bacchides* into something resembling their original order. Four further plays (*Cistellaria, Epidicus, Persa,* and *Stichus*) begin with songs and accordingly deviate from this structure:

> *Cist.* song (1–37), recitative (38–58 ia[7], 59–119 tr[7]), spoken (120–202 ia[6])
>
> *Epid.* song (1–98), recitative (99–165 tr[7], ia[8]), song (166–195), recitative (196–305 tr[7])

---

[66] See especially Law 1929; Bader 1970; Gaiser 1970:65–69; Barsby 1986:93–97; De Melo 2011:365–367.

Persa   song (1–52),[67] spoken (53–167 ia[6]), song (168–202), recitative (203–250 tr[7])

Stich.   song (1–47),[68] recitative (58–154 tr[7]), spoken (155–273 ia[6])

These four plays have not been taken into account sufficiently as possible alternative models on which to reconstruct the opening scenes of the *Bacchides*. The *Persa*, in particular, would provide a useful possible framework that would account for the scenes and meters that have long been reconstructed as the beginning of *Bacchides*, while *Cistellaria* provides a model for song or recitative verse before a delayed prologue.

I shall leave this issue momentarily in suspense in order to turn to the implicit view that our sources are a reliable guide to the meter of the extant fragments. Such an assumption is problematic. Of 20 fragments from the beginning of the *Bacchides* (excluding the fragment presently under discussion), only the bacchiac tetrameters in fr. XI are guaranteed by the methods of the source that quotes them.[69] In a few other cases we may be reasonably certain that our sources incidentally preserve complete metrical units.[70] The majority of these fragments, however, derive from sources that do not reliably quote complete metrical units and it should not be assumed that what scans as, for example, a partial iambic senarius was in fact written in that meter in the complete script.

---

[67] I take, with Questa 1995:282, *Persa* 43–52 to be the conclusion of the song and not a distinct passage of recited verse; note especially the position and pyrrhic scansion of *fuas* (*Persa* 51).

[68] The interpolated senarii at *Stich.* 48–57 are excluded from consideration.

[69] The last verse of that fragment is quoted by Nonius Marcellus p. 474.35 from list 26 ("Gloss. iii"), which source, together with its counterparts ("Alph. Verb" [27] and "Alph. Adverb" [28]), never quotes less than a complete metrical unit, and occasionally extends such a quotation to include an adjacent partial verse in order to produce complete units of sense; see Welsh 2012.

[70] Fr. I seems to be a trochaic octonarius, which admits of few other possible interpretations; fr. X is either from Nonius' "Plautus i" list and so is quoted strictly according to sense, or from the "Alph. Verb" list and so is quoted according to both sense and meter (see n. 69), but the suspicion that the fragment belongs to the reading (or reporting) from a contract makes its setting as iambic senarii secure. Cf. n. 13, above, on incidentally complete verses given by lexicographers who normally quote by sense.

The two fragments whose content permits assigning them to a house-cleaning scene must be considered afresh in view of this last point. Iulius Romanus, who is Charisius' source for fr. III, so regularly paraphrased a text, omitted words, and quoted incomplete verses both generally and from the *Bacchides* in particular, that his quotations cannot be taken to reveal with any reliability their meter in the complete script.[71] Verrius' methods could hardly be more different, but that fundamental point seems never to have been considered in connection with the problem of the beginning of *Bacchides*.

Fragment III, *conuerrite scopis, agite strenue*, cannot yield an iambic senarius without a supplement that also eliminates the exposed resolution in *conuerrite*. Editors have accordingly set a lacuna after that word. Iulius Romanus could have omitted the missing word that would produce a senarius without violating his methods. But those same methods mean that other possibilities cannot be excluded. It is no less possible that we have in this fragment the meager remains of a long iambic verse,[72] which is quite easy to justify, since it is widely believed that this fragment was originally a senarius and since it shows strong iambic rhythms. So too could this fragment have belonged to a lyric passage, with one or more words omitted between or around *conuerrite scopis*; in that connection it is noteworthy that *agite strenue* could scan as a cretic colon, although certainty about a lyric setting for *conuerrite scopis* is impossible. In any case, there is no justification either for thinking that the fragment could only have come from a scene in iambic senarii or for relying on that belief to reconstruct the beginning of *Bacchides*.[73] Other possibilities must be taken into account.

Fragment IV ought, on Verrius' usual methods, to consist of one or more metrically complete units. Once the fragment is no longer

---

[71] Iulius Romanus' imprecise quotations of the *Bacchides* are listed at Welsh 2010:275.

[72] Particularly illuminating is the quotation of *Bacch.* 186–187 at Charisius p. 275.7 Barwick.

[73] Nor can we appeal to dramatic convention to justify setting these fragments as senarii. Comparable house-cleaning scenes occur in a variety of meters. Cf. Plautus *Stich.* 347–355 (tr[7]); Titinius 36 (apparently ia[6], but also from a source whose methods do not guarantee metrical completeness), 130 (an[8], *ut uid.*). Related are Ballio's song at Plautus *Pseud.* 163–164 (tr[8]) and the verses given as Plautus *fr.* 146–147 (ia[8] with a verse that scans as an ia[6] but may be incomplete).

shackled to the belief that fragment III is an iambic senarius, a number of other scansions are available. First, the opening words *ecquis euocat* also scan without difficulty as a cretic colon, and although the meter of the remaining seven words would be obscure it remains just possible that both fragments III and IV derive from a lyric canticum. A second and more plausible solution is to set fragment IV as an iambic octonarius, as part of a *mutatis modis canticum* or as an iambic line in a lyric canticum:

ĕcquĭṣ euŏçat cum ṇassĭ̆terna et çŭm | ăqua isṭum impuṛissĭ̆ṃum.

The scansion of *ēcquĭs/ĕcquĭs* is a grand problem of Plautine prosody; I will not repeat the details here[74] but will note simply that the pyrrhic scansion given above obviates the need to set this fragment as two verses, thereby restoring Verrius' usual methods. Reconstruction of this scene ought to proceed along these lines; for Verrius' methods of quotation are so regular, and Iulius Romanus' so unpredictable, that it is quite unmethodical to allow Romanus' quotation to guide our views on the meter of Verrius'. The exact metrical nature of the house-cleaning scene must be left undetermined, since both lyric and long iambic meters are possible, although it is certain, from Verrius' methods, that the scene was not in senarii.

From the evidence of the sources' methodologies we may return to the argument about the metrical sequences of the beginnings of Plautine comedies, since a home for such a scene must also be found in the outline of the beginning of the *Bacchides*. The beginnings of *Persa* and of the other "irregular" scripts make it possible that the *Bacchides* also began with a canticum. The passage of long iambic verses at *Persa* 43–52 which concludes that play's opening song would provide another possible model against which to reconstruct the house-cleaning scene of *Bacchides*. Although the description of the scene must remain uncertain, it seems necessary to adopt a small but significant modification to the widely accepted reconstruction of *Bacchides*. The play's first scene will have contained a short song or recitative passage about cleaning the house; those instructions were not delivered in spoken senarii.

---

[74] For examples, references, and discussion, see Questa 2007:163–171.

It should be noted that such a modification reveals further sources of doubt about the traditional siftings and sortings of the fragments of this play. First, the remains of the other canticum in the lost scenes suggest that it, too, contained many cretic verses; if the house-cleaning scene contained cretic verses (admittedly the less plausible of the two possibilities suggested above), it is possible that some fragments of the other canticum have been assigned to the wrong scene.[75] Second, a few other fragments assigned to the Athenian Bacchis in the first scene have long been treated as the remains of iambic senarii. Greater skepticism is necessary. Nothing in the methodology of the sources that preserve them guarantees that either *sicut lacte lactis simile est* (fr. V) or *illa mea cognominis fuit* (fr. VI) were originally delivered as spoken iambic senarii. Other possibilities must be entertained. Doubts of course will remain about the precise nature of this scene and its delivery, but there are good reasons to think that the *Bacchides* was another play with an unusual opening song, in which this fragment, most likely an iambic octonarius, occurred.

II.4. Plautus *fr.* 68

At p. 174.17, Festus preserves some words attributed to Plautus' *Dyscolus*, which are quoted to illustrate the meaning of the phrase *nupta uerba*. That phrase, the reader is told, was used in republican Latin to indicate words *quae uirginem dicere non licebat*. The quotation was set by Lindsay and by other editors[76] as an acephalous trochaic septenarius:

⟨ – ⟩ uirgo sum, nondum dı̆dı̆ci nuptă ŭerbă dı̆cĕre.

Apart from the violation of Verrius' method of quotation, that text is unproblematic and the logic of its utterance (where a descriptor is corroborated or expanded in the second part of the verse) can be equipped with good parallels, most notably Plautus *Curc.* 57 *at illa est*

---

[75] Frag. XVII *quae sodalem atque me exercitos habet* (cr² crᶜ) could similarly belong to the proposed first canticum. If sung by Pistoclerus, as has long been thought, it would respond to Athenian Bacchis' mentioning her identical twin, rather than to that twin's appearance on stage.

[76] See Leo 1895–1896: vol. 2, 533; Monda 2004:70; and Aragosti 2009:150–152.

pudica neque dum cubitat cum uiris, Poen. 350 *pura sum, comperce amabo me attrectare, Agorastocles,* and *Rud.* 239 *socia sum nec minor pars meast quam tua.* The parallels argue against any serious alteration of the fragment and suggest that it has simply lost a metrical element in transmission. Fontaine (2005) has pointed out, on rhythmical grounds, that it would probably be preferable to set the lacuna as *uirgo ⟨ – ⟩ sum,* but the Plautine parallels make it desirable to leave *uirgo sum* together, and so one might instead consider setting the lacuna still later in the verse. I would therefore suggest restoring the septenarius, with a palaeographically simple conjecture, as:

ụirgo ṣum, ⟨si⟩ ṇondum ḍïdïci ṇuptă ụerbă ḍicĕṛe?

It is difficult to equip this conjecture with a legitimate Plautine parallel but the usage is similar to the substantive *si*-clauses common in republican Latin after *miror* and related words. The fragment would mean something like "Am I (to be considered?) a *uirgo,* if I haven't yet learned to speak *nupta uerba?*" A similar, and similarly contorted, utterance is provided by Afranius 123, *puella non sum, supparo si induta sum?* ("am I not a *puella,* since I am wearing a *supparum?*").[77]

II.5. Trag. inc. 211

At Festus (apogr.) p. 206.22, an unattributed quotation, set by Ribbeck as an acephalous trochaic septenarius from an unidentified tragedian, is introduced as a *uersus:*

OBORITVR, agnascitur; nam praepositionem ob, pro ad,
solitam poni, testis hic uersus:
⟨ – × ⟩ *tantum gaudium oboriri ex tumultu maximo.*

---

[77] This quotation cannot be treated as an example of the "*ruri* type," since dividing the text as *uirgo ⟨...⟩ | sum ...* produces an enjambment that is quite intolerable. I have perhaps let Afranius guide this conjecture too much; the anonymous reader has rightly offered up other plausible solutions, including ⟨*ego*⟩ *uirgo sum, nondum ...* and *uirgo sum,* ⟨*nam*⟩ *nondum ...*

The term *uersus* is significant, for elsewhere in the extant text of Festus the word is used to introduce a metrically complete verse.[78] Parallels for this strict usage of *uersus* are found in the technical writings of ancient grammarians, rhetoricians, metricians, and lexicographers,[79] although many less precise writers were not similarly scrupulous about their usage of the term.[80] The interpretation of *ob* as *ad* provides further support for the view that Verrius was responsible for this entry and, presumably, for excerpting this quotation.[81] Strikingly, however, the quotation violates Verrius' methods and contradicts the claim that it is a *uersus*.

Emendation is therefore necessary, but no secure guidance in this instance can come from the *sermo tragicus*, since the hypothesis that this fragment comes from a tragedy is not guaranteed. The solution nevertheless seems quite clear. Restoring a genitive in the place of the apographs' *gaudium* would give a complete iambic senarius, as:

> tanṭum gauḍi ŏbŏriṛi ex tŭmultu maxĭmo!

---

[78] Cf. Festus p. 160.23, 226.4, 306.8, 446.9, 514.15; the only instance where *uersus* is used to introduce an incomplete verse, at p. 292.7, seems to belong to the category of quotations shortened by Festus when refuting Verrius' opinion.

[79] See the diverse expressions at Caesius Bassus fr. 2 Mazzarino (= Rufinus, *Gramm.* VI 555.27) *est in Eunucho Terentii statim in prima pagina hic uersus trimetrus 'exclusit reuocat, redeam? non, si me obsecret'*; Probus fr. 20 Aistermann (= Serv. auct., Verg. *Aen.* 4.418) *si hunc uersum* (Commelinus : *uerbum* FG) *omitteret, melius fecisset*; Probus fr. 66 (= Gell. *NA* 13.21.4) *uerba e uersibus eius haec sunt*: (Verg. *G.* 1.25–26) "*urbisne inuisere Caesar* | *terrarumque uelis curam*"; Sen. *Controv.* 7.1.27 (contrast *illos optimos uersus*, introducing the two hexameters of Varro Atacinus fr. 10 Courtney, with *solebat Ouidius de his uersibus dicere potuisse fieri longe meliores si secundi uersus ultima pars abscideretur et sic desineret 'omnia noctis erant'*); Quint. *Inst.* 6.3.86; Donatus, Ter. *An.* 68; Priscian, *Gramm.* II 292.18–25 (*uersus* is not otherwise a part of Priscian's terminology for introducing quotations; note the logic underpinning his illustration of the *praesens imperfectum* at *Gramm.* II 414.21–24).

[80] Gellius does not invariably observe the strict sense of the word, although some of his sources do; contrast, e.g., *NA* 3.14.11, 4.16.6, 6.7.4, 6.17.9, 6.20.1, 10.11.6, 18.5.4, and 18.5.10 with the more precise appellations at 1.22.16, 2.29.20, etc. Thus his testimony tells us nothing about the metrical shape of Ennius *trag.* 2–3, above; the contrast between Gellius' studied *negligentia* and the precise terminology he quotes from Probus (see preceding note) is informative.

[81] For Verrius' somewhat obsessive remarks about *ob* in the sense of *ad*, see Festus p. 186.31, 218.21, 220.13; Festus doubts Verrius' opinion at p. 218.21.

Cf. Terence *An.* 963 *quid illud gaudist?* It is clear how the error occurred even though we cannot now identify when it entered the tradition. The origin of the verse must also remain uncertain; such a sentiment could as easily come from a comedy as from a tragedy.[82]

II.6. Pacuvius 208–209 (= fr. 153 Schierl)

Considerable effort has been expended on the last two words of the fragment of Pacuvius' *Iliona* preserved at Festus p. 238.4:

> făç, ut coepisti, hanç ŏpĕram mĭhĭ des perpĕṭem,
> ŏcŭlis traxĕrim

Although all the conjectures recorded by Schierl and Ribbeck aim to restore some sense and meter to *oculis traxerim*, none addresses the essential problem that *oculis traxerim* cannot be made to connect logically with the preceding verse. In the rare instances where Festus preserves an incomplete quotation of the type printed by editors here, the target-word is invariably found in the partial verse, since, it would seem, Festus was reducing to its essentials a long quotation given by Verrius.[83] This setting is accordingly suspect.

The method of quotation visible in the text of Festus would at first seem, therefore, to suggest that the text should be set as an iambic octonarius, in which *oculis traxerim* would have been preserved solely for the sake of meter. But an obstacle to such an arrangement immediately presents itself, since the forms of *perpes*, unlike those of its more common counterpart *perpetuus*, are confined to a few specific positions in iambo-trochaic verse. These positions are the end of such verses, the equivalent cretic sequences at the opening of the trochaic septenarius, and the mid-line break of long verses.[84] The same restriction applies generally to tenacious archaisms such as the passive infinitive

---

[82] For similar comic remarks, cf. Plautus *Poen.* 207–209 *quid istuc tumultist, Milphio? :: em amores tuos,* | *si uis spectare. :: o multa tibi di dent bona,* | *quom hoc mi optulisti tam lepidum spectaculum;* further, Plautus *Stich.* 295–296; Terence *Heaut.* 679–680, *Hec.* 816–817; Pomponius 141.

[83] See on the "*ruri* type" above, Section I.3.

[84] Cf. Plautus *Amph.* 280, 732; *Truc.* 278; Pacuvius 188. Lindsay's (1913:239) tentative conjecture *perpetem* ⟨ | ... *perpetem*⟩ *oculis traxerim* therefore cannot be accepted, since it

forms in -*ier*, and to other rare counterpart forms such as adverbs in -*iter* formed on first- and second-declension adjectives (e.g., *blanditer* against *blande*). These restrictions are strong throughout dramatic verse, being neglected only in cantica, and later loosened from the time of Pomponius.[85] There are therefore two possible solutions to this text. The first is to set it as an iambic octonarius deriving specifically from a canticum:

făç, ut coepisti, hanç ŏpĕram mĭhĭ des perpĕṭem, ŏcŭlis
       ṭraxĕṛim

In the context of a canticum no real difficulty would be posed by the setting of *perpetem* outside of its customary positions in iambotrochaic verse.[86] The other option is to set the verse again as an iambic octonarius, but to transpose *perpetem* to an earlier position in it, as:

făç, ut coepisti, hanç perpĕṭem ŏpĕram mĭhĭ des, ŏcŭlis
       ṭraxĕṛim

The first option is less invasive and is perhaps, therefore, to be preferred. I do not wish to exclude the second from consideration entirely, although transpositions are exceptionally rare in **F** and ought not to be adopted lightly.[87] Unless a justification for the exceptional manner of quotation can be produced, however, it is unmethodical to set this fragment as iambic senarii, and one or the other of these solutions ought to be adopted.

---

introduces a new difficulty by setting the second instance of *perpetem* at a position in the interior of a senarius.

[85] See further, Welsh 2013:259n26, 261n33.

[86] Cf. above, n. 67.

[87] Bergk 1884:323; Skutsch 1985:37. For a possible (no more than that) example of transposition in **F** compare the first three words of Plautus *Curc.* 110 at p. 312.14 (*anus haec sitit*) with the version in the direct tradition of Plautus (*sitit haec anus*); see also above, n. 14. In each instance Festus himself, rather than his scribes, may have transposed the words.

II.7. Titinius 131–132

At p. 334.4 a fragment of Titinius' *Setina* is adduced to illustrate the usage of *rediuia*, together with a complete scazon that is attributed by editors to Laevius (fr. 25 Courtney; †*Liui*† *F*). The setting of the fragment of Titinius is vexed. In his three editions of the fragments of republican drama Ribbeck set the text as two partial iambo-trochaic verses:

⟨ ... ⟩ lassitudo
conseruum, rediuiae flagri! ⟨ ... ⟩

In the second and third editions he recorded some suggestions to restore an incomplete trochaic septenarius (*lassitudo ⟨tu⟩ conseruum...*) or a complete iambic senarius (with Buecheler's *conseruum lassitudo*, but with no attention to the rarity of transpositions in **F**). Ribbeck's successors have adopted similarly diverse settings.[88] Verrius' working methods and the tradition represented by **F** suggest that none of these solutions are acceptable.

At some point before the appearance of his second edition Ribbeck entertained doubts about the iambo-trochaic scansion of this fragment, preferring at least temporarily to set it as a cretic tetrameter.[89] Neukirch (1833:134) was more confident about the correctness of that scansion.[90] This scansion is preferable from the point of view of Verrius' methods, inasmuch as it yields the metrically complete verse that the lexicographer normally cites.

Such a scansion is not without difficulty, although the problem is ultimately illusory. The second feet of Plautus' abundant cretic tetrameters are, almost without exception,[91] pure, whereas setting these four

---

[88] Guardì (1984) printed Ribbeck's text, scanning it as iambo-trochaics; López López (1983), dividing the text in the same way, analyzed it as cretics. Daviault (1981) adopted Ribbeck's ⟨*tu*⟩.

[89] I make this inference from Ribbeck's hesitant description of this fragment as both iambo-trochaics and cretics in the index (see Ribbeck 1873:508), and the repudiation of a cretic scansion in the Corollarium (see Ribbeck 1873:lxiii).

[90] Hermann (1834) did not object to treating this fragment as a cretic tetrameter. I have not yet met with success in tracking Ribbeck's (1898) report that Lucian Müller advocated the cretic scansion.

[91] The exceptions are Plautus *Amph.* 231 and *Most.* 723; see Questa 2007:420.

words of Titinius as a cretic tetrameter gives a second-foot molossus, in violation of that apparent rule of Plautine lyric:

lassĭtudo conseruum, rĕdĭuĭae flăgri!

– ᴗ – – – – – ᴗ ᴗᴗ – ᴗ –

The rule is so strong in Plautus' cretics that such a setting could hardly be accepted as unproblematic for that author. But we know too little about the cretic tetrameters of other dramatists to apply that rule to Titinius. Some support for this "license" comes from a fragment set as cretic tetrameters and printed as Turpilius 66–67 (= 68–69 Rychlewska):

set quis[92] est qui interrumpit sermonem meum
obitu suo?

– ᴗ – – – – – – – – ᴗ –

ᴗᴗ–ᴗᴗ

Leaving aside other possible treatments of Turpilius' fragment,[93] it will be clear that the complete tetrameter likewise has a second-foot molossus. Unless and until that scansion is rejected, Titinius' fragment ought to be treated as a single cretic tetrameter, in keeping with Verrius' methods.

II.8. Pacuvius 345–346 (= fr. 246 Schierl)

Editors set this fragment, preserved at Festus p. 334.8 (s.v. *redhostire*), as iambic senarii:

⟨ × – × – × – × ⟩ nĭsĭ cŏẹrcĕọ
prŏțeruĭțatem ațque hostĭọ fĕṛ̣ocĭạm.

This fragment seems to fit none of the categories of exceptions that have been described in the text of Festus; it is quoted in the company

---

[92] Rychlewska (1971:21) printed Lindsay's *ecquis est* (itself prompted by Bentley's *ecquis hic est*).

[93] The rhythm of Turpilius' cretics would seem to be somewhat improved by dividing the fragment instead as ... *set quis est* | *qui interrumpit sermonem meum obitu suo*, which is similar to the cretic pentameter (*sic*) given by Lindsay in his edition of Nonius (p. 357.22). This setting, too, gives a second-foot molossus (-*pit sermo*-).

of several metrically complete, albeit sometimes slightly corrupted, verses, making it difficult to justify an exception here. The same fragment is quoted at Nonius p. 121.13, from a source whose methods, similar but not identical to those of Verrius, would permit scanning the text either as it is set above or as a single complete verse.[94] Verrius' methods would seem to demand the latter. As with the pairing of fragments deriving from Verrius and Iulius Romanus in the opening scenes of Plautus' *Bacchides*, the stricter methodology ought to be taken as the editor's guide. Scanning *coerceo* with synizesis, as in Pacuvius 47 (= fr. 41 Schierl) *grădĕṛe atque ăṭrocem ço̧erce ço̧nfḭdentĭạm*,[95] makes it possible to set Pacuvius 345–346 as a single iambic octonarius.

II.9. Pacuvius 26 (= fr. 30 Schierl)

Editors set the quotation illustrating *reapse* that occurs at Festus p. 348.14 as an acephalous trochaic septenarius:

⟨ – × ⟩ ṣi noṇ est ingratum ṛeapsĕ quod feçi bĕṇe.

Nothing in this short entry suggests that Verrius' methods should have been abandoned here. In this instance the solution seems fairly straightforward. The reading *si non* comes from Paulus' epitome; **F** gives only *sino*. Taking that variation into account together with the problem posed by the metrically incomplete verse, I would propose instead this senarius:

siṇ[o] est ingratum ṛeapsĕ quod feçi bĕṇe.

"But if what I have done well is, in fact, unpleasing [...]." This conjecture strengthens the contrast implicit in *ingratum* and *feci bene*; the latter is itself an emphatic expression.[96]

---

[94] See above, n. 69. The version of the quotation given at Nonius p. 490.17 is transmitted in such a disastrous state that no secure conclusions may be drawn from it.

[95] The source of this fragment, quoted at Nonius p. 262.5, is obscure. Lindsay (1901:67) considered it a marginal annotation in Nonius' copy of Turpilius. All editors set it as a senarius.

[96] The word order *feci bene* is strikingly rarer than *bene feci* in republican verse, as in all tenses of this expression; the type *feci bene* is, as here, elevated in tone compared to the more colloquial or at least unmarked tone evident in *bene feci*; note especially the

II.10. Pacuvius 191–193 (= fr. 143 Schierl)

One of the more difficult quotations preserved in the text of Festus comes at p. 350.13, where some words of Pacuvius are quoted in the entry *repotia*. This quotation has at least two textual problems from the point of view of Verrius' methods. Since those problems seem to be independent of one another, the explanations offered here are necessarily tentative. The quotation must be taken in the context of the entire entry (I give the fragment as it has been set by editors of Pacuvius):

> REPOTIA postridie nuptias apud nouum maritum cenatur,
> quia quasi reficitur potatio. Pacuuius in Iliona:
>> *ab eo* ⟨...⟩
>> *depulsum mamma paedagogandum accipit*
>> *repotialis Liber.*

The two problems come in the incomplete verses at the beginning and end of the fragment. The conjunction of two incomplete verses in a single fragment is unparalleled in Festus and is considerably more difficult for an editor to justify than would be just one partial verse joined to the complete senarius *depulsum mamma paedagogandum accipit*. Since Verrius elsewhere seems to have cited complete verses without regard for sense from Pacuvius' *Iliona*[97] and since there are no indications that this fragment came to Verrius from any of the secondary sources discussed in the first half of this paper, it is difficult to appeal to such a source to justify the peculiar method of quotation that has been assumed by editors.

The stated explanation of *repotia* makes the word the proper term for a dinner on the day after a wedding, which is provided with the etymology *reficitur potatio*. In the quotation of Pacuvius *repotialis* is

---

contrast between the two expressions in Plautus *Epid.* 136–137, with further examples at Plautus *Asin.* 945, *Bacch.* 402, *Capt.* 416, *Cist.* 242, *Epid.* 209, *Men.* 1021. The same pattern applies to the distribution of phrases like *bene gesta (est)* as against *gesta (est) bene.*

[97] Cf. the discussion of Pacuvius 208–209 (Section II.6, above). Two further fragments of the play are preserved in the apographs, at p. 512.12 and 514.28; the former gives incomplete sense.

distant from that definition in terms of both sense and morphology. The quotation begins with two words that will not scan as the end of a senarius, and a lacuna must be set after them to rescue the meter. But *ab eo* is quite pointless in this quotation and it is difficult to explain why, if the quotation was abbreviated, these two words were preserved.

Elsewhere in the extant text of Festus *ab eo* is normal phrasing for introducing a lexicographical or morphological explanation, as at p. 206.19 OPPORTVNE *dicitur ab eo, quod nauigantibus maxime utiles optatique sunt portus.*[98] That phrasing suggests that *ab eo*, long taken by editors as Pacuvius' own words, may belong instead to Festus and would have formed part of a further lexicographical comment explaining the form *repotialis*. A similarly structured entry occurs at Festus p. 514.22 (apogr.) VRVAT *Ennius in Andromeda significat circumdat, ab eo sulco, qui fit in urbe condenda uruo aratri.* Although I can produce no certain supplement for the resulting lacuna, I would suggest that the text ought to be set as:

Pacuuius in Iliona ab eo de⟨... ...⟩:
de⟩pulsum mamma paedagogandum accipit
repotialis Liber.

The scribe's eye would have jumped ahead to the second *de-*, thereby causing him to omit the rest of the explanation with which the quotation was introduced. Although it is impossible to know how to supplement the lacuna, it seems better to assume that some words explaining *repotialis* have been lost, than that a peculiar manner of quotation was introduced by either Verrius or Festus in order to preserve some colorless words of Pacuvius. Plausible supplements include some form of either *declinare* or *deducere*, or, allowing for a less precise error, the simple *ducere*.[99] Since Pacuvius' *repotialis* is itself somewhat obscure, it is difficult to know how Verrius or Festus might

---

[98] Cf. Festus p. 162.17 (restored from Paulus), 196.9, 212.15, 314.11, 346.14 (restored from Paulus), 354.29, 370.35 (conjectural), 374.19 (restored from Paulus), 516.19. The fragment of Cato quoted at Festus p. 144.14 provides an interesting parallel.

[99] *declinare*: Festus p. 220.2, 346.14 (restored from Paulus); for this usage of *declinare*, see *TLL* 5,1 194.6–19. *deducere*: Festus p. 484.14; *ducere*: Festus p. 166.32, 194.2, and passim.

have explained it; the lost remark may have taken a form similar to *Pacuuius in Iliona ab eo declinatum (deductum, ductum) repotialis ait: "depulsum ..."*[100] That conjecture restores a form of quotation that is somewhat easier to accept, even though it still violates Verrius' methods. Precise parallels for metrically incomplete quotations where the partial verse contains the target-word were discussed above (the *"ruri* type"), and *repotialis Liber* could be justified by that pattern.

II.11. Pacuvius 400 (= fr. 277 Schierl)

At Festus p. 350.25, **F** presents the following text from an unidentified script of Pacuvius:

> REPEDARE, recedere. Pacuius:
> *paulum recede, gnate, a uestibulo gradum.*

Noting that the quotation does not record a form of the target-word *repedare*, Ursinus replaced the transmitted *recede* with *repeda*, producing an acephalous iambic senarius:

⟨ × ⟩ paulum ṛĕpĕda, gnate, a ụestĭbŭḷo grădum.

C. O. Müller and Ribbeck proposed to expand *paulum* as *pauxillum* or *pausillum*, restoring a complete senarius. Although that expansion tidily brings the fragment into line with Verrius' usual methods, linguistic usage does not support such a conjecture, since there are no instances of any form of *pauxillus* or *pausillus* in the remains of republican tragedy against 25 examples in republican comedy. These lexical items therefore seem to have been quite thoroughly avoided in republican tragedy and ought not to be restored to it by conjecture.

Against this approach it should be noted that the text of **F** scans as a complete senarius (*pauḷum rĕçĕdĕ, gnate, a ụestĭbŭḷo grădum*). The

---

[100]For a similar case of what are probably Festus' words being mistaken for words of a Pacuvian quotation see Festus p. 334.19 and the differing treatments of *promerenda gratia* (Ursinus : *proaererenda gratia* F) as either words of Pacuvius (Ribbeck) or, better, of Festus (D'Anna 1967:81, 201, whose correction *pro rependenda gratia* is accepted by Schierl 2006:221–222).

connection between that verse and Verrius' methods ought not to be discarded hastily; it is worth asking whether Ursinus' conjecture is correct. I would tentatively propose that this quotation properly belongs to the "*ruri* type" but its affinities with that group of exceptions have been obscured by the omission of (probably) *repeda* at the head of the quotation. The text could thus be restored as:

REPEDARE, recedere. Pacuius:
⟨...rĕpĕda...⟩
pauḷum rĕçedĕ, gnate, a ụestĭbŭḷo grăḍum.

repeda or another form of that word will have been omitted through simple scribal confusion, while Festus' text will have preserved, as in other examples of the "*ruri* type," a relevant word followed by a complete verse that illustrates the meaning of that target-word. As sometimes happens elsewhere, the lexicon's definition would employ a word that occurs in the quotation itself.[101] Certainty about the precise form of *repedare* to be restored is quite impossible.[102]

II.12. Plautus *fr.* 77

At p. 388.7, Festus preserves, together with a complete quotation of Plautus *Rud.* 820, a fragment of Plautus' *Friuolaria* whose meter has long remained uncertain. Lindsay set the fragment as a trochaic octonarius lacking its first two elements[103]:

⟨ – × ⟩ sĕquĭmĭni me hac sultis lĕgĭoņes omņes Lăụernae.

---

[101] Festus offers far fewer instances of this feature than does (e.g.) Nonius, but it is noteworthy that each of the quotations of the "*ruri* type" illustrates a definition that is itself based on the content of that quotation. For further, sometimes doubtful, examples, cf. Festus p. 226.26 (from Lucilius 1298), 240.9 (from *purus*, twice), 240.18 (from *stultior* in Plautus *Bacch.* 123, if Paulus may be trusted as evidence for Festus' definition), 256.4, 320.24, 386.27, and 430.26.

[102] The anonymous reader suggests an alternative solution, which is to retain Ursinus' view that *recede* represents a gloss that has ousted not *repeda*, but *repedato* (which form similarly gives a complete senarius), since nothing requires that such a gloss have been in precisely the same form as the original text.

[103] Lindsay's setting of the text shows that he scanned *sequimini* as *ddaB*. Aragosti's (2009:160–161) discussion of this fragment contains a number of errors.

This setting and Monda's (2004:72) preferred iambic septenarius (lacking its first element, with hiatus after *me*) both violate Meyer's Law (*lĕgĭōnēs* with word-end after the eleventh element of a trochaic octonarius; *ōmnēs* with word-end after the twelfth element of an iambic septenarius). Although the nature of this principle of iambo-trochaic versification means that similar but acceptable "violations" of it can be found in the scripts of Plautine comedy,[104] the conjunction of the irregular rhythms and the violation of Verrius' methods makes it difficult to accept either setting without reservation. Leo (1895–1896: vol. 2, 535) offered the possibility of scanning the fragment as two partial trochaic octonarii divided after *sultis*, which avoids the metrical problem but violates Verrius' methods even more outrageously.

Editors have long suspected that this fragment derives from the same scene as Plautus *fr.* 78 (*ubi rorarii estis? :: adsunt. :: ubi sunt accensi? :: ecce. .*) and *fr.* 79 (*agite nunc, supsidite omnes, quasi solent triarii*), in view of the military terminology that they share.[105] *Fr.* 79 is a complete trochaic septenarius; *fr.* 78 lacks its conclusion and so may be either a trochaic septenarius or a trochaic octonarius. Lindsay remarked in his apparatus that the trochaic meters of *fr.* 78 and 79 prohibited scanning *fr.* 77, by bracketing *omnes*, as a bacchiac tetrameter:

> sĕquĭmĭni me hac sultis lĕgĭones [omnes] Lăuernae.
>
> ◡ ◡◡ ‒ ‒ ‒ ‒ ◡◡ ‒ ‒ ◡ ‒ ‒

But the boundaries between these metrical schemes are not nearly so impermeable, and Lindsay's complete exclusion of this possibility cannot be supported. Several parallels for cantica containing intermingled long trochaic verses and bacchiacs are available in the scripts of Plautus.[106] The metrical evidence therefore does not rule out this

---

[104] See Ceccarelli 1988:80–81 and 116.

[105] With varying degrees of confidence, Leo 1895–1896: vol. 2, 535; Lindsay 1904–1905: ad loc.; Monda 2004:72; and Aragosti 2009:161, following Scaliger 1565:159.

[106] Adopting, only for the sake of testing Lindsay's metrical argument, Scaliger's suggestion that the fragments can be joined with no intervening material lost, I note these instances of at least one trochaic septenarius or trochaic octonarius followed immediately and with no interruption of sense by at least one bacchiac tetrameter, or vice versa (as printed in Questa 1995): Plautus *Cas.* 151–152, 681/3–684, 705–706, 859–860, 918/20–921; *Cist.* 18–20, 33–34; *Merc.* 354/5–356, 358–363; *Most.* 887a–888, *Pseud.* 243–256,

conjecture, which would bring the quotation into compliance with Verrius' methods.

On this conjecture, *omnes* will be the result of an uncorrected dittography of the ending of *legiones*. Examples of that error are common elsewhere in **F**, which is otherwise generally carefully copied.[107] There can obviously be no definitive proof of the correctness of this conjecture, although a number of features are in its favor, including its adherence to Verrius' methods and the admixture, elsewhere in Plautus, of trochaics and bacchiacs. Although of no evidentiary value by itself, the uninterrupted alliteration *legiones Lauernae* is attractive. The resulting bacchiac tetrameter seems unobjectionable, for although resolved ancipitia are somewhat rare in that meter in general in Plautus, they are considerably more common in the first and third ancipitia than in the second and fourth.[108] This conjecture or one like it ought to be preferred, unless an explanation can be produced for the irregular form of quotation suggested by the iambo-trochaic scansions of this verse.

II.13. Ennius *Ann.* 98

At p. 432.20 Festus expresses doubts about Verrius' interpretation of *sas*, illustrated with a quotation of Ennius' *Annales*:

> SAS Verrius putat significare EAS, teste Ennio, qui dicat in lib. I:
>
> > *uirgines; nam sibi quisque domi Romanus habet sas;*

1106–1107, 1125–1126, 1282–1283. Allowing, as Scaliger did not, that some verses may have intervened between the extant fragments would add several more passages to this list. (The list excludes, e.g., Plautus *Bacch.* 1119–1120, *Most.* 803–804, *Persa* 856–858, *Rud.* 258–259, and *Truc.* 574–575, where the change of meter attends a marked change in topic or speaker; however, I would not rule out such a shift occurring amid the material in *Friuolaria*.)

[107] Errors of dittography are strikingly more prevalent than, e.g., haplography or transposition; cf. the entries at Festus p. 150.4 *a mente [mente] abierit*; 306.25 *quianam genus isti. et in Satyra [quianam genus isti. et in Satyra]*; 400.27 *subcenturia[cen]tum*; 416.13 *[quam] quam*; 460.24 *cohibet [et]*; 468.16 *iudicareque esse [esse]que oportet*; perhaps also p. 362.28 *reque eapse [saepe]* and 398.31 *paene uuidum [dum]*.

[108] See Welsh 2013:259n27.

cum SVAS magis uideatur significare. sicuti eiusdem lib.
VII fatendum est EAM significari, cum ait (*Ann*. 211–212):

> *nec quisquam [philo]sophiam*
> (quae doctrina latina lingua no⟨me⟩n habet)
> *sapientia quae per⟨h⟩ibetur*
> *in somnis uidit prius quam sam discere coepit.*

As we have seen, when Festus disagreed with Verrius (as he did over the interpretation of Ennius' *sas* but not that of *sam*), he sometimes shortened the quotation that Verrius gave.

I shall not add to the attempts to defend or emend the cretic word *uirgines* as the beginning of an Ennian hexameter, which can be traced in Skutsch's commentary. Most are unconvincing, and on the evidence then available the only rational solution was to obelize *uirgines*. Skutsch ruled out the possibility (suggested by Terzaghi)[109] of treating *uirgines* as an interpolated gloss by appealing both to plausibility and to Festus' standard practice of quoting whole verses. The second point may now be discarded, since Festus expresses doubts about Verrius' interpretation. Skutsch's first objection nevertheless seems cogent, since it is difficult to see either why *sas* should have been glossed specifically by *uirgines* in the tradition of Festus, or why that gloss should not have appeared nearer to *sas*, if it is interpolated. If we cannot reject that possibility outright (for interpolation of the putative gloss at an unusual point is not impossible), it will, I think, be possible to solve this problem by another method that takes fuller consideration of Verrius' entry.

A hint about the likely shape of Verrius' original discussion of *sas* is provided by the two complete hexameters quoted from *Annales* VII to illustrate *sam*. It is noteworthy that Festus does not disagree with Verrius on the interpretation of *sam*, and has apparently preserved the entirety of Verrius' illustrative quotation there. In that quotation the meaning of the target-word *sam*, treated as equivalent to *eam*, is made clear by *sophiam* in the preceding verse. Verrius must be presumed to have been quoting generously here; for if his intent were solely to

---

[109] See Timpanaro 1946:72.

illustrate *sam*, he could have quoted no more than *in somnis uidit prius quam sam discere coepit*, in keeping with his method of quoting incomplete units of sense elsewhere.

To return to *Ann.* 98, *uirgines* must be regarded as suspect since that form will not scan at any point in a hexameter. But since Festus may have shortened Verrius' original quotation, it is worth noting the possibility that the original quotation, just like *Ann.* 211–212, instead ran for two verses as something like:

⟨ ... *uirginibus* ... ⟩
⟨ – ◡◡ ⟩ nam sibi quisque domi Romanus habet sas.

I am not arguing that the form *uirginibus* is specifically to be restored to Ennius, but am merely suggesting one way in which this word could have been integrated into a now-lost verse, along the lines of *sophiam* in *Ann.* 211. In this instance, Festus would have reduced the quotation from, we may hypothesize, two complete hexameters to just one partial verse. But, in such circumstances, Festus presumably would not have found it desirable to eliminate the Ennian word that clarified *sas*, just as Verrius found it desirable to include *Ann.* 211, especially *sophiam*, in his illustration of *sam*. The two different approaches of Verrius and Festus will, I think, allow us to understand the transmitted *uirgines*, even if we cannot know what form properly belongs to Ennius. I would suggest that what Festus wrote is:

SAS Verrius putat significare EAS, teste Ennio, qui dicat in lib. I ⟨pro⟩ VIRGINES:
⟨ – ◡◡ ⟩ *nam sibi quisque domi Romanus habet sas.*

The omission of the nota for *pro*, a simple enough error by itself, would have been even easier if at some stage of the transmission *lib. I* were written not as a cipher but as ⟨*libro*⟩ *primo*.[110] Whatever the form of *uirgo* that appeared in a preceding verse, for the sake of clarity it would naturally have been rewritten, in Festus' explanation, to bring it into line with *sas* and *eas*. There is no significant difference between Festus'

---

[110]The assumption of such a stage is not guaranteed; Skutsch (1985:35) assembles the evidence for the book-numbers in **F**.

usage of *pro* with an unmarked case-form (for example, *pro uirgines* equivalent to *pro illo* VIRGINES, "in the place of the word *uirgines*") and that of *pro* with the ablative.[111] This solution takes full account of Festus' methods when dissenting from Verrius; of Verrius' concern in this entry for the clarity of his quotations, apparent from *sophiam* in *Ann.* 211; and indeed of the constraints of Ennius' versification. In connection with the last point, it is noteworthy that Festus will have preserved a complete sense-unit beginning with *nam*, omitting or rewriting what preceding material he judged irrelevant; it remains reasonable to understand a full stop before *nam* (see Skutsch for references and brief discussion).

II.14. Afranius 1

At p. 454.27 Festus records an apparently corrupt verse of Afranius, illustrating its adjective *senticosa* with reference to the common meaning of *sentes*:

> Sentes cum constet esse spinas et Afranius in Abducta dixerit:
>> *quam senticosa uerba pertorquet †turba*
> pro spinosis accipi debet.

Corruption of the fragment seems almost certain, since the verse appears to be an iambic senarius but *turba* will not scan as a verse-end in that meter. Nothing in the entry suggests that Verrius took this quotation from an earlier lexicographical source, while the appeal to established consensus (*constet*) rather seems to rule out such an origin. Without justification it would be unmethodical to set the transmitted text as two incomplete verses.[112]

---

[111]Contrast, e.g., Festus p. 132.3 (*pro boni*), 140.32 (*pro mihi*), 152.16, 232.4 (*pro molitum*), 254.7 (*pro celer*), 384.25 (*pro eum*), 386.32 (*pro eos … pro suos*) with the usage of the ablative at, e.g., p. 182.12, 204.24, 214.3, 230.18, 236.4, etc.

[112]Neukirch (1833:176–177) suggested, as one of two possibilities, setting the fragment as two partial iambic septenarii (*quam senticosa uerba* | *pertorquet turba*), which Daviault (1981:142) adopted. Neukirch's other solution was to treat the transmitted text as a complete scazon or catalectic iambic trimeter, which López López (1983:97) adopted.

Early students proposed conjectures that are palaeographically close to *turba* but give a sense that is generally uncompelling.[113] Ribbeck suggested instead that *turba* represented a dittography of *uerba*.[114] If that argument is correct, something far removed from the *ductus litterarum* of *turba*, like Ribbeck's own tentative supplements *sua* or *puer*, Hermann's *tua*, or even Brakman's *pater*, has a claim to consideration and could be correct.[115] However, the underlying argument is difficult to accept, since it requires assuming that *uerba* was repeated after the intervening *pertorquet* (itself not repeated), that the word ousted the original ending of the senarius, and that the second *uerba* was then corrupted into *turba*. Even allowing the possibility that some of these errors happened simultaneously it is nevertheless the case that other errors of duplication in the tradition of Festus are considerably simpler.[116] But since errors of repetition, of one variety or another, are otherwise so common in this tradition, Ribbeck's general approach ought not to be rejected out of hand.

In view of the corruption of *subcenturia[cen]tum* (Festus p. 400.27), where an internal syllable is repeated in a situation that mimics word-division (for *[cen]tum* occurs on a new line of **F**), I would set *uerba* aside, and suggest instead that *turba* repeats the medial syllable of *pertorquet*. That explanation would, if correct, require a conjecture that maintains –*ba* at the end of the senarius, since only *tur*- would be inauthentic. Words ending in –*ba* are rare in scenic verse, and most disyllables either will not scan as the end of a senarius (*alba, balba, barba, herba, orba, scriba, uerba*) or will give nonsense in this context (*faba*). The shining exception is the adjective *proba*:

quam sĕntĭcŏsă ụerbă pertorquet prŏḅa.

---

[113]E.g. *lupa* (Scaliger and Augustinus; see Dacerius 1699:497–498), *tuba* (Bothe 1824:160), *truo* (Gulielmus 1582:14), and *tripus* (Anon. *apud* Ribbeck 1873:lxiv).

[114]First in the apparatus at Ribbeck 1855:140–141, retained at Ribbeck 1873:164 and Ribbeck 1898:193.

[115]Hermann 1834:278; Ribbeck 1873:164; Brakman 1935:63.

[116]See above, n. 107.

That conjecture gives good sense in this fragment: "what thorny words the good (woman) hurls!"[117] It also makes it easier to explain the error that gave rise to *turba*. A scribe, when faced with the two similar initial syllables of *pertorquet proba*, produced instead *pertorquet turba*, repeating the wrong syllable from the first word.[118] That the word immediately following the quotation is *pro* could only contribute to making the error more likely.

II.15. Afranius 410–411

At Festus (apogr.) p. 492.18 a quotation of Afranius is preserved without the title of its script. All of Afranius' editors have set the fragment as partial trochaic septenarii:[119]

> TANNE eo usque, ut Aelius Stilo et Opillus Aurelius inter-
> pretantur. Itaque Afranius:
> ⟨ – × – × – × – × – ⟩ tanne arcŭla
> ṭŭă plena est ăranĕarum. ⟨ – × – × – ◡ – ⟩

Such an arrangement would require more explanation than has yet been provided for it. It seems not to be justified by any of the exceptional patterns of quotation that can now be traced in the lexicon. The extant text of Festus preserves no quotations of republican verse given in connection with the opinions of Aurelius Opillus or Aelius Stilo. In loose connection with the name of the latter, but not evidently deriving from his work, three quotations (at p. 226.26, 266.23, 488.7) are given apparently to illustrate alternative meanings of a word that he defined. Furthermore, no aspect of Festus' usage of *itaque* in introducing quotations requires that Afranius' words be assigned to Verrius' use of either

---

[117] A translation of this verse can be no more than tentative, given that Verrius will have quoted a complete verse without regard for completeness of sense. Since both Verrius and Festus are concerned with the meaning of *senticosa* it is quite natural that a metrically complete quotation should leave the sense of *proba* incomplete.

[118] A kind of *Perseverationsfehler*, related to the *error Wattianus*, described at Watt 2004. The error occurred early, since Paulus p. 455.22 also records *turba* in this fragment.

[119] See Bothe 1824:198; Neukirch 1833:275; Ribbeck 1898:260; Daviault 1981:246; López López 1983:146.

source.[120] Accordingly it must be assumed that Verrius, who once elsewhere seems to give a quotation of Afranius without the title of its script (p. 406.8), added this quotation from his own reading of Afranius. The transmitted words make good sense as a single utterance. They therefore seem to require simply a better explanation of their meter. In view of *arcŭlă* the text could not be set as a single iambo-trochaic verse without supposing a lacuna, which the sensibility of the text does not support, or a transposition, which the care over word order evident in **F** does not support.[121] Against any attempt to intervene in the text or to defend the traditional scansion of this verse, it should be noted that the fragment has undeniable ionic rhythms at its beginning (*tanne arcŭlă*) and end (*est ăranĕarum*). With no greater liberty, I would suggest, than is evident in the verses at Plautus *Amph.* 168–172, the fragment can be set as a catalectic ionic tetrameter:

tanne arcŭlă tŭă plenă | est ăranĕarum

The first, third, and fourth metra are perfectly regular. The second metron contains one or another questionable detail; there either the final syllable of *plena* must be treated as long before the putative hiatus signaled here (producing ‿ ‿ – –), or, equally tentatively, *tua plena* must be treated as an anaclastic metron with the first syllable artificially heavy (producing – ‿ – ‿). The rarity of this meter in dramatic scripts makes certainty quite impossible but in view of the prosodic licenses apparent in Latin ionics[122] it does not seem beyond credibility that the text should be set with one or the other of these liberties.[123] How much Afranius' ionics may have differed on technical points from Plautus' cannot be known; however Afranius 202 shows no anaclasis in its third metron, a feature that is perfectly regular in Plautus *Amph.* 168–172.

---

[120] Festus p. 190.5, 290.35, 402.2, 442.7.

[121] See above, n. 87.

[122] See Lindsay 1922:306; Bettini 1982:71–84; Questa 2007:486–488. The treatment of *libere* at Plautus *Amph.* 171 is particularly relevant.

[123] Readers not convinced that either treatment is plausible may wish to consider instead something like *tanne arcula to⟨t⟩a plena*, which restores an anaclastic second metron, for which cf. Plautus *Amph.* 171.

III. CONCLUSIONS

Examination of Festus' quotations of early Latin poetry has confirmed the widespread article of faith that Verrius Flaccus normally quoted complete metrical units. Taking the quotations of scenic verse together with the more systematically studied quotations of hexameter poetry has also made it possible to give a secure account of the exceptional and metrically incomplete quotations. Some of those citations were transcribed from earlier sources by Verrius himself, while others appear to have been produced in Festus' own process of abridging Verrius' lexicon. The secure description of those methods provides a foundation from which to correct fragments transmitted in this text, and I have suggested a number of conjectures that would reduce the number of aberrant quotations still further.

There are, inevitably, some lingering quotations, incomplete from the point of view of meter, that do not admit of easy correction or explanation. These quotations are Accius 429 (Festus p. 180.25), Pacuvius 320 (p. 258.37), Naevius *com.* 99–102 (p. 260.15), Lucilius 1255–1256 (p. 312.22), and Plautus *Cas.* 309–310 (p. 484.14). Several of them appear to be corrupt. Tentative appeals to the kinds of exceptions discussed in this paper are possible in some instances, but emendation to restore complete verses may well be required.[124] These few inexplicable items do not stand in the way, in any case, of the general principle: Verrius' quotations are so regularly given in complete metrical units, and Festus so infrequently altered those quotations except in particular and clearly recognizable circumstances, that an editor of fragments preserved in this text must habitually prefer to set Festus' quotations as complete verses, unless an exception can be securely justified.

University of Toronto

---

[124]Pacuvius 320, quoted to illustrate *plera*, is followed by an entry illustrated with Catullus 97.6 (which gives complete meter and sense), an author otherwise rarely quoted in the lexicon. Plautus *Cas.* 309–310 is also quoted in the damaged portion of F at Festus p. 318.20; textual difficulties in each passage make certainty impossible, but the pattern of transferred quotations or that of the "*ruri* type" may also be relevant.

APPENDIX 1. THE QUOTATIONS OF VERGIL

This appendix reviews the evidence for Festus' quotations of Vergil and suggests that that material cannot be used to corroborate, or to refute, claims about Verrius' typical methods of excerpting early verse.[125] Rychlewska (1948–1949:190–191) used three Vergilian quotations to corroborate her claims about Verrius' methods of citing hexameter verse, which she illustrated first from quotations of Lucretius. The text of Festus contains eleven quotations of Lucretius, of which three are incomplete due to the state of **F**.[126] The eight remaining quotations (five from **F**, three from the apographs) consist of metrically complete verses.[127] That distribution and the occasional abruptness of sense in these Lucretian quotations suggest that Verrius excerpted them in complete units of meter, rather than of sense. Similarly, Strzelecki (1932:82) pointed out that the text of Lucretius occurs at a predictable position in the order of Verrius' seventeen lists taken from republican authors, indicating that Lucretius enjoyed the same status as Ennius, Afranius, Lucilius, and others.

The text of Festus presents ten quotations from Vergil, one of which has been damaged in **F**.[128] Of the remaining nine quotations, six are metrically incomplete, while three consist of a single complete verse. The concentration of metrically incomplete verses raises some doubts about the origin of these quotations. Strzelecki (1932:83n1) pointed

---

[125] Nonius' tendencies are similar, if reversed. He quotes early Latin verse in units of sense but usually gives complete verses of Vergil without regard for sense.

[126] At p. 480.29, the quotation of Lucr. 2.1142 was certainly a complete hexameter. At p. 426.5 and p. 442.21 it is most likely that complete verses were quoted.

[127] From **F**: p. 160.18, 182.30, 238.2, 312.32, 402.19. From the apographs: p. 210.11, 226.4, 514.2. Rychlewska's (1948–1949:189–190) discussion of the Lucretian material is generally accurate.

[128] Festus p. 388.25. From the undamaged portions of **F** emerges *maxime Teu......numquam*, which Ursinus supplemented to restore the complete text of *Aen.* 8.470. That much is certainly right, but the supplement offered to fill the previous line of the manuscript, ⟨*Vergilius lib. VIII Aeneid.*⟩, is suspect, since Festus does not elsewhere give either the title or book-numbers with quotations from *Aen.* Another possibility is that the incomplete hexameter which precedes this verse (*rex prior haec, Aen.* 8.469) belongs in the gap, although there is little cause for those three words to have been quoted to illustrate *sospes*.

out that the quotations of Vergil, and of other *recentiores*, occur in no predictable order, quite unlike the text of Lucretius. Four of the six metrically incomplete quotations of Vergil can reasonably be dispatched as not being the work of Verrius himself. At p. 490.1, Vergil's *Thymbreum* comes from Rychlewska's (1948–1949:196) anonymous geographical source. At p. 292.7, the partial quotation of *Ecl.* 5.88 is an "inserted" quotation from p. 230.30. Similarly, the two metrically incomplete quotations of *Aen.* 3 at p. 218.12 have been adduced or abbreviated by Festus himself, in order to contradict Verrius' interpretation of *obscena*. Certainty is impossible about the quotations of *G.* 4.10–11 at p. 226.4[129] and of *G.* 1.242 at p. 400.17.[130]

The three metrically complete quotations are somewhat equivocal. At p. 160.18, a complete quotation of *Aen.* 1.433 is adduced to illustrate *nectar*. Rychlewska (1948–1949:190) suggested that the omission of at least *liquentia mella* from *Aen.* 1.432 guaranteed that Verrius had excerpted the quotation as a complete metrical unit without regard for sense. But this is no example of "fleeing the infant" (see most conveniently Rychlewska 1948–1949:186); the verse in isolation, *stipant et dulci distendunt nectare cellas*, still gives a reasonable sense ("they stuff and stretch the cells with sweet nectar"), since *stipare* may take as its object both the stuffing and the thing stuffed (see *OLD* s.v. *stipo* 1 and 3). It is therefore not guaranteed that the original excerpter of this quotation was paying attention to meter alone.

At p. 402.19, the quotation of *Ecl.* 4.49, given without indication of the work's title, follows a quotation of Lucretius 4.1232 which is complete (*pace* Rychlewska) in both sense and meter. The quotation of *Ecl.* 4.49 is similarly complete in both respects. Neither can be used to corroborate Verrius' methods; the absence of *Bucolicis* is in fact troubling, since elsewhere only *Aen.* is quoted without indication of the title.

At p. 230.30, *Ecl.* 5.88 is quoted as a complete verse to illustrate the noun *pedum*. This entry must be taken together with its counterpart at

---

[129]The quotation, two incomplete verses that give a complete unit of sense, is preserved only in the apographs.

[130]The quotation is, again, an incomplete verse that gives a complete unit of sense.

p. 292.7, where Verrius evidently gave a misguided interpretation of Ennius *trag.* 181–182 (= 193–194 Jocelyn); Festus, predictably, seized the chance to correct his predecessor, and probably prefaced that correction with an inserted partial quotation of *Ecl.* 5.88 (where *pedum* in fact means *baculum*). The quotation at p. 230.30 must therefore be treated with skepticism. Although it is given in keeping with Verrius' methods, it is perhaps exceptional, having been adduced specifically to prop up Verrius' tentative, and ultimately incorrect, interpretation of Ennius' words. Since doubts linger over each of the quotations and since, as Strzelecki pointed out, Verrius seems not to have used the text of Vergil in the way that he used, say, Lucretius or Accius, it is most prudent not to rely on the Vergilian quotations for evidence about Verrius' methods.

APPENDIX 2. LOST BEGINNINGS IN QUOTATIONS OF ENNIUS' *ANNALES*

Skutsch (1985:35) observed that six of Festus' fragments of Ennius' *Annales* (5, 17, 214, 246, 332, and 476) appear to have lost some initial syllables in transmission:

5	⟨ – ⌣⌣ – ⟩ desunt riuos camposque remanant
17	⟨ – ⟩ face uero quod tecum precibus pater orat
214	⟨ – ⟩ Poeni soliti suos sacrificare puellos
246	⟨ – ⟩ quianam dictis nostris sententia flexa est
332	⟨ – ⟩ ueluti, [si] quando uinclis uenatica uelox
	apta dolet si forte ⟨feras⟩ ex nare sagaci
	sensit, uoce sua nictit ululatque ibi acute
476	⟨ – ⟩ quom illud quo iam semel est imbuta ueneno

The quotation of *Ann.* 5 is obviously more deficient than the rest, and it is impossible to know with any certainty whether its deficiencies are to be attributed to the tradition or instead to Verrius' use of a scholarly source for this quotation.

Skutsch's argument that the other five quotations were damaged in transmission was reasonable. Further support for it is offered by the fact that, in Festus' quotations of scenic verse, no example of a quotation lacking an initial monosyllable can be attributed to Verrius' own excerption; in every instance the irregularity can be explained with reference to the patterns outlined in Part I of this paper, or can be emended to restore a complete verse. There would be no reason to think that Verrius would have adopted a peculiar mode of quotation in the case of one poem alone. Skutsch's explanation of simple corruption of a complete hexameter in the course of transmission therefore seems correct in the case of *Ann*. 332–334, which has suffered wounds elsewhere, of *Ann*. 476, and probably also of *Ann*. 214. In the last-mentioned fragment, judgment about *di(ui)s*, which Nonius (p. 158.13) preserves in a partial quotation of that line (*suos diuis sacrificare puellos*), must be held in suspense until a more secure explanation of the composition of that entry and of the methods of Nonius' source that lies behind it has been produced.[131]

The situation is rather more complicated in the case of *Ann*. 17 and 246. The quotation of *Ann*. 17 is complete from the point of view of sense. The possible significance of that fact has long been overlooked; for while Verrius quoted complete units of meter without regard for completeness of sense, other lexicographers were prone to quoting complete units of sense without regard for meter. The quotation is given at Festus (apogr.) p. 218.6 s.v. *orare*, in an entry that supports its definition with evidence from the word *orator*. The problems in the separate entry for *oratores* (Festus p. 196.9) have been treated briefly in Section I.2 of this paper. The procedures by which that entry was composed raise the question of whether *Ann*. 17 also came to Verrius from the source that produced the paraphrase of Terence *Hec*. 9–10 and the quotation of Afranius' *Emancipatus* (which script seems not to have been known to Verrius). Further cause for doubting that Verrius

---

[131]Lindsay's (1905:442) attribution of the quotations of Lucretius and Ennius to list 26 ("Gloss. iii") cannot be accepted, inasmuch as the manner in which each quotation was excerpted is alien to that source's methods; see n. 69. The extensive confusion within the P-section of Nonius' second book leaves much in doubt. These two quotations are redolent of the methods of "Gloss. v"; if it should prove possible both to confirm that connection and to determine the extent of the dependence of "Gloss. v" on Verrius (on which see Lindsay 1901:101–103; White 1980:165), then Müller's *dis Poeni soliti* would be all but guaranteed.

excerpted *Ann.* 17 at first hand is provided by the fact that here, atypically, a quotation of the *Annales* is given with the title of the poem (as *l. I Annalium*; see, further, Skutsch 1985:35–36). These peculiarities together suggest that Verrius transcribed, from an intermediate source, a fragment of the *Annales* that was quoted as a complete unit of sense without regard for meter.

If the quotation was not excerpted by Verrius himself, it would still be possible, as Skutsch preferred, to scan this verse as an acephalous hexameter. However, in spite of Skutsch's defense, the setting of *uero* as a second-foot spondaic word remains metrically suspect, and if the quotation is no longer shackled to Verrius' own methods, the editor is at liberty to set the quotation in a more suitable way. Skutsch's tentative suggestion of scanning the fragment as two incomplete hexameters (*face uero | quod tecum precibus pater orat*, with the archaic form *face* used to secure the fifth-foot dactyl and with no second-foot spondaic word) must be regarded as the more natural metrical setting. Significantly, nothing in the origin of this quotation precludes such an arrangement.

Certainty about the origin of *Ann.* 246, quoted at Festus p. 306.25 s.v. *quianam*, is impossible to achieve, and in any case Skutsch's setting of the fragment as an acephalous hexameter is surely right, since *sententia flexa est* can only reasonably be set as the end of a hexameter. Yet it is of some significance, for our understanding of the text and for the assessment of conjectural supplements, whether the missing monosyllable has been lost in the transmission of Festus' text or instead was never available for Festus to transcribe. The entry *quianam* is illustrated with a corrupt but apparently complete quotation from Naevius' *Bellum Punicum*, a vexed quotation attributed apparently to the same author's *Satura*, and our quotation of Ennius, which is complete from the point of view of sense. I would suggest only the possibility that this material was not excerpted by Verrius at first hand; although the evidence is inconclusive, two features could be considered peculiar against the backdrop of the rest of the lexicon: (1) the form of the title *carmen Punici Belli*;[132] and (2) the quotation, perhaps metrically incomplete (see

---

[132] Strzelecki (1935:1–5; cf. Strzelecki 1964:x) thought, on the basis of this entry, that this was Verrius' usual way of referring to Naevius' poem and inferred from the word

Courtney 2003:3), attributed to Naevius' *Satura*, a work never other-wise quoted by Verrius or any other author. Those who would prefer to make Verrius transcribe these quotations from an earlier source there-fore have much on which to lean. The question of the origin of this quotation of the *Annales* must be left open: it is as likely as not that its missing first monosyllable was never available for Verrius or for Festus to copy.

APPENDIX 3. THE TESTIMONIA-STYLE OF CITATION

In this paper I have excluded from consideration several short snippets of text, usually no more than one to three words, that are quite distinct from the usual manner of quotation evident in Festus' lexicon. These passages are nearer to testimonia than they are to the quotations given in a full and technical style, and the entries in which they occur some-times contain indications that the material they present is not original to Verrius but came instead from secondary sources.[133] Accordingly Rychlewska (1948–1949:196) briefly explained a citation of Lucilius 1292 given in this manner as deriving from a secondary source that provided Verrius with nothing more of Lucilius than the two words *Rhondes Icadionque*. Skutsch (1985:35) cast about, without certain success, for an explanation of the reference to Ennius *Ann.* 220 in the entry at Festus

---

carmen that Verrius' copy of the poem had not been divided into books. Neither of these points is corroborated by the text of Festus. On four (perhaps five) other occasions we glimpse in the mangled remains of **F** how Verrius referred to the poem's title. On no occa-sion is either *carmen* or *liber* (a guess commonly offered by Lindsay) corroborated. But in each instance the title, however inflected, is referred to in the strict order *Bellum Punicum* (p. 158.8, 406.8, 428.33, 432.9; the fifth and dubious case occurs at p. 374.25 *Belli* ⟨...⟩, where Hostius is as likely as Naevius to have been quoted), whereas the entry *quianam* gives the title in the order *Punicum Bellum*. To be sure, Verrius was not as mechanical in repro-ducing titles as someone like Nonius was, but since the form of the title *carmen Punici Belli* at p. 306.25 is so isolated, more evidence would be needed before Strzelecki's argument could be accepted without reservation. It would be more economical to attribute the unusual quotation, and perhaps the others illustrating *quianam*, to a secondary source. No clear proof of Strzelecki's argument emerges and the question of whether Verrius' own copy of the poem had been divided into books must be left open; probability, however, would not seem to favor his claim.

[133] Cf. Jocelyn's (1991:575–577) important discussion of the ultimate source of material preserved at Paulus p. 301.3–4.

p. 494.7 (see above, n. 39) but seems not to have hit upon its similarity to the citation of Lucilius 1292.

The pattern is rather more abundantly attested in Festus' material from scenic verse, and its presence there confirms the essential correctness of Rychlewska's explanation. The tralatitious descent of this material is sometimes made clear from its context; at other times it must be inferred. Relevant passages (in both the apographs and **F**) occur at Festus p. 208.36, 230.15, 236.24, 282.9 (where the peculiar attribution *Ennius in Achille Aristarchi* is significant; cf. Jocelyn 1969:161n1), 282.11, and 498.20. For the similarity to the testimonia-style of citation, cf. Festus p. 450.22 (on Afranius' *Repudiatus*) and p. 500.2 (on the script of Titinius commonly called the *Barbatus*). Although doubts remain about the origins of individual entries there is no question that this material is distinct from and even unrelated to Verrius' usual methods.

WORKS CITED

Aragosti, A. 2009. *Frammenti Plautini dalle commedie extravarroniane.* Bologna.

Bader, B. 1970. "Der verlorene Anfang der plautinischen 'Bacchides.'" *Rheinisches Museum für Philologie* 113:304–323.

Barsby, J. 1986. *Plautus. Bacchides.* Warminster.

Barwick, C. 1964. *Flauii Sosipatri Charisii Artis Grammaticae Libri V.* Corr. ed. F. Kühnert. Leipzig.

Beare, W. 1940. "The Fabula Togata." *Hermathena* 55:35–55.

Bergk, T. 1884. *Kleine philologische Schriften.* Vol. 1, *Zur römischen Literatur.* Halle a. S.

Bettini, M. 1982. "A proposito dei versi sotadei, greci e romani: Con alcuni capitoli di 'analisi metrica lineare.'" *Materiali e discussioni per l'analisi dei testi classici* 9:59–105.

Bothe, F. H. 1823. *Poetarum Latii scenicorum fragmenta.* Vol. 1 (= Vol. 5.1 of *Poetae scenici Latinorum*). Halberstadt.

———. 1824. *Poetarum Latii scenicorum fragmenta.* Vol. 2 (= Vol. 5.2 of *Poetae scenici Latinorum*). Halberstadt.

Brakman, C. 1935. "Ad fabulas togatas." *Mnemosyne*, 3rd ser., 2:62–65.

Ceccarelli, L. 1988. *La norma di Meyer nei versi giambici e trocaici di Plauto e Terenzio*. Rome.

Courtney, E. 2003. *The Fragmentary Latin Poets*. 2nd ed. Oxford.

D'Anna, G. 1967. *M. Pacuuii fragmenta*. Rome.

Dacerius, A. 1699. *Sex. Pompei Festi et Mar. Verrii Flaccii de uerborum significatione lib. xx*. Amsterdam.

Daviault, A. 1981. *Comoedia Togata: Fragments*. Paris.

De Melo, W. D. C. 2011. *Plautus*. Vol. 1. Cambridge, MA.

De Nonno, M. 1990. "Le citazioni dei grammatici." In *Lo spazio letterario di Roma antica III: La ricezione del testo*, ed. G. Cavallo, P. Fedeli, and A. Giardina, 597–646. Rome.

Fabia, P. 1894. "Remeligo." *Revue de philologie, de littérature et d'histoire anciennes* 18:139–144.

Fontaine, M. S. 2005. Review of Monda 2004. *Bryn Mawr Classical Review*. http://bmcr.brynmawr.edu/2005/2005-05-36.html.

Gaiser, K. 1970. "Die plautinischen 'Bacchides' und Menanders 'Dis Exapaton.'" *Philologus* 114:51–87.

Glinister, F. 2007. "Constructing the Past." In *Verrius, Festus, & Paul: Lexicography, Scholarship, & Society*, ed. F. Glinister, C. Woods, et al., 11–32. London.

Guardì, T. 1984. *Fabula Togata: I frammenti*. Vol. 1, *Titinio e Atta*. Milan.

Gulielmus, J. 1582. *Verisimilium libri tres*. Antwerp.

Havet, L. 1914. *Notes critiques sur la texte de Festus*. Paris.

Hermann, G. 1834. "Adnotationes ad Io. Henr. Neukirchii librum de fabula togata Romanorum, editum Lipsiae a. 1833." In idem, *Opuscula*, Vol. 5, 254–288. Leipzig.

Jocelyn, H. D. 1964. "Ancient Scholarship and Virgil's Use of Republican Latin Poetry I." *CQ*, n.s., 14:280–295.

———, ed. 1969. *The Tragedies of Ennius*. Corr. ed. Cambridge.

———. 1991. "Studies in the Indirect Tradition of Plautus' *Pseudolus* II, Verrius Flaccus' *De significatu uerborum*." In *Studi di filologia classica in onore di Giusto Monaco*, Vol. 2, 569–580. Palermo.

Keil, H. 1857–1880. *Grammatici Latini*. Leipzig.

Lachmann, C. 1850. *T. Lucreti Cari De Rerum Natura libri sex*. Berlin.

Law, H. 1929. "The Metrical Arrangement of the Fragments of the *Bacchides*." *CP* 24:197–201.

Leo, F. 1895–1896. *Plauti Comoediae*. 2 vols. Berlin.

Lindsay, W. M. 1901. *Nonius Marcellus' Dictionary of Republican Latin*. Oxford.

———. 1903. *Nonius Marcellus. De compendiosa doctrina*. Leipzig.

———. 1904–1905. *T. Macci Plauti Comoediae*. Oxford.

———. 1905. "De citationibus apud Nonium Marcellum." *Philologus* 64:438–464.

———. 1913. *Sexti Pompei Festi de uerborum significatu quae supersunt cum Pauli epitome*. Leipzig.

———. 1922. *Early Latin Verse*. Oxford.

López López, A. 1983. *Fabularum togatarum fragmenta: Edición crítica*. Acta Salmanticensia: Filosofia y letras 141. Salamanca.

Manuwald, G. 2012. *Tragicorum Romanorum Fragmenta*. Vol. 2, *Ennius*. Göttingen.

Mariotti, S. 1971. "Enn. Ann. 353 V²." In *Studi di storiografia antica in memoria di Leonardo Ferrero*, 53–56. Turin.

Marshall, P. K. 1990. *A. Gellii Noctes Atticae*. Corr. ed. Oxford.

Marx, F. 1904–1905. *C. Lucilii carminum reliquiae*. 2 vols. Leipzig.

Monda, S. 2004. *Vidularia et deperditarum fabularum fragmenta*. Urbino.

Moscadi, A. 1979. "Verrio, Festo e Paolo." *Giornale italiano di filologia* 31:17–36.

Müller, C. O. 1880. *Sexti Pompei Festi de uerborum significatione quae supersunt cum Pauli epitome*. Leipzig.

Neukirch, J. H. 1833. *De fabula togata Romanorum: Accedunt fabularum togatarum reliquiae*. Leipzig.

North, J. A. 2007. "Why Does Festus Quote What He Quotes?" In *Verrius, Festus, & Paul: Lexicography, Scholarship, & Society*, ed. F. Glinister, C. Woods, et al., 49–68. London.

P[hillimore], J. S. 1915. Review of Havet 1914. *CR* 29:188–189.

Pieroni, P. 2004. *Marcus Verrius Flaccus' De significatu uerborum in den Auszügen von Sextus Pompeius Festus und Paulus Diaconus: Einleitung und Teilkommentar (154,19–186,29 Lindsay)*. Frankfurt.

Questa, C., ed. 1995. *Titi Macci Plauti Cantica*. Urbino.

———. 2007. *La Metrica di Plauto e di Terenzio*. Urbino.

Reitzenstein, R. 1887. *Verrianische Forschungen*. Breslau.

Ribbeck, O. 1851–1855. *Scaenicae Romanorum poesis fragmenta*. 1st ed. Leipzig.

———, ed. 1871–1873. *Scaenicae Romanorum poesis fragmenta*. 2nd ed. Leipzig.

———, ed. 1897–1898. *Scaenicae Romanorum poesis fragmenta*. 3rd ed. Leipzig.

Roeper, T. 1854. "M. Terenti Varronis saturarum Menippearum quarundam reliquiae emendatae." *Philologus* 9:223–278.

Rychlewska, L. 1948–1949. "De Verriana hexametros afferendi ratione." *Eos* 43:186–197.

———. 1971. *Turpilii comici fragmenta*. Leipzig.

Scaliger, J. J. 1565. *Coniectanea in M. Terentium Varronem de lingua Latina*. Paris.

Schierl, P. 2006. *Die Tragödien des Pacuvius: Ein Kommentar zu den Fragmenten mit Einleitung, Text, und Übersetzung*. Berlin.

Skutsch, O. 1985. *The Annals of Quintus Ennius*. Oxford.

Spengel, L. 1834. Review of *Pauli Diaconi excerpta ex libris Festi de significatione uerborum et Sexti Pompeii Festi fragmenta librorum de significatione uerborum*, ed. by F. Lindemann. *Zeitschrift für die Altertumswissenschaft* 1:697–716.

Stephanus, R. and H. Stephanus. 1564. *Fragmenta poetarum ueterum Latinorum quorum opera non extant ... undique a Rob. Stephano summa diligentia olim congesta, nunc autem ab Henrico Stephano eius filio digesta ...* [Geneva?].

Strzelecki, W. v. 1932. *Quaestiones Verrianae*. Warsaw.

———. 1935. *De Naeuiano Belli Punici carmine quaestiones selectae*. Krakow.

———. 1959. "Ein Beitrag zur Quellenbenutzung des Nonius." In *Aus der altertumswissenschaftlichen Arbeit Volkspolens*, ed. J. Irmscher et al., 81–90. Berlin.

———. 1964. *Belli Punici carminis quae supersunt*. Leipzig.

Thewrewk de Ponor, A. 1893. *Codex Festi Farnesianus XLII tabulis expressus*. Budapest.

Timpanaro, S., Jr. 1946. "Per una nuova edizione critica di Ennio." *Studi italiani di filologia classica* 21:41–81.

Vahlen, J. 1903. *Ennianae poesis reliquiae*. 2nd ed. Leipzig.

Warmington, E. H. 1935. *Ennius and Caecilius.* Vol. 1 of *Remains of Old Latin.* London.

Watt, W. S. 2004. "Error Wattianus." *CQ*, n.s., 54:658–660.

Welsh, J. T. 2010. "The Grammarian C. Iulius Romanus and the *Fabula Togata*." *HSCP* 105:255–285.

———. 2012. "The Methods of Nonius Marcellus' Sources 26, 27, and 28." *CQ*, n.s., 62:827–845.

———. 2013. "Some Fragments of Republican Drama From Nonius Marcellus' Sources 26, 27, and 28." *CQ*, n.s., 63:253–276.

White, D. C. 1980. "The Method of Composition and Sources of Nonius Marcellus." *Studi Noniani* 8:111–211.

ROME IN THE *ALEXANDER ROMANCE*

BENJAMIN GARSTAD

A CCORDING TO THE *ALEXANDER ROMANCE*, the great Macedonian conqueror went to Rome and received the submission of the city and its people, who provided troops and funds in support of his campaign against the Persians. This is, of course, one of the countless details in the *Romance* tradition which does not merely deviate from reliable history but runs counter to it. This corruption of the historical record might be of no interest to those who are chiefly concerned with the career of Alexander, but it is worth the attention of those who are concerned with his legacy. The inclusion of the Romans in Alexander's empire seems to have its basis in a number of rhetorical and historical traditions: reports of Roman diplomatic contacts with Alexander, rumors about Alexander's plans for the future, the invasion of Italy by Alexander Molossus at the same time as his nephew's expedition to Asia, and Roman counterfactual speculation about what would have happened if Alexander had made war on Rome. These are worth noting as the constituents of historical data in some late antique compositions. The passages which make Rome part of Alexander's domain also tell us something of how their authors wished Rome to be seen in relation to Alexander, the goals he pursued, and the ideals he represented.

The manuscript tradition of the *Alexander Romance* is complex and involved, to the extent that the different recensions with their substantial additions and omissions often seem to represent distinct texts rather than minor deviations in transmission.[1] This welter of recen-

The author would like to acknowledge his gratitude to Richard Stoneman, who read a draft of the present paper and did much to improve it by his helpful comments, and to dedicate this paper to the memory of his aunt, Elsie Lambert (1931–2010), who knew the value of a good story.

[1] Stoneman 1991:28–32 and 2008:230–245.

sions has produced two versions of Alexander's visit to Rome. The first is found in the oldest recension of the *Romance* (α). After he fought the battle at the Granicus and subdued Asia Minor, Alexander is supposed to have proceeded to Sicily and from there to Italy:

καὶ συνθύσας τοῖς ἐκεῖ στρατηγοῖς διεπέρασεν ἐπὶ Σικελίαν καὶ τινὰς ἀπειθήσαντας αὐτῷ ὑποτάξας διαπορθμεύεται ⟨εἰς⟩ τὴν Ἰταλίαν χώραν. οἱ δὲ Ῥωμαίων στρατηγοὶ πέμπουσι διὰ Μάρκου Αἰμιλίου στρατηγοῦ τὸν τοῦ Καπιτωλίου Διὸς στέφανον πεπλεγμένον διὰ μαργαριτῶν λέγοντες· προσεπιστεφανοῦμέν σε κατ' ἔτος Ἀλέξανδρε χρυσοῦν στέφανον ὁλκῆς λιτρῶν ρ'. ὁ δὲ παραδεξάμενος αὐτῶν τὴν εὐπείθειαν ἐπηγγείλατο αὐτοὺς μεγάλους ποιήσειν. λαμβάνει δὲ παρ' αὐτῶν στρατιώτας χιλίους καὶ τάλαντα τετρακόσια· ἔλεγον δὲ καὶ πλείονας αὐτῷ δώσειν στρατιώτας, εἰ μὴ τὸν πόλεμον συνῆπτον Καρχηδονίοις.[2]

He sacrificed with his generals there and went over to Sicily and after he subdued those who were disobedient to him he crossed to the land of Italy. The generals of the Romans sent through Marcus Aemilius, the general [or consul], the crown of Capitoline Zeus, made of pearls, saying, "We crown you besides, Alexander, for the year with a golden crown of a hundred pounds' weight." When he had received their obeisance he promised to make them great. He obtained from them a thousand soldiers and four hundred talents; they said that they would have given him more soldiers if they were not engaged in the war with the Carthaginians.

If we cannot say when precisely this episode attached itself to the collection of legendary material on Alexander that made up the *Romance*, we do know that it was included in the Greek text of the

---

[2] *Al. Rom.* (α) 1.26.4–6 (Stoneman 1991 cites this passage as 1.29); ed. Kroll 1926:26.15–27.3. This and all subsequent translations are the author's own.

Romance when it was translated into Latin by Julius Valerius some time between 270 and 330.[3] The Latin is a fairly free rendering of the Greek:

> eximque Italiam transiens legatione pariter et honore potitur Romanorum. per Aemilium quippe tunc consulem corona ei auri pondo centum, insignita etiam margaritis, honoraria datur ad argumentum amicitiae perpetuo post futurae; idque Alexandro magnae gratiae fuit amicitiamque amplectitur et verbis liberalibus Aemilium honoratum remittit. Addunt tamen Romani et militum duo milia et argenti talenta quadringenta eoque amplius fore daturos sese respondent, ni sibi bellum adversus Carthaginienses intentissimum agitaretur.[4]

And then he crossed to Italy and received an embassy of the Romans on terms of equality and with honor. Through Aemilius, since he was then the consul, an honorary crown of a hundredweight of gold and distinguished with pearls was given to him as a token of friendship ever after. This was a great favor to Alexander and he embraced the friendship and sent Aemilius away honored with courteous words. The Romans, all the same, provided two thousand soldiers and four hundred talents of silver and insisted that they would give more if they were not engaged in a most protracted war against the Carthaginians.

The latest and longest of the Greek recensions, (γ), can be dated to some time after 691 when one of its sources, the *Apocalypse* of Pseudo-Methodius,[5] was composed and demonstrates the elaborations and modifications that the *Romance* underwent over the course of late antiquity. The (γ) recension includes a version of Alexander's reception of the Roman embassy, with two remarkable discrepancies from the version in the (α) recension: the ambassadors indicate that they are crowning Alexander "king of the Romans and the whole world"

---

[3] Stoneman 1999:174–180.
[4] Julius Valerius 1.29; ed. Rosellini 1993:36.783–37.792.
[5] Brock 1982:18–19; Reinink 1992:178–186.

and omit the proviso that he is crowned "for a year" (κατ' ἔτος) and the Romans are not made to excuse the size of their contribution on account of the war with Carthage.

καὶ διελθὼν ἦλθεν ἐν ᾧ ἦσαν αἱ τῶν πλωίμων αὐτοῦ δυνάμεις, καὶ διεπέρασε καὶ ἦλθεν εἰς Σικελίαν. καί τινας ἀντιτιθοῦντας αὐτῷ ὑποτάξας διεπέρασε καὶ ἦλθεν εἰς τὴν Ἰταλικὴν χώραν. οἱ δὲ τῶν Ῥωμαίων στρατηγοὶ πέμπουσι διὰ Μάρκου στρατηγοῦ αὐτῶν στέφανον διὰ μαργαρίτων καὶ ἕτερον διὰ τιμίων λίθων, λέγοντες αὐτῷ· προσεπιστεφανοῦμέν σε Ἀλέξανδρε βασιλεῦ Ῥωμαίων καὶ πάσης γῆς, προσάγοντες αὐτῷ καὶ χρυσίου λίτρας πεντεκοσίας. ὁ δὲ Ἀλέξανδρος δεξάμενος τὴν εὐχαριστίαν αὐτῶν ἐπηγγείλατο μεγάλους αὐτοὺς ποιεῖν τῇ δυνάμει. καὶ παρ' αὐτῶν λαμβάνει στρατιώτας τοξότας δισχιλίους καὶ τάλαντα τετρακόσια.[6]

He passed through and came to where his forces under sail were, and he crossed over and came to Sicily. He subdued those who were opposed to him and crossed over and came to the land of Italy. The generals of the Romans sent through Marcus, their general [*or* consul], a crown with pearls and another with precious stones, saying to him, "We crown you besides, Alexander, king of the Romans and the whole world." And they brought him in addition five hundred pounds of gold. Alexander received their expression of gratitude and promised to make them great in power. And he obtained from them two thousand soldiers, bowmen, and four hundred talents.

In the (γ) recension, however, this episode is preceded by two other passages which involve Rome. While in the (α) recension, before the death of Philip, the youthful Alexander proves himself in a chariot-race at the Olympic Games at Elis (called Pisa in the text), the chariot-race is held at Rome in the (γ) recension:

---

[6]　*Al. Rom.* (γ) 1.29; ed. Lauenstein 1962:102.10–21.

μιᾷ οὖν τῶν ἡμερῶν μετὰ τῶν συνηλικιωτῶν αὐτοῦ
συνὼν, λόγους ἐκ λόγων προτείναντος, εἰσφέρεται λόγος
ὡς ὅτι ἐν Ῥώμῃ ἁρματηλατοῦσιν οἱ εὐδοκιμώτεροι τῶν
βασιλέων παῖδες. καὶ τῷ νικήσαντι ἆθλα δίδονται ὑπὸ τοῦ
Καπετωλίου Διός· ὃς δ᾽ ἂν ἡττηθεὶς, παρὰ τῶν νικησάντων
θανατοῦται. ταῦτα ἀκούσας Ἀλέξανδρος ἔρχεται πρὸς
Φίλιππον δρομαῖος καὶ καταφιλήσας αὐτὸν εἶπε· πάτερ τὸ
ἐν ἐμοὶ καταθύμιον πλήρωσον καὶ ἐπίτρεψόν μοι ἐν Ῥώμῃ
ἀπελθεῖν, ἐπειδὴ ἀγωνίσασθαι βούλομαι.[7]

One day when he was with his age-mates, stretching
words out of words, word was brought that the especially
honored sons of kings were driving their chariots in Rome.
And prizes would be given to the victor by Capitoline Zeus,
but the loser would be killed by the victors. When he heard
these things Alexander went running to Philip and kissing
him tenderly said, "Father, satisfy the thought on my mind
and permit me to go off to Rome, since I wish to compete."

After Alexander ascends the throne and sets out on his campaigns,
and before he receives the embassy from the Romans under Marcus, he
is supposed to have gone to Rome itself and received the submission of
the city in person:

ἀπάρας οὖν τῶν ἐκεῖσε Ἀλέξανδρος ᾤχετο Ῥώμην
καταλαβεῖν. καὶ σχεδὸν προϋπαντῶσιν αὐτῷ πρέσβεις
ἐκ πάντων ἐθνῶν καὶ προσκυνοῦσιν ἔμπροσθεν αὐτοῦ,
ἄγοντες αὐτῷ δῶρα χρυσὸν καὶ ἄργυρον ὅσον οὔκ ἐστιν
ἀριθμός, συνερχόμενοι αὐτῷ πάντες εἰς συμμαχίαν. καὶ
δὴ καταλαμβάνει τὴν Ῥώμην καὶ προϋπαντῶσιν αὐτῷ
Ῥωμαῖοι μετὰ χορῶν καὶ τυμπάνων καὶ κλάδους δάφνης
ἔχοντες ταῖς χερσὶν αὐτῶν· καὶ τῷ Ἀλεξάνδρῳ ἐπεισιόντες
καὶ βασιλεῖ κοσμοκράτορα τοῦτον ἀναγορεύουσιν.

---

[7] *Al. Rom.* (γ) 1.18; ed. Lauenstein 1962:44.19–46.1. The substitution of Rome for Elis/
Pisa is maintained throughout until Alexander's acclamation on his return from Rome at
1.20 (ed. Lauenstein 1962:54.19–56.8).

εἰσελθὼν δὲ ἐν τῇ πόλει ἄπεισιν ἐν τῷ Καπετωλίῳ Διός, καὶ ὁ ἱερεὺς δέχεται αὐτόν, καὶ ξενίζεται παρ' αὐτοῦ.

διατριψάντων οὖν ἐν Ῥώμῃ ἰδοὺ καὶ Λαομέδων ὁ συναρματηλατήσας αὐτῷ σὺν χιλιάσι πεντήκοντα ἧκεν εἰς συμμαχίαν Ἀλεξάνδρου ἔχων μεθ' ἑαυτοῦ δῶρα ἔν τε χρυσίῳ καὶ λίθοις καὶ μαργάροις. δέχεται δὲ τοῦτον Ἀλέξανδρος καὶ γνησίως ἀσπάζεται καὶ, ὦ γενναῖε, εἶπεν, ἧκάς μοι μετὰ Δαρείου μαχομένῳ σύμμαχος εἶναι. ἀπάρας οὖν ἀπὸ Ῥώμης ὥρμησε κατὰ δυσμῶν καὶ οὐκ ἦν αὐτῷ ὁ ἀνθιστάμενος. καὶ προσαπαντῶσιν αὐτὸν πᾶσαι αἱ βασιλεῖαι δυσμῶν καὶ δώροις ἐκμειλίσσονται αὐτῷ καὶ παρακαλοῦσιν ἐπιβῆναι αὐτῶν τὴν γῆν· καὶ λαβὼν αὐτῶν τὰ δῶρα ἀνθυποστρέφει καταλείπων αὐτῶν πάντων κύριον τὸν Λαομέδοντα συνταξάμενοι φόρους αὐτῷ τελεῖν μέχρι καὶ χρόνων δώδεκα.[8]

Then starting from there Alexander went to conquer Rome. And nearby envoys from all nations went out to meet him and prostrated themselves before him, bringing him gifts of gold and silver, which were without number, and all agreed to an alliance with him. And presently he conquered Rome and the Romans went out to meet him with choruses and drums, holding branches of laurel in their hands; and they approached Alexander as a king and proclaimed him the ruler of the world. Going into the city he went off to the Capitolium of Zeus, and the priest received him, and he was entertained as a guest by him.

While they were staying in Rome, behold, Laomedon, who drove the chariot with him, came with fifty thousand [men] for an alliance with Alexander, and he brought gifts in gold and stones and pearls. Alexander received him and welcomed him sincerely and said, "Noble sir, you have come to be my ally as I fight with Darius." So he left Rome and marched against the regions of the west and no one

8   *Al. Rom.* (γ) 1.27; ed. Lauenstein 1962:98.1–22.

opposed him. And all the kingdoms of the west came to meet him and propitiated him with gifts and called upon him to come to their country; and taking their gifts he turned about, leaving behind Laomedon as lord of them all, and they prescribed that they pay tribute to him for twelve years.

In what follows we shall describe the influences which may have contributed to the assertion that Alexander had gone to Italy to receive the submission of the Romans, without isolating any one of them as the exclusive source of such a claim, but rather assuming that each supplied its own information to an aggregate conception. Then we shall turn to the intentions which may have led the authors of the *Romance*, the makers of the fabulous history of Alexander, to concoct such a story on the basis of these influences.

I. SOURCES

It is perhaps inappropriate to speak of sources for a fiction, but we can certainly identify the influences which might have congealed into an accepted "fact" under the right impetus. That impetus will be discussed later, but we shall now enumerate the influences and try to discern how they might have given rise to the *Romance*'s account of relations between Alexander and Rome.

There was a report in circulation in antiquity that the Romans had sent envoys to Alexander, not as he marched through Italy before setting out against the Persians, but to Babylon in the last year of his life. Arrian offers us the fullest account of the Roman embassy and is almost alone in offering us any account at all, although he does ascribe the story to two predecessors, now lost, Aristus and Asclepiades.[9] Arrian himself refuses to either vouch for the story or reject it outright, but he provides his reader with grounds for incredulity rather than evenhanded agnosticism by pointing out that the Roman embassy was referred to by no

---

[9] Arr. *Anab.* 7.15.5–6. Aristus: *FGrH* 143 F 2; Asclepiades: *FGrH* 144 F 1. Cf. Strabo 5.3.5, in which it is recorded that Alexander complained to the Romans of the piracy of the city of Antium.

Roman historian, nor by his preferred sources on Alexander, Ptolemy and Aristobulus, and that it is unlikely that the Romans would have had any truck with kings and tyrants at a time when they enjoyed freedom in the greatest degree. Pliny says that Cleitarchus mentioned the Roman embassy to Alexander, and, while some doubt has been cast on the attribution of his notice, Pliny, nevertheless, shows that the story was known beyond Arrian and his sources.[10] Other histories of Alexander which record embassies arriving at Babylon from distant nations make no mention of the Romans.[11] Considering the qualms, detachment, and silences of our ancient authorities, it should come as no surprise that modern historians have approached this account with considerable hesitancy; the latter half of the twentieth century, however, saw the preponderance of opinion shift from Tarn's rejection of the Roman embassy as a first-century BC fabrication to Bosworth's affirmation that a kernel of truth must lie at the heart of a far from immaculate report.[12] Fortunately, it is not necessary for us to determine the historicity of the report of diplomatic contacts between Alexander and the Romans. It is sufficient for our purposes to note that such a report attached itself to accounts of Alexander certainly as early as Pliny's day, perhaps a good deal earlier. We shall now turn to the highly instructive details of Arrian's version of this report.

The report of a Roman embassy to Babylon might very well have suggested, in broad terms, the eminent plausibility of the _Romance_'s account of Marcus Aemilius being sent as an envoy once Alexander had been brought to Italy itself. It would be surprising if the one story of Roman emissaries meeting with Alexander did not contribute to the other, later one. There are, moreover, specific details which indicate that the Roman embassy to Babylon reported in Arrian—or a text closely related to it—influenced the initial composition of the portion of the _Romance_ in question. The first point in this regard depends upon the context of the passage in Arrian. Arrian's discussion of the

---

[10] Pliny _HN_ 3.57–58. Cleitarchus: _FGrH_ 137 F 31. See Tarn 1948:21–26.

[11] Diod. Sic. 17.113.1–4; Just. _Epit._ 12.13.1–2.

[12] Tarn 1948:21–26, 376–377; Sordi 1965:445–450; Schachermeyr 1970:218–223; Weippert 1972:1–10; Braccesi 1975:47–72; Martin 1982–1994: vol. 2, 19–26; Sordi 1985:207–214; Bosworth 1988:83–93; Braccesi 1995:51–52; Braccesi 2006:68–75.

possible Roman embassy follows his unquestioning account of ambassadors from a number of far-flung nations, in the west and elsewhere, meeting Alexander en route to Babylon.[13] The account opens with embassies of Libyans (that is, various African peoples) "congratulating him and crowning him on the kingship of Asia" (ἐπαινούντων τε καὶ στεφανούντων ἐπὶ τῇ βασιλείᾳ τῆς Ἀσίας) and the Bruttians, Lucanians, and Etruscans from Italy following suit.[14] Arrian's two coordinated participles should undoubtedly be taken closely together and we should understand that the crown or crowns offered by the embassies were presumably intended as victor's crowns, akin in spirit to the prizes in athletic competitions, not symbols of sovereignty and tokens of submission. This reading is strengthened by Arrian's suggestion that Alexander's reception of the embassies and their gifts was not an occasion for his presumption of universal rule (φανῆναι γῆς τε ἁπάσης καὶ θαλάσσης κύριον) until certain emissaries asked him to settle disputes amongst themselves, the right of arbitration, not the receipt of crowns, being understood as indicative of sovereignty. At any rate, envoys bearing crowns for Alexander introduce Arrian's account of the embassies, and so too in the *Romance* Marcus Aemilius is commissioned primarily to present a crown to Alexander. But, in an odd mixture of apparent erudition and ignorance, the crowns in the *Romance* have a different intent from those offered by Arrian's embassies. In the days of the Republic the Romans granted golden crowns to successful generals, as the ambassadors in Arrian did, but the crown the Romans offer Alexander in the *Romance* must be something more than that inasmuch as it is granted for a year (κατ' ἔτος), the duration of the chief magistracy of Rome, the consulship, and is taken by the narrator to indicate their obeisance (αὐτῶν τὴν εὐπείθειαν). Republican consuls did not wear crowns as part of their regalia and their office was certainly not open to foreign kings, but these slips, whether anachronisms or flights of imagination, allow the author to vividly convey his point.

[13] Arr. *Anab.* 7.15.4.
[14] Diod. Sic. 17.113.1 also mentions that some of the embassies came with the intention of crowning Alexander (οἱ δὲ στεφανοῦντες).

The *Romance* is in fact closer to another text than to Arrian at this point and we are fortunately in a position to identify it. Photius notes in his summary of the histories of Memnon of Heracleia that the historian offered an account of the relations between Alexander and the Romans:

ὅπως τε ἐπὶ τὴν Ἀσίαν Ἀλεξάνδρωι διαβαίνοντι, καὶ γράψαντι ἢ κρατεῖν, ἐὰν ἄρχειν δύνωνται, ἢ τοῖς κρείττοσιν ὑπείκειν, στέφανον χρυσοῦν ἀπὸ ἱκανῶν ταλάντων Ῥωμαῖοι ἐξέπεμψαν.[15]

When Alexander was crossing over into Asia and had written [them] either to be strong, if they were able to start, or to submit to those who are stronger, the Romans sent a golden crown of a considerable weight of talents.

Here, as in the *Romance*, the Romans offer a crown to Alexander, significantly *before* he sets off against the Persians, and here the crown is taken as a sign of submission. Although both the Alexander of history and the Alexander of fiction receive crowns from Italian embassies, the crown in the *Romance* is not Arrian's crown; it is an emblem of submission to a sovereign authority.

A further instance of a particular element from Arrian's passage influencing the *Romance* also shows adjustment and adaptation, rather than simple borrowing. According to Arrian's sources, when Alexander encountered the Roman embassy he "prophesied something of their future power" (ὑπὲρ Ῥωμαίων τι τῆς ἐς τὸ ἔπειτα ἐσομένης δυνάμεως μαντεύσασθαι).[16] The presence of such a *vaticinium ex eventu* is precisely the sort of detail that casts doubt on the incident as a whole, and at least indicates that Arrian chose a rhetorically florid and obviously unreliable version for inclusion in his history.[17] The author of the *Romance*, however, does not seem to have been bothered by the implausibility of Alexander's prophecy so much as its insubstantial quality. He has Alexander not foresee Rome's greatness, but promise to make

---

[15] *FGrH* 434 F 18.2 = Photius *Bibl.* 224 (229A).
[16] Arr. *Anab.* 7.15.5.
[17] See Bosworth 1988:93.

the Romans great (ἐπηγγείλατο αὐτοὺς μεγάλους ποιήσειν). It is easy to see how a prediction of greatness from a great man could have been reworked into an impartation of greatness, but the modification is significant. In the *Romance* it is Alexander himself who made the Romans great, not the virtues of order, hard work, and freedom which he is supposed to have observed in them according to Aristus and Asclepiades. Even though the *Romance* does not indicate how Alexander fulfilled his promise, the promise itself makes the Romans heirs to Alexander, who can bestow his own greatness on them. The *Romance* may even provide a hint as to how Alexander makes the Romans great. The promise is immediately followed by a report of the Romans' contribution to Alexander's army. Perhaps it is participation in Alexander's adventures that allows Rome to share in his greatness.

If the visit of the Roman envoy to Alexander in the *Romance* is based on a specific passage in Arrian, and not merely on the general circulation of a report of a Roman embassy to Alexander, we might consider that there was not only influence from Arrian, but even allusion and response back to the passage in Arrian. For instance, Arrian offers as grounds for the implausibility of the report of the Roman embassy the fact that no Roman historian had recorded it.[18] The author of the *Romance* must also have been aware that the historical record made no mention of Alexander's reception of a Roman delegation on Italian soil. But he makes an effort to account for this fact, if only implicitly. The passage on the Roman embassy in the *Romance*, at least in the (α) recension, ends with the Romans explicitly excusing the paucity of their contribution of men and money because they are engaged in a war with Carthage. There is an obvious anachronism here; the First Punic War did not begin until 264 BC, some sixty years after the death of Alexander. But the Roman excuse may not so much exhibit sloppy historical sense as respond to an explanatory necessity. Since the Roman contribution to Alexander's army as well as the entire Roman encounter with Alexander are fictitious, the number of soldiers and talents might have been as large as the imagination was pleased to make them. The excuse of prior military obligations, however, allows

18 Arr. *Anab.* 7.15.6.

the romancer to insist on the truth of his account and explain its unprecedented deviation from the received historical record. The Romans did make a pact with Alexander, and like his other allies they contributed to his army, but because they were at war with Carthage that contribution was so small and insignificant that it was forgotten by historians. The *Alexander Romance* may include another allusion to Rome's obscurity, explaining her absence from the record of Alexander's campaigns. In one of the letters they exchange in the course of the *Romance* Darius derides Alexander's accomplishments up to the point when they first meet in battle:

καὶ ἐτόλμησας θάλασσαν διαπερᾶσαι καὶ οὐ μακάριον ἡγήσω λανθάνοντά σε βασιλεύειν Μακεδονίας χωρὶς τῆς ἐμῆς ταγῆς, ἀλλ' ἀδέσποτον χώραν εὑρὼν σεαυτὸν βασιλέα ἀπέδειξας, συλλέξας ἑαυτῷ ἄνδρας ὁμοίους σου ἀνελπίστους, καὶ ἐπεστρατεύσω πόλεσιν Ἕλλησιν ἀπειροπολέμοις καὶ εὐλαβηθείσαις τὸ δεσπόζεσθαι, ἃς ἐγὼ περισσὰς ἡγοῦμαι ὡς ἀπερριμμένας καὶ οὐκ ἐπεζήτησα φόρους παρ' ἐκείνων.[19]

And you dared to cross over the sea and did not consider yourself fortunate to rule Macedonia unnoticed under my command, but found a country without a master and you appointed yourself king, gathering to yourself men as desperate as yourself, and you led your army against Greek cities inexperienced in war and afraid of being ruled despotically, which I considered superfluous, as despicable, and did not demand tribute from them.

Appropriately enough, Darius' letter does not name the insignificant cities he did not deign to conquer; this opens the way to some ambiguous readings. In the (β) recension, derived from the (α), as well as in the (γ) recension, the last few phrases read καὶ πολεμεῖς πόλεις ἀπείρους, ἃς ἐγὼ ἀεὶ εὐλαβηθεὶς δεσπόζεσθαι περισσὰς ἡγούμην ὡς

---

[19] *Al. Rom.* (α) 1.40.3; ed. Kroll 1926:45.5–10.

ἀπορεριμμένας, καὶ σὺ ἐπεζήτησας φόρους παρ' αὐτῶν λήψεσθαι ὡς ἐρανιζόμενος[20] (and you made war on inexperienced cities, which I always refrained from overmastering because I considered them superfluous, as despised, and you demanded to receive tribute from them, as one taking up a collection). Perhaps the adjective "Greek" has been dropped to give the unnamed cities a wider field of reference; perhaps "Greek" is a later addition to the manuscript we possess of the (α) recension. At any rate, the "country without a master" could refer to Rome, whose republican status ("masterless" in the eyes of a despot like Darius) is noted in the Romance when the Roman emissary is sent by a board of generals.[21] The Roman contingent could be amongst the desperate men gathered about Alexander. And the tribute collected as if by a man soliciting subscriptions could be a decidedly unflattering way of describing the money Alexander received from the Romans. In any case, Darius' letter suggests an explanation for the failure of the histories of Alexander to mention Rome: if the King of Kings thought the cities Alexander subdued before their first meeting too negligible to name, let alone conquer, it must come as no surprise if they are not called to mind by historians. The Romance, in perhaps more than one instance, defends its own account of Alexander and the Romans and responds to Arrian's doubts about Rome's contacts with Alexander explicitly grounded in the absence of such contacts from the historical record.

The next identifiable influence on the appearance of Rome in the Romance concerns the plans which Alexander was rumored to have left unfinished at his death. A widely reported tradition held that, after his conquests in the east, Alexander intended to launch a campaign against the peoples of the western Mediterranean. This plan is supposed to have been carried out in two distinct ways. Arrian and Plutarch indicate that Alexander planned to set out from the Euphrates, circumnavigate Africa, and enter the Mediterranean at the Pillars of Hercules; Arrian

---

[20] Al. Rom. (β) 1.40.3; ed. van Thiel 1974:60.10–12; Al. Rom. (γ) 1.39; ed. Lauenstein 1962:138.17–19.

[21] Richard Stoneman, in a personal communication, has indicated that he had taken the ἀδέσποτος χώρα to be Macedonia, deprived of a king by the assassination of Philip.

adds that Alexander would then have subdued all of Libya (Africa) and Carthage.[22] Diodorus and Curtius report that a naval expedition was to set out from the ports of the north-east Mediterranean against Carthage and then proceed along the coasts of Africa, Iberia, and Italy and then home to Epirus.[23] The latter version, which has Alexander's proposed fleet coasting along the Tyrrhenian shore of Italy, might be taken to imply some action against Rome, but it is Arrian alone who includes specific mention of Rome in Alexander's final plans. He says that accounts vary regarding Alexander's intentions after the expedition to the western Mediterranean; either he planned to sail into the Black Sea or to Sicily and the Iapygian promontory (at the heel of Italy), in the latter case because "he was already concerned that the reputation of the Romans was proceeding to greatness" (ἤδη γὰρ καὶ ὑποκινεῖν αὐτὸν τὸ Ῥωμαίων ὄνομα προχωροῦν ἐπὶ μέγα).[24]

As with the embassies to Alexander, opinions as to the authenticity of Alexander's plans have varied amongst modern historians. Tarn believed that the stories of intended conquest grew out of Alexander's actual plans for exploration and the later insistence of certain jealous Greeks that what Rome had in fact (namely, dominion over the Mediterranean basin) Alexander might have had if fate had not intervened.[25] Badian considered the final plans fictions, but highly plausible fictions contemporary with Alexander's death, concocted by Perdiccas to ensure the annulment of all of the stipulations of Alexander's will, particularly his orders to Craterus.[26] Schachermeyr, on the other hand, accepted the authenticity of the plans without exception, and

----

[22] Arr. Anab. 7.1.2, cf. 4.7.5, 5.26.2; Plut. Alex. 68.1. Dion. Hal. Ant. Rom. 1.2.4 also notes the failure of the Macedonian dominion to accomplish the very projects in question in the final plans: the conquest of Libya and Europe.

[23] Diod. Sic. 18.4.4; Curt. 10.1.17–19. To be precise, Diodorus says the expedition was directed "against the Carthaginians and the others of Libya and Iberia who live by the sea and the adjacent coastland as far as Sicily" (ἐπὶ Καρχηδονίους καὶ τοὺς ἄλλους τοὺς παρὰ θάλατταν κατοικοῦντας τῆς τε Λιβύης καὶ Ἰβηρίας καὶ τῆς ὁμόρου χώρας παραθαλαττίου μέχρι Σικελίας), while Curtius says that the expedition was "to sail past the Alps and the coast of Italy, whence it is a short passage to Epirus" (praetervehi Alpes Italiaeque oram, unde in Epirum brevis cursus est).

[24] Arr. Anab. 7.1.3.

[25] Tarn 1948:394–397.

[26] Badian 1968:183–204 (191–194 esp.); cf. Badian 1985:490–491.

Bosworth found evidence in the naval activity of the Successors to suggest that the preparations for the expedition against the western Mediterranean were under way at the time of Alexander's death.[27] Once again, we are in the happy position of not having to make a determination amongst these opinions. Whether Alexander had indeed planned an expedition against the western Mediterranean or such a plan was a fabrication imputed to him and datable to the time of his death or the acme of Rome's power, the account of his plans would have had equal weight in the later period when the *Romance* was composed.

In regard to our problem, what is significant is the ease with which legend can turn an intention into an action, which is surely, in part, what has become of Alexander's final plans in the *Romance*. Alexander was said to have contemplated a campaign in the western Mediterranean which might have encompassed Rome, and in one account intended to take action against Rome's growing power, and in the *Romance* these plans are realized before, not after, he sets out for the east. Even the romancer must have conceded he couldn't have done better than Alexander's death at Babylon as a climax to the drama of his story. Apart from this general observation, the rumors of Alexander's final plans can explain a few of the details in the *Romance*'s narrative of his encounter with the Romans. In the *Romance* Alexander advances on Italy by way of Sicily. He subdues some opponents there, but it is otherwise difficult to see what necessitates this route, which is not the natural one from Greece to Italy, nor the usual one in antiquity. Sicily is, however, mentioned in two accounts of Alexander's plans. Diodorus says that his fleet would have coasted around the western Mediterranean including the shores of Sicily, and, more importantly, Arrian reports an account that Alexander intended to proceed against Rome by moving on Sicily.[28] Diodorus at least implicates Sicily in any activity Alexander might undertake in the west and Arrian lays out as

---

[27] Schachermeyr 1954:131–138 esp. and including a bibliography of previous scholarship on the subject; Sordi 1965:438–445; Schachermeyr 1970:187–194; Schachermeyr 1973:547–556; Braccesi 1975:47–72; Goukowsky 1978–1981: vol. 1, 66–68; Bosworth 1988:185–211; see also Braccesi 2006:54–68; Briant 2010:38–41.

[28] On the place that Sicily, and Syracuse in particular, may be imputed to have held in the considerations of Alexander, see Sordi 1983.

an itinerary the route Alexander is supposed to have followed in the *Romance*.

On another point, every version of Alexander's plans (except Plutarch's apparently abbreviated one) indicates that one of the primary goals of the expedition to the western Mediterranean was the conquest of Carthage. In the *Romance* Alexander does encounter the Carthaginians, immediately after meeting the Romans, and refuses to relieve them of the Roman onslaught:

> κἀκεῖθεν ἀναβὰς καὶ διαπεράσας τὸ μεταξὺ πέλαγος παρεγένατο εἰς Ἀφρικήν· οἱ δὲ τῶν Ἄφρων στρατηγοὶ ἀπαντήσαντες ἱκέτευσαν αὐτὸν ἀποστῆσαι Ῥωμαίους τῆς πόλεως. ὁ δὲ τῆς ἀδρανείας αὐτῶν καταγνοὺς εἶπεν· ἢ κρείττονες γίνεσθε ἢ τοῖς κρείττοσι φόρους τελεῖτε.[29]

And from there he went up and crossed over the intervening sea and arrived in Africa. The generals of the Africans went to meet him and supplicated him to remove the Romans from the city. But he condemned their weakness and said, "Either become stronger or submit to those who are stronger."

I intend to address the obvious affinities of this passage with the excerpt from Memnon of Heracleia below. For the present I would insist that Alexander's encounter with the Carthaginians in the *Romance* is more than another instance of Alexander's supposed intentions becoming his legendary deeds. The Romans excuse the smallness of their contribution to Alexander's forces by reference to their war with the Carthaginians. In addition to explaining the absence of the Romans from the history of Alexander's campaigns, as suggested above, there is an intimation that even before they meet the Romans are in accord with the intentions of Alexander in regard to barbarous foreigners, and that the Romans failed to distinguish themselves fighting the Persians with Alexander because they were occupied with their own oriental

---

[29] *Al. Rom.* (α) 1.30.1; ed. Kroll 1926:27.4–7. In the (γ) recension the word Ῥωμαίους has fallen out of the text and the phrase ἱκέτευον ἀποστῆναι ἀπὸ τῆς πόλεως αὐτῶν Καρταγένης has become confused and unclear.

barbarian foes, the Carthaginians. A certain equivalence between conflicts with the Persians and the Carthaginians respectively was, after all, well established by such historiographic fancies as the report (probably based on pure supposition) that before their second invasion of Greece the Persians had recruited the Carthaginians as allies to attack the Greeks in the west and the highly improbable, but deeply meaningful, synchronism—to the day—of the Carthaginian defeat at Himera with the battle of Salamis or Thermopylae.[30]

If the two points of influence identified above may be characterized as extrapolation or exaggeration, the next seems to be an example of plain confusion. Alexander III of Macedon appears to have been identified with his uncle and namesake, Alexander I of Epirus, and the deeds of the one attributed to the other. Alexander of Epirus, also known as Alexander Molossus, the brother of Olympias and a favorite of Philip, was brought up at the Macedonian court and installed on the Epirote throne by Philip. In 334 BC Alexander responded to a call from the citizens of Tarentum and came over to Italy to fight against the Lucanians and Bruttians. He enjoyed some success until he was treacherously slain by one of the Lucanian exiles in his party.[31] The two Alexanders did not merely share a name; they were close contemporaries and near relations who were both reared in the court of Philip II, both set out on ambitious foreign campaigns in the very same year, and both died young far from home.

This parallelism was not lost on the ancients. Justin remarks on Alexander's keenness as he sailed for Italy, as if the world had been divided between himself and his nephew, the West for the one and the East for the other, and each with a sphere in which to make a name for himself.[32] Livy notes in his chronology that the undertakings of Alexander of Epirus and Alexander of Macedon were contemporary

---

[30] Hdt. 7.166; Diod. Sic. 11.1.4–2.1, 24.1.

[31] Just. *Epit.* 8.6.4–8, 9.6.1–4, 12.2.1–15; Livy, 8.24. On Alexander's Italian campaign and particularly its chronology, which is more vexed than I may have suggested, see Manni 1962:344–352. See also Braccesi 1975:117–123; Braccesi 1995:52–53; Braccesi 2006:43–54.

[32] Just. *Epit.* 12.2.1–2: *ita cupide profectus fuerat, velut in divisione orbis terrarum Alexandro, Olympiadis, sororis suae, filio, Oriens, sibi Occidens sorte contigisset, non minorem rerum materiam in Italia, Africa, Siciliaque, quam ille in Asia et in Persis habiturus.*

and, in his speculation on Alexander's chances against Rome, that the
Macedonian conqueror would have been dismayed by the signs of his
uncle's discomfiture.[33] Livy and Aulus Gellius both report that Alexander
Molossus contrasted his campaign with his nephew's by saying that
while he set out against a nation of men the king of Macedon was
going to make war on a nation of women.[34] Whether this contrast was a
genuine expression of the sentiments of Alexander Molossus or a later
embellishment matters little; it came to embody the lesson offered by
his career in the history and rhetoric of the Empire.[35] With the passage
of time the significance of Alexander Molossus for the Romans also came
to be emphasized. Whereas Livy said that Alexander struck a treaty of
peace with Rome, but doubted that it would have kept the city out of the
conflict if his campaign had met with success, Pausanias indicated that
Alexander was killed before he could come to grips with the Romans, as
if it were a foregone conclusion that he would have if fate had not intervened, and Aulus Gellius maintained that Alexander Molossus set out for
Italy with the express purpose of conquering Rome.[36]

What began as a marked and pregnant parallelism seems to have
grown into a confusion of the two Alexanders. If the suggestion of such
a confusion seems far-fetched, the *Alexander Romance* tradition itself
offers an example of precisely the sort of faulty scholarship which
might produce it. Julius Valerius informs us that, immediately before
Alexander meets the Romans, "he proceeded to Lycaonia, which this
modern age has now given the name of Lucania" (*pergit ad Lycaoniam,
cui nunc aetes recens nomen Lucaniae dedit*).[37] Lucania is not, in fact, a later
corruption of Lycaonia; the two are distinct territories, one in Italy and
the other in Asia Minor. Lucania was invaded by Alexander Molossus
and Alexander the Great's route skirted Lycaonia, which he ordered

---

[33] Livy 8.3.6–7, 9.17.17.

[34] Livy 9.19.10–11; Gell. *NA* 17.21.33; cf. Curt. 8.1.37.

[35] Some doubt about the authenticity of the saying may be entertained, not least
because each of the authors who offer us a version give it a different context. Livy puts
such words into the mouth of Alexander after he was fatally wounded, although his
account (8.24.13–14) does not seem to leave him much time for dying words, while Gellius
says he made such a remark *en route* to Italy.

[36] Livy 8.3.6, 17.10, 24.18; Paus. 1.11.7; Gell. *NA* 17.21.33.

[37] Julius Valerius 1.29; ed. Rosellini 1993:36.779–780.

his general Antigonus to subdue.[38] There is, moreover, as Braccesi has pointed out, an indication that Alexander Molossus' invasion of Italy, and specifically Livy's report of it, had an influence on the *Alexander Romance* in that one of the consuls in the year before Livy's erroneous date for Alexander's landing in Italy was Lucius Aemelius Mamercus, who could have given at least the *nomen* of his *gens* to the otherwise inexplicable Marcus Aemelius in the *Romance*.[39] The confusion of the two Alexanders as an influence on the *Romance*'s fictional encounter between Alexander and the Romans did, however, commend the historical plausibility of the fabrication, inasmuch as it demonstrated that an intimate of the Macedonian court in Alexander's day did, indeed, take an interest in Italian affairs and arrived in Italy at the head of an army. *An* Alexander, at least, led an expedition not dissimilar to the one described in the *Romance*.

A final source to be noted for the *Romance*'s meeting of Alexander and the Romans seems to have been the apparently well-established Roman tradition of speculation about what would have happened if Alexander had invaded Italy and made war on Rome. There is evidence to suggest that such speculation was widespread from a very early date. In Plutarch's account of a famous speech given before the Senate by Appius Claudius Caecus in 280 BC he includes a passage which indicates that conjecture on Rome's chances against Alexander was rife amongst his contemporaries, hardly more than a generation after Alexander's death:

ποῦ γὰρ ὑμῶν ὁ πρὸς ἅπαντας ἀνθρώπους θρυλούμενος
ἀεὶ λόγος, ὡς, εἰ παρῆν ἐκεῖνος εἰς Ἰταλίαν ὁ μέγας
Ἀλέξανδρος καὶ συνηνέχθη νέοις ἡμῖν καὶ τοῖς πατράσιν
ἡμῶν ἀκμάζουσιν, οὐκ ἂν ὑμνεῖτο νῦν ἀνίκητος, ἀλλ' ἢ
φυγὼν ἂν ἤ που πεσὼν ἐνταῦθα τὴν Ῥώμην ἐνδοξοτέραν
ἀπέλιπε;[40]

---

[38] Curt. 4.5.13.
[39] Livy 8.1.1, 3.6. See Braccesi 2006:83–88.
[40] Plut. *Pyrrh.* 19.1. See Malcovati 1953: vol. 1, 1–4; Kennedy 1972:26–29; Weippert 1972:10–17.

> For where now is your speech, constantly noised about
> to all men, that, if that great Alexander had appeared in
> Italy and had met with us in our youth and our fathers in
> their prime, he would not now be praised as invincible, but
> either fleeing or falling somewhere here he would have
> left Rome more glorious yet?

There are numerous references to Claudius' speech, but Plutarch is
the only authority to mention the counterfactual speculation—though
his account is also the fullest.[41] As a consequence, there has been
some doubt as to whether the prevalence of speculation about an
invasion of Italy by Alexander belongs to Claudius' day or to Plutarch's.
Kennedy considers the reference to talk of Alexander part of Plutarch's
hypothetical reconstruction of Claudius' speech on the basis of the
rhetorical commonplaces of his own day, whereas Morello sees it as
evidence of a longstanding tradition of counterfactual speculation on
the matter.[42] In either case such speculation was early enough to have
exerted an influence on the composition of the *Alexander Romance*.[43]
The most famous example of a counterfactual history of Alexander and
Rome is undoubtedly Livy's digression in book nine of his histories.
He compares Alexander unfavorably to not only Papirius Cursor,
the avenger of the shame of the Caudine Forks, but also to a long list
of his Roman contemporaries and the whole Roman state and its
institutions.[44] Livy also indicates that his speculative history was not an
idiosyncratic exercise, but common to the musings of the supporters
and detractors of both Alexander and Rome. He makes reference to the
general agreement that Papirius was the Roman general most likely
to face Alexander if he attacked Europe, to "utterly inconsequential

---

[41] Cic. *Sen.* 16, *Brut.* 55, 61; Livy *Per.* 13; Quint. *Inst.* 2.16.7; Suet. *Tib.* 2.1; Val. Max. 8.13.5;
Appian *Sam.* fr. 10.2; Isid. *Etym.* 1.38.2.

[42] Kennedy 1972:28–29; Morello 2002:65–66. Poulsen 1993:163 esp. also considers the
Alexander passage a genuine part of Claudius' speech, and further demonstrates from
artistic evidence the impression Alexander made in Italy from a very early date.

[43] Orosius (3.15.10) shows that the discussion of Alexander's plans for Rome and how
they would have been met was still current in the fourth century.

[44] Livy 9.17–19. See Sordi 1965:435–437, 450–452; Braccesi 1975:75–113; Merkelbach
1977:218–223; Morello 2002:62–85; Spencer 2002:41–53; Braccesi 2006:52–54, 201–213.

Greeks" (*levissimi ex Graecis*) who are in the habit of saying (*dictitare solent*) that Rome would have quaked at the very name of Alexander, and to those who compared Alexander's unsullied record of victories to Rome's many defeats in battle.[45] There is reason to believe that, while there are only two surviving examples of counterfactual speculation about an invasion of Italy by Alexander, they represent a broader tradition, and neither is a specific source for the *Romance*'s invention. These historians and putative speech writers were well aware that they set armies of ink to fight on a field of paper, but even these battles, it seems, began to take on a certain reality. Perhaps the factual and counterfactual had become muddled well before his time; perhaps the distinction was clear to the author of the *Alexander Romance*. He was nevertheless intrigued by the possibility and impressed by the plausibility of Alexander marching on Italy. At any rate, it is in his text that what might have been is definitively turned into what was.

II. INTENTIONS

Having considered the *Romance*'s possible sources—none of them absolutely necessary, and each of them by no means mutually exclusive—for the encounter between Alexander and the Romans, we are in a position to draw a few conclusions. The first regards the state of historiography at the turn of the fourth century, for we should not forget that despite all its fantastic elements and generic affinities with the novel the *Alexander Romance* was presented as a work of history and received as such. The record of the past had become porous indeed. It did not merely allow speculation and conjecture on the basis of well attested fact; the passage from the *Romance* we are examining demonstrates that it permitted inventions precariously balanced on the very edges of reliable information to be asserted as fact. In this case, reports of Alexander's diplomatic contacts with the Romans and his posthumously revealed plans were exaggerated into a meeting on Italian soil, the remarkably parallel deeds of one Alexander with Molossian royal blood raised at the Macedonian court were attributed to another, and rhetor-

[45] Livy 9.16.19, 18.6, 9.

ical speculation about historical counterfactuals was transformed into history. This is a style of history with close affinities to the novelistic tradition in its gratification of an appetite for novelty so ravenous that it would countenance the addition of fabulous and invented incidents to the story of even a well-known historical figure.

It is, nevertheless, necessary to see the deplorable state of historiography in late antiquity as a circumstance rather than an explanation for the *Romance*'s account of Alexander's dealings with the Romans. The intentions behind this story's inclusion in the *Romance* and the form it takes need to be examined. The traditional response to this problem was summed up by Welles when he explained the incident as "part of the moral resistance to Rome on the part of the Greeks which served them as a compensation for their subjection" intended "to show that Alexander did (that is to say, could have) beaten [sic] the Romans."[46] A similar interpretation is found repeated in more recent works. For instance, Bounoure and Serret, in the introduction to their French translation of the *Romance*, remark, "le détour fabuleux par l'Occident et Rome qu'il fait accomplir à Alexandre pour se rendre de Macédoine en Égypte (I, 29) pourrait bien traduire les nostalgies passablement 'revanchardes' de Grecs d'Égypte tombés sous la domination romaine, c'est-à-dire après César, et surtout Auguste."[47] A closer examination of the passage in question, particularly in the (α) recension, however, indicates that it could hardly have been the composition of Livy's *levissimi ex Graecis* who, with the wounded pride of a subject nation, insisted that the Romans would have trembled before Alexander. If they were to imagine the submission of the Romans to Alexander we should expect an abject humiliation. That is not what we find in the *Romance*. Alexander receives the submission of the Romans, but instead of crowing or grinding them under his heel he promises to make them great and counts them amongst his allies by adding their troops to his army. Even if we should expect a more positive attitude to the Romans in a Latin translation of the *Romance*, it is not too much of a stretch for Julius Valerius to open his version of this passage by saying that

---

[46] Welles 1962:275 and n. 12; cf. Tarn 1948:393–394.
[47] Bounoure and Serret 2004:xviii.

Alexander treated with the Romans "on terms of equality and honor." All of this hardly seems consistent with an attempt to adjust the historical record to salve the humbled conceit of the Greeks. On the contrary, Alexander's treatment of the Romans suggests that the author of the *Romance* had assumed a decidedly positive stance toward Rome.[48] This pro-Roman attitude is most clearly demonstrated in the *Romance*'s adaptation of Memnon of Heracleia's account of Alexander's dealings with the Romans, the evidence for which has already been quoted above.[49] The message Memnon claims Alexander wrote to the Romans, "either be strong or submit to those who are stronger," and the Romans' contemptible offer of tribute is just the sort of stinging retort to Rome's might and majesty we would expect of the jealous Greeks to whom the *Romance*'s Roman episode is usually attributed. We know, moreover, that the author of the *Romance* knew this passage of Memnon, since he twice puts the same sentiment and remarkably similar words into Alexander's mouth, once, as we have seen, to the "Africans" and then to the Athenians.[50] But not to the Romans. Memnon in no way sets the tone for Alexander's encounter with the Romans. Assuming that Alexander's retort had not become proverbial by the time of the *Romance*'s composition, Memnon is rejected as a source on precisely the point he professes to record, Alexander's treatment of the Romans. Why? Not, clearly, because the author of the *Romance* considered the message uncharacteristic of Alexander, but because the exchange cast Rome in an unfavorable light.

The *Romance*'s adaptation of the passage from Memnon of Heracleia does not only indicate a positive attitude in regard to Rome, it also suggests the reason for the inclusion of Alexander's encounter with

---

[48] Cf. Braccesi 2006:76–83.

[49] *FGrH* 434 F 18.2 = Photius *Bibl.* 224 (229A); see Ballesteros Pastor 1999; on Memnon's work as a whole, see Desideri 1966; Desideri 1970/1971. Braccesi 1995:53 takes Clitarchus to be the common source for both Memnon and the *Romance* on Alexander's encounter with the Romans; I, however, assume that the author of the *Romance* adapted material he found in Memnon.

[50] *Al. Rom.* (α) 1.30.1, 2.1.11; ed. Kroll 1926:64.18–20: ἀρτίως μὲν ἢ κρείττονες γίνεσθε ἢ τοῖς κρείττοσιν ὑποτάσσεσθε, καὶ δώσετε φόρους κατ' ἔτος τάλαντα χίλια ([Alexander to the Athenians:] By all rights you should either become stronger or submit to those who are stronger, and render a tribute of a thousand talents every year).

the Romans in the first place. The adversarial and supercilious tone
which Memnon has Alexander assume toward Rome is transferred
in the *Romance* to Alexander's speech to the Carthaginians (as well as
the Athenians). This transferral puts Alexander's attitude in line with
Roman enmity toward Carthage, explicitly adduced in the immediately
preceding narrative when the Romans explain their scanty contribution with reference to their ongoing war with Carthage. But Alexander
and the Romans are not only seen to share an antagonism toward the
oriental barbarians resident in the western Mediterranean; the Romans
also have a part to play in Alexander's undertaking against the supreme
eastern enemy of the civilized world, the Persians. The Romans pay
into his war chest, their troops march in his army, and Alexander sets
out on his expedition, for all intents and purposes, in the office of an
honorary consul of Rome. Instead of restricting Roman interests to
the *imitatio* or *aemulatio* of Alexander attributed to so many prominent
Romans, the tradition represented by the *Romance* permitted a broader
participation in the enterprise of Alexander through something that
was far more substantial to most Romans than the ambition and impos-
ture of generals and emperors: the collective history of their city.[51]
Rather than being the work of sullen and resentful Greeks scoring
points against the odious power of Rome, Alexander's encounter with
the Romans in the *Romance* gives every indication of having been
included by admiring Romans—or Greeks content as Roman citizens—
who regretted that Rome had not been able to join in Alexander's great
project, a project eminently consistent with the role and purposes of
the Rome they knew.

Our discussion so far may account for the presence of Rome in the
earliest versions of the *Alexander Romance*, but we have still to address
the ways in which Rome is dealt with in the latest and most elaborated versions of the *Romance*. The shift in the location of Alexander's
adolescent victory in the chariot-race from the Olympic Games at
Elis in the (α) recension to Rome in the (γ) recension is perhaps the

---

[51] On the *imitatio Alexandri* in Roman history, see Weippert 1972; Wirth 1976; Green
1978; Martin 1982–1994: vol. 2, 296–316; Bohm 1989; Braccesi 1991; Coppola 1993; Isager
1993; Gruen 1998; Tisé 2002; Braccesi 2006:89–198, 213–225.

easiest to explain. The chariot-race at Rome, like many of the incidents in (γ), first appears in another Byzantine version, the abbreviated (ε) recension, which cannot have preceded the (γ) by many years.[52] The earlier versions of the *Romance* had included Rome within the orbit of Alexander's activity, making his presence there unsurprising. In the late empire there was also a growing tendency to associate chariot-racing less with the Panhellenic Games and the victory odes of Pindar—especially after Theodosius I's abolition of the Olympic Games in 393—and more with the spectacle and factions in the hippodrome of the imperial capital, be it Rome or Constantinople, and their imitators throughout the provinces.[53] Taken together Alexander's putative encounter with the Romans and the association of chariot-racing with Rome would make Rome the natural venue for a chariot-race, especially one which had as competitors all the promising young princes of the day, a far more likely venue, at any rate, in the late antique and early Byzantine imagination than the forgotten backwater of Olympia. Jouanno, moreover, demonstrates that not only is the location of the chariot-race changed, but so are several details to make the whole affair more consistent with Roman or Byzantine chariot-racing than with the ancient Greek variety.[54] She also draws particular attention to those details and especially the hymn of praise offered to Alexander on his return to Macedonia which are reminiscent of the ritual acclamation Byzantine emperors received in the hippodrome:

πάλιν νοστοῦσι δ' ὅμως· θαυμάζοντες τῇ συνέσει καὶ
ἀνδρείᾳ Ἀλεξάνδρου ὕμνον αὐτὸν πλέξαντες τήνδε·
αὔχει Φίλιππε, τέρπου Μακεδονία,
ὁ μὲν γεννήτης ἐντυχὼν Ἀλεξάνδρου,
ἡ δὲ πατρὶς τυχοῦσα καλλίστου τούτου.
αὐτὸν δὴ ἀπαντήσατε στεφανώμενον,
νικητὴν ἀήττητον, γεοῦχον μέγαν·
ἀνατείλας γὰρ κατεγλάισεν Ῥώμην

---

[52] *Al. Rom.* (ε) 5; ed. Trumpf 1974:15–21. See Stoneman 2008:231.
[53] See Finley and Pleket 1976:13; Humphrey 1986:438–441, 535–539, 633–638; Cotterell 2004:278–292; Spivey 2004:203–204; Meijer 2010:130, 135–136.
[54] Jouanno 2002:361–365.

— ὡς ἀνατέλλων ἤθλησεν ἐν σταδίῳ —,
καὶ πάντας ἡμαύρωσε λοιποὺς ἀστέρας.
δέχου οὖν αὐτῷ λαμπρὰ Μακεδονία,
καὶ τοὺς ἐχθροὺς ἄμυναν ἐν τούτῳ δίδου·
Ἀλέξανδρος γάρ ἐστιν ὁ κοσμοκράτωρ.
ταῦτα λέγοντες τὴν πόλιν περιεῖον δάφνην ἔχοντες ταῖς
χερσὶν ταῖς τούτων.[55]

They went back home together. Amazed at Alexander's understanding and manliness, [the Macedonians] devised this hymn then:
"Boast, Philip! Cheer, Macedonia!
The one for being the parent of Alexander,
The other for being the homeland of this most noble man.
Come to meet him, adorned with a crown,
Invincible conqueror, great lord of the land;
For he rose up and shone down on Rome
As he arose and contended in the stadium,
And consigned all the rest of the stars to darkness.
So receive him, bright Macedonia,
And deliver his enemies to him in vengeance;
For Alexander is the lord of the world."
Saying these things they proceeded around the city carrying laurel branches in their hands.

Alexander, through his victory in the chariot-race, literally enacts the metaphorical participation the emperor was supposed to share with the victorious charioteer and embodies the solar imagery and universal pretensions which characterized imperial encomia in Byzantium. So Alexander becomes a prototype of the Byzantine emperor and his life a warrant for the rhetoric and ceremonial which surrounded him.

The (γ) recension's slight modifications of the (α) recension's meeting of Alexander and the Roman embassy show more than anything else a diminishing historical awareness. In the earlier version

[55] *Al. Rom.* (γ) i.20; ed. Lauenstein 1962:54.23–56.10.

the Romans crown Alexander, but do not designate the office with which he is invested by this coronation, although he is granted rule for a year (κατ' ἔτος), as were most of the magistrates of Rome, including the consuls. The author's studied silence suggests he knew that Alexander would not have been crowned king of the Romans, as they had no king, and that under the republican constitution a man undertook a ruler's office for no more than a year; this silence also allows him to avoid the difficulty of one consul appointing another out of the regular sequence. Alexander is granted a sign of great honor, and the reader must make of that what he will. In the (γ) recension any ambiguity is discarded along with any attempt at historical verisimilitude. There Alexander is crowned "king of the Romans and the whole world" (βασιλεῦ Ῥωμαίων καὶ πάσης γῆς); that is, Alexander is given the title of the highest office in the Roman state of the romancer's own day. When both the (α) and the (γ) recensions were written his Greek-speaking subjects regularly referred to the Roman emperor as 'king' (βασιλεύς). The difference between the two recensions is not one of contemporary terminology, but rather of an awareness of the course of history.

The author of (α) understood enough Roman history to know that there were no kings in Rome in Alexander's time, that the rulers of the Republic served for a single year, and that Rome's greatness was a future prospect that Alexander was in a position to promise to a small and out of the way state which had yet to distinguish itself. The redactor at work on the (γ) recension, however, could not conceive of a time when Rome was not ruled by emperors—that is kings (βασιλεῖς)—who ruled for life, nor a time when Rome was not in a position to confer rule over the inhabited world upon whomever she chose. The former anachronism is consistent with a tendency in the Byzantine chronicle tradition, noted by Jeffreys, to gloss over or treat in the most cursory manner those periods in the history of a state, no matter how important, which were not marked by monarchial rule.[56] Such was the predominance of the principle of monarchy in Byzantine thinking and so incomprehensibly deviant were the ways of democratic and republican forms of government that even Classical Athens and Republican Rome received

---

[56] Jeffreys 1979:207, 214–215, 218, 227–228, 230–232, 237–238.

short shrift in the chronicles. The (γ) recension's perception of Rome as the perpetual mistress of the world embodies an attitude for which parallels can also be found. Even as their empire crumbled the Romans, who were more and more the Ῥωμαῖοι, the inhabitants of the Eastern Roman or Byzantine Empire, believed that the barbarian invaders who had overrun old imperial territory held their rule by the express dispensation of the Roman emperor. They even imputed this attitude to the barbarians themselves. According to Procopius, the Franks did not consider their possession of the lands they held in Gaul secure unless it was vouchsafed to them by the emperor.[57]

The (γ) redactor further specifies the contingent of soldiers the Romans place at Alexander's disposal as archers (τοξότας). This is likewise an anachronism which situates this particular alteration in the early Byzantine era while making no pretence to an offer of historical coloring. The equipment of the legionary in the days of the Republic and early Empire included swords, spears, and javelins, but not bows; archers were provided by the auxiliary regiments. In the later Empire, however, the bow became a standard weapon amongst units of the Roman or Byzantine army to such an extent that Procopius could remark on Roman battlefield skill at archery as a point of pride, proven in one instance under the very walls of old Rome.[58] The contrast between Roman ability with the bow and Gothic ineptitude, and particularly in the ancient Roman heartland, may have led to an identification of archers with the armies of Rome in the (γ) recension. Whether or not the author of the (α) recension gave much thought to the armament of the Republican legionary, it would doubtless never have occurred to him to have Roman archers march along with Alexander. In the same way, he was conscious that the most important armed struggle undertaken by Rome in the course of her rise to the greatness promised by Alexander was the series of wars fought against Carthage, whereas the author of the (γ) recension was so unmindful of the significance of the Punic Wars that he allowed all mention of them to slip from the meeting of Alexander and the Romans.

---

[57] Procop. *De bellis* 7.33.4.
[58] Procop. *De bellis* 1.18.34, 5.27.27.

Most puzzling of all is the alternative version of Alexander's encounter with the Romans offered by the (γ) recension, in which Alexander goes to Rome itself to receive the submission of the Romans. And that is how we must take it, not as an elaboration upon or reworking of the episode in the (α) recension, but as an alternative to it. The two versions cover much the same ground and provide the same basic information, but in rather different ways. I presume that the two passages were never intended to appear together in the same narrative; their joint inclusion in the (γ) recension must be the result of an editorial oversight. But to explain the contours of this alternative version we must turn our attention to a text which seems to be intermediate between the (α) and the (γ) recensions of the *Romance*.

The account of Alexander the Great in the *Excerpta Latina Barbari*, an eighth-century Latin translation of an early sixth-century Greek Christian world chronicle of Alexandrian origin, shows all the hallmarks of being principally influenced by some early version of the *Romance*; and the *Excerpta*, or rather the ideas it exhibits, seems to have exerted an influence in turn on the picture of Alexander in the (γ) recension, particularly the alternative version of the submission of the Romans.[59] For our purposes the most remarkable feature of the *Excerpta* is the close parallelism it creates between the Romans and the Jews with regard to Alexander. The *Excerpta*'s Roman king-list ends with a note saying that after the kings God delivered the land of the Romans into the hands of the "Assyrians, Chaldeans, Persians, and Medes" until such time as He raised up Alexander, who defeated these eastern powers and freed the Romans, Greeks, and Egyptians from their subjection to them.[60] The record of the kings of Israel and Judah in the

---

[59] The most recent text of the *Excerpta* is in Garstad 2012 and all citations of the *Excerpta* follow the numbering of this text. See Garstad 2011:26–27 esp. While Frick 1892:clxvi, is undoubtedly correct in saying that the *Alexander Romance* is the ultimate source for the Alexander material in the *Excerpta*, the immediate source is more likely to have been the lost fourth- or early fifth-century historian, Bouttios; see Garstad 2005:87–93.

[60] *Excerpta* 1.6.6; ed. Garstad 2012:194: *Post haec tradidit dominus deus regnum terrae Romanorum in manus Assyriorum, Chaldaeorum, et Persarum, et Midorum. Et tributaria facta est terra illa Assyriis, et mansit Roma sine regnum, usque dum suscitauit deus Alexandrum Macedonem et conditorem. Iste quidem pugnauit contra regem Persarum et superauit eum. Et*

Excerpta ends in very similar terms, with the Lord delivering the whole earth into the hands of the same conglomeration of oriental peoples.[61] Likewise, according to the *Excerpta* the kingdom of Nebuchadnezzar, who led the Jews into exile and destroyed the temple in Jerusalem, included the land of the Romans.[62] And while the *Excerpta* is not explicit that Alexander liberated the Jews from the powers of the East as he did the Romans, it does say that he went to Jerusalem and worshipped God.[63]

The (γ) recension of the *Romance* also includes an account of Alexander's visit to Jerusalem:

ὡς οὖν ταῦτα ἤκουσαν, Ἀλεξάνδρῳ ὑπείκειν κελεύονται.

ταῖς ἱερατικαῖς οὖν στολαῖς ἑαυτοὺς οἱ τούτων ἱερεῖς ἐνδυσάμενοι καθυπαντῶσιν Ἀλεξάνδρῳ σὺν παντὶ τῷ πλήθει αὐτῶν· τούτους δὲ Ἀλέξανδρος ἰδὼν ἐδεδίει τοῦ σχήματος· καὶ τούτους μηκέτι προσεγγίσαι αὐτῷ ἐκέλευσεν, ἀλλ' ἐν τῇ πόλει ἀναστρέφεσθαι. Προσκαλεσάμενος δὲ

---

tradidit dominus in manum eius regnum Assyriorum, et introiuit in potestate regnum eorum, et concussit civitates Persarum et Medorum, et liberauit omnem terram Romanorum et Grecorum et Egyptiorum de seruitute Chaldeorum ... (After these things the Lord God delivered the kingdom of the land of the Romans into the hands of the Assyrians, Chaldeans, and Persians, and Medes. And this land was made tributary to the Assyrians, and Rome remained without dominion [or a king] until the time when God raised up Alexander of Macedon, the Founder. He fought against the king of the Persians and defeated him. And the Lord delivered into his hand the kingdom of the Assyrians, and he entered into power over their kingdoms, and he overthrew the cities of the Persians and the Medes, and he freed the whole country of the Romans and the Greeks and the Egyptians from slavery to the Chaldeans ...); cf. 1.8.4.

[61] *Excerpta* 1.8.1; ed. Garstad 2012:208: *Illi uero reges qui in Israhel et in Iudea et in Samaria finierunt, et tunc tradedit dominus deus regnum terrae in manus Assyriorum et Chaldeorum et Persarum et Midorum, et tributaria facta est eis omnis terra* (These kings who were in Israel and Judea and Samaria came to an end, and then the Lord God delivered the kingdom of the earth into the hands of the Assyrians and Chaldeans and Persians and Medes, and the whole earth was made tributary to them).

[62] *Excerpta* 1.7.5, 6, 8.1.

[63] *Excerpta* 1.8.4; ed. Garstad 2012:216: *Ut enim condidit Alexander Alexandriam contra Egyptum, ueniens in Hierusolima domino deo adorauit dicens: Gloria tibi, deus solus omnia tenens, qui uiuis in saecula. Fuit autem tunc in Hierusalem princeps sacerdotum Iaddus* (For when Alexander founded Alexandria by Egypt he came to Jerusalem and worshipped the Lord God, saying, "Glory to You, Only God, grasping all things, Who liveth unto the ages." The high priest in Jerusalem was Jaddua); see Cohen 1982:59.

ἕνα τῶν ἱερέων λέγει αὐτῷ· ὡς θεοειδὲς ὑμῶν τὸ σχῆμα·
φράσον δή μοι καὶ τίνα ὑμεῖς σέβεσθε θεόν; οὐ γὰρ ἐν τοῖς
παρ᾽ ἡμῖν θεοῖς τοιαύτην εὐταξίαν εἶδον ἱερέων. ὁ δὲ φησίν·
θεὸν ἡμεῖς ἕνα δουλεύομεν, ὃς ἐποίησεν οὐρανὸν καὶ
γῆν καὶ πάντα τὰ ὁράμενά τε καὶ ἀόρατα· οὐδεὶς δὲ αὐτὸν
ἑρμηνεῦσαι ἀνθρώπων δεδύνηται. ἐπὶ τούτοις Ἀλέξανδρος
ἔφη· ὡς ἀληθινοῦ θεοῦ ἄξιοι θεραπευταὶ ἄπιτε ἐν εἰρήνῃ,
ἄπιτε· ὁ γὰρ θεὸς ὑμῶν ἔσται μοι θεὸς καὶ ἡ εἰρήνη μου μεθ᾽
ὑμῶν, καὶ οὐ μὴ διεξέλθω ὑμᾶς καθὼς καὶ ἐν τοῖς λοιποῖς
ἔθνεσιν, ὅτι θεῷ ζῶντι ὑμεῖς δεδουλεύκατε. λαβόντες δὲ
χρημάτων πλήθη ἕν τε χρυσῷ καὶ ἀργύρῳ ἤγαγον πρὸς
τὸν Ἀλέξανδρον. ὁ δὲ οὐκ ἠθέλησε λαβεῖν, εἶπεν αὐτοῖς·
ἔστωσαν ταῦτα τὰ δῶρα καὶ ἐμοὶ ἀφωρισμένος φόρος
κυρίῳ τῷ θεῷ· ἐγὼ δὲ οὐ λήψομαι ἐξ ὑμῶν οὐδέν.[64]

So when they [the Jews] heard these things [about the
strength of the Macedonian army], they desired to submit
to Alexander. Their priests clothed themselves in their
priestly vestments and went down to meet Alexander
with the whole crowd of them. When Alexander saw
them he dreaded their appearance; and he ordered them
to approach him no more, but to turn back into the city.
But summoning one of the priests he said to him, "How
godlike is your appearance! Declare to me, what god do
you worship? For I have not seen such a disposition of
priests of the gods amongst us." And he said, "We serve one
God, Who made heaven and earth and all things, seen and
unseen; no man has been able to explain Him." At these
words Alexander said, "As worthy servants of a true god
go in peace, go; for your god will be a god to me and my
peace [will be] with you, and I will not deal with you as I
did with the rest of the nations, because you have served
a living god." Taking masses of money in gold and silver
they brought them to Alexander. But he was unwilling to

[64] *Al. Rom.* (γ) 2.24; ed. Engelmann 1963:218.7–26.

take it, and said to them, "Let these gifts and the tribute
set aside for me belong to the Lord God; I, for my part, will
take nothing from you."

In addition to their both being among the few of examples of
Alexander's bloodless and amiable conquests in the *Romance* tradition,
the (γ) recension shows a number of other specific points of comparison between Alexander's receipt of the submission of the Jews and of
the Romans. In both cases there is a decision to submit to Alexander,
implicit on the part of the Romans and explicitly described on the
part of the Jews, which obviates the need for conflict and suggests a
certain agreement or accord with the purposes of Alexander on the
part of both peoples. Processions go out to meet Alexander from Rome
and from Jerusalem, making manifest the submission of the people and
the honor offered to the conqueror. And in each narrative Alexander's
encounter with a priest is presented as the most significant event in the
incident. Each account, in fact, corresponds to the formulaic conduct
of an *adventus*, the ritual of reception performed upon an eminent
person's arrival at a city, which Cohen identifies as one of the strands
in the composition of the earliest surviving version of the legend of
Alexander's visit to Jerusalem, found in Josephus' *Jewish Antiquities*.[65]
The *adventus* appeared in that initial version, just as it appears in
Alexander's meeting with the Jews and the Romans in the (γ) recension of the *Romance*, because such official visits were understood as
establishing a relationship of mutual recognition between the visiting
dignitary and the city that received him. The (γ) recension sets out
to indicate that the Romans and the Jews each enjoyed similar cordial
relations with Alexander.

To indicate the parallels between the accounts of Alexander's visits
to Rome and Jerusalem in the (γ) recension, however, is not to imply
that the stories are cognate; one, rather, was modeled on the other.
The story of Alexander's visit to Jerusalem is the emanation of a long-
standing and widespread tradition which had its origins perhaps as
early as the second century BC and whose most important purveyor

---

[65] Joseph. *AJ* 11.8.3–7 (313–347); Cohen 1982:45–49.

was certainly Josephus at the end of the first century AD.[66] The story of Alexander visiting Rome, in contrast, occurs for the first time in the (γ) recension of the *Romance*. This alternative version of Alexander's encounter with the Romans appears to be based on the legend of Alexander's meeting with the Jews, and some equivalence is suggested between the Jews and the Romans. That is not to say, however, that some syncretistic equivalence of the God of the Jews and the Capitoline Jupiter of the Romans is being made. Note that Alexander is not supposed to have made any emphatic declaration about the truth and vivacity of the Roman god. Rather, the similar patterns in the two meetings indicate that Alexander shares a relationship of mutual respect with both the Jews and the Romans. They recognize his sovereignty and he recognizes, at least implicitly, the significance that each of these peoples would have in the history of the world which came after him—but was the living reality of the author of the (γ) recension.

This sort of analogous presentation of the Jews and Romans is not isolated to the *Alexander Romance*. We have already seen a similar comparison of the two peoples regarding their relations with Alexander in the *Excerpta Latina Barbari*. In that text the parallel was included by the Byzantine court for a specific diplomatic purpose, namely to inspire the Frankish king Theudebert I (r. 534–548) to join Justinian's war against the Ostrogoths, liberate the Romans from their eastern oppressors, and restore right reverence for God in place of the Ostrogoths' Arian heresy.[67] Alexander is offered as an ancient exemplar of these endeavors, since he had defeated the peoples of the orient, freed the Romans, and acknowledged God in His holy city.[68] Alexander also serves as a nexus between two peoples who were in his day marginal, isolated, and completely separate from one another, but whose influence, like his own, would come to overshadow the world. The *Excerpta* was written for consumption by barbarian outsiders, and

---

[66] See Marcus 1937:512–532; Cary 1954:105–113; Tcherikover 1959:42–50; Momigliano 1979; Delling 1981; Cohen 1982:41–68; Bammel 1987; Cohen 1987:412–415; Goldstein 1993; Stoneman 1994; Jouanno 2002:378–381.

[67] Garstad 2011:28–34.

[68] We can already see Rome sharing Jerusalem's status as a holy city in the Christian perspective in the fifth century; see, e.g., Leo *Sermo* 82.

we might cynically be tempted to see its rhetoric as intended to play upon their naïveté, ignorance, and conceit. But the recurrence of the parallelism of Jews and Romans in regard to Alexander in the (γ) recension of the *Alexander Romance*, a work intended for popular, internal consumption, suggests that this was more than a sly rhetorical gambit and was instead consistent with the way in which the eastern Romans wished to think of themselves.

The Byzantine Empire was upheld by the twin pillars of Roman polity and Hebraic sanctity. The derivative nature of the institutions of state and church was obscured by the immediacy with which the typological models from the Bible and ancient history were regularly presented. The matched episodes in the (γ) recension of the *Alexander Romance* showed these twin pillars sustaining Alexander in his efforts to quell barbarism and defeat the great eastern enemy, goals by no means foreign to Byzantium at any stage of its history. Nothing could better demonstrate than the figures of this popular romance that the idea of Hebrew and Roman underpinnings to the whole life of Byzantium were not rarefied or abstruse theories, but part of the common understanding of the man on the street. This is further borne out by another observation of Jeffreys on the Byzantine chroniclers, that they "came to write ancient history in terms of the Bible and Rome; in their view the past seems to have been unaffected by Greece except for the forced migration of Aeneas after the sack of Troy, and for the conquests of Alexander."[69] The association of Romans and Jews in their dealings with Alexander only grew with the passage of time. In the Early Modern Greek *Phyllada tou Megalexandrou*, an immensely popular version of the Alexander legend first published in 1680, it is at Rome that Alexander receives the crown of Solomon and it is in Rome that the prophecy of Daniel is delivered to Alexander, a scene which, since Josephus, was supposed to have taken place in Jerusalem.[70]

The *Excerpta Latina Barbari* goes some way to explaining another detail in the (γ) recension of the *Alexander Romance*. In this alternative

---

[69] Jeffreys 1979:237.
[70] *Phyllada* pp. 67–76; ed. Veloudis 1977:32–36. See Stoneman 2012:41–44. Cf. Joseph. *AJ* 11.8.5 (337).

version of Alexander's encounter with the Romans he proceeds from
Rome to march unopposed against the western regions and receive
their subjection. We have already seen that in later renditions of the
Romance the Romans proffer to Alexander kingship "of the Romans
and the whole world," but here Rome seems to be key to the rule of the
west; once the Romans acknowledge Alexander's suzerainty all of the
other kingdoms of the west fall into line. Likewise, the *Excerpta* presents Rome, from earliest times, even from before her foundation, as
the lynchpin of rule over the west and suggests that rule over Rome
entails rule over all the west.[71] The euhemerized god-kings who establish cities and kingdoms in the west rule over the western regions, but
their power and activities are centered in Italy, particularly the future
site of Rome.[72] The Alban kings, the forebears of the Romans, are apparently said to rule from Alba over the west.[73] The Roman king-list in
the *Excerpta* ends with the most explicit statement of this idea of rule
in the west devolving from Rome: *Isti reges, qui regnauerunt in Romam
et in omnem occidentalis parte terram* (These kings ruled in Rome and
in all the western part of the earth).[74] Taken alongside these intima-
tions, Alexander's triumphant progress through the kingdoms of the
west in the *Romance* suggests that Old Rome held a significance for the
Byzantines that was somehow more than symbolic. Possession of the
city of Rome meant not merely rule in the west, but rule over the west,
and this concept helps to explain why the Byzantines fought so long
and hard to reconquer Rome and held it so tenaciously as their other
western territories dwindled to a few marginal provinces.

The Romans were included in the *Alexander Romance* with a benign
intention and one very positive to Rome. Against all the historical testimony to the contrary—or perhaps we might more generously say, in
spite of the silence of the historical record—the *Romance* maintained
that the Romans had participated in the mission and the undertakings
of Alexander which they admired so much, subduing the barbarian

---

[71] Garstad 2011:23–24.

[72] *Excerpta* 1.6.1, 2.

[73] *Excerpta* 1.6.4; ed. Garstad 2012:192: *Reges autem qui regnauerunt ab Alba in occiduum
sunt isti.*

[74] *Excerpta* 1.6.5.

and laying low the might of the Orient. True, Alexander received the submission of the Romans, but this was not some vindictive literary reprisal for the humiliation the Greeks had suffered at the hands of the Romans, but rather an opportunity for Alexander to march east as something of a Roman magistrate and for the Romans to march alongside him. Later ages accepted the submission of the Romans to Alexander as part of Alexander's legend and elaborated upon it.[75] The two versions of Alexander's encounter with the Romans, however, must each be seen as products of their times and indicative of the historiography of the periods in which they were composed. The account in the (α) recension belongs to the end of the third and beginning of the fourth century when writers were not unaware of the historical record, but neither were they averse to augmenting it or filling in its gaps with fictions, be they elaborations on verifiable material or simple flights of fancy. The (γ) recension offers, in addition, an alternative version of this same encounter which is much more an example of Byzantine history writing, especially the popular kind represented by the chronicle tradition, which tended to cast the reality of its own day back upon a past which consequently became an authoritatively legitimating model for the institutions and world-view of Byzantium.

MacEwan University

WORKS CITED

Badian, Ernst. 1968. "A King's Notebooks." *Harvard Studies in Classical Philology* 72:183–204.

———. 1985. "Alexander in Iran." In *The Cambridge History of Iran*. Vol. 2, *The Median and Achaemenian Periods*, ed. Ilya Gershevitch, 420–501 and 897–903. Cambridge.

[75] See, for example, Gaullier-Bougassas 2000. There were, nevertheless, plenty of followers of the historical, as opposed to the legendary, tradition in the Middle Ages who continued to consign Alexander's conquest of Rome to the realm of possibility and intention; see Walter of Châtillon *Alexandreis* 1.5–10, 5.491–509, 7.373–378, 10.168–90, 322–9 (the last passage cited mentions the crown offered by the Romans through Emilius, but maintains that the Romans still need to be subdued); Meyer 1933:108–113; Cary 1950:52–53; Cary 1956:285–286; Braccesi 2006:225–266.

Ballesteros Pastor, Luis. 1999. "Marius' Words to Mithridates Eupator (Plut. *Mar.* 31.3)." *Historia* 48:506–508.

Bammel, Ernst. 1987. "Der Zeuge des Judentums." In *Zu Alexander dem Grossen: Festschrift G. Wirth*, ed. W. Will, vol. 1, 279–287. Amsterdam.

Bohm, Claudia. 1989. *Imitatio Alexandri im Hellenismus: Untersuchungen zum politischen Nachwirken Alexanders des Großen in hoch- und späthellenistischen Monarchien*. Munich.

Bosworth, A. B. 1988. *From Arrian to Alexander: Studies in Historical Interpretation*. Oxford.

Bounoure, Gilles, and Blandine Serret, trans. 2004. *Pseudo-Callisthène. Le Roman d'Alexandre*. 2nd ed. Paris.

Braccesi, Lorenzo. 1975. *Alessandro e i romani*. Bologna.

———. 1991. *Alessandro e la Germania: Riflessioni sulla geografia romana di conquista*. Rome.

———. 1995. "Alessandro e Roma." In *Alessandro Magno: Storia e mito*, 51–53. Milan.

———. 2006. *L'Alessandro occidentale: Il Macedone e Roma*. Rome.

Briant, Pierre. 2010. *Alexander the Great and his Empire: A Short Introduction*. Trans. Amélie Kuhrt. Princeton.

Brock, Sebastian. 1982. "Syriac Views of Emergent Islam." In *Studies on the First Century of Islamic Society*, ed. G. H. A. Juynboll, 9–21. Carbondale.

Carlsen, Jesper, et al., eds. 1993. *Alexander the Great: Reality and Myth*. Rome.

Cary, George. 1950. "Petrarch and Alexander the Great." *Italian Studies* 5:43–55.

———. 1954. "Alexander the Great in Mediaeval Theology." *Journal of the Warburg and Courtauld Institutes* 17:98–114.

———. 1956. *The Medieval Alexander*. Ed. D. J. A. Ross. Cambridge.

Cohen, Shaye. 1982. "Alexander the Great and Jaddus the High Priest According to Josephus." *AJS Review* 7:41–68.

———. 1987. "Respect for Judaism by Gentiles According to Josephus." *Harvard Theological Review* 80:409–430.

Coppola, Alessandra. 1993. "*L'imitatio Alexandri in Trogo e in Livio: Un confronto aperto*." In *L'Alessandro di Giustino: Dagli antichi ai moderni*, 45–69. Rome.

Cotterell, Arthur. 2004. *Chariot*. London.

Delling, Gerhard. 1981. "Alexander der Grosse als Bekenner des jüdischen Gottesglaubens." *Journal for the Study of Judaism* 12:1–51.

Desideri, Paolo. 1966. "Studi di Storiografia Eracleota, I: Promathidas e Nymphis." *Studi Classici e Orientali* 16:366–416.

———. 1970/1971. "Studi di Storiografia Eracleota, II: La guerra con Antioco il Grande." *Studi Classici e Orientali* 19/20:487–537.

Engelmann, Helmut. 1963. *Der griechische Alexanderroman, Rezension Γ, Buch II*. Meisenheim am Glan.

Finley, Moses, and H. W. Pleket. 1976. *The Olympic Games: The First Thousand Years*. London.

Frick, Carl. 1892. *Chronica Minora*. Leipzig.

Garstad, Benjamin. 2005. "The Tyche Sacrifices in John Malalas: Virgin Sacrifice and Fourth-Century Polemical History." *Illinois Classical Studies* 30:83–135.

———. 2011. "Barbarian interest in the *Excerpta Latina Barbari*." *Early Medieval Europe* 19:3–42.

———. 2012. *Apocalypse of Pseudo-Methodius: An Alexandrian World Chronicle*. Cambridge, MA.

Gaullier-Bougassas, Catherine. 2000. "Alexandre le Grand et la conquête de l'Ouest dans le romans d'Alexandre du XIIᵉ siècle, leurs mies en prose au XVᵉ siècle et le Perceforest." *Romania* 118:83–104.

Goldstein, Jonathan. 1993. "Alexander and the Jews." *Proceedings of the American Academy for Jewish Research* 59:59–101.

Goukowsky, Paul. 1978–1981. *Essai sur les origines du mythe d'Alexandre*. Nancy.

Green, Peter. 1978. "Caesar and Alexander: Aemulatio, imitatio, comparatio." *American Journal of Ancient History* 3:1–26 = 1989. *Classical Bearings*, 193–209. Berkeley.

Gruen, Erich. 1998. "Rome and the Myth of Alexander." In *Ancient History in a Modern University, I: The Ancient Near East, Greece, and Rome*, ed. T. W. Hillard, et al., 178–191. Grand Rapids.

Humphrey, John. 1986. *Roman Circuses: Arenas for Chariot Racing*. Berkeley.

Isager, Jacob. 1993. "Alexander the Great in Roman Literature from Pompey to Vespasian." In Carlsen 1993, 75–84.

Jeffreys, Elizabeth. 1979. "The Attitudes of Byzantine Chroniclers towards Ancient History." *Byzantion* 49:199–238.

Jouanno, Corinne. 2002. *Naissance et métamorphoses du Roman d'Alexandre: Domaine grec*. Paris.

Kennedy, George. 1972. *The Art of Rhetoric in the Roman World, 300 BC–AD 300*. Princeton.

Kroll, Wilhelm. 1926. *Historia Alexandri Magni (Pseudo-Callisthenes): Recensio Vetusta*. Berlin.

Lauenstein, Ursula von. 1962. *Der griechische Alexanderroman, Rezension Γ, Buch I*. Meisenheim am Glan.

Malcovati, Henrica. 1953. *Oratorum Romanorum fragmenta liberae rei publicae*. 4th ed. Turin.

Manni, Eugenio. 1962. "Alessandro il Molosso e la sua spedizione d'Italia." *Studi Salentini* 14:344–352.

Marcus, Ralph. 1937. *Josephus: Jewish Antiquities, Books IX–XI* (Loeb Classical Library Josephus, vol. 8). Cambridge.

Martin, Paul. 1982–1994. *L'Idée de royauté à Rome*. Clermont-Ferrand.

Meijer, Fik. 2010. *Chariot Racing in the Roman Empire*. Trans. Liz Waters. Baltimore.

Merkelbach, Reinhold. 1977. *Die Quellen des griechischen Alexanderromans*. Munich.

Meyer, Lucienne. 1933. *Les Légendes des Matières de Rome, de France, et de Bretagne dans le 'Panthéon' de Godefroi de Viterbe*. Paris.

Momigliano, Arnaldo. 1979. "Flavius Josephus and Alexander's Visit to Jerusalem." *Athenaeum* 57:442–448.

Morello, Ruth. 2002. "Livy's Alexander Digression (9.17–19): Counterfactuals and Apologetics." *Journal of Roman Studies* 92:62–85.

Poulsen, Birte. 1993. "Alexander the Great in Italy during the Hellenistic period." In Carlsen 1993, 161–70.

Reinink, Gerrit. 1992. "Pseudo-Methodius: A Concept of History in Response to the Rise of Islam." In *The Byzantine and Early Islamic Near East, I: Problems in the Literary Source Material*, ed. Averil Cameron and Lawrence Conrad, 149–187. Princeton.

Rosellini, Michaela. 1993. *Iulius Valerius. Res Gestae Alexandri Macedonis.* Stuttgart.

Schachermeyr, Fritz. 1954. "Die letzten Pläne Alexanders des Großen." *Jahreshefte des österreichischen archäologischen Instituts in Wien* 41:118–140.

———. 1970. *Alexander in Babylon und die Reichsordnung nach seinem Tode.* Vienna.

———. 1973. *Alexander der Grosse.* Vienna.

Sordi, Marta. 1965. "Alessandro e i Romani." *Rendiconti dell. Reale Istituto Lomabardo di scienze e lettere* 99:435–452.

———. 1983. "Alessandro Magno e l'eredità di Siracusa." *Aevum* 57:14–23.

———. 1985. "Alessandro Magno, i Galli e Roma." In *Xenia: Scritti in onore di Piero Treves*, ed. Fulviomario Broilo, 207–214. Rome.

Spencer, Diana. 2002. *The Roman Alexander: Reading a Cultural Myth.* Exeter.

Spivey, Nigel. 2004. *The Ancient Olympics.* Oxford.

Stoneman, Richard. 1991. *The Greek Alexander Romance.* London.

———. 1994. "Jewish Traditions on Alexander the Great." *Studia Philonica Annual* 6:37–53.

———. 1999. "The Latin Alexander." In *Latin Fiction: The Latin Novel in Context*, ed. Heinz Hofmann, 167–186. London.

———. 2008. *Alexander the Great: A Life in Legend.* New Haven.

———. 2012. *The Book of Alexander the Great: A Life of the Conqueror.* London.

Tarn, W. W. 1948. *Alexander the Great, II: Sources and Studies.* Cambridge.

Tcherikover, Victor. 1959. *Hellenistic Civilization and the Jews.* Trans. S. Applebaum. Philadelphia.

Thiel, Helmut van. 1974. *Vita Alexandri Magni: Recensionem Graecam codicis L/Leben und Taten Alexanders von Makedonien; Der griechische Alexanderroman nach der Handschrift L.* Darmstadt.

Tisé, Bernadette. 2002. *Imperialismo romano e imitatio Alexandri: Due studi di storia politica.* Galatina.

Trumpf, Juergen. 1974. *Vita Alexandri Regis Macedonum.* Stuttgart.

Veloudis, Giorgos. 1977. Ἡ Φυλλάδα τοῦ Μεγαλέξαντρου: Διήγησις Ἀλεξάνδρου τοῦ Μακεδόνος. Athens.

Weippert, Otto. 1972. *Alexander-Imitatio und römische Politik in republikanischer Zeit*. Augsburg.

Welles, C. Bradford. 1962. "The Discovery of Sarapis and the Foundation of Alexandria." *Historia* 11:271–298.

Wirth, Gerhard. 1976. "Alexander und Rom." In *Alexandre le Grand: Image et réalité*, 181–221. Geneva.

THE LATIN OF THE MAGERIUS (SMIRAT) MOSAIC

JAMES N. ADAMS

INTRODUCTION

THE MAGERIUS MOSAIC is from the village of Smirat in Tunisia, near Thysdrus, modern El Djem. It was first published by Beschaouch (1966). There have been many discussions since then, a number of which will be mentioned here (see also AE 1967.569). It is thought to date from the mid-third century AD,[1] and probably decorated a villa (that of Magerius: see below), though the details of the findspot are not known. The mosaic represents a *uenatio*, or beast hunt, and four named hunters are depicted killing four leopards, also named. One of the hunters, called Spittara, is on stilts.[2] In two places the vocative *Mageri* occurs, on each side of the mosaic. Magerius was the presenter of the show, or *editor* (twice the verb *edes* occurs in the acclamations to be discussed here), and *Mageri* must express a repeated chant of the crowd. In one corner, under one of these vocatives, there is a man the lower part of whose body has been lost. He has usually been taken to be the *editor* Magerius, but recently arguments have been advanced against this identification,[3] and it is now suggested that he may be a fifth *uenator*, possibly the *magister* of the troupe. There are three other figures in the mosaic, one usually taken to be the goddess Diana and

I am greatly indebted to a number of people who have supplied me with bibliography and other types of information, and have read and criticized drafts of the paper: Angelos Chaniotis, Katherine Dunbabin, Giuseppe Pezzini, Harm Pinkster, William Slater, Andrew Wilson, but above all Kathleen Coleman, who has repeatedly dropped everything to answer my ill-informed queries. None of them can be assumed to agree with the interpretations advanced in the paper.

[1] Beschaouch 1966:147–150.

[2] For the significance of which, see Hanoune 2000:1571–1572.

[3] See Hanoune 2000:1572–1574; Corbier 2006:109n67.

another, a naked youth, usually identified with Dionysus.[4] In the very center, between two extended pieces of Latin, stands a boy holding a silver tray with four bags of money, each with the symbol for 1,000. On his right are the words of the *curio*, or herald, addressed to the people and asking that the *uenatores*, who belong to a group called the Telegenii, be given 500 *denarii* (per leopard?; see below, 515). On his other side are acclamations of the crowd. The symbol for 1,000 shows that more than the amount requested was given.

The texts and image do not depict a moment of time but contain scenes from different points in the day. The leopards are shown as either still resisting or in their death throes, yet night has fallen according to one part of the Latin, and the boy with the money must have appeared right at the end, when the leopards had already been dispatched. The indifference to an exact chronology that is a mark of the whole artistic composition ought to prompt caution in accepting any claim that there must be a precise chronological relationship between the speech of the herald and the acclamations of the crowd (see the commentary below).

The Telegenii are discussed with a good deal of evidence by Beschaouch.[5] It is concluded that they were an African sodality (a *familia uenatorum*) with a recurrent emblem and a tutelary deity (Dionysus), and that they were available for hire for the mounting of shows (*uenationes*). Beschaouch found evidence for other sodalities in Africa.[6]

This paper does not set out to discuss details of the images on the mosaic. It is concerned with the pieces of Latin, particularly the acclamations. These belong to a formulaic popular genre attested in both Greek and Latin of the Empire (though traceable well back before then) from the circus, the arena, the senate, and gatherings of other sorts, including religious. There has been a good deal of interest in acclamations in recent decades,[7] but no comprehensive collection of the texts

---

[4]   See, however, Hanoune 2000: 1574–1576; could they be secondary persons in the show dressed as mythological figures?

[5]   1966:150–156.

[6]   1985:458–475; 2006:1405–1413.

[7]   See e.g. the general book of Aldrete 1999.

in either Greek or Latin. The acclamations on the mosaic (I believe that there are about three, not one, and spread over the whole day of the show) are conspicuously difficult to interpret, and the difficulties have tended to be glossed over, not least in translations. An interpretation will be put forward here, and the character of the Latin discussed. There are constant ambiguities caused by the elliptical style of acclamations. I will attempt to identify in such cases all possible interpretations, instead of opting for one and suppressing mention of the others.

TEXTS AND TRANSLATION

The first text below (which is on the left-hand side of the mosaic) is the request of the herald. The acclamations that follow (on the right-hand side) are printed with the line divisions that appear on the mosaic. The translation of the second part is split into paragraphs representing what I take to be the different acclamations.

> per curionem
> dictum: domini mei, ut
> Telegeni
> pro leopardo
> meritum ha-
> beant uestri
> fauoris, dona-
> te eis denarios
> quingentos.

> adclamatum est:
> exemplo tuo mu-
> nus sic discanp [*sic*]
> futuri, audiant
> praeteriti. unde
> tale, quando tale?
> exemplo quaesto-
> rum munus edes,
> de re tua mu-
> nus edes.

sta dies.
Magerius do-
nat. hoc est habe-
re, hoc est posse,
hoc est ia. nox est:
ia munere tuo
saccis missos.

Through a herald it was said: "My lords, so that the Telegenii may have the reward of your favor for (each) leopard, give them 500 *denarii*."

It was shouted forth: "By your example let future generations/benefactors (?) learn that a show is like this, and let past generations/benefactors (?) hear (that it is like this). By whom (has a show) such as this (ever been presented), when (has a show) such as this (ever been presented)? On the example of the quaestors (of Rome) you will present a show, from your pocket you will present a show. This is the day! It is Magerius who is presenting it!"

"This is to have the wherewithal, this is to have power, this is the moment!"

"It is night: now discharge (the Telegenii) from your show by (award of) the bags of money!"

THE SPEECH OF THE HERALD

It again emerges, from the words of the herald alongside the depiction of the boy carrying money bags (the boy is not to be confused with the herald, but, as Beschaouch puts it, is "un jeune serviteur"),[8] that the mosaic does not present a moment in time during the show. The herald asks for 500 denarii per leopard (see further below on this phrase), but the boy is bearing twice that amount. The request for 500 denarii and the appearance of the boy with a much greater sum cannot be simulta-

---

[8] Beschaouch 1966:143.

neous. Having heard the request of the herald the generous Magerius seems to be presented as doubling the payment, and the boy must have come forth after the initial reference to 500 denarii or else the drama of the increased award would have been lost. Beschaouch notes that "[n]ous sommes ici à la fin du combat,"[9] but even so there is a sequence of events at this late stage, with the boy appearing after the herald. The passing of time is implicit in both texts.

Commentary

per curionem dictum: Beschaouch notes that this formula (with impersonal passive verb) is found in a similar context (a description of a *uenatio*) in the *Historia Augusta* (*Gall.* 12.4, *ille per curionem dici iussit*; so again at 12.5).[10] The point of the *per*-construction is that the herald was merely the mouthpiece of the Telegenii, who spoke "through" him, or at least that is how things are presented: the herald's speech might well have been stage-managed by Magerius himself, in such a way as to highlight his generosity. *Curio* originally meant "priest of the *curia*" (*TLL* IV.1489.29ff.). The new meaning "herald" (*praeco*) appears first in Martial but mainly rather later (1489.43ff.).

It will be seen below that the formula introducing the acclamations themselves is also standard in the *SHA*. In both cases the composer of the texts on the mosaic must have adopted current phraseology for introducing words uttered at shows.

domini: the crowd here are addressed as *domini*, "lords," a form of address used by Claudius of arena crowds (Suet. *Claud.* 21.5).[11] Since *dominus* was also a term regularly addressed to the emperor himself, there was arguably a pretense of equality at such events. Aldrete observes that "this habit of Claudius represented a dramatic inversion of the social order."[12] Fagan notes that the spectators would themselves pay the *uenatores* nothing, since payment would come from the *munerarius*, but crowds "regularly demanded payment for winners"

---

[9] Beschaouch 1966:136.
[10] Beschaouch 1966:136.
[11] On this point, see Fagan 2011:130.
[12] Aldrete 1999:121.

(citing Juv. 7.243, *accipe, uictori populus quod postulat, aurum*). The crowd and *editor* are assimilated, and the "spectators imagined themselves as lords for the day."[13]

ut Telegeni ... habeant: Fagan wonders whether this *ut*-clause expresses purpose or cause.[14] Cause seems very unlikely. If cause is dismissed, two possibilities remain.

First, this could be the old use of *ut* introducing a wish ("may they have"), followed here by an imperative expressing in concrete terms the favor required. This use of *ut* is found in early Latin (e.g. Plaut. *Poen.* 912; Cato *Agr.* 1.2), and did not die out as a stylized way of presenting a wish or instruction. It occurs at Vitr. 1.1.3 (*et ut litteratus sit, peritus graphidos, eduditus geometria*), is common in curse tablets,[15] and is found even in very late texts of low register, as at *Mul. Chir.* 691 (*si collectionem fecerit, ut eum ossum fractum eximas*).[16] Here the construction might seem suited to the formal presentation of a request (*meritum ... uestri fauoris* is itself abstract and high-flown), which is then picked up by a more direct imperatival construction containing a specific demand.

However, it is better to take the clause in the conventional way as expressing purpose. This pattern occurs in acclamations, and although the speech is not strictly an acclamation, it is a public exchange with the crowd. For preposed *ut*-clauses expressing purpose in acclamations, followed by an imperative, see *SHA, Comm.* 18.7 (*ut salui simus, Iuppiter optime maxime, serua nobis Pertinacem*) and 18.15 (*ut securi simus, delatoribus metum. ut salui simus, delatores de senatu, delatoribus fustem* [with ellipse of the imperatives]). Similarly throughout the next chapter of *Comm.* there are preposed relative clauses, followed by imperatival verbs. The emphatic imperative, which is the essence of the acclamation or request, is put in final position, and the preposed subordination implies that an imperative demand is to follow.

---

[13] Fagan 2011:130 (both quotes).
[14] Fagan 2011:131n22.
[15] See Adams 1992:6.
[16] See further Hofmann and Szantyr 1965:331; and for late Latin, see Svennung 1935:511–512.

pro leopardo: this phase is unambiguously in the *ut*-clause, and not in the second clause attached to *denarios quingentos*, as it is always taken in translations ("500 denarii per leopard"). The Telegenii (or Magerius?; see above) through the herald have expressed themselves imprecisely: "so that they may have the reward of your favor for (each) leopard" might be interpreted to mean either 500 denarii divided by the number of leopards, or 500 for each leopard. If the Telegenii were themselves responsible for the speech, might the ambiguity have been deliberate?

THE ACCLAMATIONS OF THE CROWD

The first part of the text on the right, from *exemplo tuo* to the second *munus edes*, has proved particularly difficult to interpret, and the various possibilities have not been clearly separated. There are at least three ways of taking these lines. First, they may have been uttered late in the day, in response to the herald's request for payment. This is the usual interpretation, but it is open to serious objections. Second, this part might have been spoken early in the day, as the show was about to get under way. On this view it cannot be directly related to the request of the herald, as this must have been towards the end of the day; as a consequence there would have been a time lapse between the first acclamation and the last, which is uttered as night falls. Third, is it possible that the phrase *munus edes* means not "you will present a show," but something like "you will become presenter of the show in the full sense (if you agree to pay the *uenatores*)"? I take each of these in turn. In my opinion the second possibility is almost certainly right.

(1) It is clearly stated, for example, by Dunbabin that the acclamation (singular) is a direct response to the herald's speech: "it is possible to say that it [i.e. the inscription] records the *adclamatio* made in answer to the herald's appeal by the audience attending the spectacle, calling upon Magerius to perform the functions of a *munerarius*, that is, to pay the *venatores* for the show they have put on, and applauding his munificence when he does so."[17] A similar statement that the whole text (including by implication the first part) replies to the herald's

---

[17] Dunbabin 1978:68.

speech is made by Roueché, who sees the Latin as falling into the category of what she calls an "acclamatory request."[18] She continues: "It records, verbatim, the request from the *bestiarii* through a herald for payment, and *then records the crowd's response*" (my emphasis). Lane Fox notes similarly that the herald called on the "local big-wigs ... to pay 500 denarii to each hunter as the reward for each dead leopard," and adds: "The crowd then started a chanted acclamation, to encourage a possible donor" (which is not the point, as the *munerarius* was obviously long since known).[19] Bomgardner writes, imaginatively and mixing up the herald's speech and the acclamations:

> From the indiscriminate pronouncement ... of the herald ... the intensity of the moment builds and builds. The multiple harangues of the crowd ... urging the would-be *munerarius* to consider the glory to be attained by giving the *Telegenii* their well earned (*meritum*) reward, contribute to the increasing tension. Finally, the climax: Magerius comes forward and agrees to pay.[20]

The phrase *munus edes* seems not to be taken in the general sense of sponsoring the whole show, but as referring merely to the rewarding of the victors, even though Bomgardner was well aware that there was far more to the financing of a show than paying prize money. Thus he remarks: "it is generally assumed that most, if not all of the arrangements for such a spectacle were previously agreed between the contractor(s) and the *munerarius*, who was paying for it: the number of performers, the number of wild animals, prices, scenery, props, etc."[21]

The punctuation to be assigned to the words *Magerius donat* encapsulates the problem of interpreting this first part of the text. The text Beschaouch prints has the words from the start of the text (*exemplo tuo*) down to *sta dies* enclosed in inverted commas.[22] The words *Magerius donat* are outside quotation marks. Then the quotation resumes, from

[18] Roueché 1984:183.
[19] Lane Fox 2005:667.
[20] Bomgardner 2009:169.
[21] Bomgardner 2009:169.
[22] Beschaouch 1966:139.

hoc est to the end (*missos*).[23] Thus *Magerius donat* is not regarded as part of the acclamations but as a sort of editorial insertion. On this view the first acclamation is a demand that Magerius pay (but for what?). Then he succumbs to the pressure, an editorial aside states "Magerius pays up," and a celebratory acclamation begins. The same punctuation is accepted (by implication or explicitly) by Roueché (1984:183), Vismara (2007:110), Chaniotis (2009:214), and Fagan (2011:131). Lane Fox (2005:667) and Cooley (2012:210) by contrast translate *Magerius donat* as part of the acclamation.

There are various difficulties raised by the punctuation of Beschaouch and the others.

First, the whole text, including the words *Magerius donat*, comes under the heading *adclamatum est*. There is a symmetry to the layout of the two texts, in that each is introduced by a passive verb. *Per curionem dictum* on the left-hand side introduces the herald's speech, which is obviously not thereafter interrupted by editorial asides, and it would be odd to find insertions in the parallel text, which is similarly introduced.

Second, the two editorial statements that are definitely in these texts (*per curionem dictum, adclamatum est*) are both in the perfect tense. It was open to the drafter to make *Magerius donat* unambiguously into an editorial comment by putting it in the past tense, but this has not been done. We will see below (531) that Beschaouch also takes the later phrase *nox est* to be editorial,[24] but there even more clearly a past tense (*erat*) would be required to make clear that the phrase was an editor's explanation.

Third, Magerius cannot possibly be paying for the full show at this point, as the outlay incurred even before the show got under way, for example by the provision of an arena and animals, would have been considerable. All that he could be financing now are the rewards of the *uenatores*. But if we take the point to be that the crowd has been demanding precisely that, viz. the rewarding of the *uenatores*, then *munus* could hardly (without special pleading: see the section

---

[23] Beschaouch's later presentation of the text (2006:1403–1405) and the translation there are much the same, but see below, 531 on *nox est*.

[24] Beschaouch 2006:1404, which he had not done in the edition of 1966.

numbered 3 below) have its usual meaning "show," but would seem to mean something like "payment." Beschaouch, inserting a sentence into his translation that is not in the Latin, writes this verb phrase: "tu auras payé le présent munus." *Munus* characteristically is here not rendered into French at all (so elsewhere in the translation), but with the verb *payer* it might refer to a payment or sum of money, not to a show. The problem is that *payer* in French admits of the two meanings, "pay for (something)" and "pay (a sum of money)," and if *munus* itself is left untranslated the intended meaning of the phrase is unclear. The meaning "payment, reward" vel sim. is unequivocally ruled out for *munus* by the repeated verb *edes*. *Edo* does not mean anything like "pay" (see the thirteen categories of meaning in the *OLD* entry). It means rather "display, exhibit, hold" (see meanings 11, 12), and thus while it is suited to *munus* meaning "show" in general, it is not suited to some such meaning as "payment." The conclusion cannot be avoided that *munus edes* has to mean what the verb phrase elsewhere means (see below, 527), namely "you will present a show," and any interpretation of the sequence of events that is attempted must be in line with that point.

It is preferable to take *Magerius donat* not as an editorial description of the actual handing over of money, but as part of the acclamation, that is as the climactic naming of the benefactor who is responsible for the show that is about to unfold (= "it is Magerius who is granting the money for the show!," i.e. "Magerius is the benefactor"). There is no difficulty about giving both *munus* and *edo* their usual meanings, if the future tenses are taken to mean that the show has not yet begun but is about to (= "you will now present a show").

(2) If we adopt the view adumbrated in the last sentence the future tense verb *edes*, which occurs twice, becomes crucial, though it has to be said that the tense has been lost on some commentators. Wiedemann translates it as a perfect ("You have provided a *munus* as an example to the quaestors; you have provided a *munus* from your own resources"),[25] and Cooley as a present ("You provide a show according to the example

of the quaestors, you give a show at your own expense").[26] *Edes* cannot be a misspelling for *edidisti*, but it might just be a misspelling for the present *edis*, a possibility that will be considered below in the final conclusions.

The right-hand text thus would not express a single acclamation uttered at one moment of time, but several acclamations spread over the day. There is, on this second interpretation, a time lapse between the words of the first part of the text and those of the last few lines, when night has already fallen. At the start the show has not begun, as is suggested by the repeated refrain *munus edes*, "you will present a show." There is a drama built into the presentation of the acclamations.

The first acclamation, it is suggested, runs from *exemplo tuo* to *Magerius donat*. The crowd addresses in the second person (*tuus* occurs twice and *edes* twice) the benefactor who has mounted the *uenatio*, at first without naming him. Everyone knows that it is Magerius who has financed ("from [his] own pocket") the show, but the naming of him is dramatically postponed until the penultimate word of this section. It is likely that the acclamation was uttered as the *editor* Magerius ostentatiously took his seat in the crowd, a dramatic moment in any spectacle.[27] This part looks forward to the show that is to begin, and presents Magerius as the *editor* of the whole event. This acclamation is thus not a request to Magerius to pay the *uenatores* a reward, but a prediction that he is about to present a show, the total costs of which would far exceed the prize money.

Arguments in favor of this interpretation were already stated in the previous section: *munus edere* does not mean "make a payment" but "present a show," and that show will only be presented when it gets under way, which is not the case yet. But there is a second argument, and that lies in the words *exemplo quaestorum* preceding the first instance of *munus edes*, "you will present a show on the example of the quaestors." Beschaouch himself collects the evidence for the history during the imperial period of quaestors presenting shows at their own

---

[26] Cooley 2012:210.

[27] For the reactions of the crowd, e.g., to the entry of celebrities in the late Republic, see the material collected by Parker 1999:169–170.

expense to the people, that is whole events.[28] He cites, e.g., from the
SHA, Alex. Sev. 43.3 *quaestores candidatos ex sua pecunia munera populo dare
iussit*, comparing it to our phraseology *exemplo quaestorum munus edes de
re tua.*[29] If Magerius is to act on the model of the quaestors, clearly he is
about to mount a show, and is not requested simply to reward the *uenatores*. The whole phraseology of this section is appropriate to a show.
De re tua is reminiscent of *ex sua pecunia* in the *HA* above. The rhetorical
questions *unde tale, quando tale*, if they mean, as they must (see below,
524–527), "who has ever given such a *munus* or when" would be appropriate in reference to the anticipated grandeur of the event, but seem
unlikely to refer to the size of the victors' prizes. It should also be noted
that the second *munus edes* is immediately followed by the phrase *sta
dies*, i.e. in the context "this is the day when you will present a show."
The phrase would not be appropriate if it referred in a limited way to
the mere granting of prizes.

(3) Finally we might contemplate the possibility of somehow
combining the ideas present in the two interpretations set out above.
Could *munus edes* have its proper meaning "you will present a show,"
but nevertheless allude (at the end of the whole performance) in a
restricted way to the granting of rewards? That is probably the view of
Beschaouch, though he is far from explicit. Could the meaning be "you
will become the presenter of the show (when you have paid the prizes
demanded by the herald)"? Beschaouch speaks of acclaiming Magerius
"comme un véritable *'editor muneris'* ... dans la mesure où Magerius aura
fait ce qu'on va lui demander."[30]

Such an interpretation is not convincing. There is no such reservation expressed in the Latin (we noted above that Beschaouch adds
a complete clause to his translation that is not in the original), and
munus edes is a banal formulaic expression with an established meaning
in such contexts; we would need overt indicators to consider giving it
a highly allusive emphasis. There is not the slightest hint in this first

---

[28] Beschaouch 1966:145–146.
[29] Beschaouch 1966:146.
[30] Beschaouch 1966:140.

acclamation that the phrase *munus edes* has to be interpreted in the light of the herald's speech.

I therefore think it most likely that the first eleven lines form an acclamation uttered early in the day. The crowd is assembled and the *uenatio* is about to start. The crowd celebrates the benefactor as he enters, at first anonymously but with use of the second person addressed to one about to provide something special. Then at the end of this acclamation there is a naming of Magerius.

The second acclamation on my division consists of the triumphant three-line celebration of the wealth and power of Magerius, with each clause introduced by *hoc est*. The show is no longer simply foreseen, but a demonstration of wealth must be before the spectators, possibly as the performers enter the arena (note particularly the phrase *hoc est ia*). The third acclamation runs from *nox est* to the end of the text. It is night and the show is now over, and payment is made to the *uenatores*. The syntax here is particularly problematic (see below), but it is likely that there is a request for payment or a statement of payment being made in the words *saccis missos*. *Saccis* obviously alludes to the image of the boy carrying money bags, and thus this last acclamation is indeed linked directly to an adjoining part of the mosaic.

It should not be assumed that these were the only acclamations uttered during the day, or that they had precisely the form presented here. They are almost certainly a selection, chosen to glorify Magerius and no doubt simplified. Acclamations by their very nature are repetitive, and the same refrain might be repeated many times over (see the conclusions below for some figures from an African ecclesiastical assembly showing just how often a phrase might be repeated). We should not think that the crowd at this *uenatio* were as much to the point as the text might imply.

Commentary

adclamatum est: a standard way of introducing an acclamation in the *Historia Augusta* (e.g. *Alex. Sev.* 7.1, 8.2 (without *est*), 9.4, 10.3; *Gord.* 5.7; *Tac.* 7.4); see also the conclusions below on the same usage in *acta ecclesiastica* reported in Augustine *Epist.* 213. The verb goes well back in application to public acclamations, and is attested in the impersonal passive, as here: note e.g. Suet. *Dom.* 13.1 *adclamari etiam in amphitheatro epuli die libenter audit: "domino et dominae feliciter."*[31] There was however no fixed way of referring to acclamations in either Latin or Greek.[32]

sic discanp: Bomgardner translates "may future benefactors (*munerarii*) understand the spectacle."[33] But that is to disregard *sic*, which is predicative, with *esse* understood.[34] *Sic* with *est/esse* "is so" is potentially ambiguous, as it may look back (= "is as previously indicated, seen") or forward (= "as is about to be indicated/seen": see *OLD* s.v. 2, 3). Since on the interpretation adopted here the show is yet to begin, *sic* is prospective ("let them learn that this is what a show is like"). Beschaouch offered a different explanation of *sic*, based on a passage from Riemann's *Syntaxe latine* (1927).[35] *Sic* is said to place a restriction on the wish (for examples of this use, see *OLD* s.v. *sic* 8d), which will only be realized when Magerius has done what is going to be demanded of him. Riemann is cited for such a use of *sic* (or *ita*),[36] but a whole clause of the citation is omitted: Riemann was referring primarily to a use of *ita/sic* picked up by a restrictive *ut*-clause ("suivi d'une proposition avec *ut*"); there is nothing of that sort here, and no hint in the Latin that anything is understood. The restrictive use of *sic*, to judge from the examples cited by the *OLD* above, is placed right at the head of its clause, and usually with the restriction expressed. Beschaouch, as noted above, supplies in his translation after the rendering of *discant futuri* a complete clause that is not present in the Latin, but is, I take it, to be understood ("dans la mesure où tu auras payé le présent *munus*").[37] But if *sic* is given this use anticipatory of an understood restrictive clause,

---

[31] See *TLL* s.vv. *acclamatio, acclamo* for many examples from about the Ciceronian period onwards.

[32] For this point see Roueché 1984:181, mentioning for Latin *conclamatio, uox*, and *acclamatio*; also 182, referring to fragmentary Greek acclamations introduced by the Latin *succlam(atum) est*.

[33] Bomgardner 2009:168.

[34] For predicative *sic* with *esse*, see *OLD* s.v. *sic* 5a.

[35] Beschaouch 1966:140.

[36] Riemann 1927:301n2.

[37] Beschaouch 1966:139.

a major semantic difficulty arises. *Sic* ceases to be the predicate with *munus* and an understood *esse* (= "let them learn that a show is like this"), and *munus* is left as a solitary direct object of *discant*. But what sense would *munus discant* have?—"let them learn of/understand a *munus*, on condition that you pay up"(?). This has no clear point.

Beschaouch takes *futuri* and *praeteriti* as referring to benefactors (understanding *munerarii*).[38] Such terms are used in the nominative plural without an understood noun in a general sense, usually in oppositions resembling this, of past, present, or future generations.[39] However, generations of the past could hardly learn of anything from the grave, whereas some past benefactors might still be around to learn that they had been surpassed by Magerius. And so ellipse of *munerarii/editores* looks an attractive possibility—not that a formulaic and sonorous opposition need be precisely meaningful.

Discanp is not a normal type of misspelling. It may be a mere slip, with the craftsman getting into a mess over production of the letter and unable to correct, or alternatively it might be due to damage when the mosaic was moved.

It ought to be mentioned for the sake of completeness that it could also at a pinch be explained as a sort of phonetic spelling. Final -*t* in verb forms, particularly when it is part of a threefold consonant cluster across a word boundary, was frequently subject to an assimilatory loss.[40] The next word *futuri* begins with a bilabial fricative, and it is possible that the craftsman heard the final stop of *discant* as bilabial with assimilation of place of articulation to the following *f*. This would not be the only phonetic spelling in the acclamations (cf. *sta, ia* twice), but the others, unlike this one, are in significant contexts (see the final conclusions below).

The expression *exemplo tuo ... discant* ("by your example let them learn") recalls a remark by Ammianus at 28.4.33 that at every show (*in omni spectaculo*) every performer (in a long list *uenator* itself occurs)

---

[38] Beschaouch 1966:139, 140.

[39] See *TLL* X.2.1017.56ff., citing this example among others.

[40] See Adams 2013:147–157 for examples and discussion of such omissions, with conclusions at 156–157.

is constantly hailed with the cry *per te illi discant* "through you let them learn."[41] I take it that *illi* refers not to the spectators but to other performers or to opponents (= "you show them"). Magerius is to show other *editores* what a show should be like. The phrase in such a context was possibly a sort of greeting as the performer entered, and is certainly here suited to the moment when the show is about to get under way. Ammianus wryly comments "what ought to be learnt no one is able to explain" (*quid autem debeat disci, nemo sufficit explanare*).

unde tale, quando tale: it is natural here to take *unde* in the sense *a quo* (i.e. with personal reference, "by whom"), with Magerius implicitly being compared to other benefactors. This personal use is as old as Plautus and Cato, with various nuances.[42] Cf. e.g. Cato *Agr.* 5.3, *duas aut tres familias habeat, unde utenda roget* (*unde* = *a quibus* "from whom"); Sall. *Jug.* 14.22, *quamquam tibi inmaturo et unde minume decuit uita erepta est* ("from whom"); Hor. *Sat.* 1.6.12, *contra Laeuinum, Valeri genus, unde Superbus / Tarquinius regno pulsus fugit* ("by/from whom"). Note particularly Plaut. *Men.* 782–783 *ludibrio, pater, habeor. :: unde? :: ab illo quoi me mandauisti, meo uiro.*[43] A Ciceronian example (= "by whom") is cited in the next paragraph but one. Beschaouch, glossing with *ex quo* and citing Ernout and Thomas (1953:334), identified the usage correctly,[44] but there have been all sorts of vague renderings since then (notable being that of Wiedemann 1992:17, "*where* has such a thing been heard of?" [my emphasis]). *Munus* has to be understood with *tale*, and there is verbal ellipse too (see below).

There are two ways of construing these clauses. First, they may be free-standing direct questions, with ellipse of the verbs. That is the way they seem always to have been taken. If this view is accepted one must address the question in what tense the understood verbs would be (see further below). The second possibility is that these might be indirect questions (with some such verb as *editum sit* understood) dependent on *audiant*, "let past *editores* hear by whom such (a show)

---

[41] Drawn to my attention by William Slater.
[42] *OLD* s.v. 2, Hofmann and Szantyr 1965:208–209; Väänänen 1981:126.
[43] Drawn to my attention by Harm Pinkster.
[44] Beschaouch 1966:141 with n. 1.

(has been presented), and when." The whole part from the first *unde* to the second *tale* is enclosed by interpuncts, but these have no decisive bearing on the interpretation of the syntax. Interpuncts are used haphazardly in later Latin, sometimes to mark syntactic units, sometimes irrationally.[45] Whether *unde ... tale* is a free-standing sentence (i.e. a pair of direct questions) or a double dependent clause, it is still a syntactic unit. For *unde* "by whom" introducing an indirect question (with the subjunctive part of the verb in ellipse), see Cic. *Att.* 15.13a.2, *sed perscribe, quaeso, quae causa sit Myrtilo ... et satisne pateat unde corruptus* ("But pray tell me all about Myrtilus' case ... and whether it is sufficiently clear who suborned him").[46] Ellipse of the verb is not unusual in indirect questions: e.g. Cic. *Planc.* 62, *quaeris num disertus*; *Att.* 4.11.2, *perscribe ad me ... quid censores*; *Att.* 12.51.2, *hoc tamen uelim scire, quando auctio*; *Att.* 13.51.2, *Quintus cras; sed ad me an ad te nescio*.[47]

The advantage of this second interpretation is that it would supply a complement for *audiant*, which otherwise is either left free-standing or has to be given the same complement as *discant*. On the other hand it is not convincing to introduce unnecessary subordination into acclamations, which are not complex syntactically and rely on a staccato effect. Moreover the two clauses if taken as direct questions, with the understood verbs in the past tense, would seem to be a suitable follow-up to the words *audiant praeteriti* (= "let past *editores* hear of it—after all, who in the past ever put on a show such as this is to be?"). *Tale* is prospective on the interpretation of the acclamation adopted here (= "of such a kind as we are about to see before us").[48]

A verb of doing, offering, presenting (*facio, do, dono, edo*, or the like) has to be supplied, almost certainly in the past tense (but on the tense, see further the next paragraph), probably *edo* given the phraseology of the acclamation elsewhere (see further below on *edes*). The old dissertation of Heidemann shows that verbs such as *facio* and *do* are constantly omitted in Cicero's letters.[49] Note too, e.g., Hor. *Sat.* 1.2.90, *hoc illi recte*

---

[45] See Adams 1996.
[46] Shackleton Bailey 1965–1970: VI.185, changing the passive to active.
[47] See Heidemann 1893:41, 55, 60.
[48] See *OLD* s.v. 2b.
[49] Heidemann 1893:57–63, 69–71.

(sc. *fecerunt*)—an ellipse that incidentally has the interest that *hoc ille* (with *fecit* understood) is the etymology of the French word for "yes," *oui/oil*.[50] Verbal ellipse is a feature of acclamations, and probably occurs later in this text itself (see below on *saccis missos*). A classic example is *Christianos ad leonem*.[51] Note too Suet. *Tib*. 75.1, *morte eius ita laetatus est populus, ut ad primum nuntium discurrentes pars: "Tiberium in Tiberim!" clamitarent*. Here is a small selection of acclamations with verbal ellipse from the *Historia Augusta*: *Pesc. Nig*. 2.2, *"illum principem superi et illum Augustum" populus adclamaret*;[52] *Comm*. 18.5, *gladiatorem in spoliario* (part of a long acclamation: "cast the gladiator in the charnel-house"); *Comm*. 18.15, *delatoribus metum. ut securi simus, delatoribus metum. <ut> salui simus, delatores de senatu, delatoribus fustem*; Ant. Diad. 1.7, *Iuppiter optime maxime, Macrino et Antonino uitam*; *Maxim*. 26.2, *Iuppiter optime, tibi gratias. Ap[p]ollo uenerabilis, tibi gratias. Maxime Auguste, tibi gratias. Balbine Auguste, tibi gratias*. An acclamation tends to be formulaic, like a proverb or *bon mot*, and expressions of these latter types also show ellipses, e.g. *SHA, Verus* 5.1, *cum sit notissimum dictum de numero conuiuarum "septem conuiuium, nouem uero conuicium,"* ("though there is a very well-known saying about the number of diners, that 'seven make a dinner but nine make a din'" [*facere* understood]).

Finally, the possibility ought at least to be considered that the verbs understood might be future, "by whom will such a show be presented, when will it be presented?" In support of such a view it could be suggested that both questions might seem to be answered in what follows. *Magerius donat* might be taken to answer *unde tale*, and *sta dies* might pick up *quando tale*. For the question-and-answer format in acclamations (well known in modern political rallies), see Cic. *Q. fr*. 2.3.2.[53] There are however factors against such an idea. First, the addressee of the preceding part of the acclamation is clearly known, if not yet explicitly named. Magerius is addressed here, and the question "by

---

[50] See Bloch and von Wartburg 1968:330 s.v. *il, ils*.

[51] See e.g. Tert. Apol. 40.2; cf. *SHA, Comm*. 18.10, *exaudi Caesar: delatores ad leonem. exaudi Caesar: Speratum ad leonem*.

[52] Understand *seruent*; cf. e.g. Ant. Pius 3.1, *inter alias adclamationes dictum est "Auguste, dii te seruent."*

[53] Also Lintott 1968:10.

whom will such a show be presented?" would seem inappropriate, though it might just be taken to be a lead-in to the dramatic naming of the benefactor. Second, the *quando*-question would be weak, given that the crowd is already assembled to see the show. Third, and more decisively, the two questions are separated by two full clauses from the possible answers, and the elements do not look closely connected. In public chants a rhetorical question would normally receive an immediate answer.

For the type of context in which *tale* is used here, cf. Sen. *Thy.* 1047 *tale quis uidit nefas?*[54]

munus edes: this is a regular expression of the mounting of a spectacle, particularly gladiatorial (*OLD* s.v. *munus* 4; *TLL* V.2.94.27ff.): e.g. Livy 28.21.1, *Scipio Carthaginem ad ... munus ... gladiatorium ... edendum rediit*; Vell. 2.93.1, *magnificentissimo munere aedilitatis edito*; Juv. 3.36, *munera nunc edunt*; *CIL* VIII.7969 *munus gladiat(orium) et uenat(ionem) ... M. Cosinius ... Celerinus ... edidit*. *Munus* was not a neutral term simply denoting a show in the manner of *spectaculum*. It implies that that show has been mounted at someone's expense as a civic duty or public benefaction. It focuses on the role of the *editor*, whereas the focus of *spectaculum* is on the spectators. As for *edere*, this is the "verbe le plus commun, et de loin, pour exprimer l'organisation d'un spectacle."[55] Chamberland notes that he has found about 125 to 130 attestations, from the first century onwards but mainly in the second and third centuries.[56] It implies that the subject has put on the show at his own expense, as distinct from drawing on public funds.[57]

The repetition of the phrase is a refrain, and such refrains are typical of acclamations, usually in the imperial period with invariant word order. There are some strikingly repetitive acclamations in the *Historia Augusta*, with verb phrases recurring with the same word order. At *Comm.* 18-19 a long senatorial acclamation is reported. Among

---

[54] Drawn to my attention by Harm Pinkster.
[55] Chamberland 2012:275.
[56] Chamberland 2012:276.
[57] See Chamberland 2012:276 and particularly 277, making a distinction between *edere* and *curare*.

other repetitive elements it has at 18.5–6 a sequence of four instances of *unco trahatur*, and then at 19.2–6 a further sixteen instances of the same phrase with the same order. Three times in successive sentences at 18.10 there is the expression *parricida trahatur*, and then at 19.9 two instances of *parricidae cadauer trahatur*. There are other such refrains in the examples quoted in the last note (*delatoribus metum*; *tibi gratias*). Another repeated refrain with the same word order is at *Pass. Perp.* 21.2 *populus ... reclamauerit: "saluum lotum! saluum lotum!"* Aldrete notes that repetitions in senatorial acclamations in the *Historia Augusta* range from a few to "an astounding eighty iterations."[58]

An old type of public chant was the practice known now as *flagitatio*, whereby a creditor chanted (possibly with supporters) a demand for his money back in the street to bring disgrace (*flagitium*) on a debtor.[59] A few extant *flagitationes* have a refrain, as those found at Plaut. *Most.* 603 (*cedo faenus, redde faenus, faenus reddite*) and Catull. 42.11–12 (*moecha putida, redde codicillos, / redde, putida moecha, codicillos*). Fraenkel noted that the reversals of word order found in both of these refrains "belonged to a very old popular custom as a means of intensifying the demand."[60] That may be so, but the imperial refrains seen above have all but entirely abandoned such variation. This is hardly surprising, as large crowds needed to know what was coming next if they were to chant in unison, and variations of word order might not easily be predicted. That said, there is a series of acclamations at the Council of Chalcedon (*ACO* II.1.2, 110) quoted by Roueché (1984:189) in another connection that have a similar chiasmus in a refrain to that in the *flagitationes*: πολλὰ τὰ ἔτη τῶν βασιλέων· τῶν μεγάλων βασιλέων πολλὰ τὰ ἔτη ... πολλὰ τὰ ἔτη τῶν ἀρχόντων· τῶν ὀρθοδόξων πολλὰ τὰ ἔτη. A proper analysis of the word order of refrains would only become possible if a comprehensive corpus of Greek and Latin acclamations were compiled.

---

[58] Aldrete 1999:138. See further the general conclusions below on a text recording the numbers of such repetitions on a particular occasion.

[59] See e.g. Lintott 1968:8–10.

[60] Fraenkel 1961:48 = 1964: II.119.

The phrases accompanying the repeated *munus edes* are varied in the two clauses (*exemplo quaestorum; de re tua*). Such variation is typical of the complements of refrains in acclamations; see e.g. the Greek inscription (*SEG* 34.1306) from Perge in Pamphylia of the late third century AD quoted and discussed by Kuhn 2012:306–308, in which a single refrain (αὖξε Πέργη) is accompanied by more than a dozen different phrases.

sta dies: this phrase may be explained in two ways. First, *sta* may be for *ista*. Aphaeresis of the *i* (the inverse or hypercorrect variant of the prothetic vowel that often developed before *s* + stop, as in *estercus* for *stercus* or *iscola* for *schola*) in this pronoun is well attested in late Latin.[61] This explanation is almost certainly the right one.[62] *Iste* is not infrequently used in a temporal meaning of the present time (*TLL* VII.2.509.79, "spectat ad ipsum tempus praesens"), with *dies* itself (masculine or feminine) or a synonym (*lux*) or with *nox*.[63] *Iste dies* at Lucan 6.158 (*non paruo sanguine Magni iste dies ierit*) means "today," and *nox ista* at Val. Flacc. 1.670 means "tonight." The form *sta* survives in some comparable expressions in Italian (*stamattina, stasera, stanotte*).

Alternatively *sta* might just be imperative of *sto*, with the day, personified, instructed to stop (cf. Hor. *Odes* 3.28.6, *ueluti stet uolucris dies*), i.e. not to pass (into night), so that the show can last as long as possible. The reference a little later to night bringing things to a close might be thought to give some support to this view. However, before we get to *nox est* the present moment is stressed by *hoc est ia*, "this is the moment," and that phrase should surely be seen as underlining the idea behind *ista dies*.

Magerius donat: on the punctuation of these words see the introduction above.

hoc est posse: for the substantival use of *posse*, see *TLL* X.2.153.62ff. (sometimes in classical Latin and common in late Latin). There are for instance two examples (dependent on prepositions) in the school

---

[61] For examples, see Adams 2013:464; for aphaeresis in general, Sampson 2010:56–58.

[62] So Beschaouch 1966:141.

[63] See the examples of these and comparable phrases at *TLL* 510.1ff.

exercise edited by Dionisotti (1982), *pro posse* at 39 and *iuxta posse* at 70 (Dionisotti's numbers); see now Dickey (2015: **C**39c, **C**70e).

hoc est ia. nox est: this punctuation seems necessary, rather than *hoc est. ia nox est*. If the latter, *hoc est* on its own would not be meaningful. After the two instances of *hoc est* + predicate another such construction is required, and it seems to be provided by *iam* as predicate. Adverbs are not infrequently used as predicates of the verb "to be" in Latin, where an English speaker might expect an adjective or noun. Adverbs used thus include *palam, frustra, recte, bene*, and *procul* (e.g. Cic. *Pis.* 11, *quae sunt palam*).[64] However, in the present context *iam* would have to be substantivized, = "this is the precise moment" (?), which would be very odd. Salonius cites examples of the adverbs *mane, tarde*, and *sero* from later Latin that are close to substantival,[65] but these are not good parallels for the present case. Such words refer or may refer to periods in the day, and a term meaning e.g. "late (in the day)" could be reinterpreted to mean "in the evening." It is indeed the adverb *sero* that lies behind the masculine nominal reflex = *soir* "evening" in French.[66] Other types of adverbs supposedly used substantivally are usually supported by the determinative pronoun *ille* (e.g. Cic. *Luc.* 89, *illa deinceps*) or something else (e.g. Livy 6.22.1, *omnia ... inde*), or, if unsupported, may be open to alternative explanations (so *palam* at Tac. *Hist.* 1.10.2).[67] An alternative in the present passage might seem to be to understand a noun such as *munus* as predicate (= "this is the show now," i.e. "this is it now"), but the problem is that the third *hoc est* would not have an expressed predicate, which in this rhetorical tricolon it surely needs. The expression remains a real difficulty, but it is possible that here we have an extremely rare instance of a substantival use. For the adverbial use of *iam* in the sort of meaning required (= "de tempore praesente et instante"), see *TLL* VII.1.102.74ff. Could it be that there was a single

---

[64] See e.g. Salonius 1920:208; Adams 1976:92; Hofmann and Ricottilli 2003:337.

[65] Salonius 1920:209–211.

[66] See Bloch and von Wartburg 1968:595.

[67] Examples from Harm Pinkster, to be discussed in his forthcoming *Oxford Latin Syntax*.

word acclamation *iam!*, uttered right at the start as the performers appeared? If so the meaning here might be "this is the 'now.'"

Beschaouch also takes *hoc est ia* together, but then punctuates the next bit as *nox est ia. "munere tuo ..."* rather than as *nox est: ia munere tuo ...*[68] The punctuation shows that *nox est ia* is taken, like *Magerius donat*, as an editorial insertion. In his earlier paper, Beschaouch also treated *nox est ia* as a unit, but included these words in the acclamation.[69] I would prefer to see this second phonetic spelling *ia* standing in an exclamatory acclamation rather than in an aside (see the general conclusions below), and the temporal adverb looks particularly suited to initial position in its clause, introducing a conclusion to be drawn from the fall of night: *nox est: ia munere ...* ("it is night: now release the money/behold the release of the money!"). (See *OLD* s.v. *iam* 6, and see further below.) The present tense in such a phrase as *nox est (iam)* does not look at all like an editorial comment, which would surely have needed a past tense (*erat*).

ia munere tuo saccis missos: this is the most difficult phrase in the acclamations, and it has attracted some unconvincing attempts at translation.

I leave aside for the moment the syntax of *missos* and the meaning of *munus* and deal first with *saccis*. This ablative cannot convincingly be rendered "(sent off) with the bags of money," as it has constantly been taken (see further below), because such a meaning would require the presence of *cum*. Accompaniment is not expressed by the plain ablative without *cum* except in phrases, mainly military, of a certain type, viz. when the noun is accompanied by an adjective, as e.g. *omnibus copiis* and similar (e.g. Caes. *Gall.* 3.11.5, *ipse eo pedestribus copiis contendit*).[70] *Cum* is obligatory with *mitto* even when the noun is accompanied by an adjective.[71]

---

[68] Beschaouch 2006:1404.

[69] Beschaouch 1966:139.

[70] See further Ernout and Thomas 1953:87; Hofmann and Szantyr 1965:114–115.

[71] See Hofmann and Szantyr 1965:114, citing Caes. *Civ.* 2.38.1, *cum mediocribus copiis missum*.

For renderings of *saccis* that disregard the absence of *cum*, note e.g. Wiedemann (1992:17) "By your *munus* they were dismissed with money-bags"; Lane Fox (2005:667) "may the Telegenii be sent back from your *munus* with their bags full of money"; Bomgardner (2009:169) "By your gift, they've taken their leave with bags of money"; Fagan (2011:131) "They have been sent away from your *munus* with their sacks (of money)"; Cooley (2012:210) "The performers have been dismissed with money-bags from your show." It may be noted incidentally that three of these translations treat the problematic accusative participle *missos* as if it were a finite verb in the perfect tense, passive, which is out of the question, and the other (that of Lane Fox) is also hard to account for. This translation of *saccis* goes back to Beschaouch, who renders "que les Telegenii soient renvoyés de ton munus avec des sacs."[72] He did however, unlike others, address the syntax, describing *saccis* as "ablatif d'accompagnement,"[73] and he also paid attention to the problem of *missos*.

If *saccis* does not express accompaniment, what could it express? There are two possibilities.

First, *saccis* stands next to *missos*, and might be taken closely with it, as an ablative of separation (= "released from the bags"). The separative ablative is common with *mitto* in its basic meanings "send, release, throw."[74] A typical use, for instance, is at Hor. *Sat.* 1.1.114, *carceribus missos ... currus,* of chariots released from the traps (starting barriers).[75]

Clearly the Telegenii cannot be released from the bags. But the herald in putting his request to the crowd asked them to "give 500 *denarios*," and it may be the *denarios* that are now released, perhaps by a symbolic unsealing of the bags. The acclamation itself typically does not make explicit the referents, but those would be clear from what was unfolding before the spectators. This last acclamation, uttered as night falls after the show is over, is the one part of the right-hand text that

---

[72] Beschaouch 1966:139.
[73] Beschaouch 1966:143.
[74] See *TLL* VIII.1172.45, 1178.30f., in both places with cross references.
[75] See further *TLL* VIII.1174.1ff.

might be directly related to the text and image alongside, where we see both the word *denarios* and the bags of money.

Second, *saccis* might be instrumental, with *missos* referring not to the *denarii* but to the Telegenii, who are "released," i.e. "discharged" from the show by means of the grant of the money-bags. *Mitto* is regularly used of the discharge of someone from some duty or office (see *OLD* s.v. 3a–b, *TLL* VIII.1173.51ff., especially 1174.1ff.). More importantly, *mitto* (and the noun *missio*) had a technical meaning in reference to gladiators. Coleman on Mart. *Spect.* 31.3 puts it thus: "*missio* represents discharge from the authority of the editor who has sponsored the spectacle, so that a gladiator who is *missus* will return to his barracks to train for future engagements; it does not mean discharge from service as a gladiator."[76] Coleman goes on to state the two circumstances under which such a *missio* or reprieve might be granted (a gladiator who had surrendered might sometimes be granted a reprieve, or if two gladiators had fought to a draw both might be deemed worthy of a reprieve), and adds that this sort of *missio* is not to be confused with the unconditional release from service of a victorious gladiator.[77] It is important to note that *mitto* in the sense of "discharge" from some sort of service, including the gladiatorial use of a reprieve, is attested in the idiom *missum facere* (= *mittere*).[78] We will return to this idiom below.

The Telegenii were clearly not (at least in their entirety) gladiators in the conventional sense of, e.g., condemned criminals or prisoners of war.[79] They were a professional guild characterized by Beschaouch in a series of papers (1966, 1985, 2006) as a *sodalitas uenatorum* (though sodalities of this type seem to have undertaken other activities as well).[80] Bomgardner calls them "the best known troupe of itinerant *venatores* of antiquity," and remarks that a "spectacle given by a professional troupe in the hopes of attracting payment at the end is something new in our

---

[76] Coleman 2006:221.

[77] Coleman 2006:232.

[78] See below 537, with n. 92 on the inscription *CIL* VI.10194 = *ILS* 5088, cited and discussed by Coleman 2006:221–222.

[79] For these and other types, see the rich discussion of Ville 1981:228-46.

[80] See Beschaouch 2006:1414–1417 for details.

repertoire of spectacles."[81] Whatever the status of the *uenatores* themselves, slaves or free,[82] they must have been chosen and esteemed for their expertise in killing dangerous animals, as payment is demanded precisely for that. Pride was obviously taken in demonstrating that expertise under handicap, as we see from the behavior of Spittara, on stilts, and the best performers would not readily have been let go by the managers of the sodality. Conventional gladiatorial terminology of reprieve or release from service would therefore not be appropriate of the members of such a guild, but it may well be that old terminology had been given a slightly new twist in reference to such a professional troupe; they were "discharged" from the show at the end by means of the formal award of payment. The force of the instrumental *saccis* would be clearer if we rephrased with the addition of a past participle (e.g. *saccis donatis*).

In fact the expression on the mosaic (*missus* along with the ablative of *saccus*) recurs, and looks like an African formula applied to professional troupes on such occasions. On a stone preserved in the Museum of Tebessa in Algeria, there is a three-line inscription *Sadunti / ob merita / missos sacco* (*CIL* VIII.1884; *ILAlg.* I.3079; *AE* 1986.726), which has been discussed in this connection by Beschaouch, who takes *Sadunti* to be the vocative of a name *Saduntius*, which, like the vocative *Mageri* on the Smirat mosaic, must belong to the *editor*.[83] *Missos* is regarded as an accusative of exclamation, as he also takes it in the Magerius mosaic (see immediately below), and *sacco* like *saccis* is interpreted as an ablative of accompaniment (note the translation, "Qu'en récompense de leur vaillante prestation ils (= les bestiaires) quittent l'arène avec un sac d'argent chacun").[84] Again this rendering of the ablative will not do, but again the ablative may refer to the discharge of the combatants by means of the award of a bag of money.

---

[81] Bomgardner 2009:169.

[82] The engagement of free men for the gladiatorial arena or for *uenationes* was in fact an ancient practice; see Ville 1981:246 and the whole discussion to 262, with abundant documentation. On the other hand, for *uenatores* as usually of low status and as sometimes freed, see Fagan 2011:126 with n. 12.

[83] Beschaouch 1985:454–458.

[84] Beschaouch 1985:457–458.

On this view of the verb phrase in the two African documents, the *saccus* or *sacci* might have come to symbolize the discharge from the show of the professional *uenatores*, at least at this time in N. Africa, just as the *rudis* or wooden rod symbolized the release of gladiators.[85] An instrumental ablative is well suited to this idea: the bag of money discharges them, or they are discharged by it. Crucial to this interpretation is the meaning of *missos* in this context. I am not taking it merely in the sense "sent away," which might indeed require a complement expressing accompaniment, but rather in a technical sense, of discharging. The symbolism of the sack can be paralleled in a different connection in some modern languages, such as French and English, in the phrase "get the sack," of dismissal, which referred originally to a dismissed worker being given his possessions in a sack. Ideologically reference to prizes of hard cash had long caused problems in the Roman period,[86] but representations of moneybags on the prize table do appear in Roman works of art depicting contests.[87] The highly elliptical character of the expression *saccis missos* makes it certain that it must have been commonplace (or it would not have been understood), and it was probably regional and expressive of a local custom in the signing off of such professional guilds at the end of a performance.

There are at least three arguments in favor of taking *saccis missos* of discharge by the sack(s) rather than of release (of *denarii*) from the sacks.

First, *mitto* is widely used of discharging in various applications, and discharging, if of different types, had an association with shows. *Mitto* looks far more likely to refer to discharge in this quasi-gladiatorial context than to a release of coins, for which, as far as I am aware, there is no evidence.

Second, if the phrase refers to the releasing of money from the bags, the fourth instance of *munus* in the text, immediately preceding *saccis missos*, must be given a different meaning from the other three.

---

[85] On which see Coleman 2006:232.

[86] Note Dunbabin 2010:343: "explicit allusion to monetary awards was discouraged long after they had in fact become common."

[87] See Dunbabin 2010, especially 343–344 with n. 77, and figures 11, 12, 19, 33, 36, 37; also, for literary evidence, see Coleman 2006:230.

The other three mean "show." Here *munere* would have to be taken as an ablative of means or cause, with a sense shading into that of "benefaction." It was noted above that *munus* does not mean merely "show," but "show representing someone's duty or benefaction," and this latter abstract notion would have to be brought to the fore here. The idea would be along the lines that the *denarii* are "released from the bags thanks to the benefaction of this show you have presented/thanks to your generous show." It is not satisfactory to have to vary the meaning of *munus*. On the second interpretation above, the sense would be "discharged from your show by the award of the bags of money." ·

Third, the other instance of the formula, *ob merita missos sacco*, favors giving *missos* a personal reference. *Ob merita* cannot but have a personal complement understood ("on account of their deserts"), and once that is accepted it becomes difficult to believe that *missos* does not have the same personal reference ("on account of their deserts release them by the sack").

Something must now be said about the syntax of *missos*, another question usually passed over in silence. There are two ways of explaining it, and I start with the possibility that it is an accusative of exclamation.[88]

The common use of the exclamatory accusative is a marked stylistic feature of acclamations. A vivid example is recorded in the *Pass. Perp.* (21.2), at the point at which the martyr Saturus becomes the victim of a leopard. He is covered with blood by a single bite, and the crowd call out in irony *saluum lotum! saluum lotum!* This is an accusative of exclamation, and it might be rendered "look at him healthy and washed, healthy and washed!" (or "washed healthy," with *saluum* perhaps predicative, and expressing the consequence of the washing). Moreover *saluum lotum*, like *missos*, is elliptical, in that no name, noun, or pronoun is expressed with it, such as *Saturum*. The point is that at a public show everyone knows who and what the participants are, and there is no need to spell everything out, and not least since gesturing would have been taking place. *Saluum lotum* is an acclamation that was used in the bath house of someone "washed healthy," without specification of the

88 So Beschaouch 1966:143; and see above.

referent.[89] The meaning of our passage might then be "behold them discharged by the bags!" (or, on the other interpretation, "behold the money released from the bags!").

For another exclamatory accusative in an acclamation see *SHA, Comm.* 18.12, *hostis statuas undique, parricidae statuas undique, gladiatoris statuas undique* ("behold the statues of the enemy everywhere, the statues of the parricide everywhere, the statues of the gladiator everywhere"; one might in such cases suggest ellipse of, e.g., *uidete*, but that is unnecessary, as the exclamatory accusative on its own draws attention to the presence of something.

The second possibility is to understand *fac* with *missos. Facio aliquem/aliquid missum* is an idiom equivalent to *mitto* on its own (= e.g. *mitto aliquem*) in various of its senses.[90] Moreover sometimes in the *facio missum* construction *facio* is omitted, and indeed when it would be imperatival.[91] On this view *missos (fac)* would be an instruction shouted to Magerius, "discharge (them) from your show." The expression *missum fecit* is indeed used in a gladiatorial context of the granting of a reprieve at *CIL* VI.10194 = *ILS* 5088,[92] *Rom(ae) mun(eris) eiusd(em) die VIIII Fimbriam lib(erum), (pugnarum) VIIII, miss(um) fe(cit)*, and it would not be out of place in the present context, of discharging performers.

This second explanation is almost certainly right, partly because the Ciceronian examples just quoted show that ellipse of *fac* (or another jussive form) was idiomatic with such uses of *missum*, and partly because at the very end of the day and of the performance a directive by the crowd to Magerius to pay the *uenatores* seems particularly appropriate. Indeed in the Algerian text discussed above the phrase *missos sacco* is preceded by vocative address of the *editor* (*Sadunti*), and that

<hr>

[89] See the school exercise edited by Dionisotti 1982 at 64, and now Dickey 2015: **Mp**16e; also *CIL* V.4500 = *ILS* 5725 *bene laua. saluu lotu.*

[90] See *OLD* s.v. *mitto* 3a–b, 4a, 5; also the brief comment at *TLL* VI.1.119.59–60. For, e.g., *facio missum* = *mitto*, "release," see *OLD* s.v. *mitto* 3b: note in a letter of Caesar *ap.* Cic. *Att.* 9.7C.2, *et eum statim missum feci* (in reference to a capture followed by release: "and I immediately released him").

[91] See Heidemann 1893:60. Note Cic. *Att.* 15.20.3, *sed acta missa*, (where Shackleton Bailey 1965–1970: VI.269 allows omission of either *sint* or *faciamus*); and *Fam.* 9.7.2, *sed ridicula missa* (sc. *fac*).

[92] Quoted and discussed by Coleman 2006:221–222.

vocative would be better suited to an implied imperative intended for him than to an exclamation. One can imagine a stage-managed finale to the day such that the herald makes his request and is followed immediately into the arena by the boy with the bags, met by a demand from the crowd for the discharge of the Telegenii by the award of the bags of money. It is this last acclamation that is the response to the herald.

CONCLUSIONS

The Latin particularly of the acclamations is distinctive but not substandard.

Whoever drafted the texts allowed the inclusion, in what is a very elaborate and skilled work of art, of three definite phonetic spellings, namely *iam* without the final *-m* twice and *sta* for *ista*. Otherwise in the two texts final *-m* is correctly written five times. Such inconsistency is typical of countless late inscriptions, but there may be a point to all three of these misspellings in this text. All are in what might be called exclamatory phrases (which some editors might well be tempted to punctuate with exclamation marks). By contrast the two very short editorial introductions (*per curionem dictum* and *adclamatum est*) contain three of the five correct spellings with *-m*, and both of the other instances of *-m* correctly written are in formal phrases (*meritum ... uestri fauoris*; *exemplo quaestorum*). I would not suggest that the pronunciation of the two groups of terms would necessarily have differed, but it is possible that the phonetic spellings were admitted in the exclamatory phrases to capture the authentic sounds of the crowd's shouts at these heightened moments. All three of the phonetic spellings are in the acclamations, whereas the herald's speech is impeccably spelt and in places formal in style.

Discamp is of a different order, and may be a mere slip.

I come to *edes*, which, it was pointed out, has been taken as a present tense. The misspelling *e* for *i* in a verb ending is perfectly possible at this period,[93] but does not seem likely in these cases. It was just suggested that the certain phonetic spellings, all of them in the

---

[93] See Adams 2013:51–60 for the evidence.

acclamations, look to be deliberate rather than illiteracies, and it might be added that none is grammatically significant. *Edes* for *edis* would by contrast have grammatical significance. What would the consequence be of accepting *edes* as a present? The possible interpretations numbered 1 and 3 above (515, 520) would be ruled out, because both positively require a future tense, but possibility 2 could stand, with the slight modification that the show would be just beginning rather than about to begin, and the verb would be continuous ("you are presenting ...").

What are the stylistic features of the acclamations?

It tends to be assumed that acclamations are "rhythmical," but usually without discussion of the details.[94] An exception in this last respect is Cameron (1976:329–333), who expresses reservations about the metrical character of acclamations in general, and suggests (329) that they are "intermittently rhythmical rather than metrical," and then analyses some Greek acclamations with this generalization in mind. The acclamations on the mosaic are not rhythmical in any meaningful sense, in that they do not contain *cursus* or quantitative rhythms.

The three most distinctive stylistic features to be seen here are (1) a rough and ready rhetoric, (2) the use of refrains, and (3) ellipse.

(1) In the first acclamation there are two clauses, *discant futuri* and *audiant praeteriti*, of which the final words are antithetical, and the clauses are of ascending length. Ascending length of juxtaposed or balanced clauses is not, however, characteristic of these acclamations. The tricolon with each of its clauses introduced by *hoc est* shows a descent from five to four to three syllables in the three clauses. The two clauses ending with *munus edes* have introductory phrases balancing each other (*exemplo quaestorum* and *de re tua*), but these are of descending length; the second phrase might be interpreted as an explanatory gloss on the first, with the order thus semantically rather than rhetorically determined.

On the evidence of this text the final words of clauses had particular weight in acclamations. Short as the text is it contains two cases of antistrophe, that is the repetition of a word at the end of juxta-

---

[94] See e.g. Roueché 1984:189–190; Aldrete 1999:128, 134.

posed clauses or phrases (*tale/tale*, *edes/edes*), both of them moreover
in the same acclamation, and in four successive clauses. (Note too the
threefold repetition of *undique* in the acclamation at *SHA, Comm.* 18.12,
quoted in the last section.) The first acclamation also has the semantic
opposition noted above (*futuri/praeteriti*) expressed at the ends of
clauses. In a later acclamation the semantically important infinitives
habere and *posse* expressing the attributes of the benefactor are both at
the ends of (juxtaposed) clauses.

The starts of clauses have similar effects, though not as markedly
so. Twice in the first acclamation a sentence begins with *exemplo*, but
that is not particularly striking because the repeated terms are five
lines apart. More distinctive is the tricolon with *hoc est* introducing its
elements.

(2) I use the term "refrain" to refer to a whole phrase repeated.
There are two refrains in this text. The first acclamation again has
munus edes at the ends of juxtaposed clauses.[95] Later *hoc est* occurs
three times. The format of the mosaic and the small space allowed to
the Latin almost certainly mean that the element of repetition uttered
on the day itself has been drastically reduced in the record. We saw
above (528) the extent of the repetitions in the late imperial senate
as emerges from the *Historia Augusta*. Another text that graphically
illustrates the place of repetitions in acclamations is at Augustine
Epist. 213 (*CSEL* 57). This text records *acta ecclesiastica* and describes the
election of a bishop, Eraclius. Augustine delivered a speech that was
constantly interrupted by acclamations of the *populus*, and the record
states in each case the number of repetitions. I quote just one group
of these acclamations and the numerical insertions (*Epist.* 213.6, pp.
378.15–379.3):

> "de hac accessione aliquid adclamate." a populo adclamatum
> est: "fiat, fiat" (dictum est uicies quinquies); "dignum et
> iustum est" (dictum est uicies octies); "fiat, fiat" (dictum
> est quater decies); "olim dignus, olim meritus" (dictum

---

[95] We commented earlier (528) on the tendency to invariant word order of refrains
in acclamations; also (529) on the tendency for a refrain to be accompanied by varied
complements.

est uicies quinquies); "iudicio tuo gratias agimus" (dictum tredecies); "exaudi, Christe, Eraclium conserua" (dictum est octies decies).

It will be seen that *fiat, fiat* alone was repeated thirty-nine times at this point. A few other features of this passage are incidentally worth noting: the phrase *adclamatum est* at the start, the address of Augustine in the second person by the crowd (note *tuo*), and the naming of Eraclius, the key figure, only at the end, as the second-last word (cf. *Magerius donat*), though he is alluded to earlier. This last feature is also to be seen in another of the groups of acclamations, that at *Epist.* 213.3, p. 376.8–10.

(3) Acclamations tend to be elliptical partly because events are unfolding before the spectators and sometimes only key words need to be expressed, and partly because they are formulaic. We commented above on ellipse, and gave examples from acclamations elsewhere. In this text the clauses *unde tale, quando tale* have both nominal and verbal ellipse, and *saccis missos* has an imperative omitted, and is also without a noun. The same is true of the other instance of this formula, *missos sacco*.

WORKS CITED

Adams, J. N. 1976. *The Text and Language of a Vulgar Latin Chronicle (Anonymus Valesianus II)*. London.

———. 1992. "British Latin: Notes on the Language, Text and Interpretation of the Bath Curse Tablets." *Britannia* 23:1–26.

———. 1996. "Interpuncts And The Enclitic Character Of Personal Pronouns In Latin." *Zeitschrift für Papyrologie und Epigraphik* 111:208–210.

———. 2013. *Social Variation and the Latin Language*. Cambridge.

Aldrete, G. S. 1999. *Gestures and Acclamations in Ancient Rome*. Baltimore.

Beschaouch, A. 1966. "La mosaïque de chasse à l'amphithéâtre découverte à Smirat en Tunisie." *Comptes rendus: Académie des inscriptions et belles-lettres* 110:134–157.

———. 1985. "Nouvelles observations sur les sodalités africaines." *Comptes rendus: Académie des inscriptions et belles-lettres* 129:453–475.

————. 2006. "Que savons-nous des sodalités africo-romaines?" *Comptes rendus: Académie des inscriptions et belles-lettres* 150:1401–1417.

Bloch, O., and W. Von Wartburg. 1968. *Dictionnaire étymologique de la langue française*. 5th ed. Paris.

Bomgardner, D. 2009. "The Magerius Mosaic Revisited." In *Roman Amphitheatres and Spectacula: A 21st Century Perspective* (BAR International Series 1946), ed. T. Wilmott, 165–177. Oxford.

Cameron, A. 1976. *Circus Factions: Blues and Greens at Rome and Byzantium*. Oxford.

Chamberland, G. 2012. "La mémoire des spectacles: L'autoreprésentation des donateurs." In *L'organisation des spectacles dans le monde romain* (Fondation Hardt: Entretiens sur l'antiquité classique 58), 261–303.

Chaniotis, A. 2009. "Acclamations as a Form of Religious Communication." In *Die Religion des Imperium Romanum: Koine und Konfrontationen*, ed. H. Cancik and J. Rüpke, 199–218. Tübingen.

Coleman, K. M. 2006. *M. Valerii Martialis Liber spectaculorum*. Oxford.

Cooley, A. E. 2012. *The Cambridge Manual of Latin Epigraphy*. Cambridge.

Dickey, E. 2015. *The Colloquia of the Hermeneumata Pseudodositheana*. Volume 2. Cambridge.

Dionisotti, C. 1982. "From Ausonius' Schooldays?: A Schoolbook and its Relatives." *JRS* 72:83–125.

Dunbabin, K. M. D. 1978. *The Mosaics of Roman North Africa: Studies in Iconography and Patronage*. Oxford.

————. 2010. "The Prize Table: Crowns, Wreaths and Moneybags in Roman Art." In *L'argent dans les concours du monde grec: Actes du colloque international, Saint-Denis et Paris, 5-6 décembre 2008*, ed. B. Le Guen, 301–345. Saint-Denis.

Ernout, A., and F. Thomas. 1953. *Syntaxe latine*. 2nd ed. Paris.

Fagan, G. G. 2011. *The Lure of the Arena: Social Psychology and the Crowd at the Roman Games*. Cambridge.

Fraenkel, E. 1961. "Two Poems of Catullus." *JRS* 51:46–53. (Repr. Fraenkel 1964, vol. 2, 115–129.)

————. 1964. *Kleine Beiträge zur klassischen Philologie*. 2 vols. Rome.

Hanoune, R. 2000. "Encore les Telegenii, encore la mosaïque de Smirat!" *Africa Romana* 13:1565–76.

Heidemann, A. 1893. *De Ciceronis in epistulis verborum ellipsis usu.* Berlin.

Hofmann, J. B. 1951. *Lateinische Umgangssprache.* 3rd ed. Heidelberg.

Hofmann, J. B., and L. Ricottilli. 2003. *La lingua d'uso latina.* 3rd ed. Translation with supplements of Hofmann 1951 by L. Ricottilli. Bologna.

Hofmann, J. B., and A. Szantyr. 1965. *Lateinische Syntax und Stilistik.* Munich.

Kuhn, C. T. 2012. "Emotionality in the Political Culture of the Graeco-Roman East: The Role of Acclamations." In *Unveiling Emotions: Methods for the Study of Emotions in the Greek World,* ed. A. Chaniotis, 295–312. Stuttgart.

Lane Fox, R. 2005. *The Classical World: An Epic History from Homer to Hadrian.* London.

Lintott, A. W. 1968. *Violence in Republican Rome.* Oxford.

Parker, H. N. 1999. "The Observed of All Observers: Spectacle, Applause, and Cultural Poetics in the Roman Theatre Audience." In *The Art of Ancient Spectacle,* ed. B. Bergmann and C. Kondoleon, 163–179. New Haven.

Riemann, O. 1927. *Syntaxe latine d'après les principes de la grammaire historique.* 7th ed. revised by A. Ernout. Paris.

Roueché, C. 1984. "Acclamations in the Later Roman Empire: New Evidence from Aphrodisias." *JRS* 74:181–199.

Salonius, A. H. 1920. *Vitae partum: Kritische Untersuchungen über Text, Syntax und Wortschatz der spätlateinischen Vitae partum (B. III, V, VI, VII).* Lund.

Sampson, R. 2010. *Vowel Prosthesis in Romance: A Diachronic Study.* Oxford.

Shackleton Bailey, D. R. 1965–1970. *Cicero's Letters to Atticus.* Cambridge.

Svennung, J. 1935. *Untersuchungen zu Palladius und zur lateinischen Fach- und Volkssprache.* Lund.

Väänänen, V. 1981. *Introduction au latin vulgaire.* 3rd ed. Paris.

Ville, G. 1981. *La gladiature en Occident des origines à la mort de Domitien.* Rome.

Vismara, C. 2007. "Amphitheatralia Africana." *Antiquités africaines* 43:99–152.

Wiedemann, T. 1992. *Emperors and Gladiators.* London.

The Smirat Mosaic. Photograph by Andrew Wilson (Professor of Roman Archaeology, University of Oxford, and Fellow of All Souls College), reproduced with the permission of Samir Aounallah, Directeur de la division du développement muséographique, Institut National du Patrimoine.

THE CONSTRUCTION OF A HOMOEROTIC
DISCOURSE IN THE *EPIGRAMS* OF AUSONIUS

Lucia Floridi

I. SATIRIZING SAME-SEX RELATIONSHIPS

IN AUSONIUS' GENERICALLY and thematically varied collection of epigrams, several poems deal with erotic and sexual matters. But while erotic motives are given a heterosexual treatment (see e.g. *Epigr.* 14, 39, 40, 88, 89, 102, 103 Green),[1] homosexuality—with a single (partial) exception that we are soon to examine—is the realm of the scoptic. *Epigr.* 74 regards a certain Castor, who would like to perform *fellatio*, but, for lack of men, practices *cunnilingus* instead, on his wife. Here Ausonius is following in the footsteps of Martial, and of the Roman tradition in general,[2] where satiric comments on oral sexual practices are common. The same holds true for *Epigr.* 99, 100, 101, variations on the theme of "receptive" homosexuality. *Epigr.* 99—a somewhat obscure poem—criticizes an adulterous lawyer for being a *semivir* (verse 3); *Epigr.* 100 deals with the traditional subject of male depilation as an indication of passive homosexuality; *Epigr.* 101 targets a pathic significantly called Zoilus—one of Martial's favorite names for indicating an unpleasant character[3]—who has taken an adulterous wife so that they

This essay is based on a talk given at the international conference "Romosexuality: The Reception of Rome and the Construction of Western Homosexual Identities," organized by Jennifer Ingleheart in Durham, April 16th–18th, 2012. I am very grateful to the audience for the feedback I received on that occasion, and to the anonymous referee of HSCP for her/his useful comments. The section on Glaucias is greatly indebted to discussion with Prof. Gianpiero Rosati, whom I would like to thank.

[1] Ausonius' works are quoted according to Green's 1999 edition and numeration.

[2] See also Williams 1999:200: "Ausonius is clearly reflecting classical notions" (although this is rephrased in Williams 2010:221 as "Ausonius continues a long tradition").

[3] See Fusi 2006:260–261; Fusi 2008:271.

can exchange male lovers. Up to this point Ausonius' attitude is traditional: his sceptic poems show contempt of *pathici*, in accordance with a widespread motif both in Greek and Latin literature.[4] The attitude shown towards homosexuality is thus "safe": Ausonius is making fun of traditional targets, and he keeps a distance from what he describes. The satirist is morally superior to the corrupt behaviors about which he writes. Similar observations are prompted by *Epigr.* 43, a puzzle-epigram, translated from the Greek, about three men performing four sexual acts. This poem is particularly significant, as it is often quoted by those scholars who wish to show that even in a period of ever-increasing asceticism, as the fourth century was, obscene themes found in the poetry of the Greeks and in Martial could still be treated with freedom.[5] Here is the text of *Epigr.* 43:

"Tris uno in lecto; stuprum duo perpetiuntur
  et duo committunt." "Quattuor esse reor."
"Falleris: extremis da singula crimina et illum
  bis numera medium, qui facit et patitur."

"There are three in one bed. Two are passive, and two are active." "I think there are four people." "You are mistaken: give one offence each to the ones on the outside, and count the one in the middle twice, since he is both active and passive."[6]

---

[4] Cf. e.g. Henderson 1991:209-215; Williams 2010:197-200 and 338n109.

[5] See, for instance, Boswell 1980:132: "Ausonius kept in his library volumes of homosexual literature which were considered scandalous even by Roman standards and took delight in translating from Greek to Latin such tidbits as Strato's puzzle about four sex acts being performed simultaneously by three men." As regards the "scandalous" literature, Boswell is referring to sotadean verses: while describing to a friend the contents of his library Ausonius mentions, among other things, Σωταδικόν τε κίναιδον (see *Epist.* 8.29 Green). But this reference is hardly significant: the catalogue is clearly idealized and, although probably not completely irrealistic, it does not necessarily reveal the actual contents of Ausonius' library (see Mondin 1995:182-183). Moreover, Ausonius' description has a clear literary character: it is written in Greek and the expression used to indicate sotadean verses is traditional (compare Mart. 2.86.2 *nec retro lego Sotaden cinaedum*).

[6] Translations of Ausonius' epigrams are slightly adapted from Kay 2001; translations of other authors, unless otherwise stated, are my own.

The poem is based on two epigrams[7] on the same theme by Strato, *AP* 11.225 and *AP* 12.210 = 51 and 52 Floridi.

Ἡ κλίνη πάσχοντας ἔχει δύο καὶ δύο δρῶντας,
οὓς σὺ δοκεῖς πάντας τέσσαρας· εἰσὶ δὲ τρεῖς.
ἢν δὲ πύθῃ, πῶς τοῦτο; τὸν ἐν μέσσῳ δὶς ἀρίθμει
κοινὰ πρὸς ἀμφοτέρους ἔργα σαλευόμενον.

The bed holds two passive and two active people, who you would think were four in all. But they are three. If you ask "how so?", count the one in the middle twice, since he is copulating with the other two.

Τρεῖς ἀρίθμει τοὺς πάντας ὑπὲρ λέχος, ὧν δύο δρῶσιν
καὶ δύο πάσχουσιν. θαῦμα δοκῶ τι λέγειν·
καὶ μὴν οὐ ψεῦδος· δυσὶν εἷς μέσσος γὰρ ὑπουργεῖ
τέρπων ἐξόπιθεν, πρόσθε δὲ τερπόμενος.

Count three for all those on the bed, of whom two are active and two passive. It looks like I am speaking of a miracle. But it's really no lie. The middle one is involved with the other two, giving pleasure behind, getting pleasure in front.

Although it is true that Ausonius' poem is overtly obscene, commentators have not failed to notice that the most striking difference between his treatment of the theme and Strato's is the moral attitude shown towards the act described. The neutral, "paganally" hedonistic Stratonian scenario is replaced by a morally charged picture, in which words such as *stuprum* (verse 1)[8] and *crimina* (verse 3) give the

---

[7] This is the prevailing view among scholars (see Benedetti 1980:62–63; Green 1991 and Kay 2001 *ad* Aus. *Epigr.* 43; Steinbichler 1998, Giannuzzi 2007, and Floridi 2007 *ad* Strato *ll.cc.*); others, such as Lossau 1973:21–30 and González Rincón 1996:11–12, think that Ausonius' variation is based only on *AP* 11.225, while Boswell 1980:133n38 claims that "there is no way to be certain which of the two [models] Ausonius was translating (or if he knew both)."

[8] The most detailed discussion of the word is provided by Williams 2010:103–136, who shows how, in Republican and Early Imperial Rome, "the concept of *stuprum* served to idealize the inviolability of the Roman bloodline, to maintain the distinction between

act described "illegal" connotations,[9] thus "advertising" the "virtuosa presa di distanza"[10] of the poet with respect to his subject.[11] In addition, the very fact that Ausonius is translating from the Greek is significant: even when dealing with heterosexual themes, Ausonius' epigrams are mostly traditional variations based on Greek originals and/ or on Martial's models (cf. e.g. *Epigr.* 14, whose opening reworks Rufinus *AP* 5.21 = 7 Page; *Epigr.* 39, particularly close to Martial 9.32). It has to be added that commonplace erotic themes—such as the expression of one's erotic preferences or the *carpe diem* theme—are consistently given heterosexual interpretations, even when one can suspect reminiscences of homoerotic poems: this is the case, for instance, in *Epigr.* 39 and 40,[12] where Ausonius could have had, among his models, a pederastic poem, Strato *AP* 12.200 = 41 Floridi.[13] In other words, erotic or overtly sexual themes are allowed, provided they are made "safe" by the filter of literature;[14] but, even when such a filter is used, a consistent attitude towards homosexuality is detectable: it is the target of satire.

---

free and slave" (104), regardless of sex distinction. Such a concept was still basically alive in Ausonius' time: from the third century onwards, the word "was used by Roman jurists to describe sexual behaviour—either active or passive—which was unbecoming the status of a Roman citizen and not covered under another legal rubric such as rape, adultery, etc." (Boswell 1980:122; see also nn. 7-8).

[9] This can be connected to the attempt, seen for the first time in the later empire, "to translate the social sanctions against male *impudicitia* into legal prohibitions" (Kuefler 2001:92, with discussion of this epigram).

[10] The expression is borrowed from Lentano 2010:309.

[11] Boswell 1980:133n38 warns that "the use of the word 'stuprum' in the epigram should be interpreted cautiously; its ramifications are probably juridical rather than moral"; but filtering the description through the language of the law, in my view, is *per se* a clear assessment of the morality embraced by Ausonius' poetic *persona*.

[12] Still printed by Peiper as a single poem, *Epigr.* 56.

[13] This is the view of Peiper 1880:230; Stahl 1886:29-30; Munari 1956:310n2. Traina 1989:175 admits that Ausonius had in mind Strato *AP* 12.200.6 = 41.6 F. καὶ μὴ παρέχειν εἰδότα καὶ παρέχειν, "he who knows both how not to give himself and how to give himself", at least when writing *Epigr.* 40.6 *quod "volo nolo" vocant*, "what they call 'Yes and No'"; doubts are expressed by Benedetti 1980:74-78, while Kay 2001 *ad* 40 just mentions Strato's epigram as a parallel dealing with the same theme, together with Rufinus *AP* 5.42 = 15 Page.

[14] As aptly observed by Hunink 2002, "the obscene poems in Priapean or Martial fashion seem rather detached from the cultural climate in which Ausonius lived, with its increasingly strict sexual rules and morals. In his days, a series of epigrams on cunnilingus

So, what about pederasty, i.e. love for boys? It is a well-known fact that while "passive" homosexuals were criticized in both Greece and Rome, love for boys was admitted as a normal erotic option. Martial and his contemporaries wrote epigrams in praise of young boys, and this was a widespread theme in Greek epigram, to which Ausonius is greatly indebted.[15]

Only one epigram in Ausonius' collection openly deals with pederasty: *Epigr.* 73, which is condemnatory, as it satirizes a certain Marcus, who uses deceit and violence in order to coerce his unwilling young partners. According to Kay 2001 ad loc., the fact that Marcus is "an odious character" does not allow us to conclude that Ausonius' overall attitude towards pederasty is one of contempt. But it should be noted that male prostitution, with which pederasty was often associated, had already been made illegal in the West in the third century,[16] and that homosexuality, on the other hand, started to be equated to child molesting in the fourth century, something that contributed to the increasing intolerance towards homosexuality detectable from this time onwards.[17] Ausonius' epigram fits perfectly into such a context: Marcus, described with colorful language, at least in part borrowed from Lucilius, as *feles nuper pullaria dictus, / corrupit totum qui puerile secus, / perversae Veneris postico vulnere fossor / Lucili vatis † sub pilo pullo premor †,* "the one called the chicken-chasing polecat, who corrupted

---

or pederasty could perhaps only be defended as traditional literary exercises. Any suggestion of realism would have caused serious problems." The poet himself, in *Epigr.* 1—most probably the proem of the *libellus*—remarks that he, as a man, has nothing to do with the most obscene contents of his collection, according to the common motif of the distinction between *pagina* and *vita* (cf. e.g. Cat. 16.5-6; Mart. 1.4.8 with Citroni 1975 ad loc.; Mart. 11.15.11-13 with Kay 1985 ad loc.; Hadr. fr. 2 with Mattiacci 1982 ad loc. The commonplace is recalled in connection with Ausonius' obscene poetry also by Lossau 1973:30).

[15] On Ausonius and Greek epigram, see especially Munari 1956; Benedetti 1980 (with Traina 1989); a good synthesis of the problem in Kay 2001:13-19; some observations also in Floridi 2013.

[16] By Philip the Arab (AD 244-249): cf. Hubbard 2003:444 (and, in general, 443-447 for a synthesis of the different attitudes towards homoeroticism between the second century AD and the beginning of the fourth, with further bibliography).

[17] Cf. Boswell 1980:143-145. For a discussion of the shifts in attitudes towards pederasty in the later empire see Kuefler 2001:92-96 (and more generally ch. 3, 70-102, for the narrowing of the notion of male *pudicitia*).

all the boy gender, the digger of unnatural sex by violence at the back entry, the 'chicken-plucker and molester' of the bard Lucilius" (5-8),[18] is a corruptor of boys (*corrupit*), devoted to *perverse* sexual acts (*perversae Veneris*). Moreover, it is a fact that this negative example is not counterbalanced by others, in spite of the rich epigrammatic tradition of praise of love between man and boy. Therefore, it seems sensible to conclude that this thematic omission should not only be interpreted as the result of personal taste,[19] but also of the "inopportunity" of the subject matter. Scoptic epigrams on homosexuals are "excusable" as literary exercises, and also provide an occasion to "advertise" the poet's moral virtue. Traditional poems on the beauty of *pueri delicati* were perceived as unbecoming even as mere literature. But this theme had played an important role in the poetry of the previous centuries; Ausonius does not miss the opportunity to pay homage to the tradition he draws from.

II. LOVE FOR BOYS: THE CASE OF GLAUCIAS (*EPIGR.* 53)

Epigr. 53 is an epitaph for a boy named Glaucias, with clear homoerotic overtones:

> Laeta bis octono tibi iam sub consule pubes
>   cingebat teneras, Glaucia adulte, genas.
> Et iam desieras puer anne puella videri,
>   cum properata dies abstulit omne decus.
> 5 Sed neque functorum socius miscebere vulgo
>   nec metues Stygios flebilis umbra lacus,
> verum aut Persephonae Cinyreius ibis Adonis
>   aut Iovis Elysii tu Catamitus eris.

A resplendent dawn was beginning to cover your smooth cheeks when you were just entering your sixteenth year,

---

[18] On the textual problems of verse 8, where Ausonius quotes Lucilius' words, see Green 1991 and Kay 2001 ad loc.

[19] Ausonius is the poet who introduced, for the first time in epigram, the theme of marital love: see especially *Epigr.* 20, where love for Sabina is described in language echoing Catullus (cf. verse 1 *Uxor, vivamus*, modeled on Cat. 5.1 *Vivamus, mea Lesbia, atque amemus*) and love elegy; also *Epigr.* 19, 27-29 feature Sabina.

grown-up Glaucias, and you were already ceasing to look like either boy or girl, when an untimely death took away all your glory. But you will neither be mixing with the common throng of the dead, nor will you fear the Stygian lakes as a weeping shade, but you will either be an Adonis son of Cinyras to Persephone, or the Ganymede of Elysian Jove.

This poem, "entirely pagan in expression,"[20] concludes with a homo-erotic allusion: the boy is so beautiful that in the underworld he will be either an Adonis to Persephone, or a Ganymede (*Catamitus*)[21] to the Elysian Jove (i.e. Hades). As has been duly noted by scholars,[22] the epigram is based on two literary models: Martial 6.28-29 and Statius *Silvae* 2.1, both lamenting, in their different ways, the passing of Atedius Melior's favorite, a young boy whose name was precisely Glaucias. Defined by Martial as *cari deliciae ... patroni* (6.28.3),[23] Melior's *delicatus* clearly added a homoerotic dimension to Statius' poem.[24] This homo-erotic dimension is preserved throughout: the mention of the first down covering the youth's cheeks (1-2) has specific connotations in ancient pederastic poetry, as it indicates the end of the time for being loved and the beginning of adulthood, i.e. the acquisition of a sexually active role.[25] At the end of the epigram, the allusion to the Zeus–Ganymede couple makes the pederastic reference even more explicit, stressing,

---

[20] Kay 2001 ad loc.

[21] *Catam(e)itus* is the Roman form for Ganymede, mediated by the Etruscan *catmite*: cf. Paul./Fest. p. 7 M. = 7.8-9 L. *Alcedo dicebatur ab antiquis pro alcyone, ut pro Ganymede Catamitus*, p. 44 M. = 38.22 L. *Catamitum pro Ganymede dixerunt, qui fuit Iovis concubinus*; Serv. *Aen.* 1.28 *hic Ganymedes latine Catamitus dicitur* (for references, see *TLL Onom.* II 255, s.v. *Catamitus*; a discussion of the name is provided by Williams 2010:60-61 and 332n230. For the iconography, see Sichtermann 1988b).

[22] The possibility of mere coincidence is generally ruled out: cf. e.g. Green 1991 ad loc.; Kay 2001 ad loc.; Grewing 1997 *ad* Mart. 6.28; Van Dam 1984 *ad* Stat. *Silv.* 2.1.183.

[23] See also Stat. *Silv.* 2.1.71 and 200 (with Asso 2010:679-682); on the terms *delicia/deliciae* and on their erotic meaning, see Van Dam 1984:72-73; Rawson 2003:261.

[24] As has long been recognized (cf. Van Dam 1984 ad loc.; La Penna 1996; Asso 2010).

[25] It is well known that in the Greco-Roman world's "sexual ethic" there was a time for being loved and a time for loving: the boy, once he had reached maturity, stopped being the passive partner and started to play a sexually active role (with *pueri delicati* and girls alike): see Dover 1978:84-87; Buffière 1980:603-613; Cantarella 1988:58-65; Vattuone 2004:61-72; for the Roman world, see especially Williams 2010:84-93. In homoerotic

at the same time, the "literariness" of this theme: Zeus' interest in the Phrygian boy was commonplace in literature—especially in Greek epigrams—as a symbol for homoerotic love, and as a model for poets' accounts of their own erotic desires.[26] Nevertheless, as I have tried to show in greater detail elsewhere,[27] Ausonius is clearly attempting to "tone down" the homoerotic theme, so as to make it "acceptable" to a contemporary audience. I summarize here my points, in order to clarify the poem's literary genesis[28] and its thematic position in Ausonius' collection.

Ausonius' primary model is not Martial, as one may have expected given the generic similarities between the two poets, but Statius: several linguistic (compare e.g. 5, *sed neque functorum* with *Silvae* 2.1.209-210, *omnia functa / aut moritura vides*; 6, *nec metues* with *Silvae* 2.1.183, *pone metus*) and narrative details (Glaucias' entering the underworld and the good reception he receives are already in *Silvae* 2.1.183-207, where they serve a consolatory purpose) derive directly from him.

This, I suggest, is not accidental: Ausonius' choice is particularly appropriate because Statius had dealt with the difficult task of writing a consolation for a man who had lost a boy with whom he had had a relationship that was problematic from the standpoint of contemporary Roman morality.[29] Glaucias was Atedius Melior's foster-son, but the man/boy relationship also encompassed an erotic dimension. Existing paradigms of consolatory poems did not accommodate Melior's desire for the dead boy: Melior was a man of superior social status whose grief for the loss of an inferior was excessive by moral standards.[30]

---

poetry, the end of adolescence is marked by the growth of beard and hair: on the motif of εἰσὶ τρίχες, see Tarán 1985.

[26] For this motif in Greek epigram, see Tarán 1979:7-51; Sánchez Ortiz de Landaluce 2006. On Roman reception of this Greek mythic tradition, see Williams 2010:59-64.

[27] Floridi 2012.

[28] Defined as "strange" by Kay 2001 ad loc., who adds: "the recasting of an epitaph/consolation for a real person in a fictive guise, with the introduction of themes—the boy as Pluto's catamite— ... are hardly delicate, to put it no more strongly."

[29] As pointed out by Asso 2010.

[30] As observed by Asso 2010:666, who comments on the nature of the relationship between Melior and Glaucias and on the reasons that may have led Statius to adumbrate its erotic nature in a very cautious and elusive manner, "what might have required Statius' discretion and nuanced language is not the actual bond that Melior and Glaucias

Statius succeeded in creating a consolatory strategy able to convey a sense of empathy for Melior's loss, while respecting, at the same time, social decency and public expectations for the ways in which grief and love between a man and a boy should be expressed. Statius achieved this goal by exploiting widely known myths: the relationship between Glaucias and Melior was hinted at obliquely, by mentioning Hercules and Apollo, together with their respective paramours, Hyacinth and Hylas.[31] Thus, Statius' poem firstly provides Ausonius with an intertextual paradigm of decent and socially acceptable pederastic love—that between Melior and Glaucias; secondly, it indicates the allusive code of mythical paradigms as a means of expressing this love. With this in mind, I will comment on several details in Ausonius' poem.

The most significant difference between Ausonius' Glaucias and the "historical" boy is that Melior's favorite was twelve or thirteen at the time of his death,[32] while Ausonius' Glaucias is sixteen. Ausonius' modification of the boy's age is crucial: sixteen is the ideal age for homoerotic love in Greek epigram.[33] At the same time, it is a liminal age: a boy aged sixteen is about to become a man, i.e. to assume an active role in an erotic relationship. Glaucias is thus living the paradoxical moment of life in which someone is no longer a boy, but is still not a man. This allows Ausonius to stress the gender ambiguity of this figure: Glaucias is described as looking like either a *puer* or a *puella* (verse 3), and the theme is picked up at the conclusion of the epigram, where he is presented as desirable for both a female and a male divinity. In other words, by way of the focus on his androgynous appearance, Glaucias is transformed into the erotic object *par excellence*, attractive to women and men alike (or better, to goddesses and gods alike). In so doing, Ausonius distances himself from *Silvae* 2.1, where Glaucias is described

---

might have shared but the effeminate style (*mollitia*) of Melior's mourning and the lavish funerals to grieve for the loss of a socially inferior person."

[31] See Asso 2010:683-687.

[32] Mart. 6.28.8-9; Stat. *Silv.* 2.1.124-125 with Van Dam 1984 ad loc. and Newlands 2011 ad loc.

[33] Cf. Scythin. *AP* 12.22.2-3; for Strato of Sardis, who dedicates a whole poem to the subject of the appropriate age for homoerotic love (*AP* 12.4 = 4 Floridi), the sixteenth year is that of the gods.

as a child.[34] At the same time, the poet cleverly exploits a theme for which Statius himself had a predilection, that of the *puer/puella*:[35] starting from Achilles in the *Achilleis*, a boy disguised as a girl[36] and thus characterized by an *ambiguus ... sexus* (*Achill.* 1.337),[37] Statius often plays with the theme of adolescence as a period of sexual nondifferentiation, which he draws from Ovid.[38] Ausonius' verse 3—*et iam desieras puer anne puella videri*—can in fact be compared with several Ovidian descriptions: see e.g. *Met.* 4.378-379 (Hermaphroditus) *nec femina dici / nec puer ut possit, neutrumque et utrumque videntur*, "(they were) not such as to be called one, woman, and one, man"; 8.322-323 (Atalanta) *facies, quam dicere vere / virgineam in puero, puerilem in virgine possis*, "a face which you could truly say was maidenly for a boy or boyish for a maiden"; 9.712-713 (Iphis) *cultus erat pueri; facies, quam sive puellae / sive dares puero, fuerat formosus uterque*, "the child was dressed like a boy; his face would have been counted lovely whether you assigned it to a girl or to a boy." The very theme of sixteen years old as a liminal age is paralleled by Ovid: Narcissus is sixteen, and he is presented as a boy suspended between the status of *puer* and that of *vir*, desired by both men and women[39] (exactly like Ausonius' Glaucias); Hermaphroditus, for whom Narcissus is a kind of "prototype,"[40] is only one year younger

[34] Although precociously mature, according to the consolatory motif of the *puer-senex*: cf. Van Dam 1984:93-94.

[35] Cf. Van Dam 1984:413-4; Rosati 1994:30 and n. 46.

[36] It should also be noted that Statius had to deal with the difficult issue of the legitimization of Achilles' transvestism—the epic hero *par excellence* had to be portrayed as a *puella* without him losing his honor (see Rosati 1992:251; Rosati 1994:35-36; Fantuzzi 2012:71-88). Although Ausonius uses the image of sexual indistinction in a different way, as it serves the purpose of removing Glaucias from his exclusively homoerotic dimension, Statius was, also in this case, an important model as regards the legitimization of a somewhat "embarrassing" sexual *status*.

[37] On Achilles' sexual ambiguity, see especially Rosati 1992; Rosati 1994:11-19; Feeney 2004; Heslin 2005, especially 182-184.

[38] On this point, see especially Rosati 1992:247-248 (with further bibliography); Rosati 1994:28-30; Hinds 1998:135-142; Ripoll-Soubiran 2008:24-25.

[39] Cf. Ov. *Met.* 3.351-353 *Namque ter ad quinos unum Cephisius annum / addiderat poteratque puer iuvenisque videri: / multi illum iuvenes, multae cupiere puellae*, "for Narcissus had reached his sixteenth year and might seem either a boy or a man. Many boys and many girls desired his love."

[40] The expression is borrowed from Anderson 1996:444.

(Ovid *Met.* 4.292). Glaucias is thus portrayed by Ausonius not simply—and inappropriately for his time—as a *puer delicatus*: he is a beauty, regardless of sexual tastes and predilections. Crucially, such a beauty is defined as *decus*, a term which recalls the expression *decore felix* used by Martial 6.28.7 for Glaucias, but which is an especial favorite of Statius, who uses the word *decor* for Achilles, describing his *ambiguus ... sexus* (*Achill.* 1.335-337 *superest nam plurimus illi / invita virtute decor, fallitque tuentes / ambiguus tenuique latens discrimine sexus,* "for an abundant charm remains to him, although his manhood is unwilling, and he deceives viewers by the puzzle of his sex that by a narrow margin hides its secret"), and *decus* and cognates several times in *Silvae* 2.1, where they are key terms contributing to the idealization of the virtuous and modest relationship between Melior and Glaucias (cf. 103, 136 *decor*; 44, 115 *decorus*; 155 *decus*).[41] In Ausonius' epigram, attention is similarly drawn to what seems to be the essence of the boy: his *decus*, which is at the same time "beauty, grace, splendour",[42] and also "dignity, decorum."[43] In other words, Ausonius seems to indicate an idealized beauty, removed from the terrestrial realm and sexual consummation.

It is now time to analyze the conclusion of the epigram, where the mention of Ganymede serves to make explicit the pederastic motif underlying the first lines. Ganymede's example is coupled with Adonis'. Both mythical paradigms fit the context in several ways: not only are they examples of love, but they also reflect Glaucias' adolescence and the boy's gender ambiguity, as we will see presently; in addition, they are appropriate for an epitaph—the form taken by this epigram. The choice of epitaphic form is significant: Ausonius is exploiting his knowledge of Greek epigram, in which erotic and funerary motifs are often associated, in a generic and metaphoric game;[44] in particular, pederastic epigrams often describe the end of a boy's beauty as a metaphorical death.[45] Here metaphor is replaced by (literary) reality, and

[41] Cf. Van Dam 1984 *ad* vv. 36-136.
[42] Cf. *OLD* 495, s.v. 5.
[43] Cf. *OLD* 495, s.v. 4.
[44] Magini 2000; Gutzwiller 2007.
[45] Cf. e.g. Meleager *AP* 12.33 = *HE* 4480-4483; Strato *AP* 12.178 = 19 Floridi (with note *ad* loc.); Tarán 1985:95-98.

Glaucias' beauty is not dying, but attaining immortality through death (and through literature: Ausonius' epigram grants the boy a form of immortality, as Martial's and Statius' poems had somewhat "eternalized" the "historical" Glaucias).[46] The closing mythical paradigms—serving, respectively, as an example of heterosexual and of homoerotic love—should be read in the light of this generic ambiguity. Adonis, the youth loved and pursued by two goddesses, Venus and Persephone,[47] is always characterized by an intrinsic sexual ambiguity in classical literature.[48] In Theocritus 15.128-130 (ὁ ῥοδόπαχυς Ἄδωνις. / ὀκτωκαιδεκετὴς ἢ ἐννεακαίδεχ' ὁ γαμβρός· / οὐ κεντεῖ τὸ φίλημ'· ἔτι οἱ περὶ χείλεα πυρρά, "rosy-armed Adonis. Eighteen or nineteen years old, the bridegroom: his kiss does not scratch; reddish down still lies upon his lip" [trans. Burton]), for instance, he appears "at that liminal moment of boyhood when he still can look sexually ambiguous; the first down is spreading from his temples; he has not yet shaved ... this is the threshold of gender definition."[49] Ovid himself, from whom the adjective *Cinyreius* applied by Ausonius to the boy at verse 7 derives (see *Met.* 10.712 and 730),[50] underlines the sexual ambiguity of the boy, making Venus draw a comparison between Atalanta's face and body and Adonis' (and her own: cf. *Met.* 10.578-579).[51] Adonis is also an example of premature death, as the motif of the beard in Theocritus stressed:[52] the first beard

---

[46] As aptly observed by the anonymous referee, in pederastic love, in a way, "death is the only option, as beautiful boys do not stay beautiful boys, and they cannot take on a second 'stage' as wives/mothers/mistresses etc." Thus, pederastic love "has to be ephemeral, unless it is frozen."

[47] For details regarding this myth, cf. Fantuzzi 1985 *ad* Bion *Epit. Adon.* 54.

[48] Burton 1995:85.

[49] Burton 1995:57-58; on this point, see also Burton 1995:61, 85.

[50] The adjective alludes to a version of the myth according to which Cinyras was Adonis' father by an incestuous liaison with his daughter Myrrha; it is used again by Ausonius in *Epist.* 13.42 Green *Cinyreia proles* (see Mondin 1995:95 ad loc.).

[51] *ut faciem et posito corpus velamine vidit, / quale meum, vel quale tuum, si femina fias*, "but when he saw her face and her disrobed form, such a beauty as mine, or as yours, if you were a woman."

[52] Cf. Burton 1995:86. For the role of the paradigm of Adonis in funerary contexts, see Wypustek 2013:121-124 (for whom Ausonius' epigram, together with an inscription of the first century found on a tomb from Aphrodisias, *SGO* 02/09/33, would hint at the

is topically mentioned in connection with young people who died before reaching an adult age, in literature (see e.g. *Od.* 11.319-320) as well as in epitaphs for ἄωροι.[53] The presentiment of an untimely death is thus retrospectively cast on the image of Glaucias' androgynous seduction evoked, at verses 1-3, by the mention of the beard spreading over his cheeks.

Ganymede is a good match for Adonis, with whom he is actually often associated:[54] he is a beautiful adolescent boy who is desired, and kidnapped, by a divinity. Moreover, like Adonis, he can serve as an example of untimely death. In the Imperial age the myth of Ganymede started to be used in funerary iconography in connection with the ἄωροι, as shown by archeological finds[55] and inscriptions, where the dead boy is sometimes compared to Ganymede,[56] according to an allegorical reading of the myth clearly formulated by Eustathius *Il.* 1205.10 (4.396.5 Van der Valk) ἡ δὲ τοῦ Γανυμήδους ἁρπαγὴ ἄωρον αἰνίττεται

---

possibility that Adonis was "a sort of prototype of the deceased male taken by a goddess" [123], but this is far from certain).

[53] Cf. Vérilhac 1978-1982: vol. 2, 160-163.

[54] See e.g. Theocr. 15.124, with Burton 1995:137-138; Pl. *Men.* 143-144 *Dic mi, enumquam tu vidisti tabulam pictam in pariete, / ubi aquila Catameitum raperet, aut ubi Venus Adoneum?*, "Tell me, have you never seen a painting on a wall where the eagle snatches Catameitus or Venus Adonis?".

[55] Several examples in Cumont 1942:27, 97-98 and fig. VII.2; cf. also Sichtermann 1988a nos. 105, 109-110, 181-184, 260 (sarcophaguses of various provenance; none of them seems to be datable before the Imperial age); Boyancé 1952:286-287; Lambrechts 1957; Vérilhac 1978-1982: vol. 2, 317-321; Zanoni 2005:380; Wypustek 2013:134-155.

[56] See *GVI* 1318 = I 198 Vérilhac = *SGO* 16/23/06, Aizanoi, AD 247-248, lines 10-11 Ζεύς με νέον Φρύγιον Γανυμήδην κτλ., "Zeus (abducted) me, the new Phrygian Ganymede"; and *GVI* 1765 = I 199 Vérilhac = *SGO* 05/01/64, Smyrna, third century AD: here Ganymede is not explicitly mentioned, but one is obliged to identify the dead with him (see in particular lines 13-16 καί με παρὰ τριπόδεσσι καὶ ἀμβροσίῃσι τραπέζαις / ἡδόμενον κατὰ δαῖτα θεοὶ φίλον εἰσορόωσιν, / κρατὸς ἀπ' ἀθανάτοιο πατρῇσι μειδιόωντες / νέκταρ ὅτ' ἐν προχοαῖσιν ἐπισπένδω μακάρεσσι, "they kindly glance at me as by the tripods and tables I feast on ambrosia, and smiles lift the cheeks of those immortal heads when a libation of nectar for the blessed ones I pour"); *CIL* VI 35769 = *CLE* 1994 (lines 10-12 *Nunc quia non licuit frunisci nostrum ave raptum Ganymeden, / velim quidem facerent caelestia fata ut / iremus properes ad nostrum inmaturum tuendum*, "Now, because we were denied joy from our Ganymede, abducted by the bird, I would like at least for heavenly destiny to be fulfilled, so that we may soon arrive in the same place, to look after our prematurely deceased [child]"); on Ganymede in verse inscriptions, see now Wypustek 2013:130-134 (whose translations of the epitaphs are here taken).

τοῦ παιδὸς θάνατον, "the rapture of Ganymede hints at the death of the boy." His abduction became the symbol of the dead's ascension to Heaven, as the result of a symbolic idealization that was already implicit in the Platonic reading of the story (*Phaedrus* 255c), and that would become common in later religious interpretations.[57] When used in such a context, Ganymede is deprived of his erotic allure and simply becomes a paradigm of premature death. Ausonius exploits here the ambiguity between erotic abduction and death[58] as a means of making acceptable to a contemporary audience the pederastic theme. Although no proper mention of the abduction is to be found in the epigram,[59] the tradition of Ganymede as a symbol of the ascent to Heaven is necessarily evoked in an epitaph for an ἄωρος at a time when this theme was common in funerary contexts. Through a clever conflation of erotic and funerary themes, Ausonius thus "tones down" the homoerotic theme in presenting it to his contemporaries. Indeed, it is as if the fourth-century poet was writing an epitaph for the very tradition of literary praise of pederastic love, a theme that was not possible anymore.[60] Things had changed. This is a final, tactful allusion, a sort of swan song for a centuries-long tradition.

---

[57] Cf. Sichtermann 1953:33-36; Bruneau 1962, especially 196; on the eschatological meaning of the myth of Ganymede, see also Davidson 2007:189 (and in general Davidson 2007:169-200 for a survey of the different accounts of the story, both in literature and visual arts, until Humanism and the Renaissance, with a focus on Christian and Neo-Platonic interpretations).

[58] In funerary contexts, the death of young people is often represented as an abduction on the part of underworld creatures, such as Charon, Hades, the Nymphs, etc. (see Vérilhac 1978-1982: vol. 2, 173-185).

[59] Glaucias is not a passive victim of a god, but he willingly goes towards his new condition (*ibis/eris*, 7-8): this serves the purpose of intensifying the celebration of a *decus* that is more than human, and thus destined to a somewhat superhuman dimension.

[60] "Pederastic desire seems still to have existed in adult men, but they were no longer able to act on it with impunity" (Kuefler 2001:94; *Epigr.* 53 is among the documents examined to reach this conclusion).

III. REFLECTING ON OVID'S SEXUALLY AMBIGUOUS FIGURES: NARCISSUS AND HERMAPHRODITUS

Glaucias is thus modeled, at least to some extent, on Ovid's sexually ambiguous figures.[61] In Ausonius' epigrams, Ovidian characters, such as Narcissus and Hermaphroditus, do in fact appear: *Epigr.* 108-110 are devoted to the myth of Narcissus; 111-112 to Hermaphroditus. In the manuscripts of Ausonius, one series follows the other: they thus seem to betray an Ovidian continuity also by their position, and they seem to be, more generally, inserted into an Ovidian context, as they are followed by two epigrams on Daphne's pursuit by Apollo, itself a theme treated by Ovid (cf. *Met.* 1.452-567).

Here are the epigrams on Narcissus:

Epigr. 108

> Si cuperes alium, posses, Narcisse, potiri;
> nunc tibi amoris adest copia, fructus abest.

> If you desired another, Narcissus, you could possess him; as it is you have every opportunity for love, but no enjoyment of it.

Epigr. 109

> Quid non ex huius forma pateretur amator,
> ipse suam qui sic deperit effigiem?

> What would a lover not suffer from this boy's beauty, who loves his own reflection to distraction in this way?

Epigr. 110

> Commoritur, Narcisse, tibi resonabilis Echo,
> vocis ad extremos exanimata modos,

---

[61] Ganymede and Adonis, for their part, to whom the boy is explicitly compared, are often associated with Narcissus in Imperial literature: see Barchiesi and Rosati 2007:175-176. The myths of Adonis and Narcissus—coupled by Ausonius himself in *Cupid. Cruciat.* 10-11 and *Techn.* 10.2-3—form a pair also in the recently discovered elegiacs contained in *P.Oxy.* 4711. In his *editio princeps* of this piece, Henry 2005 cautiously suggests Parthenius as the author of the lines. Parthenius' authorship is supported by Hutchinson 2006 (see also Hutchinson 2008:200-205) and Luppe 2006a (see also Luppe 2006b) and is not denied by Magnelli 2006:10-11; Reed 2006 is skeptical, while Bernsdorff 2007 argues against this possibility.

et pereuntis adhuc gemitum resecuta querellis
ultima nunc etiam verba loquentis amat.

Resounding Echo dies with you, Narcissus, gasping her
last at the final sounds of your voice; up to now she has
followed your sighs with her lament as you withered away,
and now she too loves the last words of you as you speak.

If these texts were inspired by works of art, as is sometimes assumed,[62]
it should be noted that they lack descriptive elements: in particular,
there is no account of the boy's physical appearance. The poet simply
comments on single details of this well-known story.[63] *Epigr.* 108,
following Ovid *Met.* 3.466 *Quod cupio, mecum est: inopem me copia fecit,*
"What I desire is with me: richness has made me poor," plays on the
concept of *copia*, i.e. sexual opportunity, frustrated by the boy's self-
absorption, which prevents him from seizing this opportunity. The
epigram, where homoerotic love is alluded to (*si cuperes alium ...* [sc.
puerum]), thus remarks on the dangerous and sad side of the myth of
the boy in love with himself. In *Epigr.* 109 verbs such as *pateretur* and
deperit are used: the poem celebrates the exceptional beauty of the boy,
but the drawbacks of that beauty, ruined by the obsessive, homoerotic
desire of the youth for himself, are stressed. The sexual ambiguity of the
myth is preserved by *amator*, which can refer both to a female or male
lover. The last epigram of the series, 110, calls attention to the heterosexual side of the story: the love of Echo for Narcissus. As in Ovid (*Met.*
3.494-501), Echo picks up on Narcissus' dying words (and the language
of the epigram, in general, is reminiscent of the *Metamorphoses*).[64]

---

[62] See Kay 2001 *ad Epigr.* 108; Green 1991 *ad Epigr.* 109 comments: "this is, or at least
imitates, a *subscriptio* of a painting, as *sic* (l. 2) shows."

[63] After Ovid the story of Narcissus became very popular, and was one of the most
frequently represented in visual arts: see e.g. Bettini and Pellizer 2003:94-95; *LIMC*, VI.1,
s.v. *Narkissos*.

[64] *Resonabilis Echo* (verse 1) is taken from Ov. *Met.* 3.358 (for the importance of the
adjective for the characterization of Echo in Ovid, see Raval 2003); *Echo* at the end of the
hexameter is a typical Ovidian position (Barchiesi and Rosati 2007:185-186 define this as
a "scelta quasi-formulare"; Ovid introduces this word-placement at 358 and repeats it six
times, "facendone quasi un'icona metrica della funzione assegnata al personaggio"); *resecuta* (verse 3), although not used by Ovid (but see *Met.* 3.371, 372 *sequitur*), is a compound

But unlike in Ovid, she dies herself at the very moment when he dies through repeating his dying words (verse 1, *conmoritur ... tibi*). Ovid's account, which distinguishes the fading of the nymph (*Met.* 3.396-401) and her reappearance as mere voice lamenting Narcissus' death (*Met.* 3.491-501), is thus condensed, and the analogy between the fate of Echo and that of the boy is stressed. It is as if, through their overlapping voices (verse 2, *vocis ad extremos exanimata modos*), the two characters could fuse the one into the other, prefiguring to a certain extent the fate of Hermaphroditus and Salmacis.

Each poem thus deals with a different aspect of the story: frustrated homoerotic love (*Epigr.* 108); dangerous androgynous beauty (*Epigr.* 109); death and (heterosexual) love (*Epigr.* 110). Ruinous homoerotic ambiguity is implied in the first two epigrams. The last poem, dealing with the heterosexual side of Ovid's account, provides a conclusion to the series, thus redirecting the reader's attention to heterosexual love, made in its turn ruinous and hopeless by Narcissus' homoerotic self-obsession.

More generally, Ausonius' engaging with this myth may be significant from the point of view of the reflection on homoeroticism: Narcissus, with his frustrated erotic desire, seems to (literally) embody an interpretation of the homoerotic relationship as inequality and lack of fulfillment. Love between man and boy is traditionally characterized by asymmetry, as it involves the presence of an active and dominant partner, the adult ἐραστής, and a passive and dominated one, the young ἐρώμενος.[65] *Reciprocity*, so crucial in heterosexual love, is thus prevented by the very nature of the relationship,[66] as is pointedly stressed by the supporters of heterosexual love in texts debating whether love for women is to be preferred to love for boys.[67] Narcissus,

---

in *re-*, a favorite prefix with Ovid for Echo (see Barchiesi and Rosati 2007:185); *ultima ... verba* (4) might echo Ovid's *ultima vox* (*Met.* 3.499). On the similarities between Ausonius' epigram and Ovid, see also Bonadeo 2003:108-109.

[65] Dover 1978:91-98.

[66] On pederastic love as being traditionally based on "sexual inequality," see Floridi 2007 *ad* Strato 53.7-8 = *AP* 12.211.7-8.

[67] See e.g. Meleager *AP* 5.208 = *HE* 4046-4049; Ov. *A.A.* 2.683-684 *Odi concubitus qui non utrumque resolvunt; / hoc est cur pueri tangar amore minus*, "I hate intercourse which does not relieve both; this is why I find less pleasure in love of boys." The "hetero vs.

who is both ἐραστής and ἐρώμενος, personifies such an asymmetry: he is doomed to pursue an erotic object that is always elusive. The impossibility of his fulfilling his desire can thus become a symbol of homoerotic frustration. The two epigrams on Hermaphroditus read as follows:

Epigr. 111
    Mercurio genitore satus, genetrice Cythere,
    nominis ut mixti, sic corporis Hermaphroditus,
    concretus sexu, sed non perfectus, utroque,
    ambiguae Veneris, neutro potiendus amori.

    Hermaphroditus, born with Mercury as father, Cythera as mother, composite in body as in name, embodying both genders but fully formed in neither, of ambiguous sex, who can be possessed by neither kind of love.

Epigr. 112
    Salmacis optato concreta est nympha marito;
       felix virgo, sibi si scit inesse virum.
    Et tu, formosae iuvenis permixte puellae,
       bis felix, unum si licet esse duos.

    The Nymph Salmacis has fused together with the husband she yearned for; she is a happy maid if she knows her husband is inside her. And you are a twice happy youth, having mixed with this beautiful girl, if it is possible for one person to be two.

Epigr. 111 takes Hermaphroditus, "embodying both genders but fully formed in neither," as a model of imperfection, incompleteness, thus inverting the Platonic myth of perfection deriving from the recomposition of a disrupted primigenial unity (*Symp.* 189c–193e),[68] which was in the background of Ovid's depiction of Salmacis' desires, as often

---

homo" debate is a common topic in philosophical prose, ancient novel, and poetry (especially epigram): see Floridi 2007 *ad* Strato 7 = *AP* 12.7 and 87 = *AP* 12.245 for parallels and bibliography.

[68] See Labate 1993:61.

remarked by scholars.[69] *Epigr.* 112 seems to give a positive interpretation to the story, as it portrays happiness in the physical union between man and woman. The nymph Salmacis has fused together with the youth she desperately longed for, and this fusion is supposed to incarnate happiness, to "double" it (3-4 *tu ... iuvenis ... / bis felix*). But Ausonius' *makarismos* ominously echoes Salmacis' prayer to Hermaphroditus in Ovid (see in particular 4.322-326 *qui te genuere, beati, / et frater felix ... / sed longe cunctis longeque beatior illa, / siqua tibi sponsa est,* "happy are they who gave you birth, blessed is your brother ... but far, far happier than they all is she, if any be your promised bride," trans. Miller),[70] and the conclusion of the epigram is ambiguous, as it places a condition that must be met if this happiness is to be attained: *unum si licet esse duos.* To put it in Kay's words, "this joint entity will be doubly happy *provided it can still function as two people*" (my emphasis).[71] Ausonius, who knew his Ovid, expresses doubts about this possibility, thus cruelly reversing the hyperbole of *bis felix.*[72] One is inevitably reminded of Narcissus' desperate and unfulfillable wish, as it is expressed by Ovid *Met.* 3.467-468 *O utinam a nostro secedere corpore possem! / Votum in amante novum: vellem, quod amamus, abesset!* "Oh, that I might be parted from my own body! Strange prayer for a lover: I wish that what I love were absent from me!".

Ausonius thus stresses the dangerous side of Ovidian myths about sexual indistinction: it is certainly not a coincidence that *Epigr.* 72, a playful poem dealing with changes of sex, explicitly recalls the Ovidian predilection for stories of sexual metamorphoses.[73] The irony displayed there by Ausonius serves as a humorous comment on these myths of gender ambiguity.

---

[69] See e.g. Frécault 1972:264; Labate 1993:59-62; Anderson 1996:452-453; Robinson 1999:222; Barchiesi and Rosati 2007:285.

[70] I would thus not say, with Green 1991 ad loc., that Ausonius is "independent" from Ovid.

[71] Cf. Kay 2001 ad loc.

[72] Green 1991 ad loc.

[73] See Rosati 1994:29.

We do not know how Ausonius' book of epigrams—if such a book did indeed exist, as seems likely[74]—was organized; it is nonetheless worth noting that, if the mythical sequence *Epigr.* 106-114 was arranged more or less as it appears in our manuscripts, it could be significant that its conclusion is represented by a myth that is exclusively heterosexual—the story of Apollo and Daphne—as if to direct the reader's mind to the "right" path after offering homoerotic/gender-indistinguished "deviancy."

IV. CONCLUSIONS

In Ausonius' epigrams passive homosexuals are satirized, something that is not at all surprising: Ausonius is following in the footsteps of the literary tradition he is drawing from. Love for boys is banned: the theme, which had played such an important role in the literature of the previous centuries, especially in epigrams, can be "saved" only if it is aptly "toned down," through the clever conflation of erotic and funerary themes, and through the filter of literature. Glaucias is a literary creation: he is a *puer* of ambiguous status, modeled on Ovidian archetypes such as Narcissus or Hermaphroditus. Several epigrams in the collection are devoted to these mythological figures, which are paradigms of gender ambiguity: Ausonius deals with the theme of their sexual indistinction, pointing out the ambiguous, dangerous, and deviant sides.

That Ausonius is the last uninhibited and careless singer of a pagan *eros*, as is often assumed, is thus true only up to a certain point: especially when dealing with homoerotic themes, the difference with respect to earlier literary views of the subject is clear, and it contributes to the sense that this was a time of increasingly strict sexual rules and morals.

UNIVERSITÀ DEGLI STUDI DI MILANO

---

[74] On the problem, see e.g. Kay 2001:11-12; Mondin 2008:412-413.

WORKS CITED

Anderson, W. S. 1996. *Ovid's Metamorphoses: Books 1-5.* Norman, OK.

Asso, P. 2010. "Queer Consolation: Melior's Dead Boy in Statius' *Silvae* 2.1." *AJP* 131:663-697.

Barchiesi, A., and G. Rosati. 2007. *Ovidio. Metamorfosi.* Vol. II (Libri III-IV) a cura di A. B. Testo critico basato sull'edizione oxoniense di Richard Tarrant; traduzione di Ludovica Koch; commento di A. B. e G. R. Milan.

Benedetti, F., 1980. *La tecnica del 'vertere' negli epigrammi di Ausonio.* Florence.

Bernsdorff, H., 2007. "P.Oxy. 4711 and the Poetry of Parthenius." *Journal for Hellenic Studies* 127:1-18.

Bettini, M., and E. Pellizer. 2003. *Il mito di Narciso: Immagini e racconti dalla Grecia a oggi.* Turin.

Bonadeo, A. 2003. *Mito e natura allo specchio: L'eco nel pensiero greco e latino.* Pubblicazioni della Facoltà di Lettere e Filosofia dell'Università di Pavia 103. Pisa.

Boswell, J. 1980. *Christianity, Social Tolerance, and Homosexuality: Gay People in Western Europe from the Beginning of the Christian Era to the Fourteenth Century.* Chicago.

Boyancé, P. 1952. "Funus acerbum." *Revue des études anciennes* 54:275-289.

Bruneau, P. 1962. "Ganymèdes et l'aigle: Images, caricatures et parodies animales du rapt." *Bulletin de correspondance hellénique* 86:193-228.

Buffière, F. 1980. *Eros adolescent: La pédérastie dans la Grèce antique.* Collection d'études anciennes. Série grecque 132. Paris.

Burton, J. B. 1995. *Theocritus's Urban Mimes: Mobility, Gender, and Patronage.* Berkeley.

Cantarella, E. 1988. *Secondo natura: La bisessualità nel mondo antico.* Rome.

Citroni, M. 1975. *M. Valerii Martialis Epigrammaton Liber I.* Florence.

Cumont, F. 1942. *Recherches sur le symbolisme funéraire des Romains.* Paris.

Davidson, J. 2007. *The Greeks and Greek Love: A Radical Reappraisal of Homosexuality in Ancient Greece.* London.

Dover, K. J. 1978. *Greek Homosexuality.* London.

Fantuzzi, M. 1985. *Bionis Smyrnaei Adonis Epitaphium.* ARCA, Classical and Medieval Texts, Papers and Monographs 18. Liverpool.

————. 2012. *Achilles in Love: Intertextual Studies*. Oxford.

Feeney, D. 2004. *"Tenui ... latens discrimine*: Spotting the Differences in Statius' *Achilleid.*" *Materiali e discussioni per l'analisi dei testi classici* 52:85–105.

Floridi, L. 2007. *Stratone di Sardi. Epigrammi.* Hellenica 24. Alexandria.

————. 2012. "*De Glaucia inmatura morte praevento*: Riflessioni su Auson. *ep.* 53 Green." *Eikasmós* 23:283–300.

————. 2013. "*Ludificata sequor verba aliena meis*: Jeux avec les conventions et conscience de l'artifice dans quelques épigrammes d'Ausone inspirées de la tradition grecque." In *La renaissance de l'épigramme dans la latinité tardive: Actes du colloque international La fabrique de l'épigramme dans la latinité tardive, 6-7 octobre 2011— UHA, Mulhouse,* ed. M. F. Guipponi-Gineste and C. Urlacher-Becht, 89–106. Paris.

Frécault, J.-M. 1972. *L'ésprit et l'humour chez Ovide.* Grenoble.

Fusi, A. 2006. *M. Valerii Martialis Epigrammaton Liber Tertius.* Hildesheim.

————. 2008. "Marziale 3, 82 e la *Cena Trimalchionis.*" In Morelli 2008:267–297.

Giannuzzi, M. E. 2007. *Stratone di Sardi. Epigrammi.* Satura 7. Lecce.

González Rincón, M. 1996. *Estratón de Sardes. Epigramas.* Seville.

Green, R. P. H. 1991. *The Works of Ausonius.* Oxford.

————. 1999. *Decimi Magni Ausonii Opera.* Oxford.

Grewing, F. 1997. *Martial Buch VI: Ein Kommentar.* Hypomnemata 115. Göttingen.

Gutzwiller, K. J. 2007. "The Paradox of Amatory Epigram." In *Brill's Companion to Hellenistic Epigram,* ed. P. Bing and J. S. Bruss, 313–332. Leiden.

Henderson, J. 1991. *The Maculate Muse: Obscene Language in Attic Comedy.* 2nd ed. New York.

Henry, W. B. 2005. "Editio princeps of P.Oxy. 4711: Elegy (Metamorphoses?)." *The Oxyrynchus Papyri* 69:46–53.

Heslin, P. H. 2005. *The Transvestite Achilles: Gender and Genre in Statius' Achilleid.* Cambridge.

Hinds, S. 1998. *Allusion and Intertext: Dynamics of Appropriation in Roman Poetry.* Cambridge.

Hubbard, T. K. 2003. *Homosexuality in Greece and Rome: A Sourcebook of Basic Documents*. Berkeley.

Hunink, V. 2002. Review of Kay 2001. *Scholia Reviews* 11:14.

Hutchinson, G. O. 2006. "The Metamorphosis of Metamorphosis: P.Oxy. 4711 and Ovid." *Zeitschrift für Papyrologie und Epigraphik* 156:71–84.

———. 2008. *Talking Books: Readings in Hellenistic and Roman Books of Poetry*. Oxford.

Kay, N. M. 1985. *Martial Book XI: A Commentary*. London.

———. 2001. *Ausonius: Epigrams*. London.

Kuefler, M. 2001. *The Manly Eunuch: Masculinity, Gender Ambiguity, and Christian Ideology in Late Antiquity*. Chicago.

Labate, M. 1993. "Storie di instabilità: L'episodio di Ermafrodito nelle *Metamorfosi* di Ovidio." *Materiali e discussioni per l'analisi dei testi classici* 30:49–62.

Lambrechts, P. 1957. "L'enfant dans les religions à mystères." In *Hommage a W. Déonna*, 322–333. Brussels.

La Penna, A. 1996. *Modelli efebici nella poesia di Stazio*. In *Epicedion: Hommage à P. Papinius Status*, ed. F. Delarue et al., 161–184. Poitiers. (= *Eros dai cento volti: Modelli etici ed estetici nell'età dei Flavi*, Venice, 2000:135–168).

Lentano, M. 2010. "Sbatti il mostro in fondo al mare: Caligola e le *spintriae* di Tiberio." *I quaderni del ramo d'oro on-line* 3:292–319.

Lossau, M. 1973. "*Quod nobis superest ignobilis oti*: Zur παιδικὴ Μοῦσα des Ausonius." In *Verführung zur Geschichte: Festschrift zum 500. Jahrestag der Eröffnung einer Universität in Trier, 1473-1973*, ed. G. Droege, W. Frühwald, and F. Pauly, 20–34. Trier. (= J. M. Lossau 1991. *Ausonius*. Darmstadt. 283–303).

Luppe, W. 2006a. "Die Verwandlungssage der Asterie im P.Oxy. 4711." *Prometheus* 32:55–56.

———. 2006b. "Die Narkissos-Sage in P.Oxy. LXIX 4711." *Archiv für Papyrusforschung und verwandte Gebiete* 52:1–3.

Magini, D. 2000. "Asclepiade e le origini dell'epigramma erotico greco." *Acme* 53:17–37.

Magnelli, E. 2006. "On the New Fragments of Greek Poetry from Oxyrhynchus." *Zeitschrift für Papyrologie und Epigraphik* 158:9–12.

Mattiacci, S. 1982. *I frammenti dei "poetae novelli."* Edizioni dell'Ateneo, Testi e commenti 7. Rome.

Mondin, L. 1995. *Decimo Magno Ausonio. Epistole.* Venice.

———. 2008. "La misura epigrammatica nella tarda latinità." In Morelli 2008:397–494.

Morelli, A. M., ed. 2008. *Epigramma longum: Da Marziale alla tarda antichità; From Martial to Late Antiquity; Atti del Convegno internazionale di Cassino, 29-31 maggio 2006.* Cassino.

Munari, F. 1956. "Ausonio e gli epigrammi greci." *Studi italiani di filologia classica* 27-28:308-314 (= G. Pfohl, ed. 1969. *Das Epigramm.* 187-194. Darmstadt).

Newlands, C. E. 2011. *Statius.* Silvae Book II. Cambridge.

Peiper, R. 1880. "Die handschriftliche Ueberlieferung des Ausonius." *Jahrbücher für classische Philologie,* supplement 11:189-353.

Raval, S. 2003. "Stealing the Language: Echo in *Metamorphoses* 3." In *Being There Together: Essays in Honor of Michael C. J. Putnam on the Occasion of his Seventieth Birthday,* ed. F. Thibodeau and H. Haskell, 204-221. Afton, MN.

Rawson, B. 2003. *Children and Childhood in Roman Italy.* Oxford.

Reed, J. D. 2006 "New Verses on Adonis." *Zeitschrift für Papyrologie und Epigraphik* 158:76-82.

Ripoll, F., and J. Soubiran. 2008. *Stace. Achilléide.* Louvain.

Robinson, M. 1999. "Salmacis and Hermaphroditus: When Two Become One (Ovid, *Met.* 4.285-388)." *CQ,* n.s., 49:212-223.

Rosati, G. 1992. "L'*Achilleide* di Stazio, un'epica dell'ambiguità." *Maia* 44:233-266.

———. 1994. *Stazio. Achilleide.* Milan.

Sánchez Ortiz de Landaluce, M. S. 2006. "El motivo de Ganimedes en el epigrama griego posthelenistico." *Eikasmós* 17:215-242.

Sichtermann, H. 1953. *Ganymed, Mythos und Gestalt in der antiken Kunst.* Berlin.

———. 1988a. *Ganymedes.* In *LIMC* IV.1, 154-169. Zurich.

———. 1988b. *Catmite.* In *LIMC* IV.1, 169-170. Zurich.

Stahl, F. F. S. 1886. *De Ausonianis studiis poetarum Graecorum.* Diss. Kiel.

Steinbichler, W. 1998. *Die Epigramme des Dichters Straton von Sardes: Ein Beitrag zum griechischen paiderotischen Epigramm.* Berlin.

Tarán, S. L. 1979. *The Art of Variation in the Hellenistic Epigram.* Leiden.

———. 1985. "εἰσὶ τρίχες: An Erotic Motif in the *Greek Anthology.*" *Journal for Hellenic Studies* 105:90–107.

Traina, A. 1989. *Poeti latini (e neolatini): Note e saggi filologici.* Vol. 3, 171–177. Bologna (= Traina, A. 1982. "Su Ausonio 'traduttore.'" *Rivista di filologia e istruzione classica* 110:111–115).

Van Dam, H.-J. 1984. *P. Papinius Statius. Silvae Book II: A Commentary.* Leiden.

Vattuone, R. 2004. *Il mostro e il sapiente: Studi sull'erotica greca.* Bologna.

Vérilhac, A.-M. 1978–1982. ΠΑΙΔΕΣ ΑΩΡΟΙ: *Poésie funéraire.* 2 vols. Athens.

Williams, C. A. 1999. *Roman Homosexuality: Ideologies of Masculinity in Classical Antiquity.* New York.

———. 2010. *Roman Homosexuality: Ideologies of Masculinity in Classical Antiquity.* 2nd ed., with a Foreward by M. Nussbaum. New York.

Wypustek, A. 2013. *Images of Eternal Beauty in Funerary Verse Inscriptions of the Hellenistic and Greco-Roman Periods.* Mnemosyne Supplement 352. Leiden.

Zanoni, V. 2005. "Noterella in margine alla iconografia di Ganimede." *Acme* 58:377–380.

EMPEROR THEODOSIUS' LIBERTY AND THE ROMAN PAST

MASSIMILIANO VITIELLO

I. INTRODUCTION:
THE EMPEROR WHO LOVED HISTORY

EMPEROR THEODOSIUS'[1] FERVOR for the Roman past and interest in the *exempla maiorum* were celebrated by his contemporaries. It is clear from the sources that the emperor appreciated literary talents. He requested Ausonius to send him a copy of his works,[2] and he appointed authors of historical and literary works to prestigious positions. In the year 384, Themistius was promoted to the urban prefecture of Constantinople,[3] and in the year 389, Aurelius Victor, who published an historical work during the reign of Julian, was raised to the urban prefecture of Rome.[4] Two years later, in 391, Theodosius appointed the

I am grateful to the anonymous reader for the valuable critique and advice, as well as to Michel Festy (Rennes), Matthias Haake (Münster), and Johannes Hahn (Münster). I dedicate this article to the memory of Carl Harris, Wake Forest University (d. 2011).

[1] Among the recent literature on Theodosius see especially Ernesti 1998; Leppin 2003; Errington 2006; Cameron 2011.

[2] Cf. Ausonius *Epistula Theodosii Augusti* (in *Codex Parisinus* 8500; Peiper 1886:3): *Amor meus qui in te est et admiratio ingenii atque eruditionis tuae ... fecit ... ut ... sermonem autographum ad te transmitterem, postulans pro iure non equidem regio, sed illius priuatae inter nos caritatis, ne fraudari me scriptorum tuorum lectione patiaris ... Quae tu de promptuario scriniorum tuorum, qui me amas, libens imperties, secutus exempla auctorum optimorum, quibus par esse meruisti.* (see below, note 102). On the relationship between Ausonius and Symmachus prior to the victory of Theodosius against Maximus, see PLRE 1:140–141; Bowersock 1986; Bruggisser 1993:135–330 passim; Sogno 2006:5–8.

[3] Themistius was appointed prefect shortly before Theodosius visited the West, and he was entrusted with the care of Arcadius: cf. PLRE 1:892. Cf. below note 9, referring to this event.

[4] Cf. PLRE 1:960 and Nixon 1991, who does not dismiss the possibility that the work was dedicated to Julian; Dessau, *ILS* 2945, the inscription of Aurelius Victor urban prefect

famous orator Quintus Aurelius Symmachus to the consulship.[5] During this period he also brought Virius Nicomachus Flavianus to his court, first as quaestor and later as praetorian prefect, commissioning him to write an historical work which would be dedicated to the emperor.[6] The resulting history, Nicomachus Flavianus' *Annales*, has become in recent years perhaps the most frequently discussed work of the lost late antique historiographies.[7] Scholars disagree on the date of publication of this lost source, generally placing it between 388–389 and 391. There is no general consensus on the length of the original work, on its chronological scope, or on its connections with other histories like Ammianus Marcellinus' *Res Gestae* and the *Historia Augusta*. The only element upon which scholars generally agree is that the *Annales* were intended to satisfy the interests of Theodosius, as is clear from the inscription *CIL* 6.1783, which records the commissioning of Flavianus' *History* during his political appointment at court.[8]

Of course Theodosius' interest in history was not a unique case, nor was he the only emperor to whom an historical work was dedicated. To consider only the extant literature of the fourth century, emperor Julian, possible addressee of Aurelius Victor's work, had offered a parody of the history of Rome in his *Caesares*, while Eutropius and Festus had written their *Breuiaria* at the request of and in order to dedicate them to emperor Valens. Yet Theodosius' passion for history was not based only on his enjoyment of the subject. As it did for his predecessors, history played an important role in his political agenda.

The following contribution intends to prove that behind Theodosius' purported interest in Roman history and *exempla maiorum* hid the ambitions of pagan senators who came closer to the emperor and his entourage soon after the defeat of Maximus. Theodosius'

---

located in the forum of Trajan, in which Theodosius is described as *[u]eterum principum clementiam [sa]nctitudinem munificentiam supergresso*.

[5] Cf. PLRE 1:865–870.

[6] Cf. PLRE 1:347–349, also the bibliography below, note 83.

[7] The question has been recently discussed in detail for example by Zecchini 1993:51–64; Baldini 2005; Festy 2007; Ratti 2010; Cameron 2011:627–690.

[8] *CIL* 6.1783: *quos consecrari sibi a quaestore et praefecto suo uoluit*. Cameron hypothesizes that "the entire project was both begun and completed in his spare time as a busy bureaucrat over a period of less than three years" (Cameron 2011:631–632); cf. note 83.

interest in the Roman past became an instrument of these aristocrats to praise the ruler in a traditional way, while at the same time expressing a nostalgic view of the past in their political dialogue with the emperor during the years 388–391. A careful analysis of senatorial literature from the late fourth and early fifth centuries suggests that elements of this propaganda were contained in the lost panegyrics of Symmachus to Theodosius and possibly in the lost *Annales* of Flavianus: these works were produced in those same years, 388–391, to further Theodosius' ambitions to rule over the West as a traditional *princeps*, first as a new Augustus, later as Trajan. As they attempted to strengthen their relationship with the emperor, Roman aristocrats once again made a political use of the historical motifs of *libertas Romana* and the restoration of peace following the civil war. Only one generation later, with the disappearance of the so-called "Last Pagans of Rome," these motifs reappeared, in the footsteps of Seneca the Elder and Tacitus, as a way to mourn the lost glorious past of Rome.

II. THEODOSIUS' INTEREST IN THE *EXEMPLA MAIORUM* AND THE *LIBERTAS ROMANA*

Many contemporary writers attested to Theodosius' passion for Roman history, among them Themistius, who alluded to it in a *Dankesrede* to the emperor for his political appointment.[9] Some years later the anonymous author of the *Epitome de Caesaribus* also testified to this, as did Claudian, still later. This interest is also indirectly confirmed by Pacatus in his panegyric. Our information about Theodosius' interests in history is on the whole secondhand, depending on what could be creations of the authors. However, a close examination of these texts reveals common elements that should be considered in parallel and that may reflect the contours of imperial-senatorial propaganda.

In the lengthy eulogy of Theodosius that concludes the *Epitome de Caesaribus*, the anonymous author states that despite his average literary education, the emperor was profoundly interested in the deeds of the ancients, which he enjoyed reading:

[9] Them. *Or.* 17.215A. Cf. Hartke 1940:143–144, 156.

Litteris, si nimium perfectos contemplemur, mediocriter
doctus; sagax plane multumque diligens ad noscenda
maiorum gesta. E quibus non desinebat exsecrari quorum
facta superba, crudelia libertatique infesta legerat, ut
Cinnam, Marium Syllamque atque uniuersos dominantium, praecipue tamen perfidos et ingratos.

If we should compare him to the exceedingly polished,
he was moderately learned; he was obviously intelligent
and very keen with regard to becoming acquainted with
the deeds of our ancestors. From these he never ceased to
censure the acts of which he read that were haughty, cruel,
and inimical to liberty, as Cinna, Marius, and Sulla, and
everyone holding *dominatio*, but especially the treacherous
and ungrateful.[10]

It is possible that Theodosius' interests included literature *de uiris
inlustribus*.[11] It is intriguing, however, that in this context of eulogy and
interest in the *maiorum gesta*, the anonymous author does not focus
on the strong and legendary figures of Roman history who inspired
Theodosius. Rather he emphasizes those figures whose cruelty the
emperor despised, and those bad rulers of the *uniuersi dominantium* who
had been *perfidi* and *ingrati*. Only a few paragraphs before, the *Epitome*
had praised Theodosius as *propagator rei publicae atque defensor eximius*
for his successful wars against the Huns and the Goths, the peace
with the Persians, and especially for his victories against the usurpers
Maximus and Eugenius (AD 388 and 394, respectively). Between these
two sections of Theodosius' eulogy is included a comparison of the
emperor with Trajan. Scholars think with good reason that this assimilation, which was the result of a *manipulation généalogique* (Chausson)
that Theodosius (who considered himself a descendant of Nerva,
Trajan, and the Antonines) used in court propaganda in the East, did

---

[10] *Epit. de Caes.* 48.11–12 (Festy 1999). The translation is from Banchich 2009:234.
[11] Theodosius I—or more likely II—is the addressee of a poem of dedication of the
works of Cornelius Nepos; the question has been recently discussed by Burgersdijk
2007:106–107.

not circulate until 389–391 in the West, where it was well known that this ancestry claim was baseless, and in any case the idea would have been distasteful during the reigns of Gratian and of Maximus (see below, Section IV).[12] Importantly, this comparison to Trajan is not referenced by Pacatus, despite his use of Pliny's panegyric to Trajan as a model for his oration.[13] On the other hand, as we shall see, allusions to Theodosius' interest in the past do find strong parallels in Pacatus' oration of the year 389. The reason is simple: the eulogy of Theodosius in the *Epitome de Caesaribus* 48.8–18 contains many layers of political propaganda deriving from the years 388 to 391.

Claudian, too, alludes to Theodosius' passion for history in his pane-gyric, delivered in Rome in the year 398 on the occasion of the fourth consulship of Honorius. Here, in a long digression, Claudian included a prosopopoeia, writing in the guise of the dead emperor speaking to Honorius, his son and successor in the West, to advise him in matters of good rule. Theodosius warns Honorius to keep history always in mind, and advised him to look to the examples of the past, particularly those figures that represented models of virtues: "Meanwhile cultivate the Muses while you are still young; read of deeds you soon may rival; never may Greece's story, never may Rome's, cease to speak with you. Study the lives of the heroes of old to accustom yourself for wars that are to be. Go back to the Latin age."[14] These lines are followed by a list

---

[12] The comparison is briefly referenced by Them. *Or.* 16.205A, which dates to January 1, 383 (ὁ σὸς πρόγονος καὶ ἀρχηγέτης); more widely in *Epit. de Caes.* 48.5–10, and 48.1, in which Theodosius is *originem a Traiano principe trahens*. More important is Them. *Or.* 34.7, dated to ca. 385, according to which Hadrian, Antoninus Pius, and Marcus Aurelius are Theodosius' ancestors and founders of his line. On this question cf. esp. Chausson 1998 and 2007:62–73, 240–255; also Festy 1997; Festy 1999:xxxvi–xxxvii (on the source of *Epit. de Caes.* 48), 227n2; Festy 2003.

[13] Cf. *Pan. Lat.* 12.11.6 (Mynors 1964), the very generic *finibus Traianus augeret*. Trajan's name was frequently used as a model; cf. Auson. *Grat. act.* 16–17; Amm. Marc. 30.9, comparing Valentinian I to Trajan and Marcus Aurelius. Cf. also below, note 89, on the assimilation of Julian with Trajan. On Pacatus and the collection of panegyrics, cf. recently Rees 2012. Cf. also Lunn-Rockliffe 2010, on the image of Maximus in Pacatus' panegyric.

[14] Claud. *IV cons. Hon.* 414–438, part. 414–418 (trans. Platnauer 1922, slightly adapted): *Interea Musis animus, dum mollior, instet / et quae mox imitere legat; nec desinat umquam / tecum Graia loqui, tecum Romana uetustas. / Antiquos euolue duces, adsuesce futurae / militiae, Latium retro te confer in aeuum.*

of illustrious personages, events, and traditional republican virtues (among them *paupertas*) that he recommends that Honorius exercise.[15] Here especially the figures who distinguished themselves for their merits are evoked—the *exempla maiorum* recurrent in late antique literature—while there is no mention of those wicked leaders of the late republic.[16] Claudian used his deep knowledge of ancient authors[17] to celebrate the emperor and his passion for the history of Rome. However, in addressing the son of the deceased ruler, Claudian built his eulogy with a different purpose and in a different way than the anonymous author of the *Epitome de Caesaribus*, whose praises of Theodosius, as we shall see, draw from a different repertoire.

Theodosius' interest in good and bad examples drawn from the past are clearly reflected in the panegyric of Pacatus, which predates that of Claudian by nine years, and which was recited during the emperor's sojourn in Rome, between June 13 and August 30 of year 389, to celebrate his *aduentus* and triumph one year after the victory over the usurper Maximus. Besides the usual mention of the emperors traditionally loved by the Roman senate (Nerva, Titus, Antoninus Pius, Augustus, Hadrian, and Trajan),[18] the multiple references to the Roman republic in this document are connected by scholars to the interest of Theodosius in historical models, as discussed above. Scholars such as Matthews and Barnes therefore have speculated that Nicomachus Flavianus' work too, which was dedicated to the emperor, had as its focus the history of the republic. Schlumberger, on the other hand, identifies in these sources the rhetoric of the *exempla maiorum*.[19] However, as we shall see, his

[15] Claud. *IV cons. Hon.* 431 and 438: *haec genitor praecepta dabat.*

[16] On the same occasion Theodosius advises his son to follow the example of Trajan: Claud. *IV cons. Hon.* 328–332 (quoted below, in text). Cf. Ernesti 1998:388–389.

[17] Cf. Cameron 1970:331–343.

[18] *Pan. Lat.* 12.11.6. For a translation and commentary of the panegyric, see Nixon and Rodgers 1994:437–519.

[19] Matthews 1975:231n3; Barnes 1976:268; this hypothesis has been dismissed by Schlumberger 1985. On the propaganda in this panegyric, cf. Lippold 1968; Brodka 1998:13–24; Ernesti 1998:323–350; Lunn-Rockliffe 2010. The significance of the *exempla maiorum* in the literature of this period has been discussed by Portmann 1988; Felmy 2001:88–124 (Brutus), 231–280 (Marius, Sulla, Caesar); Sehlmeyer 2009:174–178.

perspective needs to be reconsidered. Viewed through a different lens, the evidence leads to other conclusions.

II.1 Restoring *Libertas*: The Republic and the End of the Civil Wars

In his panegyric, Pacatus makes abundant references to the history of Rome. Amongst them are the devastations of Cinna, Marius, and Sulla—the names that would later figure in the *Epitome*—whose cruelty he condemns together with that of Caesar:

> Tu [Roma], quae experta Cinnanos furores et Marium post exsilia crudelem et Sullam tua clade Felicem et Caesarem in mortuos misericordem ad omne ciuilis motus classicum tremescebas; quae praeter stragem militum utraque tibi parte pereuntium exstincta domi senatus tui lumina, suffixa pilo consulum capita, Catones in mortem coactos truncosque Cicerones et Pompeios fleueras insepultos.

> You, who experienced the raging of a Cinna, and Marius made cruel by exile, and Sulla, "fortunate" by your destruction, and Caesar, merciful to the dead, used to quake at every trumpet blast of civil war; for in addition to the slaughter of soldiers perishing for you on both sides, you had wept for the leading lights of your Senate, extinguished at home, the heads of the consuls were stuck upon pikes, Catos forced to die, Ciceros mutilated and Pompeys unburied.[20]

Panegyrical literature does not lack of examples of the trilogy Cinna–Marius–Sulla, which was traditionally associated with the civil war and with the loss of Rome's *libertas*. An anonymous panegyrist who possibly was one of Pacatus' models had used these names decades earlier to eulogize Constantine in his victory over Maxentius.[21]

---

[20] *Pan. Lat.* 12.46.1–2, cf. 3 (trans. Nixon and Rodgers 1994).

[21] See *Pan. Lat.* 9.20.3–21.1, dating to the year 313: *Inrupit olim te* [i.e. Roma] *Cinna furiosus et Marius iratus, qui non solo se Octauii consulis capite satiarunt sed luminibus ciuitatis exstinctis exempla, quae nunc toto sexennio passa es, reliquerunt. Vicit iterum tibi ante portam Collinam Sulla, felix si se parcius uindicasset; ⟨sed⟩ enim multis capitibus rostra compleuit;* the

However, Pacatus makes an intentional use of these motifs *only* in the final part of his long panegyric when, immediately before announcing the *aduentus* and triumph of Theodosius, he celebrates the emperor as the one who ended the civil war, reconquered Italy, and restored lost *libertas* to Rome: "now you have seen a civil war (*ciuile bellum*) ended with the slaughter of enemies, a peaceful soldiery, the recovery of Italy, and your liberation (*tua libertate finitum*); you have seen, I repeat, a civil war ended (*finitum ciuile bellum*) for which you can decree a triumph."[22] At the time of Pacatus' panegyric, the civil war had just ended and the people of Rome could finally breathe a sigh of relief.[23]

Panegyrists occasionally used the motif of *libertas Romana* to recall the origins of the consulship and its importance in the foundation of the republic. The case of Mamertinus (the oldest in the extant literature), who addressed his gratitude to emperor Julian for the consulship, is a good example:

> Will anyone believe that the ancient freedom of former ages has been given back to the republic after such a long time (*illam priscorum temporum libertatem rei publicae redditam*)? I do not think that the consulship of Lucius Brutus and Publius Valerius, who were the first to preside over the citizens with annual power after the kings were expelled, is to be preferred to ours ... They accepted their

---

name of Caesar is not mentioned. Cf. also Ausonius' use of the example of Sulla Felix and of Metellus Pius in *Grat. act.* 8.38. For other possible uses by Pacatus of this panegyric see below, notes 23 and 33. Cf. Festy 1999:234; Lippold 1968:239–240n72. It is noteworthy that the same trilogy is used by Valerius Maximus 2.8.7, 5.6.4, 6.9.6, and also by Plutarch in the beginning of the *Life of Caesar* (1.1); however here they are historically contextualized.

[22] *Pan. Lat.* 12.46.4 (trans. Nixon and Rodgers 1994); cf. also 47.3, in the description of the *aduentus*, and 9.20.3–4 (quoted above, note 21). Cf. Ambr. *De obit. Theod.* 56 (*PL* 16): *Italia ... concelebrat suae libertatis auctorem.*

[23] Pacatus may here be using as a literary model the anonymous panegyric to Constantine, which had referred to the joy of Rome after the emperor's *ciuilis uictoria* over Maxentius; cf. *Pan. Lat.* 9.20.3–21.3, in which also: *O tandem felix ciuili, Roma, uictoria! ... Constantinus uictoriae licentiam fine proelii terminauit; gladios ne in eorum quidem sanguinem distringi passus est quos ad supplicia poscebas...* (see above, note 21). Cf. Nixon and Rodgers 1994:325n127: "this is the first extant appearance of the theme in Latin panegyric ... Roman history afforded many examples of a civil victory bloodily used, and any victory of one emperor over another was followed by trepidation." See also Euseb. *Vit. Const.* 1.40.

consular power through the people, we received it through Julian. In their year freedom came into being, in ours it was restored (*Illorum anno libertas orta est, nostro restituta*).[24]

More frequently, panegyrists evoked *libertas Romana* to celebrate the end of usurpations or to announce the beginnings of new dynasties, as we see in the well-known example of Constantine's victory over Maxentius (cf. at note 23). Inscriptions in the name of Constantine, Constantius II, and especially Magnentius do not lack this motif, and expressions like *propagator / restitutor Romani status / rei publicae et libertatis* are not unusual.[25] Two inscriptions dedicated to Julian that contain the main elements of his political agenda celebrate him among other things respectively as ⟨*ph*⟩*ilosofi[ae] magistro ... uictorios[iss]imo Augusto, propagatori libertatis et rei publ[i]cae, also omn[i] genere pollenti uirtutum, inuicto principi, restitutori libe[r]t[at]is et Ro[manae] religion[is] a[c] tr[iumfat]ori orbis.*[26]

The most common allusions to Roman *libertas* refer to the beginning as well as the end of the republic. As we shall see in Section IV, imperial historiography has a tradition of raising this important theme, which is

---

[24] *Pan. Lat.* 11.30.3–4 (trans. Nixon and Rodgers 1994:433–434 with n. 180): *Credet aliquis tanto post ueterem illam priscorum temporum libertatem rei publicae redditam? Neque enim ego Lucii Bruti et Publii Valerii, qui primi exactis regibus potestate annua ciuibus praefuerunt, consulatum nostro anteponendum puto ... Illi consularem potestatem per populum acceperunt, nos per Iulianum recepimus. Illorum anno libertas orta est, nostro restituta.* Cf. also Symmachus' words to Gratian as in *Or.* 4.12–15, part. 13 and 15 (Callu 2009): *Bene igitur aput uos locata est tutela rei publicae: pacem innocentiae reddidistis, abrogata est externis moribus uis nocendi. Creuit principatus, quia liberis imperatis; tantum potestatibus quantum legibus licet ... Haec est illa Latii ueteris aetas aureo celebrata cognomine, qua fertur incola fuisse terrarum necdum moribus offensa Iustitia. Pie regimur et quaedam pignora principum sumus, neque alia inter ciues quam inter filios iudicii discretio est: dignus amore praeponitur et tamen, quisquis displicet, non necatur; praemiis uirtutis corrigitur ignauia. Quantos iste ad optimam frugem rapiet consulatus! Dum alios honoratis, alios eruditis; nam quibus ab natura recti amor defuit, spem sequentur.*

[25] Cf., for example, referring to Constantine, *CIL* 8.7010, 15451; *CIL* 14.131, 1145; *ILTun* 813; referring to Maxentius, cf. *IRT* 464, 465; for Magnentius, see *AE* 1987, 433; *AE* 1992, 741 and 783; *AE* 1993, 712b; *AE* 1997, 525; *CIL* 5.8061, 8066; *CIL* 9.5937, 5940, 5951; *CIL* 11.6640, 6643; *CIL* 13.9135; *InscrAqu* 2.2900; *Miliar.* 11, *regio* 9 and 26; *SuppIt* 5–S, 6, 9–A, 27, 9–T, 12; for Gratian, cf. *AE* 1965, 15b; *CIL* 6.1180 (together with Valentinian I); for Honorius, cf. *CIL* 6.1193.

[26] *CIL* 3.7088 (Pergamum); *CIL* 8.4326 (Numidia); cf. also *AE* 1937, 145 (Numidia); *CIL* 8.1432 (Africa Proconsularis); *CIL* 11.6669 (Etruria).

echoed by panegyrists. In the age of Theodosius this old motif appears again in Claudian's panegyric, where the emperor, speaking from beyond the grave to Honorius, reminded his son of the bad examples set by Tarquin the Proud and Julius Caesar—that is, at the beginning and the end of the republic—whose lack of moderation provoked tragic reactions (see below).[27] Indeed, Theodosius' first admonition to his son concerns Brutus and *libertas*.[28] It is noteworthy that both historical situations are also evoked by Pacatus in his panegyric, in which the motif of *libertas* is central. In fact, while the leaders of the civil wars are mentioned at the end of the panegyric, in the middle Pacatus evokes the idea of *libertas* in the well-known story of Brutus and Tarquin the Proud. Remarkably, the reference to this *exemplum* does not appear in any panegyrics of the Gallic collection, which in several places served as a model for Pacatus. Even more interesting is the fact that this notorious legend is not used to evoke the origins of the consulship, but to eulogize Theodosius as the long-awaited restorer of *libertas*:

> Denique ipsum illum Tarquinium *exsecratione* postrema hoc
> damnauere maledicto, et hominem *libidine* praecipitem,
> *auaritia* caecum, immanem *crudelitate*, *furore* uecordem
> uocauerunt *Superbum*, et putauerunt sufficere conuicium.
> Quod si per rerum naturam liceret *ut ille Romanae liber-*
> *tatis adsertor, regii nominis Brutus osor*, precariae redditus
> uitae saeculum tuum cerneret studiis uirtutis parsimoniae
> humanitatis imbutum ac refertum, nullum toto orbe
> terrarum *superbiae libidinis crudelitatis* exstare uestigium,
> iam te ipsum *qua publice qua priuatim* uideret priscorum
> duritia ducum, castitate pontificum, consulum modera-
> tione, petitorum comitate uiuentem, mutaret profecto

---

[27] Claud. *IV cons. Hon.* 309–311. For this motif, cf. Eutropius *Brev.* 6.25, referring to Caesar (Hellegouarc'h 1999): *Agere insolentius coepit et contra consuetudinem Romanae libertatis. Cum ergo et honores ex sua uoluntate praestaret, qui a populo antea deferebantur, nec senatui ad se uenienti adsurgeret aliaque regia et paene tyrannica faceret, coniuratum est ... Praecipui fuerunt inter coniuratos duo Bruti, ex eo genere Bruti qui primus Romae consul fuerat et reges expulerat, et C. Cassius et Seruilius Casca.* Cf. also the ironic words put in the mouth of Maximinus Thrax (symbol of tyranny) in SHA *Maxim.* 18.2.

[28] Claud. *IV cons. Hon.* 401: *libertas quaesita placet? Mirabere Brutum.*

sententiam tanto post suam et, cum *Romanam dignitatem ac libertatem probaret meliore in statu imperatore te esse quam consule se fuisse,* necessario fateretur Tarquinium submoueri debuisse, *non regnum.*

Finally they damned the notorious Tarquin, in an ultimate curse, with this malediction, and a man unbridled in his lust, blinded by greed, a monster of cruelty and insane in his ferocity, they called "the Arrogant," and considered that reproach sufficient. But if Nature permitted that champion of Roman liberty, Brutus, hater of the name of king, to be restored briefly to life, and to observe your age, imbued and overflowing with enthusiasm for virtue, thrift and humanity, with no trace anywhere in the world of arrogance, lust or cruelty, and to see you yourself, now, living both in public and in private with the austerity of leaders of old, the chastity of pontiffs, the moderation of consuls and the affability of candidates for office, he would surely change his mind after so long a time, and, when he found that Roman dignity and liberty were in a better condition with you as Emperor than they were in his consulship, he would of necessity confess that it was Tarquin who should have been removed, and not the monarchy.[29]

The "republican" rhetoric used to introduce Theodosius' elevation to emperor announces the tone of the panegyric,[30] and not by coincidence the censure of Tarquin rather than of the kingship itself can be found in two of Cicero's most well-known works, *De legibus*

---

[29] *Pan. Lat.* 12.20.4–6 (trans. Nixon and Rodgers 1994), cf. also par. 3: *Nam cum indiscreta felicium pedisequa sit superbia, uix cuiquam contingit et abundare fortuna et indigere adrogantia. Cuius quidem ita maiores nostros pertaesum est, ut grauiorem semper putauerint seruitute contemptum, eiusque impatientia sint coacti post bellatores Tullos Numasque sacrificos et Romulos conditores regnum usque ad nomen odisse.* The adjective *superbus* used as a noun is also in *Pan. Lat.* 3.20.4 although not in reference to Tarquin.

[30] *Pan. Lat.* 12.3.5–6, in which Theodosius is elected in order to *tantam molem subire et nuntiata Romanae rei fata suscipere,* and where there are some anachronistic references to the Roman assemblies of the republic. For further references to the republican assemblies, cf. *Pan. Lat.* 11.3.16 and 19; Symmachus *Or.* 1.9 and 4.7; Auson. *Grat. act.* 3.13–15, 9.2 and 4.

and *De republica*.[31] Theodosius, now part of this story, is eventually compared with Brutus. Unlike Brutus, Theodosius obtained *libertas* not as a consul but as an emperor. After all, as Pacatus claims, under Theodosius' empire, *Romana dignitas* and *libertas* were in better shape than at the time of Brutus' consulship (this motif is also announced in the introduction of the oration with reference to Rome, par. 1.2: *cuius et libertatem armatus adseruisti et auxisti dignitatem togatus*). Theodosius embodied both in public and private (*publice et priuatim*) the austerity of leaders of old, the chastity of pontiffs, the moderation of consuls, and the affability of candidates for office; but most of all, he was exalted for his triumph over *superbia*. This word appears in the panegyric on this occasion in reference to Tarquin, and then does not appear again until the conclusion, in a sentence that also refers to the behavior of the emperor as prince and as *ciuis* (again, *publice et priuatim*): "triumphant now in war, now over pride (*superbia*); how you showed yourself to all as a ruler (*principem*), to individuals as a senator (*senatorem*)."[32] Maximus is attributed with a list of vices similar to Tarquin, including *perfidia* (a term that in rhetoric often accompanies *superbia*), *impietas*, *libido*, and *crudelitas*. As Maximus parallels Tarquin, Theodosius in opposing him becomes Brutus, savior of liberty:

> Postremo tecum fidem, secum *perfidiam*; tecum fas, secum nefas; tecum ius, secum iniuriam; tecum clementiam pudicitiam religionem, secum *impietatem libidinem crudelitatem* et omnium scelerum postremorumque uitiorum stare collegium?

> In conclusion, on your side there was loyalty, on his, treachery; you had right on your side; he, wrong; you had justice, he injustice; you had clemency, modesty, religious scruple, he impiety, lust, cruelty and a whole company of the worst crimes and vices.[33]

---

[31] See Cic. *Leg.* 3.7.15; *Rep.* 2.30.52. Cf. Lippold 1968:242; Felmy 2001:103–104.

[32] *Pan. Lat.* 12.47.3 (cf. *superbe* in 12.36.3), trans. Nixon and Rodgers 1994. See below, with note 55.

[33] *Pan. Lat.* 12.31.3 (trans. Nixon and Rodgers 1994). Such a contraposition is occasionally found in the panegyrists of Constantine, with reference to Maxentius; *Pan. Lat.* 9.4.4:

The comparison is based on virtues and vices, and justifies the associations Theodosius–Brutus, Maximus–Tarquin the Proud, as well as the oppositions Brutus–Tarquin the Proud, Theodosius–Maximus. The criticisms of Tarquin the Proud and Maximus as tyrants and oppressors of *libertas* are formulated with similar substantives. Careful observation of the terminology in both the above-quoted passages (italicized) reveals that it is the same as that used a few years later in the *Epitome de Caesaribus* to condemn the leaders and bad rulers despised by Theodosius:

> E quibus [i.e. maiorum gesta] non desinebat *exsecrari* quorum facta *superba, crudelia libertatique infesta* legerat ... atque uniuersos dominantium, praecipue tamen *perfidos et ingratos.*

These comparisons, in which the panegyric wording dominates, in conjunction with the above-discussed trilogy Cinna–Marius–Sulla referenced in both the documents, does not dismiss the possibility that the 'common source' or link was one of the lost orations of Symmachus to Theodosius, who knew Pacatus personally and was familiar with the panegyrical tradition. Symmachus' panegyric of 388, which was an apology for having supported Maximus, is a possibility; so is the oration delivered in 391 for his consulship,[34] where Symmachus may have used these motifs in his eagerness to please the audience as much as Theodosius. Symmachus' deep attachment to the *exempla maiorum* is well attested in his works, including the extant fragments of his

---

te, Constantine, paterna pietas sequebatur, illum ... impietas; te clementia, illum crudelitas; te pudicitia soli dicata coniugio, illum libido stupris omnibus contaminata; te diuina praecepta, illum superstitiosa maleficia; illum denique spoliatorum templorum, trucidati senatus, plebis Romanae fame necatae piacula, te abolitarum calumniarum, te prohibitarum delationum; Pan. Lat. 4.31.3: Duci sane omnibus uidebantur subacta uitiorum agmina quae Vrbem grauiter obsederant: Scelus domitum, uicta Perfidia, diffidens sibi Audacia et Importunitas catenata. Furor uinctus et cruenta Crudelitas inani terrore frendebant; Superbia atque Adrogantia debellatae, Luxuries coercita et Libido constricta nexu ferreo tenebantur. These texts could be Pacatus' models. On Maxentius' abuses against the senators and their wives, which also recall Tarquin's behavior, cf. Euseb. Vit. Const. 1.33–35.

[34] Cf. Seeck 1883:vi, lvii. For this hypothesis see Festy 1999:xxxvii–xxxviii. About the relationships between Symmachus and Pacatus see below, note 85.

panegyrics, the only surviving examples of the senatorial production of the fourth century. He also stressed the importance that Roman institutions and the senate should have in the elections of emperors and consuls, and often uses a "republican" language.[35] During his urban prefecture, he addressed Theodosius in one of his *Relationes* in which he defended the right to use the old and modest carriage of the prefect against the new luxurious ones ordered by Gratian: in defending the traditional image of Rome, he appealed to the past, remembering the importance for Rome of *libertas* and how the old city of the ancestors was traditionally intolerant of *superbia* and bad actors such as Tarquin.[36]

The above-discussed repertoire of motifs was convenient for panegyrists and historians to use as a rhetorical instrument to justify intervention in civil wars by emperors who claimed to restore liberty to the old capital. Although on one hand it is likely that the panegyrical literature influenced the final eulogy of Theodosius in the *Epitome de Caesaribus*, on the other hand it is also true that the emperor's interest in reading history as referenced by the anonymous author is not directly connected to the victories over Magnus Maximus and Eugenius. If we compare the two situations, we notice an important difference: Pacatus evoked the *libertas* and the leaders of the civil war to celebrate the Roman triumph of the emperor, while the author of the *Epitome* limited his use of these motifs to highlight Theodosius' interest in history and his contempt for the enemies of *libertas*. How can we evaluate the significance of these perspectives, given that they belong to two different genres, historical and panegyrical? If, as most scholars assume, the anonymous author of the *Epitome de Caesaribus* knew Nicomachus Flavianus' *Annales*, and even used it in his abridgment,[37]

---

[35] For example Symmachus *Or.* 1.8.9 and 16, also *Or.* 4.2.4–6 (see also below, notes 36 and 51). Cf. Sogno 2006:8–21.

[36] Symmachus *Rel.* 4.3: *Inritamentum superbiae Roma Vestra non patitur memor scilicet bonorum parentum quos Tarquinius fastus et ipsius Camilli currus offendit. Nam tanto illi uiro albentes quadrigae exilium triste pepererunt. At contra Publicolae decus tribuit inclinatio potestatis; submisit enim contioni ciuium consularem securem et honoris sui culmen infregit, ut libertatem ciuitatis erigeret. Ergo moribus potius quam insignibus aestimemur. Non culpamus nouum beneficium, sed bona nostra praeferimus* (Callu 2009). To the same subject is dedicated *Relatio* 20 (cf. Sogno 2006:44–45); cf. also Claud. *IV cons. Hon.* 309–311.

[37] The question is discussed in Schlumberger 1974 and Festy 1999:xv–xx, xxvii–xxxv.

then were the *Annales* imbued with the same motifs?[38] We shall return to this question.

In his edition of *Epitome de Caesaribus* Festy remarks that: "Après sa victoire sur Maxime en 388, Théodose établit une distinction entre la guerre civile qu'il a entreprise contre lui et celles de la période républicaine, qu'il juge criminelles." He also points out that the same judgment appears in the eulogy of Theodosius made by Augustine,[39] who years later would refer to the same motif and probably a common source to celebrate Theodosius in the conclusion of Book 5 of *De ciuitate Dei*: *Bella ciuilia non sicut Cinna et Marius et Sulla et alii tales nec finita finire uoluerunt, sed magis doluit exorta quam cuiquam nocere uoluit terminata* ("Unlike Cinna, Marius, Sulla, and others who fought civil wars and kept up a battle of hate even after the heat of battle was over, Theodosius always began his wars with reluctance, and never ended them with rancor").[40] Augustine already discussed these examples in Book 3, referring to the atrocities of the sack of Alaric and reflecting on the history of Rome, and also discussing Cicero and Lucan.[41] In Book 5 Augustine widely uses examples from the Roman republic, including Tarquin the Proud and Julius Caesar, accusing the latter of compromising *libertas* on account of his own vanity.[42] He introduces the vicissitudes of Gratian's death and of the usurpation of Maximus, and he does not omit the examples of Pompey and Cato, recalling once more the civil wars.[43] Despite some similarities, Augustine's eulogy does not appear

---

[38] That could explain the influences on the anonymous author from the panegyrical literature. However, Festy (1997 and 1999:xxxv–xxxvi) suggests that the influence on the anonymous author of Flavianus' *Annales* did not concern Theodosius' eulogy of *Epit. de Caes.* 48.

[39] Cf. Festy 1999:234.

[40] Aug. *De civ. D.* 5.26 (Dombart and Kalb 1955); trans. Zema and Walsh 1950:300.

[41] Aug. *De civ. D.* 3.27–30.

[42] Aug. *De civ. D.* 5.12 passim.

[43] Aug. *De civ. D.* 5.25: *Gratianum ferro tyrannico permisit* [sc. *Deus*] *interimi, longe quidem mitius quam magnum Pompeium colentem uelut Romanos deos. Nam ille uindicari a Catone non potuit, quem ciuilis belli quondam modo heredem reliquerat; iste* [sc. *Gratianus*] *autem ... a Theodosius uindicatus est, quem regni participem fecerat.* Cato and Pompey are also mentioned by Pacatus in *Pan. Lat.* 12.46.1–2, quoted above. In any case, authors like Claudian and Augustine did not use the eulogies of Flavianus to Theodosius, because at that time Flavianus' work was banned.

to use either Pacatus or the author of the *Epitome* as direct sources. In *De civ. D.* 5.26 Augustine used different sources of imperial propaganda, both pagan and Christian, including some lines of Claudian's panegyric for Honorius' third consulship.[44] His main source of Theodosius' eulogy is Rufinus' account, as Duval has demonstrated.[45] However, unlike Augustine, Rufinus' description of the historical events does not include any reference to the republic, and his account lacks completely the propaganda of *libertas*.[46] The same can be said for Orosius' description of Theodosius' war against Maximus, in which the question of the civil wars of the Christian emperors is discussed without reference to the republic.[47] Like Rufinus and Orosius, Augustine too was interested in celebrating the victory of Christianity; nevertheless, in the *City of God* he took a broader view of the events of Roman history, also considering panegyrical sources in order to celebrate the emperor's victory against paganism. It is clear that, despite the similarities in the motifs, Augustine's treatment of Theodosius is unlike those of Pacatus and the anonymous author of the *Epitome*.

Augustine emphasized that Theodosius never provoked wars, unless situations obliged him to intervene. This characterization is also found in the *Epitome de Caesaribus* as a part of the comparison of Theodosius with Trajan that, as we have seen, postdated the year 389: unlike Trajan, Theodosius was not eager for triumphs and war, but he was confronted with them during his rule.[48] Claudian too made refer-

---

[44] Aug. *De civ. D.* 5.25: *Vnde et poeta Claudianus, quamuis a Christi nomine alienus, in eius tamen laudibus dixit: O nimium dilecte Deo, cui militat aether.*

[45] Duval 1966.

[46] Rufin. *HE* 11.14–17, which ends with Theodosius' triumph in Rome. The reference to Theodosius in *HE* 11.19 is also interesting (*PL* 21): *accessu facilis et absque imperiali fastu ad colloquium se humilibus praebere* (cf. *Epit. de Caes.* 48.18: *miscere colloquia pro personis, studia dignitatibus, sermone cum grauitate iocundo*). The expression *absque imperiali fastu* can be compared with the behavior of the emperor in Rome as described by Claudian (see below, note 56).

[47] Oros. *Adv. pag.* 7.35.6–9 (Arnaud-Lindet 1991): *Ecce regibus et temporibus Christianis qualiter bella ciuilia, cum uitari nequeunt, transiguntur: ad uictoriam peruentum est, inrupta est ciuitas, correptus tyrannus ... Formidulosissimum bellum sine sanguine usque ad uictoriam.*

[48] *Epit. de Caes.* 48.10: *Illa tamen quibus Traianus aspersus est, uiolentiam scilicet et cupidinem triumphandi, usque eo detestatus ut bella non mouerit, sed inuenerit*, on which see Festy 1999:233.

ence to the comparison with Trajan in the above-mentioned pane-gyric of 398: from beyond the grave, Theodosius praised Trajan as an example worthy of imitation, more on account of his excellent qualities as a statesman than his success as a conqueror. He also admonished his son Honorius not to repeat the mistakes of Tarquin, of Caesar (thereby raising the question of Roman *libertas*), and of Julio-Claudian emperors like Tiberius, whose cruelty was immortalized in the *annales ueterum* that "tell the ill deeds" (*delicta loquuntur*) of the ancestors (Eutr. 2.311). Although we do not know his sources, Claudian's polemical attitude in the following passage brings to mind Tacitus, who criticized the Julio-Claudian age and eulogized Trajan's new era:

> Thou must govern Romans who have long governed the world, Romans who brooked not Tarquin's pride nor Caesar's tyranny. History still tells of our ancestors' ill deeds; the stain will never be wiped away. So long as the world lasts the monstrous excesses of the Julian house will stand condemned. Will any not have heard of Nero's murders or how Capri's foul cliffs were owned by an aged lecher? The fame of Trajan will never die, not so much because, thanks to his victories on the Tigris, conquered Parthia became a Roman province, not because he broke the might of Dacia and led their chiefs in triumph up the slope of the Capitol, but because he was kindly to his country. Fail not to make such as he thine example, my son.[49]

Nor was Theodosius' propaganda of *libertas* limited to the events of the late republic, but included criticism of those rulers who had not been able to establish political concord with the Roman senate. This motif appears in the passage from the *Epitome de Caesaribus* discussed above (*exsecrari ... uniuersos dominantium, praecipue tamen perfidos et ingratos*). It can also be detected in Pacatus' comparison of Theodosius

---

[49] Claud. *IV cons. Hon.* 323–334 (trans. Platnauer 1922): it is significant that this admonition follows the critique against Tarquin and Caesar (see above, in text). Cf. also Claud. *In Eutr.* 2.61–69.

and Brutus, the first consul, in the statement that it was not necessary
to have abolished the monarchy.[50] The image of the emperor is that of
an advocate of peace.

II.2 *Libertas* and *Adventus Principis*

We find another important key for understanding Theodosius' attitude
toward the civil war in the panegyrists' descriptions of his *aduentus* in
389. In the fourth century, the *aduentus principis* was the best (if not
practically the only) occasion for a ruler to visit Rome and to meet the
members of the senate in person. In February 369, Symmachus traveled to Trier to read his panegyric to Valentinian I, with which he probably wanted to convince the emperor to come to Rome and celebrate
his triumphs for the victories achieved on the frontier.[51] This attempt,
which was intended to benefit the senate, failed, and the last emperor
before Theodosius to honor Rome with a visit was in fact Constantius
II, who more than thirty years earlier, in 357, had celebrated his victory
over the usurper Magnentius in the old capital. Constantius II's *aduentus*
is described thoroughly by Ammianus Marcellinus, who pointed out
that the emperor was impressed by the old and monumental city of
Rome. However Ammianus, in his distaste for Constantius II, also criticized the *aduentus*, denouncing the triumph as pompous and unjusti-
fied because it celebrated a victory in civil war, in which only Roman
blood had been shed:

> Constantius, as if the temple of Janus had been closed
> and all his enemies overthrown, was eager to visit Rome
> and after the death of Magnentius to celebrate, without
> a title, a triumph over Roman blood (*absque nomine ex*

[50] *Pan. Lat.* 12.20.6, quoted above.
[51] Symmachus *Or.* 1.16–18, with reference to Scipio Africanus, Lucullus, and Antonius
as *triumfales uiri, delicatis negotiis frequentibus occupati, amoena litorum terrarumque opima
sectantes*, also to Augustus, Tiberius, Antoninus Pius, and Marcus Aurelius (*proximae
aetatis exempla*), to conclude: *Tibi nullae sunt feriae proeliorum ... Tibi nullas necessitas remittit
indutias ... Lustrum imperialium iam condis annorum ubi caelo et terris horror aequalis est, sub
crassa nube iugi frigore, feroci hoste, latissima uastitate. Quietem tibi negas quam ceteris praestas.
Inter tot milia laurearum nondum digrederis ad triumfum et, cum sis maior Augusto, delegisti tibi
prouinciam de qua Caesares querebantur.*

sanguine Romano triumphaturus). For neither in person did
he vanquish any nation that made war upon him, nor learn
of any conquered by the valour of his generals; nor did he
add anything to his empire; nor at critical moments was he
ever seen to be foremost, or among the foremost.[52]

Of course, it is methodologically problematic to compare an account
of an historian hostile to an emperor with the work of panegyrists, and
public inscriptions testify that both Constantius II and Theodosius were
officially celebrated in Rome as *exstinctores tyrannorum*.[53] Nevertheless,
if we analyze parallel elements of Ammianus, Pacatus, and Claudian,
the contours of Theodosius' propaganda concerning his triumph in a
civil war become clearer. According to Ammianus, Constantius II had
come to Rome with the desire "to display an inordinately long procession, banners stiff with gold-work, and the splendor of his retinue, to
a populace living in perfect peace and neither expecting nor desiring
to see this or anything like it." He had not been able to distinguish
his victory in a civil war from the one against an enemy, and he had
ignored the past and also the traditions of Rome: "perhaps he did not
know that some of our ancient commanders in time of peace were
satisfied with the attendance of their lictors, but when the heat of
battle could tolerate no inaction ... various among them became famous
through splendid deeds, so that they commended their glories to the
frequent remembrance of posterity."[54] Although some senators may
have disliked the emperor's behavior in Rome, it is still important to
note that both Pacatus and Claudian eulogize Theodosius by using the
same motifs, which are in direct contrast with Constantius II's conduct
as described in Ammianus' account.

According to Pacatus, Theodosius during the *aduentus* presented
himself to the people as a prince in the traditional manner, but to
the senators he showed himself as an equal, mingling with them and

[52] Amm. Marc. 16.10.1-2 (for the whole event 16.10.1-17), trans. Rolfe 1935.
[53] Cf. esp. Dessau, *ILS* 731 (Constantius II); *CIL* 6.3791A-B, 36959, respectively dedicated to Valentinian II, to Theodosius, and to Arcadius as *exstinctori tyrannorum ac publicae
securitati⟨s⟩ auctori.*
[54] Amm. Marc. 16.10.2-3 (trans. Rolfe 1935).

visiting their houses.[55] And even if we cannot imagine Theodosius freely walking through Rome without any bodyguards (*remota custodia militari*), Claudian would remark some years later upon this, reminding Honorius that his father behaved as a *ciuis* during the visit to Rome, like the *meliora exempla* of the past.[56] Clearly, even apart from the testimony of the panegyrists, Theodosius likely knew of recent events and of Constantius II's behavior in Rome; and, as a connoisseur of history, he was aware of the risk a Roman triumph in a civil war represented, and of how historically dangerous this association was. Therefore, he did not ignore the traditional values of the Roman world and the *exempla maiorum*, and he did not commit the "sins" of arrogance and pomposity. Rather he visited the houses of the senators as a *ciuis* and with humility,[57] and he showed mercy to the senators who had supported his enemies. This *clementia* was an expression of what has been called "Theodosius' encouragement of Roman senators,"[58] which also included appointments to prestigious political positions of some elite pagans, such as Aurelius Victor and Symmachus.

Theodosius' efforts to forge an alliance with the pagan aristocracy of Rome is clear. "Er übt die Tugend der *civilitas*, der bürgerlichen Normalität, er ist einer 'von uns,'" writes Leppin, who also declares, "Theodosius wurde auf diese Weise kulturell in die Welt der Senatoren aufgenommen."[59] Bleckmann had the same impression, explaining the historical elements in the panegyric of Pacatus as well as the description

---

[55] Pacatus *Pan. Lat.* 12.47.3: *ut pompam praeeuntium ferculorum curru modo, modo pedibus subsecutus alterno clarus incessu nunc de bellis, nunc de superbia triumpharis; ut te omnibus principem, singulis exhibueris senatorem; ut crebro ciuilique progressu non publica tantum opera lustraueris sed priuatas quoque aedes diuinis uestigiis consecraris, remota custodia militari tutior publici amoris excubiis.* On Trajan's entrance and conduct in Rome, cf. Plin. *Pan.* 22–24.

[56] Claud. *VI cons. Hon.* 58–62: *cum se melioribus addens / exemplis ciuem gereret terrore remoto, / alternos cum plebe iocos dilectaque passus / iurgia patriciasque domos priuataque passim / uisere deposito dignatus limina fastu* (generic is Amm. Marc. 16.10.13, in which Constantius II *dicacitate plebis oblectabatur*), also 543–561, with the praise of Honorius as *ciuis* in comparison to the previous tyrants (*hunc ciuem, dominos uenisse priores*). Cf. Cameron 1970:382–389; Ernesti 1998:395–396.

[57] Cf. *Pan. Lat.* 12.47.3 and Claud. *VI cons. Hon.* 55–65, quoted in part at notes 55 and 56.

[58] Errington 2006:135–138, quoting 138. For the political picture, cf. Matthews 1975:227–238; Leppin 2003:135–167; Sogno 2006:68–71.

[59] Leppin 2003:145 and 147.

of the emperor's *aduentus* as "daß Theodosius bereit war, in der Rolle eines *princeps* alten Stils den Vorstellungen der Senatoren, deren Häuser er als Zeichen seiner *civilitas* besuchte, entgegenzukommen."[60] In this way pagan senators, including those pardoned (like Symmachus),[61] had enough reasons to accept Theodosius in their cultural world. They also had reason to celebrate Theodosius as an *exemplum* and his Roman triumph as a victory over a tyrant who had strong similarities to the vicious leaders of the late republic, leaders who, according to Pacatus and the author of the *Epitome*, the emperor despised for fomenting the civil wars and irreparably damaging the *res publica*. Theodosius was presented as being above the political factions, not a part of them; he gave back to the suffering *res publica* the long expected *libertas*, and therefore he deserved the triumph: "you [Rome] have seen a civil war ended with … your liberation (*tua libertate*); you have seen … a civil war ended for which you can decree a triumph," declaimed Pacatus (above).

These motifs were particularly appealing to the senate, which was still smarting from Constantius II's treatment during his Roman sojourn. Constantius had ordered the altar of Victory removed from the senate-house, a symbolic act that inflamed the senate and that had long-lasting repercussions.[62] Ammianus did not mention this event, about which he surely knew—on the contrary, he recorded that Constantius presented Rome with a gigantic obelisk![63]—nor did he note the fact that the altar was later returned to the senate-house, before finally being removed by Gratian. After all, this was a particularly delicate matter. The issue had been brought to the attention of the emperor Valentinian II just a

[60] Bleckmann 1995:96. On these events, cf. Leppin 2003:143–146; Errington 2006:133–141.

[61] Theodosius spared Symmachus, who had hidden in a church (Socr. *HE* 5.14.3–9). Cf. Pacatus *Pan. Lat.* 12.45.6–7: "The property of none was confiscated, no one's liberty was forfeited, no one's previous rank diminished. No one was branded with censure, no one subjected to abuse, or indeed reproof … All were restored to their homes, all to their wives and children, all finally … to innocence. See, Emperor, what the consequences of this clemency are for you: you have so managed things that no one feels that he has been conquered by you, the victor" (Nixon and Rodgers 1994:513). See also Aug. *De civ. D.* 5.26.

[62] Symmachus *Rel.* 3.4–8. On the question, see more recently Lassandro 2007:232; Lizzi Testa 2007.

[63] Amm. Marc. 16.10.17 and 17.4.

few years earlier by Symmachus in the famous *Relatio* 3, in which, in his effort to have the altar returned, he had even emphasized Constantius II's positive attitude toward the Roman tradition during his *aduentus*.[64] Ammianus' omission therefore is not surprising, especially because part of his work was publically recited.[65] It is very likely that Constantius II's *aduentus* was a favorite subject of the Roman audience because it was such an important and recent event, and one that caught general attention. We do not know whether and to what extent Ammianus' description of Constantius II's *aduentus* carried an implicit comparison with the recent visit of Theodosius in Rome, though we have reason to suspect that it did.[66] However, it is interesting that Theodosius' *aduentus* took place around the time Ammianus was publishing or at least publically reciting his historical work. Nicomachus Flavianus, whose possible relationship with Ammianus (through the so-called "circle" of Symmachus) has been the object of speculation by scholars,[67] was also involved in this event (cf. Section III).

II.3 Contemplating the Past:
Adulatio, "*Principatus et Libertas*"

An important question is whether, and in what form, the common elements in the authors discussed above appeared elsewhere in pagan literature of those years, and whether, to the more conservative Roman circles nostalgic for *libertas*, such propaganda gave hopes for a freedom of expression, of thought, and therefore of religion. A good example is the case of Symmachus, who had supported the side of Maximus, but

---

[64] Symmachus *Rel.* 3.7: *Accipiat Aeternitas Vestra alia eiusdem Principis facta quae in usum dignius trahat. Nihil ille decerpsit sacrarum uirginum priuilegiis, repleuit nobilibus sacerdotia. Romanis caerimoniis non negauit inpensas et per omnes uias Aeternae Vrbis laetum secutus Senatum uidit placido ore delubra, legit inscripta fastigiis deum nomina, percontatus templorum origines est, miratus est conditores, cumque alias religiones ipse sequeretur, has seruauit imperio.* Cf. Vera 1981:31–38, part. 35–36.

[65] Lib. *Epist.* 1063, of the year 392. Cf. Matthews 1975:228.

[66] For the possibile influence of Pacatus on Ammianus' description of Constantius' *aduentus*, cf. Sabbah 1978:327–332. Matthews 1989:11–12 does not deny the impact of Theodosius' visit on Ammianus' account and on its public recitation; see also Lunn-Rockliffe 2010:332–336.

[67] For the question, cf. Cameron 2011:362, who opposes this view.

whom Theodosius had pardoned during his *aduentus* in Rome. He would be appointed to the consulship for the year 391, when he also traveled to the court to beg the emperor through a panegyric to relocate the altar of Victory in the senate-house.[68] On that occasion, his close friend Nicomachus Flavianus was serving at the palace as praetorian prefect. Scholars generally date the publication and dedication of Flavianus' *Annales* to the time between the Roman sojourn of Theodosius and the following two years, during which Nicomachus Flavianus was at the imperial court.[69] While the chronological end of the work is unknown, it is likely that in his dedication Flavianus expressed praise for the emperor, celebrating the imperial propaganda of those years during which his career at the imperial court flourished. And if it is true, as some scholars assume, that Flavianus' *Annales* ended with Gratian's death and therefore with the usurpation of Maximus,[70] then it is possible that a final (or initial) eulogy of Theodosius in this work included the intervention of the emperor and the end of the civil war with the restoration of *libertas*.

It is clear from the inscription *CIL* 6.1783 that Nicomachus Flavianus had already held the quaestorship and was praetorian prefect at Theodosius' court when he dedicated his *Annales* to the emperor. Although the years of his quaestorship (ca. 388–390) are still considered by scholars as a possible starting date of the work, Flavianus dedicated it as praetorian prefect. The wording of the inscription may imply that Flavianus, because of his work, was accused of *adulatio* by Theodosius' entourage. This work had in fact increased the emperor's *beneuolentia* to Flavianus, which had already been demonstrated in his prestigious appointments at the court: "It was the kindness that the emperor showed upon him and tendered even to his *Annales* (he wanted his quaestor and prefect to dedicate to him) which excited the jealousy

---

[68] Prosper *De promissionibus Dei* 3.38.2; cf. Seeck 1883:vi, lvii–lviii; Sogno 2006:72–73.

[69] Cf. above, note 8. Belckmann 1995 does not dismiss the possibility that Flavianus' *Annales* were dedicated to the emperor during his sojourn in Rome.

[70] Cf. Paschoud 1980:158–160; Schlumberger 1985:221–222; Zecchini 1993:57–59, suggests the years 388/89 (the work celebrated Theodosius' victory against Maximus). For the question and the references, cf. Festy 1997:466 and Festy 1999:xvii (with notes 31 and 32), xix.

of scoundrels (*liuorem inproborum*)."[71] It is interesting that the motif of *adulatio* occurs in the most prestigious works of ancient historiography, and especially in connection with *libertas*. Tacitus expressed it in the introductions to the *Historiae* and the *Annales*, referring to the *libertas* lost because of an empire that had compromised the freedom of expression. In fact, already at the time of Augustus (but even more under his successors) the great *ingenia* were replaced by *adulatio*.[72] Considered in this context, Pacatus' words about the freedom of expression in Theodosius' age—which allude to the times of Maximus and maybe to Symmachus' panegyric delivered the year before—are even more significant:

> And indeed what has impelled me to speak is that no one was coercing me to do so (*non enim iam coacta laudatio*). For panegyric is not extorted any more ... Let it be a thing of the past, now done away with, that dire compulsion of a servile rhetoric, when false flattery gratified a harsh tyrant courting every breath of public approbation by empty popularity, when victims would give thanks, and not to have praised the tyrant was considered an accusation of tyranny (*et tyrannum non praedicasse tyrannidis accusatio uocabatur*). Now there is equal freedom to speak or keep silent (*Nunc par dicendi tacendique libertas*) and it is as safe to have said nothing about the leader as it is easy to praise him.[73]

---

[71] *CIL* 6.1783; *cuius in eum effusa beneuolentia et usque ad Annalium quos consecrari sibi a quaestore et praefecto suo uoluit prouecta excitauit liuorem inproborum* trans. Hedrick 2000:2, an exhaustive study of this document.

[72] Besides *Agric.* 2–3, see *Hist.* 1.1–2 (Heubner 1978): *postquam bellatum apud Actium atque omnem potentiam ad unum conferri pacis interfuit, magna illa ingenia cessere; simul ueritas pluribus modis infracta, primum inscitia rei publicae ut alienae, mox libidine adsentandi aut rursus odio aduersus dominantis ... Sed ambitionem scriptoris facile auerseris, obtrectatio et liuor pronis auribus accipiuntur; quipped adulationi foedum crimen seruitutis, malignitati falsa species libertatis inest*; also *Ann.* 1.1 (Jackson 1931): *temporibusque Augusti dicendis non defuere decora ingenia, donec gliscente adulatione deterrerentur. Tiberii Gaique et Claudii ac Neronis res florentibus ipsis ob metum falsae, postquam occiderant, recentibus odiis compositae sunt.* Cf. Plin. *Pan.* 24.1. See also Sussman 1978:142–143n16; Festy 2007:188n13.

[73] *Pan. Lat.* 12.2–4, trans. Nixon and Rodgers 1994:449 with note 5, who also notice: "Symmachus will have been in the audience, and Pacatus' insistence on the element of

Tacitus' work was still an important model for senatorial literature: his negative view of the Julio-Claudian dynasty and of Domitian was also connected with the end of Roman liberty. Tacitus referred to the loss of *libertas Romana* in introducing the *Historiae* and the *Annales*, a work that interestingly begins with the same sequence of events and names found in the panegyrical and historical sources discussed above (Pacatus and the *Epitome de Caesaribus*) with reference to the beginning and to the end of *libertas*: Brutus, the first consul and institutor of *libertas*, Cinna, Sulla, Julius Caesar, and the civil wars that were concluded by Augustus at the price of liberty:

> Vrbem Romam a principio reges habuere; *libertatem* et consulatum *L. Brutus instituit*. Dictaturae ad tempus sumebantur ... Non *Cinnae*, non *Sullae longa dominatio*; et Pompei Crassique potentia cito *in Caesarem*, Lepidi atque Antonii arma *in Augustum cessere*, qui cuncta *discordiis ciuilibus* fessa nomine principis sub imperium accepit.

> Rome at the outset was a city state under the government of kings: liberty and the consulate were institutions of Lucius Brutus. Dictatorships were always a temporary expedient ... Neither Cinna nor Sulla created a lasting despotism: Pompey and Crassus quickly forfeited their power to Caesar, and Lepidus and Antony their swords to Augustus, who, under the style of "Prince," gathered beneath his empire a world outworn by civil broils.[74]

On the other hand, in *Agricola* Tacitus eulogized the contemporary emperors Nerva and Trajan for having been able to mix oil with water, that is, *principatus* with *libertas*: "from the first, from the very outset of this happy age, Nerva has united things long incompatible, the

---

compulsion will have warmed the senator to him." See Lunn-Rockliffe 2010:335. An echo of this motif can be found in Cassiod. *Var.* 9.25.5, with reference to Cassiodorus' activity as panegyrist of the Gothic kings: *Gloriosis quippe dominis gratiora sunt praeconia quam tributa, quia stipendium et tyranno penditur, praedicatio autem nisi bono principi non debetur* (Mommsen 1894).

[74] Tac. *Ann.* 1.1 (trans. Jackson 1931); cf. also *Hist.* 1.1. On the motif of *libertas* in this period, see for example Wirszubski 1950:124–171.

principate and liberty (*res olim dissociabilis miscuerit, principatum ac libertatem*); Trajan is increasing daily the happiness of the time (*augeatque cotidie felicitatem temporum*); and public confidence (*securitas publica*) has not merely learned to hope and pray, but has received assurance of the fulfillment of its prayers and so has gained strength."[75] In previous times (e.g. under Domitian) the panegyrics for Thrasea Paetus and Helvidius Priscus, eulogizers of Cato Uticensis, Brutus, and Cassius during the Julio-Claudian dynasty, had been forbidden and burned, and the voice of the senate and people of Rome had been repressed together with freedom of expression. Masters of philosophy had been expelled from Rome, and the senate had known servitude and repression.[76] But under the reigns of Nerva and Trajan, Tacitus saw a return to better times, and *Agricola* became probably one of Pliny's models in the panegyric to Trajan, which showed hostility toward Domitian and in which we read the interesting expression *eodem foro utuntur principatus et libertas.*[77]

This utopic association between republican *libertas* and Trajan's civility was particularly beloved in senatorial circles, and centuries later it was still well suited for praising the good emperor. Symmachus used this combination *principatus–libertas* in 376 to thank Gratian for granting the consulship to his father: "the principate (*principatus*) grew, because you rule over free people (*liberis*). It unites as much with offices as with laws."[78] The same motif is repeated in another oration referring to the emperor's support of senatorial decisions, in which the author expresses the distinction between prince (*primus*) and dominus (*solus*): "In fact he keeps free the state (*rem publicam liberam*), under which the power of the senate has something enviable. Therefore you are great, you are famous, because you prefer to be first (*primum*)

---

[75] *Agr.* 2–3, quoted 3.1 (trans. Hutton 1970).

[76] *Agr.* 3.

[77] *Pan.* 36.4 (Radice 1969); cf. also 66.2 and 4: *nunc singulos, nunc uniuersos adhortatus es resumere libertatem, capessere quasi communi imperii curas ... Te uero securi et alacres, quo uocas, sequimur. Iubes esse liberos: erimus.* For Pliny's use of Tacitus and vice versa, cf. Bruère 1954.

[78] Symmachus *Or.* 4.13: *creuit principatus, quia liberis imperatis. Tantum potestatibus quantum legibus licet*; cf. also *Or.* 4.5: *Quam raro huic rei publicae, patres conscripti, tales principes contigerunt, qui idem uellent, idem statuerent quod senatus!* On the use of Pliny to celebrate Gratian's *nouum saeculum*, cf. recently Kelly 2013:274–286.

rather than only (*solum*). Whatever good men receive, this profits your age."[79] Symmachus' expression of the old values and the Trajanic "freedom" that the senate was experiencing perfectly suited a ruler like Theodosius, who claimed to restore the *res publica* from the usurpation of a tyrant, while at the same time boasting to be a descendant of Trajan.

This ensemble of motifs (including the *annales ueterum* that Claudian evoked in the above-quoted words of Theodosius to Honorius, with specific reference to the scandals of the Julio-Claudian family) could suggest that Theodosius may have read authors like Pliny the Younger and Tacitus.[80] And if Ammianus' work, which was also published in those years, continued that of Tacitus, it is possible that Tacitus was also one of the models of Flavianus (independently from the literary nature of the *Annales* and from the exact title of his work); and maybe Hartke was not far from the truth when he imagined his style as "sallustisch—also taciteisch gefärbt."[81] Perhaps the above-noticed similarities in historical examples between the beginning of Tacitus' *Annales* and the eulogy of Theodosius' interest in history (including the comparison Theodosius–Augustus in *Epit. de Caes.* 48.16–17, on which see Section IV) are more than coincidental. Could then Flavianus' *Annales* provide the connection, particularly since this work was probably intended to celebrate Theodosius as a restorer of *libertas* and new ruler over the West?

To summarize, a series of elements connects the work of the anonymous author of the *Epitome*, Pacatus, and Claudian, all texts that are connected to Theodosius' propaganda of 389 to justify the triumph after the civil war: namely, the respect Theodosius showed to Rome as a *ciuis* friendly to the senators, and the motif of *libertas* in connection with criticism of the leaders of the late republic and of bad emperors. This ideology, as used by the authors, promoted the relationships of the emperor with members of the senate and, although based on the

---

[79] Symmachus *Or.* 5.3: *Is enim rem publicam liberam tenet, sub quo aliquid inuidendum ⟨in⟩ potestatem senatus. Ideo magnus, ideo praeclarus es, quia primum te mauis esse quam solum. Quicquid adipiscuntur boni saeculo tuo proficit.*

[80] On Theodosius' interests in reading classic authors, see his letter to Ausonius as in notes 2 and 102.

[81] Hartke 1951:401.

ancient values of pagan Rome, it was persuasive enough to influence the eulogy of Theodosius made years later by a Christian intellectual like Augustine. The similarities between Pacatus and the anonymous author of the *Epitome* reveal the effort of some Roman senators close to Theodosius to celebrate in those years 389–391 the emperor who loved history and who was building his propaganda as ruler over the West by using the motifs of *libertas* and of a return of peace after the civil war. At this point we have reason enough to reject the perspective of Schlumberger, who attributes the evidence of Theodosius' interest in the history of the republic solely to the traditional rhetoric of the *exempla uirtutum et uitiorum*.[82] While rhetorical devices no doubt shaped the author's choices among the texts, the use of these motifs was clearly deliberate, and the connections between the texts are significant.

These explorations in *Quellenforschung* lead to the same impression: senators close to Theodosius used traditional motifs including *exempla maiorum*, *libertas Romana*, the end of the civil war, and the restoration of peace in their celebration of the emperor's victory over Maximus in the troubled years 388–391. In this period Theodosius was consolidating his rule over the West, and these associations (as well as associations with Augustus and Trajan that we shall discuss in Section IV) probably suited his political purposes. It is significant that Flavianus' historical work was presumably published in that brief span of time that separated the work of Pacatus (389) from Ammianus (ca. 392–395), Claudian (398), the *Epitome de Caesaribus* (ca. 400), and also from Symmachus' two lost panegyrics to Theodosius (388 and 391). The emperor who loved history and who commissioned a high senator to write *Annales* could not ignore the long tradition of *libertas Romana*.

III. THE LAST HOPE OF *LIBERTAS ROMANA*?

Theodosius' interest in history and Nicomachus Flavianus' activity at the court seem interconnected, beginning with the emperor's victory over Maximus and developing during his *aduentus* and sojourn in Rome,

---

[82] Schlumberger 1985:326–327 (see above, note 19).

which occasion allowed the emperor to come in contact with many senators and to publically celebrate *libertas* and the end of the civil war. These motifs, as we have seen, represent the most significant connection between the panegyrists Pacatus and Claudian, the anonymous author of the *Epitome*, and very likely Symmachus as well. The elements that united these authors between 388–389 and ca. 400 belonged to a program of propaganda at court that was supported by Roman senatorial circles and that represented Theodosius as a humble *ciuis*, merciful to former supporters of his enemies (one of whom was Symmachus).

If the beginning of the redaction of Flavianus' *Annales* can be placed in the years 388–389, and its publication some time before summer 391 (Theodosius' return to the East), then it is easy to believe that the motif of *libertas Romana* in those same years could have been used to celebrate Theodosius not only by Pacatus and by Symmachus in his panegyrics but also by Flavianus *adulator* in his historical work dedicated to the emperor. It seems likely that Flavianus supported this senatorial view during his intensive political activity. A close look at his career shows us that for the full period 388–391, when he presumably wrote the *Annales*, he was constantly at the side of Theodosius, first as quaestor and then as praetorian prefect. He was with the emperor in Milan (October 388–May 389), then in Rome (June–September 389), and again in Milan (November 389–June 390), the places from which he issued the thirty-eight laws from the *Theodosian Code* attributed to him as quaestor.[83] Not by coincidence, the first law of his quaestorship concerns the condemnation of the acts of the tyrant Maximus.[84] Soon after this quaestorship, he was appointed praetorian prefect for the years 390–392. If we accept this sequence of events, then Pacatus read his panegyric for Theodosius while the quaestor Flavianus was with Theodosius in Rome and working on his *Annales*. It would be interesting to determine the relationship between Flavianus and Pacatus at that time, since it is probable that

[83] Cf. the study of Honoré 1998b:58–70, part. 63–65 on the praetorian prefecture. Cf. also PLRE 1:347–349; Honoré 1989; Errington 1992; Matthews 1997; Honoré 1998a; Leppin 2003:137; Matthews 2006:138–139; Cameron 2011:631–632.

[84] October 10, 388. *C.Th.* 15.14.7 (Mommsen 1905): *Omne iudicium, quod uafra mente conceptum iniuriam non iura reddendo Maximo infandissimus tyrannorum credidit promulgandum, damnabimus*; cf. Honoré 1998b:59.

they met in Rome during Theodosius' sojourn; the possibility should not be dismissed, particularly considering that Pacatus was in touch with Symmachus at least since the year 390, as Symmachus' letters to him testify.[85] At that time, Pacatus was proconsul in Africa, while Nicomachus Flavianus held the praetorian prefecture of Italy. Pacatus' emphasis on the events of the republic does not necessarily reveal the contents of Flavianus' work, and the panegyric predates the publication of the *Annales*. Nevertheless, the hypothesis that the history of the late republic was included in the *Annales* should be considered, since authors such as Livy were models of the Symmachi and Nicomachi in their nostalgic view of the past.[86] If this is the case, then we can assume that Nicomachus Flavianus' account of the late republic was probably brief and limited to the exemplary figures, in the style of the fourth-century epitomes, rather than a narrative history. This becomes even more significant if—as I believe—the reference in *Epit. de Caes.* 48.11–12 that describes Theodosius as a reader of the *exempla maiorum* is related to the propaganda of the years 388–391, the period in which the *Annales* were published.

At this point we have reasons enough to believe that the image of Theodosius as the one who concluded the civil war and restored *libertas* was not limited to Pacatus' panegyric but, as the *Epitome de Caesaribus* leads us to suspect, was welcomed by Symmachus in his two panegyrics and by Nicomachus Flavianus in his *Annales*.[87] It was probably from the pen of senators of this caliber (who were related and who both benefited from the emperor's *beneuolentia*) that arose the representation of Theodosius with those traditional motifs we have considered, in a magnetic as well as utopic combination of republican *libertas* and Trajanic civility. Symmachus was probably around 391 the first in the

[85] Symmachus *Epist.* 9.61 and 64 (ca. 390), also 8.12 (after 397?); cf. Matthews 1971:1078–1082; PLRE 1:272; Roda 1981:194–197; Sogno 2006:68–69; Cameron 2011:227–230.

[86] Cameron 2011: 498–526 is the latest of several scholars to discuss the pagan literary revival, which included the edition by the Symmachi and Nicomachi of Livy's monumental work (the "Livian revival").

[87] These authors would be celebrated by their descendants respectively as *orator disertissimus* and *historicus disertissimus*; respectively, *CIL* 6.1699 (= Dessau, *ILS* 2946) for Symmachus and *CIL* 6.1782 (= Dessau, *ILS* 2947) for Flavianus.

West to celebrate the assimilation of Theodosius with Trajan—already established in the East—that circulated in western senatorial literature only after Theodosius became the real ruler of the *pars Occidentis*.[88] In the same period Flavianus may have eulogized the emperor's new era of peace in the same traditional way authors like Tacitus had done with reference to Nerva and Trajan. In their eulogies and historical accounts, both Symmachus and Flavianus may have invoked the motif of *libertas*, which at that time was particularly beloved by the elite of the pagan Roman aristocracy, who tried to improve their relationships with the emperor in order to have the altar of Victory returned to their senate-house and who probably also attempted to convince the emperor to adopt a milder attitude toward paganism. But these hopes would prove to be no more than illusions. If thirty years earlier Julian (who, with his Persian campaigns in the footsteps of Alexander and his talent as emperor, compared himself to Trajan)[89] could be celebrated as *philosophiae magister, propagator libertatis et rei publicae*, and as *restitutor libertatis et Romanae religionis*,[90] the same formula was now not entirely applicable to Theodosius. His views on paganism never wavered, and he continued to restrict the rights of pagans. The panegyric that Symmachus delivered before the emperor to thank him for his consulship at the beginning of the year 391, and that accompanied the senate's petition to have the altar returned, was unsuccessful. On February 24 of the same year Theodosius prohibited sacrifices and the worship of idols, and also worship in temples (Mommsen 1905: 16.10.10).[91] The

---

[88] Cf. above, note 12. Festy 1997; Festy 1999:xxxvii, who with convincing arguments excludes the oration of 388 and suggests that of 391. He also explains the lack of circulation in the West of this assimilation when Gratian was still ruling on the basis of the deteriorated relationship between the two emperors. Gratian in fact probably did not recognize Arcadius' nomination by Theodosius in January 19, 383 (as from the coins issued).

[89] Julian's admiration for Trajan is clear from Ammianus, who on several occasions compares the two emperors: cf. Amm. Marc. 16.1.4; 23.5.17; 24.3.9. Cf. also Julian's words about Trajan and the assimilation with Alexander the Great, in *Caes.* 327B–328B, 335D. It is very likely that the emperor himself encouraged this assimilation.

[90] *CIL* 3.7088 and 8.4326, quoted above.

[91] This law is addressed to the urban prefect of Rome. Together with *C.Th.* 16.10.11 (Mommsen 1905) this is the only law against pagans Theodosius addressed before returning to Constantinople.

praetorian prefect Nicomachus Flavianus had no choice but to support this program. Only one year later, the death of Valentinian II and the usurpation of Eugenius, together with the cryptic *liuor inproborum* of *CIL* 6.1783, drove Flavianus to change his position and eventually to support Eugenius as a new rival against Theodosius, persecutor of paganism. The subsequent events are well known.[92] Unlike Symmachus, who as a former supporter of Maximus had been forgiven by the emperor a few years earlier, Flavianus had little hope for *clementia*, and the understanding between the "last pagans" of Rome and the emperor were irreparably compromised. Flavianus' choice to commit suicide probably appeared to him the only solution to save the good name of his family.[93]

IV. THEODOSIUS, AUGUSTUS, AND SENATORIAL LIBERTY

Despite the similarities in motifs and wording between some sections of Pacatus' panegyric declaiming the *libertas* of Theodosius and the anonymous author of the *Epitome de Caesaribus* celebrating Theodosius' interests in history, for the anonymous author (unlike Pacatus), whose work focused entirely on the empire, it was surely uncomfortable to include Julius Caesar among the bad leaders of the late republic. Because of his significance to the empire and his relationship with Augustus and the imperial power, reference to Caesar as the assassin of Roman liberty through the civil war was inconvenient. Emperor Julian offers instead a different view in his parody of the *Caesares*, in which he critiques (through Constantine's mouth) Caesar and Octavian for

---

[92] Reference to these events and to Theodosius' religious policy in Rome and Italy can be found in Matthews 1975:238–252; Leppin 2003:169–187, 201–220; Errington 2006:237–245; Sogno 2006:71–85; Cameron 2011:56–131.

[93] On Nicomachus' properties, which were given back to his offspring probably by Honorius, cf. Seeck 1883:lxxi, cxix, clxii; cf. also PLRE 1:345–347. See Symmachus *Epist.* 4.19.1 (Callu 1982): *Flauianus uir inl. commune pignus diu eluctatus fortunae aspera, sed diui principis beneficio in tranquillum reductus, soluere salarium patris iussus est*; and *Epist.* 4.51.1 (both dated to 395); also *Epist.* 6.12, of the year 396. Theodosius' mercy toward the defeated and their offspring is eulogized by Aug. *De civ. D.* 5.26: *Inimicorum suorum filios, quos, non ipsius iussu, belli abstulerat impetus ... Christianos hac occasione fieri uoluit et christiana caritate dilexit, nec priuauit rebus et auxit honoribus.*

having led a revolution against good citizens, while Trajan, his model, was successful for his victories against the barbarians.[94] In this context, it is interesting to note that the only other mention of the word *libertas* in the *Epitome* refers to Augustus. Although he was well eulogized, his reign, which ended gloriously, started in a questionable way:

> Nam et in adipiscendo principatu *oppressor libertatis* est habitus, et in gerendo *ciues sic amauit* ut, tridui frumento in horreis quondam uiso, statuisset ueneno mori si e prouinciis classes interea non uenirent; *quibus aduectis felicitati eius salus patriae est attributa* ... Qui certe numquam aut rei publicae ad se potentiam traxisset, aut tamdiu ea potiretur, nisi magnis naturae et studiorum bonis abundasset.

> For in pursuing the principate he was held an oppressor of liberty and in ruling he so loved the citizens that once, when a three-day supply of grain was discerned in the storehouses, he would have chosen to die by poison if fleets from the provinces were not arriving in the interim. When these fleets had arrived, the safety of the fatherland was attributed to his felicity ... Certainly he never would have drawn the power of the state to himself or retained it so long if he had not possessed in abundance great gifts of nature and of conscious efforts.[95]

This motif essentially puts Augustus on much the same level as the other leaders of the late republic, whom Theodosius despised for their crimes against *libertas* (*Epit. de Caes.* 48.12). A similar sentiment is found

[94] *Caes.* 329B–C (Constantine's words): "In the following respects I am superior to these others; to the Macedonian in having fought against Romans, Germans, and Scythians, instead of Asiatic barbarians; *to Caesar and Octavian in that I did not, like them, lead a revolution against brave and good citizens*, but attacked only the most cruel and wicked tyrants. As for Trajan, I should naturally rank higher on account of those same glorious exploits against the tyrants, while *it would be only fair to regard me as his equal on the score of that territory which he added to the empire, and I recovered*; if indeed it be not more glorious to regain than to gain" (trans. Wright 1913).

[95] *Epit. de Caes.* 1.29–31 (trans. Banchich 2009). In *Pan. Lat.* 12.11.6 Pacatus describes Rome as decorated by Augustus' *mores*.

at Tacitus' *Annales* 1.1 (*cuncta discordiis ciuilibus fessa nomine principis sub imperium accepit* [sc. *Augustus*]). Of course there is a sharp contrast with Augustus' self-representation in the *Res Gestae* (*rem publicam a dominatione factionis oppressam in libertatem uindicaui*—paradoxically, Theodosius made use of the same propaganda of *libertas* to justify his intervention in the civil war against Maximus).[96] Nevertheless, it is noteworthy that Theodosius is eulogized with similar elements at the end of the *Epitome*, when, after having specified his interest in history, the emperor is also directly compared with Augustus!

> Habuitque a natura quod Augustus a philosophiae doctore ...
> *Melior* haud dubie, quod est rarae uirtutis, *post auctam* annis
> *potentiam regalem* multoque maxime *post ciuilem uictoriam.*
> Nam et annonae curam *sollicitius* attendere, et auri argen-
> tique grande pondus sublati atque expensi *a tyranno* multis
> e suo restituere, cum *benigni principum* et quidem uix fundos
> solerent nudos ac deformata praedia concedere.

> And he possessed by nature what Augustus possessed from
> a teacher of philosophy ... What is of rare virtue, he was
> doubtless better after his regal power increased with the
> years, and better by far after his victory in civil war. For he
> was very solicitous both to attend to the care of the grain
> supply and to return to many from his own the great mass
> of gold and silver borne off and expended by the tyrant,
> while the benign of the *principes* were, in fact, almost
> accustomed to concede denuded farms and devastated
> estates.[97]

---

[96] *Res gestae* 1.1, referring to the year 44 BC; cf. Festy 1999:67n30. See *Pan. Lat.* 12.46.4, as in Section II.

[97] *Epit. de Caes.* 48.14.16–17 (trans. Banchich 2009), but cf. also § 13 (*Irasci sane rebus indignis, sed flecti cito; unde modica dilatione emolliebantur aliquando seuera praecepta*) and § 15 (*Qui cum uidisset eum facile commoueri, ne asperum aliquid statueret, monuit, ubi irasci coepisset, quattuor atque uiginti Graecas litteras memoria recenseret, ut illa concitatio, quae momenti est, mente alio traducta parui temporis interiectu languesceret*). For the comparisons, cf. *Epit. de Caes.* 48.13–18 and 1.21–22.

This comparison and the similarities in the motifs (which include *libertas* and civil war) used to describe the first and the last emperors do not seem coincidental in the structure of the *Epitome*. Although the historical circumstances were different, Theodosius too had increased his *regalis potentia* during the years after his victory in the civil war. It was then that, together with guarantees of supplies (which the anonymous author also attributed to Augustus), he gave back from his own pocket a remarkable quantity of gold and silver, which the tyrant Maximus had previously confiscated. In doing this he proved himself better than the *benigni principum*, who often limited their charity to giving back useless plots of land. The reference is to the period following the victory over Maximus until the year 391 (*post ciuilem uictoriam*).[98] Once again, we cannot dismiss the possibility that senators like Symmachus and Nicomachus Flavianus may have used these motifs in their eulogies. In fact, like the motif of *libertas*, the assimilation Theodosius–Augustus as found in the *Epitome*, which could also address the theme of pacifism,[99] *predates* the events of Eugenius and belongs to *the same* western propaganda of the years 388–391. More intriguing is the fact that this comparison between Theodosius and Augustus (*Epit. de Caes.* 48.13–17) occurs soon after the author refers to Theodosius' above-discussed interest in history (*Epit. de Caes.* 48.11–12), and it follows the assimilation of the emperor with Trajan (*Epit. de Caes.* 48.8–10). This twofold comparison with Augustus and Trajan is interesting, and could even evoke the senatorial acclamation for the emperors as noted by the contemporary Eutropius: *usque ad nostram*

---

[98] Cf. Festy 1999:xxxvii and 235, referring to the famine of the year 389—which is also mentioned by Symmachus in *Epist.* 3.55 and 3.82—and also to the confiscations made by Maximus in Gaul, on which see Pacatus, *Pan. Lat.* 12.25–28.3. The confiscations were annulled with *C.Th.* 15.14.6–8 (Mommsen 1905). The source postdates the fall of the year 389 and predates Eugenius' usurpation. I wonder whether this situation is also evoked by Symmachus *Epist.* 2.31 (in which he also refers to his panegyric to Theodosius of the year 388): *Non puto eam causae meae bonis temporibus condicionem futuram, quae sub tyranno fuit, cuius litteris ad Marcellini suggestionem datis homines meos scis esse multatos. Quod in panegyrici defensione non tacui.* This would be another possible connection between a lost panegyric of Symmachus and Theodosius' eulogy at *Epit. de Caes.* 48.

[99] *Epit. de Caes.* 1.10–12, referring to Augustus, in which see: *Adeo denique turbas, bella, simultates exsecratus est ut nisi iustis de causis numquam genti cuiquam bellum indixerit.*

aetatem non aliter in senatu principibus adclametur, nisi "Felicior Augusto, melior Traiano."[100]

We have one more reason to believe that a panegyrical source, possibly the lost panegyric of Symmachus of 391, lay behind this section of the *Epitome*. Apart from the question of their shared Spanish origins[101] (one of the main reasons for the association, therefore likely inappropriate in the West during the usurpation of the Spaniard Magnus Maximus), the assimilation of Theodosius with Trajan in the *Epitome* is based on his manners and physique, as well as on his intellect and his love for his citizens, while the comparison with Augustus has a political connotation and is connected to the civil war. What role did the figure of Augustus play in Theodosius' propaganda? We understand from his letter to Ausonius that the emperor found in Augustus one of his models.[102] Was then Theodosius seeking to be assimilated to the first emperor of Rome because he also ended a civil war? If this is the case, the difference is that contemporaries eulogized Theodosius for his *uictoria ciuilis*[103] while they condemned Augustus for putting an end to the long civil wars by becoming an *oppressor libertatis*. And while the expression *libertate oppressa* is frequently used by authors like Cicero, *oppressor libertatis* as used by the anonymous author of the *Epitome* is extremely rare and lacks apparent comparisons.[104] Is it possible that the senators of Theodosius' entourage wanted to assimilate the emperor to Augustus, while at the same time styling him as a restorer, not an *oppressor libertatis*? This is the image that emerges from the other sources. In the *Epitome* Theodosius despised the treacherous rulers as enemies of *libertas*. Pacatus revealed a similar view in his comparison between Theodosius and Brutus, in claiming that it would not have been necessary to abolish the monarchy if only the tyrant Tarquin had

---

[100]*Brev.* 8.5.3, referring to Trajan.

[101]Cf. Festy and Chausson as above at note 12; cf. also note 48.

[102]Augustus is evoked by Theodosius as a model in his letter addressed to Auson. *Epist.* 1.3 (cf. above, note 2): *qui* [i.e. *auctores optimi*] *Octauiano Augusto rerum potienti certatim opera sua tradebant, nullo fine in eius honorem multa condentes. Qui illos haut sciam an aequaliter atque ego te admiratus sit, certe non amplius diligebat.*

[103]Compare this eulogy with *Pan. Lat.* 9.20.3, quoted at note 23.

[104]Cf. *Thesaurus Linguae Latinae* 9.2:783, s.v. '*oppressor*'; the only other reference is by Ennod. *Dict.* 18.2.

been removed (see Section II). Both authors justify Theodosius' reign using the motif of *libertas*.

In Theodosius' time, the idea that *libertas Romana* had ended with the collapse of the republic was over four hundred years old; it was also traditionally connected to theories of the ages of Rome, from the city's birth to its old age. This topic has been the subject of many important discussions and it is too complex to be considered here; nevertheless, one element should be noted. In the *Historia Augusta*—written probably about one generation after Flavianus' *Annales*—the word *libertas* is used rarely as a reference to the republic and the freedom of the Roman senate.[105] In this work Augustus is one of the model emperors and, as in the *Epitome*, he generally excites the sympathy of the author.[106] Scholars have remarked upon a passage in the introduction to the *Vita* of Carus, which describes the ages of Rome. Here Augustus is remembered as the one who, by bringing an end to the civil wars, also put an inevitable end to *libertas*:

> Creuit deinde uicta Carthagine trans maria missis impe-
> riis, sed socialibus adfecta discordiis extenuato felic⟨it⟩
> atis sensu usque ad Augustum bellis ciuilibus, adfecta
> consenuit. Per Augustum deinde reparata, si reparata dici
> potest *libertate deposita*. Tamen utcumque, etiamsi domi
> tristis fuit, apud exteras gentes effloruit.

> Next, having conquered Carthage and extended its
> empire over the seas, it waxed great, but afflicted by strife
> with allies it lost all sense of happiness, and crushed by
> civil wars it wasted away in weakness until the time of
> Augustus. He then restored it once more, if indeed we
> may say that it was restored when it gave up its freedom.
> Nevertheless, in some way or other, though mourning at
> home, it enjoyed great fame among nations abroad.[107]

---

[105] Cf. SHA *Macr.* 7.1, *Maxim.* 15.3, *Maximus* 17.4, *Claud.* 9.6; cf. also the reference to the conspiracy in *Heliogab.* 16.5.

[106] Cf. Von Haehling 1985: part. 212–214, for the reference to the quotation considered here.

[107] SHA *Car.* 3.1–2 (trans. Magie 1932).

A short list of good and bad examples follows, which includes the principal emperors until Probus, and which focuses especially on the first two centuries.[108] This paragraph has been re-examined by Paschoud, who is the last of several scholars to make a comparative analysis of the descriptions of the ages of Rome that appeared also in the works of Seneca the Elder, Florus, and Ammianus Marcellinus.[109] However, Florus interpreted the same events differently: he did not emphasize the end of *libertas* after the civil wars and the subsequent decline of Rome *in patria*. Rather he wrote of a reinvigoration and resurgence of Rome after the establishment of the empire.[110] Ammianus also, although with some pessimism, went in another direction. Instead of taking a nostalgic view of the old *res publica*, he believed that it found its true legacy in empire.[111] Even without considering the open question of how deeply Ammianus was connected with the senatorial pagan circles, it is clear that his vision of the ages of Rome did not touch on the loss of *libertas*. The closest model to the *Historia Augusta* is probably that of Seneca the Elder,[112] who, in his lost historical work, described the old age of Rome and the end of *libertas*. Seneca wrote in roughly the same period under Tiberius that Cremutius Cordus in his *Annales* eulogized Brutus and Cassius as *ultimi Romanorum*, and he preceded by not many years the works of Thrasea Paetus and Helvidius Priscus,

---

[108]SHA *Car.* 3.2–8, in which: *passa deinceps tot Nerones, per Vespasianum extulit caput. Nec omni Titi felicitate laetata, Domitiani uulnerata inmanitate per Neruam atque Traianum usque ad Marcum solito melior, Commodi u[a]ecordia et crudelitate lacerata est.*

[109]Paschoud 2001a; Paschoud 2001b:323–337. Cf. also Hartke 1951:388–402; Archambault 1966; Jal 1967:lxix–lxxix.

[110]Flor. *Epit. praef.* 1–4, in which: *A Caesare Augusto in saeculum nostrum haud multo minus anni ducenti, quibus inertia Caesarum quasi consenuit atque decoxit, nisi quod sub Traiano principe mouit lacertos et praeter spem omnium senectus imperii quasi reddita iuuentute reuiruit.*

[111]Amm. Marc. 14.6.5: *ideo urbs uenerabilis post superbas efferatarum gentium ceruices oppressas latasque leges fundamenta libertatis et retinacula sempiterna uelut frugi parens et prudens et diues Caesaribus tamquam liberis suis regenda patrimonii iura permisit*; cf. 6.2–4, the references to *Virtus* and *Fortuna*, on which also Flor. *Epit.* 1.2. See also Amm. Marc. 14.6.7–12, on the bad costumes of the senators and the comparison with the highly moral during the republic.

[112]I agree here with Chastagnol 1994:1135–1137; cf. also Paschoud 2001b:329.

mentioned above.[113] Seneca the Elder's history survives only in the fragment transmitted to us by Lactantius, yet this fragment does shed light on the perspectives of the original source. After the destruction of Carthage and the annexation of several kingdoms and states,

> cum iam bellorum materia deficeret, uiribus suis male uteretur, quibus se ipsa confecit. Et haec fuit prima eius senectus, cum *bellis lacerata ciuilibus atque intestino malo* pressa rursus *ad regimen singularis imperii reccidit* quasi ad alteram infantiam reuoluta. *Amissa enim libertate*, quam *Bruto duce et auctore defenderat*, ita *consenuit*, tamquam sustentare se ipsa non ualeret, nisi adminiculo *regentium* niteretur.

> when material of wars began now to fail, she [sc. Rome] used her own strength and resources badly, and with these she exhausted herself. This was the first old age, when, torn with civil wars and oppressed with intestinal evil, she fell back upon rule by a single command, as though she had been revolved to another infancy. For when the liberty was lost which she had defended under the leadership and authority of Brutus, she grew so old that she was, as it were, not able to support herself without leaning upon the prop of those ruling.[114]

Lactantius was presumably not the only one who still read this work, and we have reason to think that the pagan senatorial circles were also familiar with this history. This idea is supported by the existence of a palimpsest (*Codex Vaticanus Palatinus* 24), probably dating to

---

[113] On the vicissitudes of Cremutius Cordus, cf. Suet. *Tib.* 61.3; Tac. *Ann.* 4.34. Cf. also Juv. *Sat.* 5.36–37: *quale coronati Thrasea Eluidiusque bibebant / Brutorum et Cassi natalibus* (Braund 1994); and in general Plin. *Epist.* 1.17.3: *Est omnino Capitoni in usu claros uiros colere; mirum est qua religione, quo studio imagines Brutorum, Cassiorum, Catonum domi ubi potest habeat* (Radice 1969).

[114] Lactant. *Div. inst.* 7.15.14–16, quoted 15–16 from Freund 2009:156 (trans. McDonald 1964). Lactantius introduces this passage in the following way (§ 14): *Non inscite Seneca Romanae urbis tempora distribuit in aetates.* Cf. the recent detailed commentary of Freund 2009:420–439.

the early sixth century, which contains fragments of classical authors, among them Seneca, Lucan, Livy, Cicero, Gellius, and Fronto.[115] Here we find mention of the *Life* of Seneca the Elder and of the significance of his historical work on the civil wars, *ab initio bellorum ciuilium, unde primum ueritas retro abiit*.[116] This expression should be considered in parallel to the quotation above: *cum bellis lacerata ciuilibus atque intestino malo pressa*. These excerpts voice criticism of the moral decadence and luxury associated with the late republic after the third Punic war. This theme had been discussed by Sallust (and referenced by other authors, including Livy, Velleius, Lucanus, Florus, Appianus, and Ammianus)[117] and it can be detected behind the above-quoted words of the *Vita* of Carus referring to the illness of Rome in the late republic following the victory against Carthage. If the *Historia Augusta*—a work that certainly was not intended to celebrate a ruler—was influenced by the philo-republican conservative model of the ages of Rome, we can assume that Symmachus and Nicomachus Flavianus, who probably wrote a generation earlier, had taken a more moderate view of the history of the republic in their dialogue with the emperor.

Independent from the differing views on Augustus discussed above, the condemnation of the leaders of the late republic was unanimous. As restorer of peace, Theodosius was more successful than Augustus, who had contributed to compromising Roman liberty. Flavianus' work served Theodosius' political agenda in its use of the propaganda of *libertas* in 388–391, the same years he was operating at the court.

---

[115]For a study of this palimpsest, cf. Fohlen 1979.

[116]Peter 1967:98, in which among the fragments of Seneca the Elder: *quisquis legisset eius historias ab initio bellorum ciuilium, unde primum ueritas retro abiit, paene usque ad mortis suae diem, magno aestimasset scire, quibus natus esset parentibus ille qui res Roman[as]*. Cf. Fohlen 1979:212.

[117]See Fairweather 1981:16–17. Cf. Sussman 1978:137–152, esp. the references at 142–143 with notes 16–17: the beginning of this moral decadence and luxury are the destruction of Corinth and the period of the Gracchi, on which Sall. *Cat.* 10.1; *Hist.* 1, fr. 11–12; cf. also Liv. *Praef.*; Luc. *Bell. civ.* 1.173–182; Flor. 1.47.2, 2.1–2; Vell. 2.1.1–2; App. *Bell. civ.* 1.2; Amm. Marc. 14.6.8.

V. CONCLUSION:
MOURNING *LIBERTAS ROMANA* FOR THE LAST TIME

Theodosius' generation was the last in which the motif of *libertas* played an important role in the complex dialogue between emperor and Roman senate. More than a century later, in the Italy ruled by Goths, *libertas* was associated with the *nomen Romanum*, which had to be protected.[118] At that time Cassiodorus, quaestor and master of the office at the Gothic court, wrote a *History* at the order of king Theoderic to celebrate not the Roman past, but the deeds of the Goths and of the Amal royal family.[119] Nevertheless this king, who desired to rule Italy by following the footsteps and mirroring the examples of the famous emperors, wanted to hear about the ancients, whom he was zealous to imitate; and Cassiodorus entertained him with dialogues on wisdom.[120] Although in this new context *libertas Romana* did not have any immediate relevance to the relationship between Roman senate and king, its loss would be mourned once more and for the last time in antiquity by Boethius in the *Consolatio philosophiae*. In his invective against the tyrant Theoderic, through wording that deliberately evoked Tacitus, Boethius accused the king for having believed the *improbi*, the jealous courtiers who had impugned Boethius' name in the only year he was employed at the palace.[121]

> Nam de compositis falso litteris, *quibus libertatem arguor sperasse Romanam*, quid attinet dicere? Quarum *fraus aperta* patuisset, si nobis ipsorum *confessione delatorum*, quod in omnibus negotiis maximas uires habet, uti licuisset. *Nam quae sperari reliqua libertas potest? Atque utinam posset ulla! Respondissem Canii uerbo, qui cum a Gaio Caesare Germanici*

---

[118] Cf. Moorhead 1987.

[119] *Anec. hold.* lines 20–21 (Galonnier 1996); Cassiod. *Var.* 9.25.4–6, *praef.* 11; Jord. *Get.* 1 and 215. Cassiodorus began to write the *Historia Gothorum* as quaestor, 507/11, or at latest in 523/27, as master of the offices.

[120] *Var.* 9.24.8: *sententias prudentium a tuis fabulis exigebat, ut factis propriis se aequaret antiquiis.*

[121] *Anonymus Valesianus* 85–87; Proc. *BG* 1.1.32–39. About the references to the *improbi* and the *damnatio*, cf. Vitiello 2011. For more bibliography see below, note 126.

filio conscius contra se factae coniurationis fuisse diceretur: "Si ego," inquit, "scissem, tu nescisses" ... Sed fas fuerit nefarios homines, qui bonorum omnium totiusque senatus sanguinem petunt, nos etiam, quos propugnare bonis senatuique uiderant, perditum ire uoluisse ... Meministi ... Veronae cum rex, auidus exitii communis, *maiestatis crimen* in Albinum *delatae* ad cunctum senatus ordinem transferre moliretur, uniuersi innocentiam senatus quanta mei periculi securitate defenderim ... nunc ... ob studium propensius in senatum morti proscriptionique damnamur ... Et ego quidem bonis omnibus pulsus, dignitatibus exutus, existimatione foedatus ob beneficium supplicium tuli.

I think it unnecessary to speak of the forged letters through which I am accused of "hoping for the freedom of Rome." Their falsity would have been apparent if I had been free to question the evidence of the informers themselves, for their confessions have much force in all such business. But what avails it? No liberty is left to hope for. Would there were any! I would answer in the words of Canius, who was accused by Gaius Caesar, Germanicus' son, of being cognisant of a plot against himself: "If I had known of it, you would not have." ... Again, let impious men, who thirst for the blood of the whole Senate and of all good citizens, be allowed to wish for the ruin of us too whom they recognise as champions of the Senate and all good citizens: but surely such as I have not deserved the same hatred from the members of the Senate too? ... I think you remember what happened at Verona. When King Theoderic, desiring the common ruin of the Senate, was for extending to the whole order the charge of treason laid against Albinus, you remember how I laboured to defend the innocence of the order without any care for my own danger? ... But here am I ... condemned to death and the confiscation of my property because of my too great zeal for the Senate ... For kindness I have received persecutions;

I have been driven from all my possessions, stripped of my honours, and stained for ever in my reputation.[122]

Of course Boethius did not consider the Roman senate any less responsible for his misfortune for turning their backs and failing to defend him,[123] even if in this passage he evoked the Julio-Claudian tyranny in the figure of Caligula and in the allusions to *delatores*, and later hurled his invective against the infamous Nero, to whom Theoderic is likened.[124] And while his contemporary Cassiodorus still linked the consulship with the preservation of liberty and considered this office the primary reason for the growth of Rome,[125] Boethius referred instead to the loss of *libertas* by pointing his finger at the *superbia* of the consuls who many centuries earlier had obtained *libertas* after having chased out the similarly *superbi* kings. In this discussion, he connects for the last time the beginning of the Roman republic with its end by referring to the motif of *libertas*:

Certe, uti meminisse te arbitror, consulare imperium, quod *libertatis principium* fuerat, *ob superbiam consulum* uestri ueteres abolere cupiuerunt, qui *ob eandem superbiam* prius regium de ciuitate nomen abstulerant.

---

[122]Boeth. *Cons.* 1.4.26–45 passim (Moreschini 2000), trans. Cooper 1902. For a commentary on this passage, cf. Gruber 2006:129–138.

[123]Boeth. *Cons.* 1.4.23 and 31; *Anonymus Valesianus* 87. Boethius was officially condemned by the *iudicium quinqueuirale*, although this fulfilled the will of Theoderic.

[124]Boeth. *Cons.* 1.c.4, 11–18 and 3.c.4. It is worth noting that, apart from *Cons.* 3.4.4 (referred to his enemy at court Cypranus), Boethius concentrates the use of the word *delator* in the *apologia*: *Cons.* 1.4.16–24.32.46. Cf. Vitiello 2011:358n50. Interesting also in the above-quoted passage is the unusual espression of *crimen maiestatis delatae*. On the tradition of *delatores* in the first century, starting with Tiberius, cf. Rutledge 2001.

[125]Cassiod. *Var.* 6.1.1–2 and 4 (*formula consolatus*): *Statum rei publicae Romanae uiri fortis dextera tuebatur, fortunas omnium ac liberos ciuis consilia uindicabant: et tot magnis debitis sola erat huius retributio dignitatis, reperta in libertatis ornatum, inuenta ad generale gaudium. Per illam nimirum status imperii iugiter creuit, illam semper felix Roma suscepit. Merito pridem genus habebatur imperii: merito supra omnes ciues poterat, qui ab hoste patriam uindicabat ... Hinc tanta largitas profluebat, ut illa dextera, quae sanguinem copiose fuderat hostium, uitae auxilium ciuibus manaret irriguum. Sic quos felices per bella fecerat, studio largitatis explebat. In argumentum etiam publicae gloriae soluebat famulos iugo seruili, qui libertatem tantae dederat ciuitati.*

I am sure you remember how your forefathers wished to do away with the consular power, which had been the very foundation of liberty, because of the overbearing pride of the consuls, just as your ancestors had too in earlier times expunged from the state the name of king on account of the same pride.[126]

Obviously, in his solitary complaint Boethius did not have reason to specify the names of Tarquin the Proud, of Cinna, of Marius, of Sulla, and of Julius Caesar, to whom he probably referred here and whose *exempla*, as we have seen, had been used widely in imperial literature.

The rest of the story is well known: Boethius was a victim at the court of the same kind of *liuor inproborum* that Nicomachus Flavianus had experienced, and he was condemned to death.[127] The same bad fate was shortly thereafter suffered by his father-in-law Symmachus the Younger. The memory of the Symmachi-Anicii of the sixth century did not fare better than that of the Symmachi-Nicomachi of the late fourth / early fifth century. The medieval tradition, perhaps derived from Cassiodorus, would remember Boethius and Symmachus as the last defenders of the *Romana res publica*, emphasizing this through etymologies of their names, the importance of which lay in their Greek meaning.[128] And if Boethius was the last of a long line of senators who lived with the illusion of *libertas Romana*, the same illusion of a lost past had haunted Symmachus the Younger, who was the first to use, after

---

[126]Boeth. *Cons.* 2.6.2 (trans. Cooper 1902); cf. also Symmachus *Rel.* 4.3 (quoted at note 36). On *libertas* in Boethius and on the possible influences of Tacitus, see Matthews 1981:35–36; Magee 2005 and 2007. The case of Symmachus the Younger is discussed in Vitiello 2008.

[127]Cf. for example *Cons.* 1.4.9 (*Inde cum improbis graves inexorabilesque discordiae*), 1.4.46; Proc. *BG* 1.1.34 (ἄνδρας ἐς φθόνον τοὺς πονηροτάτους ἐπηγαγέτην). About this motif, see Vitiello 2011, which discusses some possible parallels with Cassiodorus and Procopius.

[128]*Vita Boethii* (from the edition of Troncarelli 1981:27): "Anicii": *Anicius dictus est Boetius quia de genere Aniciorum fuit: qui duo fuisse legunt⟨ur⟩, pater uidelicet et filius eiusdem fuerunt: et Decii qui ambo pro salute rei publicae morti se deuouerunt ...* "Boetii": *BOITOS grece, latine dicitur adiutorium. Hinc Boetius adiutor interpretatur, qui publicam rem multum iuuauit et suo auditorio muniuit ⟨ac⟩ defendit ...* "Symmachus": *compugnans uel compugnator interpretatur. SYN grece con; MACHIA dicitur pugna: quia cum Boetio pro re publica defendenda iste sollerter laborabat.* Boethius' *Vitae* show a strong influence from the same source as *Anecdoton Holderi*.

more than a century, the writings of his *parentes* Nicomachi, the *Historia Augusta*, and maybe even the *Annales* to celebrate one last time the illustrious and symbolic history of Rome.[129]

UNIVERSITY OF MISSOURI–KANSAS CITY

WORKS CITED

Archambault, P. 1966. "The Ages of Man and the Ages of the World: A Study of Two Traditions." *Revue des études Augustiniennes* 12:193–228.

Arnaud-Lindet, M. P. 1991. *Orose. Histoires (Contre les Païens)*. Vol. 3, *Livre VII - Index*. Paris.

Baldini, A. 2005. "Considerazioni in tema di *Annales* e di *Historia Augusta*." In *Historiae Augustae Colloquium Barcinonense* (Historiae Augustae Colloquia, n.s., 9), ed. G. Bonamente and M. Mayer, 15–46. Bari.

Banchich, T. M., trans. 2009. *A Booklet About the Style of Life and the Manners of the* Imperatores. Buffalo.

Barnes, T. 1976. "The *Epitome de Caesaribus* and its Sources." *Classical Philology* 71:258–268.

Bleckmann, B. 1995. "Bemerkungen zu den 'Annales' des Nicomachus Flavianus." *Historia* 44:83–99.

Bowersock, G. W. 1986. "Symmachus and Ausonius." In *Colloque Genevois sur Symmaque: À l'occasion du mille six centième anniversaire du conflit de l'autel de la Victoire*," ed. F. Paschoud, 1–12. Paris.

Braund, S. M. 1994. *Juvenal and Persius*. Cambridge, MA.

Brodka, D. 1998. *Die Romideologie in der römischen Literatur der Spätantike*. Frankfurt am Main.

Bruère, R. T. 1954. "Tacitus and Pliny's *Panegyricus*." *Classical Philology* 49:161–179.

Bruggisser, P. 1993. *Symmaque ou le ritual épistolaire de l'amitié littéraire: Recherches sur le premier livre de la correspondence*. Fribourg.

---

[129] *Anecdoton Holderi* lines 7–8 (Galonnier 1996); Jord. *Get.* 83–88.

Burgersdijk, D. 2007. "Nepos in der *Historia Augusta.*" In *Historiae Augustae Colloquium Bambergense* (Historiae Augustae Colloquia, n.s., 10), ed. G. Bonamente and H. Brandt, 95–107. Bari.

Callu, J. P. 1982. *Symmaque. Lettres.* Vol. 2, *Livres III-V.* Paris

———. 2009. *Symmaque.* Vol. 5, *Discours - Rapports.* Paris.

Cameron, A. 1970. *Claudian: Poetry and Propaganda at the Court of Honorius.* Oxford.

———. 2011. *The Last Pagans of Rome.* Oxford.

Chastagnol, A. 1994. *Histoire Auguste: Les empereurs Romains des IIᵉ et IIIᵉ siècles.* Paris.

Chausson, F. 1998. "Remarques sur les généalogies impériales dans l'*Histoire Auguste*: Le cas de Théodose." In *Historiae Augustae Colloquium Argentoratense* (Historiae Augustae Colloquia, n.s., 6), ed. G. Bonamente, F. Heim, and J.-P. Callu, 105–114. Bari.

———. 2007. *Stemmata aurea: Constantin, Justine, Théodose: Revendications généalogiques et idéologie impériale au IVe siécle ap. J.-C.* Rome.

Cooper, W. V. 1902. *Translation of Boethius'* Consolatio Philosophiae. London.

Dombart, B., and A. Kalb. 1955. *Augustinus. De Civitate Dei: Libri I-X.* Corpus Christianorum, Series Latina 47. Turnhout.

Duval, Y. M. 1966. "L'éloge de Théodose dans la 'Cité de Dieu' (V.26.1): Sa place, son sens, et ses sources." *Recherches augustiniennes* 4:135–179.

Ernesti, J. 1998. *Princeps christianus und Kaiser aller Römer: Theodosius der Große im Lichte zeitgenössischer Quellen.* Paderborn.

Errington, R. M. 1992. "The Praetorian Prefectures of Virius Nicomachus Flavianus." *Historia* 41:439–461.

———. 2006. *Roman Imperial Policy from Julian to Theodosius.* Chapel Hill, NC.

Fairweather, J. 1981. *Seneca the Elder.* Cambridge.

Felmy, A. 2001. *Die Römische Republik im Geschichtsbild der Spätantike: Zum Umgang lateinischer Autoren des 4. und 5. Jahrhunderts n.Chr. mit dem* exempla maiorum. Berlin.

Festy, M. 1997. "Le début et la fin des 'Annales' de Nicomaque Flavien." *Historia* 46:465–478.

———. 1999. *Pseudo-Aurélius Victor. Abrégé des Césars.* Paris.

———. 2003. "De l'*Epitome de Caesaribus* à la *Chronique* de Marcellin: L'*Historia Romana* des Symmaque le Jeune." *Historia* 52:251–255.

———. 2007. "L'*Histoire Auguste* et les Nicomaques." In *Historiae Augustae Colloquium Bambergense* (Historiae Augustae Colloquia, n.s., 10), ed. G. Bonamente and H. Brandt, 183–195. Bari.

Fohlen, J. 1979. "Recherches sur le manuscript palimpseste Vatican, *Pal. Lat. 24*." *Scrittura e Civiltà* 3:195–222.

Galonnier, A. 1996. "*Anecdoton Holderi* ou *Ordo generis Cassiodororum*: Introduction, édition, traduction et commentaire." *Antiquité Tardive* 4:299–312.

Freund, S. 2009. *Laktanz. Divinae institutiones. Book 7, De vita beata: Einleitung, Text, Übersetzung und Kommentar*. Berlin.

Gruber, J. 2006. *Kommentar zu Boethius, De Consolatione Philosophiae*. 2nd expanded ed. Berlin.

Haehling, R. von. 1985. "Augustus in der *Historia Augusta*." In *Bonner Historia-Augusta-Colloquium 1982/1983*, ed. J. Straub, 197–220. Bonn.

Hartke, W. 1940. *Geschichte und Politik im spätantiken Rom*. Leipzig.

———. 1951. *Römische Kinderkaiser: Eine Strukturanalyse römischen Denkens und Daseins*. Berlin.

Hedrick, C. W., Jr. 2000. *History and Silence: Purge and Rehabilitation of Memory in Late Antiquity*. Austin.

Hellegouarc'h, J. 1999. *Eutrope: Abrégé d'histoire romaine*. Paris.

Heubner, H. 1978. *P. Cornelii Taciti libri quae supersunt*. Vol. 2, fasc. 1, *Historiarum Libri*. Stuttgart.

Honoré, T. 1989. *Virius Nicomachus Flavianus: Mit einem Beitrag von John F. Matthews*. Xenia 23. Konstanz.

———. 1998a. "L'*Histoire Auguste* à la lumière des constitutions impériales" In *Historiae Augustae Colloquium Argentoratense* (Historiae Augustae Colloquia, n.s., 6), ed. G. Bonamente, F. Heim, and J.-P. Callu, 191–212. Bari.

———. 1998b. *Law in the Crisis of the Empire 379-455 AD*. Oxford.

Hutton, M., and W. Peterson. 1970. *Tacitus. Agricola, Germania, Dialogus*. Cambridge, MA.

Jackson, J., trans. 1931. *Tacitus. Histories Books IV–V, Annals Books I–III*. Trans. C. H. Moore and J. Jackson. Cambridge, MA.

Jal, P. 1967. *Florus. Oeuvres, Livre I, Tome I: Tableau de l'Histoire du people romain, de Romulus à Auguste.* Paris.

Kelly, G. 2013. "Pliny and Symmachus." *Arethusa* 46:261–287.

Lassandro, D. 2007. "Una disputa religiosa tra il prefetto pagano Simmaco ed il vescovo Ambrogio sul finire del IV secolo d.C." *Euphrosyne* 35:231–240.

Leppin, H. 2003. *Theodosius der Große: Auf dem Weg zum christlichen Imperium.* Darmstadt.

Lippold, A. 1968. "Herrscherideal und Traditionsverbundenheit im Panegyricus des Pacatus." *Historia* 17:228–250.

Lizzi Testa, R. 2007. "Christian Emperor, Vestal Virgins and Priestly Colleges: Reconsidering the End of Roman Paganism." *Antiquité Tardive* 15:251–262.

Lunn-Rockliffe, S. 2010. "Commemorating the Usurper Magnus Maximus: Ekphrasis, Poetry, and History in Pacatus' Panegyric of Theodosius." *Journal of Late Antiquity* 3:316–336.

Magee, J. 2005. "Boethius' *Consolatio* and the Theme of Roman Liberty." *Phoenix* 59:348–364.

———. 2007. "Boethius, Last of the Romans." *Carmina Philosophiae* 16:1–22.

Magie, D. 1932. *Historia Augusta. Vol. 3, The Two Valerians; The Two Gallieni; The Thirty Pretenders; The Deified Claudius; The Deified Aurelian; Tacitus; Probus; Firmus, Saturninus, Proculus and Bonosus; Carus, Carinus and Numerian.* Cambridge, MA.

Matthews, J. 1971. "Gallic Supporters of Theodosius." *Latomus* 30:1073–1099.

———. 1975. *Western Aristocracies and Imperial Court, AD 364–425.* Oxford.

———. 1981. "Anicius Manlius Severinus Boethius." In *Boethius: His Life, Thought and Influence*, ed. M. Gibson, 15–43. Oxford.

———. 1989. *The Roman Empire of Ammianus.* London.

———. 1997. "*Codex Theodosianus 9.40.13* and Nicomachus Flavianus." *Historia* 46:196–213.

McDonald, M. F. 1964. *Lactantius. The Divine Institutes.* Washington.

Mommsen, T. 1894. *Cassiodoris Senatoris Variae.* Monumenta Germaniae Historica, Auctores Antiquissimi 12. Berlin.

———. 1905. *Codex Theodosianus.* Berlin.

Moorhead, J. 1987. "*Libertas* and *Nomen Romanum* in Ostrogothic Italy." *Latomus* 46:161–168.

Moreschini, C. 2000. *Boethius. De Consolatione Philosophiae, Opuscula Theologica*. Munich.

Mynors, R. A. B. 1964. *XII Panegyrici Latini*. Oxford.

Nixon, C. E. V. 1991. "Aurelius Victor and Julian." *Classical Philology* 86:113–125.

Nixon, C. E. V., and B. S. Rodgers. 1994. *In Praise of Later Roman Emperors: The* Panegyrici Latini. Berkeley.

Paschoud, F. 1980. "Quand parut la première édition de l'Histoire d'Eunape?" In *Bonner Historia-Augusta-Colloquium 1977/1978*, ed. A. Alföldi, 149–162. Bonn.

———. 2001a. "Une réponse païenne au providentialisme chrétien." *Comptes-rendus des séances de l'Académie des Inscriptions et Belles-Lettres* 145:335–346.

———. 2001b. *Histoire Auguste*. Vol. 5, *Vies de Probus, Firmus, Saturnin, Proclus et Bonose, Carus, Numérien et Carin*. 2nd ed. Paris.

Peiper, R. 1886. *Decimi Magni Ausonii Burdigalensis opuscula*. Leipzig.

Peter, H. 1967. *Historicorum Romanorum Reliquiae*. 2nd ed. Stuttgart.

Platnauer, M. 1922. *Claudian. Opera*. Cambridge, MA.

PLRE 1. = Martindale, J. R. 1971. *The Prosopography of the Later Roman Empire*. Vol. 1, *AD 395-527*. Cambridge.

Portmann, W. 1988. *Geschichte in der spätantiken Panegyrik*. Frankfurt am Main.

Radice, B. 1969. *Pliny. Letters and Panegyricus*. Vols. 1–2. London.

Ratti, S. 2010. *Antiquus error: Les ultimes feux de la résistance païenne; Scripta varia argumentés de cinq études inédites*. Turnhout.

Rees, R. 2012. "Bright Lights, Big City: Pacatus and the *Panegyrici Latini*." In *Two Romes: Rome and Constantinople in Late Antiquity*, ed. L. Grig and K. Kelly, 203–222. Oxford.

Roda, S. 1981. *Commento storico al libro IX dell'epistolario di Quinto Aurelio Simmaco: Introduzione, commento storico, testo, traduzione e indici*. Pisa.

Rolfe, J. C. 1935. *Ammianus Marcellinus. History*. Vol. 1, Books 14–19. Cambridge, MA.

Rutledge, S. H. 2001. *Imperial Inquisitions: Prosecutors and Informants from Tiberius to Domitian.* London.

Sabbah, G. 1978. *La méthode d'Ammien Marcellin: Recherches sur la construction du discors historique dans les* Res Gestae. Paris.

Schlumberger, J. 1974. *Die* Epitome de Caesaribus: *Untersuchungen zur heidnischen Geschichtsschreibung des 4. Jahrhunderts n.Chr.* Munich.

———. 1985. "*Die verlorenen Annalen des Nicomachus Flavianus: Ein Werk über Geschichte der römischen Republik oder der Kaiserzeit?*" In *Bonner Historia-Augusta-Colloquium 1982/1983,* ed. J. Straub, 305–329. Bonn.

Seeck, O. 1883. *Q. Aurelii Symmachi quae supersunt.* Monumenta Germaniae Historica, Auctores Antiquissimi 6, part 1. Berlin.

Sehlmeyer, M. 2009. *Geschichtsbilder für Pagane und Christen:* Res Romanae *in der spätantiken Breviarien.* Berlin.

Sogno, C. 2006. *Q. Aurelius Symmachus: A Political Biography.* Ann Arbor.

Sussman, L. A. 1978. *The Elder Seneca.* Mnemosyne Supplement 51. Leiden.

Troncarelli, F. 1981. *Tradizioni perdute: La "Consolatio Philosophiae" nell'alto Medioevo.* Padua.

Vera, D. 1981. *Commento storico alle* Relationes *di Quinto Aurelio Simmaco: Introduzione, commento, testo, traduzione, appendice sul libro X, 1-2, indici.* Pisa.

Vitiello, M. 2008. "Last of the *Catones*: A Profile of Symmachus the Younger." *Antiquité Tardive* 16:297–315.

———. 2011. "'Accusarentur saecula, si talis potuisset latere familia': Il fantasma di Severino Boezio nell'Italia dei Goti." *Historia* 60:343–382.

Wirszubski, C. 1950. *Libertas as a Political Idea at Rome during the Late Republic and Early Principate.* Cambridge.

Wright, W. C. 1913. *Julian.* Vol. 2, *Orations 6-8; Letters to Themistius, To the Senate and People of Athens, To a Priest; The Caesars; Misopogon.* Cambridge, MA.

Zecchini, G. 1993. *Ricerche di storiografia latina tardoantica.* Rome.

Zema, D. B., and G. G. Walsh. 1950. *Saint Augustine. The City of God, Books I-VII.* Washington.

BENJAMIN LARNELL, THE LAST LATIN POET AT HARVARD INDIAN COLLEGE

Thomas Keeline and Stuart M. McManus

THE TWO SURVIVING EXAMPLES of Native American Latinity from colonial New England have rightly received considerable attention from historians, as they represent a unique moment in the interaction between Native Americans and the European classical tradition.[1] To these two well-known examples by students at Harvard Indian College—the elegiac couplets in Latin and Greek by Eleazar (d. 1678) and the address to the benefactors by Caleb Cheeshahteaumuck (AB Harvard 1665)—we can now add a hitherto unrecognized work preserved in manuscript at the Massachusetts Historical Society: the

The authors would like to thank Ann Blair for her comments on an early draft of this piece, Christine Glandorf for letting us see her unpublished Senior Thesis, and the staff of the Massachusetts Historical Society for their help throughout the project and for the reproductions. In this collaborative project, Thomas Keeline took primary responsibility for the analysis of the poem and Stuart M. McManus for the historical background.

[1] On the two other examples of Native American Latinity, see Hockbruck and Dudensing-Reichel 1996:1–14; Peyer 1997:47–53. The authorship of these two pieces is also disputed, although the evidence either way is scanty, and any firm conclusion is impossible without a large amount of inference. On Native American education in general, see Szasz 2007:101–128, 173–190; Calloway 2010:ix–xxiii. The authoritative treatment of Harvard Indian College is Morison 1936: vol. 1, 340–360. Ijsewijn well defends the project of taking American writers of Latin seriously (Kaiser 1984:vii–viii): "Dixerit fortasse quispiam: cur tantopere laboras pro auctoribus istis Latinis …? Cui respondeo valere eos, immo valere multum, non quod litteras Americanas monumentis locupletaverint immortalibus, sed quia symbolum sunt et signum immortalis illius ingeniorum cultus, qui multa per saecula totum orbem occiduum educavit, ditavit et colligavit." There has also been considerable interest in the Latin verses addressed to the Governor of Jamaica (1759) by the free black poet Francis Williams. For an edition of Williams' poem and an introduction to the bibliography on him, see Gilmore 2005.

Latin versification of an Aesopic fable by Benjamin Larnell (ca. 1694–1714), the last Native American student to attend Harvard in the colonial period and the only Native American to attend after the original Indian College building was demolished in 1692.[2] Although it represents an early foray into Latin versification, it nevertheless shows a competent, if as yet undeveloped poetic genius at work, and gives us a starting point for assessing Larnell's considerable contemporary reputation as a poet. More importantly, it provides a unique window into the colonial classroom, through which we see Larnell toiling away at the same late-humanist curriculum as his "English" contemporaries on both sides of the Atlantic.

BENJAMIN LARNELL:
A BRIEF INTELLECTUAL BIOGRAPHY

Described by President Leverett as "an acute grammarian, an extraordinary Latin poet, and a good Greek one," Benjamin Larnell (perhaps a corruption of the epithet "learn-well") was born into a village of Christianized "praying Indians" near Taunton, Massachusetts, around 1694. Early in life, his intellectual talents caught the attention of the Reverend Grindall Rawson (AB Harvard 1678), then working on behalf of the Society for the Propagation of the Gospel in New England, who saw Larnell's potential as a missionary to his own people and took it upon himself to prepare the young man for the ministry.[3] To this end, Rawson carefully trained Larnell in the rudiments of Latin grammar,

---

[2] Larnell's poem survives in a single, presumably autograph, manuscript copy: Larnell *s.d.* The single folio without watermark measures 175 x 155mm and bears the marks of having been folded into quarters and having been pasted into a piece of white more recent paper. The provenance of the work has proved difficult to reconstruct. We are indebted to Anna J. Cook, Reference Librarian MHS, who looked into this for us (personal communication on September 13, 2012): "I have consulted the catalog regarding the acquisition information and the record only indicates that the document was donated to the Society by a Frederick A. Jones. No date is given." It is not recorded in the most complete census of North American Neo-Latin poetry: Kaiser 1982:197–299, although its existence is noted in passing in Sibley 1942:142n4 and is discussed briefly in Glandorf 2009. On Neo-Latin in America in general, see Blair 2014.

[3] Leverett 1723:89. The most detailed biography of Larnell is in Sibley 1942:142–144, which forms the basis of the narrative given here; for Rawson, see Sibley 1885:159–168.

probably from a simple text such as the *Sententiae pueriles, Disticha Catonis* or Aesop's *Fables*, which had been the standard introductory Latin works since the High Middle Ages.[4] After this basic training, in late January 1711 Rawson sent Larnell, then aged about 17, on foot and alone to Boston with a letter of presentation addressed to Judge Samuel Sewall, the secretary of the Society for the Propagation of the Gospel in New England, to begin the next leg of his journey to becoming a Christian minister.[5] Despite Larnell's unruly behavior and propensity to drink, which began to show itself even at this early stage, the Judge clearly took a liking to the bright but boisterous young man, whom he recommended to Nathaniel Williams, the new Master at Boston Latin School.[6]

Once at Boston Latin School, Larnell continued with the curriculum of the humanist grammar school, and it was probably there that he composed the verses that we present below. It seems that he had made good progress under Rawson, since he was put straight into the fifth of seven grades, meaning that he had already mastered the rudiments of Latin grammar and perhaps started on Greek. In the fifth grade, boys were drilled in Greek grammar and Latin prosody, "turning a fable into verse, a distich in a day," before embarking on Latin prose composition and the study of rhetoric through the orations of Cicero and Isocrates in the sixth grade. On Wednesdays of the final year they were required to "compose a Praxis on the Elegancies and Pithy sentences in their lesson in Horace in Latin verse" in the morning, and turn "a Psalm or something Divine into Latin verse" in the afternoon.[7] Although we

---

[4]   On medieval and early renaissance education, see Black 2001.

[5]   It seems Sewall at least partly funded Larnell's education under Rawson; see Blackmon 1969:165–176. Winship 1941–1944:82, 94, 107.

[6]   Judge Sewall, better known today for his role in the Salem Witch Trials two decades earlier, was one of the colony's leading minds and both the author and the subject of Latin verse. For Nehemiah Hobart's verses on Sewall and his own verses, see Kaiser 1982: no. 90 and nos. 59–120 passim. Sewall 1972: vol. 2, 297: "Mr. Williams examines Benjamin Larnell. He goes to Schoole." Larnell's drinking was a problem even before he entered Harvard. Sewall 1711–1714:57 (dated November 1712): "I spoke to Benj. Larnell about his soul's concern; desired him to beware of excessive drinking."

[7]   The curriculum under Williams is reproduced in Holmes 1935:258–260. During his short time at the grammar school Larnell seems to have skipped yet another grade, since we find him at Harvard College within two years of his arrival in Boston.

cannot be certain, the poem we present here seems to resemble most closely the requirements for the fifth grade, which would mean that it belongs to early or mid-1711.

All this careful training in Latin verse composition was in preparation for entrance into Harvard College, which required "the ability to speak and write idiomatic Latin both prose and verse by, as they say, the sweat of one's own brow" (*congrue loquendi ac scribendi facultas oratione tam soluta quam ligata, suo, ut aiunt, Marte*).[8] However, Latin versification seems to have been among the most difficult skills for aspiring *Harvardinates*, and many probably entered the College without achieving Larnell's proficiency, as John Barnard (AB Harvard 1700) attests:

> Though I was often beaten for my play, and my little roguish tricks, yet I don't remember that I was ever beaten for my book more than once or twice. One of these was upon this occasion. Master put our class upon turning Aesop's Fables into Latin verse. Some dull fellows made a shift to perform this to acceptance; but I was so much duller at this exercise, that I could make nothing of it; for which master corrected me, and this he did two or three days going. I had honestly tried my possibles to perform the task; but having no poetical fancy, nor then a capacity opened of expressing the same idea by a variation of phrases, though I was perfectly acquainted with prosody, I found I could do nothing; and therefore plainly told my master, that I had diligently labored all I could to perform what he required, and perceiving I had no genius for it, I thought it was in vain to strive against nature any longer and he never more required it of me.[9]

By December of 1712, Larnell was judged ready to enter Harvard College. As was traditional, he presented the master, usher, and students of his

---

[8]   Quincy 1860: vol. 1, 577.

[9]   Barnard 1836:180. In 1734 Harvard reduced its entry requirements to being: "skilled in making Latin verse, or at least in the rules of Prosodia."

school with a copy of verses he had composed, to which Sewall added the following lines, perhaps in reference to Larnell's drinking or his brawl with his classmate Joshua Gee, the future librarian of Harvard College:[10]

> Erroresque meos mihi condonate perosos;
> Absentique mihi precibus succurrite semper.
>
> Forgive my detestable follies
> and remember me in your prayers when I'm gone.

At Harvard, Larnell, who continued to impress and disappoint his teachers in equal measure, benefited from the Boyle fund and as a result paid no tuition, with his board seemingly being taken care of by Sewall.[11] At the time, all freshmen followed the same curriculum, spending the first part of the year reviewing rhetorical theory and the classical texts read in school (Cicero, Isocrates, Homer, Vergil, and the Greek New Testament), before beginning Hebrew and Logic in the Spring. In this, as in all his intellectual endeavors, Larnell seems to have made good progress.[12] Although Latin versification played little or no role in the curriculum after the freshman year, it seems to have been popular leisure reading among students—so popular, Cotton Mather would have us believe, that these works from "Satan's library," such as Ovid's more scandalous verses, were having a negative effect on the morality of the students![13] No doubt spurred on by the "satanic" Roman poet, Larnell quickly fell, again in the words of Cotton Mather, "into

---

[10] On Gee, see Sibley 1942:175–183.

[11] Larnell technically should have received free board under the terms of the liquidation of Indian College two decades earlier, as the President and Fellows had written to London in 1693 stating that any future Native American students "should enjoy the studies rent free" in the new building constructed from the bricks of the former Indian College (quoted in Morison 1936: vol. 1, 359). The Boyle fund, funded by the legacy of Robert Boyle, the founder of modern Chemistry, provided scholarships to students at Harvard and William and Mary who would "wholy devote themselves to the Work of the Gospel among the Natives" (Burton 1994:134).

[12] Morison 1936: vol. 1, 139–147. For an account of the contemporary curriculum in "the other Cambridge," which followed the same general pattern, see Waterland 1730.

[13] "Cotton Mather's points to be inquired into concerning Harvard College" transcribed in Quincy 1860: vol. 1, 558–560.

dreadful Snares of Sin, and of Death."[14] Within the year he was sent down in disgrace, and only returned to Boston in August 1713 thanks to "a very pathetical letter" from Rawson to Sewall, who found it in his heart to give him another chance, even paying off Larnell's debts, the origins of which remain mysterious.[15] Larnell returned to Cambridge on March 20, 1714, when he made such a theatrical show of public penitence, an act partly conducted in Latin, that President Leverett noted in his diary:

> In the publick reading of his Confession the flowing of his passions were extraordinaryly timed, and accented his Expressions, and most peculiarly and Emphatically those of the grace of God to him. Which indeed did a peculiar grace to the performance itself, And raised I believe a charity in Some, that had very little, I am Sure, and ratified wonderfully that which I had conceived for him.[16]

After these histrionics, he seems to have returned to his studies for a while, and probably followed the rest of the class of 1716 in studying Logic, Greek, Hebrew, and devoting all of Friday to rhetoric and declamation in Latin and Greek.[17] He continued to compose verses, now not only in Latin, but in Greek and Hebrew as well, examples of which Cotton Mather sent to Sir William Ashurst, former Lord Mayor of London and Treasurer of the Society for the Propagation of the Gospel in Foreign Parts, as proof of Harvard's success in educating native ministers.[18]

---

[14] Mather 1911–1912: vol. 2, 231.

[15] Sewall 1972: vol. 2, 369. Winship 1941–1944:107.

[16] Leverett 1724:88. The public confession Larnell read probably included the Latin formula instituted by President Dunster; see Quincy 1860: vol. 1, 581: *ego, S. W.* [i.e. the sinner's name], *qui a cultu divino in aula Collegii tam matutino quam vespertino toties per aliquot menses abfui (in qua absentia monitis et aliis in me animadversionum gradibus non obstantibus hactenus perstiti), nunc culpam meam agnosco, et publicae agnitionis hoc testimonio me reum profiteor, et majorem in his exercitiis pietatis diligentiam in posterum (Deo volente), dum hic egero, polliceor.*

[17] Morison 1936: vol. 1, 139–147.

[18] Mather 1971:150–151: "What I now entertain you with is a poem in the three learned languages, all formed and written by an Indian youth whom we are educating at our college for your service, not yet got beyond the standing of a Junior Sophister.

Sadly, Larnell was not destined to fulfill the mission for which he had been trained. At midnight on July 21, 1714, he died in the house of Samuel Sewall, where he was spending the summer vacation.[19] His coffin was carried to the Granary Burying Ground in Boston by his fellow students (including Gee, whom he had kicked while at school), and beside the coffin walked the President and two fellows of Harvard College, Judge Sewall, and the commissioners of the Company for the Propagation of the Gospel in New England. Grief-stricken at the loss of the promising young man in whose education he had invested so much time both financially and personally, Sewall put up the following simple note after the service: "Prayers are desired that God would graciously Grant a suitable Improvement of the Death of Benjamin Larnell, Student of Harvard College."[20]

TEXT AND COMMENTARY

Oh, Eleazar Wheelock was a very pious man;
He went into the wilderness to teach the Indian,
With a *Gradus ad Parnassum*, a Bible and a drum,
And five hundred gallons of New England rum ...[21]

Considering the person from whom it comes, it may hope for some acceptance with you ..." Unfortunately, it has not been possible to locate these verses.

[19] Sewall 1711–1714:156 (dated July 1714): "Benj. Larnell died at my father's about midnight; was delirious almost ever since he took to bed [...] he was a good scholar and had made considerable proficiency in learning; was entered upon his third year at the college ... a great frown upon the work gospelling the Indians that all attempts to educate one of their own Nation have prov'd abhortive."

[20] Sewall 1972: vol. 3, 11. Larnell's headstone does not seem to survive, if one was even erected: City of Boston, *Historic Burying Grounds Initiative*, http://www.cityofboston.gov/parks/hbgi (accessed January 12, 2013).

[21] The beginning of a late 19th-century song about the founder of Dartmouth College; for the full text see Hovey 1924:26. The song itself quickly entered into Dartmouth lore, and in the late 1930s a series of murals was even commissioned to illustrate it (Wheelock mixes rum, a Native American woman reads a *Gradus ad Parnassum* upside-down, etc.). Both the murals and the song have had a checkered history in the 20th century, on which see the online exhibition of Dartmouth's Hood Museum at http://hoodmuseum.dartmouth.edu/collections/overview/artoncampus/hovey.html (accessed February 19, 2013). For more on classical education at Dartmouth, see Vance 2013.

Verse composition was a foundational element of education in the traditional grammar school from the Elizabethan age onwards,[22] and no exception was made for American Indians in colonial New England. The original "Indian Library" of Dartmouth College, founded by Eleazar Wheelock in 1769, really did contain just such a *Gradus* to help budding bards along the rocky path to Parnassus's peak[23]—it can be seen in the Rauner library at Dartmouth today.[24] Such aids to versification also belonged to boys at Boston Latin School, and Larnell likely had such a book propped open on his desk as he undertook this composition.[25]

When reading Larnell's verses today, the classicist will immediately think of Hor. *Ep.* 1.7.29–36, the first four lines of which Larnell does us the courtesy of quoting as the finale of his own work. His version, however, is not simply a reprise of Horace, but rather, as we shall see presently, a versified version of an Aesopic fable found in Latin prose schoolbooks. Without further ado, here is the poem itself:[26]

Fabula De Vulpeculâ Et Mustelâ

Esurie longâ tenuis vulpecula quondam,
Forte per angustam tendebat repere rimam

[22] See especially Watson 1968:468–486, along with Baldwin 1944: vol. 1, 380–416.

[23] A *Gradus* is a dictionary used in Latin verse composition which provides the prosody of a word and choice verses from Latin authors exemplifying its appropriate use, sometimes with further hints and helps—epithets, synonyms, etc.—for the aspiring versifier. On the *Gradus ad Parnassum* genre in general, see the comprehensive survey of Butterfield 2010.

[24] Rauner Woodward Library 337. Whether this was literally Wheelock's *Gradus* of the song cannot be verified: it belonged to Jeremy Belknap (signed on the fore edge with the date 1758), who was one of Wheelock's early friends and staunch supporters. He either gave it to Wheelock or donated it directly to the college library. (This information was kindly supplied *per litteras* by Jay Satterfield, Special Collections Librarian at the Rauner Library. See also Torbert 1929.)

[25] Holmes 1935:262–264, 339. A copy of the 1709 London edition owned by a contemporary of Larnell, Benjamin Gibson, survives in the Gutman Education Library at Harvard (Special Collections EducT 20917.09). On Gibson (AB Harvard 1719), see Sibley 1942:310–311 and the valedictory poem quoted on p. 636 below. The 1723 Harvard Library catalog does not contain a copy of the *Gradus*, but this does not mean that contemporary Harvardians did not make use of their own copies: Bond and Amory 1996.

[26] The text as printed here aims to be a diplomatic transcription of Larnell's manuscript, complete with its vagaries of punctuation and orthography.

Frumenti ad cumeram: quando benè pasta fuisset
Corpore cum pleno rursùs discedere vellet.
Mustelâ cernente procul, tandem monet illam,
Si cupias cumerâ rursus discedere, dicens;
Macra cavum redeas arctum, quo macra subisti.
Pauperie videas laetos multosque paratos,
Quòd curis vacuos, non anxietate peritos.
Sin opulenti cùm, cernes incedere moestos,
Atque suas nunquam frontes intendere rursùm,
Et curis plenos, pressos formidine mentis.
Hanc quoque fabellam ^{sic} clarus Horatius effert,
Forte per angustam tenuis vulpecula rimam,
Repserat in cumeram frumenti: pasteᵃque rursùs
Ire foras pleno tendebat corpore, frustra.
Cui mustela procul, si vis, ait effugere isthinc,
Maᶜra cavum repetas arctum, quem macra sub^{isti}.

Benjamin Larnellus

Fable of the Fox and the Weasel

Once upon a time a fox, thin because of long-standing hunger,
happened to be striving to creep through a narrow crack
into a bin of grain. When he had eaten his fill,
he was eager to leave again with his stuffed belly.
A weasel, watching from afar, at last advised him,
saying, "You must return through the narrow hole as skinny
    as when you entered it."
You could see many people happy in their poverty and well
    supplied,
because they are free from cares and know no anxiety,
but when they are wealthy, you will see them walk in sadness
and never unfurrow their brows
and be full of cares, weighed down by fear in their minds.
Famous Horace also tells this fable as follows:
"By chance a thin fox had crept into a bin of grain
through a thin crack; having eaten he
kept trying to go outside again with his full belly to no avail.

A weasel said to him from afar, 'If you want to get out of there, you must return through the narrow hole as skinny as when you entered it.'"

Benjamin Larnell

"Fable of the Fox and the Weasel" by Benjamin Larnell, ca. 1711–1714. Original manuscript from "Fable of the Fox and the Weasel." Massachusetts Historical Society. Photo courtesy of the Massachusetts Historical Society.

The poem is plainly student work, but it compares reasonably well with what Larnell's coevals at Boston Latin School could produce.[27] There is only one metrical flaw of substance: in line 10 *sin opulenti cum*, the monosyllable before the caesura is inadmissible.[28] The unelided *atque* of line 11 is actually a Horatian predilection, although one may reasonably doubt whether Larnell was knowingly imitating it;[29] *tandem monet illam* closing line 5 is likewise well suited to Horace's hexameter. Indeed line 5 also showcases Larnell's knowledge of metrical subtleties or plain good luck, for he rightly pairs his third-foot trochaic caesura with a strong caesura in the second foot and follows it with an iambic word. In sum, the poem at least scans, and this in itself is no mean accomplishment for a tyro still struggling to conform his tottering steps to the unforgiving strictures of metrical feet.[30]

The grammar, on the other hand, is distinctly odd in places. We might initially have ascribed these blunders merely to the schoolboy's shaky grasp of the Latin language, and to be sure this must bear the brunt of the blame, but it does not tell the whole story. As previously indicated, the poem is not merely a paraphrase of Horace, but rather a versified version of a Latin prose fable that Larnell must have been assigned from a textbook, probably as part of the fifth-grade exercise described in Boston Latin School's curriculum above (see p. 623).[31] The reading of Aesop's fables in Latin was a standard part of the

---

[27] See p. 636 below.

[28] See e.g. Winbolt 1903:94

[29] On Horace's use of unelided *atque*, see Butterfield 2008:406–409.

[30] This is well known to anyone who has ever tried to learn or teach verse composition. If we compare Larnell's efforts with the elegy of Eleazar, the other American Indian Latin poet, we can see that he too has mastered the salient points of Latin metrics. (Errors have been introduced, however, by his editors.) Eleazar's Greek tetrastich, on the other hand, is not so felicitous, being replete with various metrical missteps. For the text and translation, see Hockbruck and Dudensing-Reichel 1996:7–9, which require copious correction.

[31] On the place of Aesop in the school curriculum, see Baldwin 1944: vol. 1, 607–640; Watson 1968:300, 302, and 519. In at least one school these stories were also used as a quarry for *English* verse composition: "After [the students] are thus become acquainted with a variety of metre, you may cause them to turn a fable of Aesop into whatever kind of verse you appoint them" (Hoole quoted in Watson 1968:481–482). Such fables might indeed be thought particularly useful for teaching Indians European values.

school curriculum from the 13th through 18th centuries; such assignments had the virtue of inculcating both morality and Latinity in one fell swoop. Since they were such a staple of the schoolroom, editions proliferated at an astonishing rate, with new accretions continually being encrusted on the canon. The story versified by Larnell is one such accretion, for it is not to be found in any ancient texts besides Horace, but by the 16th century it had spread throughout Latin collections of Aesop's fables.[32] Here is a version found in an edition from 1537:[33]

De vulpecula & mustela.

Vulpecula, longa inedia tenuis, fortè per angustiorem rimam in cumeram frumenti repsit. In qua cum probè pasta fuit, dein rursus tentantem egredi, distentus impediit venter. Mustela lúctantem procul contemplata, tandem monet si exire cupiat, ad cauum macra redeat, quo macra intrarat.

Morale.

Videas complures in mediocritate laetos esse, atque alacres, vacuos curis, expertes animi molestijs. Sin hi diuites facti fuerint, videbis eos moestos incedere, nunquam frontem porrigere plenos curis, animi molestijs obrutos. Hanc fabellam sic Horatius canit libro primo epistolarum,

> Fortè per angustam tenuis vulpecula rimam
> Repserat in cumeram frumenti, pastáque rursus
> Ire foras pleno tendebat corpore frustra.
> Cui mustela procul, Si vis, ait, effugere isthinc,
> Macra cauum repetas arctum, quem macra subisti.

---

[32] A related version of the story is found as Perry 24 (e.g. Babrius 1.86); in that case, however, the fat fox gets stuck inside a tree. It is not clear when the version that Larnell versifies first found its way into the Aesopic canon.

[33] *Aesopi Phrygis Vita et Fabulae a Viris Doctissimis in Latinam Linguam Conuersae ...* (Paris 1537) p. 205.

After Larnell's poem, this will all look quite familiar. Similar texts with small variations are found throughout countless contemporary editions of Aesop,[34] and it is immediately clear that Larnell's *Vorlage* must have been one of them.[35] The assignment—a typical one in the pre-modern Latin classroom[36]—was to render the Latin prose into verse a line at a time, and this is precisely what Larnell did, hewing closely to his original.

Since we have a good sense of Larnell's training and the texts he had at his disposal, we can reconstruct his thought process almost word-by-word and line-by-line, and this incidentally helps explain most of the various grammatical inconcinnities. In line 1, for example, Larnell knows that he must first place *vulpecula*. There is but one position in the hexameter where it can comfortably stand, and so there he immediately puts it. The fox is *tenuis*, and this epithet can conveniently be placed next to *vulpecula*. *Inedia* is metrically intractable, and so a synonym must be found. If Larnell consulted Aler's *Gradus*, he would have been referred s.v. *inedia* to *fames*, whose first and only synonym is given as *esuries*. (He could of course have arrived at the synonym *ex ingenio suo*, but given the level of grammatical knowledge displayed elsewhere in the poem, we might fairly doubt how many Latin words for "hunger" he would have had at the tip of his tongue.) If he retains *longa* from the original, the only admissible order is *esurie longa*. This

---

[34] E.g. H. Clarke, *Fabulae Aesopi Selectae* ... (Baltimore 1817) p. 31; see Appendix One. This edition postdates Larnell by a century, but as it is closely based on earlier versions it may stand as a witness to the sort of texts in circulation aimed at the schoolboy market.

[35] Amid the sea of possibilities we have not yet been able to identify exactly which text Larnell was using. In some ways it stands closer to the version cited in n. 34 (e.g. *angustam*), but in other ways it is clearly more analogous to the edition quoted in the text above (for example, it includes the Horatian verses as a tailpiece). We know that copies of Aesop's fables, usually published in London, were frequently imported to Boston in this period, but unfortunately the surviving records do not cast any more light on the matter of which edition Larnell was using. See Ford 1917:91, 150, 174, 175.

[36] On versification of Latin prose, see the evidence cited in Watson 1968:472–473, e.g. Wolsey's quotation (472): "It will also be of very great importance that [the students] sometimes turn verse into prose, or reduce prose into metre," a practice likely continued unbroken from the rhetorical school of antiquity. Cf. too the fifth-grade curriculum at the Boston Latin School (above p. 623) and Barnard's lament above (p. 624) about his experience versifying Aesop's fables.

leaves one hole to fill, the final spondee, and here he very reasonably invents *quondam*, a word he would have seen in countless other fables. If he did indeed proceed in such a stepwise fashion, this would explain why he did not write the slightly more elegant *esurie tenuis longa vulpecula*, with epithets and nouns paired in an interlocking arrangement. This observation may indicate that once he had a verse that scanned, he was content and required no further revision.

The next phrase, *forte per angustiorem rimam in cumeram frumenti repsit*, begins suitably enough, and so he writes *forte per*. Did his *Vorlage* contain *angustiorem* or *angustam*?[37] If the latter, he was already in business up to the caesura; if the former, then in order to avoid an intractable cretic he was forced to revert to the positive degree of the adjective, which he would have seen in Horace's poem. Having espied Horace's original and matched its opening, he doubtless seized on its final *rimam* as well. Realizing then that he needed some short vowels for a fifth-foot dactyl, *repsit* became *repere*, which produced the happy coda *repere rimam*. One gap was left to be bridged, and Larnell required a word that could take a prolative infinitive. *Tendebat* looks suspicious at first glance; the word used in the sense of "strive to" plus infinitive is rare (*OLD* s.v. 13b), but of course it is found in the very passage of Horace that he is quoting, in that same form and in that same metrical *sedes*. Thus a molossus of roughly suitable meaning and construction was at hand, and so Larnell promptly plucked it from Horace and placed it in his own composition. No doubt he smiled to himself and thought, "Two lines done."

This mechanical process of composition goes a long way towards explaining the various grammatical blemishes. In *mustela cernente procul, tandem monet illam* (line 5), for example, he begins with an ablative absolute, which immediately becomes the subject of the verb. The schoolmaster will not have been pleased. Nevertheless, the source of the solecism is clear: the original had *mustela ... contemplata tandem monet*, where the deponent perfect participle is of course active in meaning and nominative in case. Finding a synonym for *contemplari*, whether in the *Gradus* or from his own native *copia*, Larnell fitted it

---

[37] Cf. n. 35 above.

into the line as an ablative absolute: this parallels both the meaning of the original and its form, with a noun and a participle in agreement, and he could keep the adverb *procul*. He then completed the line as it is found in his exemplar, having forgotten that he used an ablative absolute up to the caesura. Similar observations will explain *quando bene pasta fuisset* (line 3) for "when he had eaten well," and *quod curis vacuos, non anxietate peritos* (line 9), where the accusatives are not governed by anything except memory of the original.

It is harder to explain away the subjunctive *vellet* at the end of line 4 or the phrase *sin opulenti cum*. In the latter case Larnell no doubt simply began with the *sin* of his model, but looked in the *Gradus* for something to replace the cretic *divites*. He was faced with choices like *locupletes* and *opulenti*, which were at first sight more promising than whatever else was on offer (*ditissimi* and *praedivites* will also have been suggested by the verse dictionary, neither of which will scan). Nevertheless he was then confronted with a problem, a monosyllabic hole at the caesura. He may have been unaware of the rule that a monosyllable cannot stand before the caesura unless preceded by another monosyllable or a pyrrhic,[38] but that will not explain the grammar of the choice. We suspect that he may not have known the precise meaning of *sin* ("but if") and so thought that it could be—or needed to be—paired with "when." Alternatively *cum* may be a slip of the pen for *tum*, which would solve the grammatical problem and give good sense, even as it left the metrical flaw untouched.[39]

Does Larnell ever seem to innovate on his model? Aside from necessary trivialities designed to make the original conform to the meter and the like (e.g. *clarus Horatius* in line 13), there is one place where he seems to show himself genuinely independent of the exemplar. In line 13 he writes *pressos formidine mentis* to replace *animi molestiis obrutos*. This is a significant difference, and he could not have gotten from the one to the other simply by flicking through pages in the *Gradus*—no, it seems likely that he remembered Verg. *Aen.* 3.47 *tum uero ancipiti mentem formidine*

---

[38] Cf. n. 28 above.

[39] The punctuation of Larnell's ms, however, militates strongly against this interpretation.

pressus and that he has varied and reproduced the tag. No doubt Larnell had read this part of the *Aeneid* with Rawson or at Boston Latin School and, recalling the phrase, saw a good opportunity to insert it here.

This is the exercise of a schoolboy. Larnell was still a tyro at Latin verse composition when he dipped his quill in the inkwell and wrote out this copy, and it would not be fair to compare his effort to the other two specimens of Native American Latinity by Caleb and Eleazar. Each of those was the product of a Harvard-educated man and shows a much higher standard of both Latinity and invention.[40] We can, however, compare Larnell's exercise to the poetic effusions of Benjamin Gibson (BLS 1715; Harvard AB 1719), who was a grade behind Larnell at the Boston Latin School.[41] Gibson composed a valedictory poem of more than 135 hexameters for the annual visit of the School's selectmen in 1715, of which the opening five will give a sufficient flavor:[42]

> Nunc annis variis vigili moderamine vestri
> laetitia suavi duxi mea tempora cuncta,
> et venio genibus ad te nunc tempore flexis
> discedens tanto fido vigilique magistro
> quo melior possit reperiri tempore nullo.

> Now for many years I have spent all my time
> In sweet happiness under your tutelage,
> And now I come to you on bended knee
> To bid adieu to such an unswerving and attentive teacher
> Than whom no better can be found in any age.

In just these first five lines, we find dubious grammar (e.g. *vestri* in line 1), prosody (*genibūs ad*), frequent repetition (*tempora* 2, *tempore* 3, *tempore* 5—all in the same metrical *sedes*; cf. too *vigili* in 1 and 4), and a general poverty of poetic imagination. This, the poem's opening, is presumably the most carefully crafted part of the most important piece

---

[40] Although they are hardly entirely free from fault themselves, particularly Eleazar's Greek. See n. 30 above.

[41] For more on Gibson, see n. 25 above.

[42] The poem is preserved only in Gibson's unpublished autograph manuscript: Gibson 1715.

of Latin poetry that the most skilled student at the Boston Latin School had heretofore written. When held up against this standard—the only standard with which it can reasonably be compared—Larnell's composition does not come off badly.

CONCLUSION

In these verses, we see Larnell at a mid-point in his academic career, sometime after he has been plucked from his village and immersed in the Latinate world of the late-humanist schoolroom, but before he had had a chance to develop fully, and probably at least a few years before he merited Leverett's high praise as "an acute grammarian, an extraordinary Latin poet, and a good Greek one." This single manuscript folio offers us a unique opportunity to get inside one Native American schoolboy's poetic workshop and watch him as he goes about his task. He shows competence at least equal to his peers' and some promise, but he has a long road ahead of him before he reaches his full potential. Sitting at his desk in Boston Latin School with a Latin prose version of an Aesopic fable before him, he turned it into passable Latin verse with the help of the *Gradus ad Parnassum,* a schoolboy's constant companion in this period and for some two centuries thereafter. In at least one instance he has gone beyond a merely mechanical process of composition by invoking his own knowledge of classical literature in his variation on a half line from Vergil's *Aeneid,* a hint perhaps at some future promise which cannot now be verified.

As recent work on late humanism has shown, Latin poetry was both a "learned recreation and a valued professional accomplishment" in the "old" Republic of Letters, that international community of scholars, which continued to cultivate the traditions and learned practices of the Renaissance into the eighteenth century, and Larnell's schoolboy composition shows him taking the first tentative steps towards acquiring the skills to participate in this world.[43] Larnell's small poem

---

[43]   Shelford 2007:2, 45–76; Grafton 2012:2–5; Haskell 2013. The continuity of the tradition into the eighteenth century is apparent from the large number of Latin poems dedicated to Benjamin Franklin in his lifetime, including a little-known example by Jakob Hendrik Hoeufft, the famous Dutch Neo-Latin poet (Hoeufft 1788:198); see Appendix Two.

is striking exactly because of its perfect concordance with the genre of early modern schoolboy versification. It shows that his training was identical to that of his "English" contemporaries and that, as far as can be ascertained, there was no attempt to adapt the curriculum for a Native American student; in fact, Larnell would have recognized almost every aspect of his English counterparts' education at Eton and Oxford, from the exercises to the editions of the texts they read.[44] Indeed, this educational program was so common in the Republic of Letters that the same introductory texts were read by students in both Boston and Peru in this period. Closer to home, just two years after Larnell went up to Harvard, Benjamin Franklin (1706–1790) would sit in the same classroom and, like generations of New England boys before him, would begin the long educational journey that led from reading Latin poetry to turning prose fables into verse.[45] Of those who attempted the same exercise as Larnell, a few would have had more success than he, but many, as John Barnard attests, would struggle to produce anything at all. In attempting to train a Native American boy as a preacher to spread the Gospel among his people, the New Englanders put Larnell through the same "Christian humanist" curriculum that Europeans had followed since the Renaissance, with little sense of the oddity of hammering hexameters and Greek conjugations in the head of a boy who was born an ocean away from Rome and Athens. Rather, they believed it provided the linguistic tools to access, appreciate, and impart the wisdom contained in the New Testament, the heroic narrative of Vergil, and the simple but instructive fables of Aesop.

WASHINGTON UNIVERSITY IN ST. LOUIS

HARVARD UNIVERSITY

---

[44] The fable of the fox and the weasel is found in a roughly contemporary school edition of Aesop printed in Lima: *Aesopi, et aliorum fabulae, latinius: quam ante hac expressae. Nunc denuo ab omnibus mendis vindicatae* (Lima, 1752), 137.

[45] Franklin was removed from Boston Latin School by his father for financial reasons and so probably never got beyond reading elementary Latin texts: Franklin 2003:52–53.

APPENDIX ONE

De Vulpecula & Mustela

Vulpecula tenuis longā inediā fortè repsit per angustam rimam in cameram (*sic*) frumenti, in quā cùm fuit probè pasta, deinde venter distentus impedit tentantem egredi rursus. Mustela procul contemplata luctantem, tandem monet, si cupiat exire, redeat ad cavum macra, quo intraverat macra.

Mor.

Videas complures laetos atque alacres in mediocritate, vacuos curis, expertos molestiis animi. Sin illi fuerint facti divites, videbis eos incedere moestos; nunquam porrigere frontem, plenos curis, obrutos molestiis animi.

H. Clarke

APPENDIX TWO

In Franklini mortem falso nuntiatam

Quem colit Europaeque obponit America toti,
    Albion ipsa hostem quem venerata fuit—
ecce Acheronteis rediit Franclinus ob oris,
    publicaque in Sophies ponit ut ante sinu.
anne igitur, superum qui tela trisulca parenti
    eripuit, Stygium vicit et ille Jovem?

Jakob Hendrik Hoeufft

WORKS CITED

Aler, P. 1699. *Gradus ad Parnassum*. Cologne. (And often reprinted.)

Baldwin, T. W. 1944. *William Shakespere's Small Latine and Less Greeke*. Urbana, IL.

Barnard, J. 1836. "Autobiography of Rev. John Barnard." *Collections of the Massachusetts Historical Society*. 3rd ser. 5:178–243.

Black, R. 2001. *Humanism and Education in Renaissance Italy: Tradition and Innovation in Latin Schools from the Twelfth to the Fifteenth Centuries*. Cambridge, UK.

Blackmon, J. L. 1969. "Judge Samuel Sewall's Efforts in Behalf of the First Americans." *Ethnohistory* 16:165–176.

Blair, A. 2014. "Neo-Latin in North America." In *The Brill Encyclopaedia of Neo-Latin*, ed. J. Bloemendal, C. Fantazzi, and P. Ford, 883-884. Leiden.

Bond, W. H., and H. Amory, eds. 1996. *The Printed Catalogues of the Harvard College Library, 1723-1790*. Boston, MA.

Burton, J. D. 1994. "Crimson Missionaries: The Robert Boyle Legacy and Harvard College." *The New England Quarterly* 67:132–140.

Butterfield, D. J. 2008. "The Poetic Treatment of *Atque* from Catullus to Juvenal." *Mnemosyne* 61:386–413.

———. 2010. "*Gradus ad Parnassum*." In *Classical Dictionaries: Past, Present, and Future*, ed. C. Stray, 71–93. London.

Calloway, C. G. 2010. *The Indian History of an American Institution: Native Americans and Dartmouth*. Hanover, NH.

Ford, W. C. 1917. *The Boston Book Market, 1679-1700*. Boston.

Franklin, B. 2003. *The Autobiography of Benjamin Franklin*. Ed. L. W. Labree. New Haven, CT.

Gibson, B. 1715. *Valedictory Poem*. Massachusetts Historical Society, Miscellaneous Bound Manuscripts, 1714-1718. Boston, MA.

Gilmore, J. 2005. "The British Empire and the Neo-Latin Tradition: The Case of Francis Williams." In *Classics and Colonialism*, ed. B. Goff, 92–106. London.

Glandorf, C. 2009. *The Mis-education of Benjamin Larnell: The Story of the Last Indian Student at Colonial Harvard*. Senior Thesis, History Department, Yale University.

Grafton, A. 2012. "The Republic of Letters in the American Colonies: Francis Daniel Pastorius Makes a Notebook." *American Historical Review* 117:1–39.

Haskell, Y. 2013. *Prescribing Ovid: The Latin Works and Networks of the Enlightened Dr Heerkens.* London.

Hockbruck, W., and B. Dudensing-Reichel. 1996. "*Honoratissimi Benefactores*: Native American Students and Two Seventeenth-Century Texts in the University Tradition." In *Early Native American Writing: New Critical Essays,* ed. H. Jaskoski, 1–14. Cambridge, MA.

Hoeufft, J. H. 1788. *Particula poetica fasc. III: Accedunt ejusdem Pericula critica. s. l.*

Holmes, P. 1935. *A Tercentenary History of the Boston Public Latin School, 1635-1935.* Cambridge, MA.

Hovey, R. 1924. *Dartmouth Lyrics.* Ed. E. O. Grover. Hanover, NH.

Kaiser, L. M. 1982. "A Census of American Latin Verse, 1625–1825." *Proceedings of the American Antiquarian Society* 91:197–299.

———. 1984. *Early American Latin Verse 1625-1825: An Anthology.* Chicago.

Larnell, B. *s.d. Latin Poem.* ms. S-143. Massachusetts Historical Society. Boston, MA.

Leverett, J. 1723. *Diary, 1707-1723.* Papers of John Leverett. UAI 15.866 Box 1. Harvard University Archives. Cambridge, MA.

Mather, C. 1911–1912. *Diary of Cotton Mather.* 2 vols. Boston, MA.

———. 1971. *Selected Letters of Cotton Mather.* Ed. Kenneth Silverman. Baton Rouge.

Morison, S. E. 1936. *Harvard College in the Seventeenth Century.* 2 vols. Cambridge, MA.

Peyer, B. C. 1997. *The Tutor'd Mind: Indian Missionary-writers in Antebellum America.* Amherst, MA.

Quincy, J. 1860. *The History of Harvard University.* 2 vols. Cambridge, MA.

Sewall, J. 1711–1716. *Diary 1711-1716.* Reel 8.4 of Massachusetts Historical Society, Pre-Revolutionary Diaries Microfilm Collection. Boston, MA.

Sewall, S. 1972. *Diary of Samuel Sewall 1674-1729.* 3 vols. New York.

Shelford, A. G. 2007. *Transforming the Republic of Letters: Pierre-Daniel Huet and European Intellectual Life, 1650–1720.* Rochester, NY.

Sibley, J. L. 1885. *1678–1789.* Vol. 3 of *Biographical Sketches of Graduates of Harvard University, in Cambridge, Massachusetts.* Cambridge, MA.

———. 1942. *1713–1721.* Vol. 6 of *Biographical Sketches of Graduates of Harvard University, in Cambridge, Massachusetts.* Cambridge, MA.

Szasz, M. C. 2007. *Indian Education in the American Colonies 1607–1783.* Lincoln, MA.

Torbert, E. B. 1929. "Here's the Original Indian Library." *Dartmouth Alumni Magazine,* November 13–15.

Vance, E. J. 2013. *Before the Alba Mater: Classics, Civilization, and Race at Moor's Indian Charity School.* Senior Thesis, Department of Classics, Dartmouth College.

Waterland, D. 1730. *Advice to a Young Student: With a Method of Study for the First Four Years.* London.

Watson, F. 1968. *The English Grammar Schools to 1660: Their Curriculum and Practice.* London.

Winbolt, S. E. 1903. *Latin Hexameter Verse.* London.

Winship, G. P. 1941–1944. "Samuel Sewall and the New England Company." *Proceedings of the Massachusetts Historical Society.* 3rd ser. 67:55–110.

SUMMARIES OF DISSERTATIONS
FOR THE DEGREE OF PH.D

Thomas John Keeline—*A Rhetorical Figure: Cicero in the Early Empire*

My dissertation investigates the reception of Cicero in the early Roman Empire, focusing on the first 250 years after his death. I show that this reception is primarily constructed by the ancient rhetorical schoolroom, where young Romans first encountered Cicero, reading his speeches and writing Ciceronian declamations. Here they were exposed to a particular version of the man, with points of emphasis often selected for political purposes. When they grew up, that schoolroom image of Cicero continued to permeate their thought and writing. My study unpacks this complex process and lays bare the early Empire's relationship with one of its most significant late Republican predecessors.

The dissertation has five chapters, along with an introduction and conclusion. In chapter 1, I triangulate among the comments of the scholia Bobiensia, Asconius, and Quintilian on the *Pro Milone* to reconstruct how a Roman *rhetor* taught a Ciceronian speech in the classroom. Careful scrutiny of the preoccupations and interests of these teachers reveals what students in the early Empire would have learned about Cicero from their closest surviving link to the man, his speeches. In chapters two and three, I look at declamations about Cicero and Ciceronian pseudepigrapha, which are also products of the rhetorical schoolroom, and compare them with the literary versions of Cicero of early imperial authors. I show that what we find in the literary authors reflects what they learned as adolescents in the rhetorical classroom. Finally, chapters 4 and 5 comprise case studies of Cicero in Pliny the Younger and Tacitus, which both pivot around the central figure of Quintilian. In chapter 4, I demonstrate that Tacitus mounts a sophisticated theoretical rejection of Quintilian's neo-Ciceronianism, particularly in the *Dialogus*, where the rejection is cloaked in remarkable Ciceronian intertextuality—Tacitus rejects Cicero by subverting Cicero's own words. Pliny, by contrast, is torn between following Quintilian's prescription to become a Cicero *rediuiuus* and the knowledge that neither his native *ingenium* nor the changed political circumstances allow him to do so. In chapter 5, I show that Pliny's *Epistulae* manifest a persistently uneasy anxiety of influence and that his relationship with Cicero remains an unresolved and unresolvable tension throughout his work. In a concluding section I draw all these threads together and provide an aperçu on the late antique and early medieval reception of Cicero, in which Christian readers begin to turn away from Cicero the orator and to focus on Cicero the philosopher.

Degree in Classical Philology 2014

ERIKA NICKERSON—*The Measure of All Things: Natural Hierarchy in Roman Republican Thought*

THIS DISSERTATION EXPLORES how writers of the late Roman Republic use the concept of nature rhetorically, in order to talk about and either reinforce or challenge social inequality. Comparisons between humans and animals receive special attention, since writers of that time often equate social status with natural status by assimilating certain classes of person to certain classes of animal. It is the goal of this study to clarify the ideology which supported the conflation of natural and social hierarchy, by explicating the role that nature was thought to play in creating and maintaining the inequality both between man and man, and between man and animal. In investigating this issue, this study also addresses the question of whether the Romans took a teleological view of human society, as they did of nature, and ultimately concludes that they did not. It proposes, rather, that the conceptual mechanism which naturalized social inequality, and which drove the assimilation of human to animal, was the belief that there is one, natural measure of worth and status for all creatures: utility to the human community.

Chapter 1 identifies some pertinent beliefs, commonly found in Republican texts, about nature, animals, humans, and the relationship of all three to each other. Chapter 2 considers whether these beliefs have a philosophical provenance, by discussing Aristotle's theory of natural slavery and Stoic views on the institution of slavery, and their possible relation to the ideas expressed in Roman sources. Chapter 3 returns to Republican texts—including Varro's *Res rustica*, Cicero's *De officiis*, and popular oratory—and examines comparisons between domestic animals and humans in the treatment of slavery and wage-earning. Chapter 4 examines comparisons between wild animals and humans in discussions about violence and primitive peoples, and in political invective.

This work aims to contribute to the study of Republican literature and history by reconstructing a pattern of thought, or ideological framework, which authors frequently drew upon in order to understand and discuss the Roman socio-political structure. The dissertation also shows that these ideas played a part in the highly charged rhetoric of class and class conflict which was prominent in public discourse of the late Republic.

Degree in Classical Philology 2015

SERGIOS PASCHALIS—*Tragic Palimpsests: The Reception of Euripides in Ovid's Metamorphoses*

THE SUBJECT OF THE DISSERTATION is the reception of Euripides' tragedies in Ovid's *Metamorphoses*. It explores the pivotal research question of what is distinctly Euripidean in the Ovidian epic by identifying tragic elements in the poem which have Euripidean provenance. In particular, the Roman poet assimilates and reconfigures in his narrative standard formal components of Euripidean tragedy, such as the expository prologue, choral lyric, the messenger report, the dramatic soliloquy, the recognition scene, and the *deus ex machina* speech. Ovid essentially reworks each Euripidean play in a different way by employing a large variety of techniques, which include "intertextual conflation," namely the organic blending of Ovid's sources; "fragmentation," a term which refers to the dismantling of a Euripidean play down to its constituent elements, such as characters, speeches, and themes, which are then refashioned and incorporated into different stories in the *Metamorphoses*; and "refraction," that is the portrayal of an Ovidian figure not as mirror image of a Euripidean character, but as his/her distorted reflection.

The first chapter offers a general survey of the afterlife of Euripidean drama in the major intertexts mediating between Euripides and Ovid, namely Hellenistic poetry, Roman Republican tragedy, and Virgil's *Aeneid*, as well as a review of the pervasive presence of the Greek tragedian in the Ovidian corpus. The second chapter focuses on the reception of Euripides' *Bacchae* in the *Metamorphoses*. The Greek play is condensed into a two-hundred-line epic narrative with four scenes which correspond to an episode or conflation of episodes of the drama. At the same time Ovid fuses his Euripidean model with the Homeric *Hymn to Dionysus* and Theocritus' *Idyll* 26 and grafts elements of the *Bacchae*, such as Dionysus' epiphany and Pentheus' dismemberment, into the Bacchic narratives of the Minyads and Orpheus by means of "fragmentation."

The third chapter begins with an investigation of Ovid's intertextual engagement with Euripides' *Medea* in the Medea narrative of Book 7, which is read as an epicized "mega-tragedy" encompassing the Colchian's mythical *res gestae* and blending together material drawn from Euripides, Apollonius, and Virgil. The appropriation of the Greek play consists in amplifying its marginal elements, such as the murder of Pelias, into full-blown narratives and conversely in compressing radically the central story of the drama thereby rendering it a peripheral narrative. In the second part of the chapter, which explores the Roman poet's reworking of the Euripidean tragedy in other episodes of the *Metamorphoses*, it is argued that Procne, Althaea, and Deianira constitute "refractions" of Euripides' Medea, in that they can be viewed as graded variants of the tragic heroine. Procne is an amplified version of Medea surpassing her in cruelty and ruthlessness; Althaea constitutes a more humanized variant of the Euripidean protagonist in terms of her profound contrition for her filicide; finally, Deianira is merely an "aspiring Medea," since she entertains a plot of dispatching her erotic rival, but eventually abandons it.

The fourth chapter examines Ovid's epic reimagining of Euripides' *Hecuba*, which he merges with Virgil's version of the Polydorus myth in

Aeneid 3. It is contended that the Roman poet emulates his tragic ante-cedent in terms of the depiction of his female protagonists. Polyxena outdoes her Euripidean counterpart both with regard to female sensuality and the adoption of male heroic characteristics, while Hecuba exceeds her tragic model in terms of the emotional inten-sity of her dirge for her daughter and the savagery of her vengeance on Polymestor. The fifth chapter is devoted to the episode of Virbius and Egeria in *Metamorphoses* 15. Ovid produces a novel version of the Hippolytus myth by conflating Virgil's Virbius vignette in *Aeneid* 7 with Euripides' two *Hippolytus* plays, the extant *Hippolytos Stephanephoros* and the fragmentary *Hippolytos Kalyptomenos*. The messenger speech of *HippS* relating Hippolytus' chariot disaster is converted into Virbius' posthumous account of his own violent death, while the opening and conclusion of Virbius' speech constitute a creative rewriting of Artemis' epilogue speech as *dea ex machina* in *HippS*. At the same time the Ovidian narrative diverges from *HippS* and echoes instead *HippK* in terms of key plot elements, such as the means of disclosure of Phaedra's passion to Hippolytus, the role played by Aphrodite, and the time of Hippolytus' death.

Degree in Classical Philology 2015

JULIAN YOLLES—*Latin Literature and Frankish Culture in the Crusader States (1098–1187)*

AFTER THE FIRST CRUSADE, who were the Europeans that remained in the Levant, and what written records did they leave behind? In this study, I propose to view all of the surviving texts, which include historiography, sermons, pilgrim guides, monastic literature, and poetry, as part of a nascent literary tradition of the Frankish Levant. The first part of this study (Chapter 1) critically reevaluates the Latin literary texts and combines the evidence, including unpublished mate-rials, to chart the development of genres over the course of the twelfth century.

The second half of the study (Chapters 2–4) subjects this evidence to a cultural-rhetorical analysis, and asks how Latin literary works, as products by and for a cultural elite, appropriated preexisting materials and developed strategies of their own to construct a Frankish cultural identity of the Levant. Proceeding on three thematically different, but closely interrelated, lines of inquiry, it is argued that authors in the Latin East made cultural claims by drawing on the classical tradition, on the Bible, and on ideas of a Carolingian golden age.

Chapter 2 demonstrates that Latin historians drew upon classical traditions to fit the Latin East within established frameworks of history and geography, in which the figures Vespasian and Titus are particularly prevalent. Chapter 3 traces the development of the conception of the Franks in the East as a "People of God" and the use of biblical texts to support this claim, especially the Books of the Maccabees. Chapter 4 explores the extent to which authors drew on the legend of Charlemagne as a bridge between East and West.

Although the appearance of similar motifs signals a degree of cultural unity among the authors writing in the Latin East, there is an abundant variety in the way they are utilized, inasmuch as they are dynamic rhetorical strategies open to adaptation to differing exigencies. New monastic and ecclesiastical institutions produced Latin writings that demonstrate an urge to establish political and religious authority. While these struggles for power resemble to some extent those between secular and ecclesiastical authorities and institutions in Western Europe, the literary topoi the authors draw upon are specific to their new locale, and represent the creation of a new cultural-literary tradition.

Degree in Medieval Latin Philology 2015